Mastering CLAIT Plus

Bernard Kane

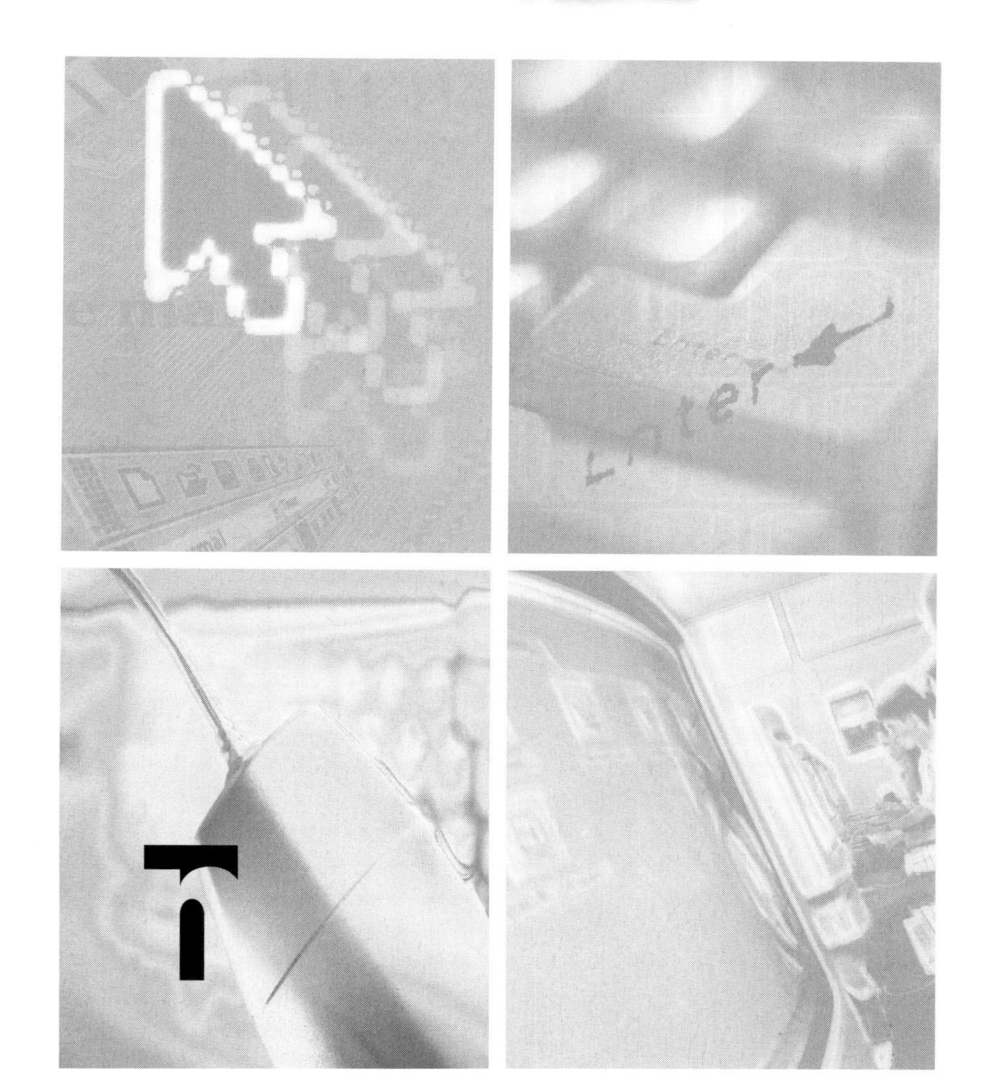

Published in 2003 by:
Nelson Thornes Ltd
Delta Place
27 Bath Road
CHELTENHAM
GL53 7TH
United Kingdom

01 02 03 04 05 06 / 10 9 8 7 6 5 4 3 2 1

A catalogue record for this book is available from the British Library

ISBN 0 7487 7078 X

Page make-up by GreenGate Publishing Services

Printed and bound in Great Britain by Scotprint

Contents

Acknowledgements v
Dedication v
Author's note v
Introduction vi

UNIT 1 **Create, manage and integrate files** 1

Managing files • How to copy, move and delete files • Opening, closing and saving files • Understanding how to format a page layout and manipulate text according to a house style • Moving, inserting and deleting text • Using headers and footers • Creating bullet and number lists • Amending documents and using the spell checker • Using special symbols and characters • Using the find and replace function • Creating and using tables • Importing and manipulating images • Importing and formatting charts • Importing datafiles

UNIT 2 **Spreadsheets** 77

Open a spreadsheet, enter/amend data, create formulae and use functions • Cell references – absolute, relative and mixed • Using Excel functions • Projecting results by changing data inputs • Modifying a spreadsheet layout and formatting text and data • Naming cells and referencing different spreadsheets • Formatting the display of a spreadsheet • Producing spreadsheet reports

UNIT 3 **Databases** 143

Introducing the CLAIT Plus unit on databases • Creating and saving databases • Entering records into a table • Interrogating a database • Creating and formatting reports

UNIT 4 **Desktop publishing** (CD) 1

Setting up a master page and style sheet • Importing and manipulating text and image files • Dealing with graphics • Working with design briefs • Creating tables in a publication • Proof correction symbols • Preparing a publication for press

Acknowledgements

This book uses two of the most widely used software packages on the market today, Microsoft Office and the Corel Corporation's CorelDRAW Suite 11. I am grateful to both Microsoft and the Corel Corporation for their software without which this book would not have been written.

I would also like to thank the members of the publishing teams from both Nelson Thornes and GreenGate Publishing Services for their help and support in getting this book off the ground, in particular James Rabson, Rick Jackman and Sarah Robertson of Nelson Thornes and Anna Carroll and David Mackin of GreenGate Publishing Services.

Dedication

This book is dedicated to my wife Wendy whose patience and understanding over months of lost evenings and weekends was only exceeded by her faith in my ability and determination to complete the project.

Author's note

This book is written for those thousands of students and potential students who recognise that being able to use a computer and associated software is but a tool to help them appreciate the benefits that accrue from becoming computer literate. To those who have undertaken the challenge I wish every success in their future careers and I hope that in some small way this book will help them use their computer more effectively in whatever they wish to accomplish. Believe in yourself and your ability to succeed and the world is your oyster. God bless and good luck.

Introduction

What is CLAIT Plus?

CLAIT Plus is the second level qualification offered by the Oxford, Cambridge and RSA examinations awarding body in the Certificate for IT Users series of qualifications. These courses are primarily designed to help you develop skills that prepare you for using IT in the workplace although you may find such skills equally useful when using your software at home, for work or for recreational purposes. CLAIT Plus replaces the previous qualification IBT II, which covered databases, spreadsheets, desktop publishing, and Cambridge Information Technology. CLAIT Plus helps to build on skills covered at level 1 in New CLAIT.

There are no formal requirements for undertaking CLAIT Plus, but if you are intending to seek accreditation you may find it helpful to have completed an IT program at level 1 related to the National Qualifications Framework such as New CLAIT. CLAIT Plus is designed to give flexibility in terms of both the extent and pace of learning that suits you. The suite of applications offered in the overall qualification covers a wide range of generic software, ranging from the traditional spreadsheets, databases, presentation and desktop publishing applications to web page creation, electronic communications, computer art and charts and graphs.

How do I get certification?

To achieve a full certificate you will need to complete a core unit covering a variety of competencies and routine tasks, plus three of the optional units that allow you to demonstrate skills in a number of software applications. You do not need to take all the units at once. You can complete a single unit and gain certification for that unit. Alternatively you can complete the core unit and three optional units to gain full certification. Before undertaking the CLAIT Plus programme it is best to seek guidance from your centre tutor as to which options are most suited to your personal circumstances.

Once you have decided which units you wish to complete and have prepared yourself for an assignment you will be given up to three hours to complete each assignment. You do not have to do the assignment at one sitting but can split your time into several shorter periods. In other words, if you start on one day but only have time to complete one hour's worth of assignment you can carry on when next you attend the centre, continuing where you left off.

What are units?

A *unit* relates to an application and group of specific skills that have been identified as being needed in the modern workplace. OCR has liaised closely with industry and commerce to establish which IT skills will be relevant over the next few years and these skills are incorporated into the units that form the qualification. Each unit has its own syllabus containing a number of broad *learning outcomes*. So, for example, in the unit on databases, a learning outcome would be: create a database file, set up fields and enter records.

Units also have *assessment objectives*, which are skills for that unit. Within each assessment objective are a number of individual skills that make up the overall objective. Taking the database unit as an example the assessment obective may be:

Create and save database

The individual skills required under this objective are:

- set up field names
- set up data types for fields
- format fields
- set appropriate field lengths
- enter records
- save table/query/report.

Once you have covered all the assessment objectives within a unit you will be ready to take the assignment for that unit. The assignment tests your knowledge and understanding of some of the learning outcomes and assessment objectives covered by the unit.

How do I know which units will suit me?

Each unit within this book starts by highlighting the relevant broad and individual assessment objectives required to achieve certification. At the end of the book in Appendix 1 is a complete list of syllabuses for each unit covered in the CLAIT Plus qualification. By examining the syllabus first you can make an informed choice about which of the optional units you would prefer to take.

How to use this book

Mastering CLAIT Plus covers the skills you will need for all main applications covered in the CLAIT Plus syllabus. The most popular units are included in the book itself whilst other optional units that you may choose to do in place of units covered in the book (other than the compulsory unit, Unit 1) are included on the CD which accompanies this book in a .pdf (read only) format. If you choose to complete one of the units contained on the CD you may find it helpful to print a hard copy of the unit before starting.

The units included either in the book or on the CD are:

Core unit:	Unit 1	Create, manage and integrate files
Optional units:	Unit 2	Spreadsheets
	Unit 3	Databases
	Unit 4	Desktop publishing (this unit is on the CD)
	Unit 5	Presentation graphics
	Unit 6	Computer art (this unit is on the CD)

Unit 7	Web page creation
Unit 8	Electronic communication (this unit is on the CD)
Unit 9	Graphs and charts

First decide which subjects you would like to complete to gain the full Level 2 Certificate for IT Users (ÇLAIT Plus). You do not need to complete the units chosen in any particular order. Each unit covers all the skills you are required to have in order to gain certification. First the skill is identified and then you will be shown how to perform that particular skill. You will be given an opportunity of checking your own understanding of the explanations given through simple 'try it out' exercises. As you go through the unit you will follow a series of build-up exercises that help you develop the range of skills needed for the whole unit. Finally, at the end of each unit, you have the opportunity of completing a full practice exercise covering many of the skills covered in the unit. The process is the same for each unit so that you can become familiar with the underlying pattern throughout the book.

- The skills are identified and this is followed by an explanation of how to complete them.
- Once an explanation for a new skill has been given you are invited to carry out a simple 'try it out' exercise.
- At the end of each particular section is a list of skills that have been covered to check that you have understood each skill. Where you are not certain about how to complete a skill it may help to revisit that particular section.
- After a range of skills has been introduced you can complete a build-up exercise to practise the skills of that section.

Accompanying CD

On the CD accompanying this book are .pdf files covering Units 4, 6 and 8. In addition you will find a number of exercise files that have been produced for you to use in various try it out, build-up or full practice exercises.

The full formal CLAIT Plus syllabus for each unit is shown in Appendix 1.

Solutions for each full practical assignment can be found in Appendix 2.

Create, manage and integrate files

Five key assessment objectives

- Manage files and directories/folders
- Enter data accurately from data input sheets and amend existing data
- Create and print an integrated document
- Format page layout and manipulate text according to a house style
- Format tabular data

Each of these broad objectives covers a number of specific skills relating to the creation and management of files. A complete list of the individual skills for each objective can be found in Appendix 1.

In this unit you will learn how to:

- create, name, rename, move, copy and delete files and folders
- understand file types and formats
- open, close and save existing files
- print a file structure
- format a page layout and set text according to specified requirements
- apply a house style
- enter text, numbers and dates accurately and in a specified format
- move and delete text
- use headers and footers
- use automatically generated fields, such as dates
- create bullet and number lists
- amend a document and understand the uses and limitations of the spell checker
- use special symbols and characters
- use the search and replace function
- insert a table, set column/cell widths and alignment
- format table borders and shading
- apply table gridlines and alignment
- specify date formats
- import and manipulate images, charts and data files into a document
- use codes for efficient data entry.

Managing files

Being able to manage the storage of your data effectively and efficiently within a well mapped out file structure is arguably the most important lesson to learn when using a computer in either a business or the home environment. Having spent time and effort creating files, the essence of good file management is arranging them so they can be found quickly when you need to use or amend them. Amongst other requirements, which will be covered as you go through the unit, is the ability to access files that have been previously stored. You will need to be able to open and amend files from different applications and then integrate them into a single document. The files you use in exercises and the assessment are, generally, provided for you.

Consider a situation where you have been working on a document or report for weeks, or even months. The document may include extracts of spreadsheets, databases or graphical files. It is important for you to know where these files are kept, particularly if they are to be regularly updated. A logical file structure will help. There are no hard and fast rules about how folders should be arranged in your file structure, but they should be organised in a way that suits your work.

Viewing file structures

You can view and manipulate files and folders using Windows Explorer, which can be accessed through the Start menu or by selecting the My Computer shortcut on the desktop (see Figure 1.1).

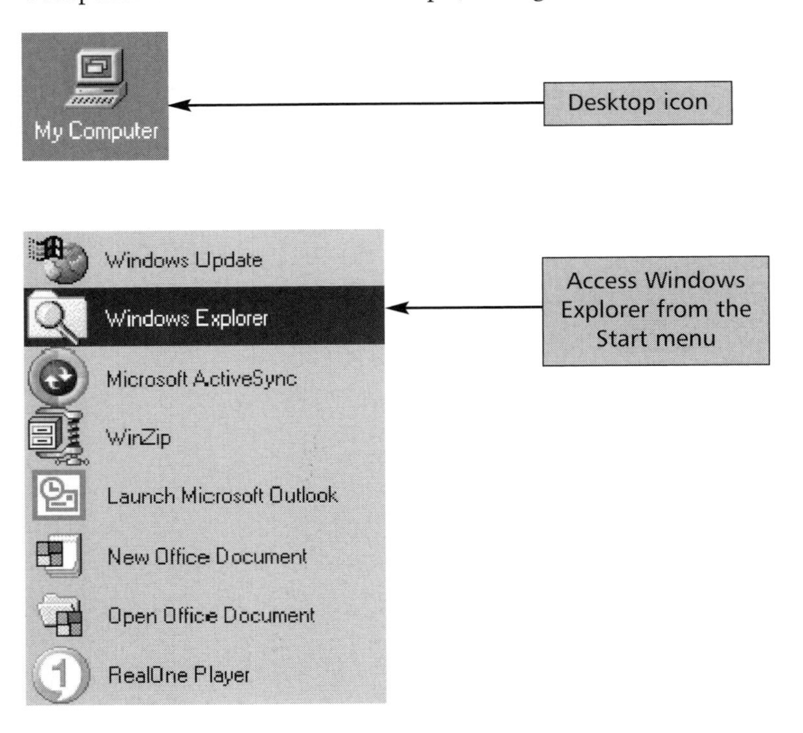

Figure 1.1

Which you choose is very much a matter of personal preference. The way in which you view the files can be altered depending on the options selected. For example, you may just wish to see the structure or folders in a particular area. Alternatively you may want to see the details of a file, such as its name, type, size or the date it was last modified. Figure 1.2 shows two fairly standard options. On the left of the picture is the Large Icon view and on the right the Details view allows more details of files contained in each folder to be seen.

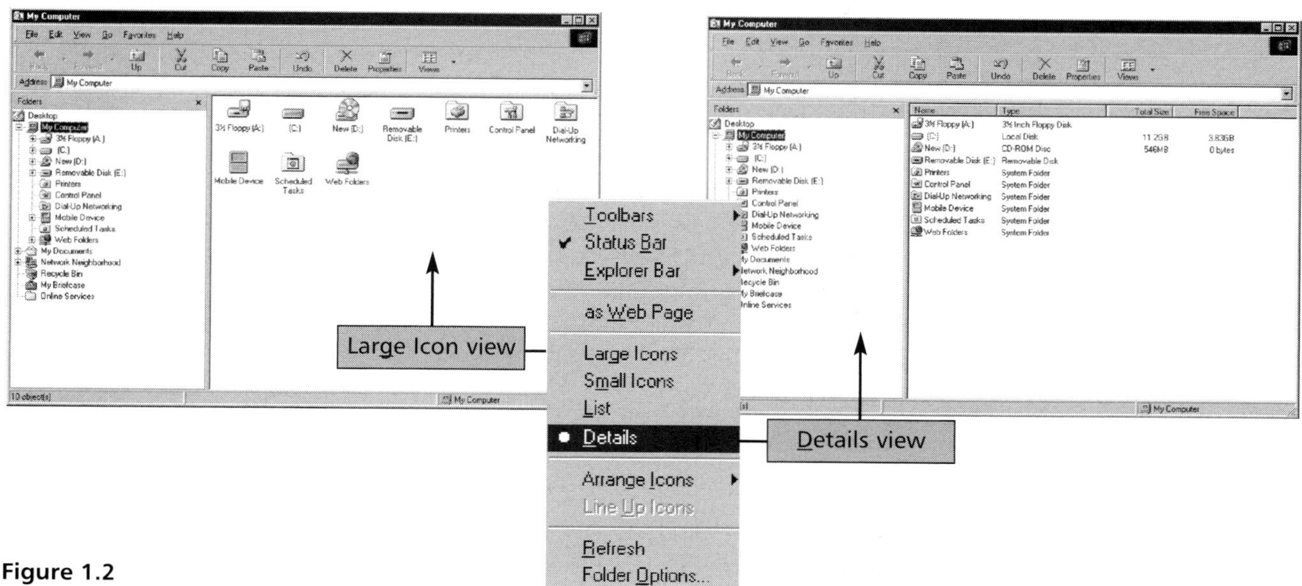

Figure 1.2

On the left-hand side of both views you can see the drive/folder structure for the whole computer. The view for your computer will differ depending largely on how it is set up and whether you have additional drive letters on your hard disk, or other external drives attached to the computer. The plus sign on the left side of the drive or folder indicates that there are further folders within that part of the file structure. Where there is a minus sign, or no sign at all, this indicates that the structure is fully expanded or there is nothing else to view.

Drive letters

In Figure 1.2 you can see four drive letters:

3½ Floppy (A:)
(C:)
New (D:)
Removable Disk (E:)

The 3½ Floppy (A:) relates to the standard floppy disk drive and the (C:) to the hard disk on the computer. New (D:) is the CD drive where the CD currently inserted into the drive contains data, but the disk itself simply has the default name 'New'. If there were no disk inserted in the drive you would just see (D:), the drive letter. Removable Disk (E:) refers, in this instance, to an external Zip drive. You may have a number of other letters depending on how your hard disk has been configured and what devices there are attached to your computer. For example, large hard disks are often divided into two or more drives and each would have its own drive letter, assigned at the time the disk was partitioned.

Folders

You can think of the drives as buildings housing your data. As with organisations, different functions can be carried out in different buildings and so it is with drives, each performing a similar but different task. In a building you would expect to see offices with filing cabinets. These hold folders that themselves contain files holding important information about the business or organisation. Folders in a file structure carry out virtually the same function where folders are created and named according to how you want to access your files. When your computer is set up a number of folders containing a variety of files will automatically form part of the folder and file structure on your hard disk. For example, when Windows is installed it creates a number of default folders such as:

- My Documents
- Program Files
- Windows

There are a number of others that you don't need to worry about now. As the name suggests, the Program Files folder contains folders for each program installed on your computer. The Windows folder similarly contains files associated with the Windows operating system. Many of the folders will have sub-folders, which in turn may have further sub-folders. In other words the structure is hierarchical. Have a look at Figure 1.3.

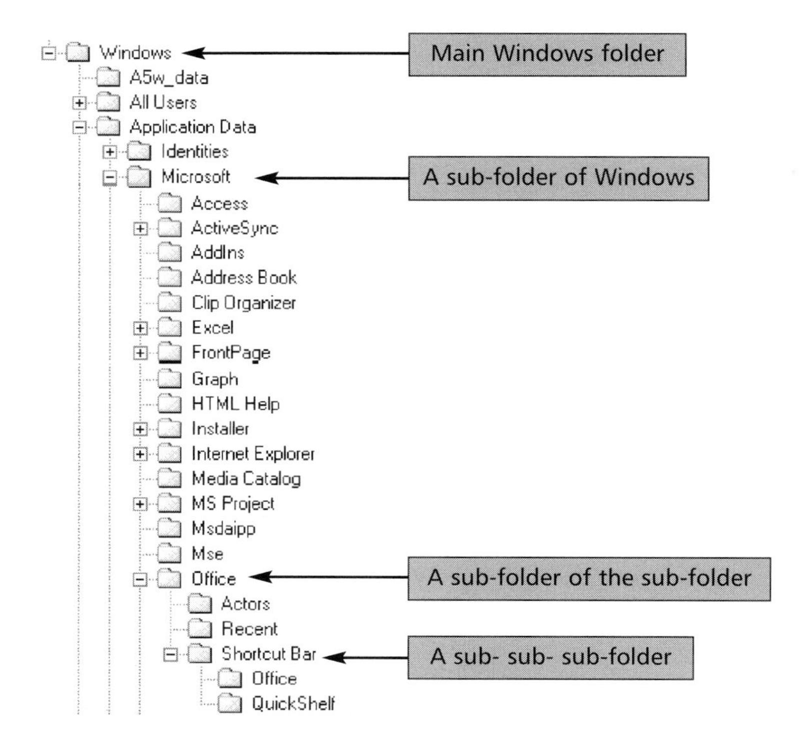

Figure 1.3

Here you have the main folder Windows and a number of sub-folders. Some of these will themselves have a number of sub-folders. The figure shows clearly the hierarchical nature of the structure. It is important that you do not try to alter, move, delete or otherwise tamper with files in these folders as you could prevent either a program, or Windows, from working properly. Most of the files in these folders are known as either program or system files and should be treated carefully if you are not familiar with how they work.

Designing a file structure

For the most part you will only be interested in managing your own data files. These are the files you create using one of the Microsoft or other software applications. Windows Explorer provides the basic folder for you to start developing your structure and this is called My Documents. You do not have to use this folder as the starting point for your file structure but you will find it much easier if you treat the My Documents as the top of your structure.

As mentioned above, how you develop your structure depends largely on your organisation, the type of data files you use and any system you design that helps you to find files quickly.

The following is offered simply as a guide on how you might approach the task of building a structure. There are no hard and fast rules. You might choose to have a structure that relates simply to topics and subject matters or you might decide that files should be separated depending on the application they are associated with or indeed a mixture of both. In Figure 1.4 the example structure is based on data separated by application and then subject. Your wordprocessing files may have a folder for financial matters called simply 'Finance', one for 'Insurance', 'Maintenance', 'Meetings' and so on. Each folder would possibly have sub-folders, similar to those shown in the 'Meetings' folder.

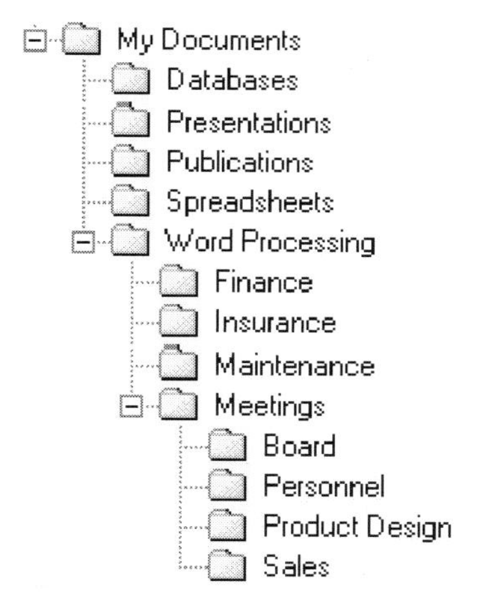

Figure 1.4

The system is flexible and can accommodate almost any structure or naming convention you need. However, you should also be careful that your structure does not cause the very problem you are trying to avoid by having too many folders. This can lead to difficulty in finding a file when you are unsure which folder it belongs in. As in all things, there is a balance to be struck.

How to create a file structure

To create a folders structure start at the top of the hierarchy. In this case My Documents will be at the top of the structure. You can check that the My Documents folder has been selected by clicking on My Documents and then looking at the Address box at the top of the window: see Figure 1.5.

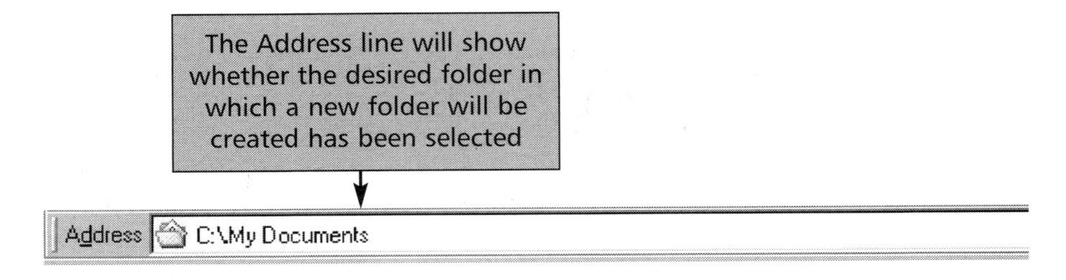

Figure 1.5

Once My Documents is selected a new folder can be added by choosing File, New, Folder from the main menu. When Folder is clicked, Windows Explorer creates a new folder with the default name 'New Folder' New Folder.

Notice how the lettering of New Folder is already highlighted ready for you to overtype the personalised name you want for the folder. If for any reason you click outside the folder box before overtyping the name it is easy to rename the folder by placing the cursor over the folder and clicking on the right-hand mouse button. This will bring up the menu list shown in Figure 1.6.

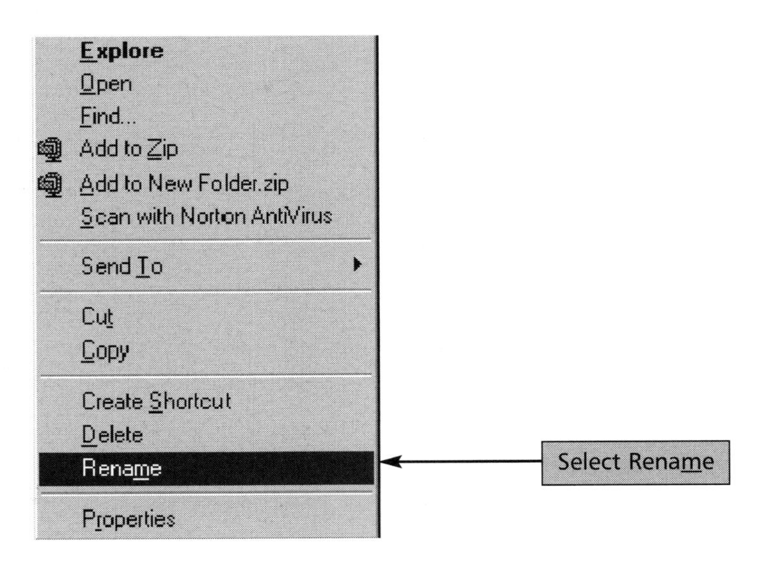

Figure 1.6

Select the Rename option and notice how the New Folder name is once again highlighted ready for you to type in the required name for the folder. By typing 'Wordprocessing' over the name New Folder a new folder has been created in My Documents called Wordprocessing. From here you can either create another sub-folder in My Documents or a new sub-folder of Wordprocessing.

Adding additional folders is equally straightforward. First ensure that the place you want to create the folder is shown in the Address box at the top of the window. If My Documents is showing and you want to create a folder in Wordprocessing simply click on Wordprocessing and when you see it showing in the Address box, repeat the same process as before.

By now you should have the general idea, so have a go at creating a new folder using a floppy disk. The principle for creating a structure on a floppy disk is exactly the same as on the hard drive.

Try it out

Scenario

Assume you have decided to set up a structure for exercises on subjects you want to cover in CLAIT Plus. For the purpose of this exercise you will set up a structure that contains the following folders:

Folder hierarchy
Main folder: CLAIT Plus
Sub-folders: Computer Art; Databases; Managing Files; Spreadsheets.

Insert a new floppy disk into your disk drive.

Click Windows Explorer (or My Computer if you prefer).

Click on 3½ Floppy (A:).

Note: if you use My Computer instead of Windows Explorer you will need to double-click on 3½ Inch (A:) Floppy Disk.

Select File, New, Folder.

Type 'CLAIT Plus' over the name New Folder.

Click outside your new folder to accept the change.

Click on your new folder CLAIT Plus.

Select File, New, Folder.

Type 'Computer Art' as your sub-folder of CLAIT Plus.

Now repeat this exercise to make new sub-folders in the CLAIT Plus folder for Databases, Managing Files and Spreadsheets.

Your structure should now look like Figure 1.7.

Figure 1.7

You now decide to change the Managing Files folder name to File Management.

Move the cursor so that it is over the folder Managing Files.

Click on the right-hand mouse button.

Select Rename.

Type 'File Management' as the new name for your folder.

How to copy, move and delete files

In the previous section you learnt how to create and rename folders. The process for copying, moving and deleting files is virtually the same as that for renaming a folder or file. There are, however, certain aspects of these processes about which it is useful to know. For example, when you copy a file from one folder to another you will end up with two versions of the same file but in different folders. The original version will still be available in the folder from where the file was copied and there will also be a copy in the folder it was copied to. What you cannot do is have two files of the same name in the same folder. When you move a folder or file, you physically move it from one location to another and therefore you end up with the same folder or file but put in a different location on your hard or floppy disk. When you delete a folder or file from your *hard disk* it is first sent to the recycle bin which gives you an opportunity of restoring it a later date, providing the recycle bin has not been emptied. If you delete a file from a *floppy disk* you cannot recover it easily as it does not go to the recycle bin.

Try it out

Insert the floppy disk containing the folder structure completed in the previous Try it out exercise. Insert the CD accompanying this book into the CD drive.

Open Windows Explorer.

Locate the file named Computer Art in the sub-folder Managing Files in Unit 1 on the CD accompanying this book.

Click on the file Computer Art using the right-hand mouse button so that the file is highlighted (see Figure 1.8).

From the menu list that appears:

Select Copy.

Open the folder called File Management on the 3½ Floppy (A:).

Click on the right-hand mouse button.

Select Paste from the menu list (see Figure 1.9).

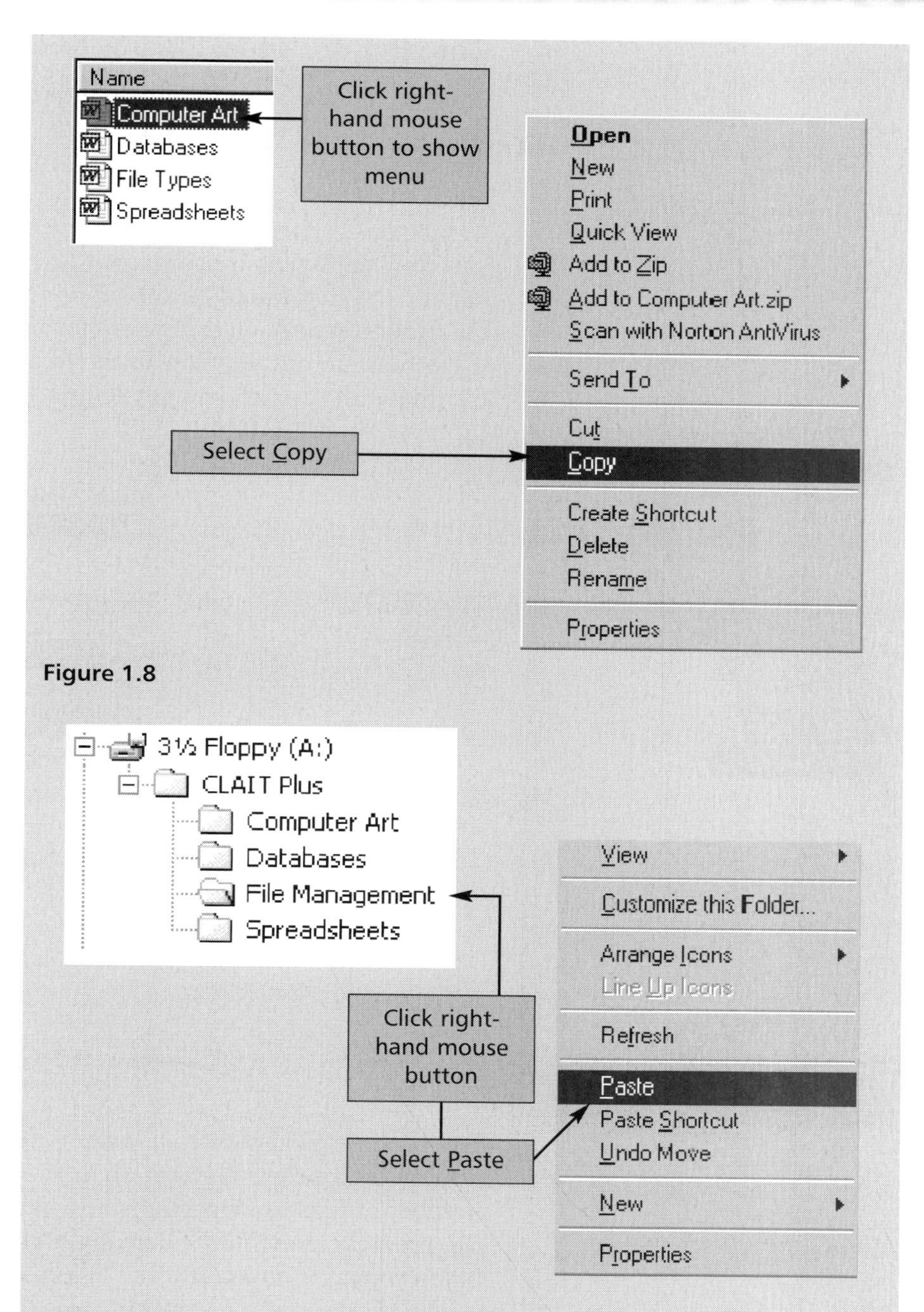

Figure 1.8

Figure 1.9

If you have the File Management folder selected you should see that the file Computer Art has been copied.

Note: remember that when a file is copied from a CD it may have a *read-only* property. In this case if you want to use and change the file you must open it and use the Save As… feature. Alternatively you can change the file's property in Windows Explorer by clicking on the file using the right-hand mouse button and selecting Properties. In the dialogue box uncheck the Read-only property and select the Apply button.

Copying multiple files in one move

Copying more than one file at a time is more or less the same as copying a single file. The benefits are mainly that if you have a number of files to copy you need only go through the copy and paste process once.

First select the files that are to be copied. If the files are all together you can use the lasso approach. Click the left-hand mouse button outside the first file to be copied and then drag the cursor over each file in turn before releasing the button. This will highlight all the files. If the files are not together in the folder then you can select the first file and with the Ctrl key pressed down select each file to be copied in turn (see Figure 1.10).

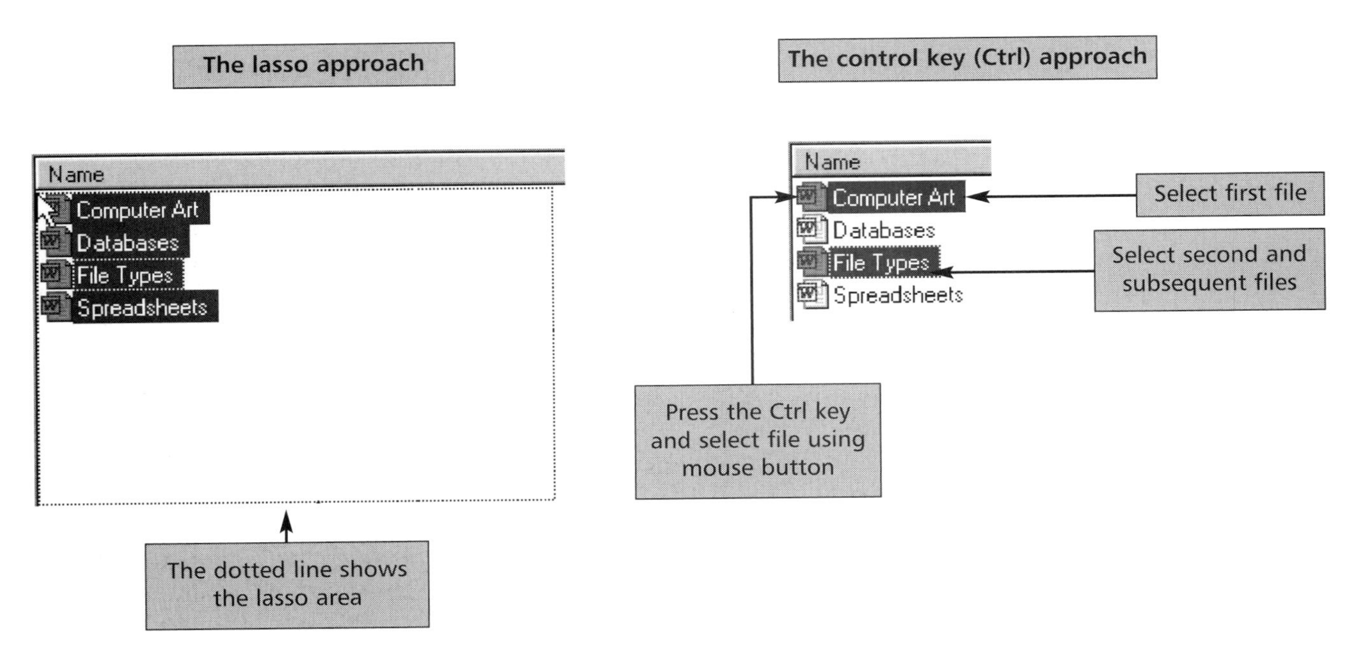

Figure 1.10

The files are then copied in exactly the same way as a single file and also pasted to their destination in the same way. When there are a number of files to be copied you will see a dialogue box that tells you the progress made in the copying cycle, and also both where the file is being copied from and to: see Figure 1.11.

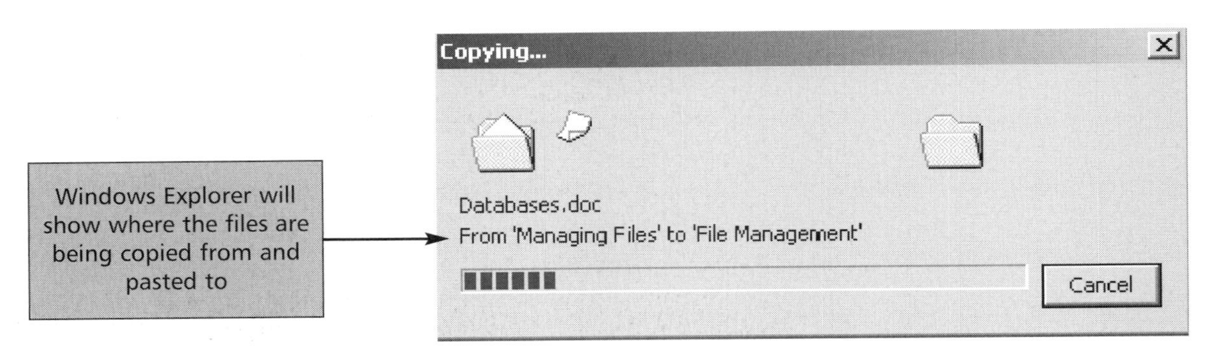

Figure 1.11

Try it out

Open the folder called Managing Files on the CD.

Copy the files called:

Databases

File Types

Spreadsheets

to the folder called File Management on your floppy disk.

Moving a file

In the last exercise you copied a number of files from the Managing Files folder on the CD to the File Management folder on your floppy disk. Suppose you now decide that you actually want each file in the appropriate folder. For example, you want the Databases file in the Databases folder and the Computer Art file in the Computer Art folder, and so on. There are a number of ways you could achieve the same result. You could copy the respective file in the Managing Files folder and paste it to the new folder and then delete the original file, but this would be time consuming. You could cut the file from the first folder and paste it to the appropriate folder, but you always run the risk of losing the file altogether. The easiest method is to highlight the file and drag it to the folder you want it to reside in.

To do this, simply highlight the file you want to move and literally drag it across to the folder you want to move it to. Have a look at Figure 1.12.

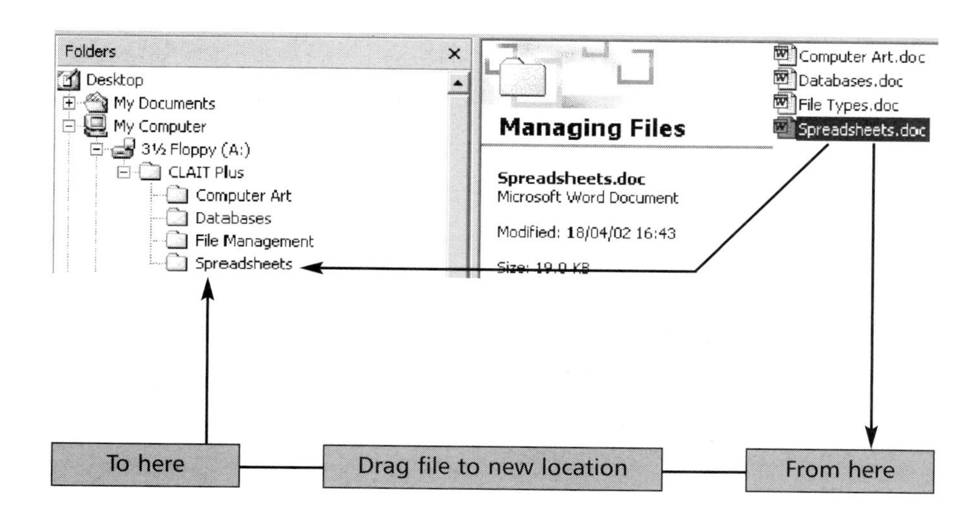

Figure 1.12

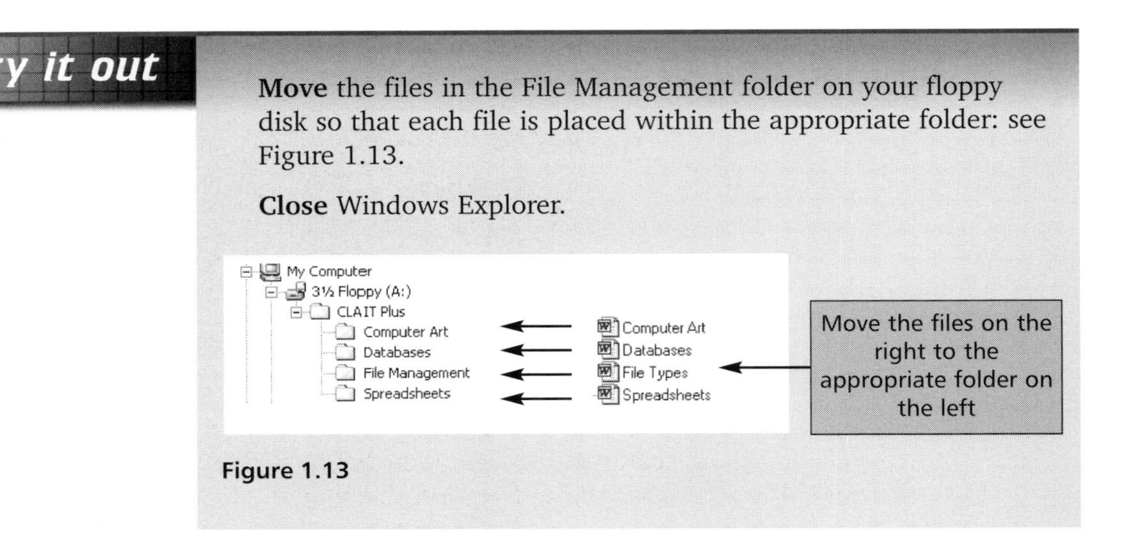

Try it out

Move the files in the File Management folder on your floppy disk so that each file is placed within the appropriate folder: see Figure 1.13.

Close Windows Explorer.

Figure 1.13

As was the case for copying files, if you have a number of files to move, and provided they are all going to the same folder, you can highlight all or selected files and drag them to their new destination.

Deleting a file or folder

To delete a file (or folder) place the cursor over the file/folder to be deleted and then press the right-hand mouse button. A menu list will appear. Select the Delete option. If it is a folder you are deleting and there are currently files in the folder, Windows Explorer will ask if you wish to delete the folder and all its contents. If it is simply a single file Windows Explorer will still offer you the chance of changing your mind by displaying the dialogue box shown in Figure 1.14.

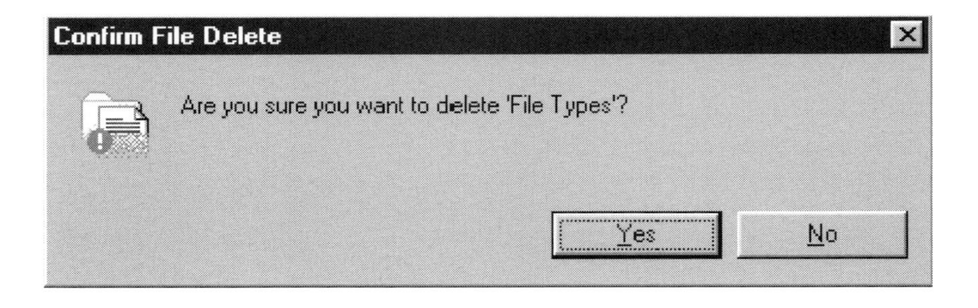

Figure 1.14

Press the Yes button to continue with the deletion and the No if you want to check if you have the correct file. Remember if you are deleting from the floppy disk you cannot reverse the process once you have confirmed the deletion.

Restoring a deleted file

To restore a deleted a file from your hard disk simply double-click on the Recycle Bin on the desktop, highlight the file that you wish to restore and then select the Restore button.

Try it out

Create a new folder called Test on your floppy disk.

Copy the file **Test File** 1 located in the Samples Files sub-folder in the Unit 1 main folder on the CD, to the new folder Test on your floppy disk.

Delete the folder and file **Test File 1** on your floppy disk.

Understanding file types and formats

Files have a variety of functions. Some deal with the systems in your computer whilst others have specific functions in running and managing programs. The majority of files you will have direct dealings with are ones that contain information relating to a particular application, such as a wordprocessor, spreadsheet or database type of file.

All files can be identified by file extensions. These extensions help to identify the type and function of a file. Extensions come at the end of a file name, separated from the name of the file by a dot similar to a full stop. An example of this may, for instance, be a wordprocessor data file such as **MyLetter.doc**. Here 'MyLetter' is the name given to the file, while the '.doc' signifies that the program associated with the file is Microsoft Word. Knowing what the file extensions of individual files mean can be useful in helping you to locate a file (or groups of files) of a particular type or program. The list of file types is virtually endless but some will become more familiar than others. Table 1.1 shows the extension identifiers for some Microsoft programs that you may come across in the course of your CLAIT Plus studies.

Table 1.1

File or application type	File extension
WORD	.doc
ACCESS	.mdb
EXCEL	.xls
POWERPOINT	.ppt
PUBLISHER	.pub
PAINT	.bmp
OUTLOOK	.pst
WEB PAGE	.htm
NOTEBOOK	.txt
WORDPAD	.rtf

As a general rule most modern, generic software packages can either read each other's formats or they will convert them into a form that can be read. For example, probably the most common type of file for the average user is the text file. Each proprietary wordprocessing package will have its own file extension. As you have already seen Word has the file extension '.doc'. WordPerfect, another popular wordprocessing package, uses a file extension '.wpd'. Most modern processors will read either format, but you also have the option of using simple text files formats such as:

- Rich Text Format (.rtf)
- text files (.txt).

Rich Text Format
Rich Text Format (.rtf) files will save your work with its formatting, and allow users of different programs to open and read or amend your document with the format you created in the original file.

Text files
Saving your work as text (.txt) files means that users of other programs will be able to open them, but none of the formatting (such as bold, underlining and so on) will be saved with the file.

Opening, closing and saving files

Opening a file

One of the benefits of understanding extensions, as has already been mentioned, is the ease with which you can identify the type of file and hence its associated application. In Figure 1.15 you can see a selection of different file types as shown in Windows Explorer. Some are graphic files and have an extension of .jpg or .gif which identifies them as pictures. A file with .sys identifies it as a system file and these should not be tampered with. The file with the extension .exe shows it is an application file; double-clicking on this type of file will open the related application.

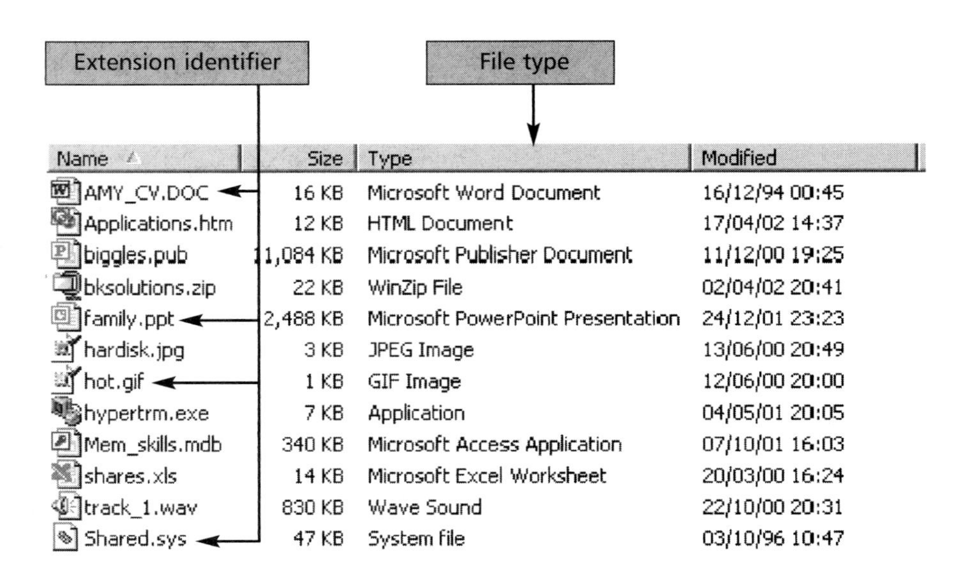

Figure 1.15

Where the file is a data file, with an extension such as .doc, .mdb or .xls, it is related to an application. By double-clicking on it the data file will be opened in the relevant application.

Normally you will open a data file from within the application to which it is related. All applications within the Microsoft Office suite of applications have a main menu bar similar to that shown in Figure 1.16.

Figure 1.16

By selecting the File option on the main menu and then Open (Figure 1.17),

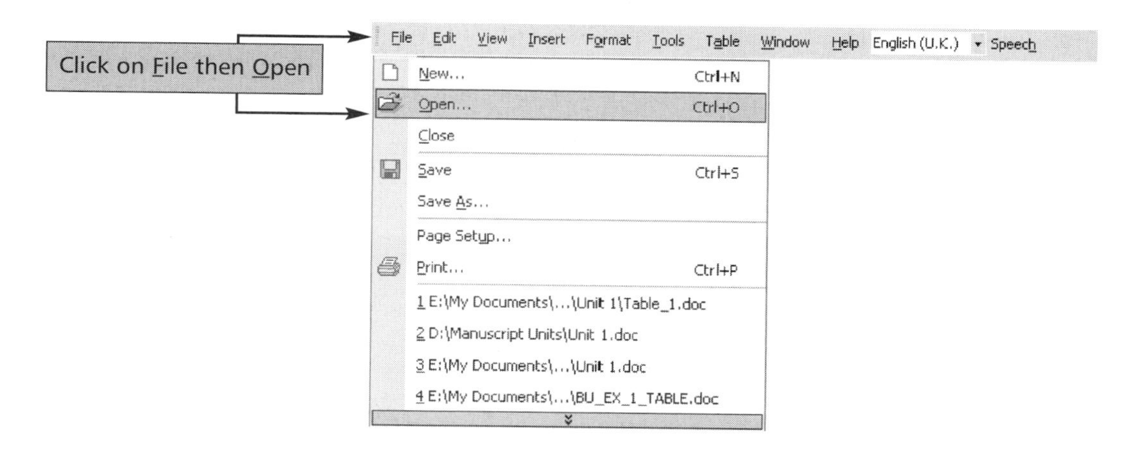

Figure 1.17

the Open File dialogue box will appear as shown in Figure 1.18. This allows you to locate and open the required file. First, the appropriate folder is selected by pressing on the down arrow to the right of the Look in: box. Next the required file from those shown in the main part of the window is highlighted and finally the Open command button located on the bottom right is pressed.

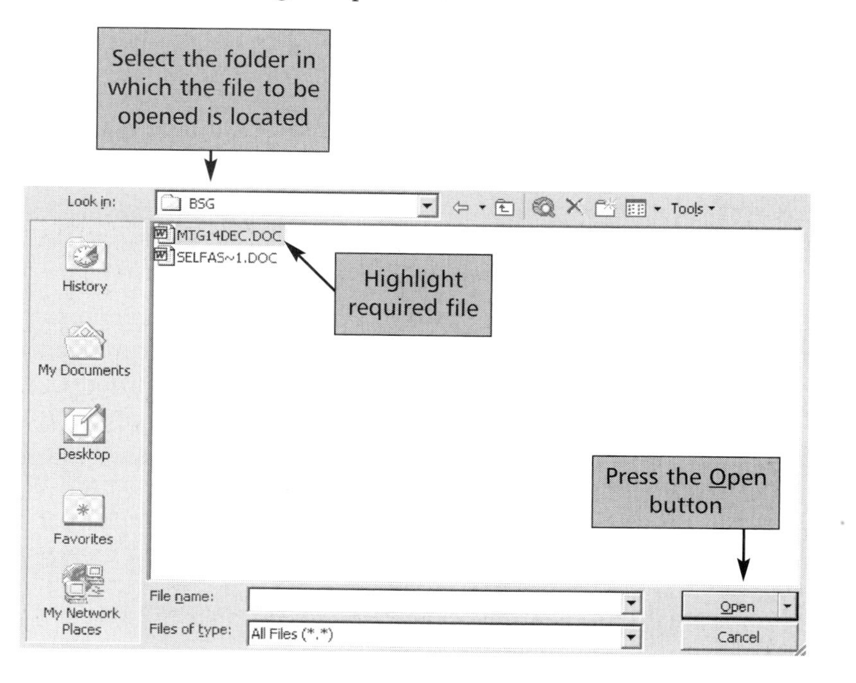

Figure 1.18

Closing a file

Generally speaking the procedure to close a file in any of the Office applications is the same, although there are minor variations for Access and FrontPage. These are covered later in the book. For programs such as Word, Excel and PowerPoint there are three standard options.

Option 1
Select Close from the File option on the main menu.

Option 2
Press the close icon on the standard toolbar.

Option 3
Press the close window button (the cross) in the top right of the screen shown in Figure 1.19.

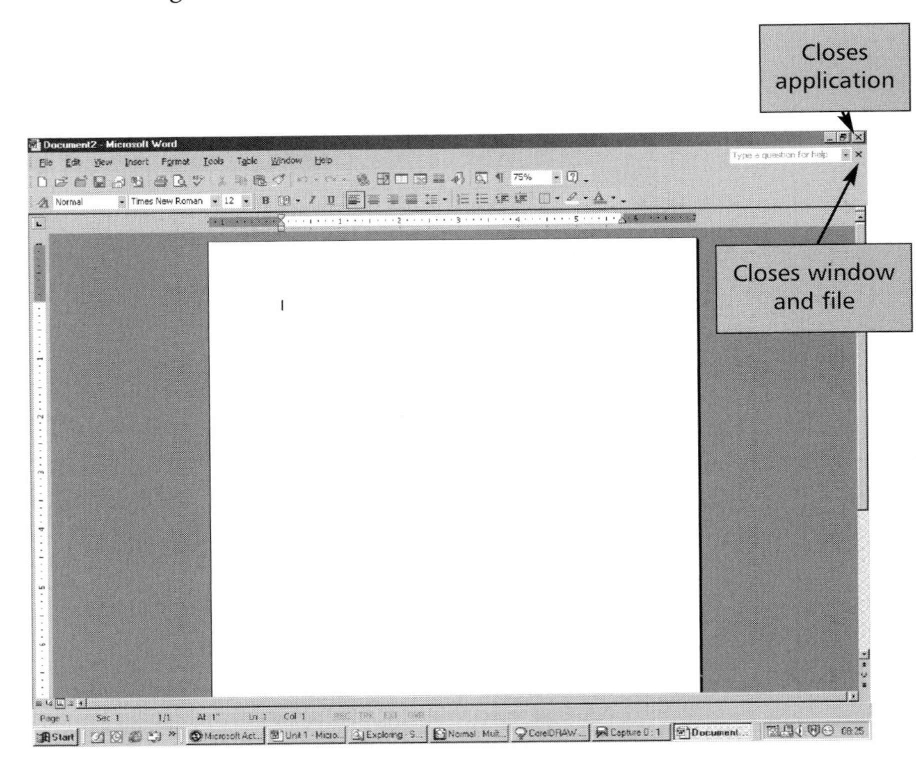

Figure 1.19

Saving files

If you have used computers previously or have completed New CLAIT, opening, closing and saving files will not be new to you. However, being able to save files properly and in such a way that they are easily located for future use is probably one of the most important skills to learn. The importance of setting up your folder structure was emphasised earlier in this unit. When you start saving files the need for this becomes very apparent.

Files can be saved and stored on a number of devices:

- the hard disk
- a floppy disk

- a CD (if you have a CD-write facility)
- a zip or tape drive.

For CLAIT Plus you will only be expected to know about saving files to a hard or floppy disk. Although the procedure for saving files in most of the Office applications (with the exception of Access and FrontPage) is the same (or similar) this unit concentrates on saving files for Microsoft Word. As you learn other applications for CLAIT Plus differences in specific programs will be explained.

Save and Save As

To save a newly created document the Save option is selected from the main menu. This opens the Save As dialogue box shown in Figure 1.20.

Figure 1.20

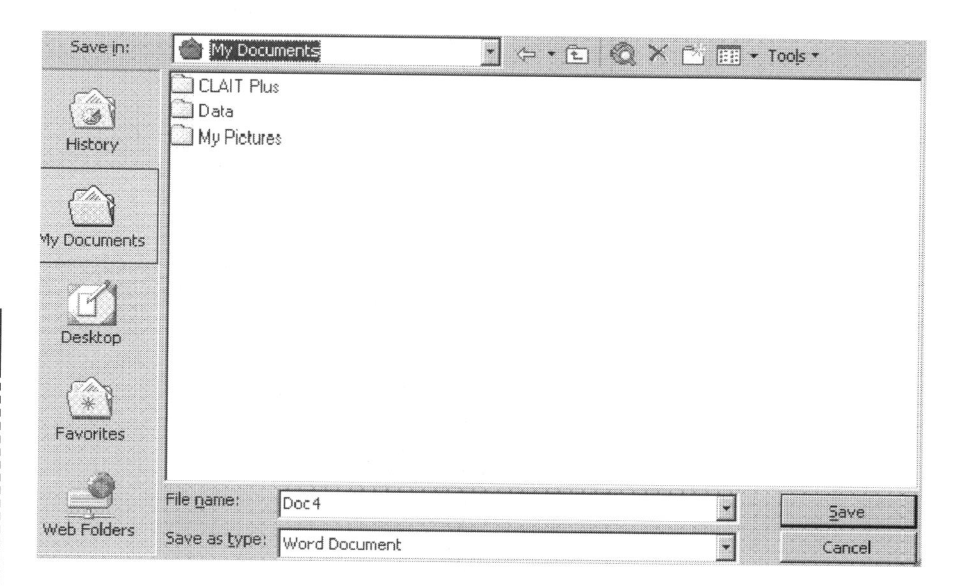

Word will, by default, offer the My Documents folder as the starting point to locate the folder you want to save your document.

> **SAVING TIP**
>
> You can always change the default folder by selecting Options... from Tools on the main menu. The Options dialogue box will appear as in Figure 1.21.
>
> Select the File Locations tab and press the Modify... button. Using the arrow to the right of the Look in: box select the folder you want Word initially to offer for saving your documents.
>
> **Note:** If you are saving to your hard disk, the folder names, other than My Documents, will be different to those shown in Figure 1.22 as they will represent whatever folder structure you have set up for your own computer.

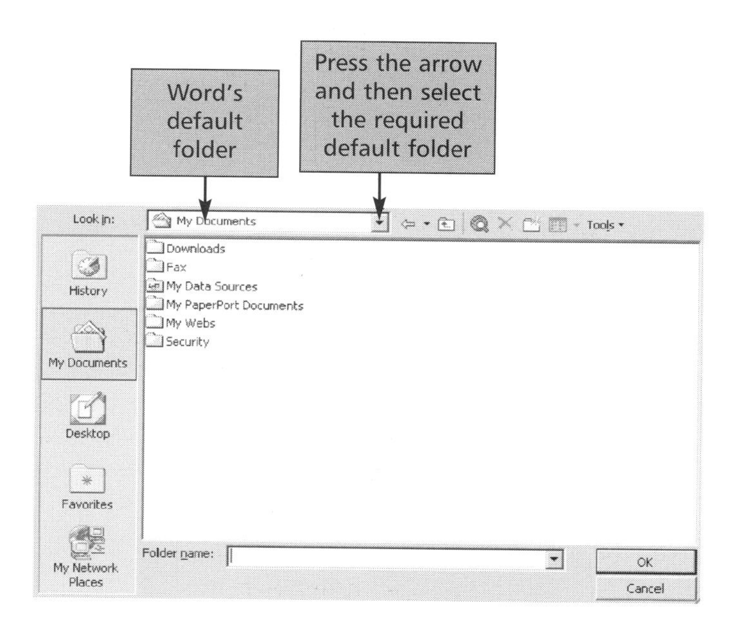

Figure 1.21

To save your file to a floppy disk, simply select 3½ Floppy (A:) from the drop-down menu shown in Figure 1.22.

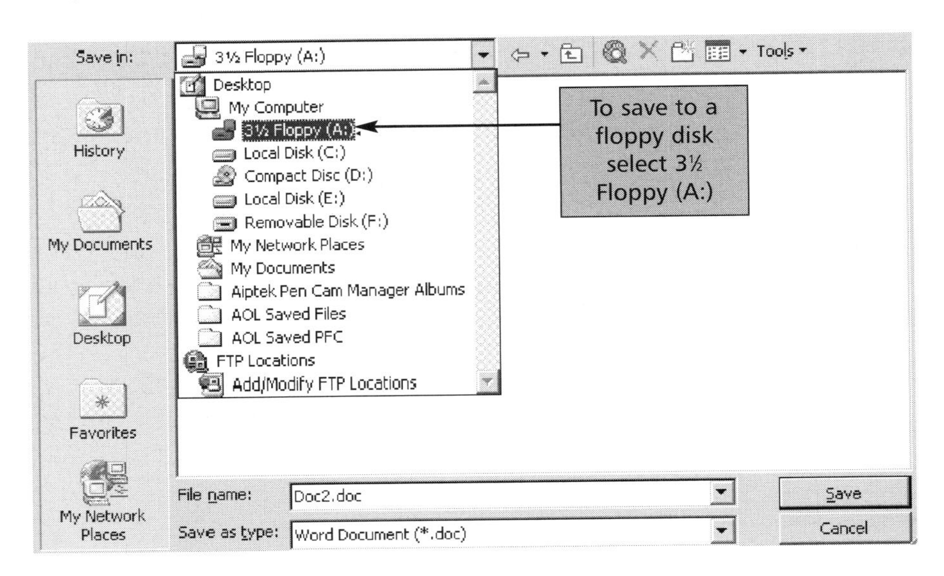

Figure 1.22

Once a file has been saved, Word will always remember its location. You should get into the habit of saving your work regularly. There is nothing more frustrating than spending a long time on a piece of work only to lose it because of a computer 'hang up' or a power failure or some similar catastrophe. To save new work on a file once it has been initially saved, simply click on the save icon or select Save from the File option on the main menu. You will not be shown the Save As dialogue box again,as Word is already aware of the file's location.

Note: If you are saving to a floppy disk keep the disk in your 'A' drive until you have finished and closed the file on which you are working.

SAVING TIP

Automatic file saving

You can set Word to save your work automatically at regular intervals. Select Options... from Tools on the main menu. Enter the interval of time that Word is to save your work as shown in Figure 1.23.

Security | Spelling & Grammar | Track Changes
User Information | Compatibility | File Locations
View | General | Edit | Print | Save

Save options
Always create backup copy
Allow fast saves
Allow background saves
Embed TrueType fonts
Embed characters in use only
Do not embed common system fonts
Make local copy of files stored on network or removable drives
Save AutoRecover info every: 10 minutes
Embed smart tags
Save smart tags as XML properties in Web pages
Prompt for document properties
Prompt to save Normal template
Save data only for forms
Embed linguistic data

Set the interval for saving here

Default format
Save Word files as: Word Document (*.doc)
Disable features introduced after: Microsoft Word 97

OK | Cancel

Figure 1.23

TIP

Opening generic files

Generic files such as '.txt' (text) or '.rtf' (Rich Text) files are opened in exactly the same way as any other file. Simply select File, Open… on the main menu. When the Open dialogue box appears make sure the Files of type: field at the bottom of the dialogue box has the relevant generic file format selected, e.g. Text Files or Rich Text Format.

Save As

There will be occasions when you wish to save your file as something other than the file you initially saved. For example, you may want to make minor changes to a document you use on a regular basis but keep the original unaltered. This could be where the main text of the original remains more or less the same with only changes to dates or figures; this may be the case for a monthly report or a repetitive message to friends or colleagues. Alternatively you may want to save a document in a different format. For example, if you opened or imported a generic file such as a text or Rich Text formatted file you may wish to save the file in a Word or other wordprocessing software format or an html web page.

To do this select Save As… from the File option on the main menu. You will see the Save As dialogue box as you did when you initially saved the file for the first time. You can now select another location or change the format of the file as shown in Figure 1.24.

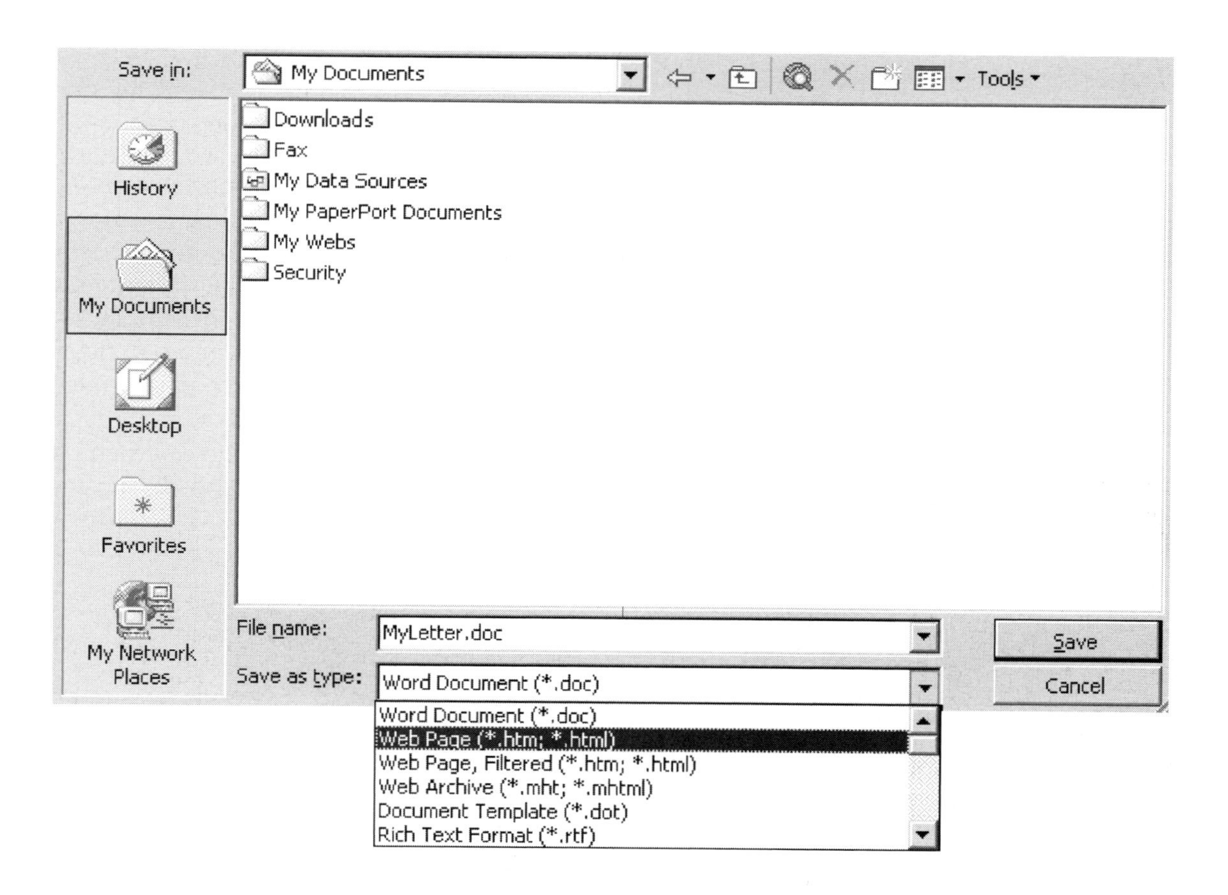

Figure 1.24

Notice how the file name now appears in the File name: box. Here you can give the file a different name from the original. If you are changing the format you can keep the original name if you wish.

Try it out

Insert the floppy disk with your file structure into the A: drive.

Create a new sub-folder called My Exercises in the File Management folder.

Copy the file **The_Village_Web_Site.rtf** from the folder Sample Files (Unit 1) on the CD to your new folder My Exercises.

Open the file **The_ Village_Web_Site.rtf**.

Save the file as **Village_Web.doc** (i.e. as a Word document).

Close the file.

Delete the file **The_ Village_Web_Site.doc** from the folder My Exercises.

Re-open the file **The_Village_Web_Site.rtf.**

Save the file with an html (webpage) format in the same folder (My Exercises).

Close the html file **Village_Web.htm**.

Printing a file structure

For CLAIT Plus you will be expected to produce a printout of your folder structure or the contents of your folders. Unlike printing a normal document there is no facility to print the structure directly using a print function in Explorer. To overcome this you can use the PrtScn button that is found on the keyboard. Pressing the PrtScn (short for 'print screen') copies an image of the complete window to the clipboard. Once the screen has been copied, the image can be pasted into a document and printed off.

As you may have found before, the image can then be manipulated in the same way as any graphic can be modified. The easiest way to find out how this works is to have a go.

WINDOWS TIP

To move between open applications press and hold down the Alt key and then use the tab key to move between the windows. As a window is shown release the Alt key and that window will become the active window.

Try it out

Insert the floppy disk containing your file structure into the A: drive.

Create a new document in Word.

Open Windows Explorer.

Make sure that all of your file structure is fully expanded. For example, if there is a + sign against a folder, click on it to expand and show the sub-folders.

Click on the sub-folder named My Exercises to view the files **Village_Web.doc** and **Village_Web.htm.**

Press the PrtScn button on your keyboard.

Tab back to your new Word document.

Select Paste from the Edit option on the main menu. (Alternatively press the right-hand mouse button to show the menu list and select Paste or press the Ctrl+V keyboard keys to paste the image.)

The screen dump picture of the file structure should look similar to that shown in Figure 1.25.

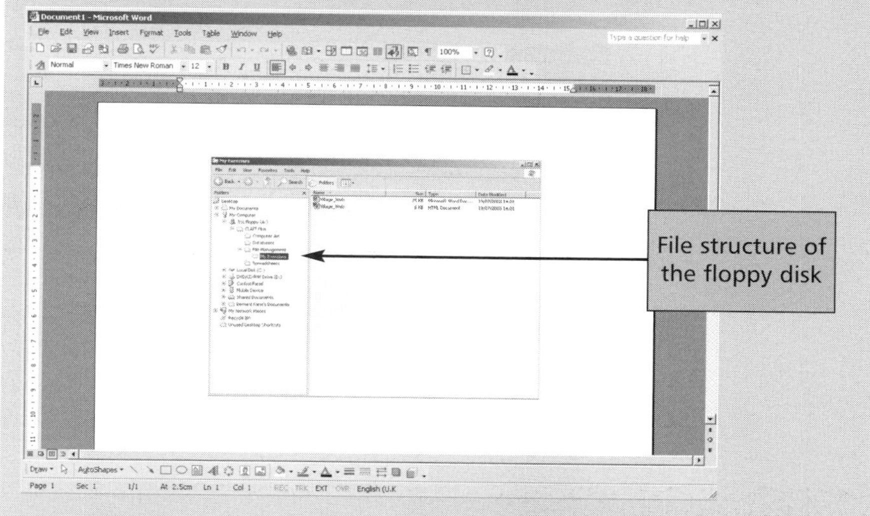

Figure 1.25

Note: your structure will be slightly different to that shown in Figure 1.25, but the structure for the floppy disk should be the same.

Cropping a picture

Whilst this printout is perfectly acceptable it includes more of the structure than is required, so for clarity it is better to crop the image to show just the relevant information. By clicking on the graphic, the Picture toolbar will activate as shown in Figure 1.26.

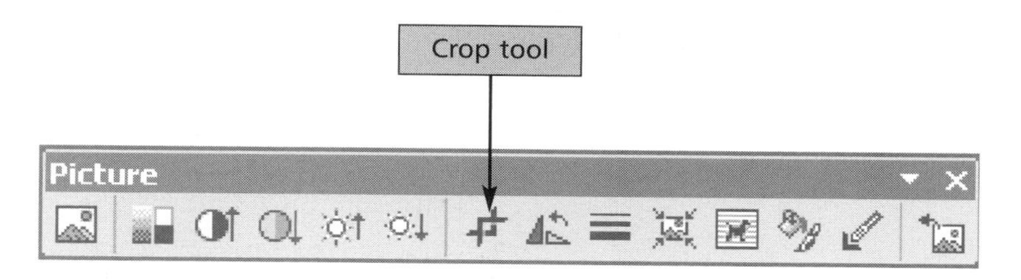

Figure 1.26

This toolbar allows you to edit a picture's contrast, brightness, orientation (rotate it), and a number of other features that you may wish to look at when you have time. However, also included on the toolbar is the crop tool which looks something like a square with overlapping sides. By highlighting the graphic and then selecting the crop tool you can adjust the area of the picture to be viewed. If you place the cursor over one of the picture's size handles and drag in the desired direction you can crop the image to suit your needs. Have a look at Figure 1.27.

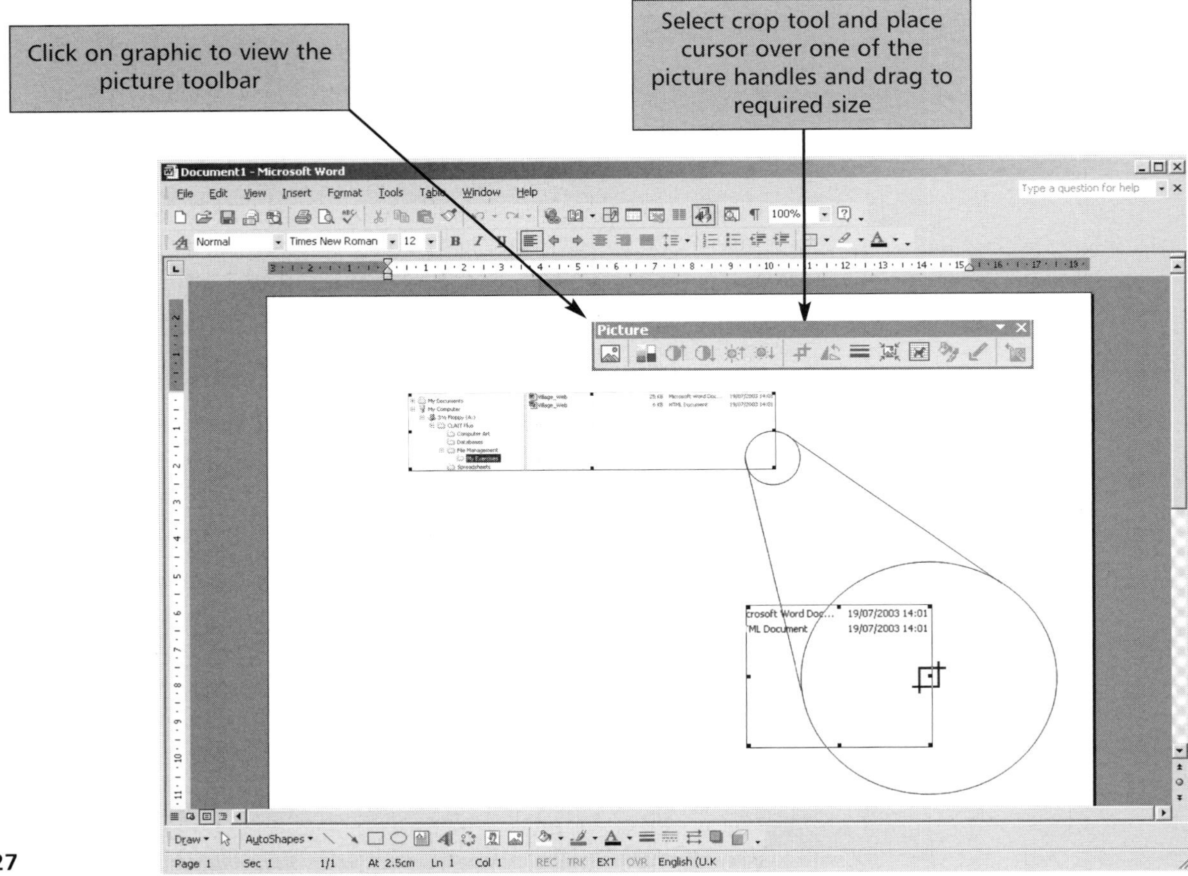
Click on graphic to view the picture toolbar
Select crop tool and place cursor over one of the picture handles and drag to required size
Document1 - Microsoft Word
Picture
Microsoft Word Doc... 19/07/2003 14:01
ML Document 19/07/2003 14:01

Figure 1.27

Here you can see that the picture has been cropped to show just the file structure of the floppy disk.

Try it out

Crop the file structure image so that only the floppy disk file structure and the files **Village_Web.doc** and **Village_Web.htm** can be viewed.

Print the document.

Save the document and image on your floppy disk as **My_Files**.

You should now be able to:

- create a folder structure
- rename a folder or file

- move and copy files to different locations
- delete a file or folder
- understand about different file formats
- open and close a file
- save a file in a required location
- save a file with a different format
- print a screen dump of a file structure and relevant files.

Understanding how to format a page layout and manipulate text according to a house style

For CLAIT Plus you will be expected to produce a single integrated document based on a specified house style. House styles are instructions describing how a document is to be presented and formatted. House style instructions will include formats such as:

- paper size
- orientation
- margin sizes
- spacing
- font type, style and size
- text alignment
- required headers and footers
- page numbering
- table formats.

In the next part of this unit you will learn how to use the page setup and format text and numbers facilities to conform to a given house style.

Page setup

The Page setup dialogue box, selected from the File option on the main menu, allows you set the basic format parameters for your document. Have a look at Figure 1.28.

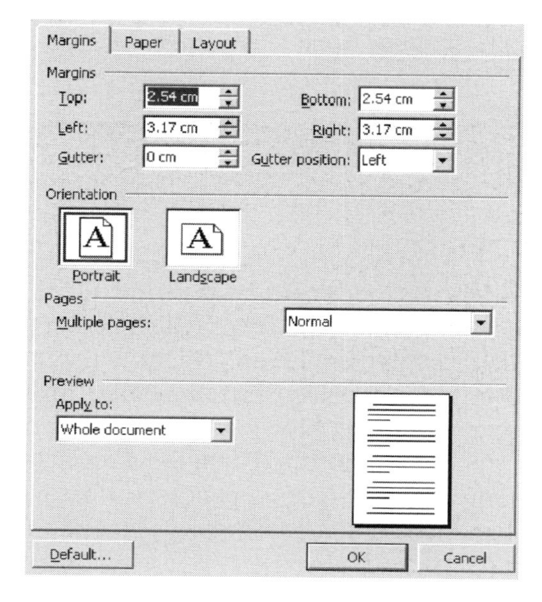

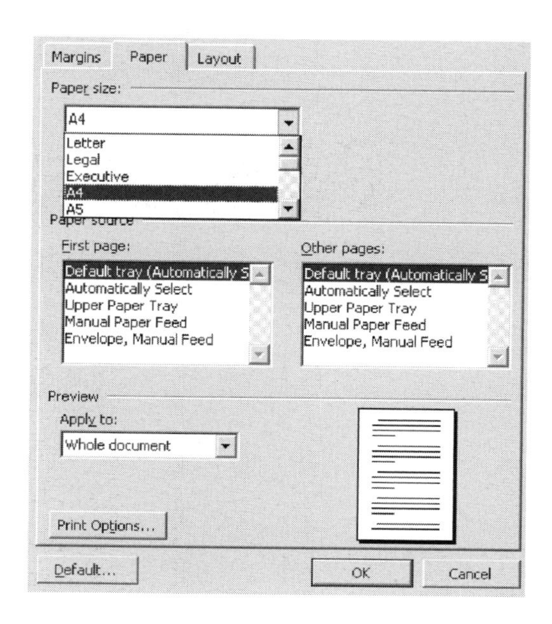

Figure 1.28

The picture on the left under the Margins tab, not surprisingly, allows you to set the top, bottom, left and right margins, the orientation (i.e. portrait or landscape) and a number of other features you do not need to worry about at this stage. The picture on the right under the Paper tab allows you to set the paper size and other features, which again you need not worry about for now. Similarly you can ignore the Layout tab for the time being.

To set a page to a required format for text which has already been prepared you must first open the document. Once the document has been opened you can use the Page setup dialogue box to set the required margins, orientation and so on.

Try it out

Scenario

You are going to apply the following house style details to a pre-prepared text document.

Paper size:	A4	
Orientation:	Landscape	
Margins:	Top	3 cm
	Bottom	2 cm
	Left	2.5 cm
	Right	2.5 cm

Open the file **Random_Text** found in the sub-folder called Sample Files in the Unit 1 main folder on the accompanying CD.

Select Page Setup… from the File option on the main menu.

Set the page size (under the Paper tab) to A4.

Set the margins (under the Margins tab) as shown above.

Set the orientation (under the Margins tab) to Landscape.

Press OK.

Save your file as **Random_Text_1**.

Close the file.

Styles and formatting

Modifying the body text style of a document

Word provides a number of built-in styles which automatically set the format of a document's text, numbering, colour, paragraph, line spacing and so on. However, these formats can be amended for individual aspects of the document. In addition you can add your own, new styles.

There are a number of options to change the format of a document's text. The option you choose largely depends on what it is you want to format – the whole document, a paragraph, just a line or individual words.

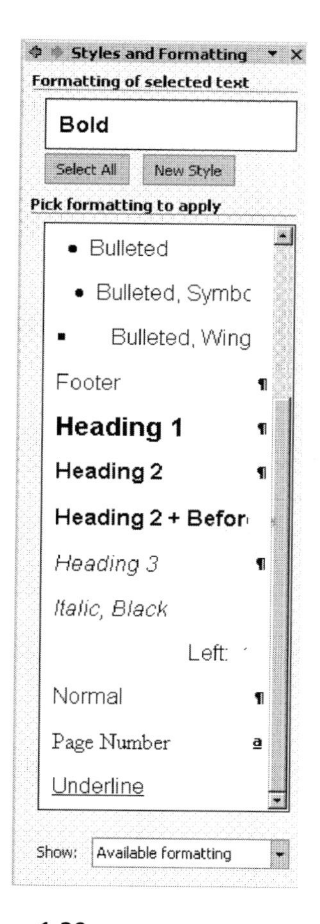

Figure 1.29

When you create a new document it is based on a template (normally the 'Normal' style template). All templates available are shown in the Styles and Formatting task pane which can be seen by either selecting Styles and Formatting... from the Format option on the main menu or pressing the Styles and Formatting... icon on the formatting toolbar. The style currently selected for the document is shown in the styles box, normally immediately to the right of the Style icon.

If the text for the whole document is to be reformatted then simply click on the arrow to the right of the Normal template in the Styles and Formatting task pane and select Modify... from the drop-down menu list. In the Modify Style dialogue box choose the font, font size, weight etc. that is required: see Figures 1.29, 1.30 and 1.31.

The font for the whole document will then follow the amended style for the template, in this case the 'Normal' template. The changes will only apply to the active document unless the formatting for the underlying template is changed by checking the Add to Template check box.

If only a paragraph is to be reformatted, then the cursor is placed in front of the first word of the paragraph and an appropriate text template selected. For example, using the Normal template will change the font for the whole document, body text templates are based on paragraphs and will reformat only the paragraph.

Alternatively, reformatting can be achieved by using the toolbar formatting icons. The text to be changed is first highlighted and the relevant toolbar icon used.

Try it out

Open Lost_Opportunities.doc from the Sample File sub-folder under the main folder Unit 1 on the accompanying CD.

Select Page Setup... and apply the following settings:

Paper size:	A4	
Orientation:	Portrait	
Margins:	Top	2 cm
	Bottom	2 cm
	Left	3.5 cm
	Right	2.5 cm

Click OK.

Now you are going to format the font for the whole document.

Select Styles and Formatting... from the Format option on the main menu.

(See note below if you are using an earlier version of Office.)

Place the cursor over the Normal style.

Press the arrow to the right of the box: see Figure 1.30.

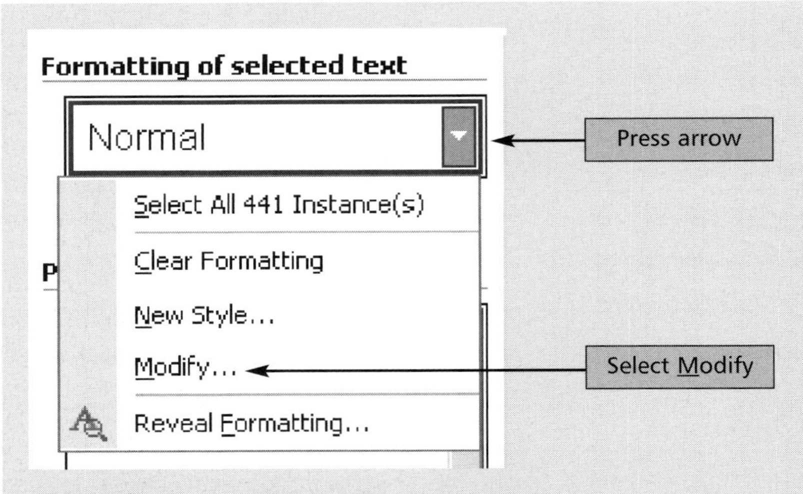

Figure 1.30

Select Modify... and the Modify Style dialogue box shown in Figure 1.31 will appear.

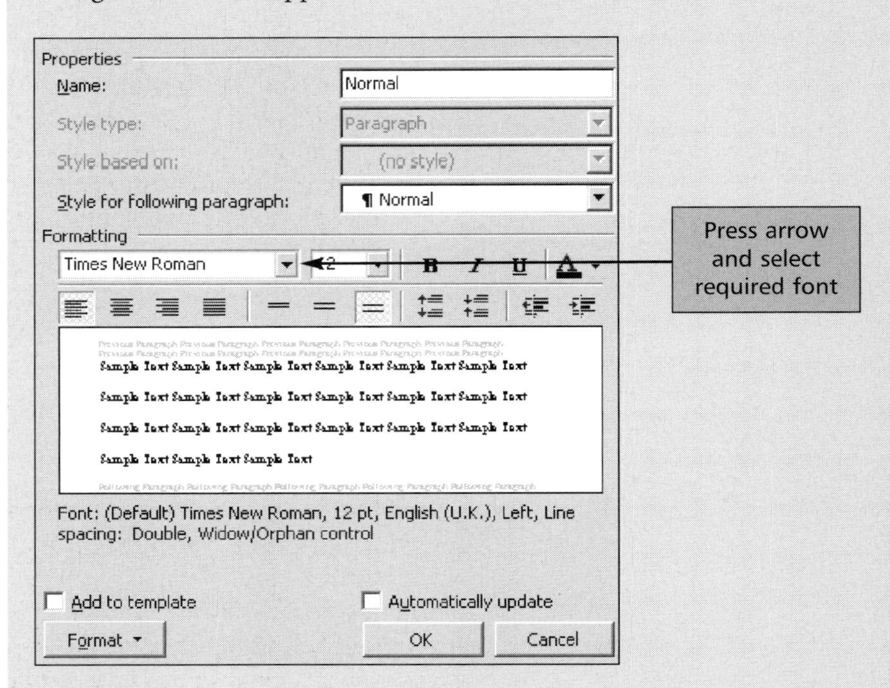

Figure 1.31

Note: if you are using an earlier version of Office to XP then select Style... from the Format option and the styles dialogue box will open. Press the Modify... button and a Modify Style dialogue box will open. It will look slightly different to Figure 1.31 (see Figure 1.32) but the principles for modifying styles are exactly the same. In Office XP there is a Formatting option on the main dialogue box to modify the font, but you can equally use the Format button to bring up the Font dialogue box. From here both versions of Office are more or less the same.

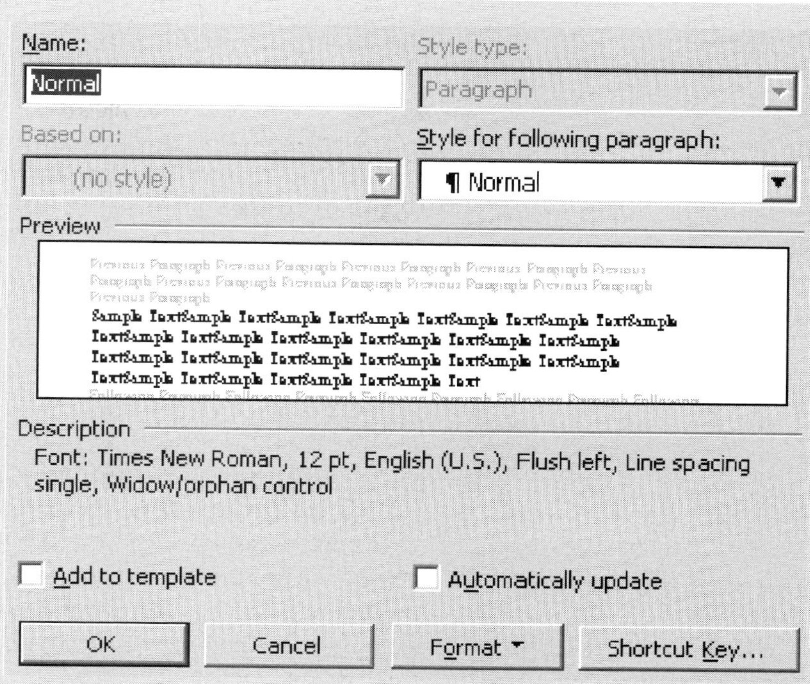

Figure 1.32

Select Arial as the font and 12 points as the font size.

Save the file as '**Lost_Opportunities**' on your floppy disk.

Close the file.

Modifying or creating heading styles for a document

CLAIT Plus requires you to follow the house style for headings and sub-headings as well as body text. Although text formats, whether body text or headings, can be reformatted using normal formatting options for fonts available on the toolbars or menu options, it is invariably easier to create your own heading styles or modify those offered by Microsoft. By doing this you can ensure you have consistency throughout a document. It is entirely a matter of personal preference how you format text to comply with a given set of house styles and using the toolbar formatting icons or options on the main menu under Format are both valid ways. However, the built-in styles do provide you with a better opportunity of maintaining consistency. The following section gives guidance on how to create (or modify) heading and text styles.

Creating a new heading style

As you learnt in the previous section, formatting text can be achieved by using the Styles and Formatting… option on the main menu or with text-related icons on the formatting toolbar. Microsoft provides a number of solutions to complete most tasks. However, students are not required to complete tasks in any specific way providing the outcome meets the OCR's standards. That said, some solutions are considered to be more appropriate than others depending on the tasks to be undertaken. Formatting headings is an example where using a built-in style may provide more benefits than simply formatting the text using the formatting toolbar icons.

For example, in a long document with many main and sub-headings it would help the reader if a table of contents were placed at the beginning of the document. A table of contents is simply a list of the headings used in the document. This book has a contents page at the beginning based on the unit and paragraph headings. By using recognised styles you can insert a table of contents. You are not expected to know how to do this for CLAIT Plus but if you learn to format your headings using styles you may find creating tables of contents easier in the future should you wish to do this.

To create a new heading style use the Styles and Formatting task pane by selecting Styles and Formatting… from the Format menu.

Click on the New Style button to bring up the New Style dialogue box.

In the Name: box a new heading name is entered e.g. Main Heading. The font is changed to the specified style, size and weight and when the OK button is pressed the new heading style is created: see Figure 1.33.

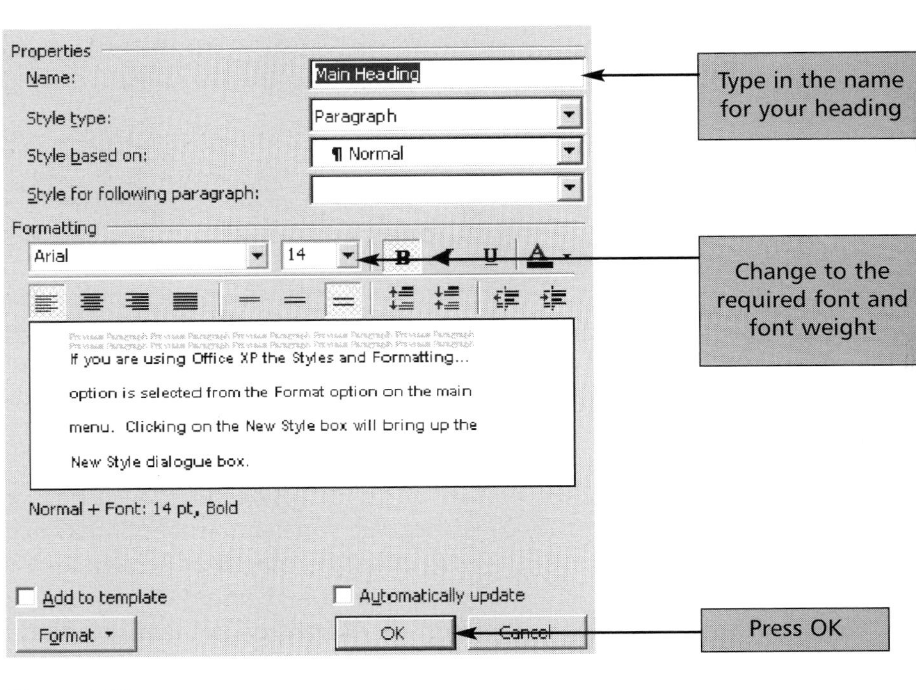

Figure 1.33

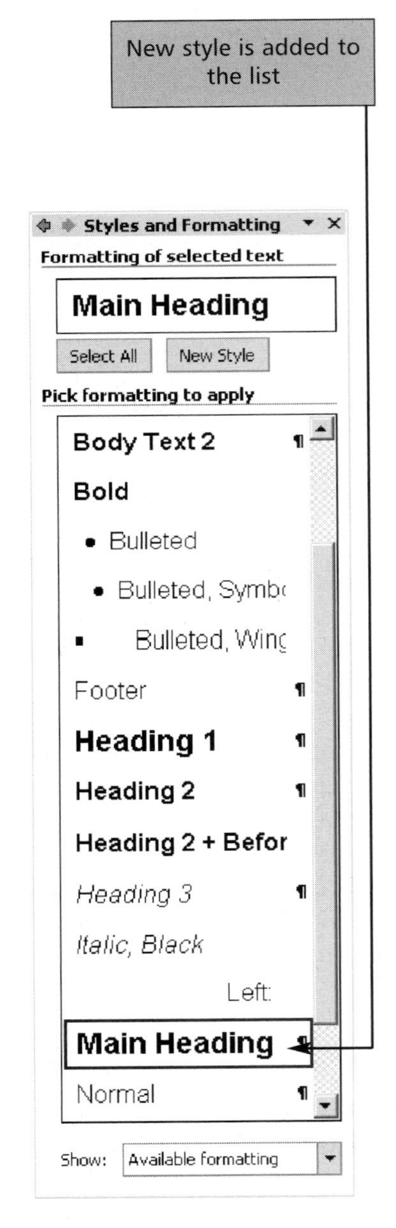

Figure 1.34

Once the new style has been created it is added to the Styles and Formatting list (see Figure 1.34) and can then be selected from the styles list icon on the formatting toolbar.

The new style that is created will only be available in the active document. If you want to add this to the Styles and Formatting task pane list for new documents then select the Add to template check box. The new style will then be available for all new documents.

To modify existing styles simply select the style from the list, press the arrow to bring up the drop down-menu list and select Modify... . Changes to the existing style are then made in exactly the same way as if you were creating a new style.

Now create three new heading styles.

Try it out

Open Lost_Opportunities.doc.

Place the cursor in front of the 'C' of Chapter 1.

Select Styles and Formatting... from the Format option on the main menu.

Press New Style in the Styles and Formatting task pane (or select Style... and New... from the Format menu if using an earlier version of Office).

Type 'Main Heading' as the name of your first new heading.

Select Font type as Arial.

Select Font size as 14.

Select Font weight as bold.

Press OK.

Select Main Heading as the heading style from the styles option on the formatting toolbar: see Figure 1.35.

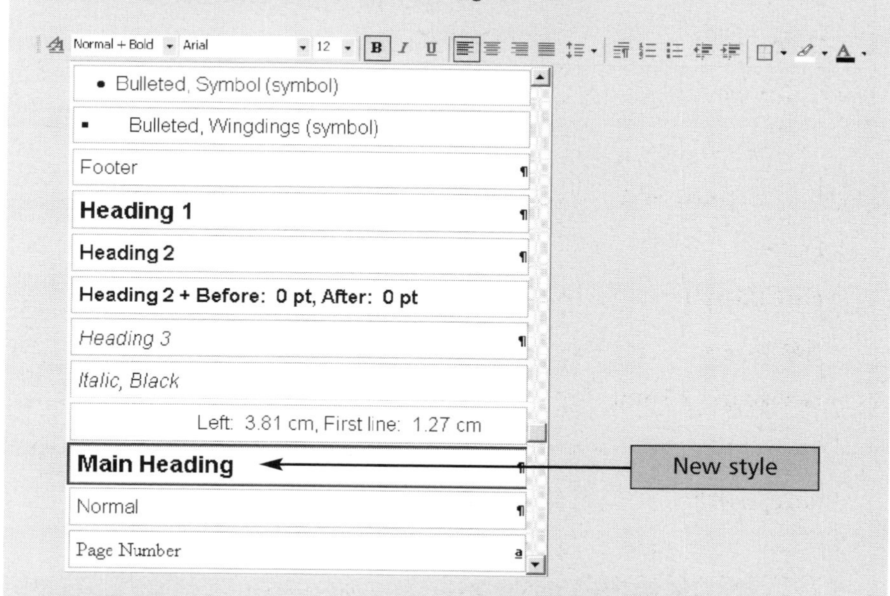

Figure 1.35

The heading 'Chapter 1' will now assume the format of your new style heading and you can then use the same style for any main heading.

Now **create** two further headings based on the following styles:

Name: Sub-heading 1
Font: Arial
Size: 12
Style: Bold, italic

Name: Sub-heading 2
Font: Times New Roman
Size: 12
Style Bold

Modify the heading 'Lost Opportunities' to the Sub-heading 1 style.

Save your file.

Close the file.

Moving, inserting and deleting text

There will be occasions when having completed a document, either for yourself or someone else, amendments will need to be made. You are likely to have come across functions such as cut, paste and delete if you completed New CLAIT. This section is included here as either a refresher or an introduction to understanding how to amend a document for those who have not completed a level 2 course.

Moving text using cut and paste

To move either a single word or a paragraph using cut and paste you must first highlight the text in question. Having highlighted the text you can cut it out of the document by using Cut from the Edit option on the main menu or alternatively use the cut icon on the formatting toolbar. Cutting data from any document sends it to the clipboard – an area of memory that allows you to keep objects or data until you want to use them again; but once the computer is switched off everything on the clipboard is lost. To view what is being stored on the clipboard, select Office Clipboard... from the Edit option on the menu (alternatively press Ctrl+C twice).

Once the item to be moved has been cut, place the cursor at the point to which the data or object is to be moved and then either select Paste from the Edit option on the menu bar, or press the paste icon found on the formatting toolbar . The object or data will then reappear.

Try it out

Open the file **Precinct_Society.doc** which can be found in the Sample Files folder of Unit 1 on the accompanying CD.

Move the final paragraph so that it becomes the second paragraph.

Reminder:

Highlight the final paragraph that starts with Professor Willow... .

Cut the paragraph using either the menu or toolbar options.

Place the cursor on the line immediately below the first paragraph.

Press the Enter key to create a new paragraph.

Paste the paragraph back into the document using either the menu or toolbar options.

Save your amendments as a new file on your floppy disk.

Close the file and application.

Deleting and restoring text

To delete text from a document first highlight the text to be deleted and then press the delete button on the keyboard. Remember that deleting text does not send it to the clipboard and therefore if you find that you have made a mistake by deleting the wrong text you will need to undo that last action. To undelete a deletion, select the Undo option from Edit on the main menu or alternatively press the undo arrow on the Standard toolbar .

Using automatically generated date fields in a specified format

To enter a date into a document select Insert, Date and Time... from the main menu. The Date and Time... dialogue box will appear, offering you a variety of formats for the date such as:

22/06/03
22 June 2003
22.06.03

You can also select the country format. The English format (the one you are required to use for CLAIT Plus) is always in the order of day, month, year. Date format codes are often shown 'dd/mmm/yy' or 'dd/mm/yy' or 'dd/mmm/yyyy' where the d is the day, m the month and y the year. American date formats reverse the month and day so 22/06/03 becomes 06/22/03. You can easily spot this where the day is greater than 12, as in the case above, but it can be easily missed if the date was, say, 05/06/03.

The date and time dialogue box also offers you the opportunity to update the date (or time) automatically. This is done by clicking in the Update automatically box in the bottom right corner of the dialogue box. If this is checked, every time you open the document the date will automatically be updated to the current date.

Once you have selected the date and country format required, simply press the OK button and the date will be inserted into the document.

Using headers and footers

Some documents need specific information on every page, such as page number, date, file information and so on. Using headers and footers allows you to include information throughout a document without the need to retype the same information onto each page of the document. Also, bearing in mind the need for accuracy and consistency, if Word reproduces repeating data, the likelihood of mistakes is reduced. Word, and for that matter most modern wordprocessing packages, provides a headers and footers function.

Headers and footers are placed in the top and bottom margin spaces of the page. You can insert text, numbers, data fields or graphics as a header or footer. Common examples of standard headers or footers are:

- page numbers
- dates
- author details
- book details
- company logos
- file names and location paths.

To insert a header or footer simply select the Header and Footer menu item found under the View option of the main menu. Alternatively, click on the header and footer icon ; it can be placed on the toolbar using Customize... from Toolbars, under View on the main menu.

Note: customising toolbars is covered in detail in the book *Mastering New CLAIT through Office.*

Once Header and Footer has been selected you will see the header box and the header and footer toolbar displayed as shown in Figure 1.36.

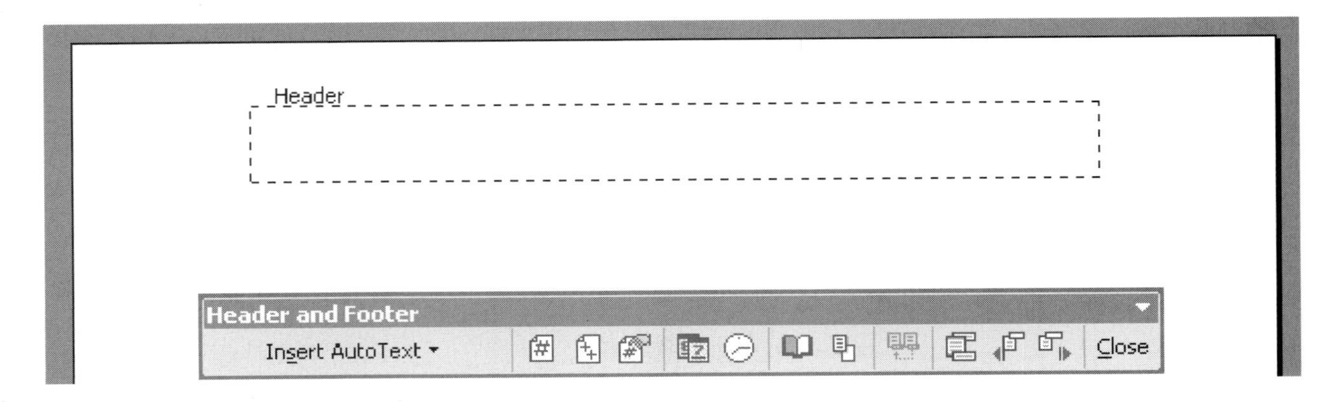

Figure 1.36

It is worth having a more detailed look at the options available on the toolbar itself, as shown in Figure 1.37.

Figure 1.37

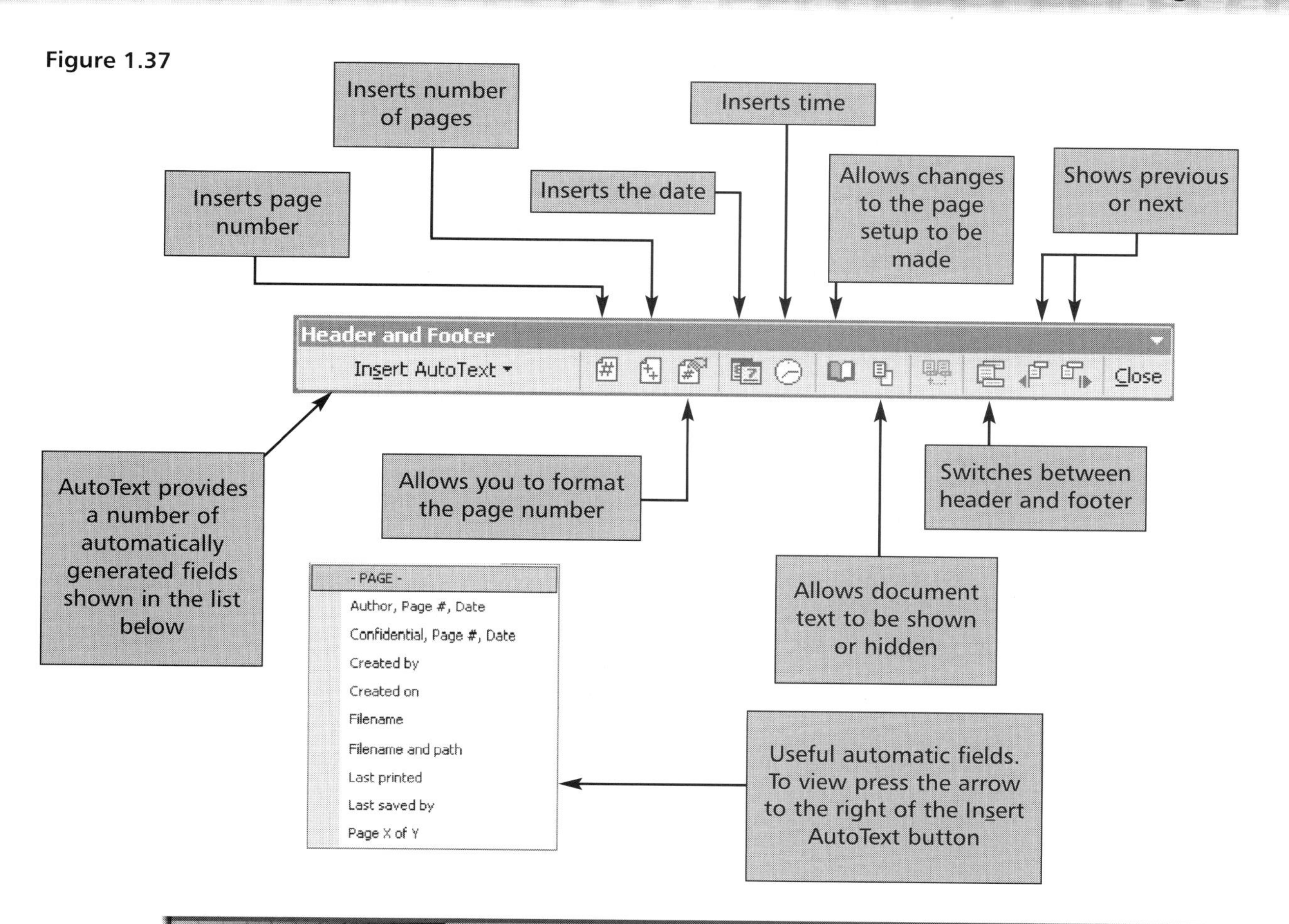

Try it out

Open a new Word document.

Type '=Rand(10,10)'.

(**Tip**: the Rand formula allows you to generate random text to avoid the need to type a lot of text when you want to try something out. The first number is the number of paragraphs you want to create and the second number represents the number of sentences in the paragraph.)

Select Header and Footer from the View main menu.

Type 'The Quick Brown Fox' in the header section.

Press the switch between header and footer icon.

Press the insert page number icon.

Once the page number has been inserted

Press the centre icon on the formatting toolbar.

Press Close.

Notice how the heading appears on both pages and that page numbers have been inserted with 1 on the first page and 2 on the second.

As you can see from the above exercise in addition to using the built-in functions such as date, time, filename etc., you can type your own text into either the header or footer. For example, you can type your name or address.

Now test your knowledge and understanding of the skills learnt so far in this unit by completing Build-up Exercise 1.

Build-up Exercise 1: Stage 1

Scenario

You are the administrative assistant for an antiques and auctioneering company called Bellings. You have been asked to prepare a leaflet on a forthcoming auction. The leaflet is also an opportunity to let people know other details about Bellings, the services they offer and events they organise.

Open the document called **Bellings**.

Set the page format as follows:

Paper size: A4
Orientation: Portrait
Margins: Top 2 cm
Bottom 2 cm
Left 3 cm
Right 3 cm

Set the text styles as follows:

Table 1.2

Feature	Font	Type size	Style	Alignment	
Body text	Sans serif	12 point	Normal	Left	
Bullet text	Sans serif	11 point	Normal	Left	
Headings	Sans serif	14 point	Bold	Centred	
Sub-headings	Sans serif	12 point	Bold, italic	Left	
Tables	Sans serif	12 point	Gridlines	Column heading	Centred, bold and shaded
				Row heading	Left
				Text	Left (wrapped)
				Numbers	Right
				Date	Right
Imported data	Sans serif	12 point	Gridlines	Column heading	Centred, bold and shaded
				Text	Left
				Numbers	Right

Note: some of the features in this table will be covered later in the unit.

Create a new main heading to the house style specification.

Create a new sub-heading to the house style specification.

Amend the Normal style to reflect the house style specification.

Apply house style to the headings and text as per the house style.

Insert the graphic file **Belling_Logo.jpg** as a header.

TIP

Inserting graphics

Inserting graphics as a header is executed in exactly the same way as a text or automatic header. Select Header and Footer from the View menu to bring up the header box. When the header box and toolbar come into view select Insert, Picture, From File... on the main menu. When the Insert Picture dialogue box appears as in Figure 1.38, locate the folder on the CD (Unit 1, Sample Files) where the graphic is stored, select the graphic and then press the Insert button at the bottom of the box.

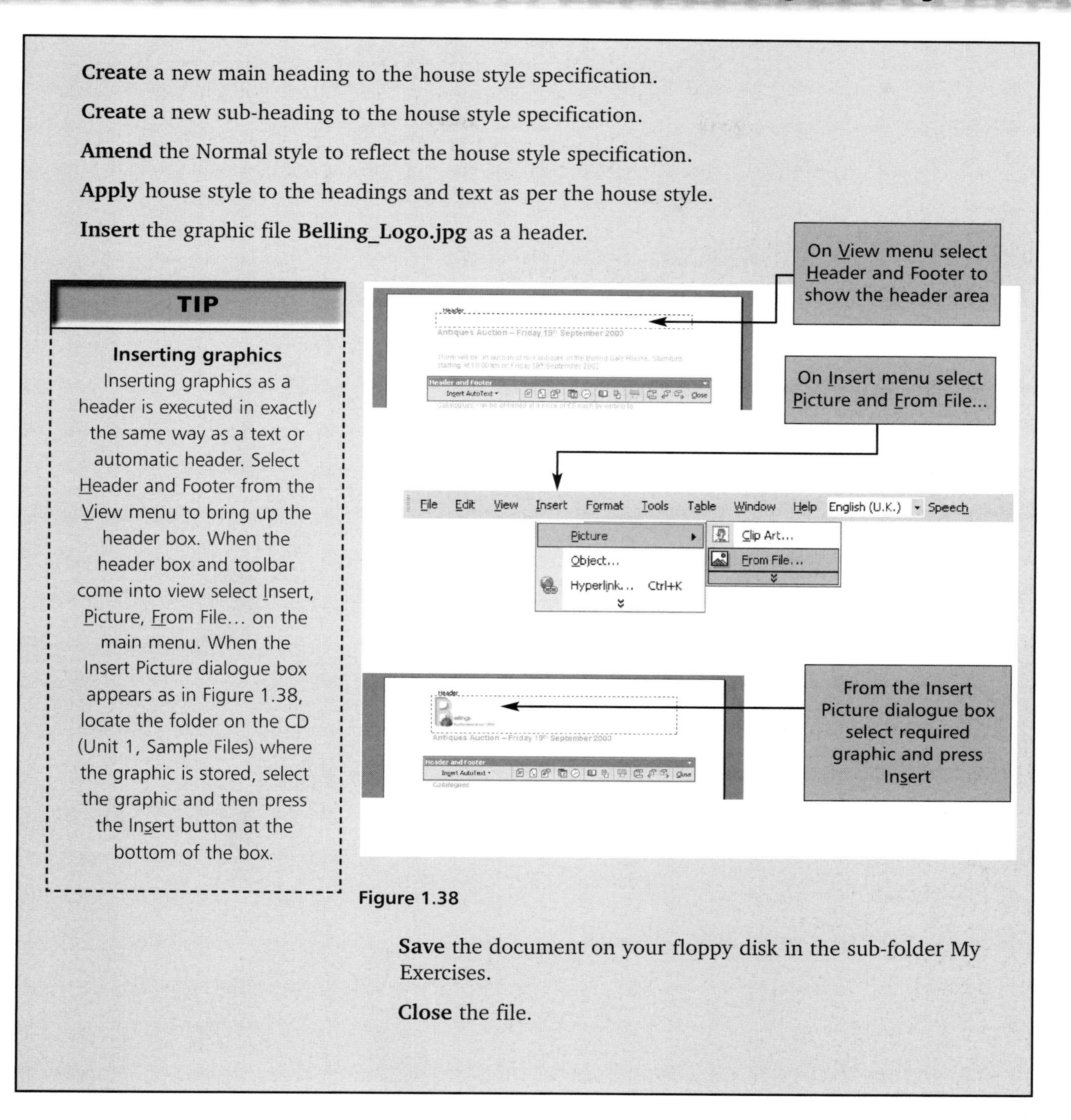

Figure 1.38

Save the document on your floppy disk in the sub-folder My Exercises.

Close the file.

Creating bullet and number lists

Word offers a variety of ways to enhance documents to emphasise major points or lists. Bullets and lists come in a number of formats. The easiest way to start a bullet or numbered list is to click on the appropriate icon on the formatting toolbar: see Figure 1.39.

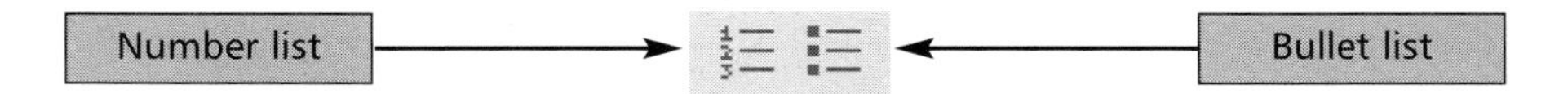

Figure 1.39

Alternatively you can select Bullets and Numbering... from the Format option on the menu. By choosing this method you can select the bullet or number style that is appropriate for your work. Have a look at Figure 1.40.

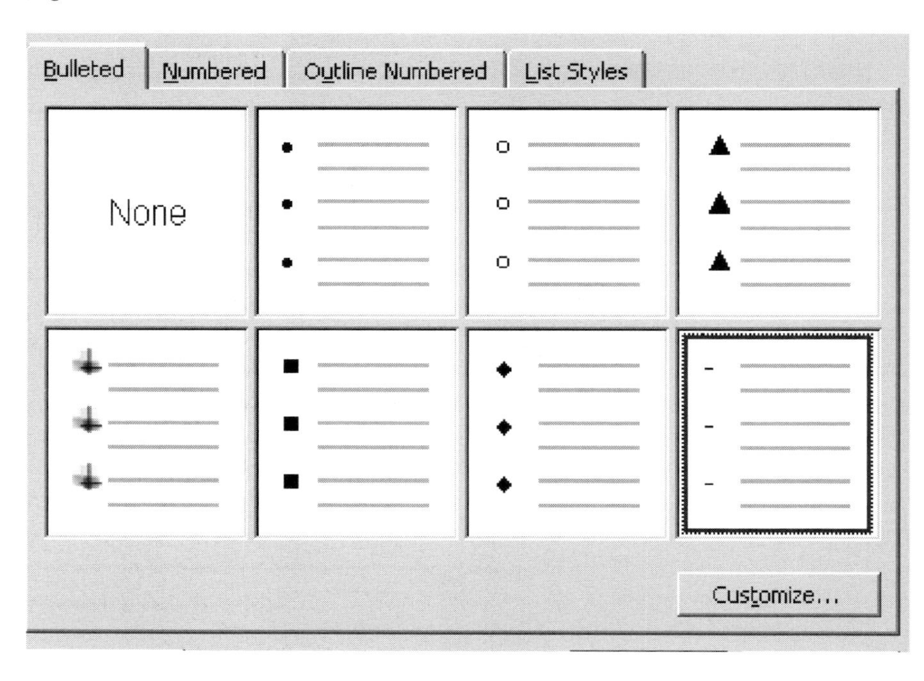

Figure 1.40

You can also convert text to a list after the text has been entered. Now have a look at Figure 1.41.

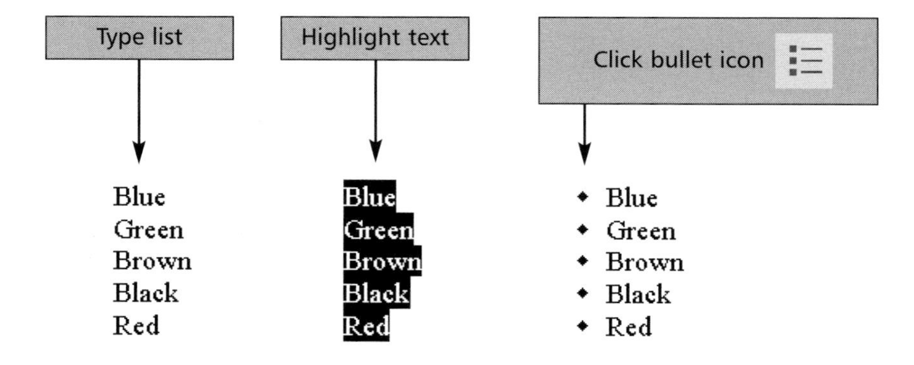

Figure 1.41

First the text for the list is typed, then the whole text is highlighted and once the bullet icon is pressed the text is converted into a bullet list. The bullets can still be reformatted by using the Bullets and Numbering... option from the Format option on the menu.

Numbered lists are created in a similar way. The cursor is placed where the list is to start. When the number icon is selected Word will start the list with the first number. After the enter key is pressed Word inserts the next sequential number. If a line is wanted between the numbers then by pressing the Shift key and then, whilst still holding the Shift key, pressing the Enter key a line will be inserted without starting a new sequence in the list. Pressing the Enter key will insert the next number on the following line. A number list can also be created by typing the number one at the beginning of a line and entering text for that line. Word will automatically assume that a number list is required and once the enter key is pressed the next number will be inserted.

Where sub-lists are required these can be achieved by pressing the increase indent icon or back to the primary number by pressing the decrease indent icon: see Figure 1.42.

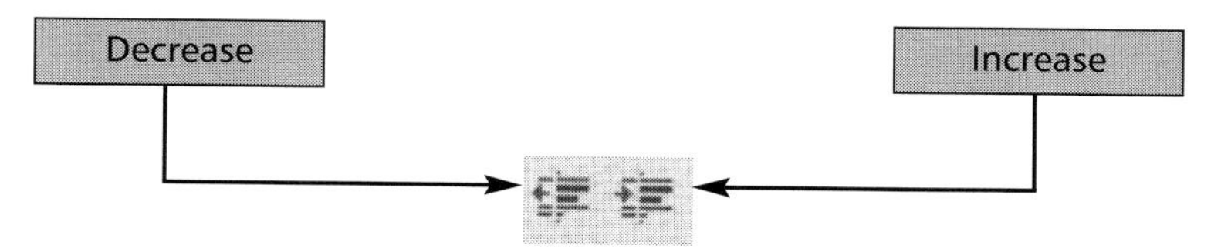

Figure 1.42

Try it out

Create a bullet list

Open a new Word document.

Click on the bullet icon.

Type 'Garden' following the first bullet.

Press Enter.

Type 'Tools' after the next bullet.

Create the remaining items in the list with:

Plants
Bulbs
Seeds

Press Enter twice.

Create a numbered list

Click on the number icon.

Type 'Large tools' after the first number.

Press Enter.

Type 'Band saw'.

Press the increase indent icon.

Press Enter.

Type 'Circular saw'.

Press Enter.

Type 'Small Tools'.

▶▶

Press the decrease indent icon.

Notice how the primary series is returned to with the next sequential number.

Press Enter.

Type 'Screwdriver'.

Press the increase indent icon.

Press Enter twice.

Close the document without saving it.

Amending documents and using the spell checker

However careful you are in preparing and presenting documents for yourself or other people, there will inevitably be a need to review the document and make amendments. These can be as a result of spelling errors, punctuation mistakes, inaccurate or changing data, inserting new information or simply the need to move text from one location in the document to another. In this section you will learn how to:

- use Word's built-in spell checker
- use search and replace data
- insert and delete text
- copy and move text from one location to another.

The spell checker

Word provides a powerful spell checker to assist you in ensuring spelling errors are minimised. The spell checker can be used in a variety of languages, although those available on your computer will depend on options selected when the software was installed. Despite the power of Word's spell checker there are a number of points you will need to consider when using it. The first is to check what default language was set when Word was first loaded. Microsoft is an American product and therefore often you will probably find that the dictionary's language is set to English (US). To reset the default language to English (UK) either select Tools, Language, Set Language... on the main menu or alternatively use the language drop list on the formatting menu. Both these options are shown in Figure 1.43.

Using the menu option allows you to set the required language as the default.

The second point to watch is the actual use of words. The spell checker will look for the correct spelling of a word. It does not determine whether the word chosen is correct for the context of the work. So, for example, if you use 'there' rather than 'their' or 'week' as opposed to 'weak', Word rightly sees no spelling error.

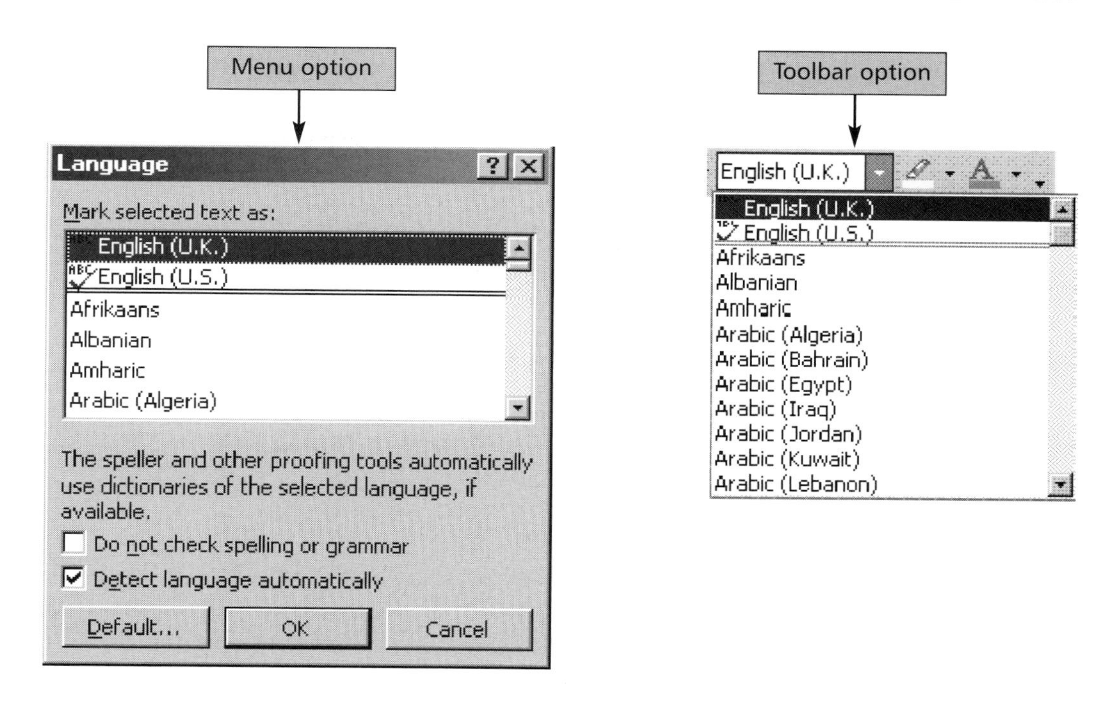

Figure 1.43

Word checks both spelling and grammar. Incorrectly spelt words will have a wavy red line underneath while questionable grammar is underlined in green. To use the spelling and grammar checker select Spelling and Grammar… from the Tools menu option. You will be shown the spelling and grammar dialogue box. At the top of the box you can see the default language. Now have a look at Figure 1.44.

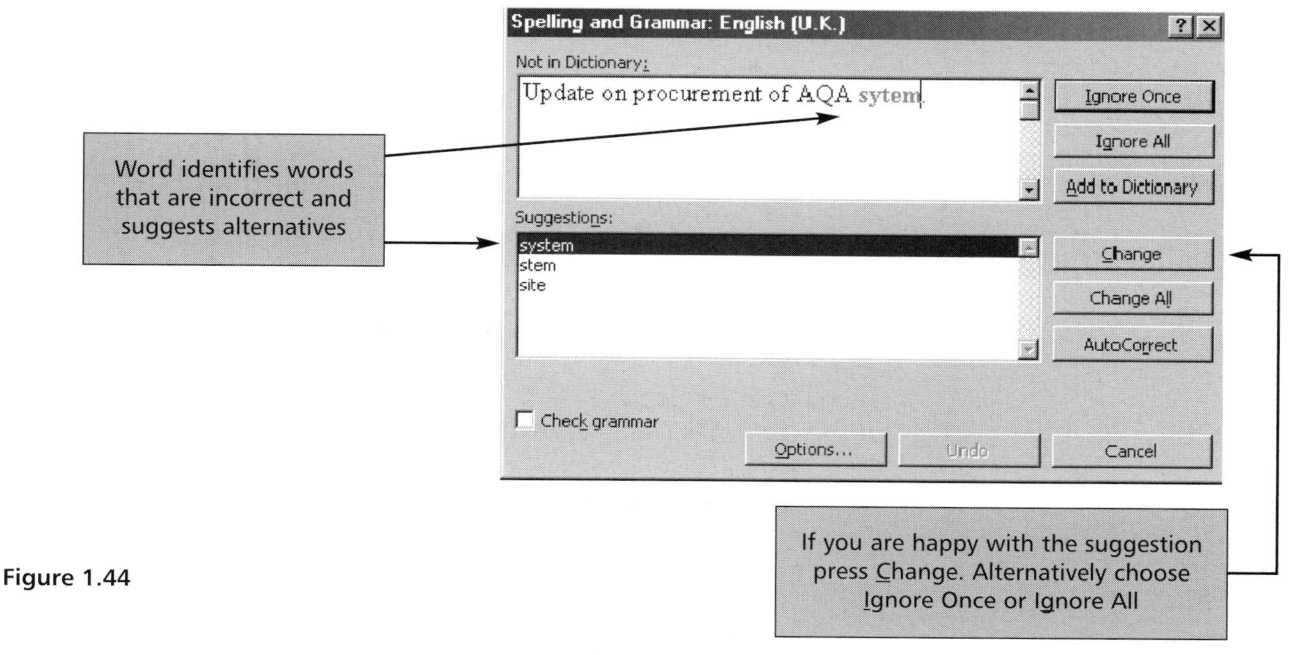

Figure 1.44

The spell checker gives you the option of accepting suggestions from a list of alternative words, or ignoring it. If you wish to accept a suggestion offered simply select the appropriate word in the Suggestions: box and then press the Change button. If there are a number of occurrences of the word then you can choose whether to change them all at once by pressing the Change All button or one at a time by pressing Change. Occasionally Word may display a word that appears to you to be correct. This will happen if the word itself is not in Word's dictionary. In this case you can choose to ignore or add the word to the dictionary for future use.

Once the spell checker has finished checking the document a dialogue box as shown in Figure 1.45 indicates the check has been completed.

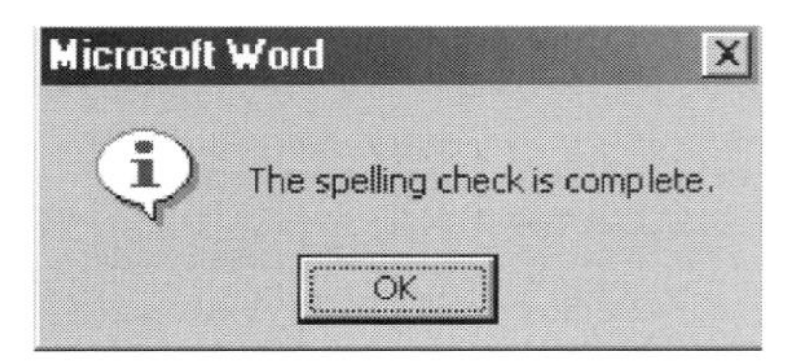

Figure 1.45

Try it out

Open the file **Company_Performance.doc** in the Unit 1 Sample Files folder on the accompanying CD.

Select Spelling and Grammar, from the Tools option on the menu.

Press Change to accept the suggested replacement words. There should be three in total.

Once the check has been completed

Close the file without saving.

Build-up Exercise 1: Stage 2

Open Bellings.doc.

Format the list of services to become bullet points as shown below:

- Best trade prices
- Valuations
- Packing and shipment of items anywhere in the world
- Insurance arranged
- Export advice and documentation
- Storage

Select Spelling and Grammar from the Tools option on the menu and spell check the document.

Note: where the spell checker highlights a word which is correct, but not in the dictionary (e.g. proper names such as Bellings), **press** the Ignore Once button.

Save the file.

Close the file.

You should now be able to:

- format the page layout of a document according to a given house style
- create and modify headings and body text styles for a document
- insert a date in a specified format
- insert headers and footers
- create bullet and number lists
- check a document for spelling mistakes using the spell checker.

Using special symbols and characters

In addition to the bullets shown in the bullets and numbering dialogue box in Figure 1.40 above, Word provides a wide range of symbols and special characters that can be used in a document's body text or alternatively used to customise bullet points. To view the characters and symbols available select Symbol… from the Insert option of the main menu. A dialogue box similar to that shown in Figure 1.46 will appear.

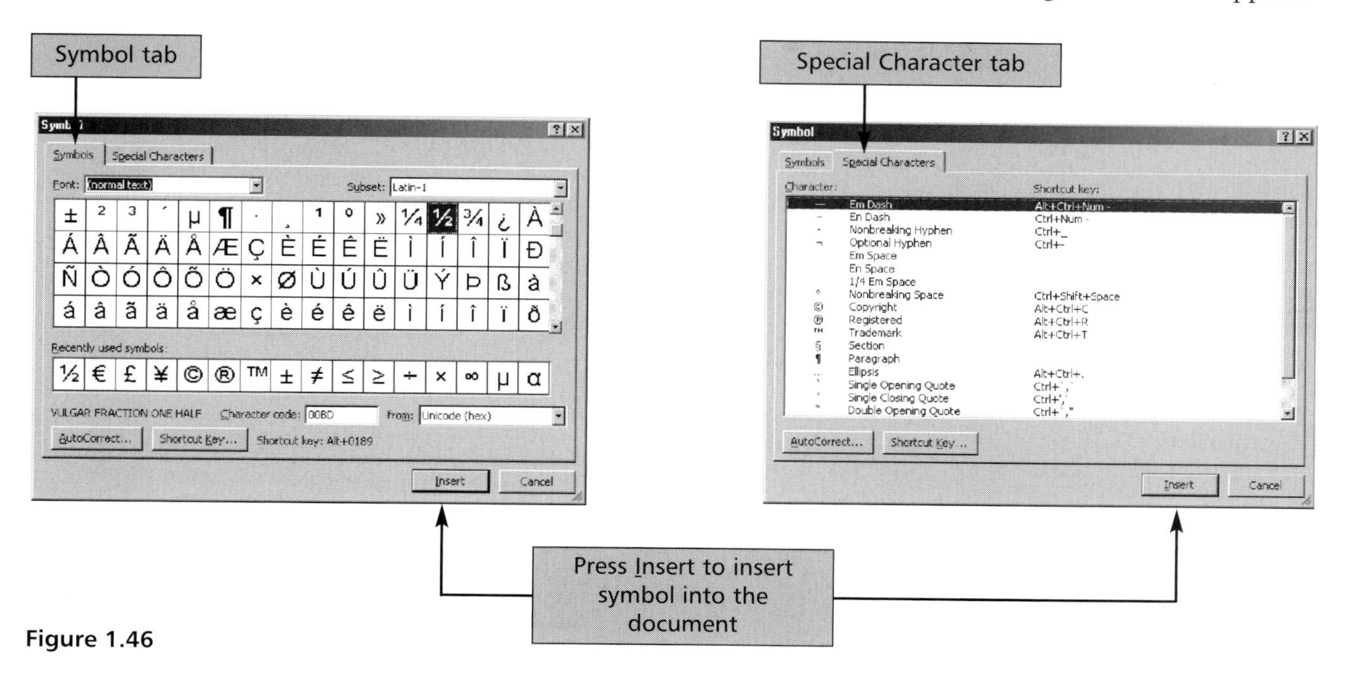
Symbol tab
Special Character tab
Press Insert to insert symbol into the document

Figure 1.46

This dialogue box has two tabs. The first, Symbols, allows you to select from a wide range of symbols. By pressing down on the arrow to the top left of the box you can select from the list of fonts available; the arrow on the right helps you to select the style of symbol you want to use. To insert the symbol into a document simply highlight the required symbol and then press the Insert button.

The second tab allows you to select from a range of special characters. A selection of these is shown in the list below:

© copyright
¶ paragraph symbol
® registered trade mark
™ trade mark

Inserting a special character is carried out in exactly the same way as a symbol, by pressing the Insert button.

Earlier you learnt how to create bullet lists using the default bullets in the bullets and numbering box. You can also use this dialogue box in conjunction with the available symbols to customise bullets.

Try it out

Open a new Word document.

Open the Bullets and Numbering dialogue box (see Figure 1.40).

Select one of the bullet boxes to be customised.

This will then enable the Customize… button.

Press the Customize button and you will be shown the Customise Bulleted List dialogue box shown in Figure 1.47.

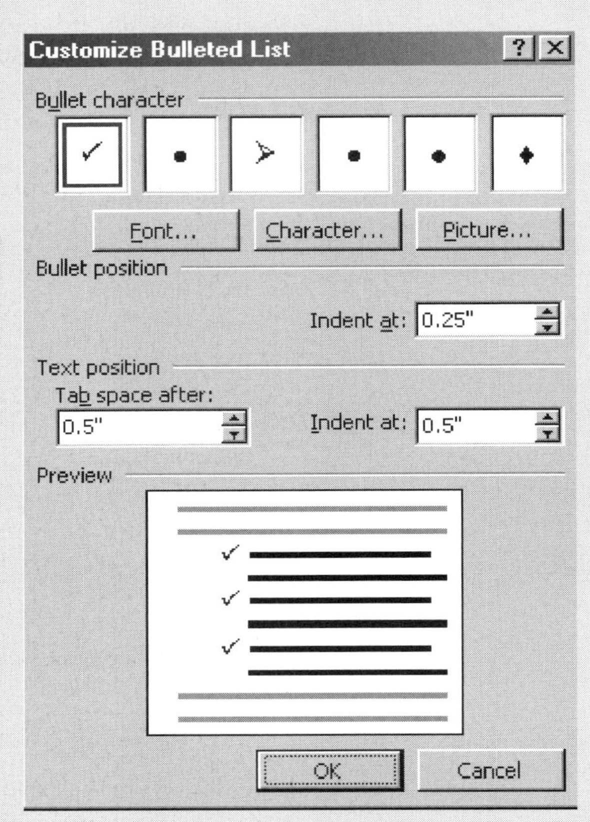

Figure 1.47

Here you have a choice of selecting the Font button to format the font of the existing bullet shape, the Picture button to select a picture as a bullet or the Character button. Pressing the character button will bring up the symbol dialogue box from which you can select the style of font and character or symbol required for the bullet.

Press the character button.

Select Wingdings from the font drop-down list.

Select a suitable Wingding to replace the bullet style.

Press OK three times to return to the active document.

A bullet to start the list will be inserted.

Type the list:

Coffee
Tea
Water
Orange juice

Close the file without saving.

Using the find and replace function

Two extremely useful functions available to you in Office applications are the Find... and Replace... options. These functions allow you to look for specific words in a document and then replace them with another word or phrase. If you completed New CLAIT you may well have already used this function.

Have a look at the following paragraph:

John returned to the centre of the town with his bicycle. The bicycle was bright red but his recent accident had severely scratched the paintwork and he wanted to find a suitable colour match to repaint the bicycle frame.

For the sake of argument let us say you want to change the word 'bicycle' to 'cycle'. Clearly in this short example it would not be difficult to find all the occurrences of the word 'bicycle'. However, had this been part of a long story then making sure you changed *all* the occurrences would have been more difficult.

Under the Edit option on the main menu is a menu item called Replace... and selecting this option will bring up the dialogue box shown in Figure 1.48.

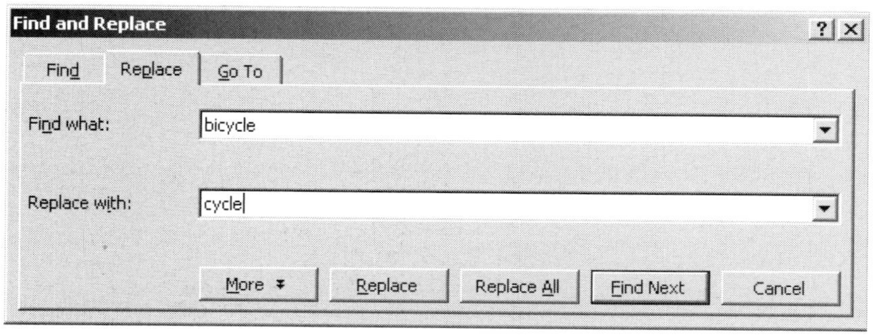

Figure 1.48

Type in the word to be replaced in the Find what: box, and the new word in the Replace with: box, and Word will find each occurrence and, depending on whether you select Replace or Replace All, change it to the new word. Once Word has changed all the words to be replaced it helpfully tells you it has finished and the number of occurrences it has changed: see Figure 1.49.

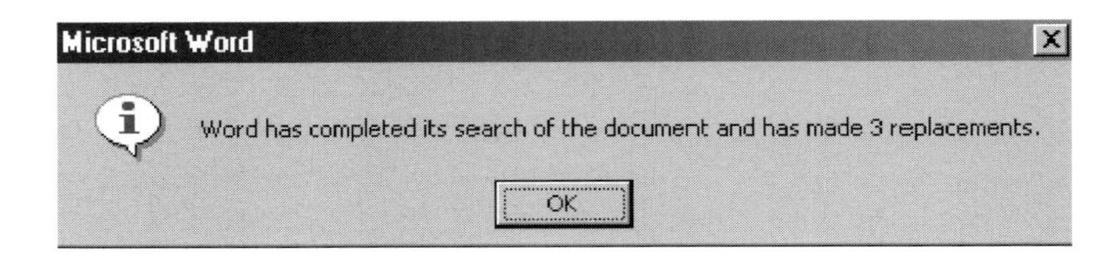

Figure 1.49

The example paragraph will now reflect the changes as shown below:

> *John returned to the centre of the town with his cycle. The cycle was bright red but his recent accident had severely scratched the paintwork and he wanted to find a suitable colour match to repaint the cycle frame.*

Try it out

Open the file **Conference_Centre.doc** in the Sample Files folder for Unit 1 on the accompanying CD.

Replace the words 'No. 24' with 'The Business Café'. There should be three occurrences in all.

Close the file without saving it.

Creating and using tables

Tables have a variety of uses, but predominantly they are used to organise and present data in an easily understandable format. Tables are made up of *rows* and *columns*. Where a row intersects a column a *cell* is formed in which data can be placed and stored. Have a look at Figure 1.50.

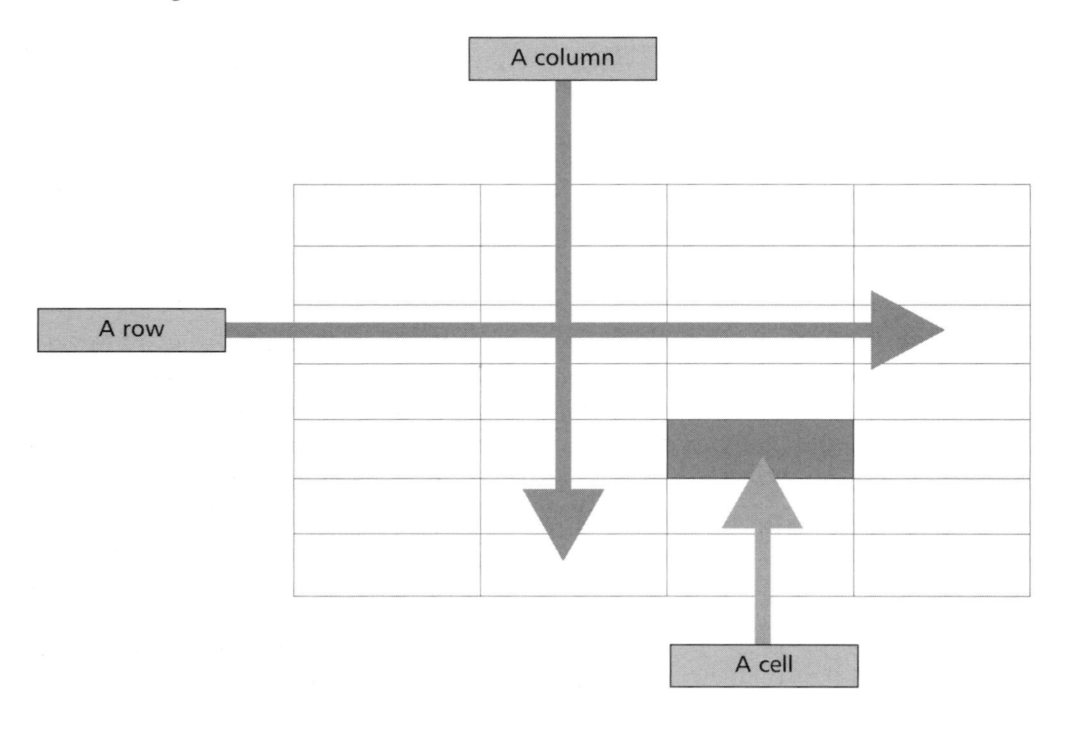

Figure 1.50

For CLAIT Plus you are required to create a table from a given set of data, change a number of the table's properties (column width, cell alignment, etc.) and insert it into a document.

Creating a basic table is simplicity itself. There are a number of ways in which this can be achieved but the two most common ways to create tables are to use the menu option or toolbar icon.

Creating a table using the toolbar

On the standard toolbar you should see the insert table icon . By clicking on the icon a table-shaped box will appear with 20 squares. By selecting the first box and dragging the cursor over the number of rows and columns required, and then releasing the cursor, a table is automatically inserted into your document at the point where the cursor is positioned: see Figure 1.51.

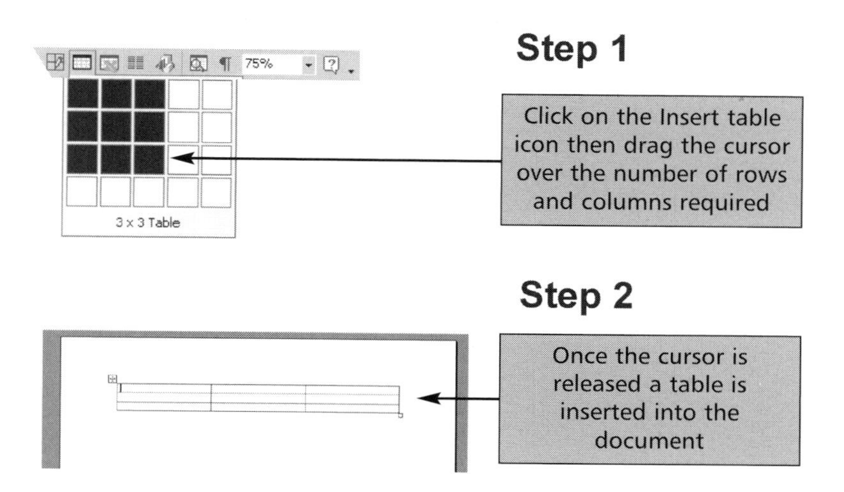

Step 1
75%
3 x 3 Table
Click on the Insert table icon then drag the cursor over the number of rows and columns required
Step 2
Once the cursor is released a table is inserted into the document

Figure 1.51

This is without question the simplest way of creating a table. However, as you will have noticed, the toolbar option limits the size of the initial table to five columns and four rows. Whilst you can add columns and rows to a table at any stage, you may prefer to dictate the number of rows and columns you want at the beginning of the process – that is providing you know the size of the table required, which is not always the case.

Creating a table using the menu

To create a table using the main menu click on Table, Insert, Table... from the menu options. Once the Table... item is selected the Insert Table dialogue box appears as shown in Figure 1.52.

By default Word offers the initial option of five columns and two rows. The number of columns and rows can be adjusted by simply typing in the required number or using the arrows to the right of the column or row boxes to add or reduce the default settings.

The default AutoFit format and Table style: are set to automatic. Again these can be changed at any stage. Word offers a wide range of styles and these can be viewed by pressing the Autoformat... button. Figure 1.53 shows the selections that can be made.

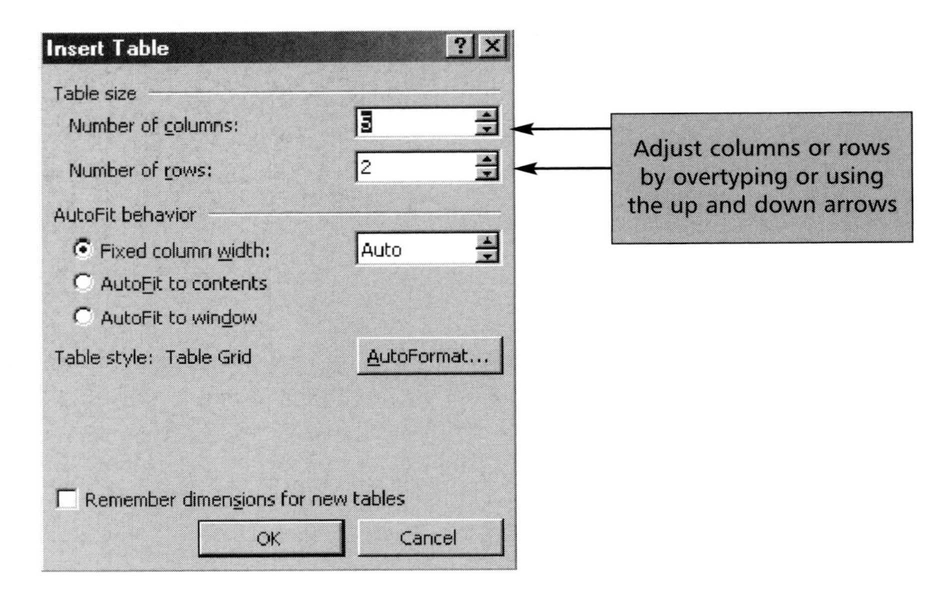

Figure 1.52

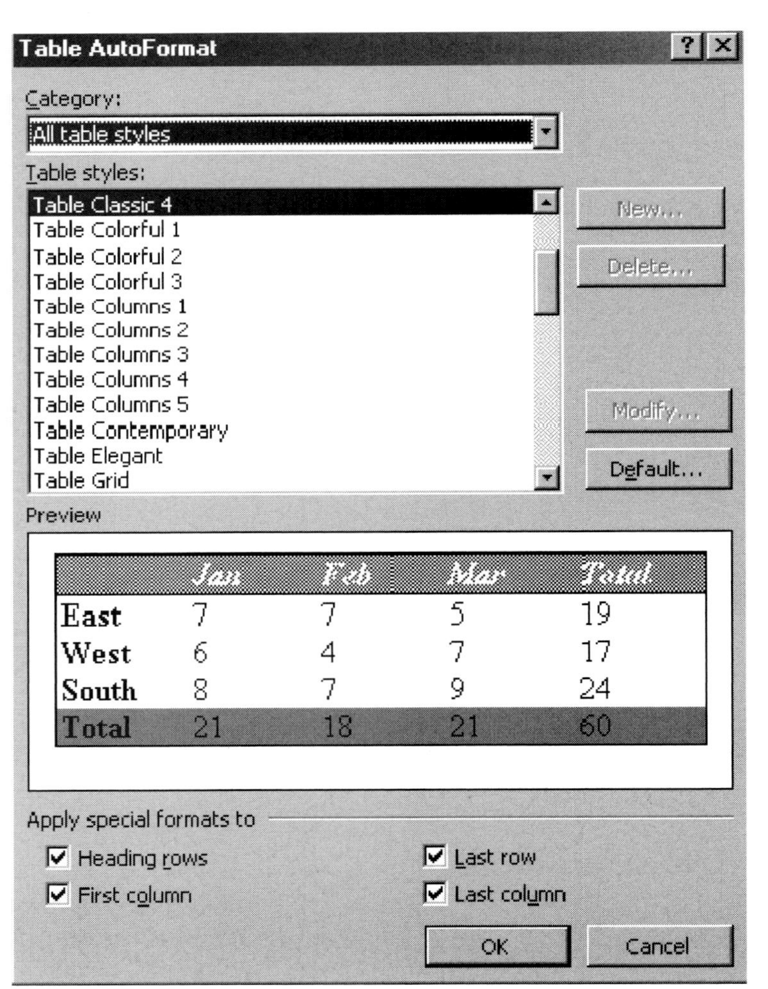

Figure 1.53

Once you have determined the size and format of the table, pressing OK will insert the table into the document.

Try it out

Open a new Word Document.

Select Table, Insert, Table... from the main menu.

Amend the default table size so that it has four columns and ten rows.

Press OK.

Print the table.

Save the file as **Table 1.**

Close the document.

Setting a table's column widths

When a new table is created and inserted into a document, Word automatically sets the column width. However, it is seldom that a table with multiple columns will need the same column widths throughout. For example, a column of text is likely to be wider than one containing numerical data.

As you will now appreciate there is more than one method available for amending the column and row widths for a table. Column widths can be changed either by amending the table properties in the Table Properties dialogue box, or alternatively by using the mouse and the drag method.

Using the Table Properties dialogue box

All objects in a Windows environment have properties, and tables are no exception. By placing the cursor over the object and pressing the right-hand mouse button the drop-down menu provides the range of options shown in Figure 1.54.

Note: for pre XP versions of Office select Table on the main menu and then Table Properties... from the list offered.

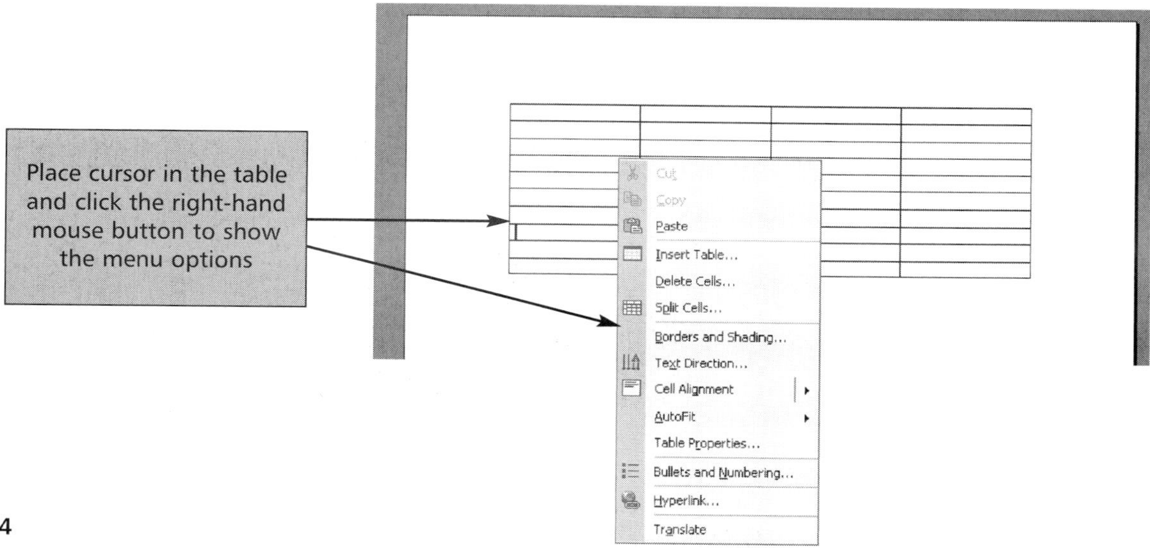

Figure 1.54

To change the properties of the table the Table Properties... item is selected and the dialogue box shown in Figure 1.55 appears.

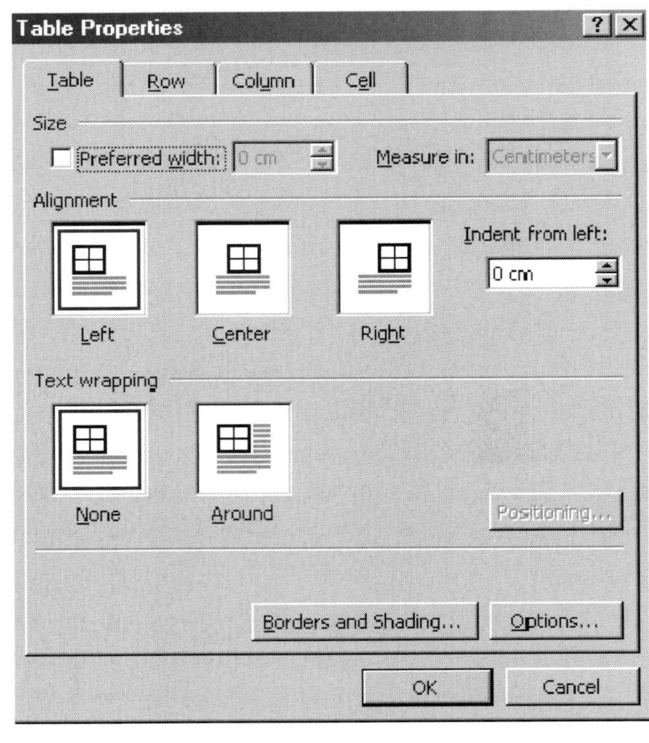

Figure 1.55

Each tab allows you to format different aspects of the table, from its columns and rows to borders and shading. To change the column width the Column tab is selected as shown in Figure 1.56.

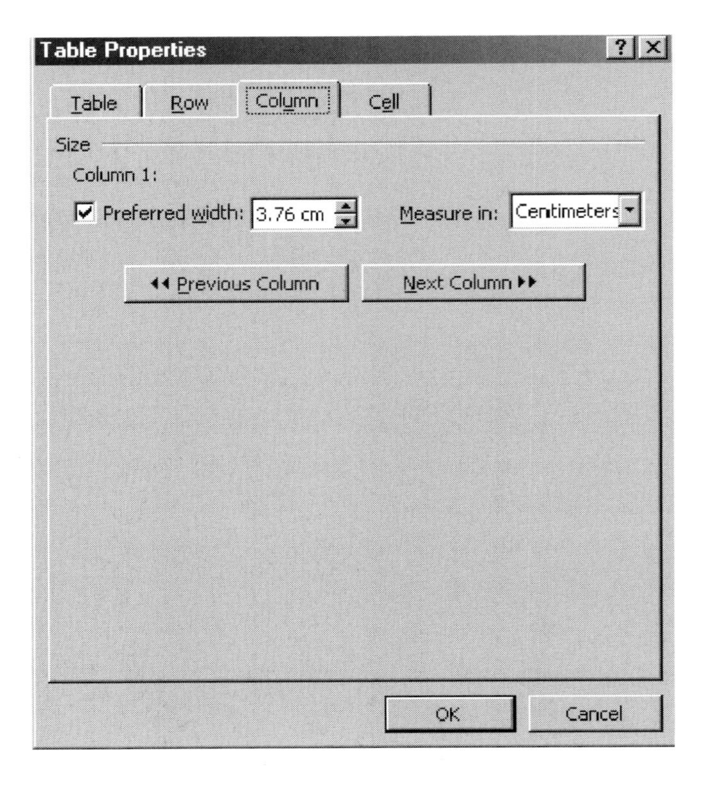

Figure 1.56

With the Column tab selected the width of the table columns can be changed. The width of the column is measured either by using a width measurement or as a percentage of the rest of the columns in the table. To change the width simply type in the required width in centimetres (or other measurement depending on the default setting) or alternatively type a percentage value (e.g. 20%) for that column.

Using the drag method

To alter the width of a column using the drag method, place the cursor over the line between the columns, and pressing and holding down the left-hand mouse button, drag the column out to the required width. As the cursor is moved over the line between the columns it will change shape to ◄||►.

Try it out

Open Table 1.

Using the Table Properties dialogue box method

Format the column widths as follows:

Column 1 5 cm

Columns 2–4 2 cm

Save the table.

Close the file.

Table borders, gridlines and alignment

Tables are immensely flexible and useful tools for presenting data in many different ways. However, the sheer range of formatting functions can in itself lead to a danger of making the end result less readable than it should be. It is beyond the scope of this book to review all the table functions available to you but having understood the basics you may feel sufficiently confident to try practising with some of the functions shown in the various dialogue boxes and menus. For CLAIT Plus you will be expected to understand how to align text and numerical data in columns, format table borders and cell borders, and also be able to turn table gridlines on and off.

Borders and gridlines

By default, when Word creates a table it does so with the borders showing. These borders can be shown either for the whole table or any part of it. Borders can be formatted using either the menu options available, or the toolbar icon. Using the dialogue box gives you greater control than the toolbar but the toolbar is perhaps easier to use and more convenient if the changes to be made do not call for complex formatting.

You may have noticed in Figure 1.55 that there was a button for Borders and Shading. These features allow you to format the borders around the table or for individual cells. They can also introduce shading to all or part of the table. Now have a look at Figure 1.57.

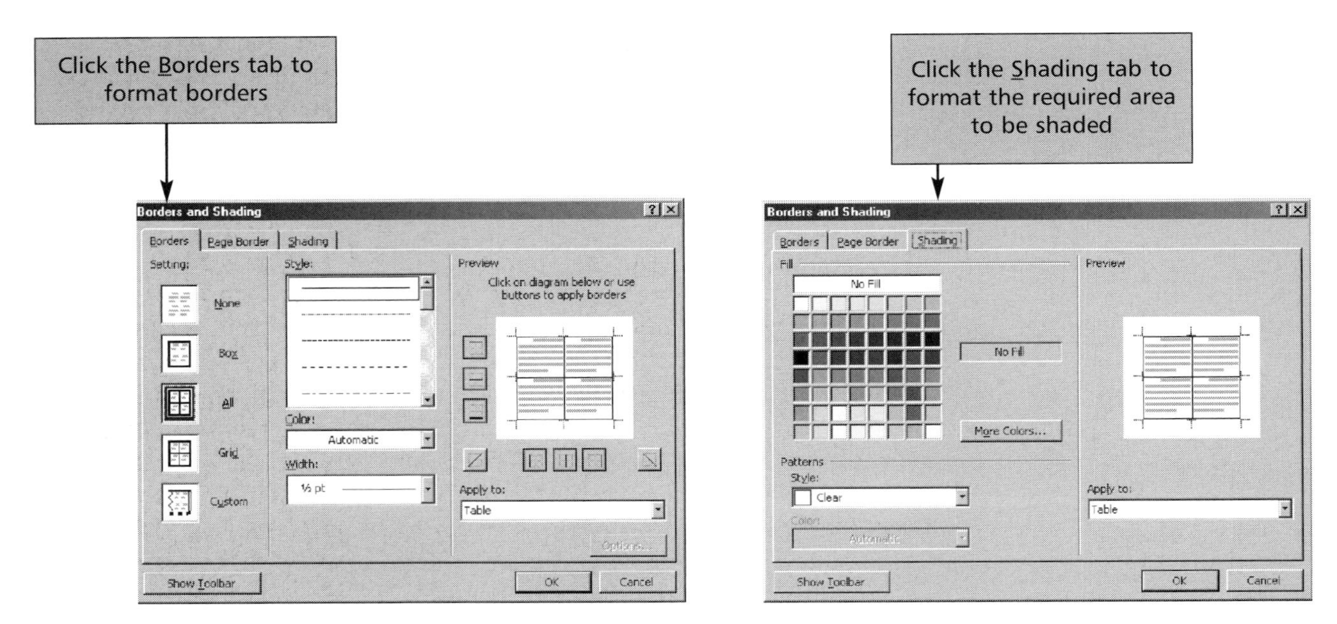

Figure 1.57

Pressing the Borders and Shading button brings up the Borders and Shading dialogue box. However, before accessing this you will need to highlight (or select) those areas of the table which are to be formatted. Have a look at Figure 1.58.

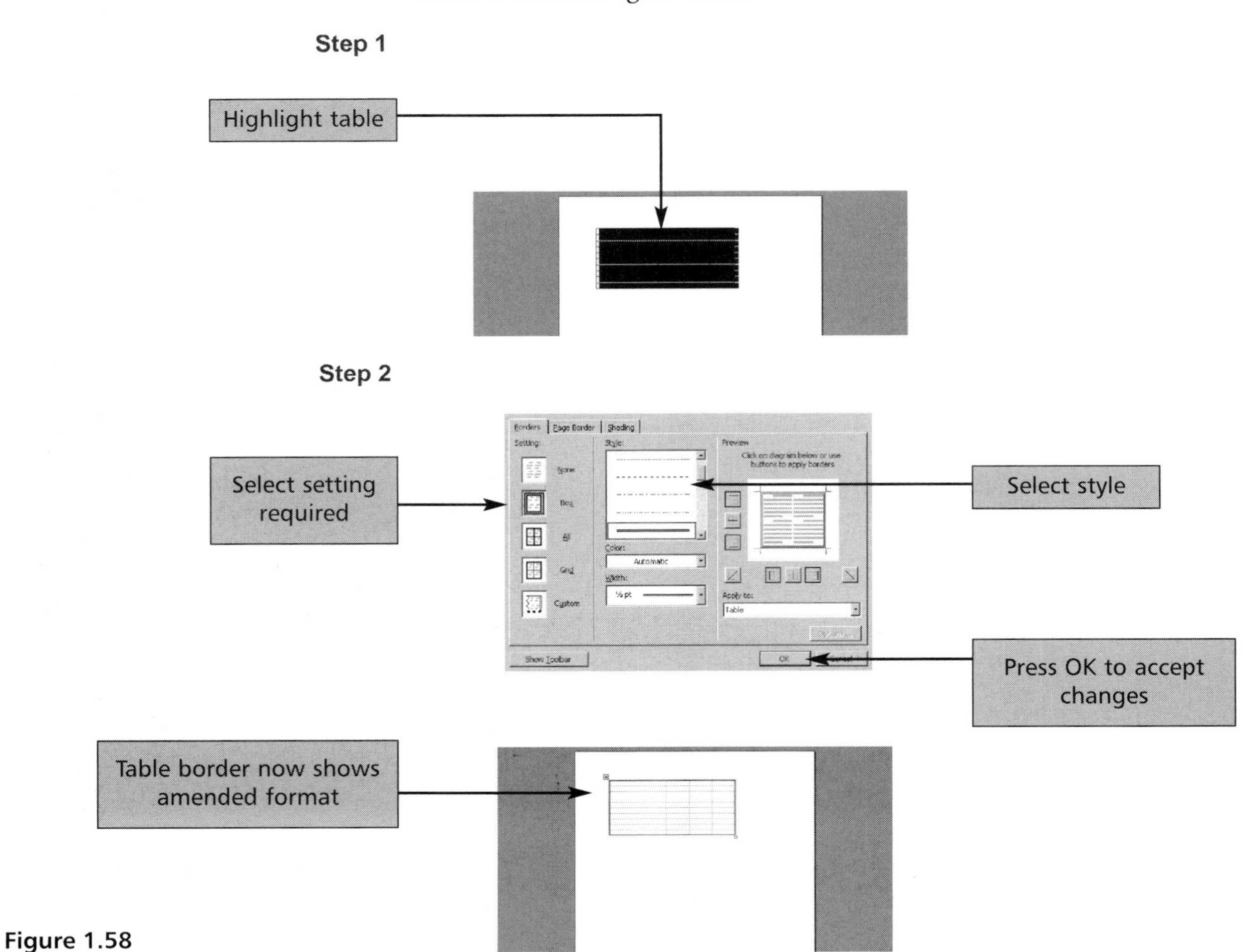

Figure 1.58

In this instance the border around the table was reformatted to a double line. If all the borders were to be reformatted in this way then the All setting could have been selected. Alternatively, if only parts of the table had been selected the Custom setting would be used.

Shading

Shading areas of a table is achieved in much the same way as reformatting the border style. First the area to be shaded is selected, then the Borders and Shading dialogue box is accessed in exactly the same way as you saw for changing the borders. However, instead of selecting the Borders tab the Shading tab is selected (see Figure 1.57). On the left side of the dialogue box is the colour palette from which the required colour is selected. If the colour you want is not shown you can create a customised colour by selecting the More Colours button and then either choosing a standard colour or creating your own by using the Custom tab.

Beneath the Fill colour palette is a further option called Patterns with a Style box underneath. In this selection you can either choose a percentage shade or a pattern: see Figure 1.59.

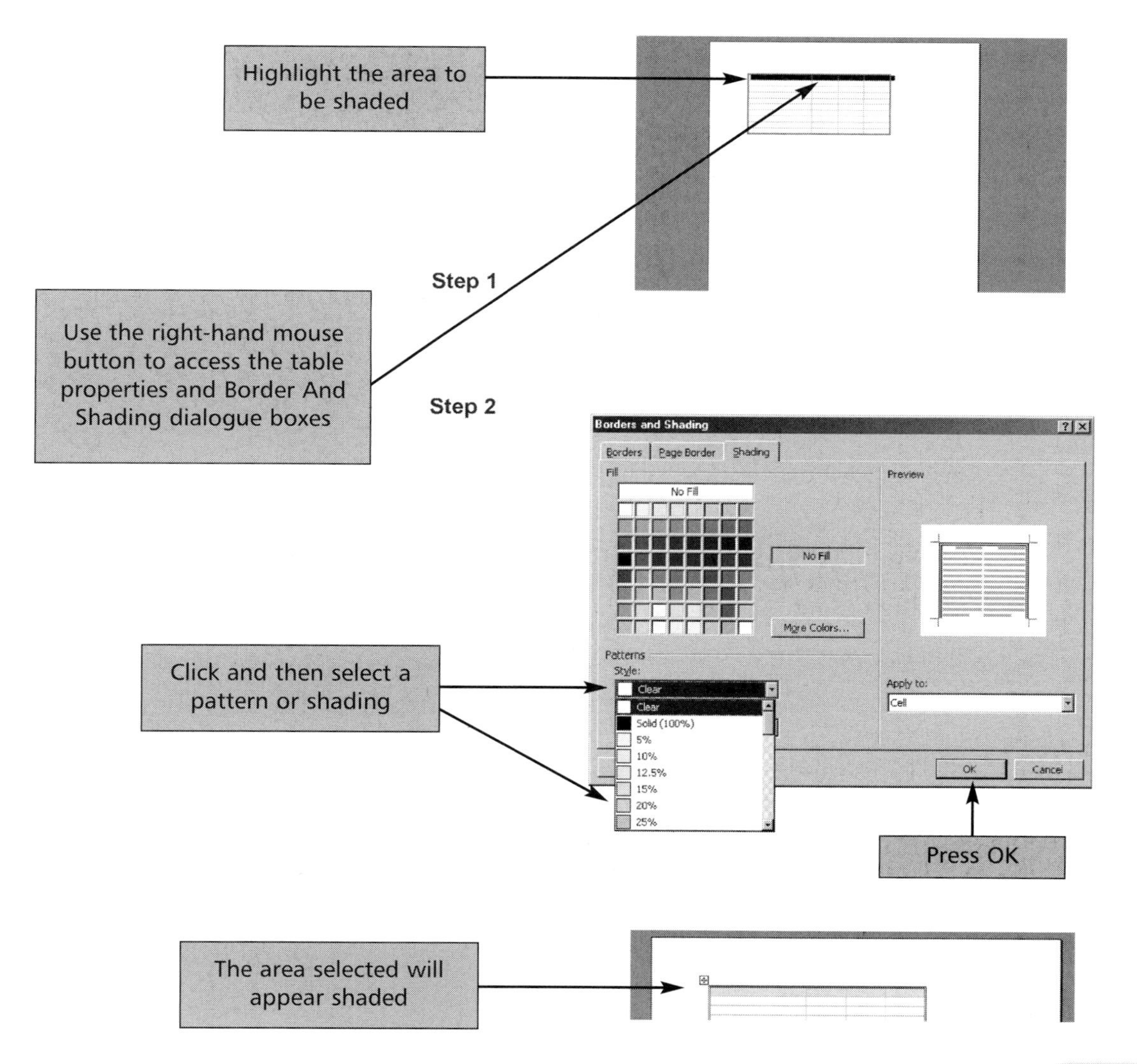

Figure 1.59

Using the toolbar

On the formatting toolbar you will see the borders icon, shown in Figure 1.60.

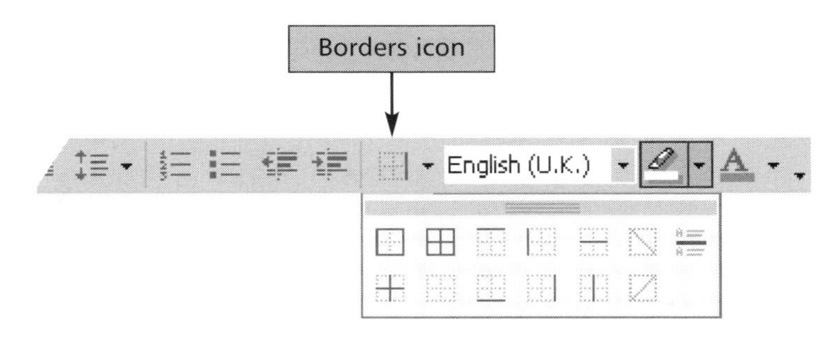

Figure 1.60

Essentially this toolbar is a facility for you to show or hide the borders for specific areas of a table. It does not provide a facility to format the lines of a border (i.e. weight, double line, etc.) and is therefore slightly less flexible than using the options within the Borders and Shading dialogue box.

To use the borders icon, first either place the cursor where you want to make changes or, if the whole table or multiple cells are to be changed, they all need to be highlighted. In Figure 1.61 notice how the border to the right of the first cell in the table is to be removed. To reinstate the border simply click on the appropriate border in the toolbar.

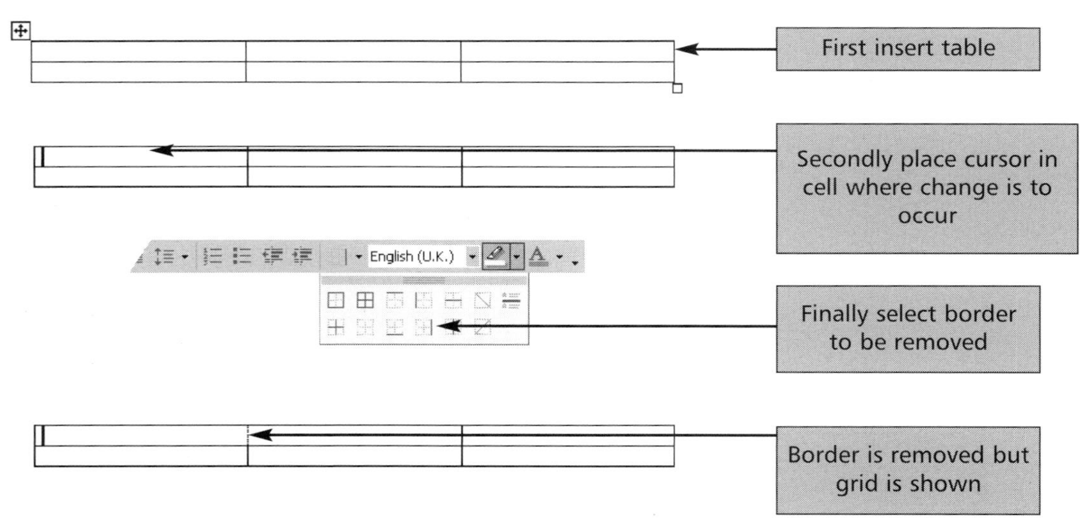

Figure 1.61

Gridlines

In some documents you may want to import a table but make it seem as if it is not a table but a part of the typed document. To achieve this you may want to remove all the printable borders, but still see the gridlines while working on the document. Gridlines help you to navigate around the table you are working on but will not print when the document is completed. Have a look at Figure 1.62.

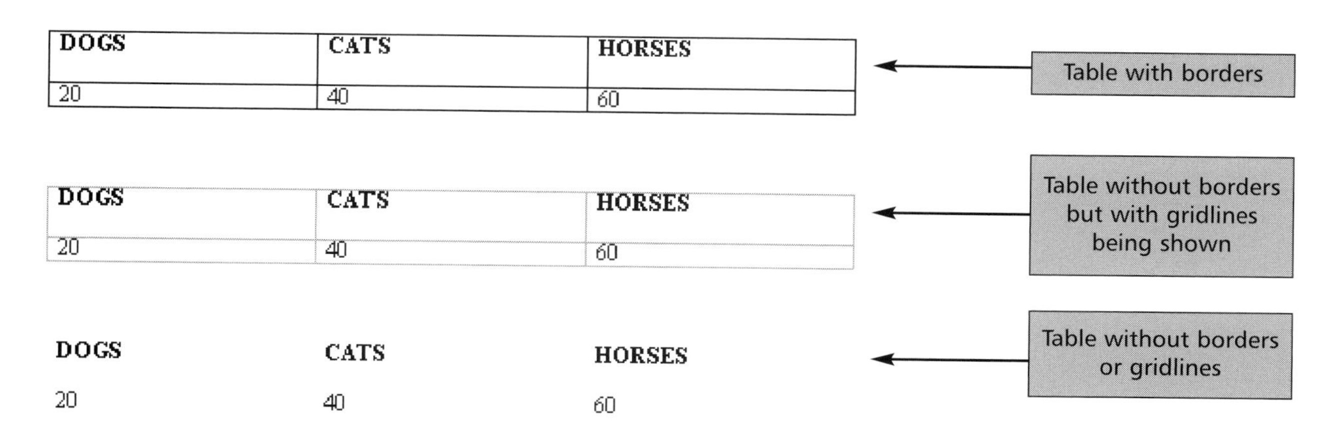

DOGS	CATS	HORSES
20	40	60

DOGS	CATS	HORSES
20	40	60

DOGS	CATS	HORSES
20	40	60

Figure 1.62

The first table above has all the borders and these will be printed. The second table has all the borders removed, but you can still see the cells, which helps you navigate round the table. The third table is how it would appear in a printed document. In fact you can also turn the gridlines off while working on the table, but this does make it more difficult to work on the table.

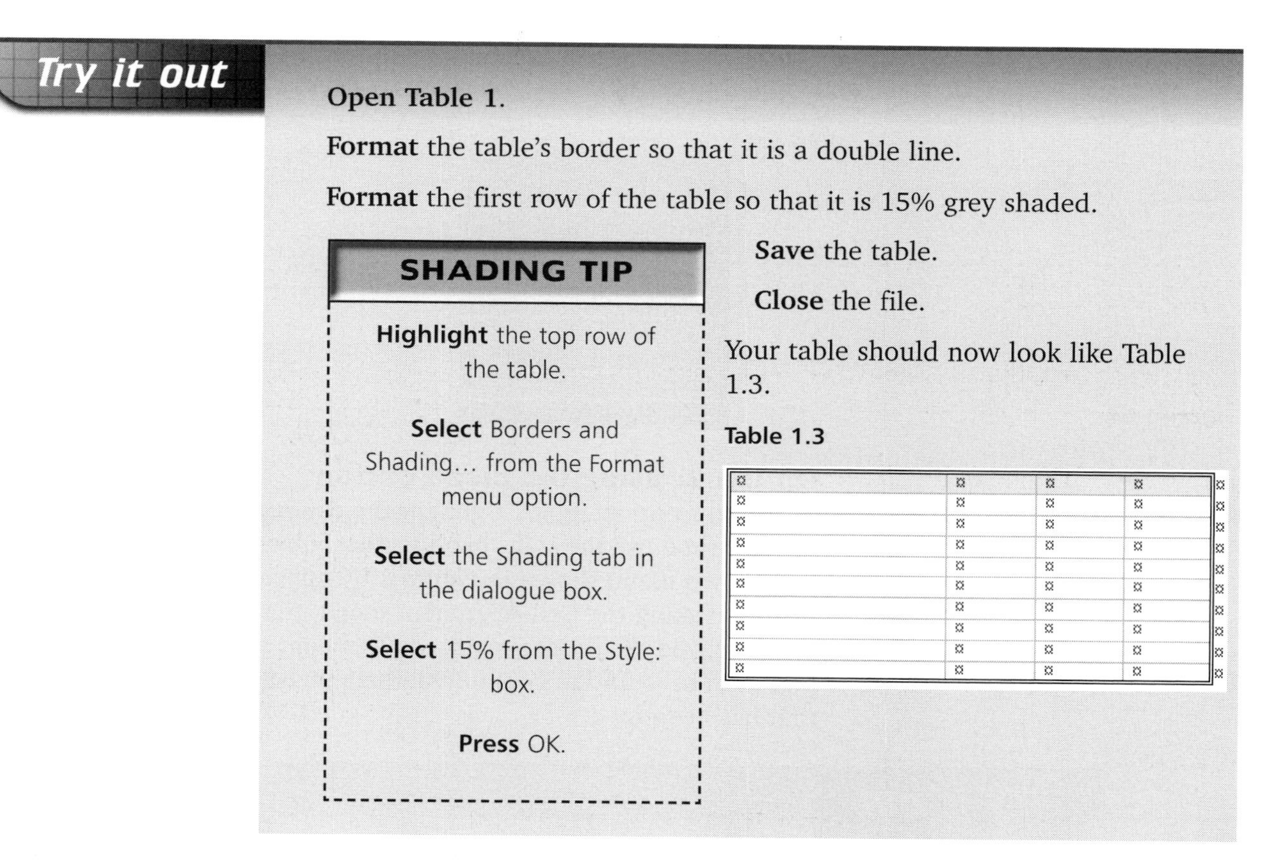

Try it out

Open Table 1.

Format the table's border so that it is a double line.

Format the first row of the table so that it is 15% grey shaded.

SHADING TIP

Highlight the top row of the table.

Select Borders and Shading… from the Format menu option.

Select the Shading tab in the dialogue box.

Select 15% from the Style: box.

Press OK.

Save the table.

Close the file.

Your table should now look like Table 1.3.

Table 1.3

¤	¤	¤	¤
¤	¤	¤	¤
¤	¤	¤	¤
¤	¤	¤	¤
¤	¤	¤	¤
¤	¤	¤	¤
¤	¤	¤	¤
¤	¤	¤	¤
¤	¤	¤	¤
¤	¤	¤	¤

Aligning text and numeric data

By default, Word aligns both text and numeric data to the left of a cell. Data can be aligned in much the same way as normal text is in a document.

There are two main ways to set the alignment for a column, row, group of cells or a single cell.

Option 1: using the toolbar

To align data in a column using the toolbar, first select the column and then press the appropriate alignment icon on the formatting toolbar (see Figure 1.63).

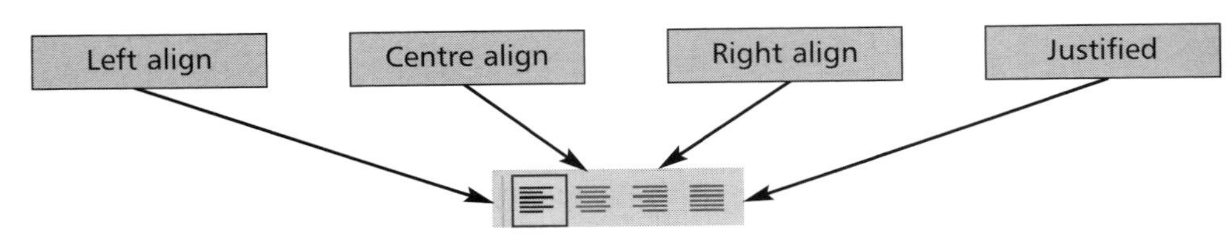

Figure 1.63

A column can be selected by placing the cursor in the first cell and while holding the left-hand mouse button, dragging down the column. More conveniently, if it is a large table, place the cursor above the column to be highlighted and, when you see an arrow appear, click on the left-hand mouse button (see Figure 1.64).

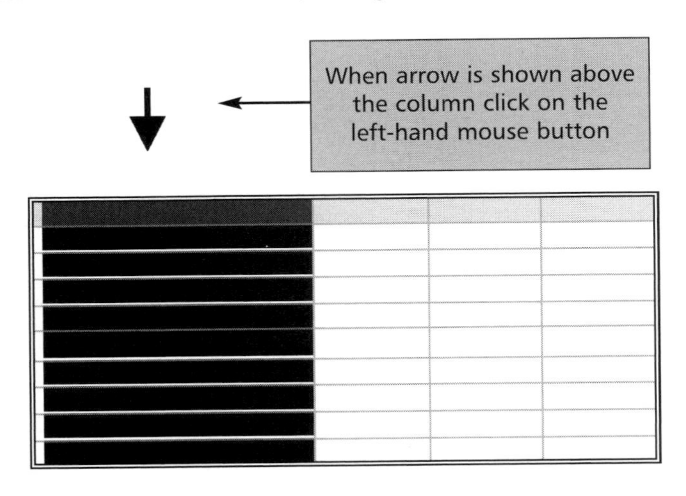

Figure 1.64

Option 2: using the menu option

To use this option, again highlight the column or cells to be aligned, but this time use the right-hand mouse button and you will see the drop-down menu shown in Figure 1.65 appear.

By selecting the Cell Alignment menu item the alignment options are displayed. Select the required alignment and any text or data placed in cells in that column will be aligned according to the selection that has been made.

Try it out

Open Table 1.

Highlight the second and third columns and using either of the above options

Format the cells so that they are right-aligned.

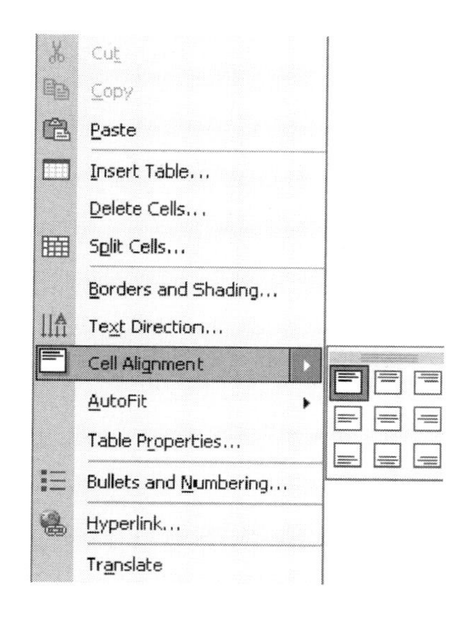

Figure 1.65

Enter the following data:

Table 1.4

Visitor categories	Qtr 1	Qtr 2	Qtr 3
Japanese	560	853	1025
French	212	198	350
German	364	520	569
American	1525	1487	1920
Chinese	105	114	96
Dutch	56	41	78
Swedish	26	45	26
Italian	115	140	267
Total	2963	3398	4331

Save Table 1.

Close Table 1.

Build-up Exercise 1: Stage 3

Open Bellings.doc.

Replace the word 'events' with 'shows' wherever it appears (four occurrences in all).

Save the file.

Close the file.

Build-up Exercise 1: Stage 4

Open a new Word document.

Create a table with three columns and six rows.

Set column widths as follows:

Column 1 5 cm

Column 2 2.5 cm

Column 3 5 cm

Insert the following data into the table:

Table 1.5

Venue	Date	Type
Birmingham	27/10/02	General
Glasgow	15/12/03	Specialist antique
Exeter	20/2/04	Specialist antique
London	24/5/04	Specialist antique
York	9/8/04	General

TABLE TIP

You may have noticed that when you draw the cursor over the table a handle similar to this ⊞ appears. By clicking on this handle you can select the whole table. This allows you to format all text and data at one go. You can also still use the drag method by clicking in the first cell and, with the left-hand mouse button held down, dragging across the range of cells to be highlighted.

Format the first row with 10% shading.

Format the date column (column 2) to be right-aligned and columns 1 and 3 left-aligned.

Format the heading row as bold.

Format the font style for all data to Arial 12.

Save the file as **Venues**.

Close the file.

You should now be able to:

- use special symbols and characters
- find and replace words and phrases
- create and use a table
- format borders and align data in a table
- understand about gridlines in a table
- shade columns, rows and cells in a table.

Importing and manipulating images

Later units in this book show how to create a variety of data files, images and charts that can then be integrated into other files. You will learn these techniques if you choose one of these as optional units. In this core unit for CLAIT Plus the files, images and charts are provided and all you need to do is import and insert them at a specified point within a document.

In this section of the core unit you will learn how to import a picture into a particular location of your document and then resize the image to meet specified formatting requirements.

Inserting an image

First put the cursor at the point in the document where you want to place the image. As you learnt in the headers and footers section, images can be imported directly into any document using the option Insert, then Picture on the main menu. Clicking on the Picture option produces a further menu list. The one you will be concerned with for CLAIT Plus is the From File... option. Selecting this opens the insert picture dialogue box shown in Figure 1.66.

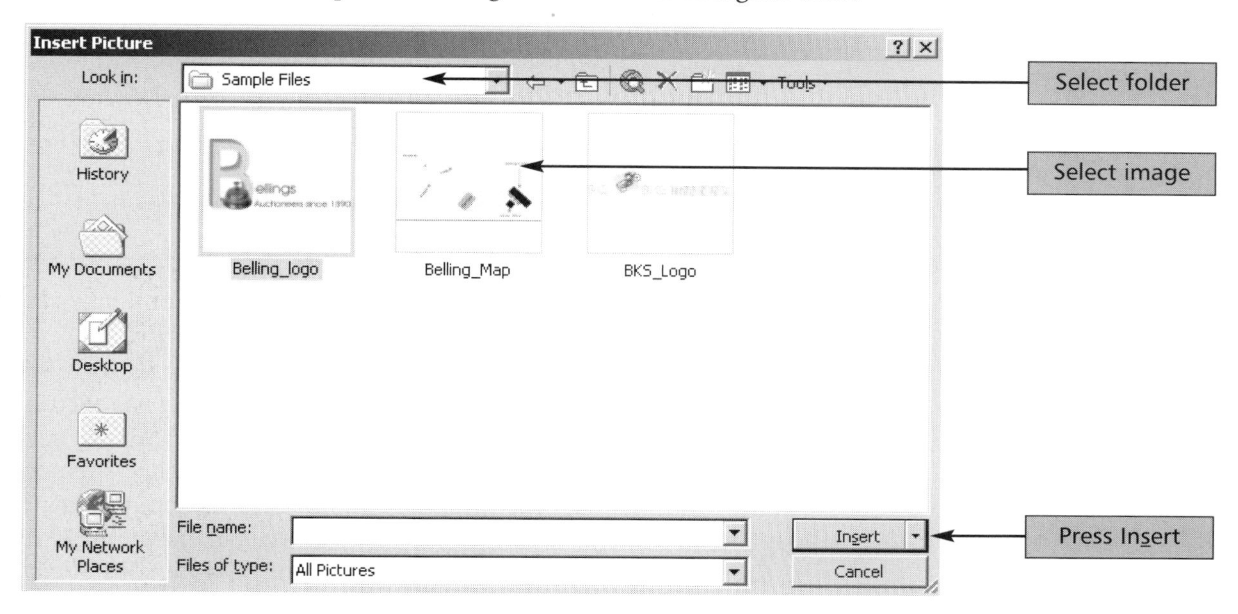

Figure 1.66

Once you press the Insert button the image is inserted into the document at the point where the cursor has been placed. By default Word imports the image so that it moves in line with the text. In this format the image will always stay with text associated with it. This is useful when you have additions to make in an earlier part of the document, since the image will then move with the text to which it applies. Clearly, when you add a new line or paragraph, text below the new insertion will move down.

Formatting an image's layout

The image can be relocated by clicking on it and dragging it to another location where it will again become locked to the text at its new position. The layout of images can be changed in a variety of ways depending on how you want them to behave with text. By pressing the right-hand mouse button with the cursor over the image that is to be reformatted, and selecting Format Picture... the formatting dialogue box will appear. If you select the Layout tab you can see the various options that are available and how these options change the way the picture behaves with any text around it: see Figure 1.67.

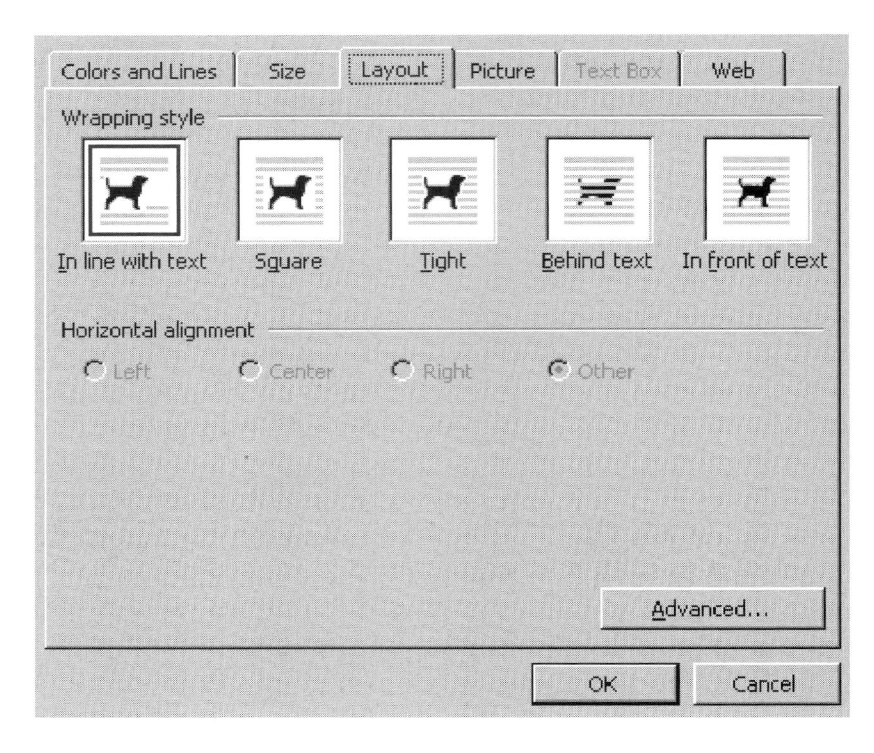

Figure 1.67

Image editing

Although Word is not designed as a graphics editing package it does offer some remarkably useful editing functions using the Picture toolbar. The toolbar can be viewed either by selecting the picture or selecting View, then Toolbars, then Picture from the main menu. This toolbar allows you to adjust the brightness, contrast, rotation, format (i.e. layout, size, etc.) and a number of other aspects of the image. Figure 1.68 shows the Picture toolbar and some of the functions available.

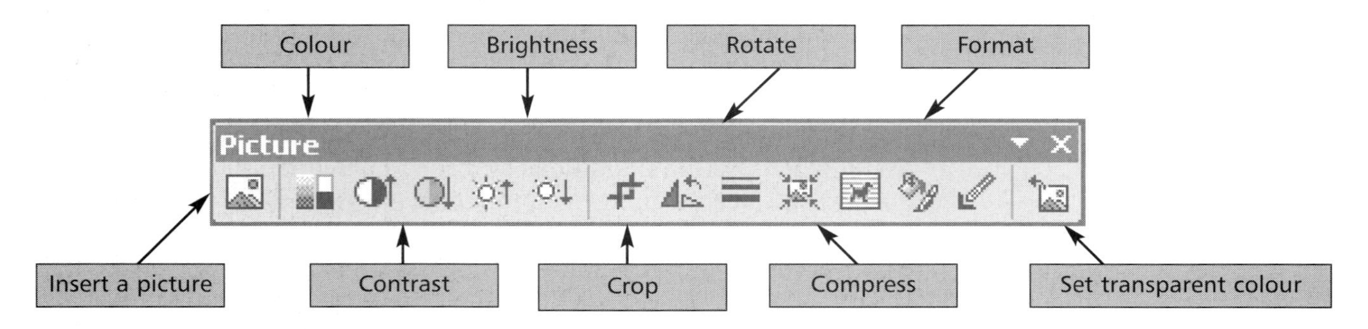

Figure 1.68

Whilst this is not a requirement for CLAIT Plus, you may wish to experiment with some of these options. You will, however, be required to ensure an image is sized correctly, maintaining the original proportions of the image.

To resize an image without changing its proportions can be achieved in two ways. First, if the precise size is not defined you can use one of the corner drag handles to drag the image to the required size. Using one of the corner drag handles will ensure that changes to the image keep the proportions the original image. If you need to change an image to an exact, specified size, use the format picture dialogue box.

To format the picture size using the dialogue box, first select the picture. Then call up the formatting picture dialogue box either by clicking on the Format picture icon on the Picture toolbar, or by selecting the picture and clicking the right-hand mouse button and selecting the Format Picture... menu option. Press the Size tab and, ensuring the Relative to original picture box is checked, enter the required dimensions in the Height: and Width: boxes. Press OK and the picture will change to the set size.

Try it out

Create a new Word document.

Type '=rand(10,10)'.

Press the Enter key.

This will produce random text as described earlier in the unit.

Place the cursor after the last word of the second paragraph.

Press Enter twice to create a new paragraph and line.

Select Insert, Picture, Clip Art... from the main menu.

Press Search to show all pictures available in the gallery.

If you see the Add Clips to Organizer dialogue press the button which says Later.

Select one of the pictures from the clip art gallery. It is not important which picture is used.

Press the arrow to the right of the selected image to view the menu list.

Select Insert.

(Alternatively, to insert the image double-click on it.)

Changing the size using the format picture dialogue box

Click on the image using the right-hand mouse button.

Select Format Picture... from the list.

Select the Size tab.

Making sure the Relative to original picture size box is checked,

Type 14.5 cm as the width of the picture.

Press OK.

The image will automatically resize, keeping its original proportions, based on the width selected. You could equally have inserted a height.

Press the undo icon on the toolbar to undo the resizing.

Changing the size using the drag technique

Click on the image to make drag handles appear.

Place the cursor over a corner handle (usually the bottom right handle) until you see the cursor change shape to a double arrow.

Click and hold down the left-hand mouse button.

Drag the image to the required size.

Close the document without saving.

Importing and formatting charts

Charts are a particularly useful feature made available in most Microsoft applications. Charts show a pictorial view of data and help the viewer understand the story behind the figures. In CLAIT Plus, unless you choose to complete the unit on graphs and charts as one of the optional units, you are not expected to be able to create a chart. However, you are expected to understand how to import and place charts (as well as datafiles and images) and also ensure that the imported object is legible. On occasions this may mean you will need to change the size of text or to alter a fill colour/pattern where, for example, a clear distinction cannot be made between two data series when the chart is printed in black and white.

Importing a chart

In this section you will learn how to import a chart pre-prepared as part of an Excel worksheet and to change a number of its properties.

Again, as with most application functions there are a variety of ways you can import chart objects. For this core unit you will use the Insert, Object... option on the main menu. Since this option is relatively straightforward it is easier to understand by doing it rather than reading detailed explanations. Have a go at following the Try it out exercise below.

Try it out

Open a new Word document.

Type '=rand(10,10)'.

Press Enter to generate random text.

Place your cursor at the end of the last word in paragraph 2. 

Press the Enter key twice.

Select Insert, Object... from the main menu.

Select the Create from File tab on the Object dialogue box.

Press Browse: see Figure 1.69.

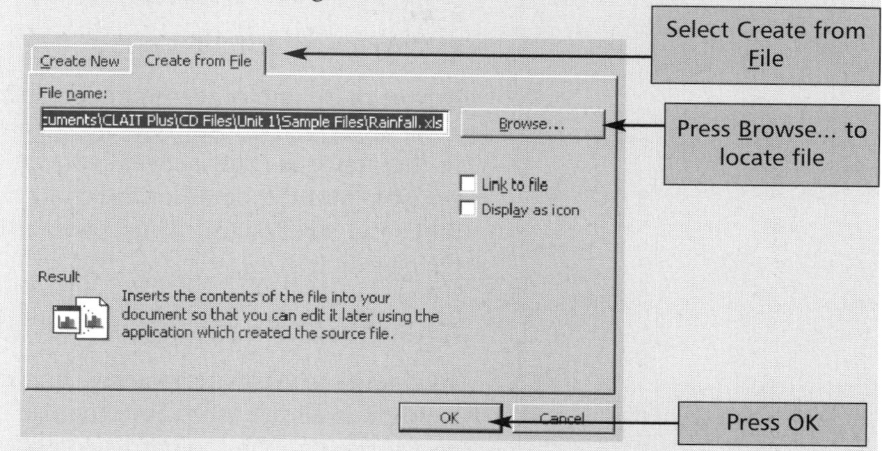

Figure 1.69

Select Rainfall.xls from the Unit 1, Sample Files folder on the accompanying CD.

Press Insert.

Press OK.

The chart from this worksheet is inserted into the document. You will notice that the size is not appropriate for the page orientation.

Click on the chart to show the size drag handles.

Reduce the size of the chart so that it fits between the margins of the document by clicking on and dragging one of the corner drag handles.

Your document should now look similar to Figure 1.70.

The quick brown fox jumps over the lazy dog. The quick brown fox jumps over the lazy dog. The quick brown fox jumps over the lazy dog. The quick brown fox jumps over the lazy dog. The quick brown fox jumps over the lazy dog. The quick brown fox jumps over the lazy dog. The quick brown fox jumps over the lazy dog. The quick brown fox jumps over the lazy dog. The quick brown fox jumps over the lazy dog. The quick brown fox jumps over the lazy dog.
The quick brown fox jumps over the lazy dog. The quick brown fox jumps over the lazy dog. The quick brown fox jumps over the lazy dog. The quick brown fox jumps over the lazy dog. The quick brown fox jumps over the lazy dog. The quick brown fox jumps over the lazy dog. The quick brown fox jumps over the lazy dog. The quick brown fox jumps over the lazy dog. The quick brown fox jumps over the lazy dog. The quick brown fox jumps over the lazy dog.

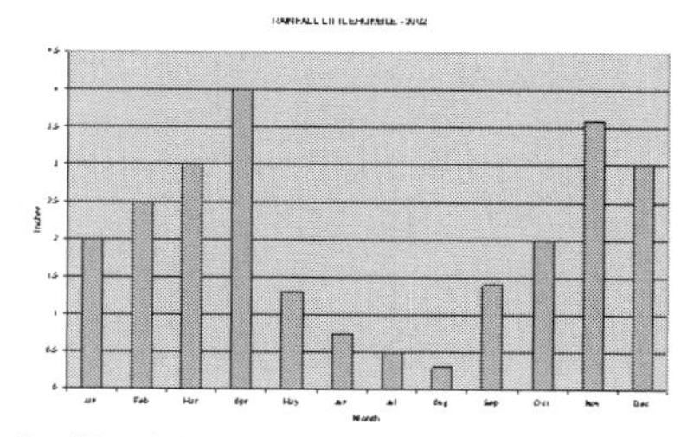

The quick brown fox jumps over the lazy dog. The quick brown fox jumps over the lazy dog. The quick brown fox jumps over the lazy dog. The quick brown fox jumps over the lazy dog. The quick brown fox jumps over the lazy dog. The quick brown fox jumps over the lazy dog. The quick brown fox jumps over the lazy dog. The quick brown fox jumps over the lazy dog. The quick brown fox jumps over the lazy dog. The quick brown fox jumps over the lazy dog.
The quick brown fox jumps over the lazy dog. The quick brown fox jumps over the lazy dog. The quick brown fox jumps over the lazy dog. The quick brown fox jumps over the lazy dog. The quick brown fox jumps over the lazy dog. The quick brown fox jumps over the lazy dog. The quick brown fox jumps over the lazy dog. The quick brown fox jumps over the lazy dog. The quick brown fox jumps over the lazy dog. The quick brown fox jumps over the lazy dog.

Figure 1.70

Save the document as **Chart_1**.

Formatting a chart

Once a chart has been created, irrespective of the application in which it was created, its properties will be set to the default of that application. Amongst properties included are:

- font colour, size and style
- scale
- colour and pattern fills.

Any of these and other formats relating to the chart can be changed to meet any given house style. Because the size of the chart you imported in the previous exercise was reduced to fit between the margins it is possible that the detail of the chart may not be clearly legible and to make the label or axis fonts easier to read it may be necessary to change their size.

Changing a heading, data label or axis font size

To change a chart's formatting, first double-click on the chart itself. Doing this allows Word to recognise that the chart was created in Excel and so change the toolbar to access the Excel menu. To change the font size, type or colour of the chart's axis heading, data label or other aspect of the chart, the relevant part of the chart has to be selected. For example, if you want to change the font size of the X-axis double-click on one of the axis labels and a Format Axis dialogue box will appear, with the font tab already selected as shown in Figure 1.71.

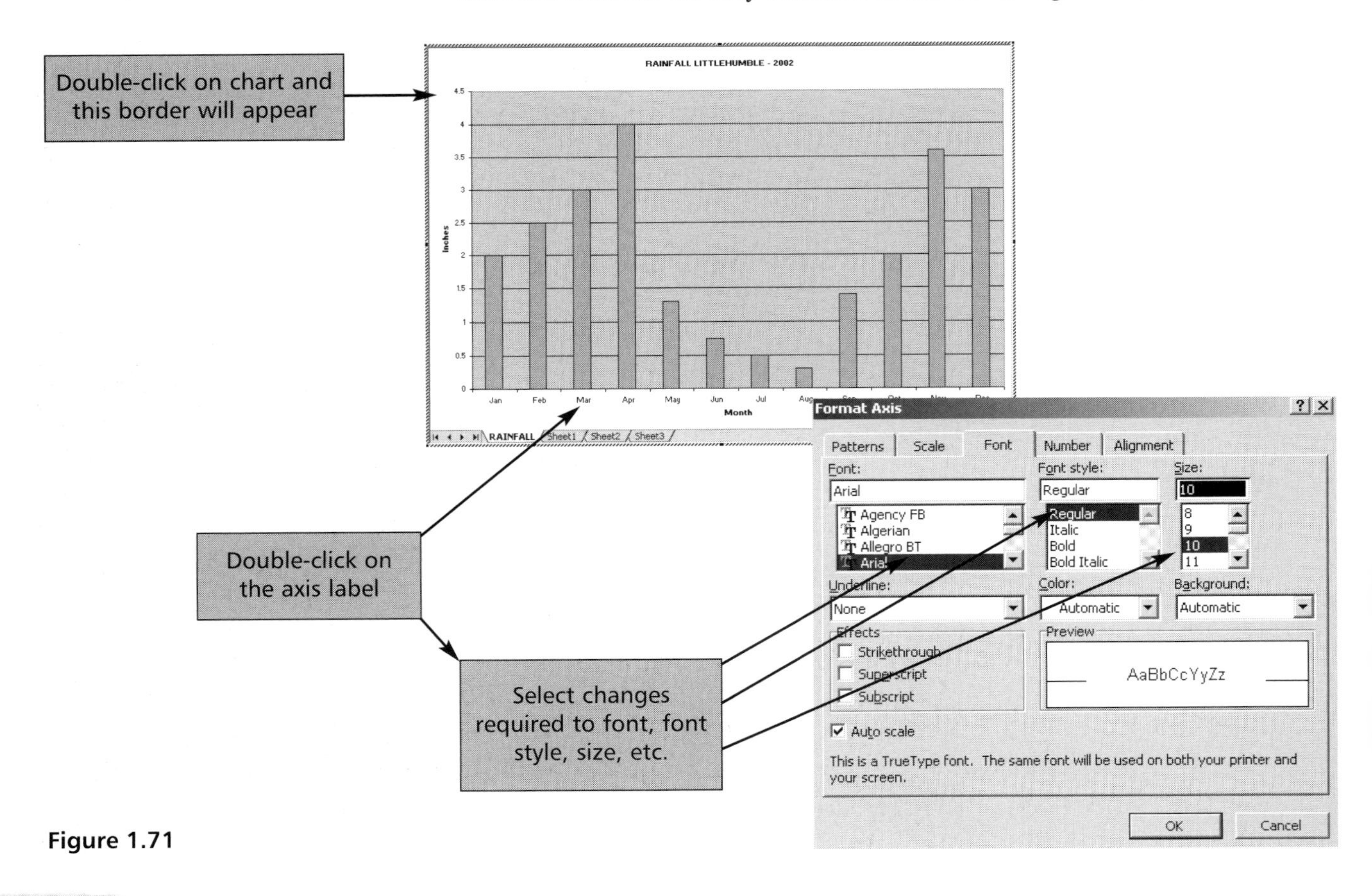

Figure 1.71

Try it out

Open your document **Chart_1** if it is not already open.

Double-click on the rainfall chart.

Double-click on the X-axis data label (any of the months will do).

In the Formatting Axis dialogue box:

Change the size of the font to 16 point.

Repeat this exercise for the Y-axis data label with a font size of 16 point.

Change the X- and Y-axis titles (Month and Inches) to font size 18 point.

Change the main heading to font size 22 point.

Save your document as **Chart_2**.

Have a look at Figure 1.72 and see how the change makes the detail of the chart more legible.

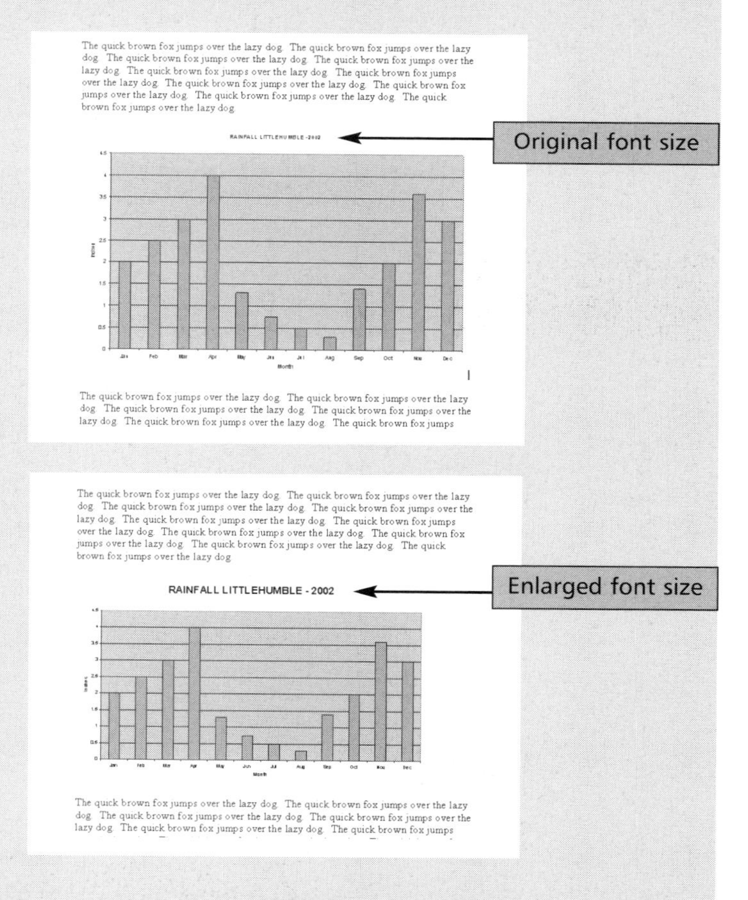

Figure 1.72

If your chart has labels attached to the data itself then the same procedure should be followed to change the properties of the data labels.

Formatting a chart's data series

The data series of a chart can also be formatted using similar techniques to those outlined above. Format a series of data (in the previous example the series would be columns in the rainfall chart) by double-clicking on the series; the dialogue box shown in Figure 1.73 now appears.

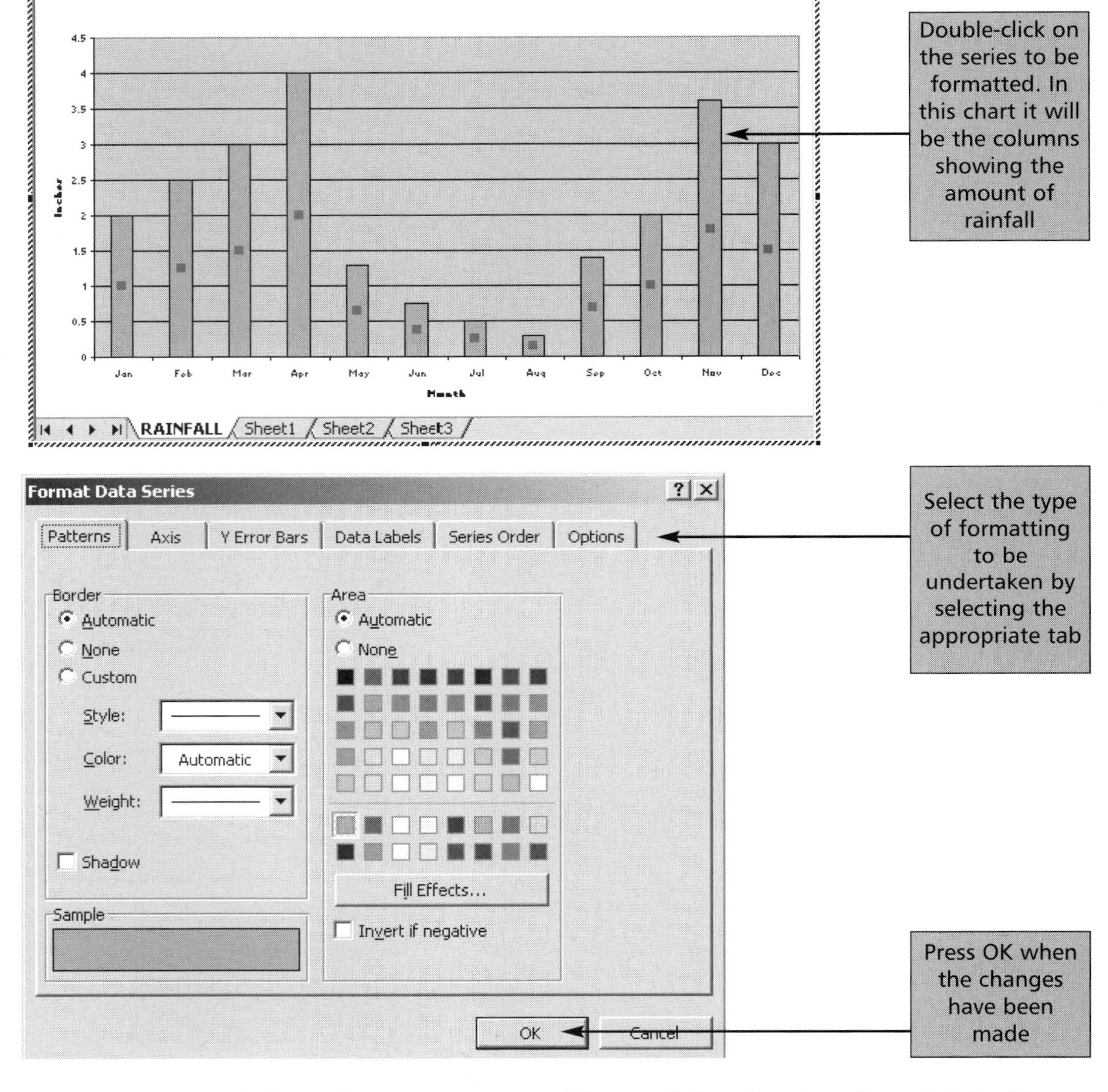

Figure 1.73

Where there are two sets of data and the chart is to be printed with a black-only printer it can be useful to change the colours to patterns so that the data sets are easily distinguishable from each other.

Importing datafiles

Since OCR does not prescribe any specific software for you to use to complete CLAIT Plus, the data files provided for you to use in assignments are in .csv (comma separated values) format. This simply means that instead of, say, having an Excel file saved in its normal .xls format the file has been saved in a way that the data is separated by commas. You will not notice any significant difference, but using a generic format such as .csv allows the file to be opened and used by a variety of packages other than Microsoft software.

The simplest and most effective way of importing a datafile is to follow this procedure:

Open the file to be imported in Excel.

Highlight the data range (or all the data) to be imported.

Select Copy from the Edit option on the main menu.

Switch to the document into which the file is to be imported (normally Word).

Postion the cursor at the point where the file is to be placed.

Select Paste from the Edit options on the main menu.

The file will now be pasted as a table into the target document. Being a table all normal formatting on the table, such as column widths, borders and shading, fonts sizing etc., can be carried out on the imported data table. Now have a go at importing a simple .csv datafile from Excel into a Word document.

TIP

Opening files in Excel

First select Microsoft Excel from the programs list on the Start menu. Select File, Open.... Locate the file from the CD, or your hard disk if you have already transferred the CD files. Make sure the All Files option is selected in the Files of type: box at the bottom of the Open dialogue box. Click on the .csv file to be used and click OK.

Try it out

Open Car_Sales.doc from the Sample Files sub-folder of the Unit 1 folder on the accompanying CD.

Open Car_Sales_July.csv in Excel.

Highlight cells A1:D9.

Copy the contents of these cells to the clipboard.

Insert the datafile after the first paragraph of **Car_Sales.doc** leaving at least one line space after the last line of the paragraph.

Paste the datafile from the clipboard into the document using Edit, Paste from the main menu.

Format the heading row in the datafile with 10% shading.

Format the heading in the table to bold.

Adjust the width of the table so that the heading is not word wrapped.

Save the file as **Car_Sales_July** on your floppy disk.

Close both working files (Word and Excel).

Your document should look similar to Figure 1.74.

TIP

Copying to clipboard

After highlighting the data

Select Edit on the main menu.

Select Copy.

You will notice an animated dotted line around the highlighted cells.

RESULTS OF THE CAR SALES COMPETITION FOR JULY

I am delighted to announce the winner of the sales competition for July. As you can see from the table below July was a good month for all the sales team but Andy managed to pip Peter to the post by one.

CAR SALES COMPETITION - JULY 2003			
CHARLIE	14		
PETER	16		
ANDY	17		
JOAN	15		
JONATHAN	10		
JED	12		
SUSAN	14		

Again many congratulations to you all and Andy in particular. The prize for this month's competition is an all expenses paid trip to Venice for a long weekend. There will not be a competition next month as a number of the team will be away on holiday and others are attending the sales convention in Brighton. Competitions will start again in September and run through to December.

Figure 1.74

You should now be able to:

- insert an image into a document
- format the layout properties of an image
- resize an image
- import a chart and change its properties
- import a datafile.

Now put together some of the skills learnt in the last section by completing the following build-up exercise.

Build-up Exercise 1: Stage 5

Open Bellings.doc in Word.

Insert Belling_Map.jpg in the Catalogues paragraph after 'A map showing how to find us is shown below.' Ensure that the size of the picture is contained within the margins of the document.

Insert the bar chart **Repeats.xls** (from Unit 1 on the CD accompanying this book) in the About Bellings paragraph after '….through repeat business shown in the chart below' ensuring that the chart is within the margins.

Format the data and axis fonts as follows:

X- and Y-axis titles	14 points
X- and Y-axis labels	14 points
Chart title font	18 points

Insert the following paragraph with a sub heading 'Range of Items' after the Catalogues paragraph:

'For this September's sale we are pleased to announce that the range of antiques on offer is excitingly broad and there should be something for most collectors and enthusiasts. The information below shows the range of antiques currently in the catalogue with a guide to the anticipated prices they may attract.'

Insert the datafile **Antiques.csv** (from Unit 1 on the CD accompanying this book) immediately below the last sentence of the paragraph Range of Items.

Insert the table 'Venues', created in Stage 4, after the last paragraph.

Finally ensure that no datafile crosses the page boundaries and that there is no more than a two-line space at the bottom of each page.

Your final document should look similar to Figure 1.75.

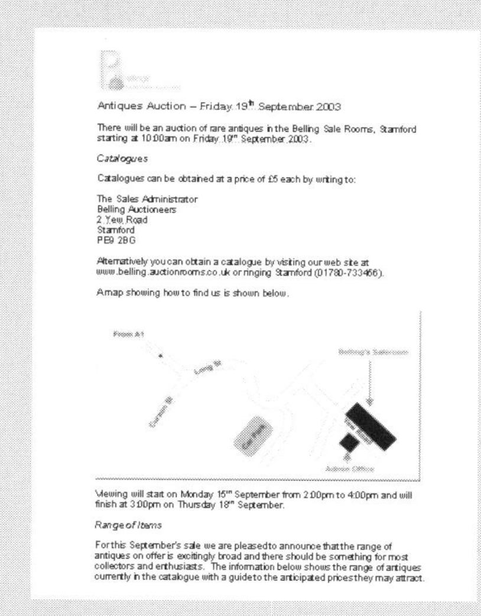
Antiques Auction – Friday 19th September 2003

There will be an auction of rare antiques in the Belling Sale Rooms, Stamford starting at 10:00am on Friday 19th September 2003.

Catalogues

Catalogues can be obtained at a price of £5 each by writing to:

The Sales Administrator
Belling Auctioneers
2 Yew Road
Stamford
PE9 2BG

Alternatively you can obtain a catalogue by visiting our web site at www.belling.auctionrooms.co.uk or ringing Stamford (01780-733466).

A map showing how to find us is shown below.

Viewing will start on Monday 15th September from 2:00pm to 4:00pm and will finish at 3:00pm on Thursday 18th September.

Range of Items

For this September's sale we are pleased to announce that the range of antiques on offer is excitingly broad and there should be something for most collectors and enthusiasts. The information below shows the range of antiques currently in the catalogue with a guide to the anticipated prices they may attract.

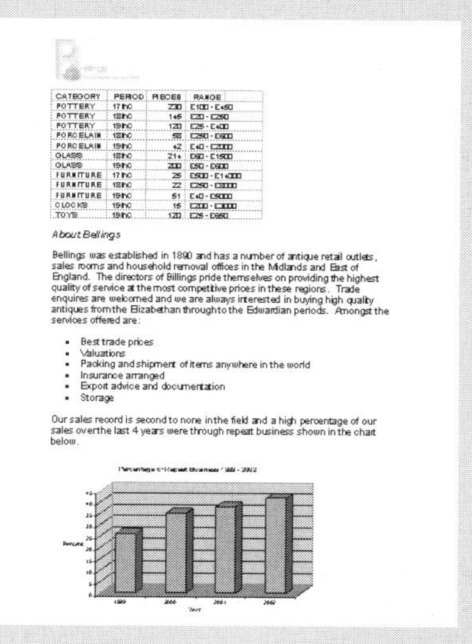

CATEGORY	PERIOD	PIECES	RANGE
POTTERY	17thC	230	£100 - £450
POTTERY	18thC	145	£20 - £250
POTTERY	19thC	120	£25 - £400
PORCELAIN	18thC	58	£250 - £600
PORCELAIN	19thC	42	£40 - £2000
GLASS	18thC	214	£60 - £1500
GLASS	19thC	200	£50 - £600
FURNITURE	17thC	25	£600 - £14000
FURNITURE	18thC	22	£250 - £8000
FURNITURE	19thC	51	£40 - £5000
CLOCKS	19thC	15	£200 - £3000
TOYS	19thC	120	£25 - £850

About Bellings

Bellings was established in 1890 and has a number of antique retail outlets, sales rooms and household removal offices in the Midlands and East of England. The directors of Billings pride themselves on providing the highest quality of service at the most competitive prices in these regions. Trade enquires are welcomed and we are always interested in buying high quality antiques from the Elizabethan through to the Edwardian periods. Amongst the services offered are:

- Best trade prices
- Valuations
- Packing and shipment of items anywhere in the world
- Insurance arranged
- Export advice and documentation
- Storage

Our sales record is second to none in the field and a high percentage of our sales over the last 4 years were through repeat business shown in the chart below.

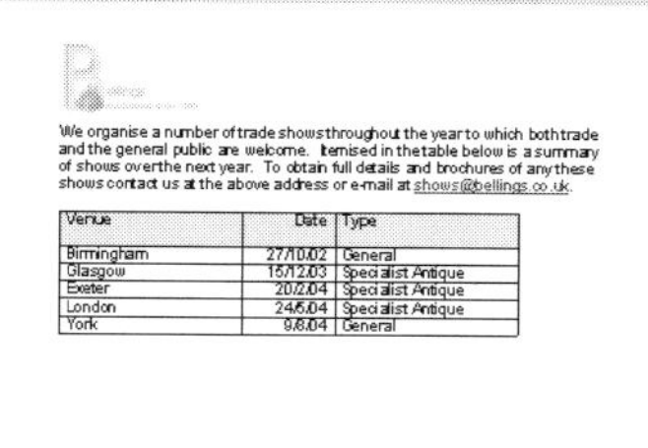
We organise a number of trade shows throughout the year to which both trade and the general public are welcome. Itemised in the table below is a summary of shows over the next year. To obtain full details and brochures of any these shows contact us at the above address or e-mail at shows@bellings.co.uk.

Venue	Date	Type
Birmingham	27/10/02	General
Glasgow	15/12/03	Specialist Antique
Exeter	20/2/04	Specialist Antique
London	24/5/04	Specialist Antique
York	9/8/04	General

Figure 1.75

You have completed all the requirements of OCR for the core unit on creating, managing and integrating files.

Now have a go at the full practical assignment below. A solution to this assignment can be found in Appendix 2.

Practical assignment 1

Create, manage and integrate files

Scenario

You are the secretary for the senior partner in a motorcycle training company called BKS. Your boss has noticed that there is a backlog of students awaiting training because the pass rate for the theory test has reduced dramatically. He has been carrying out some analysis of these results and decided to offer additional training for the theory test. Those students who decide to take up this offer will be given a discount. You have been asked to prepare a brief on the proposals for all the instructors.

To produce this brief you will need the following files:

	File location	
■ A text file that forms the basic brief to which you will need to make a number of am endments and also import a variety of files.	CD: Filename:	Unit 1\Sample Files **Theory_Test.doc**
■ An Excel spreadsheet containing a chart showing the student pass rates over a six month period.	CD: Filename:	Unit 1\Sample Files **First_Passes.xls**
■ The company logo	CD: Filename:	Unit 1\Sample Files **BKS_Logo.jpg**
■ A datafile containing details of student bookings for the month of January 2003.	CD: Filename:	Unit 1\Sample Files **Student_Bookings.csv**

In carrying out this exercise you should consult the house style sheet to ensure the document layout is as required.

Part of this exercise requires you to create a table with certain data and format. To include the relevant data you will need to consult the student booking sheets.

You will use the following software to complete this exercise:

- Word
- Excel
- Access

Your work should be saved on a new floppy disk or your hard disk.

▶▶

House style sheet

Page setup

Orientation		Portrait		
Margins	**Top**	2.5 cm		
	Bottom	2.5 cm		
	Left	3.0 cm		
	Right	3.0 cm		
Header	BKS_Logo	Left-aligned		
Footer	Date	Left-aligned	Page number	Right-aligned
Spacing	Single spacing			

Text styles

Text	Font	Text size	Style	Alignment
Heading	Sans serif	16 point	Bold, capital	Centred
Sub-headings	Sans serif	14 point	Bold, capital	Left
Body	Sans serif	12 point		Justified
Bullet text	Sans serif	12 point		
Tables	Sans serif	12 point	With gridlines	Column heading – centred, bold, 10% shading Text – left Numeric data – right-aligned Dates – right-aligned
Imported datafile	Sans serif	12 point	With gridlines	Column heading – centred, bold, 10% shading. Text – left Numeric – right Dates – right
Graph/chart	Text sans serif	Legible		

Note

Spacing between headings, sub-headings and paragraphs must be applied consistently.

Avoid widows and orphans.

Text, images, graphs and lines must not be superimposed.

Imported data is not to be split across pages.

Graphs and charts must be positioned within the margins of the page.

Spell check the document.

Practical assignment 1

Exercise brief

Assessment objectives	Stage	
		In completing this exercise you will be working with a number of files so you will need to setup a folder either on a floppy or your hard disk.
1a	1	On your floppy or hard disk create a new folder and call it BKS.
1e	2	Copy the files: **Theory_Test.rtf** **First_Passes.xls** **Student_Bookings.csv** **BKS_Logo.jpg**
		From Unit 1 on the accompanying CD to your new folder:
1b	3	Open the file called **Theory_Test.rtf** and save as a Word document.
2e	4	Using the spell checker check the document for spelling errors.
2a 2b 2c 3b 2d 2e 3c 3d 3e 4c 4d 4f 5a 5b 5c 5d	5	Referring to the draft document on pages 71–2 make the changes indicated.
4h	6	Using the search and replace function replace Theory Test with Theory Exam wherever it occurs (six occurrences in all).
4a 4b 4e	7	Apply the page layout and house style as indicated on the house style sheet – Practical assignment 1.
2e	8	Recheck for any spelling errors.
1b	9	Save your document to the newly created folder BKS using the **Theory_Test** name.
3e	10	Print the document.
1b	11	Close the document and application.
1f	12	Rename the BKS folder **BKS_Bike_Training.**
1a	13	Create a new folder in the working folder and call it **Dumps.**
1d	14	Move the files **First_Passes**, **Student_Bookings**, **BKS_Logo** to the Dumps folder.
1h	15	Produce a screen printout of the folders and the files they contain.

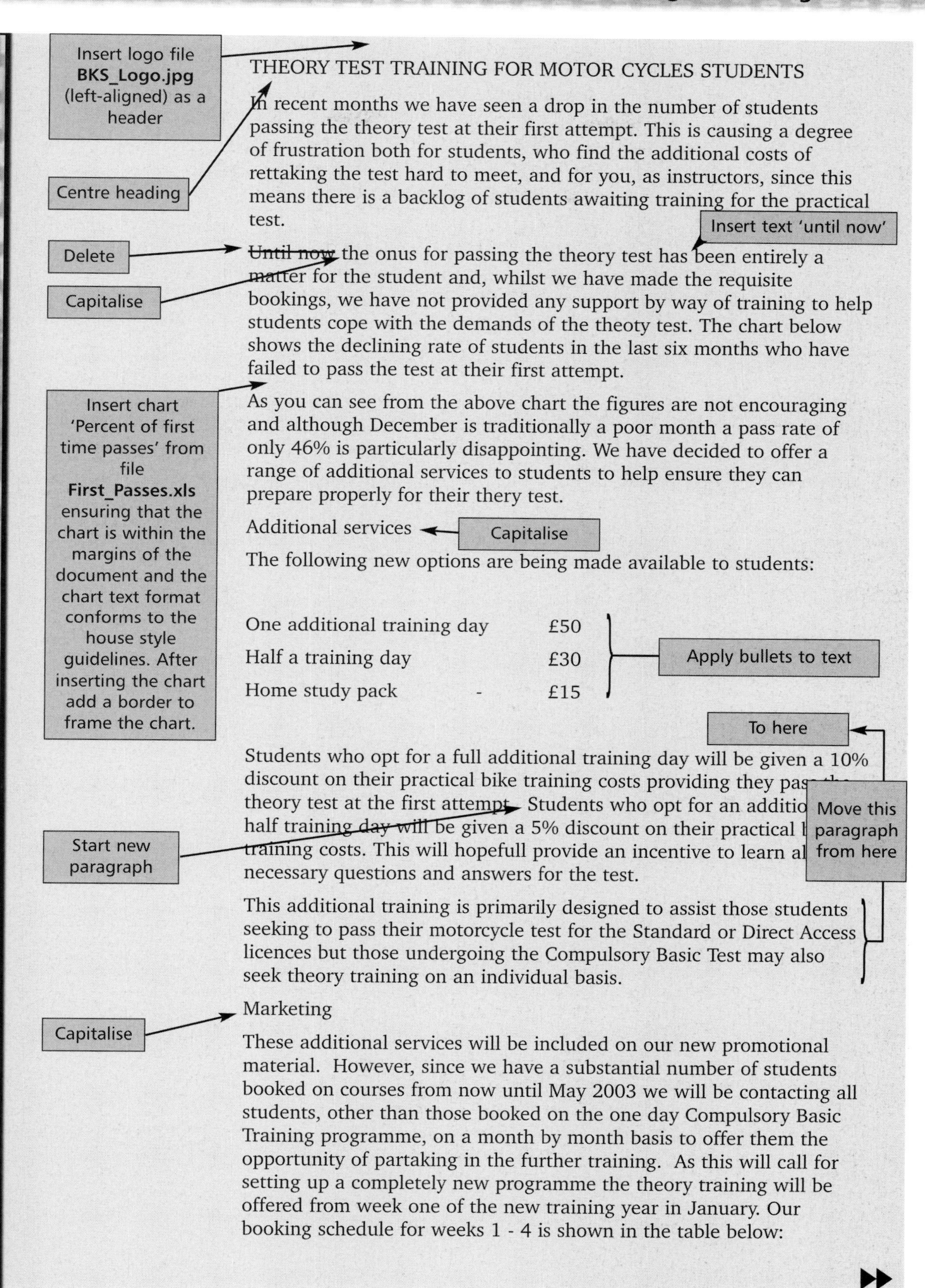

THEORY TEST TRAINING FOR MOTOR CYCLES STUDENTS

In recent months we have seen a drop in the number of students passing the theory test at their first attempt. This is causing a degree of frustration both for students, who find the additional costs of rettaking the test hard to meet, and for you, as instructors, since this means there is a backlog of students awaiting training for the practical test.

Until now the onus for passing the theory test has been entirely a matter for the student and, whilst we have made the requisite bookings, we have not provided any support by way of training to help students cope with the demands of the theoty test. The chart below shows the declining rate of students in the last six months who have failed to pass the test at their first attempt.

As you can see from the above chart the figures are not encouraging and although December is traditionally a poor month a pass rate of only 46% is particularly disappointing. We have decided to offer a range of additional services to students to help ensure they can prepare properly for their thery test.

Additional services

The following new options are being made available to students:

One additional training day £50

Half a training day £30

Home study pack - £15

Students who opt for a full additional training day will be given a 10% discount on their practical bike training costs providing they pass the theory test at the first attempt. Students who opt for an additional half training day will be given a 5% discount on their practical bike training costs. This will hopefull provide an incentive to learn all necessary questions and answers for the test.

This additional training is primarily designed to assist those students seeking to pass their motorcycle test for the Standard or Direct Access licences but those undergoing the Compulsory Basic Test may also seek theory training on an individual basis.

Marketing

These additional services will be included on our new promotional material. However, since we have a substantial number of students booked on courses from now until May 2003 we will be contacting all students, other than those booked on the one day Compulsory Basic Training programme, on a month by month basis to offer them the opportunity of partaking in the further training. As this will call for setting up a completely new programme the theory training will be offered from week one of the new training year in January. Our booking schedule for weeks 1 - 4 is shown in the table below:

Insert logo file **BKS_Logo.jpg** (left-aligned) as a header
Centre heading
Delete
Capitalise
Insert text 'until now'
Insert chart 'Percent of first time passes' from file **First_Passes.xls** ensuring that the chart is within the margins of the document and the chart text format conforms to the house style guidelines. After inserting the chart add a border to frame the chart.
Capitalise
Apply bullets to text
To here
Move this paragraph from here
Start new paragraph
Capitalise

Practical assignment 1

Insert a table containing five columns with the headings of Course, Course No, Start, End and Students. Include data contained in the sheets named BOOKINGS FOR JANUARY 2003. Only include records for Direct Access Licence and Standard Licence courses. Direct Access courses should be coded as DAS and Standard Licence courses coded as SLC. Date format should be English (short date format). Gridlines and borders on the table should be shown. Ensure that only the data asked for is included and that all data is visible and that column widths are sufficient to ensure words are not split.

As will be appreciated the extended programme will call for amendments to made to the schedule and final details will be advised to all trainers once the January uptake has been evaluated. However, it is likely that three day programes will now run from Monday to Thursday and from Tuesday to Friday.

New Booking Dates ← Capitalise

Some students may wish to change their booking dates and you should contact your individual students, once they have decided whether or not to opt for additional training, to see whether their current booking is still acceptable. A list of students and the courses they are currently booked on for January is shown in the following table.

You will be advised in the next couple of weeks whether students, once contacted, wish to undertake additional training. The central office will not be asking students whether their present booked dates are still acceptable. This will be left to individual trainers to arrange with students.

Insert here the datafile **Student_Bookings.csv** found on the CD accompanying this book.

▶▶

Practical assignment 1

BOOKINGS FOR JANUARY 2003

Serial:	1	**Training Week:**	1				
Date:	30/12/2002	**Day:**	Monday	**Duration:**	3	**End:**	1/1/2003
Course:	Direct Access Licence	**Course No:**	1201				
Bike (cc):	500	**Cost:**	300				
Students:	3	**Trainer:**	BC				

Serial:	2	**Training Week:**	1				
Date:	1/1/2003	**Day:**	Wednesday	**Duration:**	3	**End:**	3/1/2003
Course:	Standard Licence	**Course No:**	1123				
Bike (cc):	125	**Cost:**	250				
Students:	2	**Trainer:**	KL				

Serial:	3	**Training Week:**	2				
Date:	6/1/2003	**Day:**	Monday	**Duration:**	3	**End:**	8/1/2003
Course:	Direct Access Licence	**Course No:**	1202				
Bike (cc):	500	**Cost:**	300				
Students:	4	**Trainer:**	BC				

Serial:	4	**Training Week:**	2				
Date:	8/1/2003	**Day:**	Wednesday	**Duration:**	3	**End:**	10/1/2003
Course:	Direct Access Licence	**Course No:**	1203				
Bike (cc):	500	**Cost:**	300				
Students:	2	**Trainer:**	MH				

Serial:	5	**Training Week:**	2				
Date:	8/1/2003	**Day:**	Wednesday	**Duration:**	1	**End:**	8/1/2003
Course:	Compulsory Basic Training	**Course No:**	1118				
Bike (cc):	125	**Cost:**	60				
Students:	3	**Trainer:**	HI				

Practical assignment 1

Serial: 6 **Training Week:** 3
Date: 13/1/2003 **Day:** Monday **Duration:** 3 **End:** 15/1/2003
Course: Direct Access Licence **Course No:** 1204
Bike (cc): 500 **Cost:** 300
Students: 2 **Trainer:** BC

Serial: 7 **Training Week:** 3
Date: 13/1/2003 **Day:** Monday **Duration:** 1 **End:** 13/1/2003
Course: Compulsory Basic Training **Course No:** 1119
Bike (cc): 125 **Cost:** 60
Students: 3 **Trainer:** HI

Serial: 8 **Training Week:** 3
Date: 15/1/2003 **Day:** Wednesday **Duration:** 3 **End:** 17/1/2003
Course: Standard Licence **Course No:** 1124
Bike (cc): 125 **Cost:** 250
Students: 3 **Trainer:** KL

Serial: 9 **Training Week:** 4
Date: 20/1/2003 **Day:** Monday **Duration:** 3 **End:** 22/1/2003
Course: Standard Licence **Course No:** 1125
Bike (cc): 125 **Cost:** 250
Students: 3 **Trainer:** KL

Serial: 10 **Training Week:** 4
Date: 20/1/2003 **Day:** Monday **Duration:** 3 **End:** 22/1/2003
Course: Direct Access Licence **Course No:** 1205
Bike (cc): 500 **Cost:** 300
Students: 3 **Trainer:** BC

Practical assignment 1

Serial:	11	Training Week:	4				
Date:	22/1/2003	Day:	Wednesday	Duration:	1	End:	22/1/2003
Course:	Compulsory Basic Training	Course No:	1120				
Bike (cc):	125	Cost:	60				
Students:	3	Trainer:	HI				

Serial:	12	Training Week:	4				
Date:	22/1/2003	Day:	Wednesday	Duration:	3	End:	24/1/2003
Course:	Direct Access Licence	Course No:	1206				
Bike (cc):	500	Cost:	300				
Students:	3	Trainer:	DT				

Serial:	13	Training Week:	4				
Date:	27/1/2003	Day:	Monday	Duration:	3	End:	29/1/2003
Course:	Standard Licence	Course No:	1126				
Bike (cc):	125	Cost:	250				
Students:	2	Trainer:	KL				

Serial:	14	Training Week:	4				
Date:	27/1/2003	Day:	Monday	Duration:	3	End:	29/1/2003
Course:	Direct Access Licence	Course No:	1207				
Bike (cc):	500	Cost:	300				
Students:	1	Trainer:	DT				

Serial:	15	Training Week:	4				
Date:	27/1/2003	Day:	Monday	Duration:	1	End:	27/1/2003
Course:	Compulsory Basic Training	Course No:	1121				
Bike (cc):	125	Cost:	60				
Students:	2	Trainer:	HI				

Practical assignment 1

Serial:	16	Training Week:	4				
Date:	29/1/2003	Day:	Wednesday	Duration:	3	End:	31/1/2003
Course:	Standard Licence		Course No:	1127			
Bike (cc):	125	Cost:	250				
Students:	21	Trainer:	HI				

Serial:	17	Training Week:	4				
Date:	29/1/2003	Day:	Wednesday	Duration:	3	End:	31/1/2003
Course:	Direct Access Licence		Course No:	1208			
Bike (cc):	500	Cost:	300				
Students:	3	Trainer:	BC				

Spreadsheets

This unit assumes you have had some experience of using a spreadsheet and therefore does not cover all of the skills required for level 1, New CLAIT. Where, however, it is felt that a revision of the skills covered in New CLAIT would be beneficial for progression they are included in the unit.

Five key assessment objectives

For CLAIT Plus there are five main assessment objectives, each of which contains a number of skills that you will be expected to learn. When you have completed the unit you should be able to:

- **Open a spreadsheet, enter/amend data, create formulae and use functions. This includes the ability to:**
  - open and import a generic data file
  - enter, amend and delete data and enter formulae that produce correct results
  - replicate formulae into appropriate cells
  - use a range of functions that produce correct results
  - project results
  - save and name a spreadsheet.
- **Use a variety of cell references. This includes the ability to:**
  - use relative, absolute and mixed cell references
  - name and use named cell references
  - use a reference to a cell in another spreadsheet.
- **Format and present data, including the ability to:**
  - amend column widths to ensure that data is displayed in full
  - display data using a variety of formats
  - align cell data both vertically and horizontally
  - set text orientation
  - wrap cell contents
  - merge cells
  - sort data.
- **Format document display, including the ability to:**
  - alter margins and page orientation
  - insert headers and footers
  - insert automatic fields into headers and footers
  - apply cell borders and/or gridlines
  - hide columns and rows.

- **Produce spreadsheet reports, including the ability to:**
  - print a document or a selection from a document
  - fit the document to a specified number of pages
  - display row and column headings
  - print spreadsheets showing the formulae in full.

These objectives also assume a level of knowledge and understanding in respect of the broad area being covered. As you go through the unit the relevant knowledge and understanding will be explained. A complete list of the individual skills for each objective, together with the required knowledge and understanding, can be found in Appendix 1.

In this unit you will learn how to:

- Import and use a generic data file
- Enter, amend and delete data and replicate formulae
- Understand and use relative, absolute and mixed cell references
- Use a variety of spreadsheet functions
- Project results from a given data range
- Modify a spreadsheet layout and format text and data
- Sort data
- Name cells and reference cells in different spreadsheets
- Use automatic fields for headers and footers
- Change the presentation of a spreadsheet by hiding columns and rows, applying borders and gridlines
- Display and print data in a required report format

Open a spreadsheet, enter/amend data, create formulae and use functions

Importing and using generic data files

In Unit 1 you were introduced to generic files by importing a file into a Word document. For CLAIT Plus you will be expected to understand how to open/import data from generic files into a spreadsheet. You will need to appreciate what is meant by generic files and why and how they can be used.

When creating a wordprocessing document that is to be sent by electronic means to someone (i.e. transferred by e-mail) or accessed by them from a storage disk for reading or amending, you may not always know the software package being used by the future user. For example, this book covers Microsoft applications such as Word, Excel and PowerPoint. However, Word is not the only wordprocessing product so to ensure someone receiving your file can read or make amendments to it, generic file formats such as text files or Rich Text Format files can be used. Similarly, when dealing with data originating from an Excel file you want to give as much flexibility as possible to the recipient of your work, if you are not sure what software they are using. Using generic file formats helps to ensure files can be read and data contained in the file changed. Generic file formats allow you to save data in such a way as to allow receivers of your files to use them irrespective of the products being used. For example, if you are preparing an Excel file (.xls being the standard format) one format that can be used generically is the 'comma separated' file, or .csv. Such files are known as 'delimited', meaning that each item of data, or individual field value, is separated by a comma. Other delimiters include tabs, semicolons, and spaces. This is not as complicated as it may first seem. Have a look at Figure 2.1.

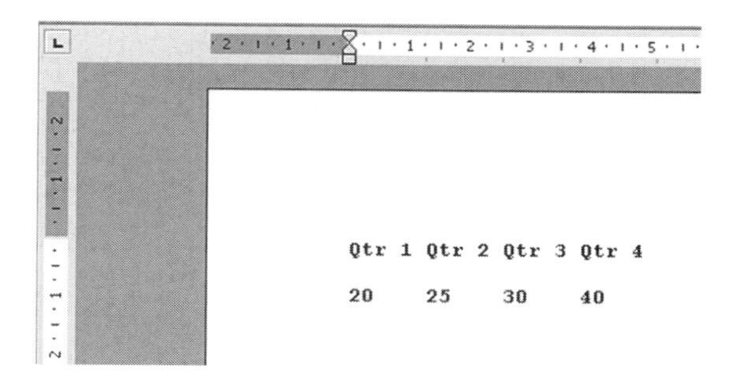

Figure 2.1

This is a text (.txt) file saved in Word, showing a series of numbers for Qtrs 1, 2, 3 and 4 – the details of what the figures mean are not important. Each Qtr is separated by a tab, and so this is therefore a tab delimited file. You can check this by pressing the non-printable character icon (¶) on the toolbar: see Figure 2.2.

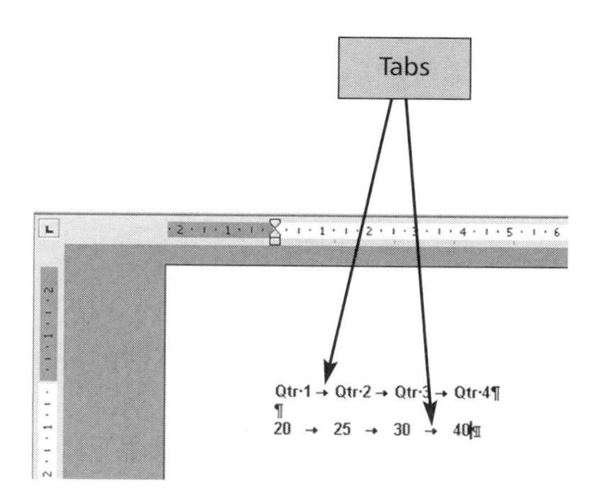

Figure 2.2

This file can be imported into an Excel workbook. The following sequence shows how data in a .txt delimited file can be opened in an Excel workbook. You can follow this process through by using the file '**Delimited_File.txt**' in the Unit 2 folder of the accompanying CD.

Try it out

Open a new workbook in Excel.

Select Data on the main menu.

Select Import External Data.

Select Import Data… .

Locate and select the text file to be imported (**Delimited_File.txt**).

Press Open.

The Text Import Wizard shown in Figure 2.3 now appears.

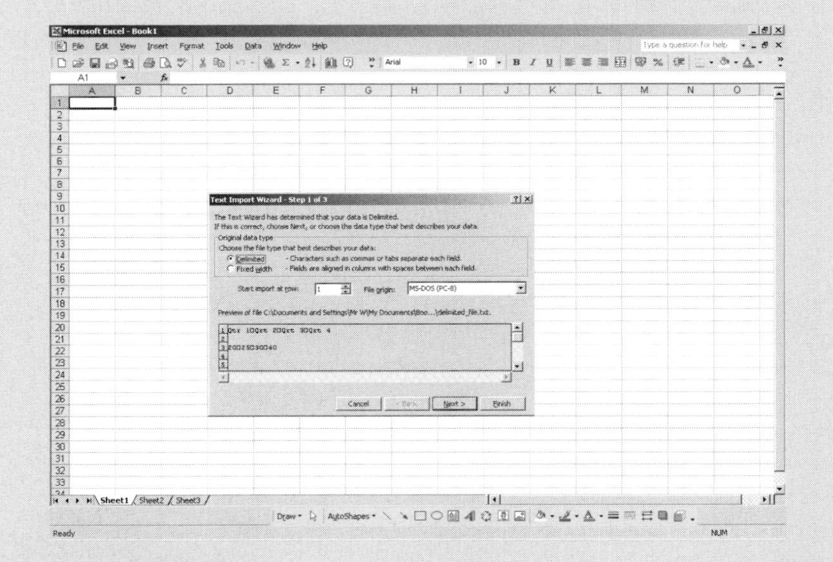

Figure 2.3

This box identifies whether or not the file to be imported is delimited.

Press the Next button.

This allows Excel to determine the type of delimiter and also gives a preview of the data to be imported: see Figure 2.4.

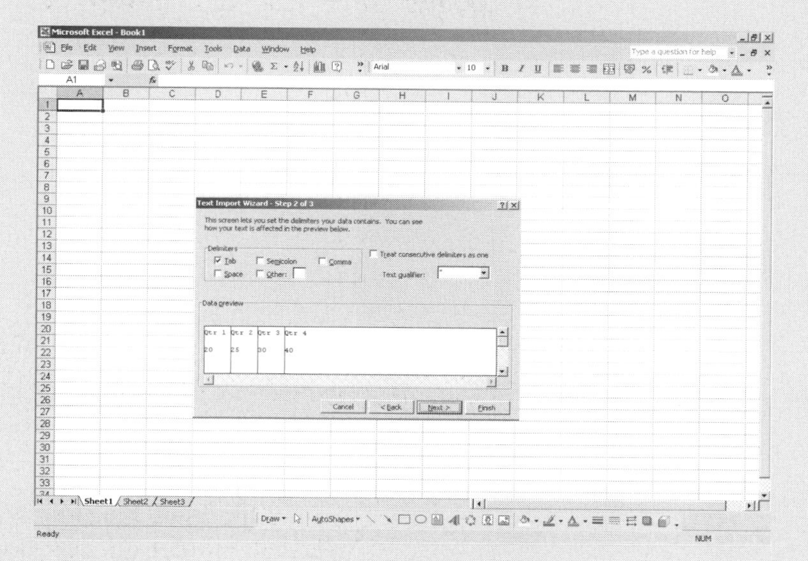

Figure 2.4

Press Next and Excel allows you to set the data format for each column: see Figure 2.5.

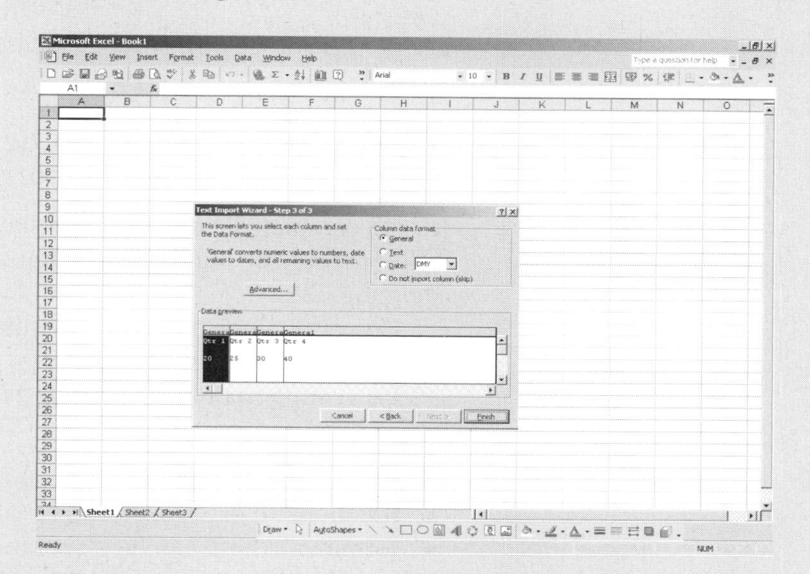

Figure 2.5

Press Finish and Excel then suggests a range where the data will be put.

Press OK to accept the default range.

The data is now imported as shown in Figure 2.6.

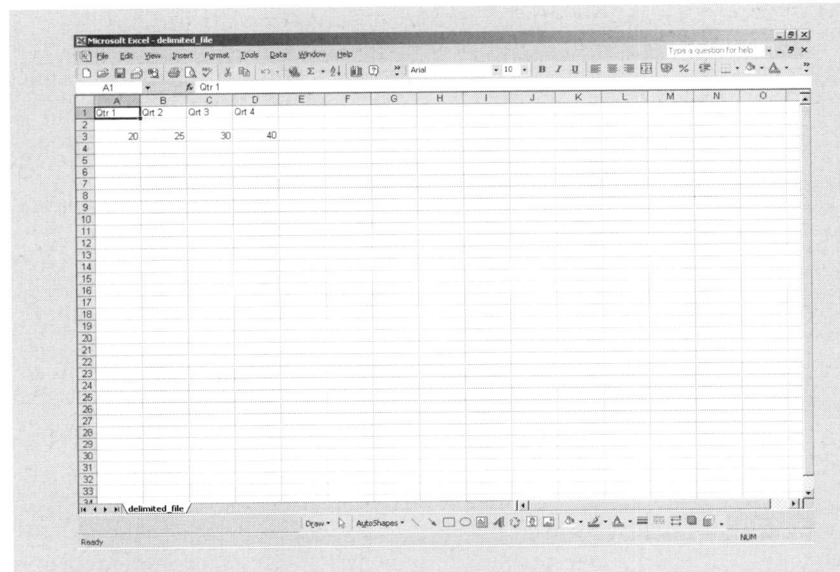

Figure 2.6

Save the file as an Excel workbook (.xls file) in your spreadsheet folder on your floppy disk, giving it a suitable name.

Entering, amending and deleting data and entering formulae that produce correct results

If you completed New CLAIT, or have used spreadsheets previously, you will probably be relatively familiar with entering, amending and deleting data.

However, since this is an essential skill for CLAIT Plus it is covered briefly in this section of the unit.

Excel supports four basic data types:

- values (e.g. numbers)
- text (e.g. headings, notes, etc.)
- functions (e.g. Sum, Average, Count)
- formulae (these can be a simple formulae such as '=A1+B1' or a combination of numbers, text and functions).

Excel recognises the type of data you input by the characters you use, for example:

- **Numbers** digits (e.g. 1, 2, 3), a decimal point (1.23), a hash sign (#), a percentage sign (%), a plus sign (+) or a minus sign (–).
- **Text** any string of characters (A1, 7FG, :8, etc).
- **Formulae** formulae are always preceded by an equals sign (=).

CELL ALIGNMENT TIP

Text and numeric data are aligned differently by default. Numbers in cells are right-justified and text is left-justified. As you type numbers into a cell they appear on the left of the cell until you click outside the cell or the Enter key is pressed to accept the changes.

Data entry methods

There are two ways to enter data into a worksheet: direct entry or via the formula bar.

Direct entry

By placing the cursor where you want to enter the data and clicking on the relevant cell you can type in the required data. The information can be seen both in the cell and in the formula bar.

Using the formula bar

First click on the cell where the data is to be stored, then click in the formula bar and type in text, numbers or a formula and it will automatically be reproduced in the cell where the cursor is located.

As a refresher complete this Try it out exercise.

Try it out

Open a new workbook in Excel.

Enter the data shown in Figure 2.7.

	A	B	C
1	**Courses**	**Women**	**Men**
2	Ramsey	284	196
3	Speed	300	323
4	Portmond	412	381
5	Manton	212	295
6	Clayborne	150	200
7	Fenney	317	365
8	Packstone	550	652
9	Sawbry	96	125

Figure 2.7

Save your workbook as **Golf_1.**

Close the workbook.

Amending and deleting text and numerical data

Being able to amend and delete data is a requirement for CLAIT Plus. You will have learnt these skills if you completed New CLAIT certification. They are covered briefly here as a reminder.

Once data has been entered in a cell, pressing the Delete key in Excel will remove the cell contents. However, this will not remove formatting. Numeric data can be formatted either as integers (whole numbers) or to a specified number of decimal places. Formatting also covers alignment, font style, emphasis, borders and so on for both text and numbers. Where a cell has formatting that you want to clear you should use Clear, then All on the Edit option of the main menu.

To amend the data in a cell simply click on the cell to be amended and then overtype either by typing directly into the cell or using the formula bar. Some care needs to be taken not to amend a cell which contains a formula that affects other cells in the worksheet. If a cell contains a long formula or text and you only want to change a part without changing the whole cell you can make amendments to the cell either by clicking on the cell and using the formula bar or by clicking on the cell and pressing the F2 function key. This allows you to make amendments directly into the cell without the need to re-type all the contents of the cell.

Try making some changes to the prepared file in this Try it out exercise.

Try it out

In Unit 1 you created a folder structure on a floppy disk.

Create a new folder on your floppy or hard disk as a sub-folder of Spreadsheets and call it 'Exercises'.

Open Clothes_Stock.xls in Unit 2 on the accompanying CD.

Click on cell A1.

Type 'PRODUCT' to replace ITEM as the heading in column 1.

Replace TOTAL in cell A9 to read 'TOTAL STOCK VALUE'.

You have received word that the new sales figures are as follows:

Table 2.1

Item	Initial stock	Sales
Jumpers	120	32
Shirts	300	75
Trousers	250	48
Socks	500	205
Ties	420	302
Gloves	115	2
Jackets	50	23

Amend the sales figures as shown in the table.

Remove the bold emphasis on the headings for columns B to F.

Save your file in the new Exercises folder as **Clothes_Stock_2**.

Close the file.

Exit the application.

Entering formulae to produce correct results

New CLAIT introduced the concept of creating and using formulae to derive results from data in a spreadsheet. CLAIT Plus extends this by introducing some standard spreadsheet functions, while still including the use of mathematical operands (+, –, *, <>) in creating spreadsheets.

Mathematical operands

You may well already be familiar with creating simple formulae using the operands shown above but you may find the following Try it out exercise a useful refresher.

Try it out

Open a new workbook in Excel.

Enter the data shown in Table 2.2, starting at cell A1.

Table 2.2

Items	Price/Ea	Qty
Oranges	0.22	6
Apples	0.2	4
Pears	0.36	6
Cherries (bag)	1.69	0
Strawberries (bag)	1.19	0
Bananas	0.19	4
Grapes (bag)	2.28	1
Melons	1.48	1
Lemons	0.19	3
Satsumas	0.22	6
Grapefruits	0.32	2

Click in cell C13.

Total the QTY column using the + operand.

(**Tip:** =C2+C3+C4 ...etc. to C12; remember that a formula must start with the equals sign.)

Press the Enter key.

Click in cell D1. Enter the heading 'COST'. Make the heading bold and right-aligned.

Click in cell D2.

Enter a formula that calculates the cost of oranges. (Multiply B2 by C2 and press Enter.)

Save the file as **Fruits** in the Exercises sub-folder on your floppy disk.

Replicating a formula

Being able to replicate formulae is both a New CLAIT and CLAIT Plus assessment objective. Excel allows you to replicate a formula into a range of cells, obviating the need to re-type the same formula in each cell in the range. Spreadsheet software uses something called 'relative referencing' (explained in the next section), when replicating a formula.

Try it out

Open the file **Fruits**.

Click on cell D2. Notice how the cell has a thick black line around it with a small square box in the bottom right corner as in Figure 2.8.

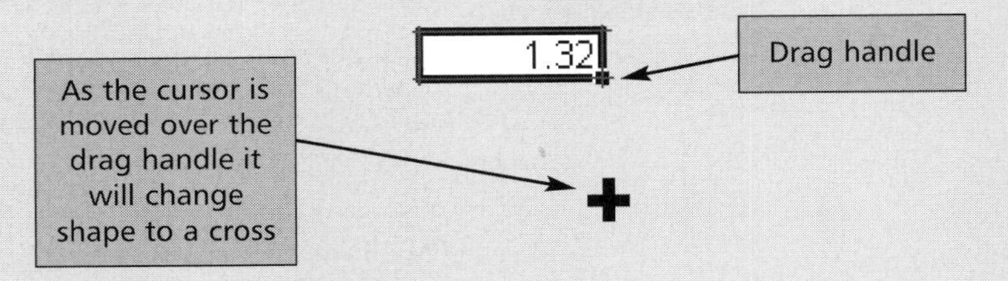

Figure 2.8

Place the cursor over the small square at the bottom right of the cell and with the left-hand mouse button pressed:

Drag the box to cell D12 as shown in Figure 2.9.

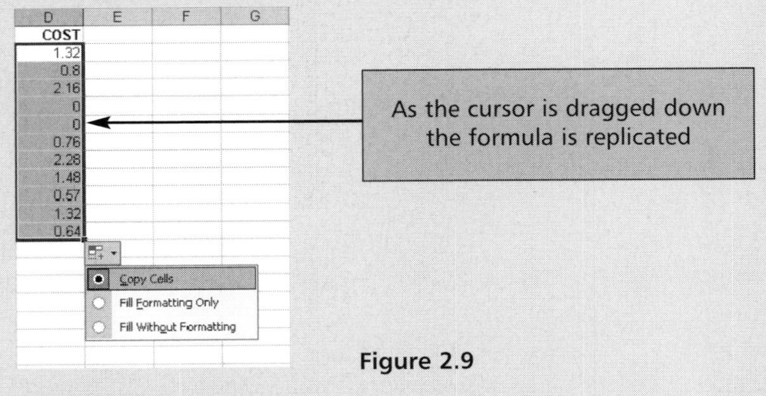

Figure 2.9

Save the file.

Cell references – absolute, relative and mixed

Relative referencing

With the Fruits file open, click on each of the cells from D2 to D12. Notice how the formula you placed in cell D2 (=C2*B2) changes to C3*B3, C4*B4, C5*B5 and so on, down to the last cell where the formula is replicated as C12*B12 (see Figure 2.10).

	A	B	C	D
1	ITEMS	PRICE/EA	QTY	COST
2	ORANGES	0.22	6	=C2*B2
3	APPLES	0.2	4	=C3*B3
4	PEARS	0.36	6	=C4*B4
5	CHERRIES (Bag)	1.69	0	=C5*B5
6	STRAWBERRIES (Bag)	1.19	0	=C6*B6
7	BANANAS	0.19	4	=C7*B7
8	GRAPES (Bag)	2.28	1	=C8*B8
9	MELONS	1.48	1	=C9*B9
10	LEMONS	0.19	3	=C10*B10
11	SATSUMAS	0.22	6	=C11*B11
12	GRAPEFRUITS	0.32	2	=C12*B12

Formula changes relative to the column and row reference

Figure 2.10

This is known as *relative referencing*. When you replicate a formula Excel automatically adjusts the references in the next cell based on the relative position of the formula. Excel makes the assumption that you want to use the reference of the new cell rather than the original cell and will continue to do this until the end of the range.

Absolute references

There are two other types of cell referencing that you will need to understand for CLAIT Plus: absolute and mixed.

An absolute cell reference in a formula always refers to a particular cell in a specific location. It is marked by using a $ sign in front of both the column and row part of its address. So if you want to refer to a cell that, for example, gives a discount rate for each fruit item, you could make it absolute by using $ signs in the address. Figure 2.11 may help to explain this.

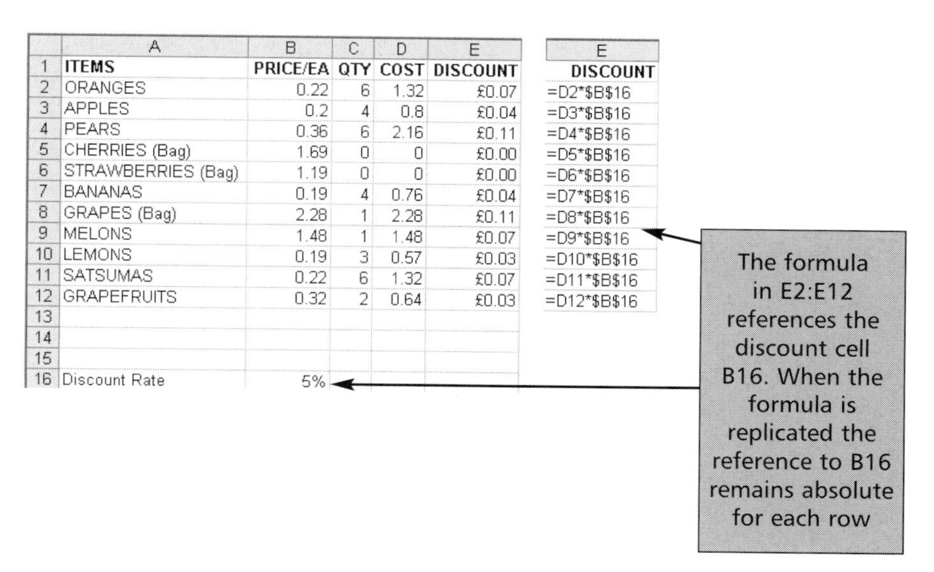

	A	B	C	D	E
1	ITEMS	PRICE/EA	QTY	COST	DISCOUNT
2	ORANGES	0.22	6	1.32	£0.07
3	APPLES	0.2	4	0.8	£0.04
4	PEARS	0.36	6	2.16	£0.11
5	CHERRIES (Bag)	1.69	0	0	£0.00
6	STRAWBERRIES (Bag)	1.19	0	0	£0.00
7	BANANAS	0.19	4	0.76	£0.04
8	GRAPES (Bag)	2.28	1	2.28	£0.11
9	MELONS	1.48	1	1.48	£0.07
10	LEMONS	0.19	3	0.57	£0.03
11	SATSUMAS	0.22	6	1.32	£0.07
12	GRAPEFRUITS	0.32	2	0.64	£0.03
13					
14					
15					
16	Discount Rate	5%			

E
DISCOUNT
=D2*$B$16
=D3*$B$16
=D4*$B$16
=D5*$B$16
=D6*$B$16
=D7*$B$16
=D8*$B$16
=D9*$B$16
=D10*$B$16
=D11*$B$16
=D12*$B$16

The formula in E2:E12 references the discount cell B16. When the formula is replicated the reference to B16 remains absolute for each row

Figure 2.11

Had cell B16 not had the $ sign in the formula at cell E2, then when the formula was replicated, B16 would have changed to a relative reference and instead of staying B16 would have become B17, B18, B19 and so on. Remember that new formulae entered in a spreadsheet have a relative reference by default and if an absolute reference is required you need to change the reference manually by placing the $ sign in front of the column and row cell address – e.g. $B$16.

Mixed references

Mixed references are a combination of an absolute reference and a relative reference. A mixed reference has either an absolute column and relative row, or an absolute row and relative column. For example, where $B$16 is an absolute reference for both the column and the row, $B16 is absolute for the column but relative for the row. Similarly B$16 would be relative for the column but absolute for the row.

You may understand this easier by trying a simple exercise.

Try it out

Open a new workbook in Excel.

Enter the following data:

Table 2.3

	A	B
1	Car	Basic
2	Jaguar	25000
3	Audi	16000
4	Mini	8600
5	Ford	7950

Type 'Delivery Charge' in cell A9.

Type '0.01' which will represent 1% of the delivery charge.

Type 'WITH DELIVERY' in cell C1.

Enter the formula '=B2*$C$9+B2' in cell C2.

This formula calculates the percentage of the cars' basic cost (1%) and adds back the basic cost to the 1%, giving the total cost including delivery charges.

Replicate the formula to cells C3:C5.

Notice that because you have made C9 an absolute reference it will take this same value for each row, as shown in Figure 2.12.

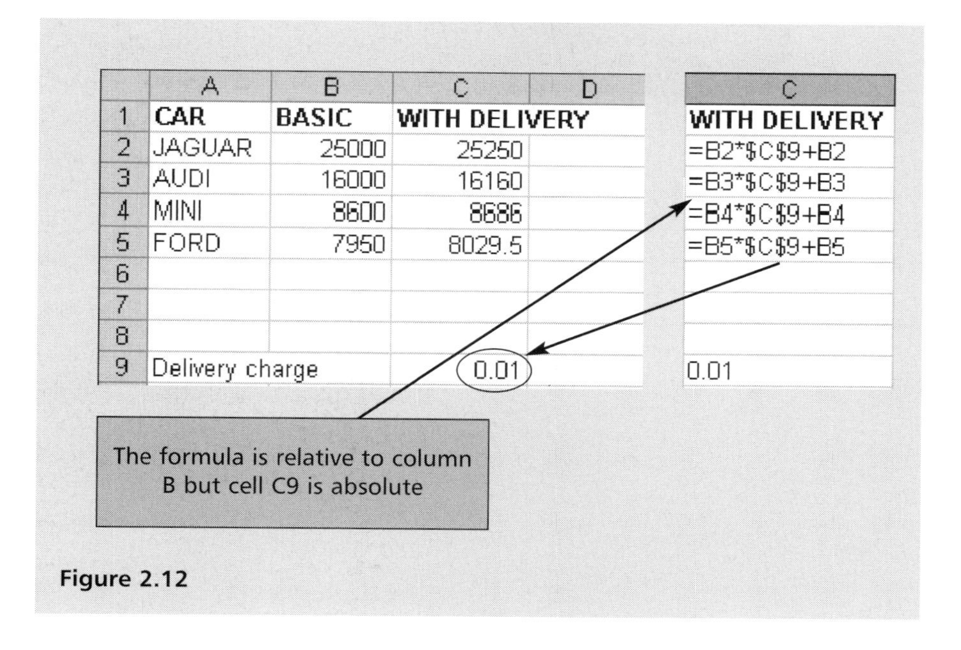

Figure 2.12

Using Excel functions

Excel offers a wide range of functions that can be used to make your spreadsheet more concise. Functions are built-in formulae that perform calculations using specific values, called arguments. They are presented in a specific order, or structure. Functions are used to perform both simple and complex calculations.

In all Excel provides over 200 functions for you to use. Many of these are of a highly specialised nature, but others are quite basic and of general, practical value.

For CLAIT Plus you are required to know and understand the following functions:

AVERAGE
COUNT/COUNTA/COUNTIF
MIN
MAX
SQRT
IF

Each of these is covered in the next section of this unit.

The AVERAGE function

The AVERAGE function returns the average or arithmetic mean of a given set of numbers. So, for example, given the following list of numbers: 2, 2, 4, 3; you can establish that the average is 2.75. This would be calculated manually by adding the numbers together (2+2+4+3) and then dividing by the number in the series (4). In a simple example such as this the calculation is not complex but if you were dealing with a large spreadsheet such a calculation would be lengthy. Excel provides a function to help you calculate the average from any size of data list.

Try it out

Open the **Average** file in Unit 2 on the accompanying CD.

To get an average you would ordinarily have to add up all the numbers in the list and then divide by the actual number of figures.

Click in cell A101.

Select Function... from Insert on the main menu.

The dialogue box in Figure 2.13 is shown.

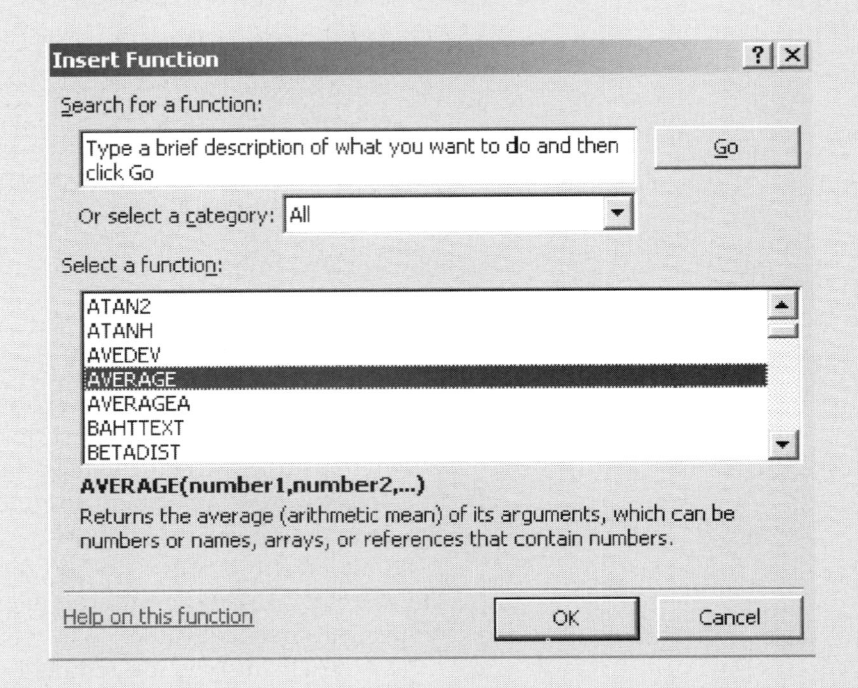

Figure 2.13

Check that AVERAGE is highlighted.

Press OK.

A second dialogue box appears, shown in Figure 2.14.

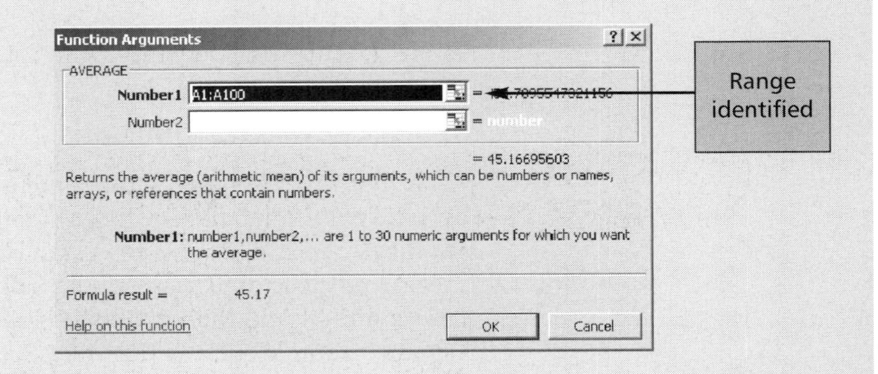

Figure 2.14

If the range identified is correct:

Press OK.

Excel will calculate the average for the range identified.

Close the file without saving.

COUNT/COUNTA/COUNTIF functions

COUNT

COUNT counts the number of *cells* in a range. You can only use count where there are numbers, so the COUNT function will not, for example, count text.

Say, for instance, that you wanted to count the number of golf competitions, but not the actual number of players. Have a look at Figure 2.15.

	A	B
13	Competition	Players
14	Medal 5 Oct	50
15	Medal 9 Nov	56
16	Medal 4 Jan	52
17	Medal 8 Feb	48
18	Medal 7 Mar	62
19	Medal 11 Apr	60
20		6

B
Players
50
56
52
48
62
60
=COUNT(B14:B19)

The COUNT function simply adds the number of items not the actual sum of players

Figure 2.15

There are only six competitions in this spreadsheet although there are many more than six players.

Try it out

Open Stock_1 from Unit 2 on the CD.

Click in cell B8.

Select Insert, Function... from the main menu.

The Insert function dialogue box shown in Figure 2.16 will appear.

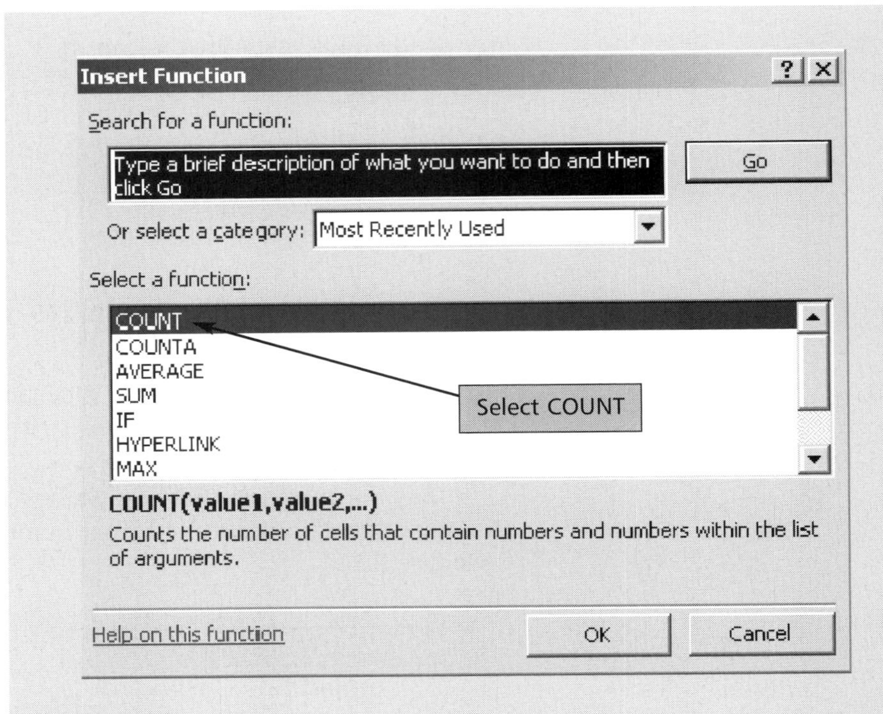

Figure 2.16

Select COUNT.

Press OK.

Another dialogue box appears, which in Value 1, suggests the range that is to be counted and the result: see Figure 2.17.

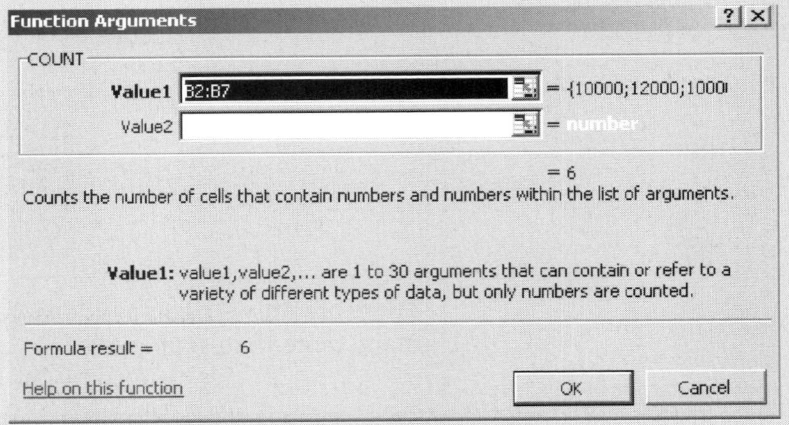

Function Arguments

COUNT

Value1 B2:B7 = {10000;12000;1000

Value2 = number

= 6

Counts the number of cells that contain numbers and numbers within the list of arguments.

Value1: value1,value2,... are 1 to 30 arguments that can contain or refer to a variety of different types of data, but only numbers are counted.

Formula result = 6

Help on this function OK Cancel

Figure 2.17

If this is correct:

Press OK.

Notice how Excel ignores Cell B1 which contains text.

Close the file without saving.

COUNTA

COUNTA operates in a similar way to COUNT, but this function counts the number of *cells that are not empty* and can be used with cells that contain *text*. Have a look now at Figure 2.18.

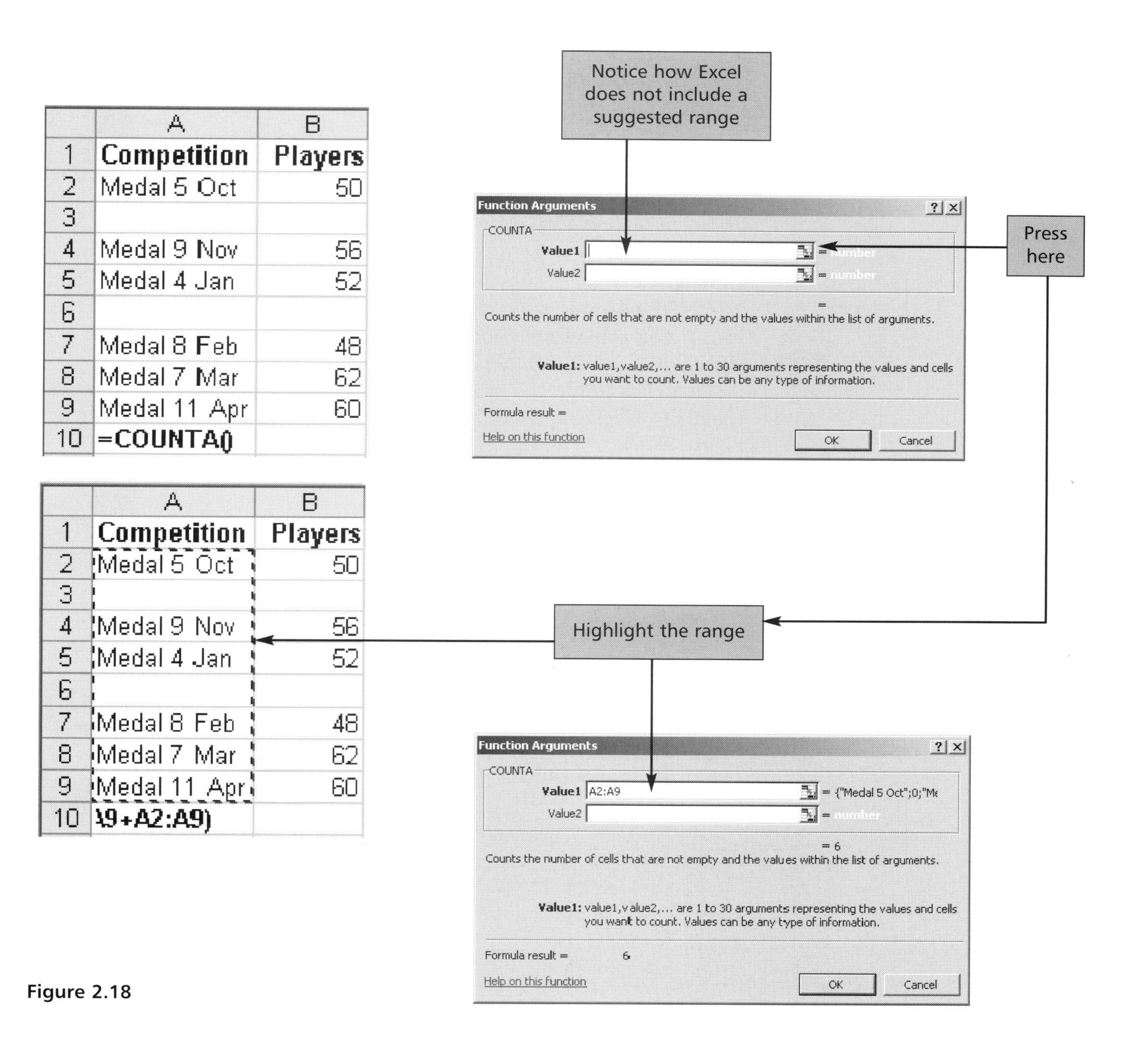

Figure 2.18

COUNTA will count all cells provided there is an entry in them, whether it is numerical or text.

Try it out

Open Stock_2.

Click in Cell A10.

Select Insert, Function... from the main menu.

Select COUNTA.

Press OK.

Highlight the range A2:A9.

Press OK.

Excel has added the number of non-blank cells in the range which, not surprisingly, still amounts to six.

COUNTIF

COUNTIF introduces a conditional argument. Say, for example, in the simple golf spreadsheet above you wanted to count the number of clubs with a total membership that was greater than 500.

First click in the cell where the result is to be placed. Next select the range on which the condition is to be based and finally press Enter (see Figure 2.19).

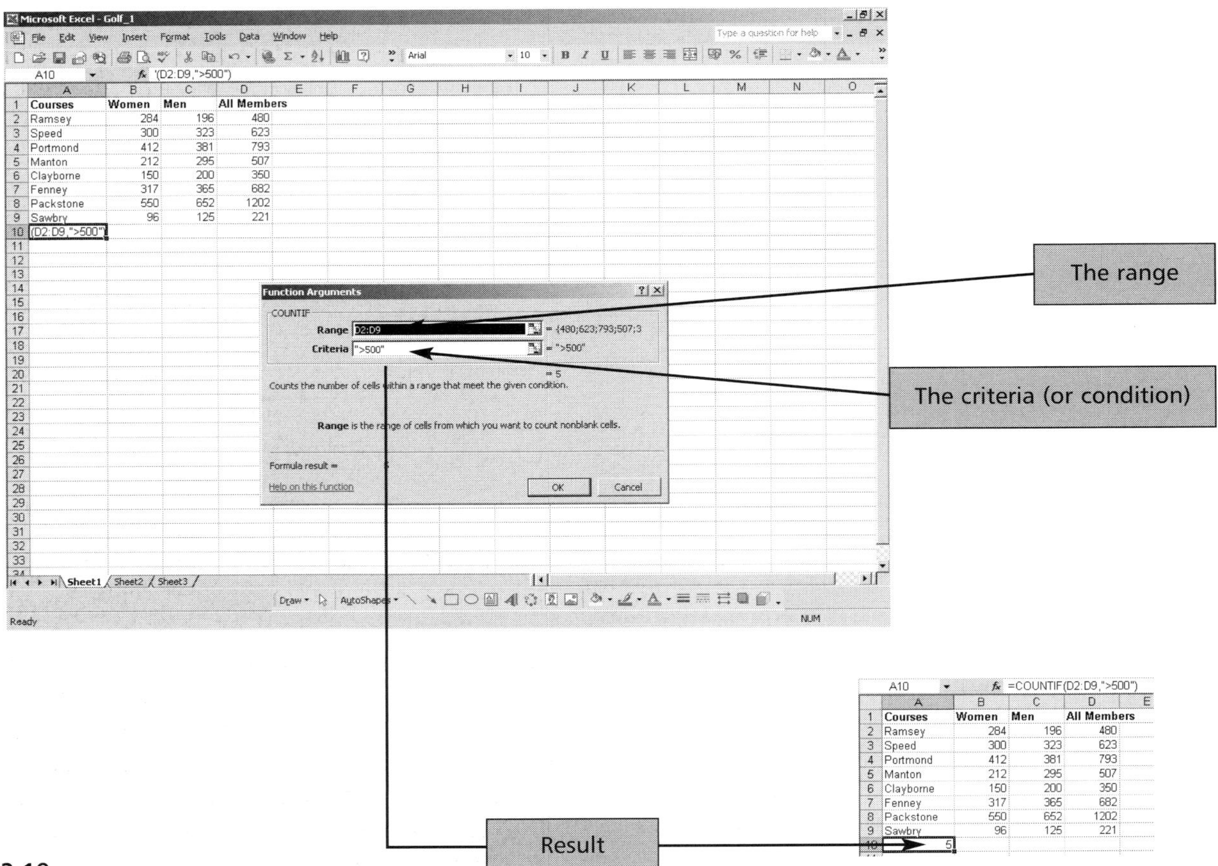

Figure 2.19

Try it out

Open Stock_3.xls.

Click in Cell A8.

Insert a COUNTIF function to determine the number of stock items that exceed 3500.

The formula bar should look like this:

=COUNTIF(B2:B7,">3500")

Press OK.

Save the file.

Exit the application.

MIN and MAX functions

The MIN function returns the smallest value in a range whereas the MAX function returns the greatest value. Both these functions ignore logical values and text.

You can try the functions out by opening a new workbook and typing in a range of numbers. At the end of the range insert a MIN and then MAX function in exactly the same way as you inserted the COUNT functions.

SQRT

SQRT is the function that finds the square root of a number. Finding the square root of a number is the inverse operation to finding the square of that number. So, for example, the square of 6 is 36 (6 × 6). Inversely, the square root of 36 is 6, because 6 multiplied by itself is 36.

SQRT operates in the same way as any other function and returns the square root of any particular value in a worksheet.

IF

The IF function is possibly one of the most useful functions in Excel. As you saw with COUNTIF, IF is a *conditional* argument. IF checks whether a condition is met and returns a value of *true* if it is and a value of *false* if not.

Using the IF function is the same as using any other function in Excel. First select the cell where you want the result of your query placed and then using the Function… option from Insert on the main menu, select the IF function from the functions dialogue box. Excel will then ask you for the arguments to be used. First is the logical test: 'IF something is true then return one result and if it is false return something else'. Have a look at Figure 2.20.

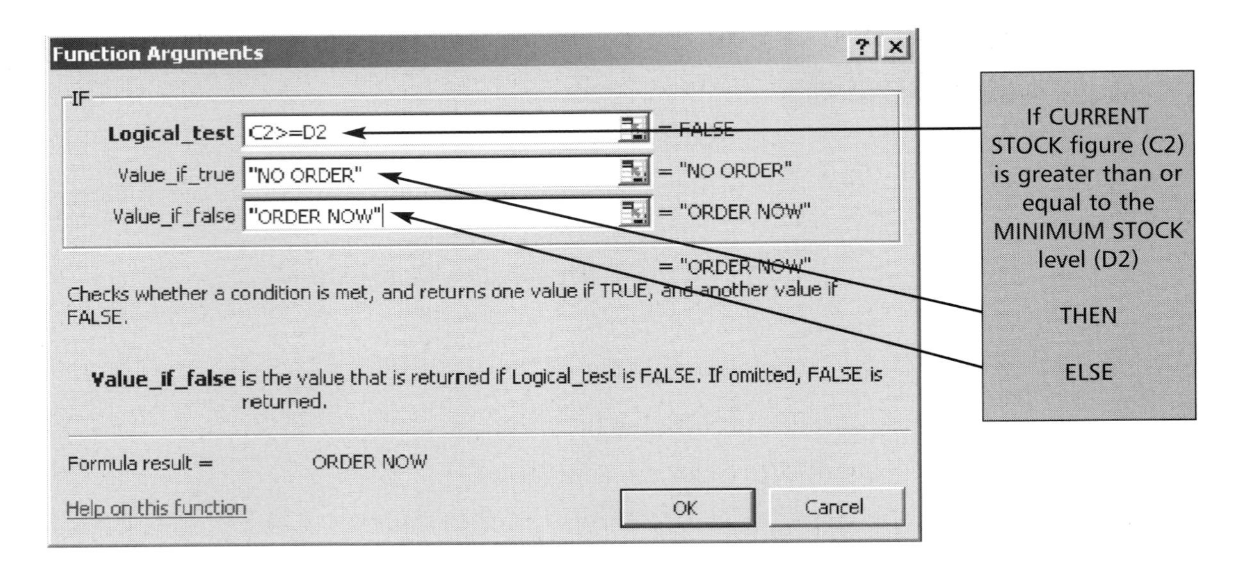

Figure 2.20

The logical test is shown as '=IF(C2>=D2,"NO ORDER","ORDER NOW")'. Let's break this down.

The question being asked is: 'IF the current stock level of the figure in C2 is greater than (>) or equal to (=) the minimum stock level in D2, then re-ordering is not required and no action need be taken. However, if the current stock level is less than the minimum level then a re-order is required.'

Excel will return the results as shown in Figure 2.21.

E2 fx =IF(C2>=D2,"NO ORDER ","ORDER NOW")

	A	B	C	D	E	F
1	**STOCK ITEM**	**MAX STOCK**	**CURRENT STOCK**	**MINIMUM STOCK**	**ORDER STATUS**	
2	Nuts	30000	10000	15000	ORDER NOW	
3	Washers	20000	12000	10000	NO ORDER	
4	Bolts	15000	10000	7500	NO ORDER	
5	Screws 1"	10000	5000	5000	NO ORDER	
6	Screws 1.5"	10000	3500	5000	ORDER NOW	
7	Screws 2"	10000	2700	5000	ORDER NOW	

Figure 2.21

Try it out

Open the file **Drink.xls** in Unit 2 on your CD.

Save the spreadsheet as **Drinks** in the Spreadsheets folder of your floppy disk or on your hard drive.

Scenario

This spreadsheet represents the stock levels in a local club of a variety of drinks. As the bar manager you are expected to maintain a level of stock that is sufficient for normal daily use, plus some extra in the event that members want to put on a party.

You decide it would be useful if you were automatically told when the stock level was such that you needed to re-order. You have set a reasonable re-ordering level.

Type a new heading for column F 'ORDER NOW'.

Right align the heading.

Click in cell F2.

Select Function from the Insert menu option.

Scroll down the list to find the IF function.

Highlight the function.

Press OK.

Click on cell D2.

After D2 is shown in the Logical Test field:

Type '<=' immediately after D2.

Click on cell E2.

The Logical Test field should now look like this:
D2<=E2

Click in the Value_if_true field below the Logical Test field box.

Type 'YES'.

Click in the Value_if_false field.

Type 'NO'.

Press OK.

Notice how Excel has now entered YES in the cell F2.

Now replicate this formula to F6.

Check the logic for each cell. So, for example, the re-order level for beer is 24. The stock level is actually eight so since the stock level is less than the re-order level the logical test must return a value of TRUE (or in this case YES).

Save the file.

Close the file.

Nested IF statements

Sometimes you may wish to evaluate more than one argument. You can test for up to 30 conditions. Have a look at Figure 2.22.

E3 =IF(AND(D3>0)*AND(D3<51),$B$8,IF(AND(D3>50)*AND(D3<101),$C$8,IF(D3>100,$D$8)))

	A	B	C	D	E	F	G	H	I	J
1										
2	**ITEM**	**Price/Kilo**	**Order/Kilo**	**Cost**	**Discount**					
3	Nails	£5.00	10	£50.00	No Discount					
4	Screws	£6.00	15	£90.00	10%					
5	Pins	£2.00	30	£60.00	10%					
6	Washers	£1.00	200	£200.00	15%					
7	Discounts	**1 - 50**	**51 - 100**	**Over 100**						
8		No Discount	10%	15%						

Figure 2.22

In the spreadsheet a discount is being offered depending on the level of sales. For sales of a value between £1 and £50 no discount is given (cell B8), between £51 and £100, 10% is offered (cell C8), and for sales above £100 a discount of 15% is given (cell D8).

Now have a look at the formula in the formula bar. The formula starts with a normal IF statement. Because there is more than one argument you need to use the AND operator. Figure 2.23 explains the logic behind the formula.

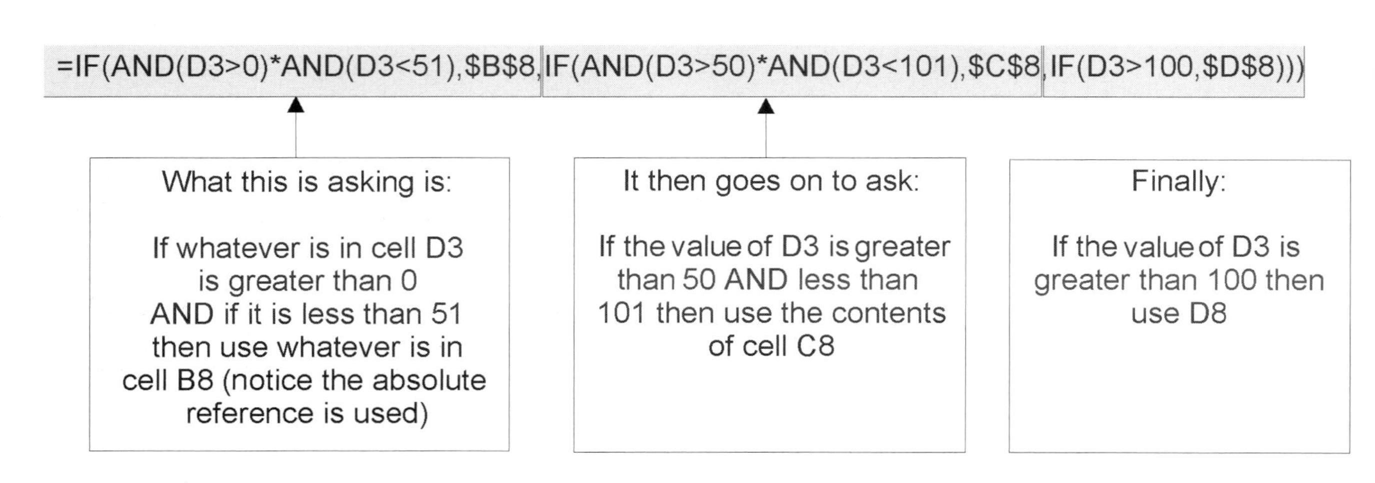

Figure 2.23

Projecting results by changing data inputs

One of the great advantages that spreadsheets offer over other software applications is their ability to allow you to project what might happen if certain aspects of your business or organisation change. Have a look at Figure 2.24.

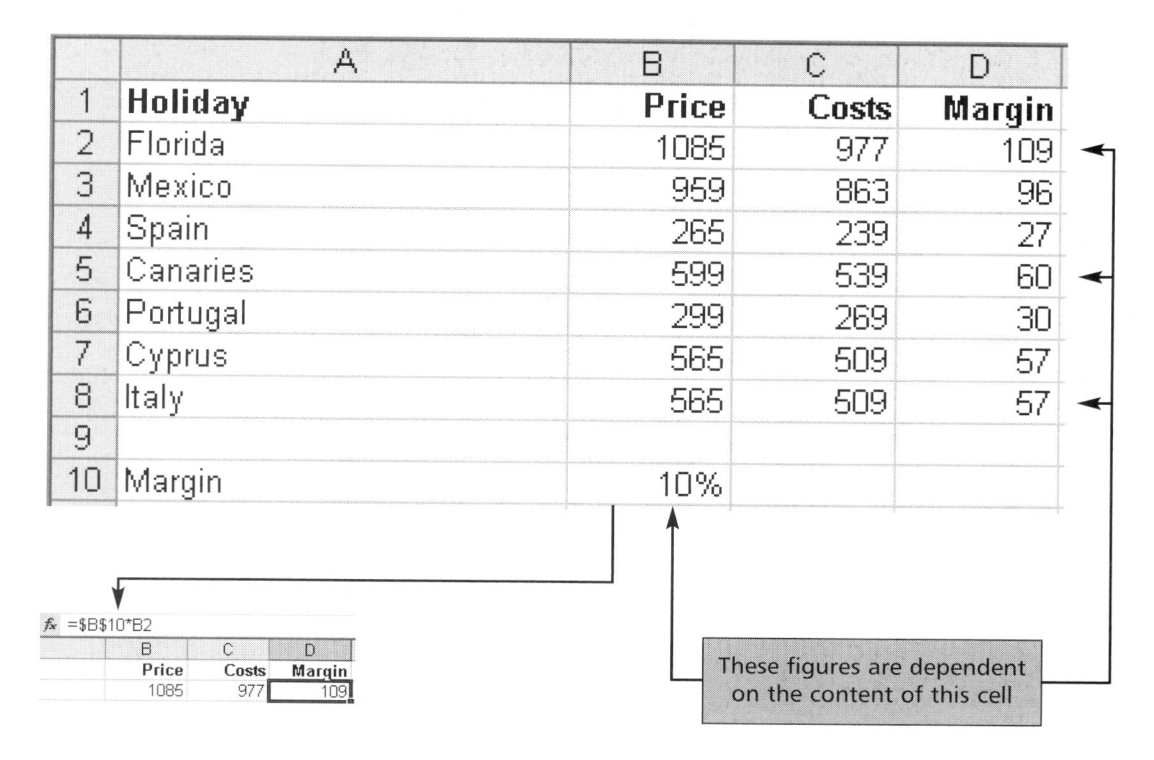

	A	B	C	D
1	**Holiday**	**Price**	**Costs**	**Margin**
2	Florida	1085	977	109
3	Mexico	959	863	96
4	Spain	265	239	27
5	Canaries	599	539	60
6	Portugal	299	269	30
7	Cyprus	565	509	57
8	Italy	565	509	57
9				
10	Margin	10%		

	B	C	D
	Price	Costs	Margin
	1085	977	109

Figure 2.24

In this example the company is looking to achieve a certain margin (profit) on each holiday. To achieve the desired margin the costs must be kept below certain levels. For example, for it to achieve the 10% margin shown in cell B10 the costs for that holiday must not exceed £977. Because the actual amount of margin shown in column D is dependent on the input in cell B10 the company can change the margin in B10 and see what level the costs must be kept at.

Try it out

The file **Holiday_1.xls** can be found in Unit 2 on your CD.

Open this file.

Now try changing the margin figure in B10. Notice how the costs and margin achieved change as the figure in cell B10 is amended.

Now put the skills learnt in the last few sections into practice by completing Stages 1–3 of Build-up Exercise 2.

Build-up Exercise 2: Stage 1

Scenario

You are the caretaker at a local boarding school. The headmaster has asked if you can give him some recommendations as to what decorating can be achieved over the holiday period within the budgets he has available. You decide that the best way of providing this information is to use the skills you learnt when you did the CLAIT Plus certificate in spreadsheets.

Open Excel.

Open the **Decorate.csv** file from your CD accompanying this book.

Save the file as **Decorate.xls** on your floppy or hard disk.

Calculate the cost of paint for Dormitory 1. (Formula: Paint*Paint Cans or B13*B2). Remember the reference at B2 must be an absolute reference.

Replicate this formula for all buildings.

Repeat this exercise for Sand Paper and Brush Sets.

For the Turps column divide the cost of the (20 ltr) can of Turps by the number of buildings to be decorated.

Calculate the total cost of materials before discount for each building.

Using the IF statement, calculate the discount available for Dormitory 1.

Formula: =IF(AND(I15>=151,I15<=200),$C$9,$B$9)

Replicate this formula for all buildings.

Now calculate the actual cost, including discount, for the decorating materials for Dormitory 1.
Formula: =I15*(1-J15)

Replicate this formula for all buildings.

Save your spreadsheet.

Your spreadsheet should now look similar to Figure 2.25.

	A	B	C	D	E	F	G	H	I	J	K	L
1												
2												
3	Brush Sets	10.5										
4	Paint	21										
5	Sandpaper	0.15										
6	Turps (20 Ltrs	18										
7												
8	Discounts	50 - 150	151 - 200									
9		0.1	0.2									
10												
11	DECORATING MATERIALS COSTS											
12												
13	Building	Paint Cans	Sand Paper (	Brush Sets	Paint Cost	Sand Paper C	Brush Costs	Turps	Total Material	Discounts	Discounted Price	
14												
15	Dormitory 1	6	20	2	126	3	21	1	151	20%	120.80	
16	Dormitory 2	6	20	2	126	3	21	1	151	20%	120.80	
17	Dormitory 3	6	20	2	126	3	21	1	151	20%	120.80	
18	Dormitory 4	6	20	2	126	3	21	1	151	20%	120.80	
19	Dormitory 5	6	20	2	126	3	21	1	151	20%	120.80	
20	Dormitory 6	6	20	2	126	3	21	1	151	20%	120.80	
21	Kitchen	4	14	1	84	2.1	10.5	1	97.6	10%	87.84	
22	Games Rm	5	16	2	105	2.4	21	1	129.4	10%	116.46	
23	Study Rm 1	3	10	1	63	1.5	10.5	1	76	10%	68.40	
24	Study Rm 2	3	10	1	63	1.5	10.5	1	76	10%	68.40	
25	Study Rm 3	3	10	1	63	1.5	10.5	1	76	10%	68.40	
26	Study Rm 4	3	10	1	63	1.5	10.5	1	76	10%	68.40	
27	Classroom 1	5	16	2	105	2.4	21	1	129.4	10%	116.46	
28	Classroom 2	5	16	2	105	2.4	21	1	129.4	10%	116.46	
29	Classroom 3	5	16	2	105	2.4	21	1	129.4	10%	116.46	
30	Classroom 4	5	16	2	105	2.4	21	1	129.4	10%	116.46	
31	Classroom 5	5	16	2	105	2.4	21	1	129.4	10%	116.46	
32	Classroom 6	5	16	2	105	2.4	21	1	129.4	10%	116.46	
33												
34												
35												

Sheet1 / Sheet2 / Sheet3

Figure 2.25

Build-up Exercise 2: Stage 2

Scenario

You have managed to find a supplier who will provide the same paint at £19.00 rather than the present £21.00.

Amend the Paint cost to £19.

Type 'Totals' in cell A33.

Calculate in cell B33 the total number of cans of paint for each building.

Replicate this formula for columns C to I.

Having negotiated a new price for paint you have also managed to negotiate a new discount range. For orders between £50 and £100 the new discount is 15% and for orders between £101 and £150 the new discount is 20%.

Amend cell B8 to show '50–100' and cell C8 to show '101–150'.

Amend the discount rate in cell B9 to 15% (0.15). The rate in cell C9 remains the same.

Amend the formula in cell J15 to reflect these changes, (=IF(AND(I15>=101,I15<=150),$C$9,$B$9)).

Replicate the formula to cell J32.

Calculate the total discounted price by inserting an appropriate formula in cell K33.

Insert a formula in cell J33 to calculate the average discount for all buildings,(=AVERAGE(J15:J32)).

Save your file as **Decorate_2.xls**.

You should now be able to:

- import a generic file and save it as an Excel file
- enter data into specified cells
- amend and delete data
- use basic mathematical functions
- replicate formulae
- use absolute, relative and mixed cell references
- use simple Excel functions
- understand about nested IF statements
- project different results by changing data inputs.

Build-up Exercise 2: Stage 3

Scenario

Having determined the material costs per building you now need to calculate the labour costs.

The cost of the painter per hour is £18.50.

Work on the basis of eight hours in a working day.

Move the heading 'DECORATING MATERIALS COSTS' to cell A1.

Enter the heading 'LABOUR COSTS' into cell E1.

Enter 'Per Hour' in cell F2.

Enter 'Painter' in cell E3.

Enter 'Hours per Day' in cell E4.

Enter the painter's rate of 18.5 in cell F3.

Enter the Hours per Day as 8 in cell F4.

Enter the heading 'Days' in cell N13.

Insert the following data:

Table 2.4

Building	Days
Dormitory 1	3
Dormitory 2	3
Dormitory 3	3
Dormitory 4	3
Dormitory 5	3
Dormitory 6	3
Kitchen	2
Games Rm	2.5
Study Rm 1	1.5
Study Rm 2	1.5
Study Rm 3	1.5
Study Rm 4	1.5
Classroom 1	2.5
Classroom 2	2.5
Classroom 3	2.5
Classroom 4	2.5
Classroom 5	2.5
Classroom 6	2.5

Insert the heading 'Labour' in cell O13.

Calculate the cost of labour for Dormitory 1 in cell O15, (=N15*$F$4*$F$3).

Replicate this formula for all rooms.

Insert a formula in cell N33 to calculate the total days for decorating all rooms.

Replicate this formula to cell O33 to calculate the total labour costs.

Your spreadsheet should now look similar to Figure 2.26.

	A	B	C	D	E	F	G	H	I	J	K	L	N	O
1	DECORATING MATERIALS COSTS				LABOUR COSTS									
2						Per Hour								
3	Brush Sets	10.5			Painter	18.5								
4	Paint	19			Hours per	8								
5	Sandpaper	0.15												
6	Turps (20 Ltrs)	18												
7														
8	Discounts	50 - 100	101 -150											
9		0.15	0.2											
10														
11														
12														
13	Building	Paint Cans	Sand Paper (Sheets	Brush Set	Paint Cost	Sand Paper Cost	Brush Cost	Turps	Total Materials	Discounts	Discounted Price		Days	Labour
14														
15	Dormitory 1	6	20	2	114	3	21	1	139	20%	111.20		3	444
16	Dormitory 2	6	20	2	114	3	21	1	139	20%	111.20		3	444
17	Dormitory 3	6	20	2	114	3	21	1	139	20%	111.20		3	444
18	Dormitory 4	6	20	2	114	3	21	1	139	20%	111.20		3	444
19	Dormitory 5	6	20	2	114	3	21	1	139	20%	111.20		3	444
20	Dormitory 6	6	20	2	114	3	21	1	139	20%	111.20		3	444
21	Kitchen	4	14	1	76	2.1	10.5	1	89.6	15%	76.16		2	296
22	Games Rm	5	16	2	95	2.4	21	1	119.4	20%	95.52		2.5	370
23	Study Rm 1	3	10	1	57	1.5	10.5	1	70	15%	59.50		1.5	222
24	Study Rm 2	3	10	1	57	1.5	10.5	1	70	15%	59.50		1.5	222
25	Study Rm 3	3	10	1	57	1.5	10.5	1	70	15%	59.50		1.5	222
26	Study Rm 4	3	10	1	57	1.5	10.5	1	70	15%	59.50		1.5	222
27	Classroom 1	5	16	2	95	2.4	21	1	119.4	20%	95.52		2.5	370
28	Classroom 2	5	16	2	95	2.4	21	1	119.4	20%	95.52		2.5	370
29	Classroom 3	5	16	2	95	2.4	21	1	119.4	20%	95.52		2.5	370
30	Classroom 4	5	16	2	95	2.4	21	1	119.4	20%	95.52		2.5	370
31	Classroom 5	5	16	2	95	2.4	21	1	119.4	20%	95.52		2.5	370
32	Classroom 6	5	16	2	95	2.4	21	1	119.4	20%	95.52		2.5	370
33	Totals	87	286	31	1653	42.9	325.5	18	2039.4	19%	1650.00		43.5	6438

Figure 2.26

Modifying a spreadsheet layout and formatting text and data

As part of the CLAIT Plus syllabus you are required to be able to format data and also present the spreadsheet in an acceptable form for viewing. As you would expect, Excel provides an array of formats for both data and text. If you have completed New CLAIT, or an equivalent level course, you will already have come across some of the options available for displaying numerical data and also how to align data in columns and cells. CLAIT Plus builds on these skills and helps you understand how to use additional options and the reasons for doing so.

Setting appropriate column widths

By now you should be familiar with using the drag technique to either widen or narrow a column. Similarly, you may have used the method of double-clicking between columns to widen the cell to accommodate the longest cell data. In addition to these methods you can also set the width of a column to specific dimensions.

To set the specific width of a column first highlight the column to be formatted and once highlighted press the right-hand mouse button to show the menu. Select the Column Width… option and a dialogue box appears as shown in Figure 2.27.

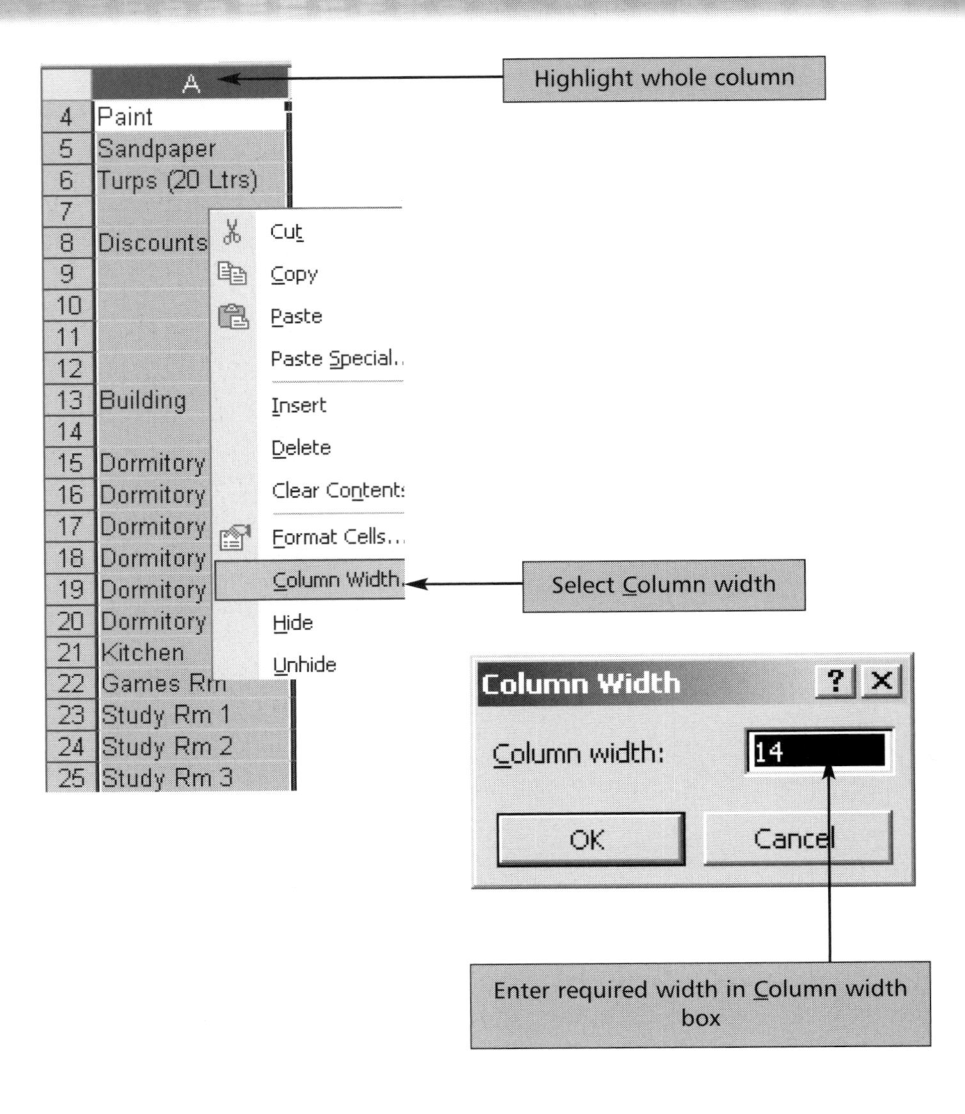

Figure 2.27

Enter the required width for the column and press OK.

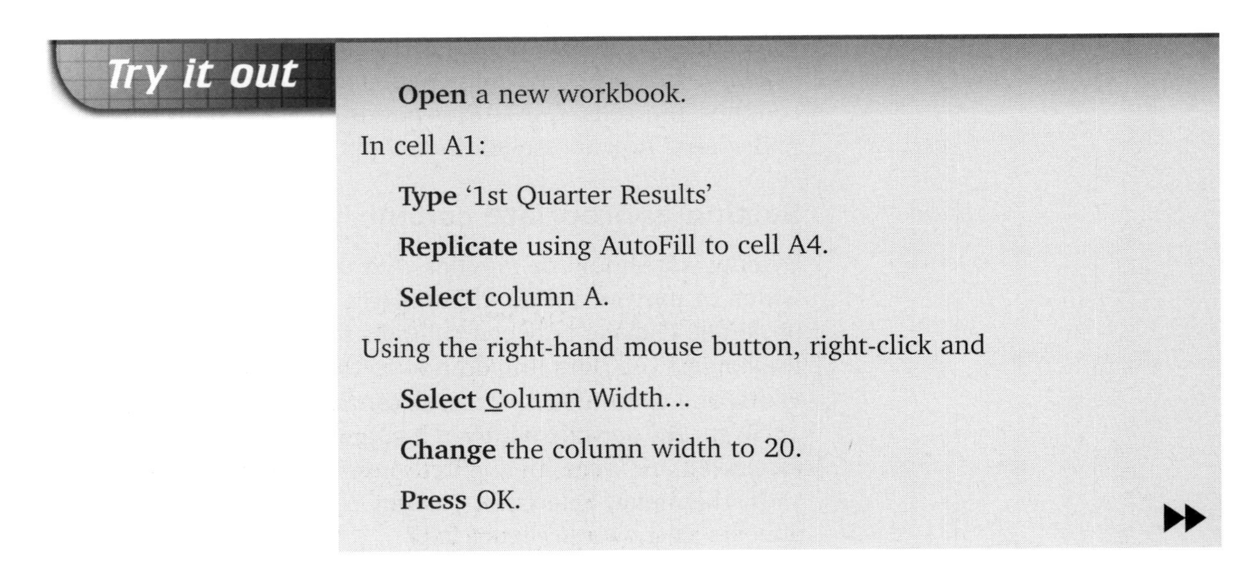

Try it out

Open a new workbook.

In cell A1:

Type '1st Quarter Results'

Replicate using AutoFill to cell A4.

Select column A.

Using the right-hand mouse button, right-click and

Select Column Width…

Change the column width to 20.

Press OK.

Save the workbook as **Number_Format**.

Notice (see Figure 2.28) how the column has widened to 20 and is now sufficiently wide to accept the row headings.

	A	B	C
1	1st Quarter Results		
2	2nd Quarter Results		
3	3rd Quarter Results		
4	4th Quarter Results		
5			
6			
7			
8			

2	2nd Quarter Results		
3	3rd Quarter Results		
4	4th Quarter Results		
5			
6			
7			
8			
9			
10			
11			

Figure 2.28

Formatting numerical data

If you completed New CLAIT or an equivalent level 1 programme you will have already used or seen how to format numeric data to different numbers of decimal places. There are, however, a number of different ways that data can be formatted, such as percentage, currency, date, time, negative and general.

Have a look at Figure 2.29.

The formatting options dialogue box is accessed by selecting Format, Cells… on the main menu or clicking the Format Cells icon on the toolbar .

Along the top of the dialogue box are six tabs: Number, Alignment, Font, Border, Patterns, Protection. Some of these will be covered later in the unit. For now you are interested only in the Number tab as shown in Figure 2.29.

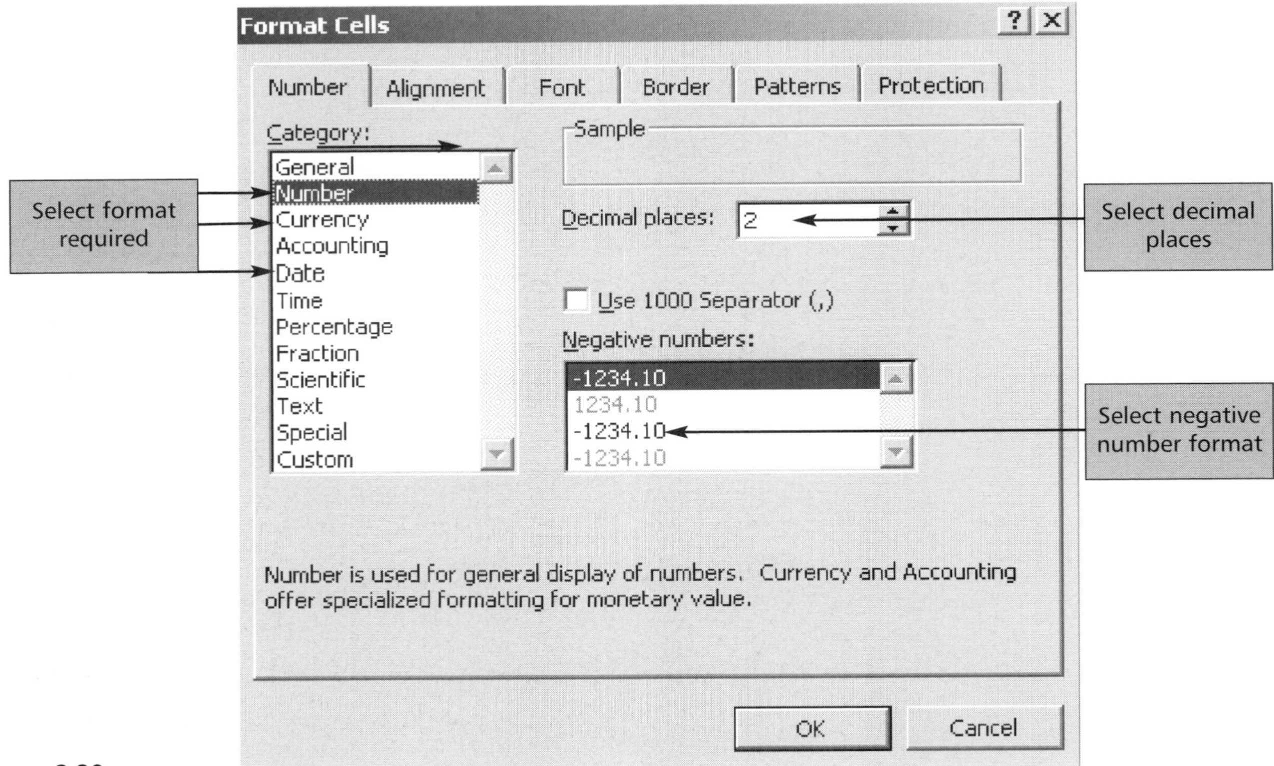

Figure 2.29

To the left of the box under Category: are the range of formats available, General, Number, Currency, and so on. When Number, Currency, Accounting, Percentage or Scientific is selected in the Category box, a field marked Decimal places: is visible on the right. Here you can select the number of decimal places any data in these cells should have. When Currency or Accounting is selected in the Category box a further field called Symbol: is visible below the Decimal places: field. Here you can select the currency symbol appropriate to the data in use, such as £, €, $, etc.

If the Date or Time option is selected in the category list then you have the opportunity to determine the date's format from the appropriate box on the right.

The principles outlined above also hold good for any of the other format styles available in the category list. Now have a go at changing the format of data in a Try it out exercise.

Try it out

Open the **Number_Format** workbook created in the last exercise.

Insert a row above 1st Quarter Results.

Enter the following headings:

A1 Period

B1 Northern

C1 Eastern

D1 Western

E1 Southern

Enter the data shown in Table 2.5:

Table 2.5

Period	Northern	Eastern	Western	Southern
1st Quarter Results	12560	5000	24125	58125
2nd Quarter Results	15240	6300	28536	65752
3rd Quarter Results	25463	8750	48712	78214
4th Quarter Results	18542	4478	26321	62147

Highlight cells B2:E5.

Format these cells as Currency to two decimal places.

Insert two columns between the Period and Northern columns.

Set the column widths of these new columns to 17.

Enter the following new column headings:

Column B Qtr Start

Column C Qtr End

Enter the new data shown in Table 2.6.

Table 2.6

Qtr Start	Qtr End
01/01/02	31/03/02
01/04/02	30/06/02
01/07/02	30/09/02
01/10/02	31/12/02

Format cells B2:C5 as Date in full, i.e. 1 January 2002.

Save the workbook.

Formatting text data

Textual (or for that matter numeric) data can be displayed or formatted in a variety of ways, using alignment, orientation, emphasis and wrapping amongst other formatting functions, to best display the data.

Have a look at Figure 2.30.

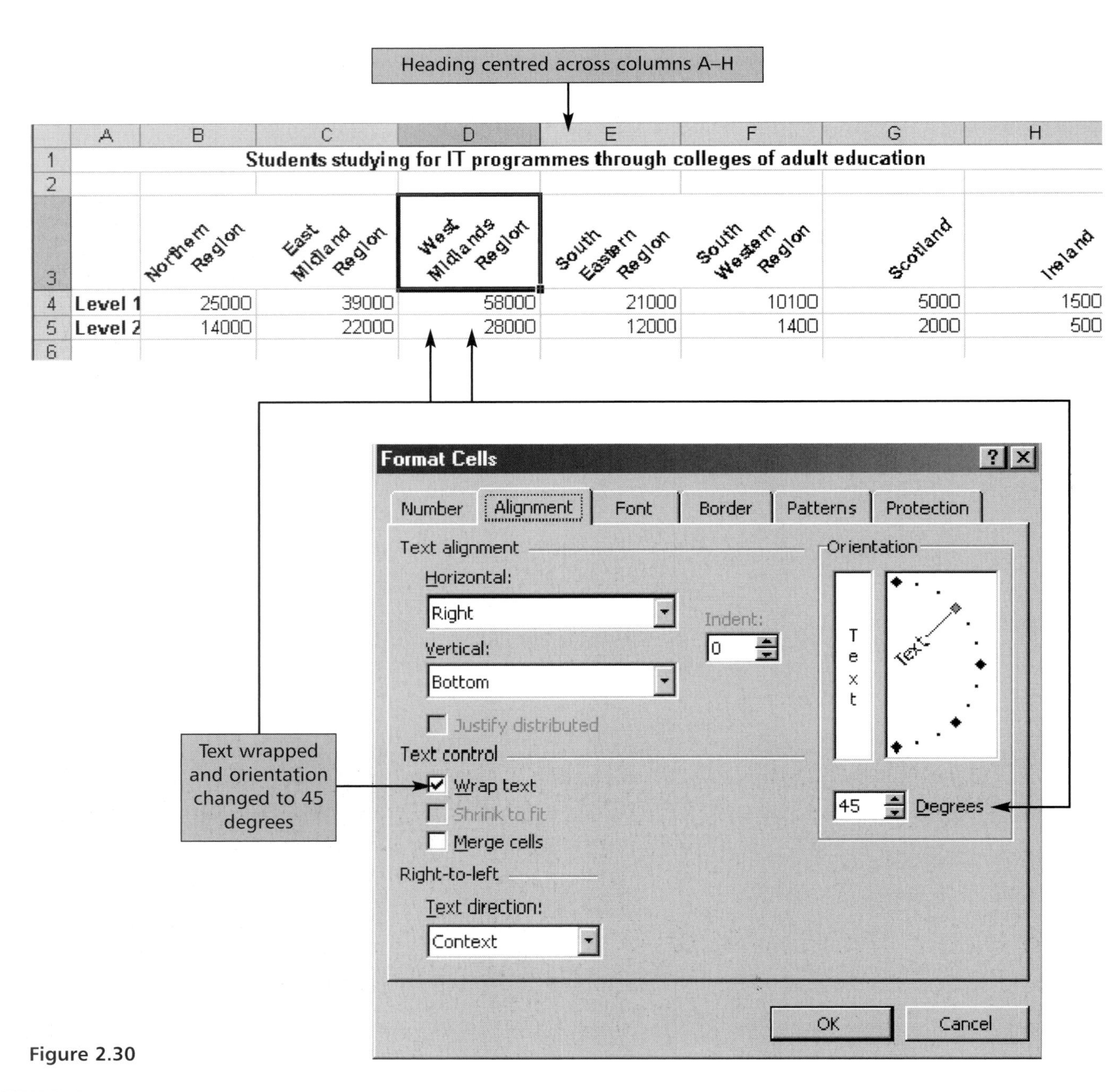

Figure 2.30

In this simple spreadsheet the main and column headings have been subjected to a number of formats. The cells across columns A to H have been merged and the heading centred. The column headings have been text-wrapped and their orientation has been changed from horizontal to an angle of 45° to the horizontal. You might ask why it is necessary to do this. The answer is, it is not, but there may well be times when the column heading is too long to just word-wrap and the appearance of the spreadsheet could be improved by changing the orientation of the text. To change the orientation, first select the cell or cells to be formatted and then using the orientation options in the Format Cells dialogue box (see Figure 2.31) make the changes required.

Similarly with wrapping the text in a single cell or in multiple cells, the cell or cells are first selected and then the Wrap text check box (see Figure 2.32) is checked.

There may be occasions when you want to present a column or row heading across a number of columns or rows, and here the merge cell option can help. Now have a go at formatting text in a simple spreadsheet.

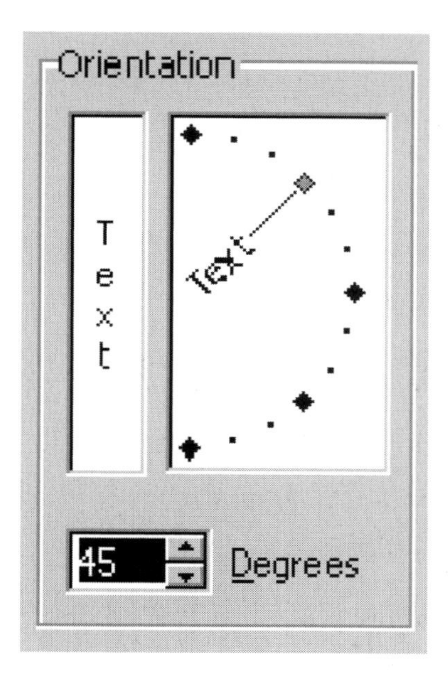

Figure 2.31

Figure 2.32

Try it out

Copy the file **Holiday_Bookings.xls** from the attached CD to your floppy or hard disk and uncheck the read-only attribute.

Open Holiday_Bookings.xls.

Notice that a number of the country column headings are too long for the width of the column. In this exercise you will use both the wrap text and orientation functions available from the Format Cells dialogue box.

Highlight cells B3:I3.

Select Format, Cells... from the main menu to show the Format Cells dialogue box.

Select the Alignment tab.

Check the Wrap text check box under the Text control options.

Press OK.

Select Format, Cells... from the main menu to show the Format Cells dialogue box.

Select the Alignment tab.

Change the orientation to 45°.

Press OK.

The row height needs to be adjusted so that the column headings are displayed in full. With cells B3:I3 selected:

Select Format, Row, Height... and change the row 3 height to 60.

Centre align the column headings. To do this ensure all heading cells are highlighted (i.e. B3:I3) and press the centre alignment icon ≡.

Change the widths of columns B:I to 10.

Highlight cell A16.

Select Format, Cells... from the main menu to show the Format Cells dialogue box.

Select the Alignment tab.

Check the Wrap text check box under the Text control options.

Press OK.

Change the width of column A to 10.

Change row 16 height to 30.

Finally you are going to vertically centre the data in row 16 so that it aligns centrally to the TOTAL BOOKINGS row heading.

Highlight cells B16:I16.

Select Format, Cells... from the main menu to show the Format Cells dialogue box.

Select the Alignment tab.

In the Vertical field under the Text alignment options:

Select Centre.

Save the changes you have made.

The spreadsheet should now look similar to Figure 2.33.

	A	B	C	D	E	F	G	H	I
1	BOOKED HOLIDAY PACKAGES BY COUNTRY								
2									
3		Egypt	Majorca	Ibiza	Minorca	Gran Canaria	Costa Brava	Costa de Almeria	Algarve
4	Jan	165	296	100	145	483	288	285	255
5	Feb	193	424	285	225	294	180	110	226
6	Mar	451	490	362	349	285	346	376	107
7	Apr	181	236	336	138	233	400	163	327
8	May	442	467	228	151	170	418	230	224
9	Jun	312	176	201	285	169	267	413	201
10	Jul	109	309	271	493	247	381	233	245
11	Aug	382	316	268	107	410	243	454	215
12	Sep	478	233	361	107	137	297	193	109
13	Oct	260	126	295	334	425	151	223	311
14	Nov	325	459	479	106	114	334	161	443
15	Dec	275	208	212	172	120	392	247	484
16	TOTAL BOOKINGS	3572	3739	3398	2611	3087	3697	3088	3147

Figure 2.33

Merging cells

Another method of aligning (text) data is to merge cells and then align the text depending on the layout sought.

Have a look at Figure 2.34. The aim is to align departments that have the same holiday entitlements. On the left the display would appear to show that the entitlements belong to Manufacturing and Senior Management. The right-hand side clearly indicates that the departments are in two groups: Administration and Manufacturing; Distribution and Senior Management. This has been achieved by merging cells C3 and C4, similarly cells C7 and C8.

To merge two or more cells highlight the cells to be merged and then check the merge cells check box in the Format Cells dialogue box under the Alignment tab. Alternatively, if you intend to merge and centre data at the same time you can use the merge and centre icon on the toolbar.

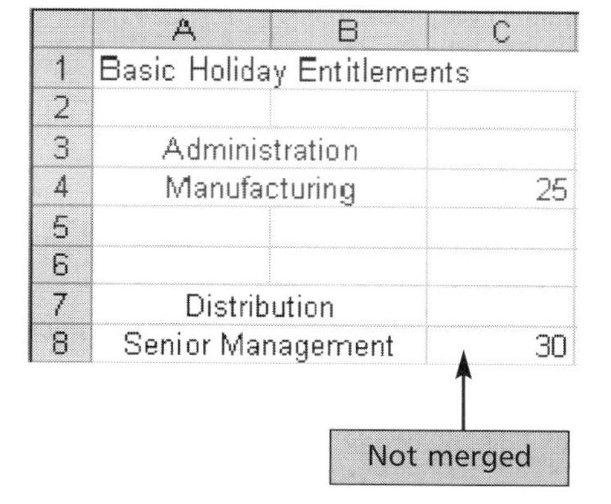

	A	B	C
1	Basic Holiday Entitlements		
2			
3	Administration		
4	Manufacturing		25
5			
6			
7	Distribution		
8	Senior Management		30

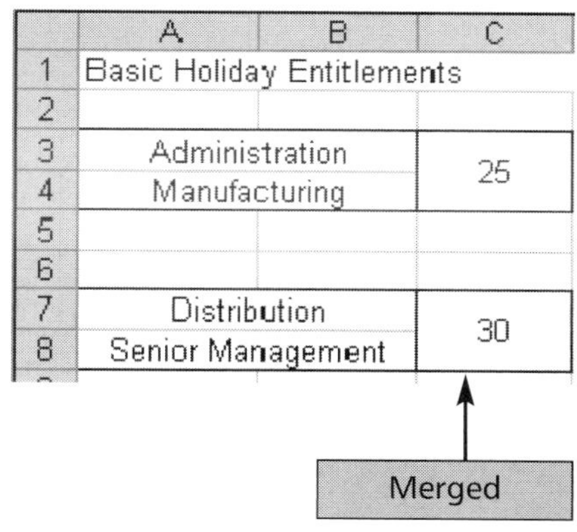

	A	B	C
1	Basic Holiday Entitlements		
2			
3	Administration		25
4	Manufacturing		
5			
6			
7	Distribution		30
8	Senior Management		

Figure 2.34

Try it out

Open Holiday_Bookings.xls.

Centre the heading BOOKED HOLIDAY PACKAGES BY COUNTRY across columns A to I inclusive. Use either of the methods explained above.

Your completed spreadsheet should now look similar to Figure 2.35.

	A	B	C	D	E	F	G	H	I
1	BOOKED HOLIDAY PACKAGES BY COUNTRY								
2									
3		Egypt	Majorca	Ibiza	Minorca	Gran Canaria	Costa Brava	Costa de Almeria	Algarve
4	Jan	165	296	100	145	483	288	285	255
5	Feb	193	424	285	225	294	180	110	226
6	Mar	451	490	362	349	285	346	376	107
7	Apr	181	236	336	138	233	400	163	327
8	May	442	467	228	151	170	418	230	224
9	Jun	312	176	201	285	169	267	413	201
10	Jul	109	309	271	493	247	381	233	245
11	Aug	382	316	268	107	410	243	454	215
12	Sep	478	233	361	107	137	297	193	109
13	Oct	260	126	295	334	425	151	223	311
14	Nov	325	459	479	106	114	334	161	443
15	Dec	275	208	212	172	120	392	247	484
16	TOTAL BOOKINGS	3572	3739	3398	2611	3087	3697	3088	3147

Figure 2.35

Sorting data in a spreadsheet

Having built the basic framework for a spreadsheet there will be occasions when you may need to re-organise the data to make an analysis of the information easier. Being able to sort data in a spreadsheet is a CLAIT Plus requirement.

Data can be sorted in a variety of ways. It can be sorted by column (top to bottom) or by row (left to right), in ascending or descending order.

Have a look at the example shown in Figure 2.36.

	A	B	C
1	BOOKS	PAGES	COPIES
2	BLUE	34	600
3	RED	45	520
4	ORANGE	56	418
5	GREEN	34	369
6	PINK	27	534
7	YELLOW	81	739

Unsorted

	A	B	C
1	BOOKS	COPIES	PAGES
2	BLUE	600	34
3	RED	520	45
4	ORANGE	418	56
5	GREEN	369	34
6	PINK	534	27
7	YELLOW	739	81

Sorted by row – left to right

	A	B	C
1	BOOKS	COPIES	PAGES
2	GREEN	369	34
3	ORANGE	418	56
4	RED	520	45
5	PINK	534	27
6	BLUE	600	34
7	YELLOW	739	81

Sorted by column – top to bottom

Figure 2.36

The data here has been sorted in a variety of ways which you can follow through in the next Try it out exercise.

Sorting by Rows

Try it out

Open the file **Books.xls** on the accompanying CD and save it as **Books_1.xls** on either your floppy or hard disk.

First you are going to sort the data by row (or left to right).

Highlight cells B1:C7.

Select Sort... from the Data option on the main menu.

The dialogue box shown in Figure 2.37 will appear.

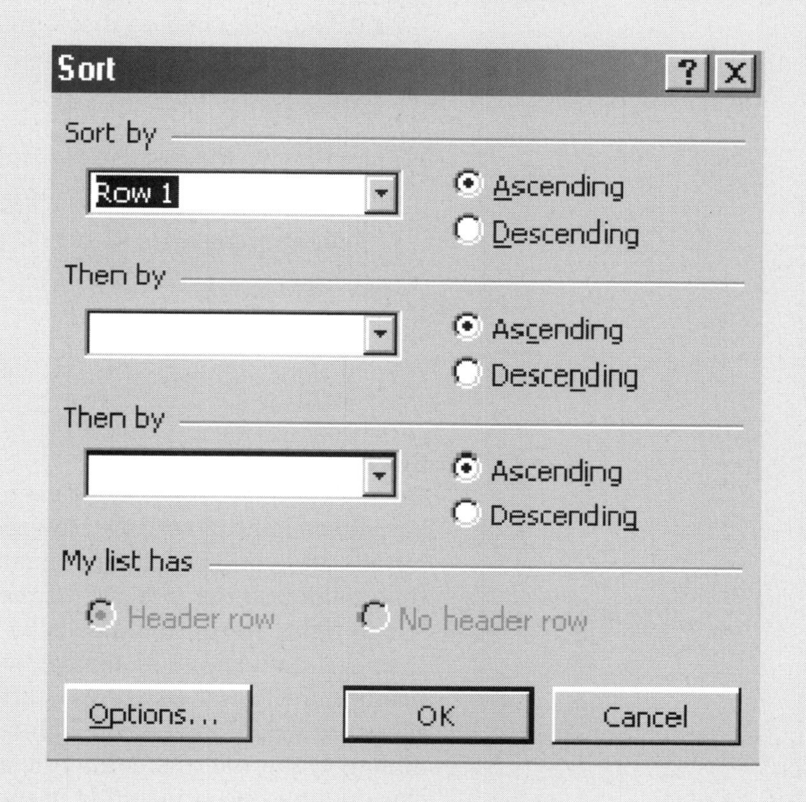

Figure 2.37

In the top left of the box is a field asking you what you want to Sort by. If the option Row 1 is shown, that is what you want, and Excel is intending to sort by row (left to right). If, however, the dialogue box shows PAGES then Excel is set to sort by column (top to bottom) which is *not* what you want. To change this option the Options... button is pressed so a further dialogue box (Sort Options) is presented as shown in Figure 2.38.

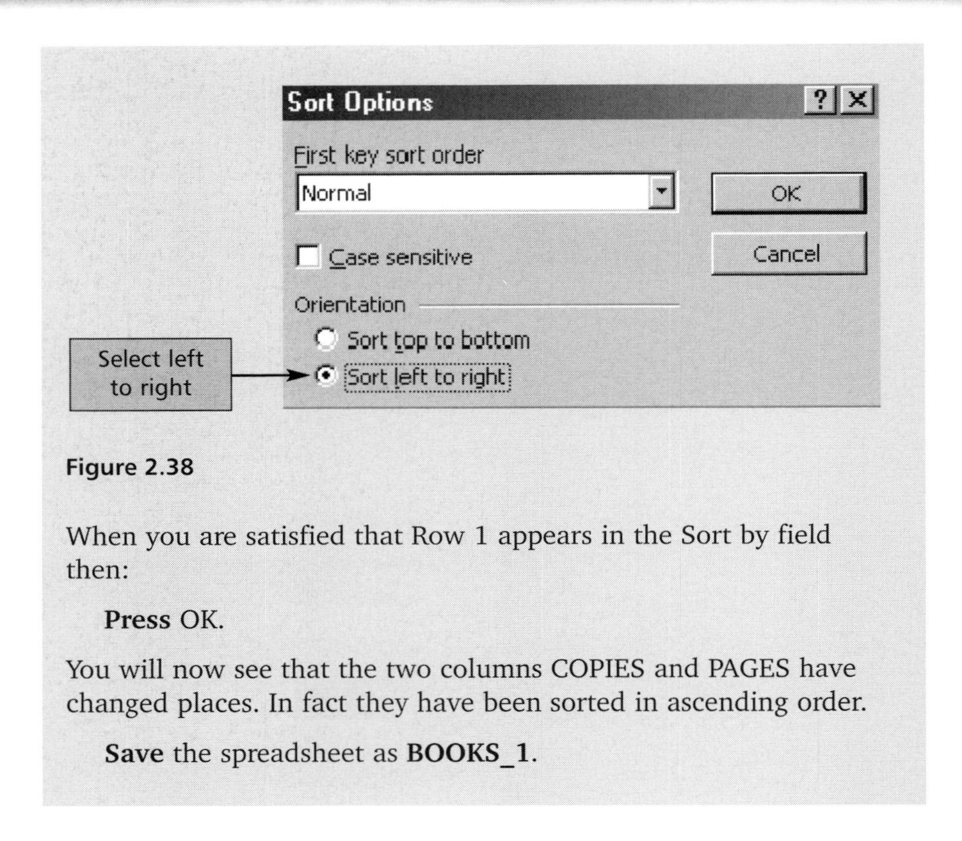

Figure 2.38

When you are satisfied that Row 1 appears in the Sort by field then:

Press OK.

You will now see that the two columns COPIES and PAGES have changed places. In fact they have been sorted in ascending order.

Save the spreadsheet as **BOOKS_1**.

Sorting by columns

Having completed the above exercise you should now understand the basic principles of sorting. However, in sorting data there can be pitfalls and you need to understand how to sort data and, at the same time, maintain the integrity of the data. When you sorted the rows, left to right, you selected cells B1 to C7. Had you included A1 to A7 then this data would also have been sorted. As it happens the heading for Row 1 in cell A1 starts with the letter B (BOOKS) and therefore would have come before COPIES as B comes before C in the alphabet. But had the column heading been, say, MANUSCRIPTS and this data had been included in the sort then it would have been placed between COPIES and PAGES. In other words you must be careful to ensure you select the appropriate data to sort. When sorting data top to bottom the pitfalls can have an even more detrimental effect.

For example, you are shortly going to sort the data top to bottom by BOOKS. Before doing so, consider what would happen if you only selected the same data as in the previous exercise, that is B1 to C7. If the BOOKS column is omitted you are actually asking Excel to sort the data in cells B1 to C7, top to bottom (ascending), and ignore column A. In effect the data would be sorted as requested, but the numbers corresponding to PAGES and COPIES would no longer relate to the name of the book. Have a look at Figure 2.39.

Instead of BLUE having 600 copies it is shown as having 369

	A	B	C
1	BOOKS	COPIES	PAGES
2	BLUE	600	34
3	RED	520	45
4	ORANGE	418	56
5	PINK	369	34
6	GREEN	534	27
7	YELLOW	739	81

	A	B	C
1	BOOKS	COPIES	PAGES
2	BLUE	369	34
3	RED	418	56
4	ORANGE	520	45
5	PINK	534	27
6	GREEN	600	34
7	YELLOW	739	81

The data is sorted in ascending order but not related to the original books

Figure 2.39

To avoid this problem ensure that all the data in the sort is selected – i.e. A1 to C7.

Now sort the spreadsheet by column, top to bottom.

Try it out

Highlight cells A1:C7.

Select Sort… from the Data option on the main menu.

Ensure the orientation check box in Sort Options indicates that 'Sort top to bottom' is checked.

Press OK in the Sort options dialogue box.

Select COPIES in the first Sort by field of the Sort dialogue box.

Press OK.

Your data should now have been sorted by COPIES.

Save your spreadsheet as **BOOKS_2**.

You should now be able to:

- change column widths and row heights
- display data using a variety of formats
- change the alignment and orientation of data
- wrap text in a single cell or multiple cells
- merge cells
- sort data by row and column.

Now return to the build-up exercise.

Build-up Exercise 2: Stage 4

Open Decorate_2.xls.

Change the column widths of the spreadsheet to 10.

Format Columns E, F, G, H, I, K and O to Currency to two decimal places.

Format cell G4 to Number with no decimal places.

Format cells B3:B6 to Number and two decimal places.

Set the headings in row 13 to Wrap text.

Adjust the column width of column A to 12.

Format the column headings in row 13 to bold.

Move the heading in F2 to G2.

Move the data in F3 and F4 to G3 and G4 respectively.

Merge cells E4 and F4.

Format cells B8 and C8 to be right-aligned.

Format cell G2 to be right-aligned.

Merge and centre the heading in E1 so that it is centred across columns E to G.

Merge and centre the heading in A1 so that it is centred across columns A to C.

Align column headings in row 13, columns A to D to be left-aligned.

Align column headings in row 13, columns E to K and N to O to be centred.

Change the orientation of the headings in row 13, columns E to K and N to O so that the headings are at a 45° angle.

Set the row height of row 13 to 45.

Format cells A1 and E1 as bold.

Save your spreadsheet as **Decorate_3.xls**.

Your spreadsheet should now look like Figure 2.40.

	A	B	C	D	E	F	G	H	I	J	K	L	M	N	O
1	**DECORATING MATERIALS COSTS**				**LABOUR COSTS**										
2							Per Hour								
3	Brush Sets	10.50			Painter		£18.50								
4	Paint	19.00			Hours per day		£8.00								
5	Sandpaper	0.15													
6	Turps (20 Ltrs)	18.00													
7															
8	Discounts	50 - 100	101 -150												
9		0.15	0.2												
10															
11															
12															
13	**Building**	**Paint Cans**	**Sand Paper (Sheets)**	**Brush Sets**	**Paint Cost**	**Sand Paper Cost**	**Brush Costs**	**Turps**	**Total Materials**	**Discounts**	**Discounted Price**			**Days**	**Labour**
14															
15	Dormitory 1	6	20	2	£114.00	£3.00	£21.00	£1.00	£139.00	20%	£111.20			3	£444.00
16	Dormitory 2	6	20	2	£114.00	£3.00	£21.00	£1.00	£139.00	20%	£111.20			3	£444.00
17	Dormitory 3	6	20	2	£114.00	£3.00	£21.00	£1.00	£139.00	20%	£111.20			3	£444.00
18	Dormitory 4	6	20	2	£114.00	£3.00	£21.00	£1.00	£139.00	20%	£111.20			3	£444.00
19	Dormitory 5	6	20	2	£114.00	£3.00	£21.00	£1.00	£139.00	20%	£111.20			3	£444.00
20	Dormitory 6	6	20	2	£114.00	£3.00	£21.00	£1.00	£139.00	20%	£111.20			3	£444.00
21	Kitchen	4	14	1	£76.00	£2.10	£10.50	£1.00	£89.60	15%	£76.16			2	£296.00
22	Games Rm	5	16	2	£95.00	£2.40	£21.00	£1.00	£119.40	20%	£95.52			2.5	£370.00
23	Study Rm 1	3	10	1	£57.00	£1.50	£10.50	£1.00	£70.00	15%	£59.50			1.5	£222.00
24	Study Rm 2	3	10	1	£57.00	£1.50	£10.50	£1.00	£70.00	15%	£59.50			1.5	£222.00
25	Study Rm 3	3	10	1	£57.00	£1.50	£10.50	£1.00	£70.00	15%	£59.50			1.5	£222.00
26	Study Rm 4	3	10	1	£57.00	£1.50	£10.50	£1.00	£70.00	15%	£59.50			1.5	£222.00
27	Classroom 1	5	16	2	£95.00	£2.40	£21.00	£1.00	£119.40	20%	£95.52			2.5	£370.00
28	Classroom 2	5	16	2	£95.00	£2.40	£21.00	£1.00	£119.40	20%	£95.52			2.5	£370.00
29	Classroom 3	5	16	2	£95.00	£2.40	£21.00	£1.00	£119.40	20%	£95.52			2.5	£370.00
30	Classroom 4	5	16	2	£95.00	£2.40	£21.00	£1.00	£119.40	20%	£95.52			2.5	£370.00
31	Classroom 5	5	16	2	£95.00	£2.40	£21.00	£1.00	£119.40	20%	£95.52			2.5	£370.00
32	Classroom 6	5	16	2	£95.00	£2.40	£21.00	£1.00	£119.40	20%	£95.52			2.5	£370.00
33	Totals	87	286	31	£1,653.00	£42.90	£325.50	£18.00	£2,039.40	19%	£1,650.00			43.5	£6,438.00
34															

Figure 2.40

Naming cells and referencing different spreadsheets

Naming and using named cell references

So far in this unit, when you have created a formula in a spreadsheet you have referred to individual cell addresses or ranges such as C4 or C5:F10. Excel also gives you the opportunity of naming cells which can be referred to by specific names rather than a cell address. Naming cells or ranges has a number of advantages. First it reduces the chance of error as it is easy to see exactly which cell you are referring to. It is easier to recognise than the meaning of a formula. For example, it is easier to refer to 'Average_Sales' rather than cell F57 or VISITORS*TICKET_VALUE. Naming ranges can make it easier to refer to areas of a large spreadsheet.

Have a look at the worksheet shown in Figure 2.41.

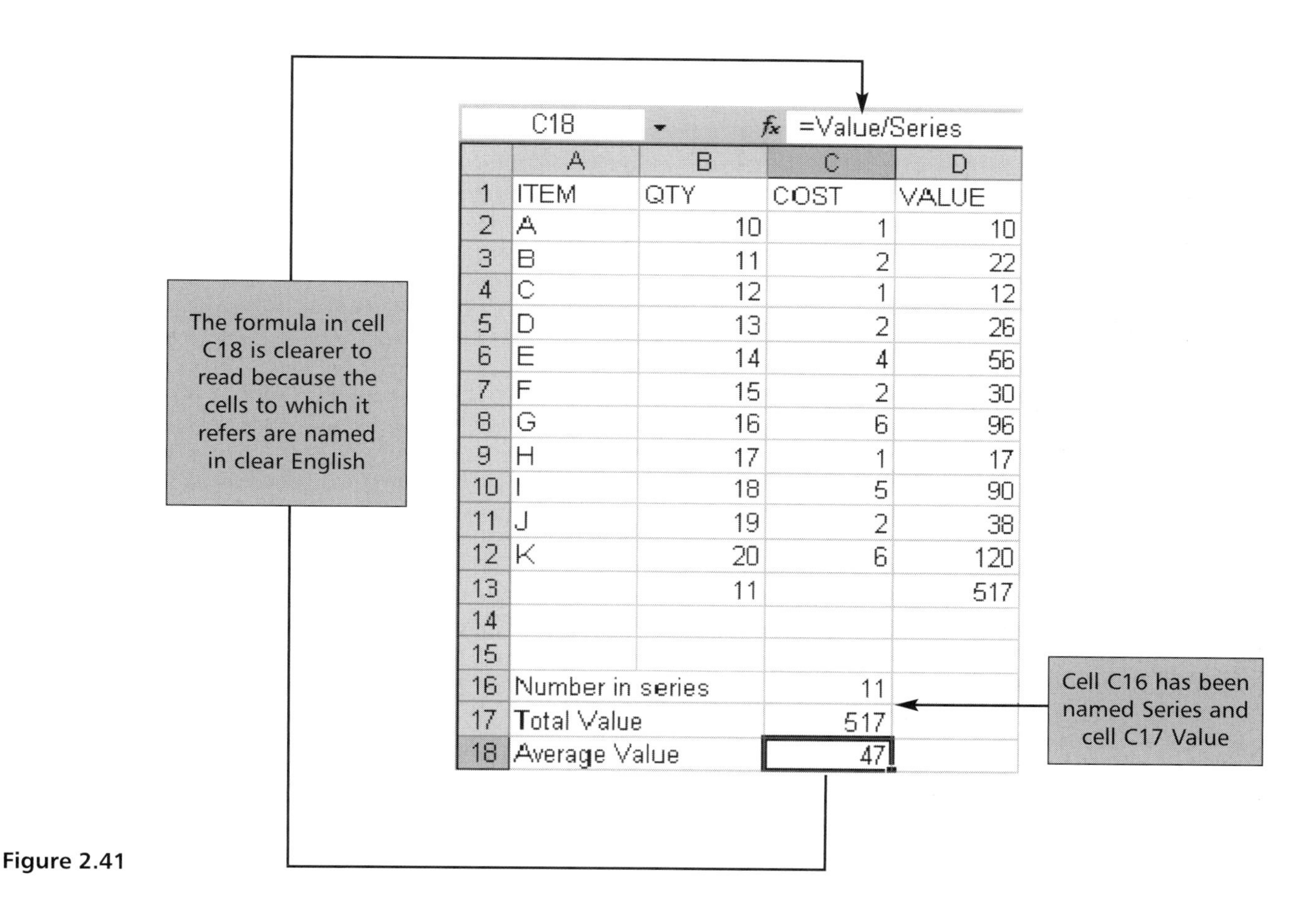
C18
=Value/Series
The formula in cell C18 is clearer to read because the cells to which it refers are named in clear English
Cell C16 has been named Series and cell C17 Value

	A	B	C	D
1	ITEM	QTY	COST	VALUE
2	A	10	1	10
3	B	11	2	22
4	C	12	1	12
5	D	13	2	26
6	E	14	4	56
7	F	15	2	30
8	G	16	6	96
9	H	17	1	17
10	I	18	5	90
11	J	19	2	38
12	K	20	6	120
13		11		517
14				
15				
16	Number in series		11	
17	Total Value		517	
18	Average Value		47	

Figure 2.41

To define (or name) a cell, select Insert, Define, Name... from the main menu. The dialogue box shown in Figure 2.42 then appears.

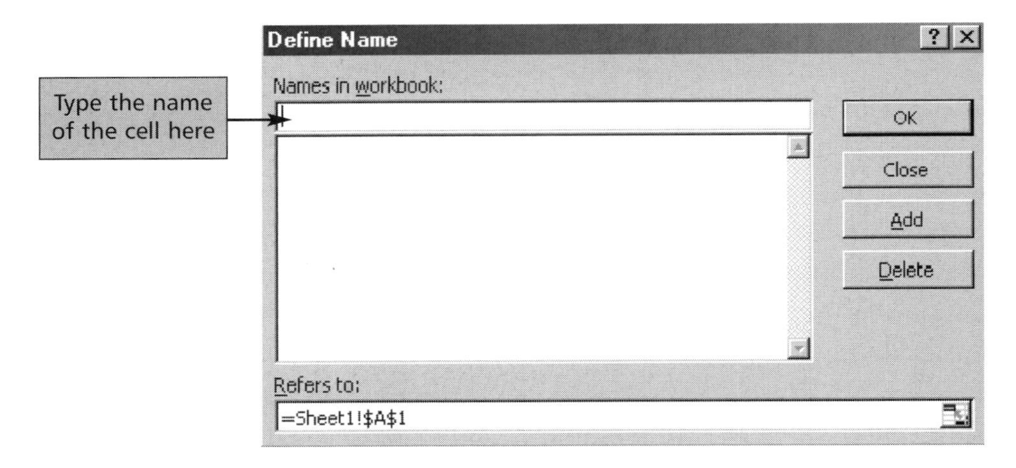

Figure 2.42

Once the cursor is on the cell you want to name, type in an appropriate name for the cell and press OK. It is as simple as that. Now try this out.

Try it out

Open the file **Reconcile.xls** from the Unit 2 folder on the CD.

Save the file as **Reconcile_1** on your floppy or hard disk.

The worksheet shows a particular range of stock, in this case adapters, the quantity of sales per week and the value of sales per week. Under the value of weekly sales is a line showing the balance of stock for each adapter by the end of the week. Your task is to create a formula using an IF statement that will identify whether there is a need to re-order.

Click on cell B30.

Define the cell's name as 'BALANCE_ADAPTER_1'.

Click on cell C30.

Define cell C30 as 'BALANCE_ADAPTER_2', D30 as 'BALANCE_ADAPTER_3' and so on until all six adapters have been named.

Warning! When defining the cell name make sure the cell that the name refers to is correct. See Figure 2.43.

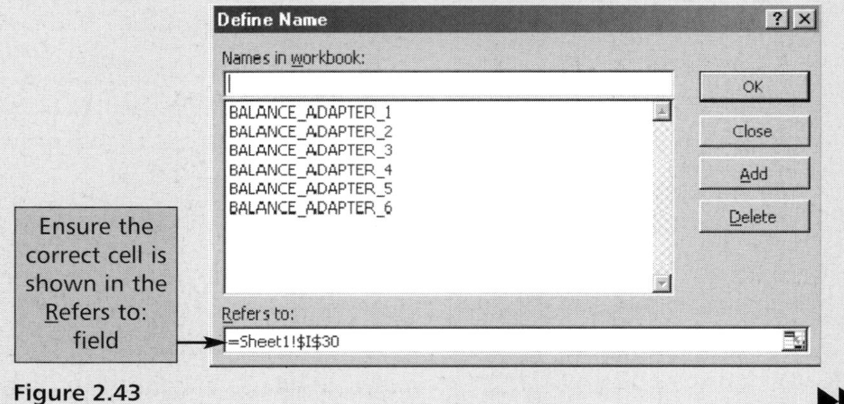

Figure 2.43

If the address is not correct there are two ways that changes can be made.

Option 1

Highlight the cell reference in the Refers to: field and overtype with the correct cell address.

Option 2

Click on the navigation box to the right of the Refers to: field. You can now click on the correct cell directly in the worksheet (see Figure 2.44).

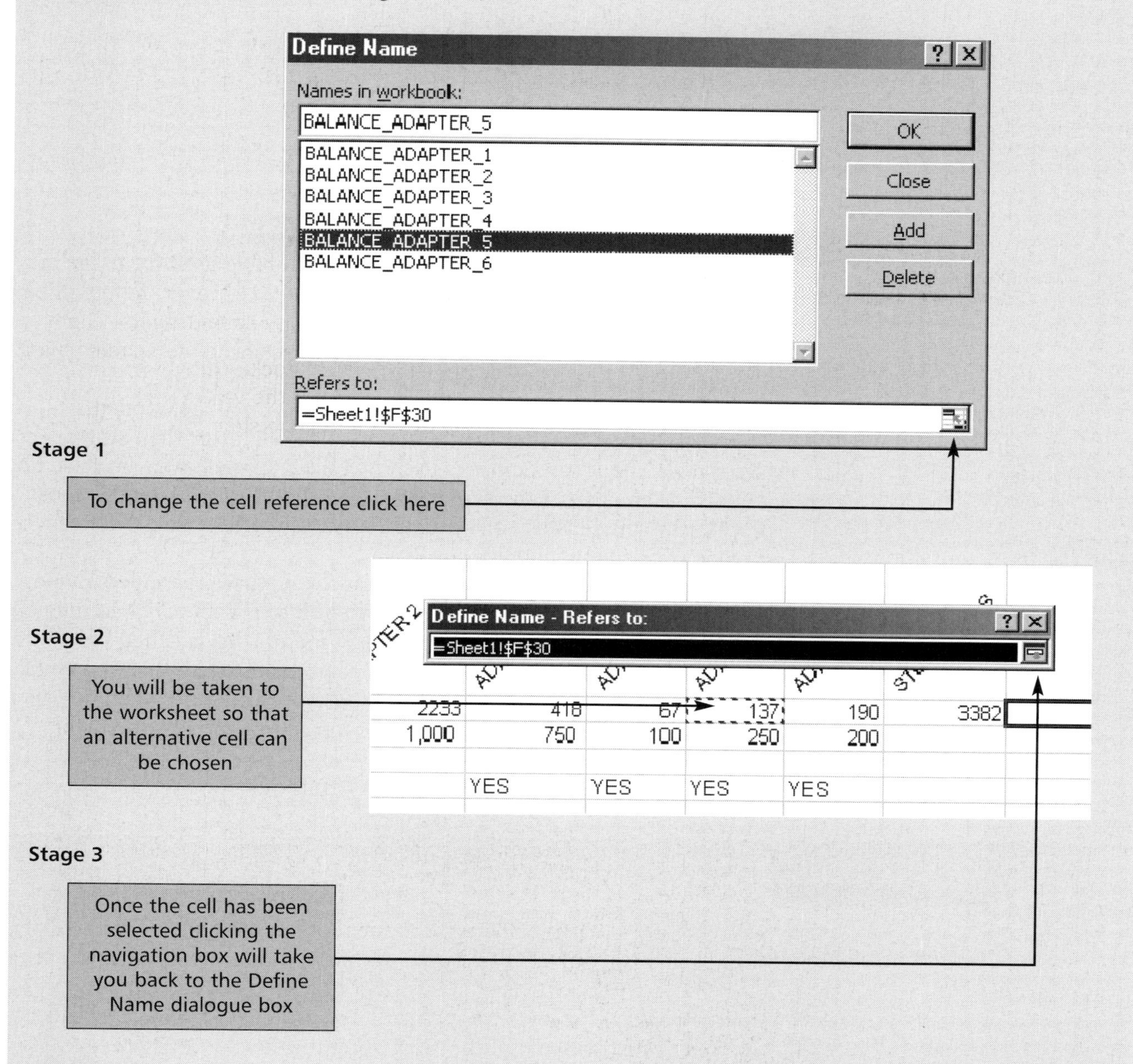

Figure 2.44

The area of the worksheet you have just changed should now look like Figure 2.45.

29	STOCK BALANCE	ADAPTER 1	ADAPTER 2	ADAPTER 3	ADAPTER 4	ADAPTER 5	ADAPTER 6	STOCK ITEMS
30		337	2233	418	67	137	190	3382
31	Re-order Level	500	1,000	750	100	250	200	
32								
33	Re-Order	YES	NO	YES	YES	YES	YES	

Figure 2.45

Save the file as **Reconcile_1**.

Referencing cells in other spreadsheets

In the exercise you have carried out so far you have used formulae to reference various parts of the same spreadsheet. However there will be occasions when it is useful to reference separate spreadsheets. There are a number of advantages to using links to separate worksheets. First it means that you do not need to work on particularly large spreadsheets, instead breaking them down into small components which are linked. Smaller worksheets recalculate faster than single, larger ones and less memory is used by linked spreadsheets because not all need to be open at the same time. Excel, and for that matter most proprietary spreadsheet software, allows you to create links between spreadsheets simply and effectively.

To create a link, open both the spreadsheet where the link is made and the one where the data you want to link to is kept. Click in the cell of the spreadsheet where the link is to be made (this is called the destination file). The spreadsheet that contains the data that you want to link is called the source file. Type '=' as you would do when building a formula, and then click on the cell of the source file to which you want to link.

Follow this through in the following Try it out exercise.

Try it out

Scenario

Having built the spreadsheet **Reconcile_1** to determine, amongst other things, whether there is a need to re-order any of the adapter products, you now want to develop a new spreadsheet for the ordering and costing department to determine how many of each adapter needs to be re-ordered to bring the stock level back to full capacity. Also you want the costing department to calculate the cost of the orders. Since there will be changes made to the spreadsheet at the retail end this will have to be a separate spreadsheet, but linked to the original.

Open Reconcile_1 if it is not already open.

Open Reconcile_2 from the CD and save it to your floppy or hard disk.

Create a link from **Reconcile_1** to **Reconcile_2** which calculates, for each adapter, whether a re-order is necessary.

Your link statement should look like this: =(Reconcile.xls)Sheet1!B$33.

Using an IF statement calculate the amount required for the order. The logic for the statement should be: IF the appropriate ORDER REQUIRED cell states an order is required then take the original stock level and subtract the total weekly sales. If an order is not required then the cell should indicate NO ORDER.

Formula: =IF(B4="YES",[Reconcile.xls]Sheet1!$B$3–[Reconcile.xls]Sheet1!$B$18,"NO ORDER")

In the COST column:

Create a link to **Reconcile_1** which calculates the cost of the orders in column D.

The logical argument for this link is: If an order is required (YES) then multiply the PRICE of the appropriate adapter by the number required in the order.

Formula: =IF(C4<>"NO ORDER",[Reconcile.xls]Sheet1!C3*C4,"NO COST")

Save the spreadsheet.

Your spreadsheet should now look like Figure 2.46.

D4 | =IF(C4<>"NO ORDER",[Reconcile.xls]Sheet1!C3*C4,"NO COST")

	A	B	C	D	E	F	G
1	RE ORDERS						
2							
3	PRODUCT	ORDER REQUIRED	AMOUNT	COST			
4	ADAPTER_1	YES	337	21,901.63			
5	ADAPTER_2	NO	NO ORDER	NO COST			
6	ADAPTER_3	YES	418	12,535.82			
7	ADAPTER_4	YES	67	1,071.33			
8	ADAPTER_5	YES	137	2,808.50			
9	ADAPTER_6	YES	190	8,645.00			

Figure 2.46

You should now be able to:

- name and use reference cells
- create links from one spreadsheet to another.

Build-up Exercise 2: Stage 5

Open the file **Decorate_3.xls.**

Type in cell A11 the heading 'General Decorating Budget'.

Enter '5000' as the budget in C11.

Create a new spreadsheet on your floppy or hard disk and call it **'Decorate_4.xls'**.

Format and set up the spreadsheet as shown in the Table 2.7:

Table 2.7

Column, row cell	Input	Data	Special instructions	Font
A1	Spreadsheet heading	Budget analysis	Capitals, centred across columns A–D	Arial 10, bold
A3	Column heading	Building	Capitals	Arial 10, bold
B3	Column heading	Total decorating cost	Capitals, word wrap	Arial 10, bold
C3	Column heading	Accumulated cost	Capitals, word wrap	Arial 10, bold
D3	Column heading	% of budget expenditure	Capitals, word wrap	Arial 10, bold
Row 3	Height		65	
Row 3	Heading orientation		45°	
Column A	Format		Width 12	Arial 10
Column B	Format	Accounting to 2 decimal places	Width 12	Arial 10
Column C	Format	Accounting to 2 decimal places	Width 12	Arial 10
Column D	Format	Percentage with no decimal places	Width 12	Arial 10

Create a link in Cell A4 to Dormitory 1 in file **Decorate_3.xls.**

Replicate the data for each building.

Create a linked formula in Cell B4 to **Decorate_3.xls** that calculates the total decorating cost for each building (use Total Decorating Cost = Discounted Price + Labour).

Type the heading 'General Decorating Budget' in Cell A26.

Create a link to the budget amount in **Decorate_3.xls** (Cell C11).

Create a formula in Cell C4 that will calculate the accumulating cost as each room is decorated. (use the Formula =SUM($B$4:B4).

Note the need to make the first cell an absolute reference.

Replicate this formula for all buildings.

Create a formula in Cell D4 that calculates the accumulating percentage spend against budget as each room is decorated (use the formula =C4/$C$26, and note Cell C26 will always be the absolute reference).

Replicate this formula for all buildings.

Sort the data by Decorating Cost.

You can now see that to use the budget to maximum effect without going over budget you can decorate all the studies, classrooms, the kitchen and games room.

Save the spreadsheet.

Formatting the display of a spreadsheet

Margins and page orientation

You may have come across margins in other application software such as Word, desktop publishing or reports in databases. Changing margins for spreadsheet printouts is very similar.

First the spreadsheet is opened and Print Preview is selected from the File option on the main menu. This activates the print preview screen (see Figure 2.47) where you have a number of options.

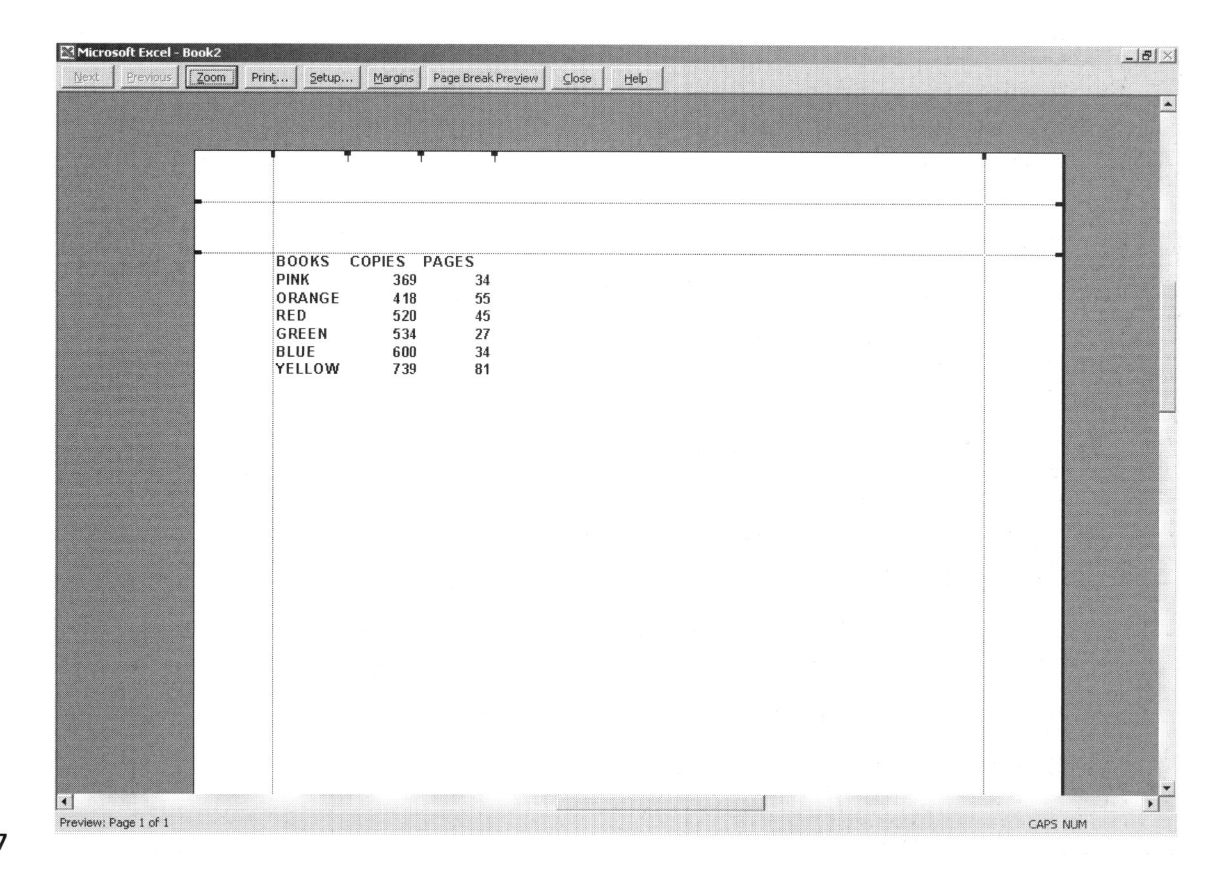

Figure 2.47

To change the margins either select the Setup... button and then the Margins tab or use the Margins button to drag the margins as shown on the screen.

Using the drag technique

Place the cursor over the margin guideline and it changes shape to a cross with double headed arrows, the direction of which depend on whether you are changing left and right margins or top and bottom (see Figure 2.48).

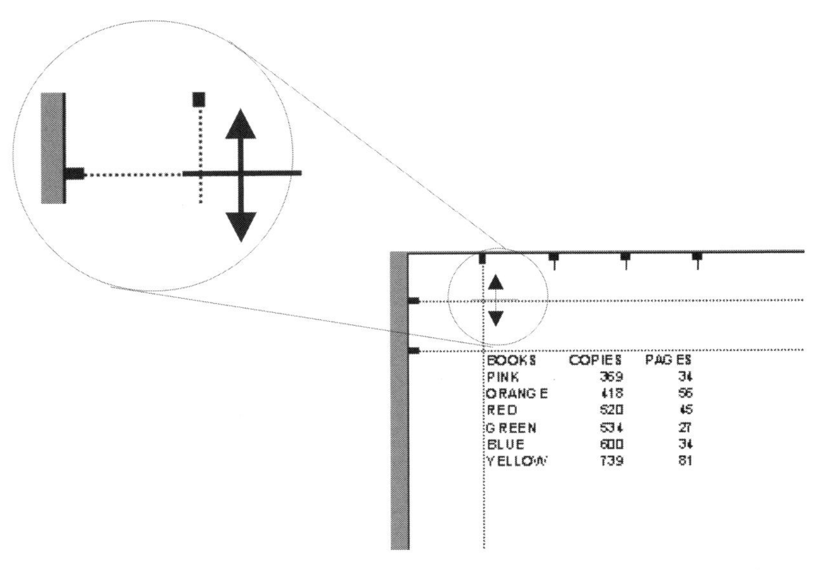

Figure 2.48

Press the left-hand mouse button and while it is still held down, drag the appropriate margin to the required position. As you drag, an indicator appears at the bottom left-hand corner of the screen to show the actual measurement for the margin position.

Using the page setup dialogue

By selecting the Setup... button the Page Setup dialogue box will appear. Press the Margins tab and then enter the required margin measurements: see Figure 2.49.

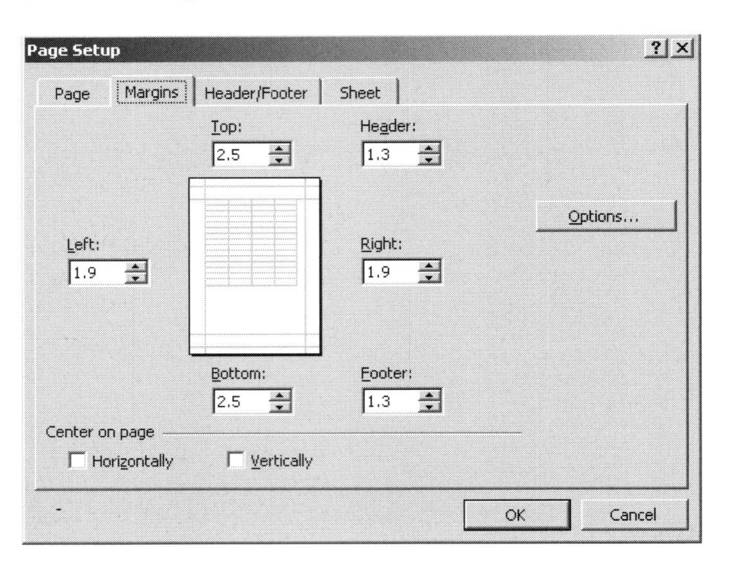

Figure 2.49

Try it out

Open your **Holiday_Bookings.xls** file.

Set the margins as follows:

Top:	2 cm
Bottom:	2 cm
Left:	2 cm
Right:	2 cm

If you chose to use the Page Setup dialogue box, notice how you also have the option of centring the worksheet vertically and horizontally.

The Print Preview dialogue box also indicates whether the page is set to a portrait or landscape orientation. Being in the preview mode it is easy to see which orientation is appropriate. Where Excel is able, it sets the orientation in a way it thinks is most appropriate for the spreadsheet.

To change the orientation simply select the Page tab on the Page Setup dialogue box and check the Portrait or Landscape orientation as required.

Headers and footers

Using the same Page Setup dialogue box and selecting the Header/Footer tab enables you to create either headers or footers in your final printed spreadsheet.

Headers and footers are of two types: automatic, such as date, page, file name and path; and custom headers and footers, where you can enter any custom text you want. Have a look at Figure 2.50.

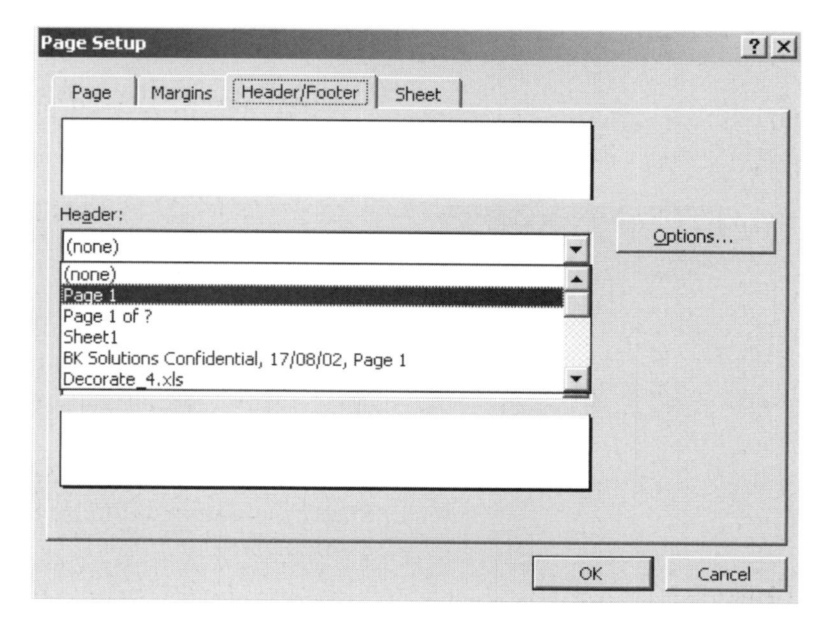

Figure 2.50

When you choose one of the selections from the header or footer field in the list, Excel places the selected automatic header or footer field in the centre on the printout.

Selecting the Custom Header… or Custom Footer… button brings up a further dialogue box, shown in Figure 2.51.

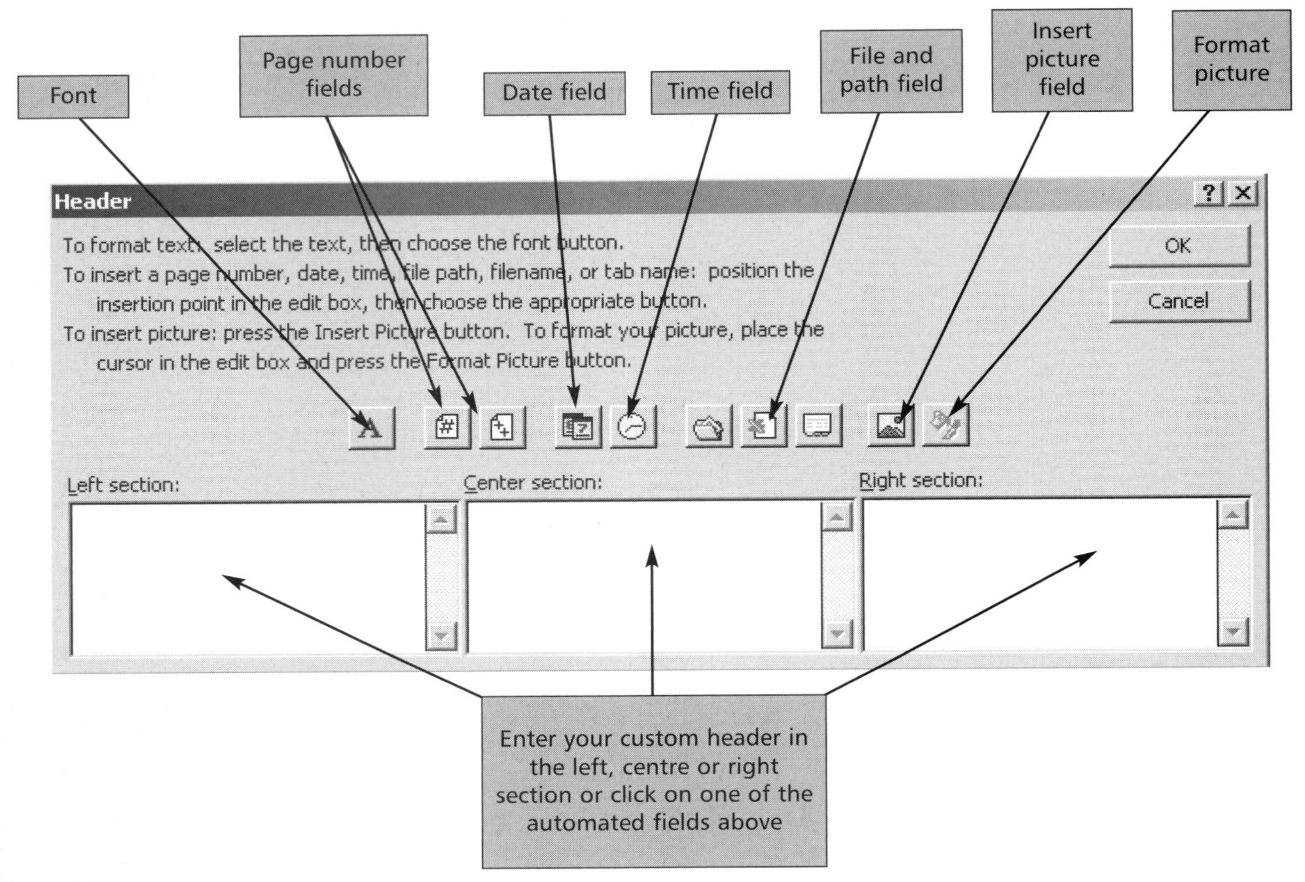

Figure 2.51

Here you have the choice of selecting one of the automated fields shown or inserting your own header or footer. Try creating a header and footer.

Try it out

Open Holiday_Bookings.xls.

Select Print Preview from the File option on the menu.

Select Setup… on the preview page.

Select the Header/Footer tab.

Select Custom Header…

Insert the automated date field in the Left section: of the dialogue box.

Insert your name in the Right section of the dialogue box.

Press OK.

Notice how the fields are now shown in the top section of the Page Setup box.

Select Custom Footer...

Insert the automated Page number in the centre section.

Press OK.

Press OK.

The headers and footers you have created are now shown in the print preview and will be printed as shown.

Save the file.

Hiding columns and rows

There may be times when you want to hide columns or rows so that they do not appear as part of the spreadsheet display – perhaps for reasons of confidentiality or because you do not want them in a printout. For CLAIT Plus you are expected to be able to hide specified columns or rows for your assignment. Hiding columns and rows is extremely straightforward.

Try it out

Open Holiday_Bookings.xls if it is not already open.

Select columns D and E.

Select Format, Column, Hide from the main menu.

Notice how columns D and E are now hidden from view. They have not disappeared, they are simply hidden.

To show the columns again:

Select Format, Column, Unhide from the main menu.

Rows are hidden in the same way, except Format, Row, Hide (or Unhide) are selected from the menu options.

Applying cell borders and gridlines

Gridlines

By default when a new workbook is created Excel displays the gridlines that show each cell of a worksheet. To some extent these are similar to grids shown in a table in Word and like in Word they can be shown or hidden. To hide gridlines in a worksheet select Tools, Options... from the main menu. A dialogue box appears with all the options available for a wide variety of defaults. For CLAIT Plus you are only interested in the options under the View tab shown in Figure 2.52.

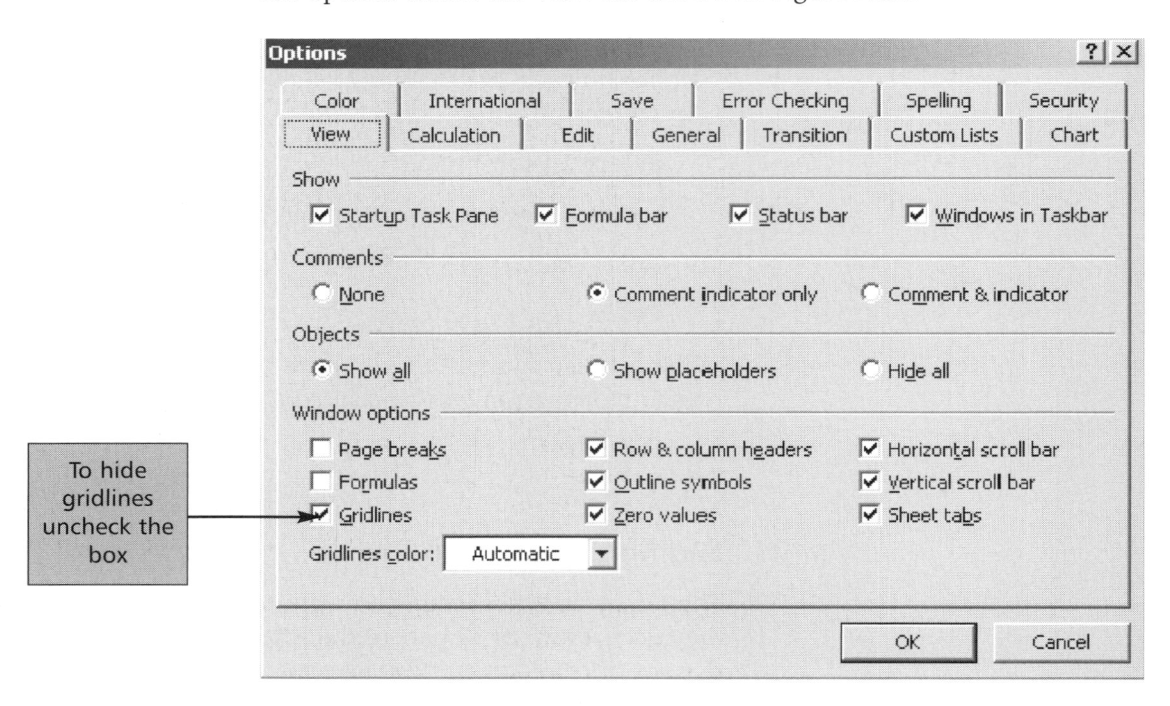

Figure 2.52

Unchecking the gridlines check box will hide the gridlines from view. Whether gridlines are in view or hidden Excel does not print the gridlines by default. If you want the gridlines to print, this option must be switched on from the Print section in the Sheet tab of the Page Setup dialogue box which is accessed by selecting Page Setup… from the File option of the main menu, then selecting the Sheet tab. By ensuring the Gridlines check box is selected the gridlines will be seen on the printout.

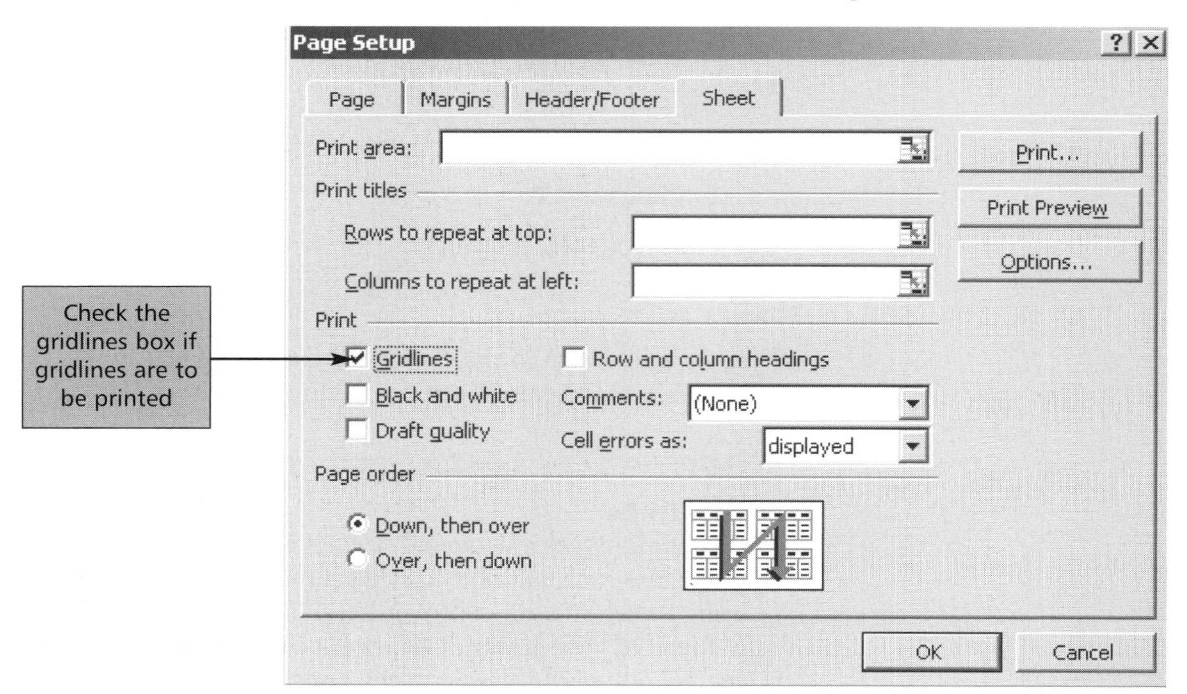

Figure 2.53

Try it out

Open **Holiday_Bookings.xls.**

Select Options from the Tools menu.

Uncheck the Gridlines check box.

Press OK.

Now reverse this action by unhiding the gridlines.

Borders

As with any document, presentation can be enhanced or areas made to stand out using borders or lines. In Excel applying borders can help the viewer focus more quickly on an area, particularly if this is a named area of the spreadsheet. When you first opened the **Holiday_Bookings.xls** file you will have noticed that the TOTAL BOOKINGS line had a single line top border and a double line bottom border. It would be fair to say that this emphasised the TOTAL BOOKINGS line more than if it had had no border.

Creating or formatting borders can be achieved in two ways. As is the case when you format any text or data, the area to be formatted has first to be identified (highlighted). Once the area to be formatted has been selected you can use the Borders box on the toolbar (shown in Figure 2.54).

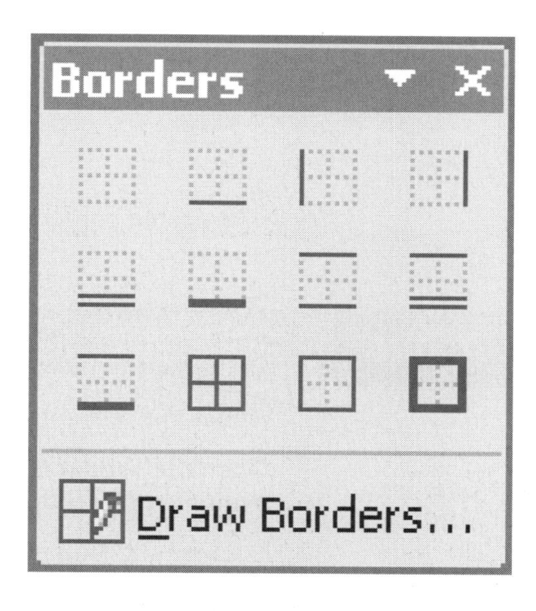

Figure 2.54

The box is fairly self-explanatory with options for selecting a single line at the top, bottom, left or right of the chosen area, all borders or just the outside borders of the selection. However, you cannot custom format the borders using this toolbar option. If you want to change the line's colour, thickness or style you will need to use the options provided on the Border tab of the Format Cells dialogue box. These options are shown in Figure 2.55.

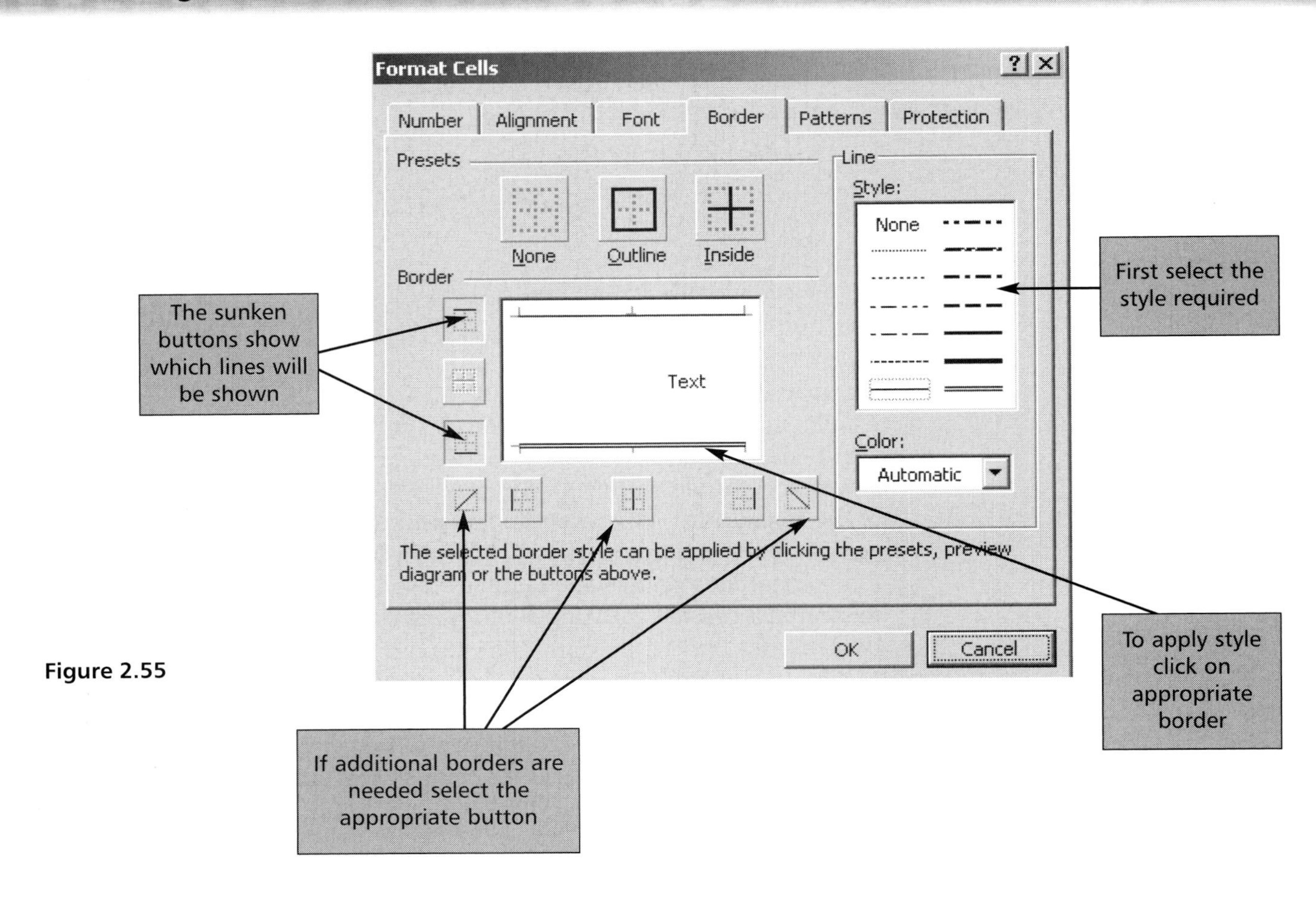

Figure 2.55

Try adding some borders to the **Holiday_Bookings** spreadsheet.

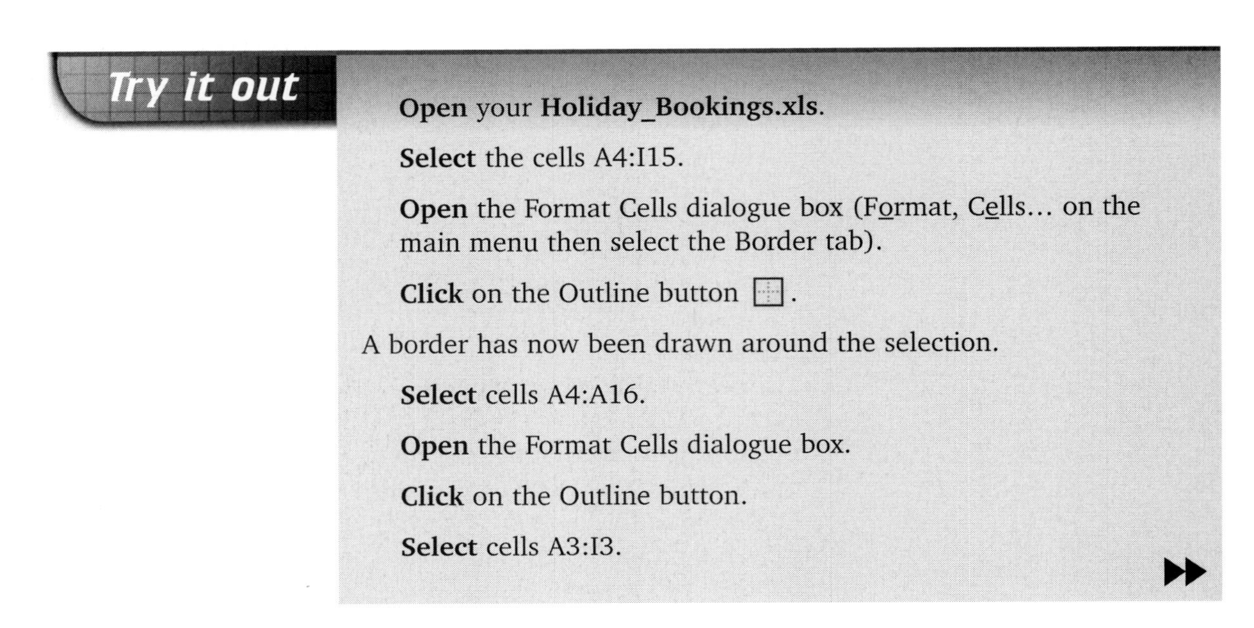

Try it out

Open your **Holiday_Bookings.xls.**

Select the cells A4:I15.

Open the Format Cells dialogue box (Format, Cells... on the main menu then select the Border tab).

Click on the Outline button.

A border has now been drawn around the selection.

Select cells A4:A16.

Open the Format Cells dialogue box.

Click on the Outline button.

Select cells A3:I3.

Open the Format Cells dialogue box.

Click on centre line in the format box as shown in Figure 2.56.

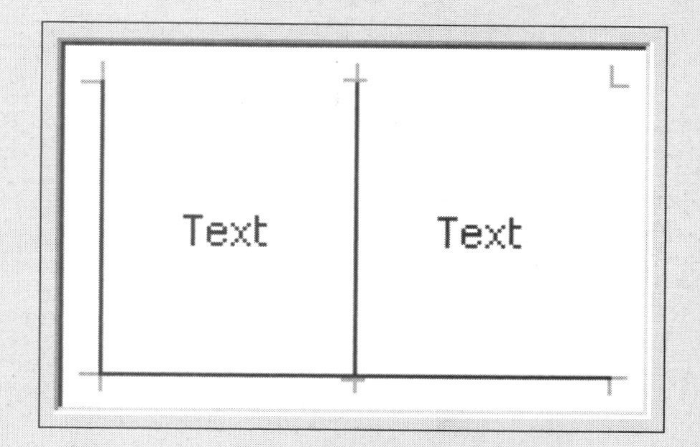

Figure 2.56

Press OK.

Notice how the lines are diagonal. This is because you changed the orientation of these cells in an earlier exercise.

Now have a look at the Print Preview (File, Print Preview on the menu bar).

Notice how the first line is vertical and rather spoils the overall impression.

Click in cell A3.

Open the Format Cells dialogue box.

Deselect the left line.

Press OK.

As you saw in the print preview, the layout would be better if cell I16 had a right-hand border.

Click in cell I16.

This time use the border toolbox and:

Click on the right border icon.

Select cells: A4:A16, B3:I3, B16:I16 and

Press the bold button on the toolbar.

(**Tip**: to select all the above cells in one go, press and hold down the Ctrl key on the keyboard and while it is still held down select each range shown above.)

Go to the Print Preview to see the end result which should look like Figure 2.57.

A	B	C	D	E	F	G	H	I
BOOKED HOLIDAY PACKAGES BY COUNTRY								
	Egypt	Majorca	Ibiza	Minorca	Gran Canaria	Cost Brava	Costa de Almeria	Algarve
Jan	165	296	100	145	483	288	285	255
Feb	193	424	285	225	294	180	110	226
Mar	451	490	362	349	285	346	376	107
Apr	181	236	336	138	233	400	163	327
May	442	467	228	151	170	418	230	224
Jun	312	176	201	285	169	267	413	201
Jul	109	309	271	493	247	381	233	245
Aug	382	316	268	107	410	243	454	215
Sep	478	233	361	107	137	297	193	109
Oct	260	126	295	334	425	151	223	311
Nov	325	459	479	106	114	334	161	443
Dec	275	208	212	172	120	392	247	484
TOTAL BOOKINGS	**3572**	**3739**	**3398**	**2611**	**3087**	**3697**	**3088**	**3147**

Figure 2.57

You should now be able to:

- change margins and the page orientation of a spreadsheet
- insert and use headers and footers
- hide (and unhide) columns and rows
- apply cell borders and gridlines.

Now test your understanding of these skills in the build-up exercise below.

Build-up Exercise 2: Stage 6

Open Decorate_3.xls.

Apply outline single line borders to cells A1:C11.

Apply outline single line borders to cells E1:G4.

Apply single top line border and a double bottom line border to cells A33:K33, and N33:O33.

Apply a bottom line border to cells A13:K13 and N13:O13 to separate the column headings from the numerical data.

Hide columns L and M.

Insert a custom heading ANALYSIS OF DECORATING COSTS. The font should be Arial 16 bold and the heading should be underlined.

Insert the date in the left section of the footer box and your name in the right section.

Save the spreadsheet.

Your spreadsheet should now look similar to Figure 2.58.

ANALYSIS OF DECORATING COSTS

DECORATING MATERIALS COSTS		
Brush Sets	10.50	
Paint	19.00	
Sandpaper	0.15	
Turps (20 Ltrs)	18.00	
Discounts	50 - 100	101 -150
	0.15	0.2
General Decorating Budget		5000

LABOUR COSTS	
	Per Hour
Painter	£18.50
Hours per day	8

Building	Paint Cans	Sand Paper (Sheets)	Brush Sets	Paint Cost	Sand Paper Cost	Brush Costs	Turps	Total Materials	Discounts	Discounted Price	Days	Labour
Dormitory 1	6	20	2	£114.00	£3.00	£21.00	£1.00	£139.00	20%	£111.20	3	£444.00
Dormitory 2	6	20	2	£114.00	£3.00	£21.00	£1.00	£139.00	20%	£111.20	3	£444.00
Dormitory 3	6	20	2	£114.00	£3.00	£21.00	£1.00	£139.00	20%	£111.20	3	£444.00
Dormitory 4	6	20	2	£114.00	£3.00	£21.00	£1.00	£139.00	20%	£111.20	3	£444.00
Dormitory 5	6	20	2	£114.00	£3.00	£21.00	£1.00	£139.00	20%	£111.20	3	£444.00
Dormitory 6	6	20	2	£114.00	£3.00	£21.00	£1.00	£139.00	20%	£111.20	3	£444.00
Kitchen	4	14	1	£76.00	£2.10	£10.50	£1.00	£89.60	15%	£76.16	2	£296.00
Games Rm	5	16	2	£95.00	£2.40	£21.00	£1.00	£119.40	20%	£95.52	2.5	£370.00
Study Rm 1	3	10	1	£57.00	£1.50	£10.50	£1.00	£70.00	15%	£59.50	1.5	£222.00
Study Rm 2	3	10	1	£57.00	£1.50	£10.50	£1.00	£70.00	15%	£59.50	1.5	£222.00
Study Rm 3	3	10	1	£57.00	£1.50	£10.50	£1.00	£70.00	15%	£59.50	1.5	£222.00
Study Rm 4	3	10	1	£57.00	£1.50	£10.50	£1.00	£70.00	15%	£59.50	1.5	£222.00
Classroom 1	5	16	2	£95.00	£2.40	£21.00	£1.00	£119.40	20%	£95.52	2.5	£370.00
Classroom 2	5	16	2	£95.00	£2.40	£21.00	£1.00	£119.40	20%	£95.52	2.5	£370.00
Classroom 3	5	16	2	£95.00	£2.40	£21.00	£1.00	£119.40	20%	£95.52	2.5	£370.00
Classroom 4	5	16	2	£95.00	£2.40	£21.00	£1.00	£119.40	20%	£95.52	2.5	£370.00
Classroom 5	5	16	2	£95.00	£2.40	£21.00	£1.00	£119.40	20%	£95.52	2.5	£370.00
Classroom 6	5	16	2	£95.00	£2.40	£21.00	£1.00	£119.40	20%	£95.52	2.5	£370.00
Totals	87	286	31	£1,653.00	£42.90	£325.50	£18.00	£2,039.40	19%	£1,650.00	43.5	£6,438.00

18/07/2003 Bernard Kane

Figure 2.58

Producing spreadsheet reports

Setting a print area

With a large spreadsheet you may only wish to print specific parts or subsets of the data. Excel allows you to set the print area to cater for this. First highlight the area to be printed. If the areas are not adjacent to each other then hide the appropriate columns or rows before highlighting the area you want to print. Now, select File, Print Area, Set Print Area. By selecting the Print Preview you can see how the report will be printed.

Try it out

Open Decorate_3.xls if it is not already open.

Hide columns B,C and D.

Highlight cells A13:I33.

Select File, Print Area, Set Print Area.

Select Print Preview.

If you want to centre the print horizontally or vertically on the page select the Margins tab from the Page Setup dialogue box and check the 'Centre on page' check boxes horizontally or vertically as required.

Select the horizontal check box.

Press OK.

Print the page.

Note: to print the page you can use the normal File, Print... options in the spreadsheet menu or press the Print... button on the toolbar of the Print Preview screen.

To clear the print area once you are satisfied with the printout produced, return to the spreadsheet by pressing the Close button in Print Preview and then select File, Print Area, Clear Print Area on the menu. To check the area has been cleared, select the Print Preview on the File menu again.

Clear the print area.

Save your spreadsheet.

Displaying row and column headings.

You have noticed in the preview page, and from your printout in the previous exercise, that the row numbers and column letters are by default excluded from the printout. However, if you need to show the row and column headings (you may need to if you are working on the hard copy of a spreadsheet to plan changes or modifications), you can show them by selecting the Sheet tab in the Page Setup... dialogue box and checking the Row and column headings box. Try it.

Try it out

Open Decorate_3.xls.

Select Page Setup... .

Click in the Row and column headings check box.

Press OK.

Select Print Preview.

The column heading letters and row numbers can now be clearly seen.

Fitting a spreadsheet to print pages

If you were to select the whole of the **Decorate_3.xls** spreadsheet for printing it would print over two pages. You can, however, use the functions in the setup options to force Excel to show all the spreadsheet on one page.

Under the Page tab of the Page Setup dialogue box there is an option to either adjust the view of the spreadsheet to a smaller (or larger) percentage of the original or if you select the Fit to: field and enter the number of pages, to let Excel fit your spreadsheet into the pages you desire.

Try it out

Open Decorate_3.xls if it is not already open.

Select the whole spreadsheet for printing.

Select Page Setup... from the File menu (or the Print Preview page).

Select the Page tab.

Click in the Fit to: check box.

Check the page(s) box shows 1 wide and 1 tall.

Press OK.

Select the Print Preview.

Your spreadsheet should now be fitted to one page.

Displaying the content of cells

If you completed New CLAIT you will already have experienced the function that allows you to display the contents of a cell other than the data. In the main this means displaying just the formulae that are built into the spreadsheet.

To show formulae select Options... from Tools on the main menu to display the Options dialogue box. Check the Formulas check box under the Windows options section of the dialogue box. Once the OK button is pressed you will be returned to the spreadsheet but instead of seeing the results of the formulae the formulae themselves are shown.

Warning: for CLAIT Plus you will be expected to show formulae (contents) of spreadsheet cells. However, each formula must be displayed *in full*, so you must be careful to check that all the formulae and other data are displayed in full, that is, none of the data is cut from view.

You should now be able to:

- set the print area of a spreadsheet
- display row and column headings
- fit a spreadsheet to a specified number of pages
- display the contents of cells in a spreadsheet
- print the results.

Build-up Exercise 2: Stage 7

Open Decorate_3.xls.

Select Options... from the Tools menu.

Select the View tab.

Check the Formulas check box under the Windows options section.

Press OK.

Adjust any columns where the formulae or data are not displayed in full.

Select the area of spreadsheet containing formulae (cells A13:O33).

Set the print area.

Select Print Preview.

Select Page Setup.

Select the Sheet tab.

Check the Row and columns headings check box.

Select the Page tab and ensure the print is set as Fit to: 1 page.

Select the margins tab and ensure the print will be centred both horizontally and vertically.

Press OK.

Print the results.

Once you have printed the results return the spreadsheet to normal data view (i.e. with the formulae showing).

Save the spreadsheet and close the file.

Exit the application.

That completes all the assessment objectives you will need for achieving certification in spreadsheets for CLAIT Plus. Now complete the practical assignment shown below. Solutions to this assignment can be found in Appendix 2.

Spreadsheets

Scenario

You are the manager of a small training and meeting room facility that has now been open for about a year. Although you have a broad understanding of the way the business is going there are a number of variable factors that affect the viability of your business. You have decided to create a spreadsheet showing all the income and expenditure for your first year of operation. The spreadsheet will allow you to change variables and project what changes can be made to ensure that no month of activity produces a result worse than breakeven and the average % profit is better than 10%.

Task 1

Your first task is to prepare the underlying spreadsheet for the exercise.

Assessment objectives	Stage	
1a 1g 3b 3c 3e 4a	1	Open the datafile **Roomhire.csv** in Unit 2 on the accompanying CD and save it as a normal Excel (.xls) file on your floppy or hard disk. Format as per the house style sheet.
3a 3e 3f	2 3	Set the column widths to 11 and wrap the cells containing the column headings in the main spreadsheet. Adjust any column where appropriate to display data clearly. In the OVERHEAD VARIABLES and the COST OF SALE VARIABLES section merge the cells where the row heading is wider than one column width.
1b 3e	4	Amend the column heading Basic to read 'Room Hire Income'. In the COST OF SALE VARIABLES section amend the heading Income to read 'Menu Prices (Per head)' and the heading Margin to read 'Target Margin'. Text-wrap both these cells.
1c 1d 2a 2b 2c	5	Using the formulae sheet complete the following calculations: Room Hire Income Average Usage Hospitality Equipment Income Total Income Staff Costs Food Cost Monthly Maintenance, Rates, Insurance and Telephone Electricity Total Expenditure.
1c 1d 1e	6	Total all columns where it is appropriate to do so (all except Month, Season and Average Usage) using the AutoSum facility or an Excel Function.
1c	7	In the Average Usage total cell use the AVERAGE function to establish the average of use for all months in the year.

4b 4c	8	Insert the date as a page footer left-aligned and the page number as a footer right-aligned.
4d	9	Apply an outline border around the OVERHEAD VARIABLES section and a line beneath the heading.
	10	Apply an outline border around the COST OF SALE VARIABLES section and a line beneath the heading.
	11	Apply an outline border around the EQUIPMENT HIRE COST section and a line beneath the heading.
	12	Apply a single top and double bottom line to the Totals row.
1b	13	Emphasise the Totals cell as bold.
4e	14	Hide column P.
3c 3e 3f	15	Realign the heading ANALYSIS OF TRAINING AND SEMINAR BUSINESS PERFORMANCE so that it is centred across columns A:O.
5a 5b	16	Set the print area for the spreadsheet so that it is printed two pages wide and one page tall with the Income on one page and the Expenditure on the other. Print the spreadsheet.
1g	17	Save the changes made to the spreadsheet.

Task 2

Having prepared the spreadsheet you will now create a linked spreadsheet that shows the effect of changing variables to achieve the objectives for the business.

1a 1g 3b 3c 3e 3f 4a	18	Open the datafile **Roomhire_Analysis.csv** in Unit 2 on the accompanying CD and save it as a normal Excel (.xls) file on your floppy or hard disk. Format as per the House Style sheet. **Note:** you will need to text-wrap and merge the heading cell to achieve a central alignment over the data columns.
3a	19	Set the column widths of columns B and C to 11 and Column A to 12.
	20	Make the Annual Profit row heading bold.
1c 1e 2d	21	Using the formula on the formula sheet create a linked formula for the Jan cell that calculates the net profit for the month. **Note:** when the link is created Excel automatically makes the link reference absolute. You will need to change this from an absolute to a relative reference by removing the $ symbols.
1d	22	Replicate the formula for the remaining months of the year.
1c 1e.	23	Using the formula on the attached formula sheet create a linked formula that calculates the percentage profit for Jan.
1d	24	Replicate the formula for the remaining months of the year.

▶▶

1e	25	In the Annual Profit row under the Dec % Profit, using the formula on the formula sheet enter a function that averages the profit over the year.
2c 2d	26	Name the cell containing the target margin in **Roomhire.xls** 'Margin'.
	27	Beneath the annual profit line, leaving one clear row, create the heading 'Target Margin in use' and emphasise it in bold.
	28	In the next available column cell create a link referencing the named cell Margin in **Roomhire.xls**.
1f 3g	29	At a target margin of 50 per cent Aug is below breakeven and the average for the year is less than 10 per cent. Altering the target margin find the target margin that produces no month less than breakeven and an overall average profit not less than 10 per cent. Sort the data by % Profit in descending order.
5a	30	Print the spreadsheet **Roomhire_Analysis**.
5d	31	Print the spreadsheet showing all formulae in use.
5c	32	Print the spreadsheet showing row and column headings.
1g	33	Save your spreadsheet changes and close the file.

House style sheet

Page setup

Page Size	A4			
Orientation	Landscape			
Margins	Top	2 cm		
	Bottom	2 cm		
	Left	1 cm		
	Right	1 cm		
Header	Date	Left-aligned	File name	Right-aligned
Footer	Your name	Left-aligned	Page number	Right-aligned

Text style

Feature	Font	Font size	Style	Alignment
Title	Sans serif	16	Bold and in capitals	Centred across all columns that contain data
Section headings	Sans serif	12	Bold and in capitals	Centred across columns of the section
Column headings	Sans serif	10	Bold	Vertical alignment: top Horizontal alignment: Text: left Numbers: right
Body	Sans serif	10	No emphasis (unless otherwise indicated)	Left

Number style

Feature	Font	Font style	Style	Alignment
Money values	Sans serif	10	Two decimal places – only show £ symbol in totals row	Right
Percentage	Sans serif	10	No decimal places	Right
Other non-currency values	Sans serif	10	No decimal places	Right

Formulae

Task 1

Note: remember that absolute and mixed references should be used where appropriate.

Room hire income	-	Bookings (days)* Daily rate rm hire
Average usage	-	Persons/Bookings (days)
Hospitality	-	(Menu 1*the price of menu 1)+ (Menu 2*the price of Menu 2) + (Menu 3*the price of Menu 3) **Note:** remember that absolute references should be used where appropriate.
Equipment income	-	(OHP Hires *OHP (in Equipment Cost section))+ (Laptop Hires *Laptop (ea) (in Equipment Hire Cost section))+ (Video Hires *Video (in Equipment Hire Cost section)).
Total income	-	= the SUM of Room hire income, Hospitality and equipment income.
Staff costs	-	To calculate this you will need to multiply the staff rate per hour by 8 (the number of hours worked in the day), then the cost of staff per hour by the percentage for On costs, by the number of staff employed and the number of Bookings days. Staff costs = Staff (per hour)*8+Staff (per hour)*On Costs*Bookings (days)*Staff **Note:** Appropriate brackets will need to be inserted to arrive at the correct calculation.
Food cost	-	The Food cost is calculated by taking the cost of hospitality and then subtracting that cost multiplied by the Target margin. Food cost = Hospitality – (Hospitality*Target cost)
Monthly maintenance, rates, insurance and telephone	-	These are calculated by referencing the appropriate annual rate in the OVERHEAD VARIABLES section and dividing by 12. The formula is then replicated for each month.

Electricity	-	You have assessed that the profile of costs for electricity throughout the year is:
		
		Winter (W) 40%
		Spring (Sp) 30%
		Summer (Smr) 10%
		Autumn (A) 20%
		
		Create an IF statement that allows for the identification of the month, its percentage profile of cost over the year and the length of the season.
		
		If the season is winter then multiply the annual electricity cost by 40% and divide the overall calculation by 4 (being the number of months this season lasts). Repeat this in a nested IF statement for each season.
		
		Electricity=IF(Season=Winter,(Electricity*.4)/4),
		IF(Season=Spring,(Electricity*.3)/3),
		IF(Season=Summer,(Electricity*.1)/3),
		IF(Season=Autumn,(Electricity*.2)/2).

Practical assignment 2

Total expenditure	-	=SUM(Staff costs, Food cost, Monthly maintenance, Rates, Insurance, Telephone, Electricity).

Task 2

Net Profit	-	Total income – Total expenditure.
% Profit	-	(Total income – Total expenditure)/Total expenditure.
Annual average profit	-	Average (Jan:Dec)

Databases

The CLAIT Plus Database unit builds on the skills required at level 1 (New CLAIT). In this unit you will build on the objectives set at level 1 and learn new competencies relating to the creation, maintenance and interrogation of a database file. In addition you will learn how to use the reporting facilities available in Access including how to format reports to meet specific requirements.

Four key assessment objectives

For the unit on databases in CLAIT Plus there are four broad assessment objectives, each of which covers a number of skills you will need to learn. You are required to complete an assignment that covers some or all of the objectives listed below:

- **Create and save a database**
  - set up field names
  - set up data types for fields
  - format fields
  - set appropriate field lengths
  - enter records
  - save a table, query and report
- **Format reports**
  - alter margins and page orientation
  - use page headers and footers
  - align data
  - insert automatic fields into headers and footers
  - insert titles and group headers
- **Import and interrogate a database**
  - import and open a datafile
  - add, amend and delete records and fields
  - use logical operators in queries
  - use a range of operators in queries
  - combine search criteria using logical operators
  - use a calculated field
- **Present and print data**
  - data displayed in full
  - data presented in a specified field order
  - data sorted
  - use search results to produce a report
  - data presented in table or list format
  - data presented in group format
  - data presented in record and columnar format for label printing
  - summaries displayed

Introducing the CLAIT Plus unit on databases

All the applications covered in the CLAIT Plus programme are designed to help you develop skills that you are likely to use in a work environment. You will find these skills equally helpful in maximising the use of your computer at home for work or for recreational purposes. Database technology is a very complex subject but thankfully Access has been designed so that database applications can be created by novices as well as experts.

If you completed the database unit for New CLAIT you will remember that the emphasis was placed on making changes to the data in terms of adding, amending and deleting records in a prepared database table, sorting data and then using the data to create queries. CLAIT Plus reinforces much of what was covered in New CLAIT but also focuses on the power that databases have to display information through the creation of reports. Whilst this unit assumes that you have covered the skills necessary for certification at level 1 (New CLAIT) or similar, some aspects will be covered again briefly as a reminder.

In this unit you will learn how to:

- create a simple database structure
- understand what primary keys are
- set specific data types for individual fields
- enter records
- import a database and use queries to interrogate data
- derive information from stored data using calculations in queries and reports
- format data in calculated fields of queries and reports
- use wild cards to search for data
- create and format simple reports
- present data in different formats and order
- display summary information.

Creating and saving databases

The heart of any database is its table structure which stores the data from which information can be derived. A database can be made up from a simple, single table or it can have dozens of tables; it depends on the use to which it is being put. The decision as to which fields a table should have or how many tables should form the database is determined at the design stage.

For CLAIT Plus you are required to build a simple data structure (or table). You also need to understand the differences between field types, their uses and how to set their format.

Using Access for the first time

When you open Access XP you will be presented with the options shown in Figure 3.1.

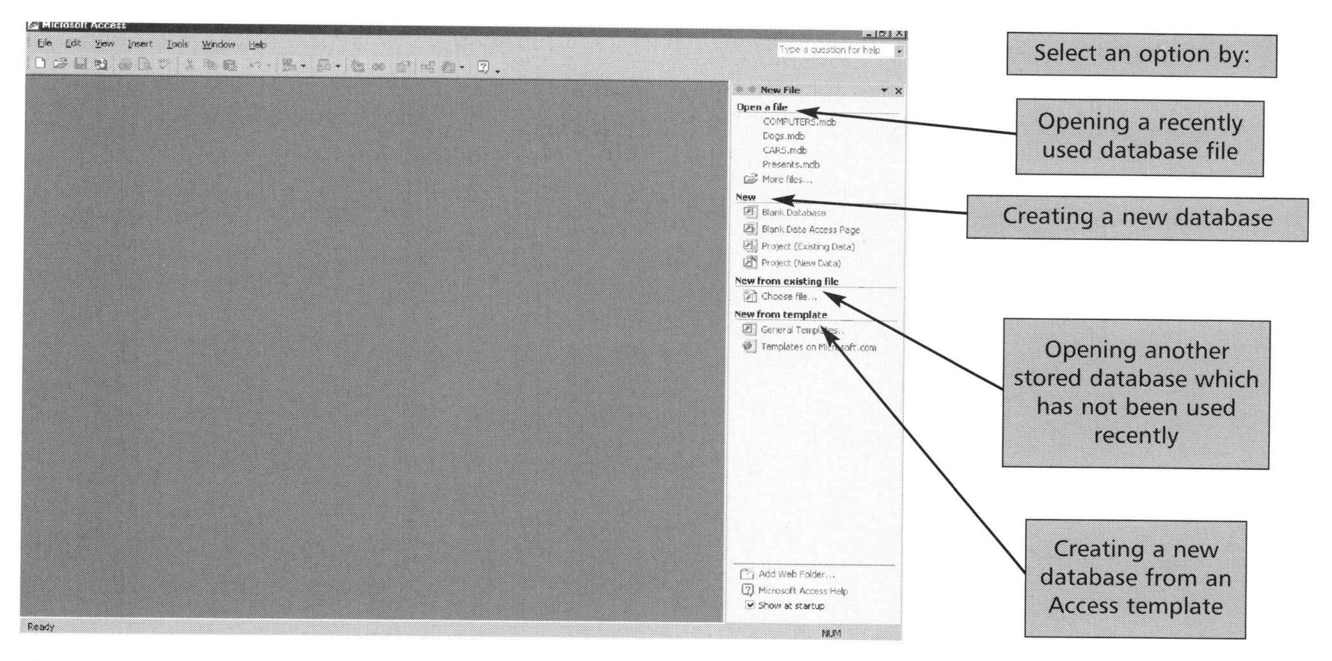

Figure 3.1

Try it out

Press Start.

Select the Programs icon.

Select Microsoft Access from the program list 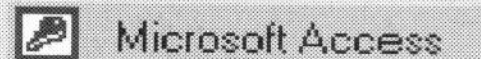.

Select the Blank Database which will bring up the File New Database dialogue box shown in Figure 3.2.

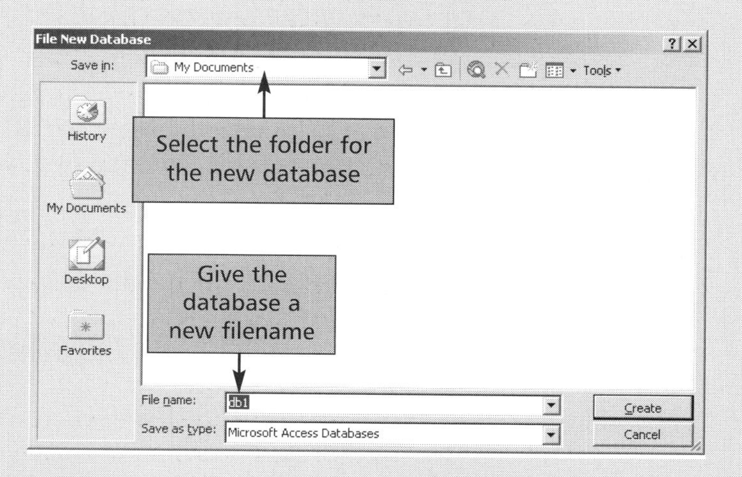

Figure 3.2

Select the appropriate folder for your database. If you set up your file structure in Unit 1 use the Databases folder. If you have not yet created a folder for your database exercises, do so now.

Type 'My Database' in the File name: box.

Press Create.

You will then see the database window shown in Figure 3.3.

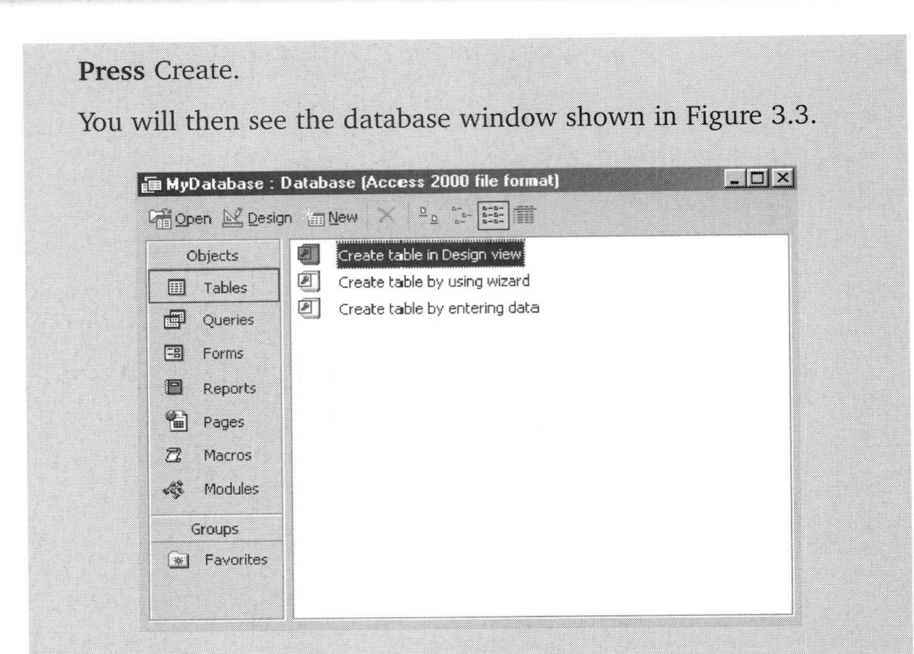

Figure 3.3

The database window may vary slightly depending on the version of Access you are using, but the basic components will be the same. On the left-hand side are the various objects that can be created (tables, queries, forms, reports, etc.). On the top you will see a toolbar that allows you to open objects, create new ones and so on.

Set up data types for fields

To create a table, first either highlight Tables in the objects list or select the option 'Create table in Design view', in the database window, where there are three options:

- Create table in Design view
- Create table by using wizard
- Create table by entering data

For CLAIT Plus you will only use the option Create table in Design view. The New button New at the top of the window is then pressed and Access presents the dialogue box shown in Figure 3.4.

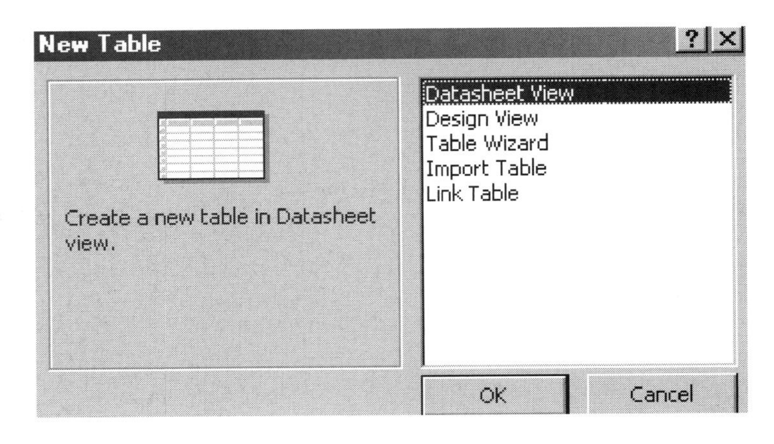

Figure 3.4

The New Table dialogue box offers you five options:

- Datasheet View
- Design View
- Table Wizard
- Import Table
- Link Table

For the time being you are only interested in Design View. Once this is selected the window shown in Figure 3.5 will appear.

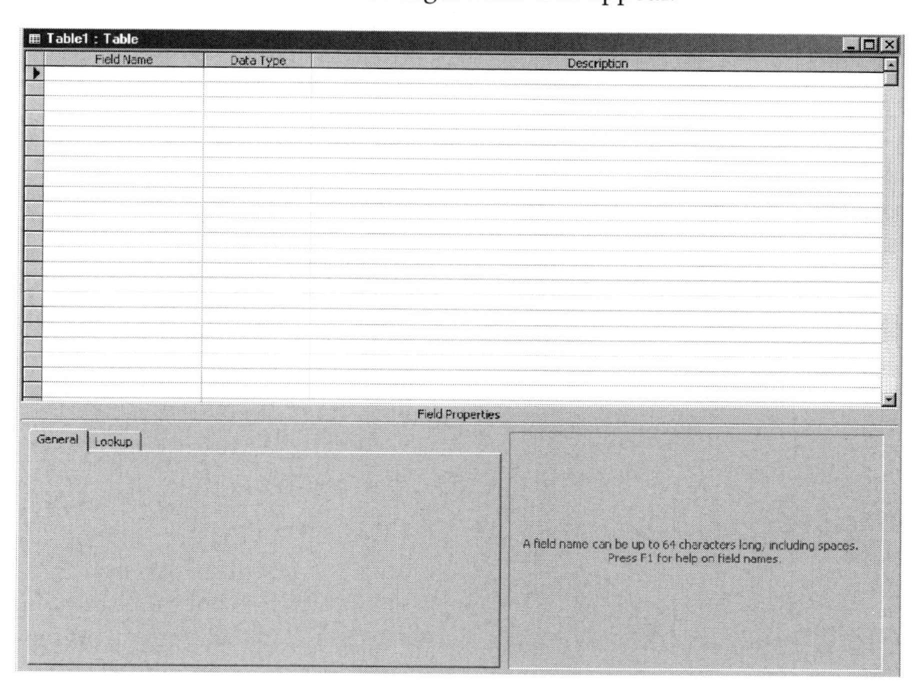

Figure 3.5

The four main elements of this window are:

- Field Name
- Data Type
- Description
- Field Properties

Let's look at each of these in turn now.

Field name

The main components of a table are the fields that contain data. Have a look at Figure 3.6.

A field

TITLE	INITIAL	NAME	ADDRESS 1	ADDRESS 2	TOWN	POSTCODE
MR	P	SMITH	THE COTTAGE	UPPER ST	STEEL	ST1 3ET

A record

Figure 3.6

Tables are made up of fields such as TITLE, INITIAL, etc. A group of fields, when holding data, form a record. So in the example above the complete record would be:

Mr P Smith
The Cottage
Upper St
Steel
ST1 3ET

Each field in a table can be up to 255 characters in length. However, it is important when designing a database to keep the length of a field to the minimum necessary to house the required data. Every character represents eight bits of storage space on your disk (this includes spaces). So, for example, it would not be sensible to have an INITIALS field with a length property of more than say three or four, since few people have more than three or four initials. You will learn about properties in more detail later.

Data types

Access supports a variety of data types for fields in a table. The full list is:

Text	AutoNumber
Memo	Yes/No
Number	OLE Object
Date/Time	Hyperlink
Currency	Lookup Wizard

Most of these are self-explanatory and indeed for CLAIT Plus you will only be interested in the more commonly used data types such as Text, Number, Date/Time, Currency, AutoNumber and Yes/No.

Description

The description field is, as the name suggests, a field where you can type in a description of the field in the database if it is not self-explanatory. You may, not unreasonably, ask why you would want to do this. Well, whilst you will do all that you can to design your database in a logical and understandable way, there may well be occasions in the future when you may want to make changes. As is often the case with learning any software, if you don't use it often you may forget some of the detail. If you have made clear notes in the description column why something is there, or why you decided to put something in, it may well help you when you return to make changes later.

Field properties

As you saw in the section on field names, fields have properties such as length in the case of a Text field. Where a field might contain a numerical data, the Number can be an integer (no decimal places) or double, a format where you determine the number of decimal places that are allowed. Similarly with a Date/Time field, there are a variety of Date formats you can use such as long, medium or short.

Access allows you to set the properties for each field as you create your database. Now try building a table.

Try it out

Open Access.

Create a database called MyDatabase in the database folder you created in Unit 1.

Select Tables from the objects list (or highlight Create table in Design view).

Select New from the toolbar.

Select Design View from the New Table dialogue box.

Press OK.

A new table in design view will appear on the screen as shown in Figure 3.7.

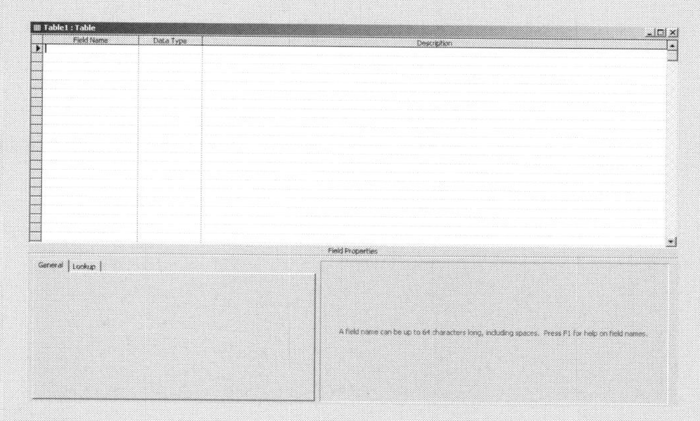

Figure 3.7

Enter the following field names in the first column:

TITLE
INITIAL
LASTNAME
COURSE
START
END
FEE

Press the Save icon or select Save from File on the main menu.

The Save As dialogue box shown in Figure 3.8 will appear.

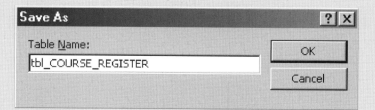

Figure 3.8

In the Table Name box:

Type 'tbl_COURSE_REGISTER'.

Press OK.

Access will now advise you that there is no primary key defined.

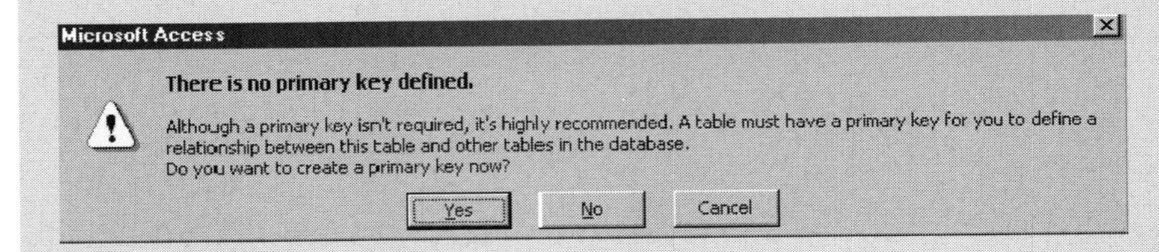

Figure 3.9

Primary keys will be covered shortly but for now:

Press NO.

Your table should now look like Figure 3.10.

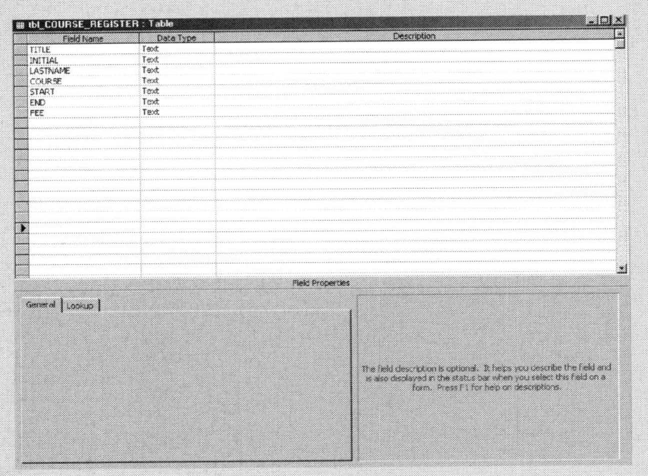

Figure 3.10

Close the table and notice how the table has been added to the database window of objects.

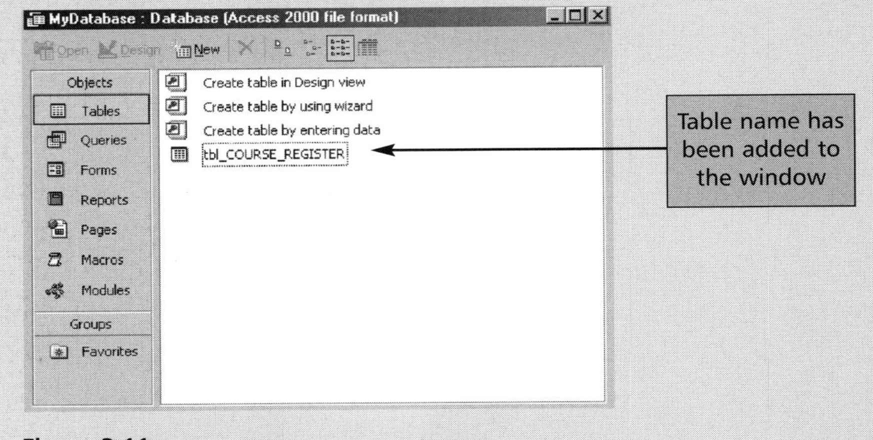

Figure 3.11

Primary keys

Understanding what primary keys are and being able to use them is not strictly a CLAIT Plus requirement, although you are expected to understand database structures. When saving a new table Access will always ask you if you want a primary key if one has not been defined. Most commercial databases have more than one table in their structure. To be of any use as a database these tables usually need to be related to one another. A primary key is a field in one table that has been identified with unique data and is also contained in another table. Have a look at the example in Figure 3.12.

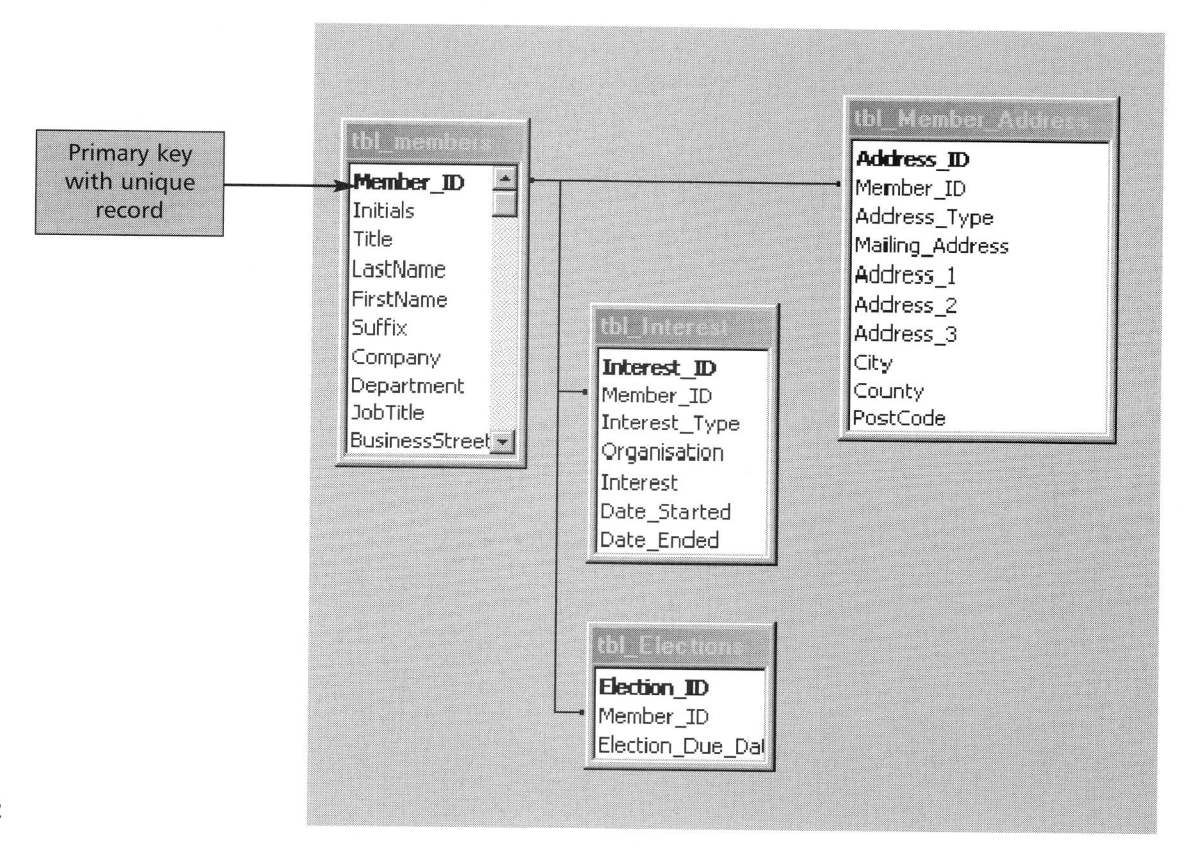

Figure 3.12

This is a view of a database structure showing the relationships between several tables. It is not important what the database itself is, but notice that the tbl_members has a field called Member_ID. This is the primary key for that table because a member can only have one ID number and it will be different to that of all other members. Now have a look at the other tables in the picture. Each table also has a field called Member_ID which is not a primary key but is known as a foreign key. This allows the table with the primary key to have a relationship with the other tables containing the Member_ID field.

Setting up data types for fields

Later in this unit you will learn how to create reports to display data contained in tables in a user friendly way. Reports provide essential information to the reader. However, not all data needs to be stored in a table. Earlier you learnt that it is important to restrict the size of fields to that which is necessary to house the data being captured so as to minimise the amount of space used for storing your database. By formatting fields in formats other than text format, Access allows you to derive additional information by using logical operators, built-in functions and other formulae. For example, take the MyDatabase database you have just created. Currently the field for fees is of a Text data type. If you wanted to calculate the total amount of fees collected you could not do so with this data type. However, if the data type was Number or Currency you could calculate the result.

Now change the data types for the MyDatabase database.

Try it out

Open MyDatabase, if it is not already open.

Open the table **tbl_COURSE_REGISTER** in design view.

Now **amend** the data types for the fields of the table as shown in Figure 3.13.

Tip: to change the data type, click in the data type field (column 2) and using the arrow on the right of the field select the appropriate data type.

Field Name	Data Type
TITLE	Text
INITIAL	Text
LASTNAME	Text
COURSE	Text
START	Date/Time
END	Date/Time
FEE	Currency

Figure 3.13

Press the save icon to save your changes to the table.

Setting the appropriate length and format properties for fields

Finally, as far as this table is concerned, you need to set sensible lengths for your fields and also appropriate formatting where required. By clicking the field name of individual fields in design view the field properties box is enabled at the bottom of the design window.

There are three different data types in this table: Text, Date/Time and Currency.

Text fields

Text fields should be no longer than is necessary to contain the anticipated data. The normal default setting for a text field is 50 characters. Clearly there may well be occasions when this is either more than sufficient or not enough. Looking at the fields in the table **tbl_COURSE_REGISTER** it is obvious, for example, that 50 characters is far too big for both the TITLE and INITIAL fields. Although there may well be exceptions you would normally expect to see titles such as Mr, Mrs, Miss, Ms, Dr, Prof (short for professor). Allowing for some exceptions where an abbreviated form of the title may be used, you would probably need no more than a field size of five. Similarly, it is unlikely that anyone would have more than four letters for their initials or even if they had you would probably only want to store a maximum of three of them. The LASTNAME field will need to be a little larger, say 25 characters. The COURSE field is likely to need a greater length than the default 50, let's say 100 characters.

Numeric fields

Generally speaking for most database applications you are likely to design and use for CLAIT Plus, numeric fields are either integer (i.e. no decimal places), double to two decimal places or currency to two decimal places. By clicking in the field in the top part of the design window to select the field that has to be formatted you can then click in the Format box in the field properties at the bottom of the window. Clicking on the arrow to the right of the Format field lists the options available as shown in Figure 3.14.

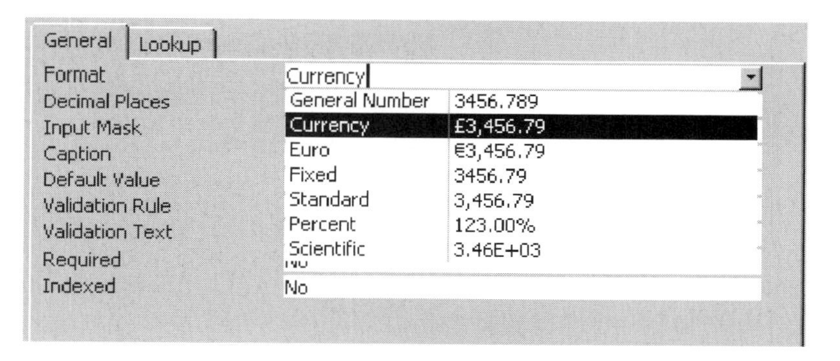

Figure 3.14

If you require more than two decimal places you can select the number of places wanted in the Decimal Places field immediately below the Format field.

Date/Time fields

Formatting Date/Time fields is carried out in exactly the same way as for Text or Numbers fields. First select the field you want to format and then click in the Format field in the field properties box and choose the appropriate date or time format (see Figure 3.15).

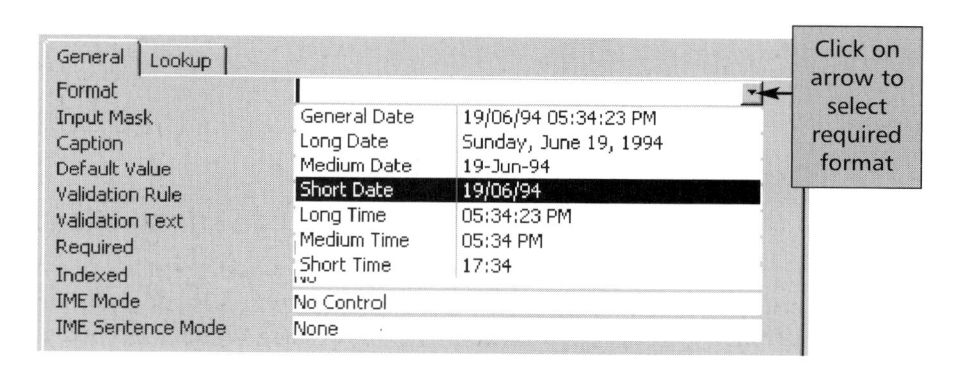

Figure 3.15

Try it out

Now change the properties of your **tbl_COURSE_REGISTER** table in MyDatabase as shown in Table 3.1.

Table 3.1

Field	Data type	Length/format
TITLE	Text	5
INITIAL	Text	3
LASTNAME	Text	25
COURSE	Text	100
START	Date/Time	Short date
END	Date/Time	Short date
FEE	Currency	2 decimal places

Save the changes to the table's format.

Build-up Exercise 3: Stage 1

Create a new database in your databases folder and call it WORKS.

Create a new table with the following fields, data types and format:

Table 3.2

Field	Data type	Length/format
Bldg_No	Text	2
Building	Text	50
Job	Text	200
Estimate	Currency	2 decimal places
Quote	Currency	2 decimal places
Start	Date/Time	Short date
Finish	Date/Time	Short date

Save the table as **tbl_BLDG_WORKS**.

Entering records into a table

There are basically two methods of entering data into a table. The first, and most common in a work environment, is to use a form. Forms are a user friendly way to enter data into a table. Building forms is not part

Click Next >.

Access confirms where it intends to place the data.

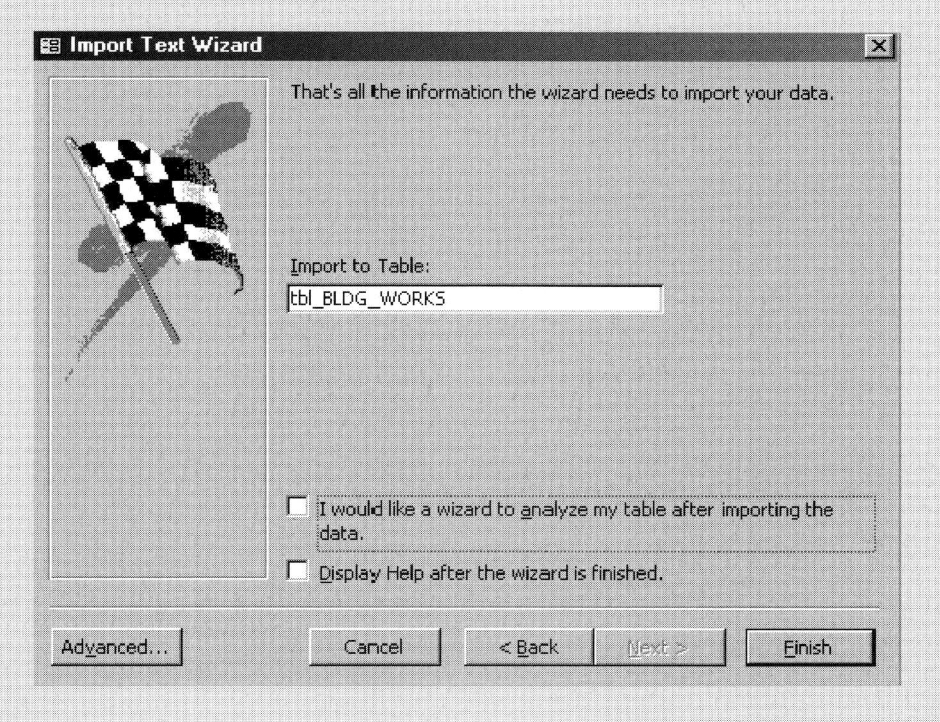

Figure 3.22

Press Finish.

Notice Access will now warn you that it has finished importing but that not all the data could be imported. However, very helpfully Access builds an errors table to show which data has not been imported (see Figure 3.23).

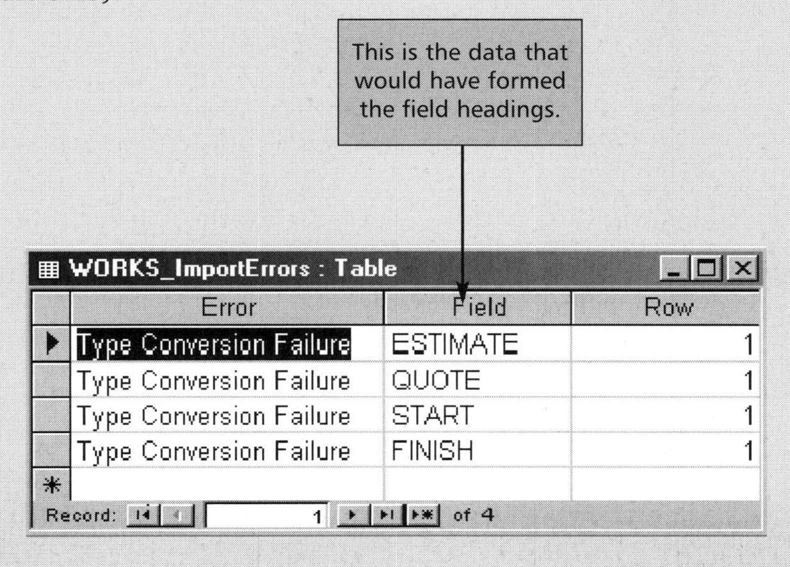

Error	Field	Row
Type Conversion Failure	ESTIMATE	1
Type Conversion Failure	QUOTE	1
Type Conversion Failure	START	1
Type Conversion Failure	FINISH	1

Figure 3.23

Press OK.

Now **open** the table created by Access called **WORKS_Import_Errors**. Access could not import ESTIMATE, QUOTE, START, FINISH because it sees these as data in fields that have data types that are not Text.

Close the table **WORKS_Import_Errors**.

Delete the table **WORKS_Import_Errors**.

Tip: to delete the table right-click on the table in the database window to bring up the list and select Delete.

Open tbl_BLDG_WORKS.

All the required data has been imported. The first record shows the remaining field headings that were imported because they were text.

Delete this record.

Tip: to delete the record select the record and either press the delete key or press the right-hand mouse button and select Delete Record from the drop-down list. Access will ask if you really want to delete the record.

Select Yes.

Note: If you had not prepared the table in advance and selected the New Table at the appropriate point in the import process, Access would have imported all the data into a new table with all the field data types as text.

You should now be able to:

- create a database structure
- set appropriate data types for fields in a table
- change the properties of fields in a table
- enter data
- delete records
- import data from a generic file into an existing or new table.

Adding fields to a table and amending records

To add a field to a table, open the table in design view. Click in the first blank row after the last entry in the Field Name column. Enter the name of the field you want to add and set the appropriate data type and properties for the field. Try adding two fields to the database named **Manifest.mdb** on the accompanying CD.

Try it out

Open Manifest.mdb in the Unit 3 folder on the accompanying CD.

Open the table Manifest in design view.

Click in the first empty field in the Field Name column.

Type the new field name 'VALUE'.

Set the data type to Currency.

Set the Decimal Places in the properties box as 2.

Save the changes to the table. To save any changes made to the table either press the Save icon on the toolbar or select Save from the File option on the main menu.

Now **add** another new field as follows:

Field name: Destination
Data type: Text
Field length: 15

Save the changes made.

Enter the following data into the table:

Table 3.4

ITEM	QTY	VALUE	DESTINATION
POWDER PAINT - BRILLIANT RED	1	£10.00	Peje
POWDER PAINT - BRILLIANT BLUE	1	£10.00	Peje
EMPTY PLASTIC TUBS	24	£20.00	Peje
BLU-TAC	4	£15.00	Decani
PAINT BRUSHES	60	£25.00	Decani
MARABU PAINT SETS	2	£50.00	Decani
PENCILS - BLACK LEAD	36	£10.00	Peje
PENCIL SHARPENERS	6	£12.00	Decani
FANCY RUBBERS	8	£15.00	Decani
STENCIL PACKS	2	£35.00	Decani
CRAYONS - VARIOUS COLOURS	180	£50.00	Decani
POWDER PAINT - BRILLIANT GREEN	4	£10.00	Peje
POWDER PAINT - WHITE	4	£10.00	Peje
POWDER PAINT - BLACK	1	£10.00	Peje
MODELLING MATERIAL	1	£65.00	Peje
WASHABLE ADHESIVE	2	£20.00	Decani
DICTIONARY	2	£25.00	Decani
SWEET BAGS	4	£5.00	Decani

You realise that the empty plastic tubs are to go to Decani and not Peje.

Amend this record to reflect the change of destination.

The sweet bags are a small gift that will be carried separately.

Delete this record from the manifest.

Your table should now look like Figure 3.24.

Manifest : Table

ITEM	QTY	VALUE	DESTINATION
POWDER PAINT - BRILLIANT RED	1	£10.00	Peje
POWDER PAINT - BRILLIANT BLUE	1	£10.00	Peje
EMPTY PLASTIC TUBS	24	£20.00	Decani
BLU-TAC	4	£15.00	Decani
PAINT BRUSHES	60	£25.00	Decani
MARABU PAINT SETS	2	£50.00	Decani
PENCILS - BLACK LEAD	36	£10.00	Peje
PENCIL SHARPENERS	6	£12.00	Decani
FANCY RUBBERS	8	£15.00	Decani
STENCIL PACKS	2	£35.00	Decani
CRAYONS - VARIOUS COLOURS	180	£50.00	Decani
POWDER PAINT - BRILLIANT GREEN	4	£10.00	Peje
POWDER PAINT - WHITE	4	£10.00	Peje
POWDER PAINT - BLACK	1	£10.00	Peje
MODELLING MATERIAL	1	£65.00	Peje
WASHABLE ADHESIVE	2	£20.00	Decani
DICTIONARY	2	£25.00	Decani
		£0.00	

Record: 18 of 18

Figure 3.24

You should now be able to:

- add a new field to a table
- set the field properties
- amend an existing record
- delete a record.

Interrogating a database

If you have already completed a level 1 certification in databases you will be familiar with the concept of querying data in a table. If you are not familiar with queries this section of the unit may help you to understand the basics of interrogating data through queries.

The query is an essential tool in any database. A query is the means by which groups of records are sorted against a defined set of criteria. For example, in the Manifest database created in the last Try it out exercise you could select only those items which are destined for Peje. This would be done through a query.

To design a new query the query tab in the database window is selected, then the New icon is pressed and a dialogue box very similar to the one shown for building a new table appears. See Figure 3.25.

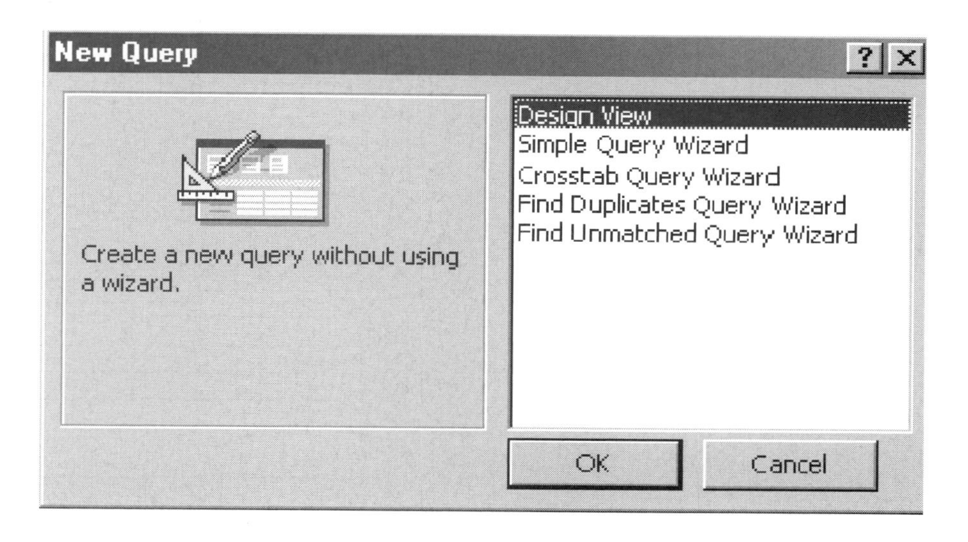

Figure 3.25

Assuming the Design View selection is highlighted the OK button is pressed to reveal the query grid and a dialogue box that allows you select the appropriate table, or query, to be used in the query grid.

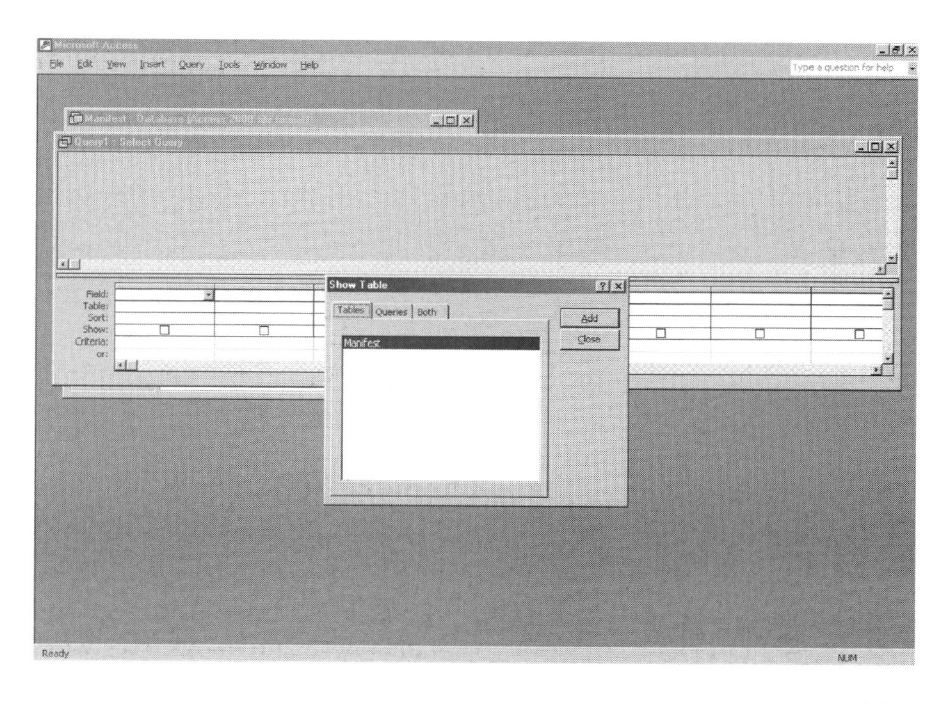

Figure 3.26

After the table or query has been added to the query window, Access waits for you to insert the field that contains the data to be interrogated.

Fields can be added to the query grid in a number of ways:

- By dragging the field from the table to the field row of the grid in the lower part of the window.

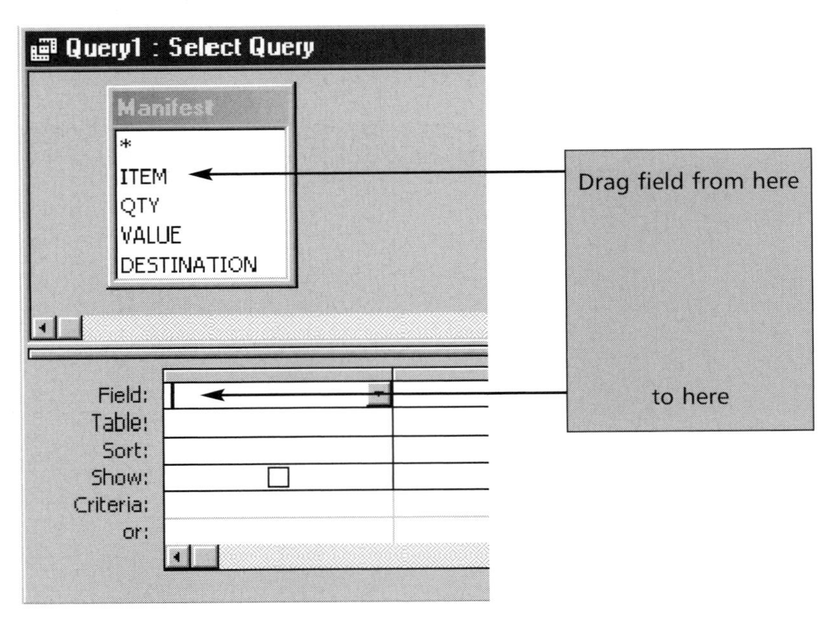

Figure 3.27

- By double-clicking on the required field in the table; this places it in the next available field cell of the query grid.

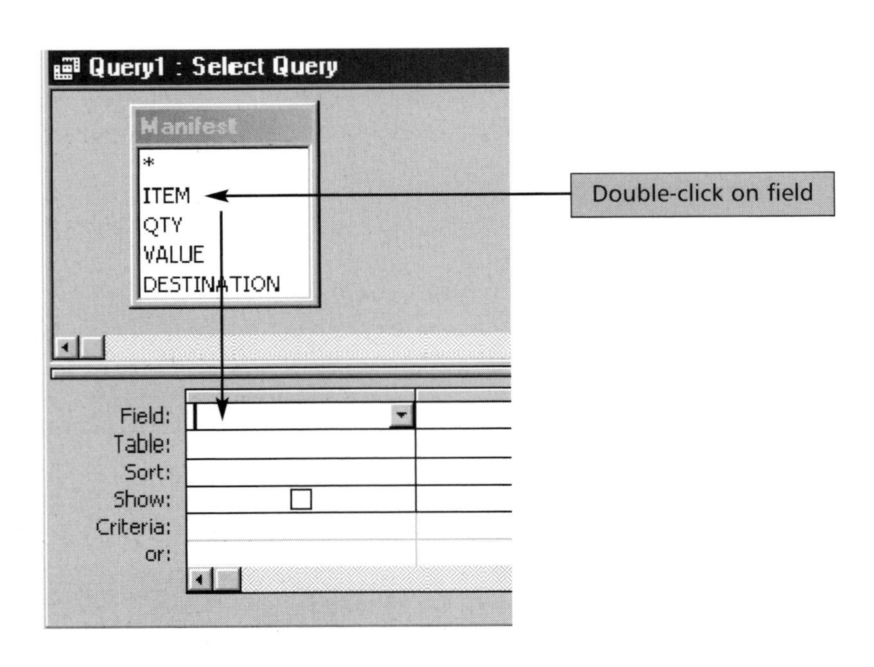

Figure 3.28

- By pressing the down arrow to the right of the cell in the field row of the query grid and selecting the appropriate field from the table.

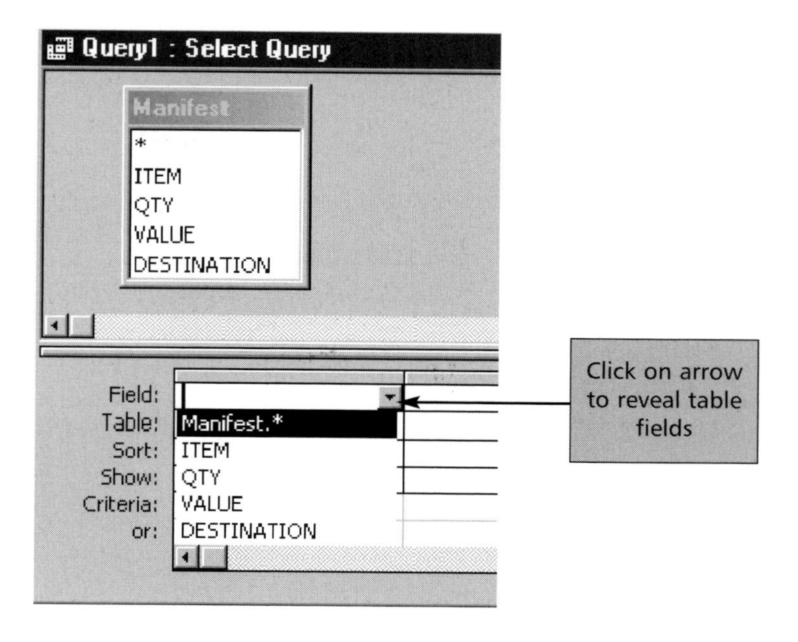

Figure 3.29

Once the required fields have been added the query can be run by either clicking the run query icon on the toolbar , or selecting Query, Run from the main menu.

Using logical operators

In CLAIT Plus you are required to use criteria to select a sub-set of data, use logical operators and also understand the use and purpose of calculated fields. To understand a little more about queries, the use of search criteria and logical operators, attempt the following Try it out exercise.

Try it out

Open the Manifest database if it is not already open.

Select the queries tab and,

Press the New query icon.

Select Design View.

Press Add to add the Manifest table to the query grid.

Press Close to close the Show Table dialogue box.

Add each of the fields from the table using any of the above options.

In the DESTINATION column and Criteria: row

Type 'Peje'.

In the QTY column and the Criteria: row

Type '<36'.

Press the Run query icon or use the Run option under Query on the main menu.

The datasheet view of your query should look like Figure 3.30.

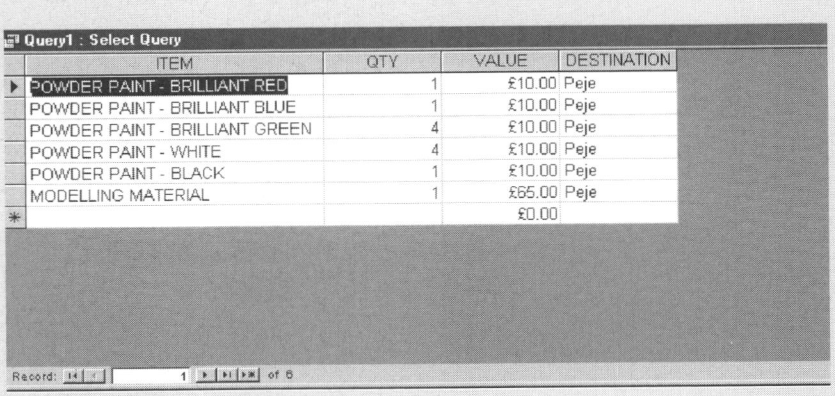

Query1 : Select Query

	ITEM	QTY	VALUE	DESTINATION
▶	POWDER PAINT - BRILLIANT RED	1	£10.00	Peje
	POWDER PAINT - BRILLIANT BLUE	1	£10.00	Peje
	POWDER PAINT - BRILLIANT GREEN	4	£10.00	Peje
	POWDER PAINT - WHITE	4	£10.00	Peje
	POWDER PAINT - BLACK	1	£10.00	Peje
	MODELLING MATERIAL	1	£65.00	Peje
*			£0.00	

Record: 1 of 6

Figure 3.30

Save the query as **qry_Peje_1**.

By using the search criteria you have selected a sub-set of data from the Manifest table. You have also used one of the logical operators (<) to select all the items where the quantity is less than 36.

Access has a number of logical (or comparison) operators you can use in queries. These are:

<	less than
<=	less than or equal to
>	greater than
>=	greater than or equal to
=	equal to
<>	not equal to

Logical operators can also be combined when defining a search criterion. For example, in the query you have just completed you might equally have decided to search for quantities <36 AND >1. This would have returned just two records as opposed to the six in your original query.

Notice that in this example AND has been used to distinguish between the two operators. When you use more than one operator in a criteria cell Access combines these by using the AND expression. Where AND is used Access will return only those records which meet both criteria. Another expression Access uses is OR. Where expressions or operators are in different rows you can use OR, which will return records that meet either of the criteria in any of the cells.

Try this out.

Try it out

Open the query **qry_Peje_1** you recently created in design view.

Amend the QTY criteria cell to read '1 AND 4'.

Run the query.

Notice that the query returns no records. This is because no cell record for Peje has 1 and 4 in the same cell. Now amend the criteria to read '1 OR 4'. Access now returns six records because Peje has this number of records that have either a QTY of 1 OR a QTY of 4.

Save your query as **qry_Peje_2**.

Tip: To save the query using a different name use the File Save As... option on the main menu.

Using the Find and Replace function

You will already have come across the 'Find and Replace' facility in the core unit. This handy function allows you to search for data and replace it with amended data without the need to manually go through a large database to find the data that requires changing. In the examples used for the CLAIT series of qualifications you could be forgiven for wondering why you would need such a function, as the databases are all relatively small. However, in a commercial environment databases may have many thousands of records and to search through the whole database would be a time consuming occupation. By selecting the Replace... option under the Edit menu (usually, but not necessarily, with either a table or query open) the Find and Replace dialogue box provides you with the opportunity to state the data you want to find and the data you want to replace it with. Have a look at Figure 3.31.

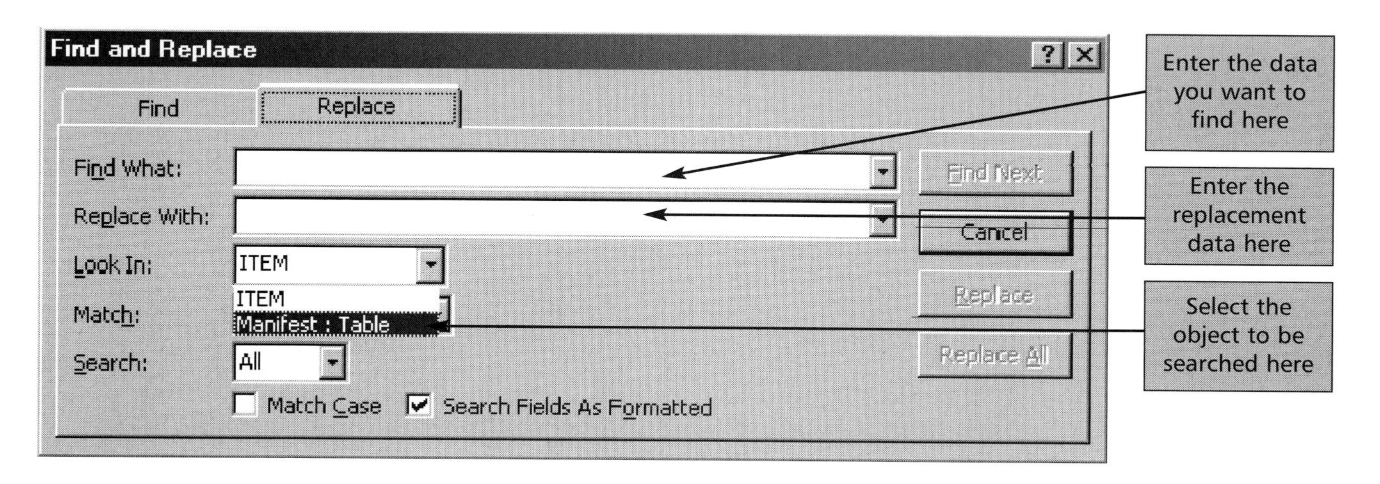

Figure 3.31

The diagram is self-explanatory. The data to be replaced is typed into the top field and below it you type in the replacement data that is to be substituted. If the object in question is not open it can be chosen from the Look in: field. The first options allow you to be more specific about the search criteria.

Now try changing some of the data in the Manifest table.

Try it out

Open the Manifest table.

Select Replace… from the Edit menu.

Type '£10.00' in the Find What: field.

Type '£12.50' in the Replace With: field.

Click in the first record or the VALUE column.

Select Find Next.

Press Replace.

Access has now replaced the second occurrence of £10.00 with £12.50.

Clearly you could go on down the table, search for each occurrence and decide if it needs changing. If you knew that all occurrences needed changing then you could just press the Replace All button.

Using wild cards

Sometimes you may want to search for specific records but may not be exactly sure what all the text or numbers are, or alternatively you want to search for a series of numbers. Wild cards can be extremely useful in helping to find data, or records, under these circumstances.

Let us say, for example, you had been asked to find the destination for all items of powder. In the Manifest database there are a number of records relating to different colours of paint powder. You may not know all the colours available but need to find all occurrences of paint powder. In these circumstances you can use the wild card * (which is also the sign for multiplication).

Try finding all the paint powder in the MANIFEST database.

Try it out

Open the MANIFEST database if it is not already open.

Create a new query containing all the fields in the MANIFEST table.

In the Criteria cell under the ITEM field

Type 'POWDER'.

Click outside the field for the input to be accepted.

Notice that Access has replaced your POWDER with Like "POWDER*".

Run the query.

Access has found all the occurrences of POWDER.

Save the query as **qry_POWDER_ALL.**

Close the query.

Using calculations in a query

Earlier in this unit the need to avoid unnecessary storage of data was emphasised. You were also told that data could be *derived* rather than storing it in a table.

Data can be derived in a number of ways, and Access provides a very wide range of functions for you to use. For CLAIT Plus you will only be required to understand how to use basic calculated fields using mathematical operators such as +, -, / and *. However, the principles can be applied to most calculations.

Try it out

Open qry_Peje_1 in your Manifest database.

Remove the criteria <36 and Peje.

Assume the VALUE shown is for all items. Let's say you wanted to create a field that showed the value for each item even though such a field does not exist in your table. You can calculate this using a mathematical operator.

Click in the Field cell immediately after DESTINATION.

Note: Expressions can be entered either by using a facility called the Expression Builder or by typing directly into the cell where the expression (or calculation) is to be made. In this instance you are going to use the Expression Builder. When you decide to use the Expression Builder (rather than entering the formula directly into the appropriate cell) remember that the query you are using should normally be saved before using the builder. By saving the query first you can use the fields entered into the query directly from the grid. If the query has not been saved the Expression Builder will not recognise the field names in the query. This does not mean you cannot use the Expression Builder without first saving, but if you do you will need to use the fields from the table rather than the query.

Press the build icon on the toolbar. The following dialogue box will appear.

SEARCH TIP

Using the wild card

You can use the wild card * in any application where you are uncertain of the full details of the data being sought. Simply place the wild card symbol immediately after the last character of the word you are searching for and the software will find any occurrences containing the letters typed. For example, if you type 'Ca*' you could find Cat, Car, Carpet, and so on, because the wild card immediately follows the 'a' of 'Ca'. You can also use the wild card in Windows Explorer or My Computer when you want to find a file, but are not sure of the exact name or type of the file. So, for example, you might ask the software to find Ca*.doc which would find all .doc files (Word) that begin with Ca. Alternatively you might search for Ca*.*. This would find all files with Ca in the name irrespective of the application.

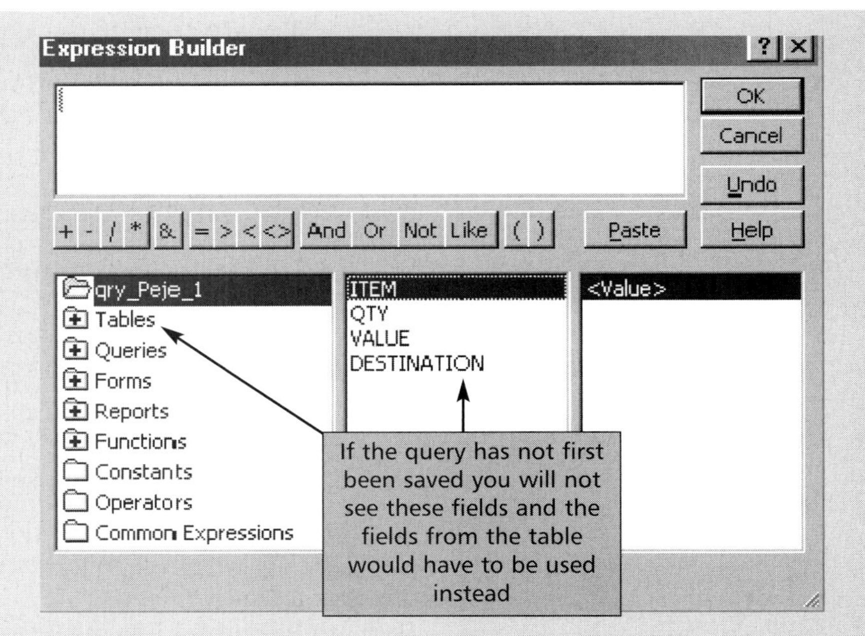

Figure 3.32

To calculate the value of each item the expression to be used would be:

VALUE/QTY

Make sure the cursor is flashing in the white area of the Expression Builder at the top of the dialogue box.

Double-click on VALUE in the central column.

Immediately below the Expression Builder area you will notice a row of icons ranging from mathematical and logical operators to icons for And, Or, Not, Like and parenthesis.

Click on the Divide operator (/).

Double-click on QTY.

Press OK and you are returned to the query grid.

Click outside the cell into which the calculation has been placed to accept the expression.

The cell will now look similar to Figure 3.33.

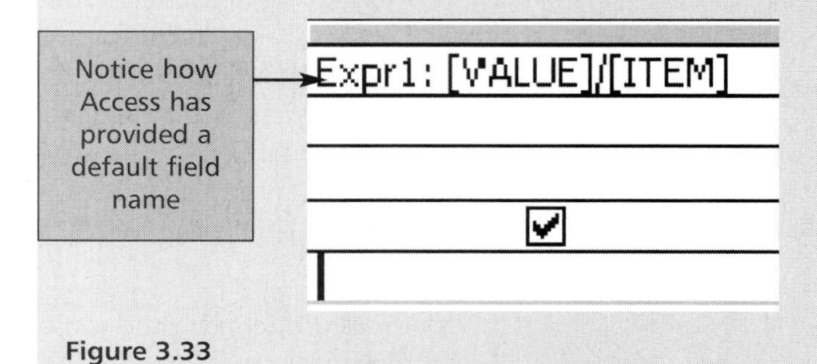

Figure 3.33

Note: Notice that in front of the formula VALUE/QTY Access has placed 'Expr:'. Effectively you are adding a new field to your query; not one based on data contained in the Manifest table but one based on the formula to calculate the cost of each item. Access uses 'Expr:' as the default name for your new field. You can alter anything in front of the colon without affecting the calculation.

Highlight Expr: in front of the formula.

Type the new name for the field 'VALUE EACH'.

Save your query as **qry_Peje_3.**

Tip: Use the Save As... option from the File menu.

Run the query.

Now you will see the value of each item to many decimal places.

Formatting field data

The procedure for formatting field data is very similar to formatting the fields of a table. However, instead of seeing the properties box as part of the design query view, you need to show the properties by clicking in the cell to be formatted using the right-hand mouse button as shown in Figure 3.34.

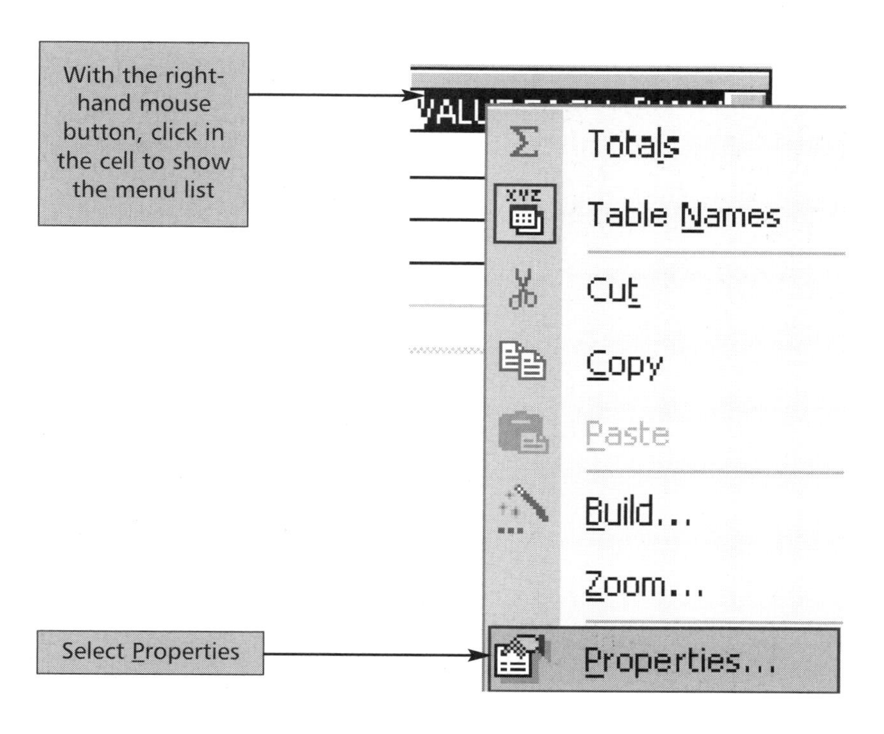

Figure 3.34

This brings up the properties available for that cell: see Figure 3.35.

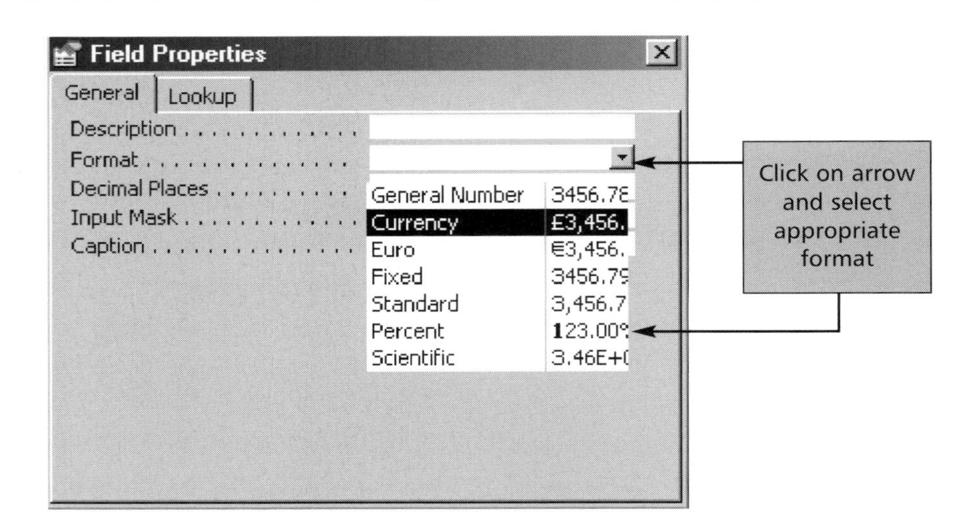

Figure 3.35

By clicking on the arrow to the right of the Format option a familiar list appears that allows you to select the appropriate number format. Below this option the number of decimal places is then selected. Now change the format of the cell into which you place your formula to calculate the value of each item in **qry_Peje_3**.

Try it out

Open qry_Peje_3 in design view.

Using the right-hand mouse button:

Click in the field cell VALUE EACH.

Select Properties… .

Select Currency for the format.

Select 2 for the number of decimal places.

Close the Field Properties box.

Run the query, which should now look like Figure 3.36.

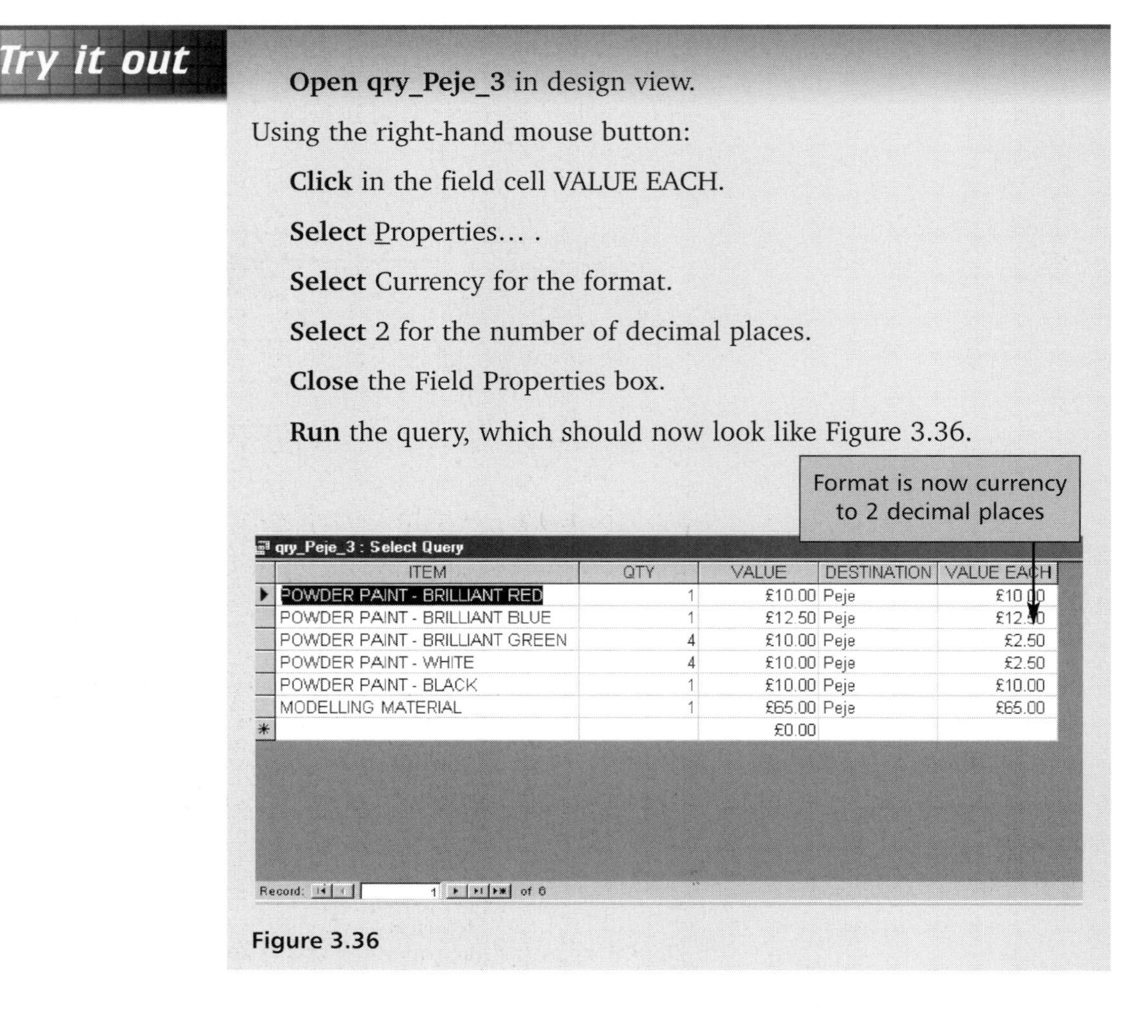

ITEM	QTY	VALUE	DESTINATION	VALUE EACH
POWDER PAINT - BRILLIANT RED	1	£10.00	Peje	£10.00
POWDER PAINT - BRILLIANT BLUE	1	£12.50	Peje	£12.50
POWDER PAINT - BRILLIANT GREEN	4	£10.00	Peje	£2.50
POWDER PAINT - WHITE	4	£10.00	Peje	£2.50
POWDER PAINT - BLACK	1	£10.00	Peje	£10.00
MODELLING MATERIAL	1	£65.00	Peje	£65.00
		£0.00		

Figure 3.36

You should now be able to:

- create a query
- use logical operators to find sub-sets of data
- use mathematical operators to calculate and derive data not stored in the database table
- find and replace specific data using the find and replace function
- use wild cards to find partly known data
- format numerical data in a query cell.

Build-up Exercise 3: Stage 3

Open the WORKS database.

Create a new query containing all the fields in the table **tbl_BLDG_WORKS**.

Run the query.

Save the query as **qry_BLDG_WORKS.**

You decide to see what the actual difference is between the builders' estimates for each job and their quotes.

Create a new query and include the following fields:

BUILDING
JOB
ESTIMATE
QUOTE

Save the query as **qry_Variation_1.**

Using the Expression Builder:

Enter a formula in the cell immediately following QUOTE that calculates the difference between the quote and estimate and shows whether the quote is higher or lower than the estimate. (To calculate the difference the formula should be QUOTE minus ESTIMATE.)

Rename the field Expr as 'Variation'.

Save the query.

Run the query.

Build-up Exercise 3: Stage 4

Using an appropriate logical operator:

Select a sub-set in the query named **qry_Variation_1** of data, that returns only those variations where the quote exceeds the estimate by £20 or more. (Formula should be >=20.)

Run the query. The query should return six records where the quote exceeds the estimate by more than £20.

Format the result of the Variation cell as a Fixed number to two decimal places.

Using Save As:

Save the query as **qry_Variation_2.**

Build-up Exercise 3: Stage 5

Using **qry_Variation_2**:

Select only those records that apply to the building called DANTE.

Two records should be returned.

Using Save As:

Save the query as **qry_Variation_3**.

Build-up Exercise 3: Stage 6

It has been decided to change the name of the BODRUM building to BECKER. Using the Find and Replace facility:

Change the name of the BODRUM building in **tbl_BLDG_WORKS** to BECKER.

There are two occurrences in all.

Build-up Exercise 3: Stage 7

Using the wild card symbol and **qry_Variation_1**:

Present all records of buildings that begin with the letter B.

There should be five records of buildings beginning with the letter B.

Close the query without saving the changes made.

Creating and formatting reports

If tables are the building blocks of a database then reports are the paint, wallpaper and furnishings that bring the building to life. Reports allow you to select sets of data, sort and group data and generally present data in a variety of ways that turn raw data into understandable and useful information.

You will not be surprised to learn that Access provides more than one way to create reports. In this section you will learn how to create a report using the Report Wizard and then how to make various adjustments to the report's format.

Creating a simple report

In the database window in Access is a tab called Reports. When this is selected you are given two options:

- to create a report in design view
- to create a report using the Report Wizard.

Creating a report in design view allows you to build a report from scratch in a blank report window. To a beginner this can be a bit daunting and even to those who have some experience in creating reports there are pitfalls if you don't have some experience in building reports from scratch. The Access Report Wizard helps you create professional reports from either tables or queries and is basically very simple to use.

Reports come in many different formats, styles and layouts. To help you understand how the Wizard works you may find it easier to try a hand-holding Try it out exercise first.

Try it out

Open the MANIFEST database.

Select the Reports tab in the database window.

Click on Create report by using wizard.

Press the New button on the window.

A dialogue box appears similar to others you have seen when building tables or queries (see Figure 3.37).

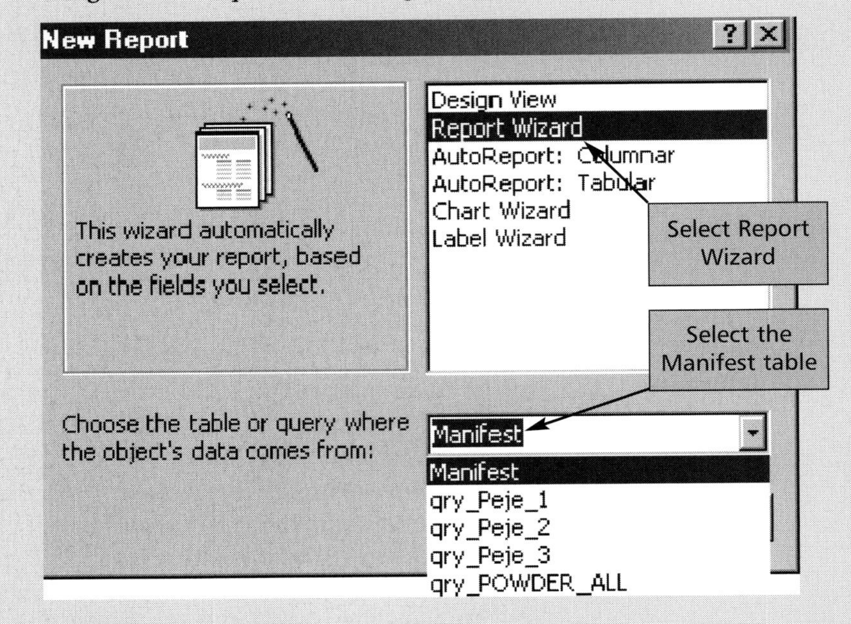

Figure 3.37

Select the Report Wizard option in the top box of the dialogue.

Select the table Manifest in the lower box.

Click OK.

Access presents the first set of choices for you to build the report; see Figure 3.38.

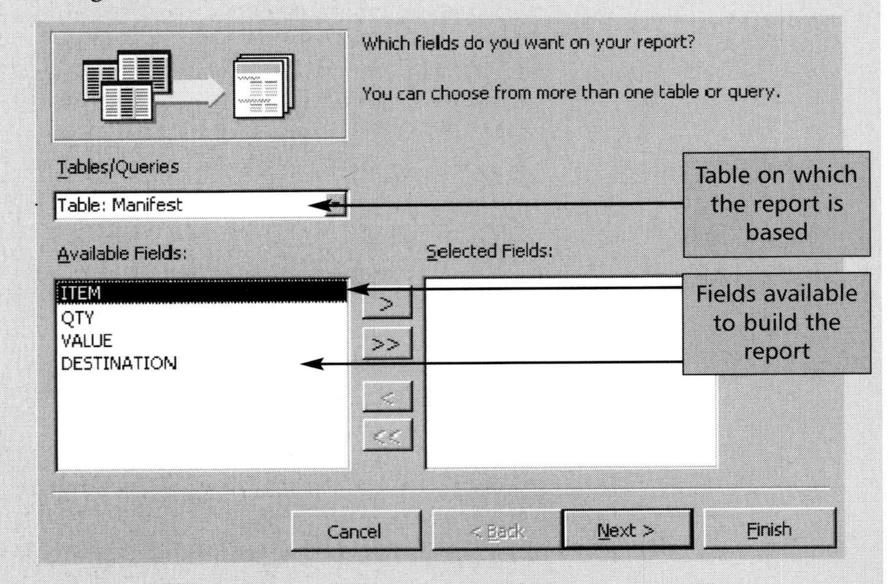

Figure 3.38

In the first box on the top left of the window, Access is telling you the table or query on which your report is going to be based.

Immediately below this are the fields from the table that can be used in the report. The right-hand box is for you to select the field you want to use (i.e. you do not have to use all the available fields).

Click the >> to select all the fields.

Notice how Access moves the selected fields from the left-hand box to the right-hand box.

Click Next >.

Access is now asking whether you want to group any of the fields for the report. This will become clearer once the report has been finished. You do not necessarily have to select any groupings at this stage as you can create groupings at any time: see Figure 3.39.

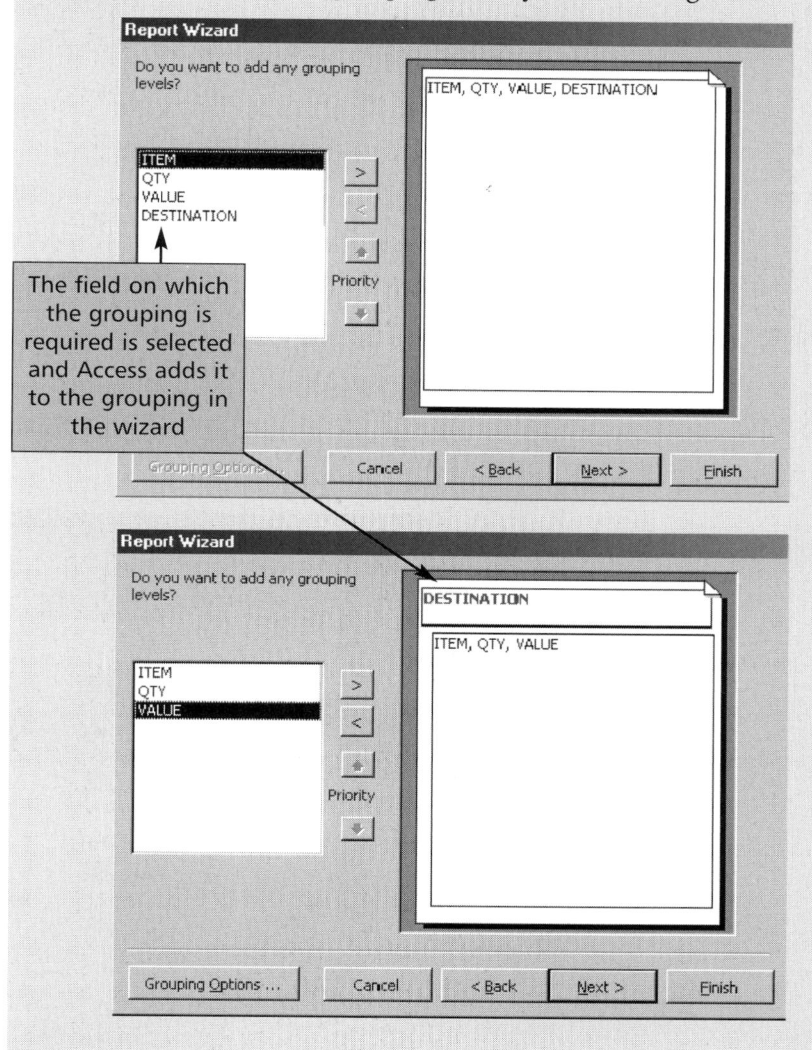

Figure 3.39

On this occasion you will sort by destination.

Select DESTINATION.

Click Next >.

Access then asks if the data is to be sorted by any specific field, as seen in Figure 3.40.

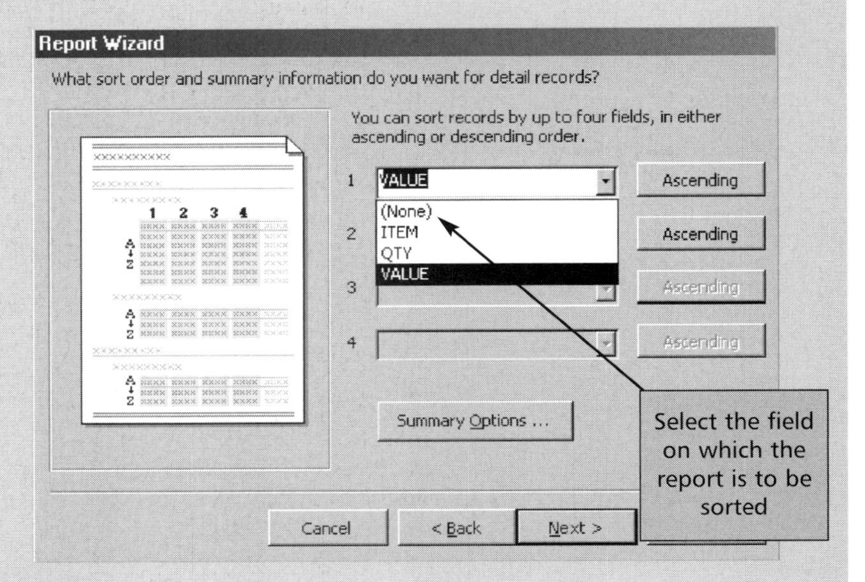

Figure 3.40

Select VALUE as the field to sort by.

Click Next >.

Access provides a variety of layouts for reports as shown in Figure 3.41.

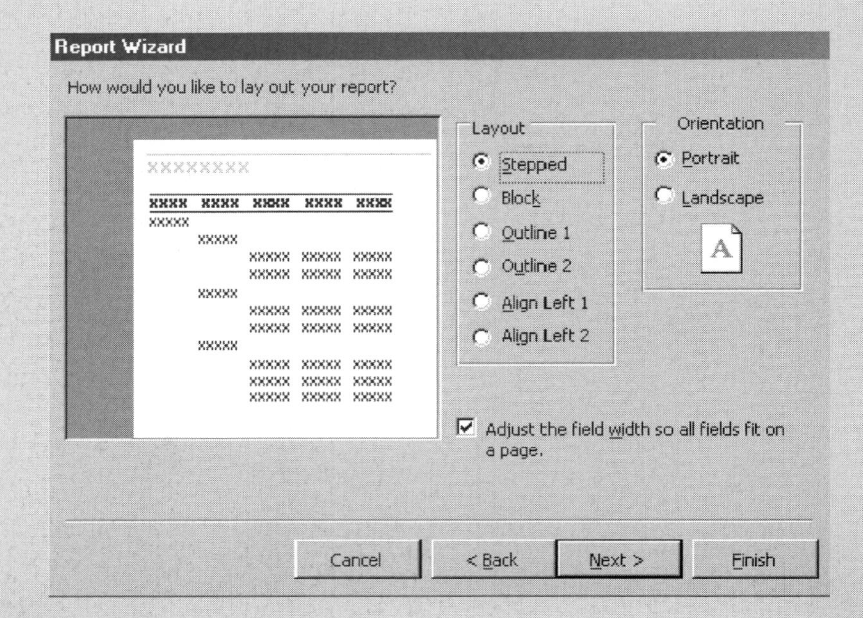

Figure 3.41

To go into all these is beyond the scope of CLAIT Plus, but you may wish to experiment at a later date. For now accept the Stepped default layout in Portrait. Ensure that the 'Adjust field width so all fields fit on a page' check box is checked.

Click Next >.

Access also provides an array of styles that you can use and these are shown in Figure 3.42.

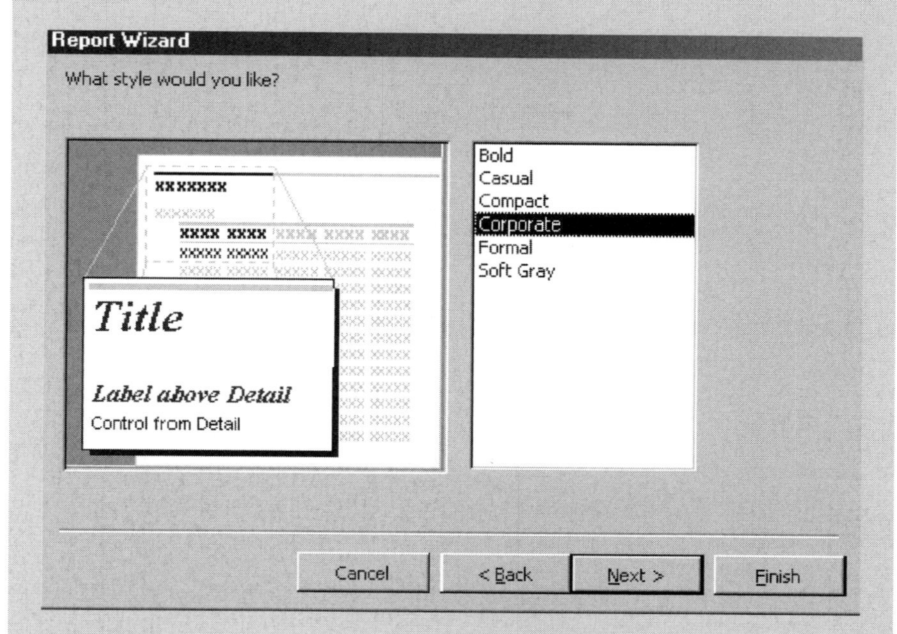

Figure 3.42

The styles provided by Access are built-in templates. Even if you choose one of these styles you can easily adjust the styling once the report has been completed. For now accept the default Corporate style.

Click Next >.

Access finally provides you with an opportunity to name your report. This is not the same as saving the report with a name. The name selected here is the one used as a heading for your report.

In the title box call your report 'MANIFEST BY DESTINATION'.

Click Finish.

Access will now go away and build the report based on the input you have given it via the Report Wizard. The results are then displayed as shown in Figure 3.43.

Notice how the report is grouped by DESTINATION (Decani and then Peje) and then sorted by VALUE. The heading for the report is MANIFEST BY DESTINATION as requested.

Close the report.

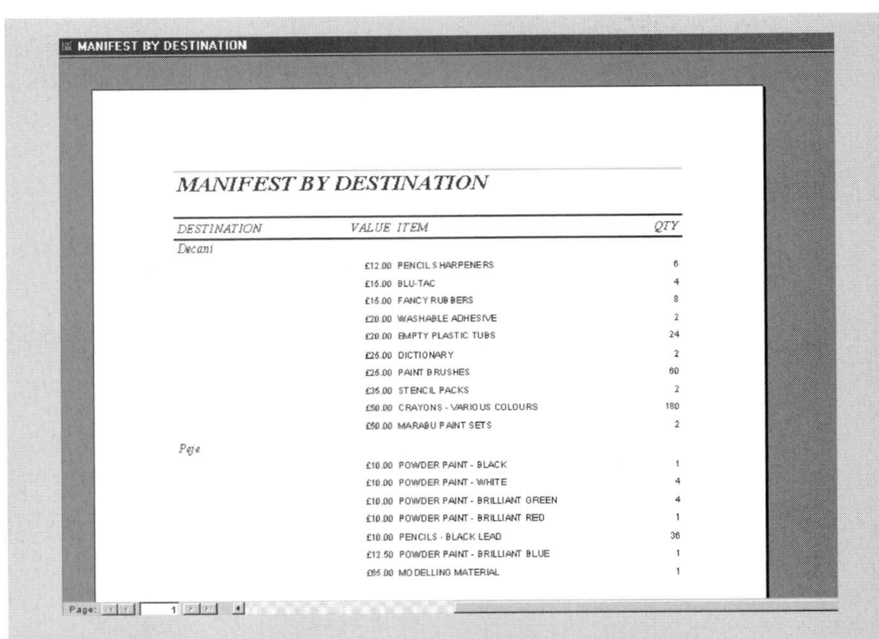

MANIFEST BY DESTINATION

DESTINATION	VALUE	ITEM	QTY
Decani			
	£12.00	PENCIL SHARPENERS	6
	£15.00	BLU-TAC	4
	£15.00	FANCY RUBBERS	8
	£20.00	WASHABLE ADHESIVE	2
	£20.00	EMPTY PLASTIC TUBS	24
	£25.00	DICTIONARY	2
	£25.00	PAINT BRUSHES	60
	£35.00	STENCIL PACKS	2
	£50.00	CRAYONS - VARIOUS COLOURS	180
	£50.00	MARABU PAINT SETS	2
Peje			
	£10.00	POWDER PAINT - BLACK	1
	£10.00	POWDER PAINT - WHITE	4
	£10.00	POWDER PAINT - BRILLIANT GREEN	4
	£10.00	POWDER PAINT - BRILLIANT RED	1
	£10.00	PENCILS - BLACK LEAD	36
	£12.50	POWDER PAINT - BRILLIANT BLUE	1
	£85.00	MODELLING MATERIAL	1

Figure 3.43

Access has assumed you want the report file's name to be the same as the heading you gave it. In the database window you can see under the Report tab that MANIFEST BY DESTINATION is the name given by Access to the report.

To change the name of the report simply click on the name using the right-hand mouse button, select Rename and overtype the name you want your report to be called.

> **Change** the name of the report in the database window to: **rpt_Manifest_By_Destination.**

Formatting reports

Looking at the report produced in the above exercise it can be said that it meets all the basic requirements and contains all the necessary data. However, the layout and format can clearly be improved. For example, it would be better if the ITEM column came immediately after the group header. The gaps between columns could be reduced to improve the overall layout of the report.

At this stage it is perhaps worth looking at the report in design view and understanding the various components of the report and the objects within it. Have a look at Figure 3.44, which is a design view of the report **rpt_Manifest_By_Destination**.

Report label fields

Labels, as the name suggests, simply indicate the name of something whether this is the data displayed in a text box or the name of a report, page or group heading. Label boxes have properties similar to any other object in the report but are limited in nature to such things as font format, position, colour, border style and so on.

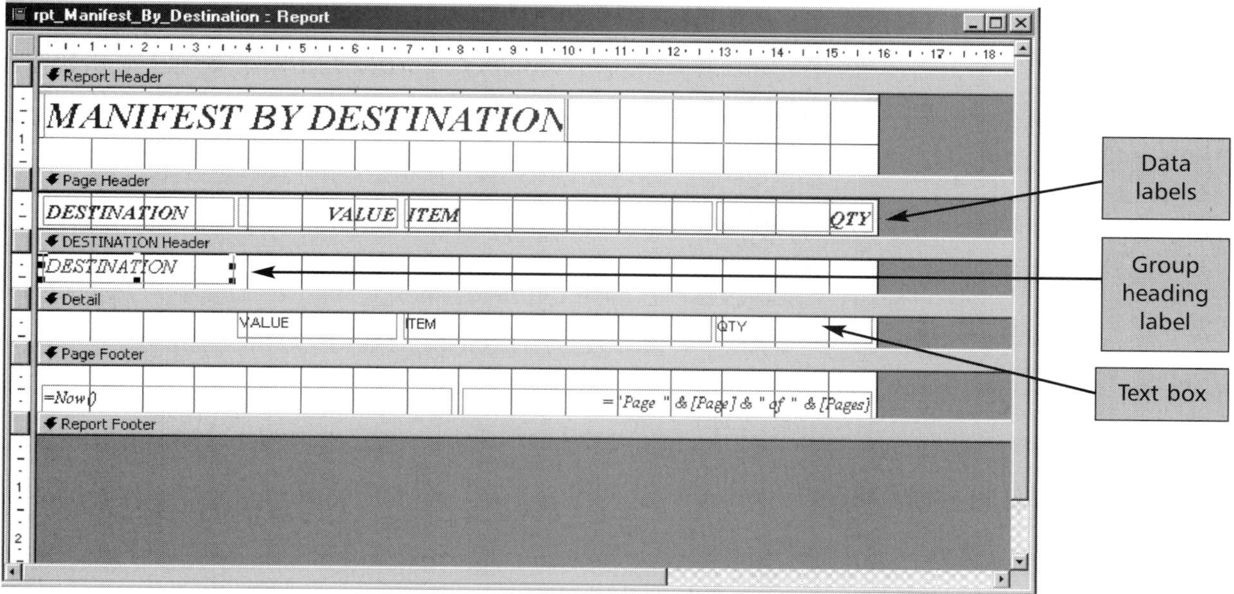

Figure 3.44

Text boxes

A text box is normally 'bound' to specific data known as the control source. For example, take a look at the text box QTY in Figure 3.45. This box is 'bound' to a control source which is the QTY field in the Manifest table.

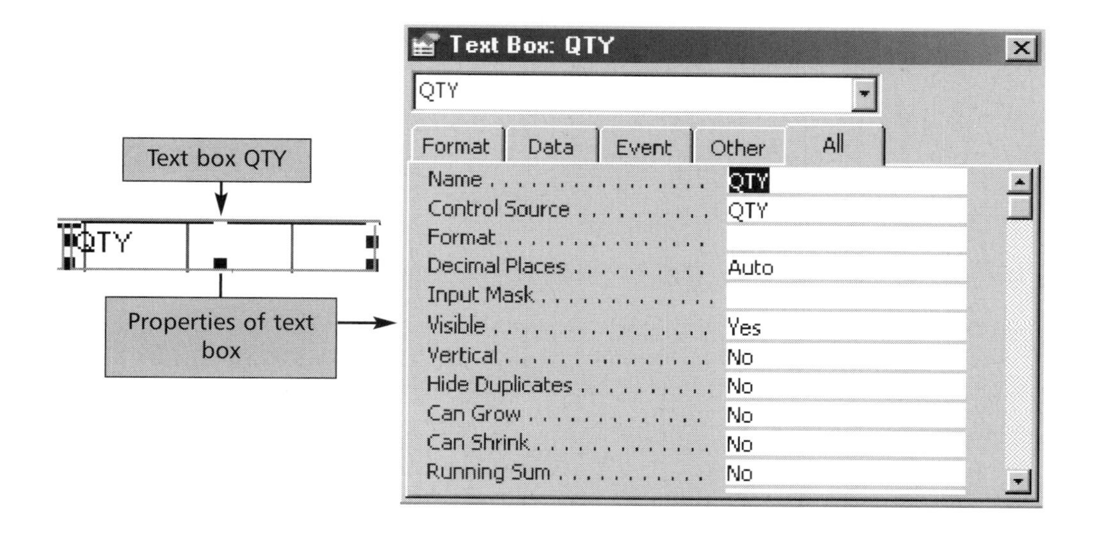

Figure 3.45

Other formats

Fortunately, you will not, for CLAIT Plus, need to know about bound and unbound controls, but it is nevertheless useful to understand the difference between various objects that are used when designing a report. You are expected to understand about group headings and why they are used, and this was covered earlier when you built the report. You are also expected to understand the use of automated fields such as file names, dates and page numbering and how to include headers and footers in a report.

Changing the layout and presentation of a report

Objects in a report window react in the same way as any other object in a Windows environment. They can be moved, resized, reformatted and so on. In an earlier Try it out exercise a report was created using the Report Wizard but now there is a need to polish the report for distribution.

To move a field, simply click on it and drag it to the desired location. In the MANIFEST BY DESTINATION report it would make more sense to have the fields shown as:

DESTINATION ITEM QTY VALUE

Try it out

Open rpt_Manifest_By_Destination in design view, if it is not already open.

Now move the fields to the appropriate positions by dragging both the Label and Text box to the location.

Select both the label and text box objects of VALUE and drag to their new location: see Figure 3.46.

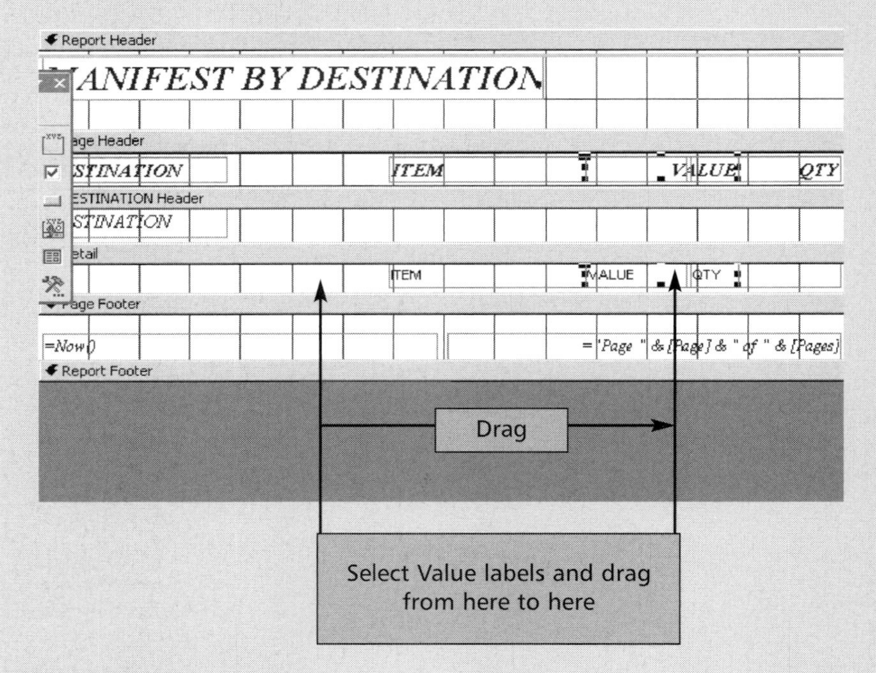

Figure 3.46

Using the same technique:

Select the label and text box of ITEM and drag it so that it is just to the right of DESTINATION.

Select the label and text box of QTY and position both between the ITEM and VALUE fields.

Your report design should now look similar to Figure 3.47.

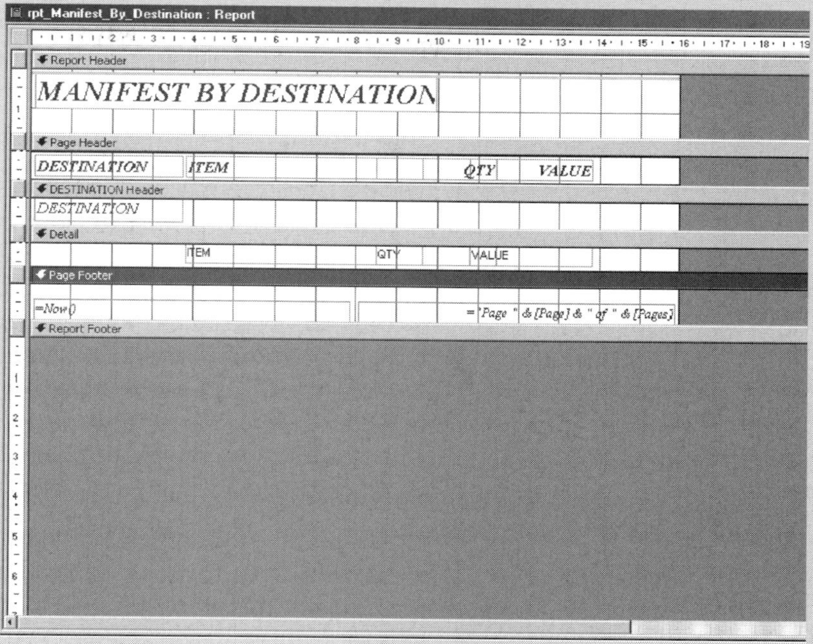

Figure 3.47

Now preview the report either by clicking on the Preview icon on the toolbar or selecting the Print Preview option from View on the main menu. Your report should now look similar to Figure 3.48.

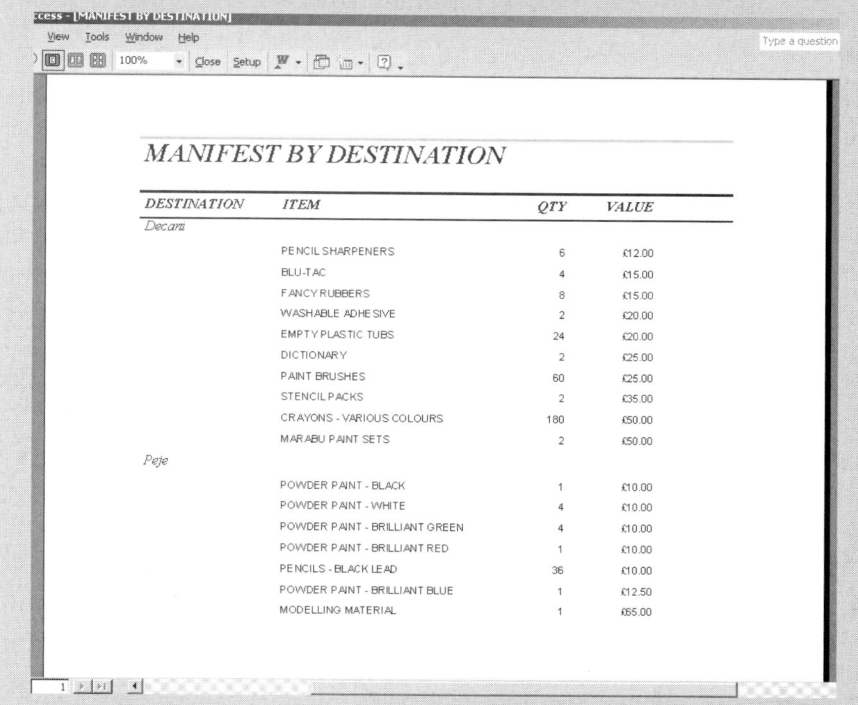

MANIFEST BY DESTINATION

DESTINATION	ITEM	QTY	VALUE
Decani			
	PENCIL SHARPENERS	6	£12.00
	BLU-TAC	4	£15.00
	FANCY RUBBERS	8	£15.00
	WASHABLE ADHESIVE	2	£20.00
	EMPTY PLASTIC TUBS	24	£20.00
	DICTIONARY	2	£25.00
	PAINT BRUSHES	60	£25.00
	STENCIL PACKS	2	£35.00
	CRAYONS - VARIOUS COLOURS	180	£50.00
	MARABU PAINT SETS	2	£50.00
Peje			
	POWDER PAINT - BLACK	1	£10.00
	POWDER PAINT - WHITE	4	£10.00
	POWDER PAINT - BRILLIANT GREEN	4	£10.00
	POWDER PAINT - BRILLIANT RED	1	£10.00
	PENCILS - BLACK LEAD	36	£10.00
	POWDER PAINT - BRILLIANT BLUE	1	£12.50
	MODELLING MATERIAL	1	£65.00

Figure 3.48

Save the report.

You now have a better separation between headings in the report.

Presenting data in different formats and order

The previous example is of a report in tabular or list format. CLAIT Plus requires that you are able to understand how to produce queries and reports in a variety of ways and also display fields and records in a specified order. You will also need to understand the differences between records displayed in a columnar, tabular or group format. You will already have seen how to sort data both in queries and reports. Also when using the Reports Wizard Access allows you to state which fields to sort by and in what order (i.e. ascending or descending). However, whilst using the wizard allows you to build the basics of a report there will be occasions when you want to change the sort order different to the default.

Columnar and tabular reports

When you want to be selective about which fields are to be included in a report the Report Wizard is a handy tool for building the basics which you can subsequently amend. This is particularly so, as you saw in the previous exercise, when you want to group data. However, Access also provides an AutoReport option where it will build a specifically formatted report based on all the fields in the source object. You can still be selective about which fields are contained in the report but, if you don't want all the fields in a table or you want to add other fields such as calculated fields, you first need to build a query based on the data you want to use.

AutoReports come in two flavours:

- columnar
- tabular.

Figure 3.49 demonstrates the difference between a columnar and tabular report.

To understand how this is achieved in the design stage of the report have a look at Figure 3.50.

Notice how in the columnar report the fields in the detail section (i.e. where the data text boxes go) are placed one underneath the other whilst those in the tabular report are positioned across the page.

Building AutoReports

Building either of the above types of report is extremely straightforward. First decide what data you want to use in your report and build an appropriate query. Next create a new report in the same way as before, but instead of using the query Wizard the appropriate AutoReport format is selected (i.e. columnar or tabular) and then the query on which the report is to be based is selected. Access will then go away and build a basic report based on the information you have provided. Try this out by creating a columnar report using AutoReport.

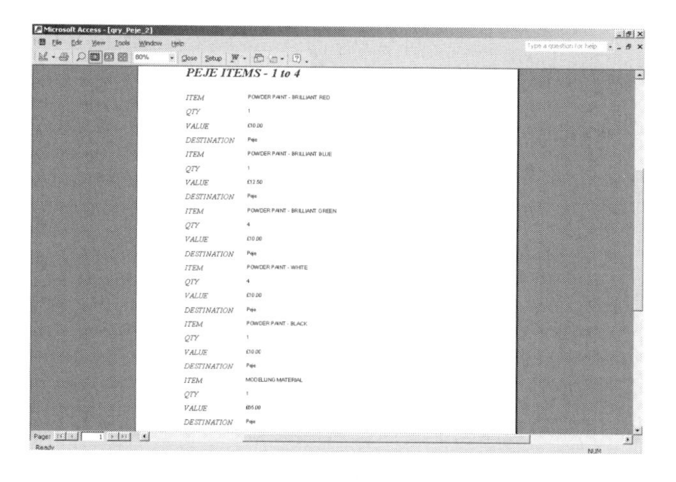

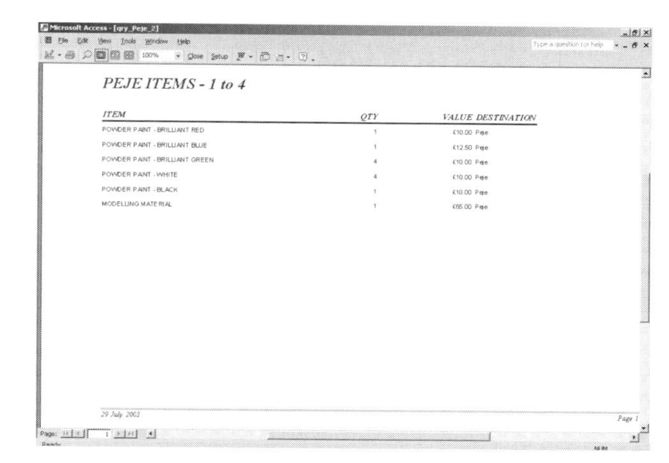

A columnar report

A tabular (list) report

Figure 3.49

Fields laid out in a column style

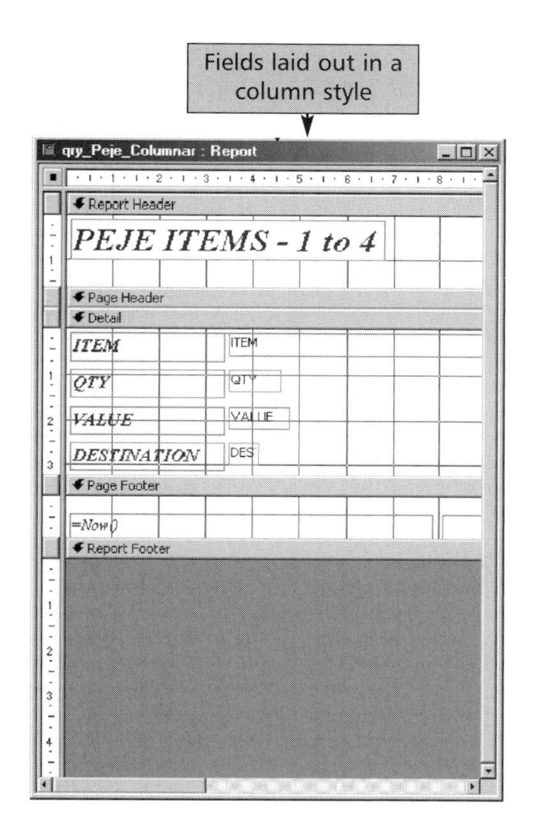

Fields laid out per a table

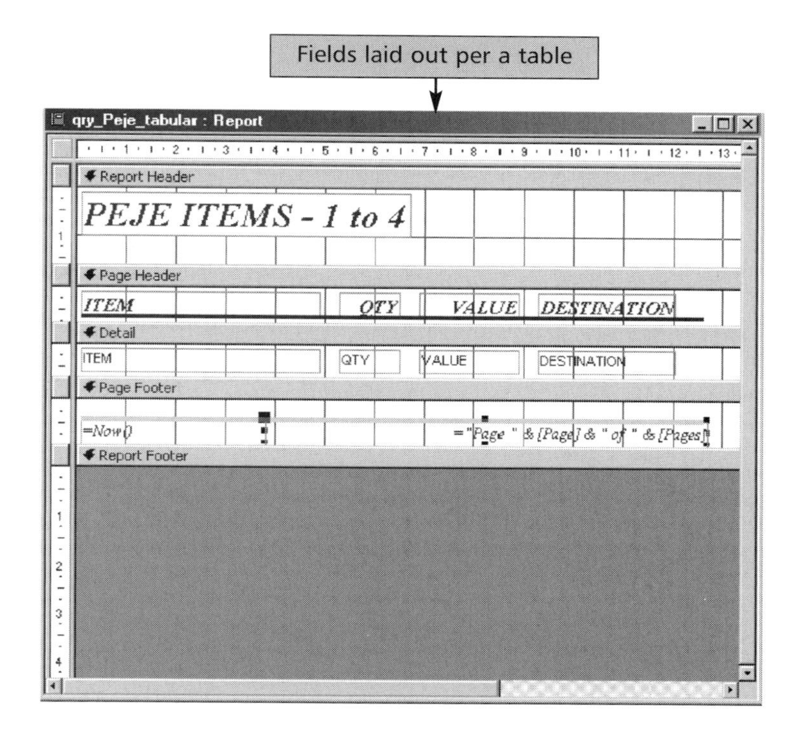

A columnar report

A tabular (list) report

Figure 3.50

Try it out

Open the Manifest database if it is not already open.

Create a new field below ITEM called **CODE** in the Manifest table.

Tip: To insert a field between two existing fields place the cursor in the row above which the field is to be added and press the insert row icon on the toolbar. Type in the name of the field and set the appropriate data type and properties.

Save the changes made to the table.

Open the Manifest table in datasheet view.

Enter the appropriate codes as shown in Table 3.5.

Table 3.5

ITEM	CODE	QTY	VALUE	DESTINATION
POWDER PAINT - BRILLIANT RED	PWDR	1	£10.00	Peje
POWDER PAINT - BRILLIANT BLUE	PWDR	1	£12.50	Peje
EMPTY PLASTIC TUBS	PT	24	£20.00	Decani
BLU-TAC	BT	4	£15.00	Decani
PAINT BRUSHES	BR	60	£25.00	Decani
MARABU PAINT SETS	PNT	2	£50.00	Decani
PENCILS - BLACK LEAD	PEN	36	£10.00	Peje
PENCIL SHARPENERS	PEN	6	£12.00	Decani
FANCY RUBBERS	RUB	8	£15.00	Decani
STENCIL PACKS	STN	2	£35.00	Decani
CRAYONS - VARIOUS COLOURS	PEN	180	£50.00	Decani
POWDER PAINT - BRILLIANT GREEN	PWDR	4	£10.00	Peje
POWDER PAINT - WHITE	PWDR	4	£10.00	Peje
POWDER PAINT - BLACK	PWDR	1	£10.00	Peje
MODELLING MATERIAL	MOD	1	£65.00	Peje
WASHABLE ADHESIVE	GLU	2	£20.00	Decani
DICTIONARY	DICT	2	£25.00	Decani

space between the group header and the data is really too large to be acceptable. By placing the cursor over the top line of the detail section the cursor will change to a cross shape ↕.

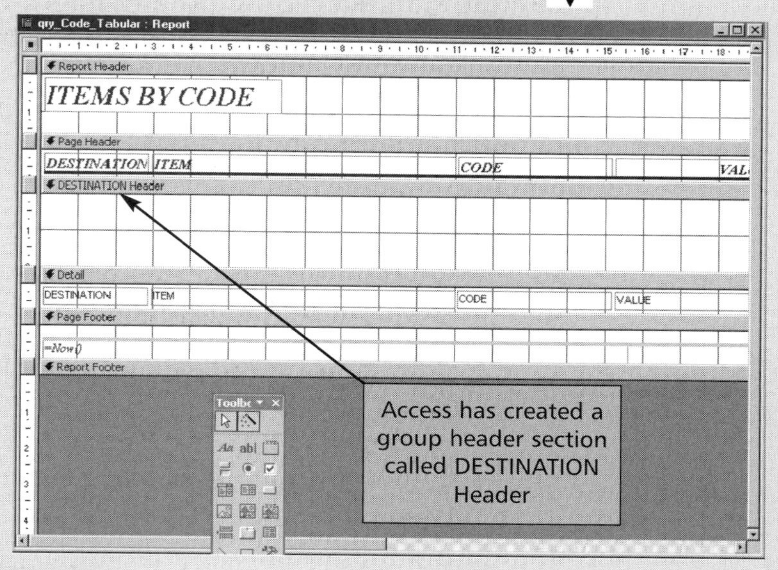

Figure 3.55

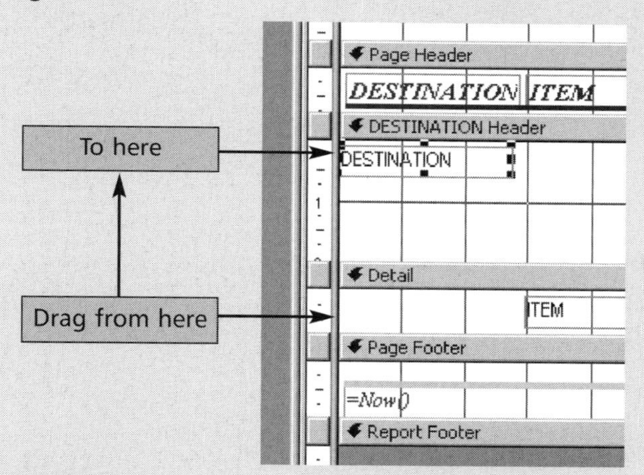

Figure 3.56

Click and hold the left-hand mouse button down and drag the Detail bar up to the base of the DESTINATION text box, leaving a small gap between the bottom of the text box and the top of the Detail bar as shown in Figure 3.57.

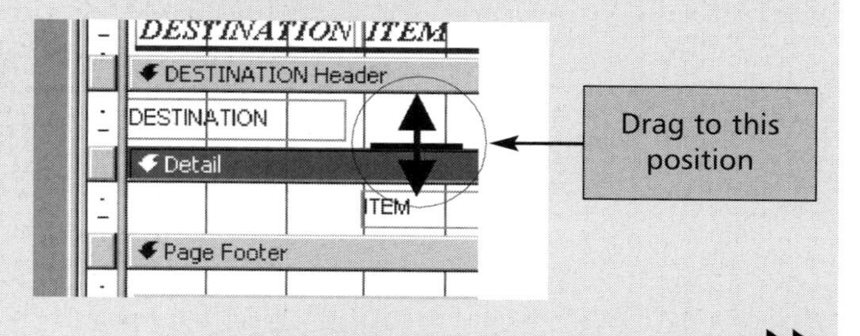

Figure 3.57

Save the report as **rpt_Code_Grouped**

Preview the report.

Now compare the report in Figure 3.53 with your grouped report. They are very similar but whereas in the normal tabular report Peje and Decani appear for each record, in the grouped report Peje and Decani only appear as a group header.

Displaying summary information

Where you have a large database it may be difficult and unwieldy to provide a report that shows all the records in the file. Grouping records and providing a summary at the end of each group can help the reader to get an overview of the information being provided. Again, there are any number of ways you can deal with summary information, but in a report you would use summary functions to provide totals etc. for each group in the report.

Try it out

Open qry_Code_Grouped in design view.

Select Sorting and Grouping from the View menu option.

Select Yes for the Group Footer.

From the toolbox shown in Figure 3.58 click on the text box icon.

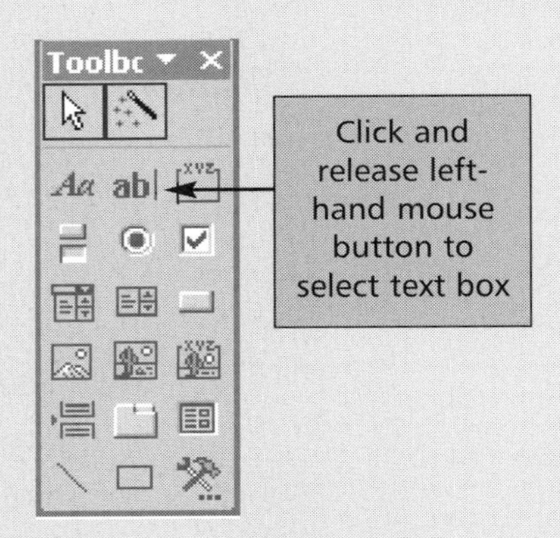

Figure 3.58

Tip: To select and insert the text box into the footer section of the report click on the text box in the toolbar with the left-hand mouse button then release the mouse button. Move the cursor to a position roughly underneath the VALUE column of the report and click the mouse button again.

Access will place an unbound text box in the report as shown in Figure 3.59.

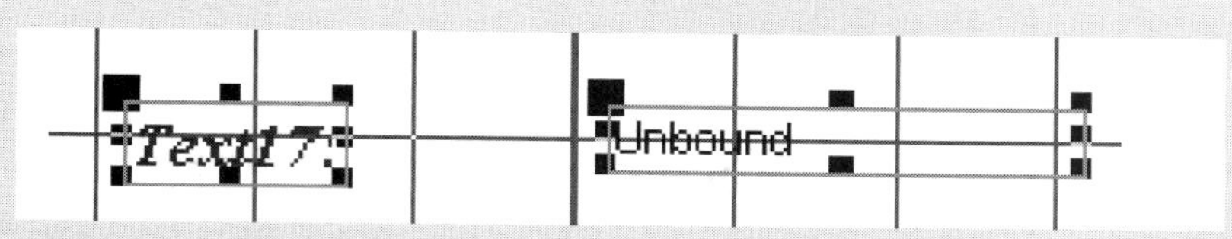

Figure 3.59

On this occasion you will need to make this box bound to a function that will total the value of the items for each group. You may recall using the Expression Builder on page 169 to calculate a cell in a query. In this case you will use the Expression Builder, but this time use one of Access's built-in functions – the sum function.

Click on the text box inserted into the report so that the resize handles appear.

Press the right-hand mouse button to show the menu list.

Select Properties.

Find the Control Source property and click in the cell so that an arrow and an ellipsis (...) are showing.

Click the ellipsis.

In the Expression Builder dialogue box click on Built-in Functions. Notice how in the right column of the dialogue box a variety of functions appear.

Find the Sum function by scrolling down the list.

Double-click on the Sum function.

This sequence is shown in Figure 3.60.

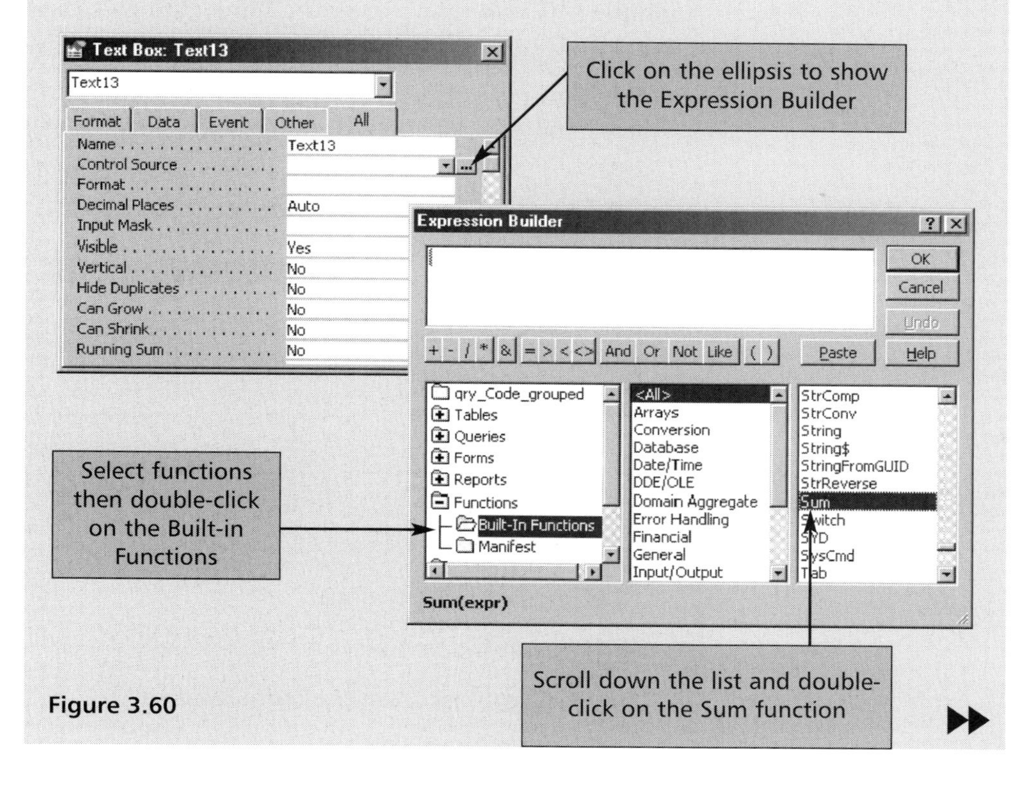

Figure 3.60

Once you have double-clicked on the function required, it is placed in the top Expression Builder box (see Figure 3.61), waiting for you to complete the expression (expr).

Expression Builder
Sum («expr»)

Figure 3.61

Click on 'expr' portion of the expression in the box and it will be highlighted.

Double-click on Reports in the left-hand column.

Double-click on loaded reports.

Click on **qry_Code_Grouped** to display the fields available.

Double-click on VALUE in the centre column.

Click OK. You will then be returned to the text box property box.

The Control Source cell now shows the following formula: =Sum([Value])

Close the property box. Notice how the text in the text box has changed from unbound to display the formula it will use.

Save your report as **rpt_Summary_Grouped**.

You now need to tidy up the position of the text box in relation to the column it is summing and at the same time give the label a more meaningful name.

Position the bound part of the text so that it is slightly to the right of the left-hand edge of the VALUE field, as shown in Figure 3.62.

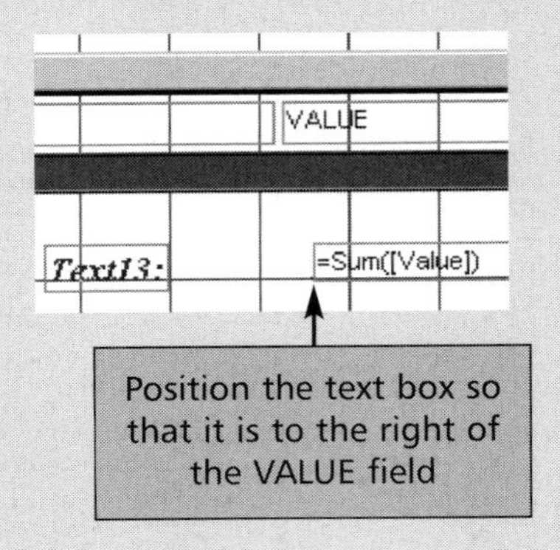
VALUE
Text13:
=Sum([Value])
Position the text box so that it is to the right of the VALUE field

Figure 3.62

Holding the shift key down:

Select both the text box and VALUE field.

Select Align, Left from the Format menu.

The text box and VALUE field are now aligned to the left.

Labels associated with text boxes are bound to the text box. To move the label independently of the text box itself you must click on the large, square handle on the top left of the label, as shown in Figure 3.63.

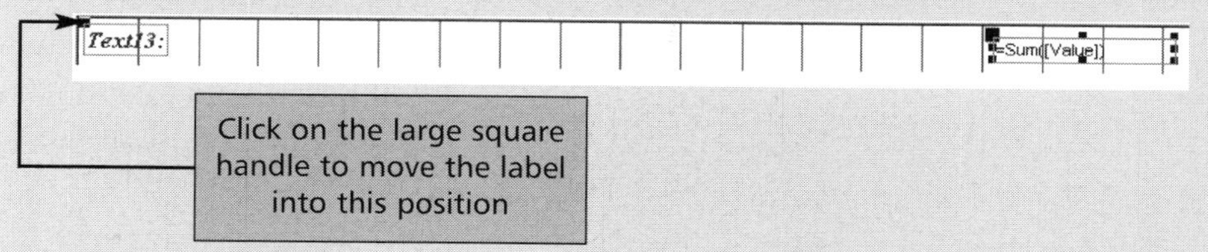

Figure 3.63

Move the label to the position shown in Figure 3.63.

To change the name of the label either click in the label itself and overtype the default text, or right-click on the box and select Properties from the list. In the property box type the required name for the label in the field labelled Caption.

Rename the label as 'Group Total Value'.

This name is now too long for the label box. To resize the box click on it and then using the right-hand central resize square, resize the label so that all the text is displayed.

Adjust the section heights so that you can display the report on one page. To do this follow the same procedure you did when you inserted the group header. You will probably have to change each of the section heights to get the report on one page.

Save the report.

Preview the report. Your report should now look similar to Figure 3.64.

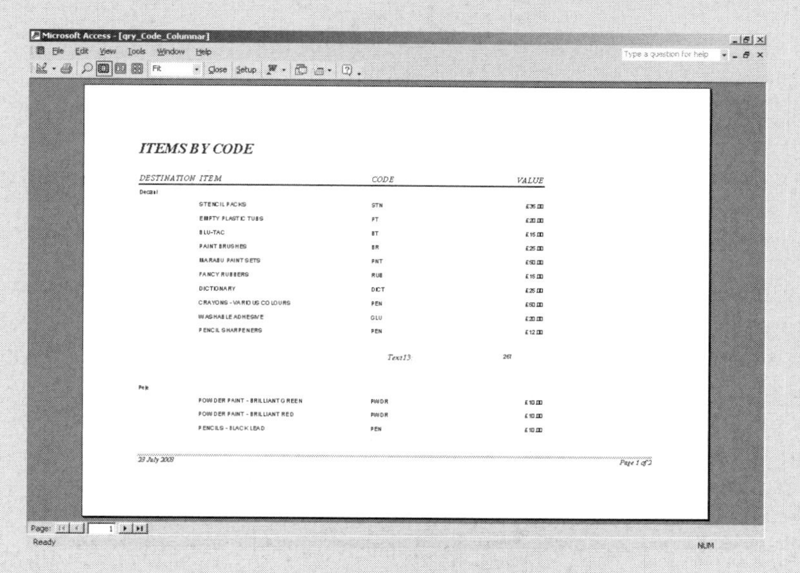

Figure 3.64

Notice that the group footers now display the total value for each group. The value is slightly offset from the actual VALUE field. If you wanted you could change the alignment in each of these fields to suit. To do this size the text boxes so that they are the same width, align them either left or right and then change the text alignment using the properties box.

Sorting data

Earlier in this unit you learnt how to sort data in a query. However, even if you are using a query, with data pre-sorted, as the source for your report you can still change the order of the data at the design stage of building the report.

Have a look at Figure 3.53, **rpt_Code_Tabular**. Remember that this report was based on **qry_Code_Columnar** although the actual report was formatted in a tabular layout. The VALUE column is currently in no fixed sort order.

You are now going to sort the VALUE field into an ascending order.

Try it out

Open rpt_Code_Tabular in design view.

Select Sorting and Grouping from the View menu.

In the first row of the Field/Expression cell:

Click on the arrow to the right of the cell to show the list of fields available.

Select VALUE.

Accept the default order of Ascending: see Figure 3.65.

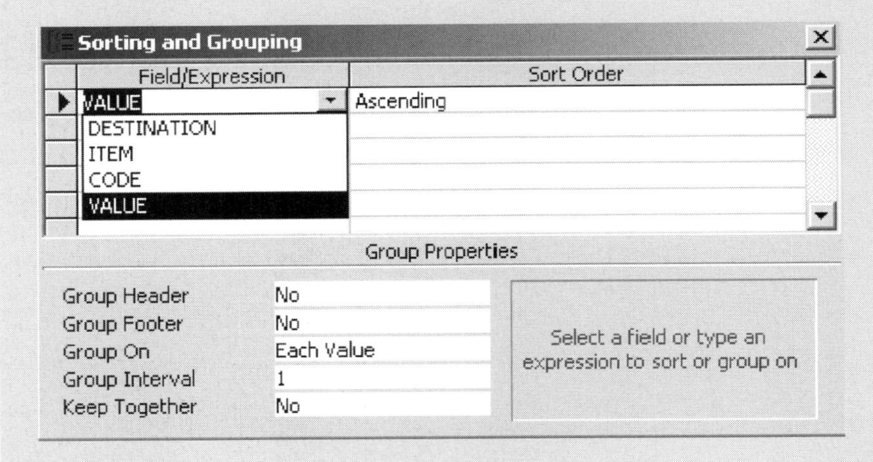

Figure 3.65

Close the dialogue box.

Preview the report.

Notice how each record has now been sorted into ascending order according to the amount in the VALUE field.

Save the report as **rpt_Value_Sorted**.

Close the report and the database.

You should now be able to:

- create a report using the Report Wizard
- change the layout and presentation of a report
- create columnar and tabular reports using the AutoReport function
- create a grouped report
- display summary information as a report
- sort data in a report.

Build-up Exercise 3: Stage 8

Scenario

As the Bursar's assistant for the school on which the WORKS database is based you included the estimated prices for the work to be done in the school budget for the year. You have a Governors' meeting coming up in the next week and the Bursar has asked you to create a report showing the amount of money that has been saved against budget.

Open the WORKS database.

Copy qry_Variation_2 and paste it as a new query with the name **qry_Savings**.

Open qry_Savings in design view and remove the >=20 in the criteria cell for the Variation field so that all variations are shown in the query.

Run the query to satisfy yourself that this is the data on which you want to build your report. The query should have 12 records.

Create a tabular report, based on **qry_Savings**, using the AutoReport function.

Save the report as **rpt_Savings**.

Change the heading of the report to read: 'WORKS SAVINGS AGAINST BUDGET'.

Create a group heading for buildings so that the heading BUILDING only appears once in the report.

Close the gap between the group heading (BUILDING header) and the detail section.

Save the report.

Build-up Exercise 3: Stage 9

Create a summary field to show the total amount of savings arising from the difference between estimate and quote for each building.

Change the default label text to read 'Total savings against budget by building', and position it on the left-hand side of the report.

Make sure that all the text in the label can be seen.

Create a summary field in the Report Footer section which shows the overall saving for all groups.

Tip: use exactly the same technique as for creating a summary in the Group Footer. Click on the text box icon in the toolbox and then click again in the dark grey section under the Report Footer section bar. The report area will increase to take the new text box. The formula is the same as for the group summary, except Access will sum all the variation figures and not just those for the group.

Move the label only of the text box so that it is positioned on the left-hand side of the report.

Change the default label text to read 'Total budget savings'.

Adjust the vertical spacing between sections so that the whole report appears on one page.

Tip: You may have to move some of the data text boxes to adjust the section heights. To move the text box simply click on it and drag it up or down. To ensure that alignment remains constant lasso all fields in a section before moving them.

Save the report.

Your report should now look like Figure 3.66.

WORKS SAVINGS AGAINST BUDGET

BUILDING	*JOB*	*ESTIMATE*	*QUOTE*	*Variation*
BECKER				
	MAKE GOOD PLASTER IN ROOM 6	£80.00	£65.00	-£15.00
	RECARPET	£3,500.00	£3,780.00	£280.00
Total savings against budget by building				265
BISMARK				
	REPAIR GUTTERING	£200.00	£210.00	£10.00
	REPAIR CHIMNEY	£100.00	£80.00	-£20.00
	REPAIR SLATE TO ROOF	£250.00	£350.00	£100.00
Total savings against budget by building				90
DANTE				
	REDECORATION GROUND FLOOR	£1,500.00	£1,700.00	£200.00
	REPAIR FLOOR BOARDS IN ROOM 2	£250.00	£315.00	£65.00
Total savings against budget by building				265
NELSON				
	CHANGE FRONT DOOR LOCK	£30.00	£36.00	£6.00
	REDECORATION FIRST FLOOR	£1,500.00	£1,650.00	£150.00
Total savings against budget by building				156
SAMSON				
	REPLACE BOILER	£1,200.00	£1,190.00	-£10.00
	REPLACE GRND FLOOR WINDOW SILLS	£650.00	£708.00	£58.00
	RENEW GUTTERING	£350.00	£366.00	£16.00
Total savings against budget by building				64
Total budget savings				840

23 July 2003 *Page 1 of 1*

Figure 3.66

Altering orientation and margins of a report

Orientation

Changing the orientation of a report is virtually the same as changing the orientation of a Word document. On the File menu option is another menu item called Page Setup… which, when opened, is fairly self-explanatory. This dialogue box has three tabs: Margins, Page and Columns. For CLAIT Plus you will only be interested in the first two of these.

When building a report through one of the Wizards Access will assess whether the page should be in landscape or portrait orientation. You have already seen how to adjust the width of a data text box and there will be times when the spaces between the fields in your report are really too large to make the report's presentation acceptable. Decreasing the width and repositioning the data text boxes can allow you to change the orientation of the report. However, you must be careful when you produce a report for CLAIT Plus that all the data is legible and can be seen. After changing the width of a text box check to see that you can still see all the contents. Also, when moving data boxes you should ensure that the data in adjoining text boxes is not obscured. Have a go at the following Try it out exercise.

Try it out

Open the Manifest database.

Open rpt_Code_Tabular.

Select Page Setup… from the File menu.

Select the Page tab.

Select Portrait.

Press OK.

Notice how the VALUE field has moved to page 2 of the report, as shown in Figure 3.67.

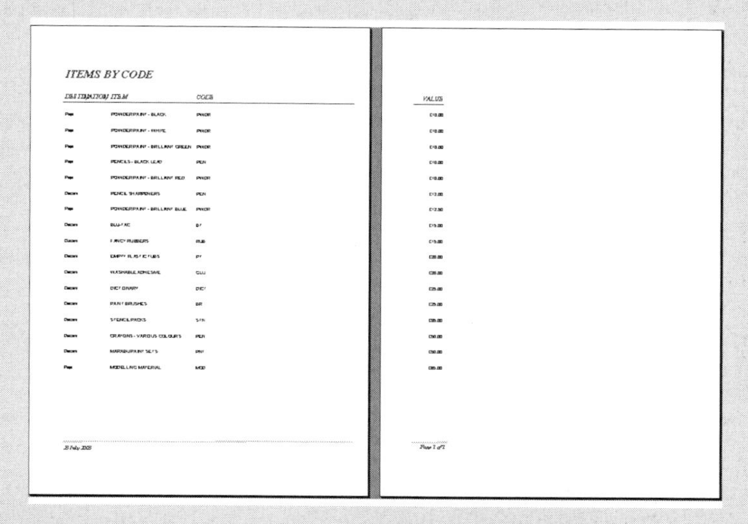

Figure 3.67

To ensure that all the data appears on one page the text box sizes will need to be reduced and repositioned.

Tip: It is always easier to resize and reposition the text boxes before changing the orientation.

Resize the width of the ITEM text box and its associated label to about 5 cm. You can always check this (and indeed change it) using the properties box width property.

Move the ITEM text box and label so that it is immediately to the right of the DESTINATION text box.

Resize both the CODE and VALUE text boxes and labels to about 1.7 cm wide.

Reposition both these boxes and labels so that they follow on immediately from the ITEM text box and label heading.

Resize the automated date field (=Now()) and the Page field.

Reposition both these fields so that the right edge of the Page field does not extend beyond the VALUE text box.

Save the report as **rpt_Code_Tabular_2.**

Lines

You will also have noticed that as part of the report format, Access has included lines to separate the page header data from the detail and the detail from the page footers. Lines are resized in the same way as text boxes. However, some patience is required if you resize them manually as they can change their shape quite easily. You may find that altering the Line Property in the properties dialogue box is an easier method of changing the length of a line. It can then be repositioned without the risk of changing its shape.

You might ask 'Why do you need to alter the line length?'. The working area of the report (that is the white area) cannot be reduced if there are objects preventing it being reduced. If the working area is not reduced it is shown as a part of the report, and when you view the report if it cannot fit onto one page the report will have a 'blank' page as well as the one containing the data. This is both unnecessary and a waste of paper.

So now let's change the line lengths in your report.

Try it out

Resize the lines in the Page Header and Page Footer sections to about 12 cm. If you are manually changing the size make them no longer than the right edge of the VALUE field text box.

Drag the report work area, or grid, as far to the left as it will go. See Figure 3.68.

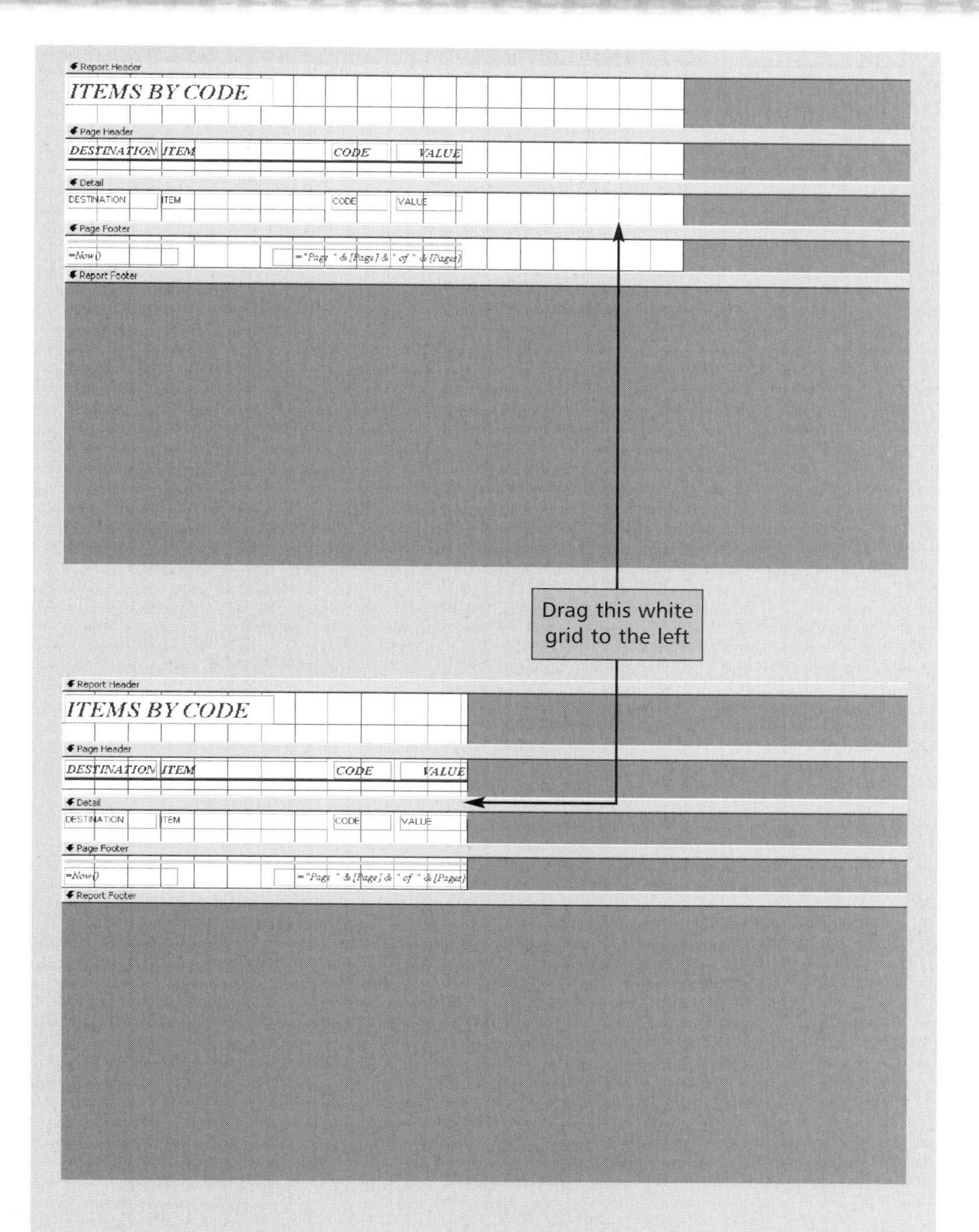

Figure 3.68

Select Page Setup... from the File menu.

Select the Page tab and click on Portrait.

Save the report.

The report should now look similar to Figure 3.69.

ITEMS BY CODE

DESTINATION	*ITEM*	*CODE*	*VALUE*
Peje	POWDER PAINT - BLACK	PWDR	£10.00
Peje	POWDER PAINT - WHITE	PWDR	£10.00
Peje	POWDER PAINT - BRILLIANT GREEN	PWDR	£10.00
Peje	PENCILS - BLACK LEAD	PEN	£10.00
Peje	POWDER PAINT - BRILLIANT RED	PWDR	£10.00
Decani	PENCIL SHARPENERS	PEN	£12.00
Peje	POWDER PAINT - BRILLIANT BLUE	PWDR	£12.50
Decani	BLU-TAC	BT	£15.00
Decani	FANCY RUBBERS	RUB	£15.00
Decani	EMPTY PLASTIC TUBS	PT	£20.00
Decani	WASHABLE ADHESIVE	GLU	£20.00
Decani	DICTIONARY	DICT	£25.00
Decani	PAINT BRUSHES	BR	£25.00
Decani	STENCIL PACKS	STN	£35.00
Decani	CRAYONS - VARIOUS COLOURS	PEN	£50.00
Decani	MARABU PAINT SETS	PNT	£50.00
Peje	MODELLING MATERIAL	MOD	£65.00

24 July 2003 *Page 1 of 1*

Figure 3.69

Margins

Margins for a report are again changed in very much the same way as in a Word document. You have already seen that the Page Setup... dialogue box has a Margins tab: see Figure 3.70.

To change the margin simply type in the appropriate top, bottom, left or right margin size and press OK. However, some care should taken when entering larger margins than the default, as you may cut off data from the report page.

Automated fields

You will have noticed that the reports you have so far produced automatically insert both the date and page number fields. Since these fields are placed in the report's Page Footer they will appear on each

Page Setup
Margins
Page
Columns
Margins (millimeters)
Top: 25.4
Bottom: 25.4
Left: 25.4
Right: 25.4
Sample
Print Data Only
OK
Cancel

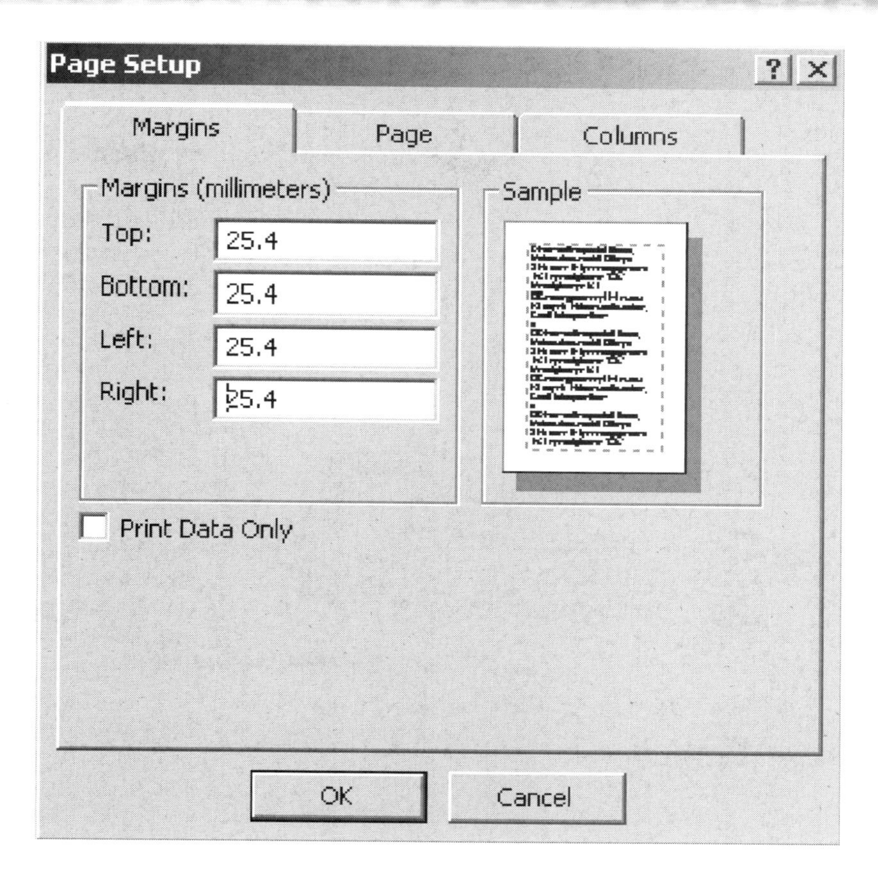

Figure 3.70

page of the report. You can, of course, remove these fields by simply selecting them and pressing the delete key. However, it is more than likely that most reports you produce will need these details as a minimum.

If you are creating a report from scratch the blank report will not already include these automated fields. To insert a page number, click on Insert on the menu bar and select the Page Numbers… option. The dialogue box shown in Figure 3.71 appears.

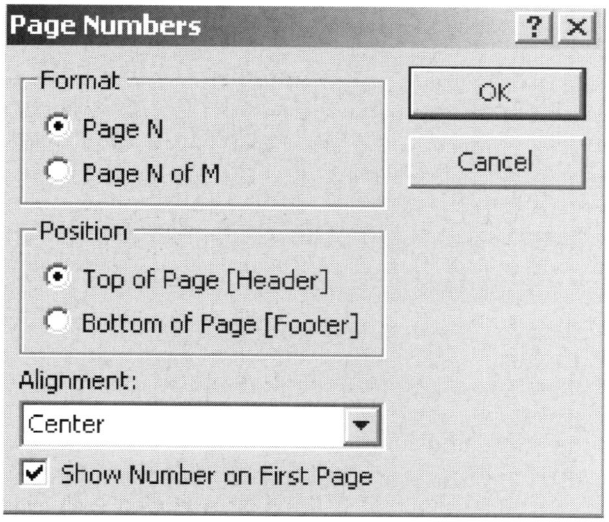

Page Numbers
Format
Page N
Page N of M
OK
Cancel
Position
Top of Page [Header]
Bottom of Page [Footer]
Alignment:
Center
Show Number on First Page

Figure 3.71

The dialogue box is fairly self-explanatory. You have the option of selecting a format with or without the number of pages, the position of the number as either a header or a footer and the alignment. In addition you can select whether or not the number appears on the first page of your report.

In a similar way automated date fields can be inserted. Again, click on Insert on the menu bar and select Date and Time.... The dialogue box shown in Figure 3.72 now appears.

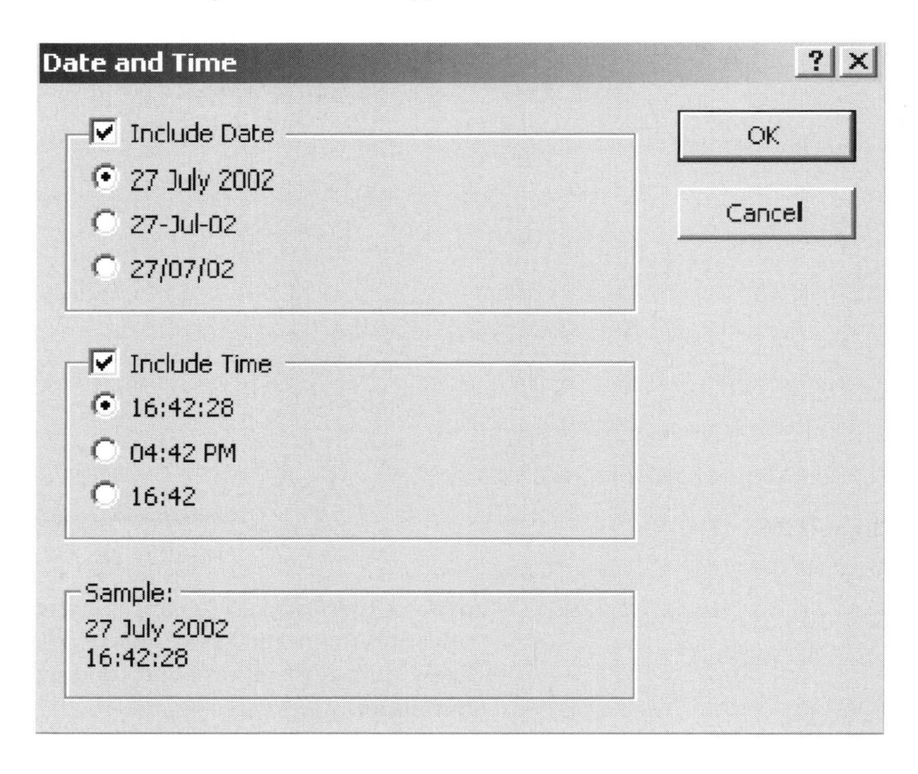

Figure 3.72

Here you are given the choice of date format and whether the time is to be included. If you review the properties of the field after it has been inserted you can see the formula is '=Now()', which is a function available in Access.

You should now be able to:

- change the orientation of a report
- change the margins of a report
- insert automated fields into a report.

Build-up Exercise 3: Stage 10

Open The WORKS database.

Open rpt_Savings in design view.

Change the orientation of the report to Portrait.

Tip: You will need to change the width and position of the fields to ensure that the data does not spread onto a second page.

Change the top, bottom, left and right margins to 2 cm

Save the report as **rpt_Savings_2**.

Your report should now look similar to Figure 3.73.

WORKS SAVINGS AGAINST BUDGET

BUILDING	*JOB*	*ESTIMATE*	*QUOTE*	*Variation*
BECKER				
	MAKE GOOD PLASTER IN ROOM 6	£80.00	£65.00	-£15.00
	RECARPET	£3,500.00	£3,780.00	£280.00
Total savings against budget by building				265
BISMARK				
	REPAIR GUTTERING	£200.00	£210.00	£10.00
	REPAIR CHIMNEY	£100.00	£80.00	-£20.00
	REPAIR SLATE TO ROOF	£250.00	£350.00	£100.00
Total savings against budget by building				90
DANTE				
	REDECORATION GROUND FLOOR	£1,500.00	£1,700.00	£200.00
	REPAIR FLOOR BOARDS IN ROOM 2	£250.00	£315.00	£65.00
Total savings against budget by building				265
NELSON				
	CHANGE FRONT DOOR LOCK	£30.00	£36.00	£6.00
	REDECORATION FIRST FLOOR	£1,500.00	£1,650.00	£150.00
Total savings against budget by building				156
SAMSON				
	REPLACE BOILER	£1,200.00	£1,190.00	-£10.00
	REPLACE GRND FLOOR WINDOW SILL	£650.00	£708.00	£58.00
	RENEW GUTTERING	£350.00	£366.00	£16.00
Total savings against budget by building				64
Total budget savings				840

23 July 2003 *Page 1 of 1*

Figure 3.73

Close the report and database.

That completes all the objectives you will need to know for the databases part of CLAIT Plus. Now try and put the skills you have learnt in this unit into practice by completing the practical assignment below. Solutions to this assignment can be found in Appendix 2.

Practical assignment 3

Databases

Scenario

You are working as a volunteer at the local Citizens Advice Bureau. Many of your recent clients are either unemployed through redundancy or are women returners. Some are reluctant to go to the nearby Job Club and so you have been asked to set up a database of jobs in the local area across a wide spectrum of specialisations.

Task 1

Assessment objectives	Stage	
1a 1b 1c 1d 1f	1	Open Access and create a new database using the field headings shown below. Once you have created the structure set the appropriate field data types. **Field heading** Company – Text Job Code – Text Job – Text Ref – Text Hours – Number (Integer) Close – Date – Short date Basic – Number (currency) – two decimal places Use the following codes for the Job Code data: Administration AD Education ED Health HLTH Management MGT Retail RTL
1e	2	Only enter data where there is a valid Ref for the job.

Table 3.6

Company	Code	Job	Ref	Hours	Close	Basic
Rutland Newspapers	AD	Admin Assistant	001/AS	37	07/03/03	£12,500.00
XEMA	AD	Support Assistant		40	09/03/03	£12,000.00
Northern Cross HCT	AD	Administrator	NCHCT/12	28	22/03/03	£15,200.00
Stainford College	ED	NVQ Assessor	STC/A/12	35	14/03/03	£20,000.00
Deepley NHS (PCT)	HLTH	Nursery Nurse	AHCT02	15	12/03/03	£13,000.00
The Retreat Café	MGT	Assistant Manager	201	40	14/03/03	£16,500.00
Caister Cement	MGT	Laboratory Manager	CCA-52	37	12/03/03	£14,750.00
Steps & Connington	RTL	Store Manager	SM110	40	14/03/03	£17,500.00
Dolphin Supplies	RTL	DIY Sales Person	33301	37	14/03/03	£12,300.00
Create Pictures	RTL	Sales Person	121	35	12/03/03	£10,750.00
Deeply Motors	RTL	Valet Operator		40	12/03/03	£9,500.00

Practical assignment 3

Criteria	Task	Instructions
1f	3	Save the table as **tbl_Jobs**.
2a 2c 2e 1f 4a	4	Produce a report showing all the jobs in the **tbl_Jobs** table. Make the heading for your report - 'Jobs Currently Available'. Save the report as **rpt_All_Jobs**. Group the data in the report in order of Job Code. Sort the jobs by Hours. Ensure all the data and label information is displayed in full.
2d 2b 4e	5	Ensure that your report contains an automatic footer containing the date and page number. Insert a label as a report header with the text: 'For further details contact: Bernard Kane on Ext 34'. Print the report in Portrait orientation.
1a 1b 1c 1e 1f	6	Create a new field in your table between Hours and Close called 'Days per Week'. Data type: Number – Integer Enter the following data for the new field:

Table 3.7

Company	Days per week
Rutland Newspapers	5
Northern Cross HCT	4
Stainford College	5
Deepley NHS (PCT)	3
The Retreat Café	6
Caister Cement	5
Steps & Connington	6
Dolphin Supplies	5
Create Pictures	5

Save the changes made to the table.

Criteria	Task	Instructions
1f 2a 3c 4a 4b 4c 4d 4g	7	Create a query that contains the fields in the following order: Company Job Job Code Close Basic Use an operator that will show only those jobs where the basic salary is equal to or above £11,000. Sort the query by Job Code in ascending order. Save the query as **qry_Jobs_Above_£11000.** Produce a report, in portrait orientation, based on the query in columnar format. Ensure all data is displayed in full.

Practical assignment 3

2b 2c 1f	8	Give your report the heading: "Jobs Available in Excess of £11,000" Ensure all data fields are left-aligned. Border style for data text fields should be transparent. Adjust the size and alignment of data text boxes so that all data can be seen on one page. Save the Report as: **rpt_Jobs_Above_11000**. Print the results of your report.
		You have been asked to find the hourly rate for all administration posts and produce a tabular report to show the results of your work.
3d 3e 4b 4c	9	Create a query that shows all records with the AD code. In your query use the following fields in the order shown: Company Ref Job Job Code Hours Basic Use mathematical operators to calculate the hourly rate for each job. Save the query as **qry_Hourly_Rate_Admin.** Give the calculated field the name 'Hourly Rate'. **Tip:** Hourly Rate is: ([Basic]/52)/[Hours].
1f 2a 2b 2c 4a 4d 4e 2d	10	Use the search results of this query to produce a tabular report in landscape orientation. Set the heading for your report as 'ADMINISTRATION – HOURLY RATES'. Ensure all data is displayed. Set the margins (top, bottom, left and right) to 22 mm. Ensure there is an automatic field footer to show the date and page number. Insert a new footer label with your name between the date and page number. Adjust the gaps between the text boxes and heading labels. Save the report as **rpt_Hourly_Rate_Admin.**

Task 2
Scenario

You are the Secretary for a local golf club. One of your responsibilities is to monitor activity relating to various competitions and make recommendations to the Handicap Committee.

Assessment objectives	Stage	
1a	1	Create a new database called 'Competitions'.
1b 1c		Import the data file called **Competitions.csv** into Access as an imported table and name the imported table **tbl_Competitions.**
1d 3a		The first row of the data file contains the field headings for the new table.
4a		No primary key is required and accept the field headings offered in the csv file.
		Set the data type and properties of fields as shown in Table 3.8.

Table 3.8

Field	Data Type	Properties
Title	Text	5
Initial	Text	5
Name	Text	25
Competition	Text	50
Handicap	Number	(Double) 1 decimal place
Entry Fee	Currency	2 decimal places
Paid	Text	3
Date Paid	Date/Time	Short date
Gross	Number	(Integer) 0 decimal places

Assessment objectives	Stage	
3b	2	It has been agreed by the Management Committee that members who have played a competition but failed to pay the entry fee should be disqualified. Delete all records where the fee has not been paid.
3b	3	You have been advised that one member who did play and has paid their entry fee was accidentally omitted from the list of players. Add this player and relevant data to the table.

Title	Mr
Initial	W
Name	Sparks
Competition	Jul Medal (M)
Handicap	18.4
Entry Fee	£2
Paid	Yes
Date Paid	12/7/03
Gross	98

▶▶

3c **3d**	4	Create a query called **qry_Hdcp_Review** which includes all fields and then add additional fields to calculate the following information: Net is Gross minus Handicap Save the query. Add a new field to the query and calculate the + or - par for each player. Par +/- is Net minus 72. Format as Fixed to 0 decimal places. Save the query. Close the query.
1a **1c** **1d** **1e** **1f**	5	Insert a new field called 'Change' in the table. Data Type is Number (Double) to one decimal place. Save the changes made to the table. Enter data as shown in Table 3.9.

Table 3.9

Title	Initial	Name	Competition	Handicap	Entry Fee	Paid	Date Paid	Gross	Change
Mrs	T	Stirling	Jul Medal (L)	35.4	£2.00	Yes	05/07/03	105	0.3
Mr	P	Gregson	Jul Medal (M)	16.6	£2.00	Yes	08/07/03	86	0.2
Mr	T	Abbott	Jul Medal (M)	15.1	£2.00	Yes	08/07/03	88	–0.1
Mr	D	Savoy	Jul Medal (M)	22.3	£2.00	Yes	10/07/03	95	–0.1
Mrs	P	Abbott	Jul Medal (L)	28.7	£2.00	Yes	10/07/03	115	–0.2
Mr	E	Spink	Jul Medal (M)	18.3	£2.00	Yes	12/07/03	102	0.1
Mr	W	Sparks	Jul Medal (M)	18.4	£2.00	Yes	12/07/03	98	0.1
Mr	R	Downs	Tets Trophy	19.2	£2.00	Yes	17/07/03	89	0.2
Mr	V	Brooks	Tets Trophy	25.9	£2.00	Yes	18/07/03	96	0.2
Mr	G	Strong	Aug Mixed 4s	11.2	£4.00	Yes	21/07/03	84	–0.1
Mrs	F	Strong	Aug Mixed 4s	24.5	£4.00	Yes	21/07/03	95	0.1
Mr	P	Oliver	Tets Trophy	28.4	£2.00	Yes	21/07/03	102	–0.1
Mr	E	Fretter	Tets Trophy	22.4	£2.00	Yes	21/07/03	98	–0.1
Mr	B	Nettle	Aug Mixed 4s	16.2	£4.00	Yes	22/07/03	84	0.3
Mrs	F	Nettle	Aug Mixed 4s	28.3	£4.00	Yes	22/07/03	99	0.1
Mr	G	Johns	Tets Trophy	24.3	£2.00	Yes	22/07/03	96	0.0
Mrs	K	Armitage	Aug Mixed 4s	21.6	£4.00	Yes	23/07/03	91	0.3
Miss	K	Young	Aug Medal (L)	26.4	£2.00	Yes	27/07/03	98	0.0
Miss	L	Good	Aug Medal (L)	18.9	£2.00	Yes	28/07/03	92	–0.2
Mrs	M	Peters	Aug Medal (L)	20.2	£2.00	Yes	29/07/03	105	–0.1
Mrs	D	Freeman	Aug Medal (L)	14.4	£2.00	Yes	30/07/03	96	–0.1
Mrs	S	Woodman	Aug Medal (L)	22.1	£2.00	Yes	30/07/03	102	–0.1

▶▶

Criteria	Task	Instructions
1f 3d	6	Open your query **qry_Hdcp_Review**. Insert the newly created field (Change) into the query. Save the query. Insert a new calculated field to calculate the new handicap. Give the expression field the name: 'New Hdcp'. New Hdcp is Hdcp + Change Print the query.
2a 2b 2c 2d 2e 3e 4b 4c 4d 4f 4g	7	You have been asked to produce a report in tabular format for the club notice board that shows those competitors with a handicap of less than 100. The report is to be sorted by handicap in ascending order. The fields to be included in the report in the order shown are: Competition Title Initial Name Handicap New Hdcp (Format Number Standard to one decimal place) **Tip:** Use the query **qry_Hdcp_Review** as the basis for your new query. Save the query as **qry_Hdcp_Review_2**. Make the appropriate changes to the query. Remember for fields not to be shown in the query (or subsequent report if you are using the AutoReport: Tabular Wizard) deselect the check boxes in the show row of the query grid for those fields that are not to be included. The heading for your report is to be 'HANDICAP CHANGES – JULY AND AUGUST' (point size 18). Group the report by the competition name and use a group header. Set the margins for the report as follows: Top 22 mm Bottom 22 mm Left 20 mm Right 20 mm Ensure your report has a date and page number footer. Insert a text label with your name between the date and page number. Adjust the size alignment of the text boxes and labels in the report so that they fit in portrait orientation onto one page.

Presentation graphics

This unit assumes you have had some experience of using presentation software in New CLAIT or an equivalent level 1 programme. Presentation graphics provides you with the opportunity of using specialist software to produce a variety of slides, from built-in or custom templates, to present data in a format that is informative and holds an audience's attention. CLAIT Plus builds on the skills you will have learnt if you completed New CLAIT or an alternative level 1 programme. The unit covers all five key assessment objectives for CLAIT Plus and the individual objectives contained within them.

Five key assessment objectives

For CLAIT Plus you will need to:

- **Use appropriate software to create a presentation**
  - create a presentation following a specified house style
  - save and name a presentation
- **Set up a master slide layout and style in accordance with a specified house style**
  - follow a specified layout for headings
  - follow specified bullet points
  - apply fonts as specified on each style
  - apply colours as specified on each style
  - apply text alignment as specified on each style
  - apply a background colour
- **Import, insert and manipulate data/graphics and slides**
  - insert or import data
  - edit text
  - insert an adjust a graphic
  - embed a chart
  - embed an organisation chart
  - use tables and columns
  - insert slide numbers
  - insert the date and time
  - find and replace data
  - add, delete or hide a slide
- **Control a presentation**
  - use build facilities
  - use transition facilities
  - apply timings
  - change the order of slides
  - create a hyperlink to access hidden slides

- **Print a presentation and supporting documents**
  - print specified individual printouts of slide(s)
  - print presenter notes
  - print handouts, thumbnails or miniatures
  - screen print to show the use of special effects and timings
  - print in outline view

In this unit you will use Microsoft PowerPoint as an appropriate presentation software.

In this unit you will learn how to:

- set up a master slide
- apply a house style
- apply a background colour or template
- apply and reapply styles
- insert and import data
- insert images into a presentation
- edit images
- import text into a presentation
- apply a bullet style
- insert a new slide in a specified location of the presentation
- use charts and tables in a presentation
- use the find and replace function to edit data
- find and replace data
- use automatic and custom fields
- control a presentation
- use the build functions
- automate build effects
- set the timings for effects
- change the order of slides in a presentation
- delete and hide slides
- create hyperlinks within a presentation to navigate to hidden slides
- use transition facilities
- print presentation support documents.

Understanding house styles and setting up a master slide

If you have already completed earlier units you should be familiar with the concept of house styles. It is unlikely that you will see a professional corporate presentation, publication or document that does not conform to a style identifying the company or organisation to which it belongs. Advertising, whether it is sportswear, cars or toiletries, relies heavily on the fact that people associate with an image. House styles are an extension of this and also ensure consistency in the presentation of information. PowerPoint provides a facility called the Slide Master which allows you to prepare a template for a presentation whereby text and images (such as logos) conform to a standard pattern throughout your presentation. It is worth remembering that using a large variety of different styles in terms of colour, text or other objects can seriously detract from the impact a presentation has on an audience.

Those watching a slide presentation want to have information imparted to them on the subject and not a demonstration of how clever the creator of the presentation is at using the software.

Setting up the Slide Master view

First create a new PowerPoint presentation. In PowerPoint XP a new blank presentation is automatically opened with a title slide ready for you to start building your presentation. To view the Slide Master, select View, Master, Slide Master from the main menu. You may have noticed that other selections include Handout Master and Notes Master. These are variations of the Slide Master and you will be introduced to handouts and presenter guidance notes towards the end of this unit when you learn about printing presentation support documents.

The Slide Master provides consistency for headings, sub-headings, text formats and styles. Placeholders are boxes with dotted or hatched borders that usually form part of slide layouts. Placeholders can include a variety of objects such as titles, body text or charts, tables and pictures.

Remember that the Slide Master is a part of the overall design template and is not used to input text or other objects directly unless they are to form part of the style for the presentation. Information included as part of the presentation is input in the normal view for a slide. This will become clearer as you go through the unit. Figure 5.1 shows the basic components of the Slide Master.

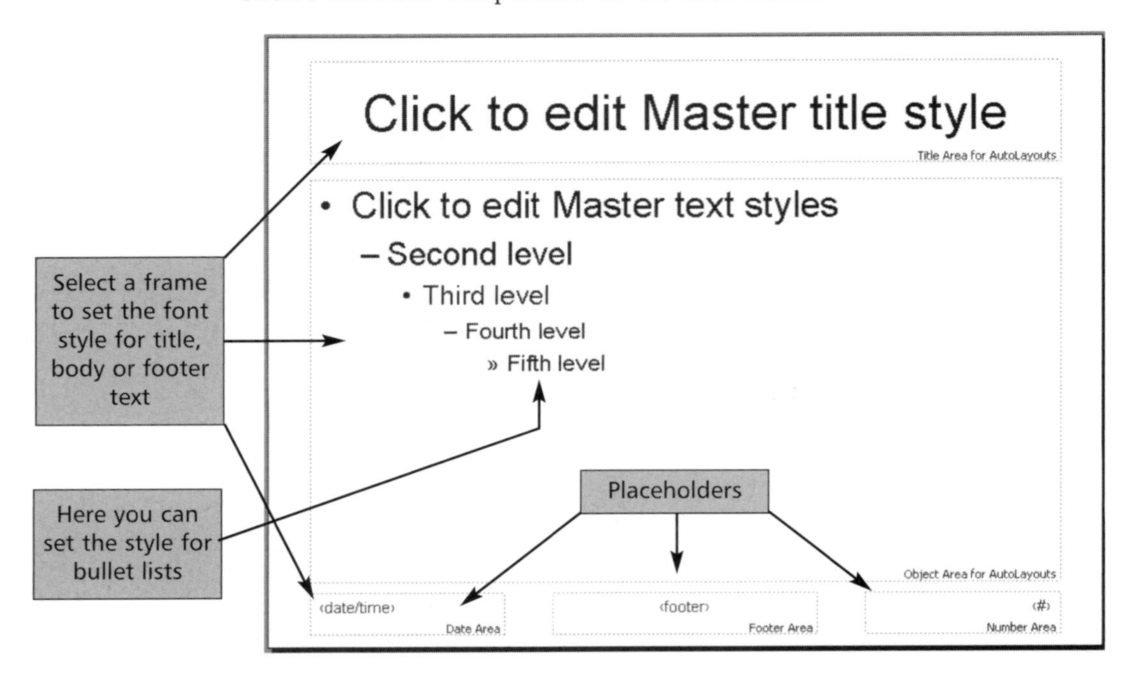

Figure 5.1

Applying a house style

For CLAIT Plus you are required to set up a Master Slide layout to a specified house style. The easiest way to understand how this is done is to follow a hand-holding Try it out exercise.

Try it out

You are going to set up a Master Slide based on the house style shown in Table 5.1.

Brief for Master Slide

Table 5.1

Style	Font style	Font size	Emphasis	Alignment
Title	Sans serif	42	Bold, underlined	Left
Bullet – level 1	Sans serif	28	No emphasis	Left
Bullet – level 2	Sans serif	24	No emphasis	Left
Bullet – level 3	Sans serif	20	No emphasis	Left
Bullet – level 4	Sans serif	16	Italic	Left
Background	Colour	RGB	R-220, G239, B240	

FORMAT TIP

Remember: To change the font for a title or level, click on the text in the title or level and the text will be highlighted. Use the toolbar or menu options to change the font.

Open a new presentation file.

Save the file as **SafeHome.ppt**.

Select the master view.

Click in the placeholder for the master title area and format the font to Arial, size 42 point, underlined and bold.

Click in the Object Area frame and amend the various bullet levels as shown in Table 5.1 but do not change the background at this stage.

Your Master Slide should now look like Figure 5.2.

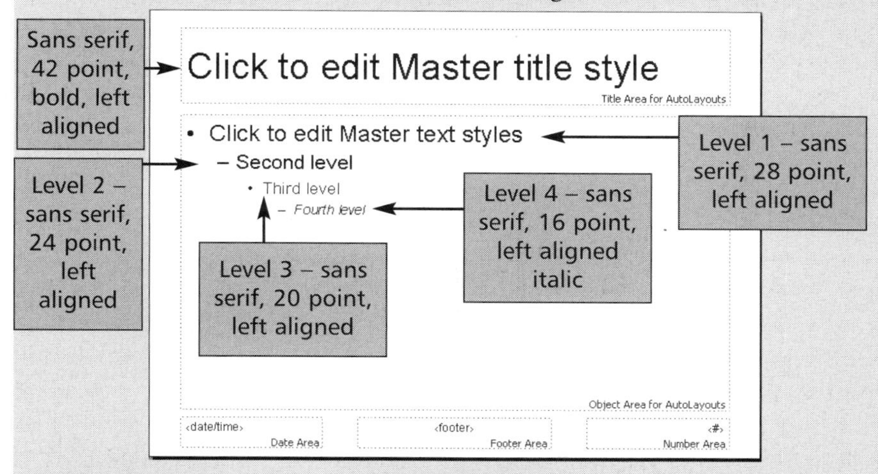

Figure 5.2

Save the presentation and return to the normal slide view by View, Normal on the main menu.

Saving a presentation

Saving a presentation is carried out in exactly the same way as saving a file in other Microsoft applications (with the exception of Access). Select File, Save from the main menu and in the Save dialogue box select the folder where the presentation is to be saved and then type in the name of your presentation in the File name: box. The file type will by default show Presentation (*.ppt). This is the file type used in PowerPoint. The equivalent in Word would be *.doc.

Applying a background colour or template

PowerPoint offers a wide range of backgrounds to your slides. These include:

- background single colour
- background, two colour or preset gradients
- patterns
- textures
- pictures

Backgrounds can either be set as part of the Slide Master template or in the Normal view of slides. If you choose to set the background in the Slide Master it will be consistently applied to all slides in the presentation unless you instruct PowerPoint to omit a background for a particular slide or group of slides. Backgrounds set in the Normal view of a slide can be applied to the single slide, or all slides as appropriate.

To access the options for the background select Format, Background... from the main menu and the Background dialogue box shown in Figure 5.3 appears.

By clicking on the arrow to the right of the fill colour option a list of choices is offered as shown in Figure 5.4.

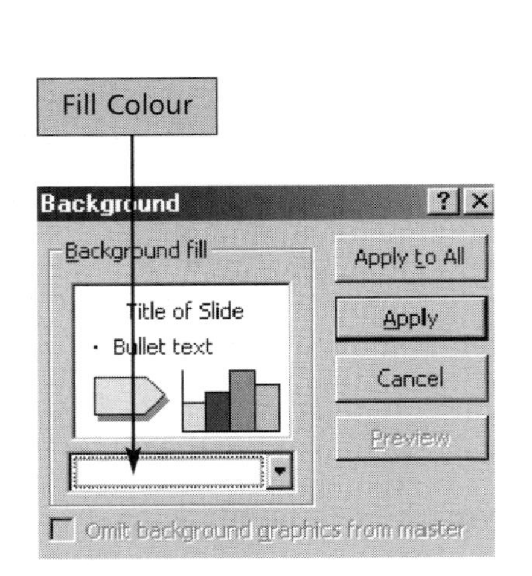

Figure 5.3

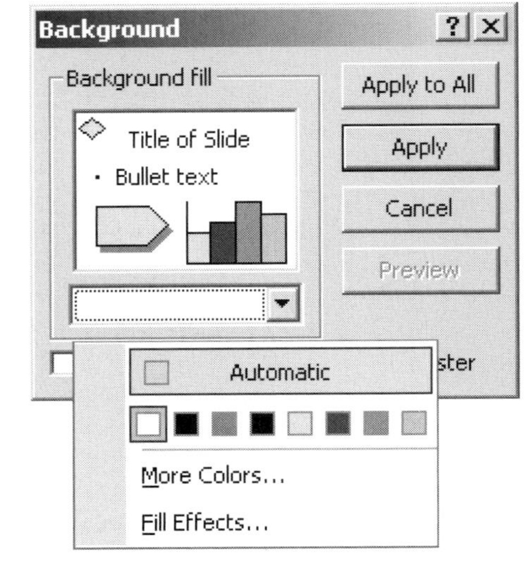

Figure 5.4

Colours

You can choose one of the colours in the top part of the box, select More Colours… or Fill Effects… . Selecting the More Colours option will bring up the colour palette which you may have seen in other applications. By clicking on a colour in the palette, using the left-hand mouse button, you can select the required colour. The box on the right of the dialogue box shows the original colour and the new one: see Figure 5.5.

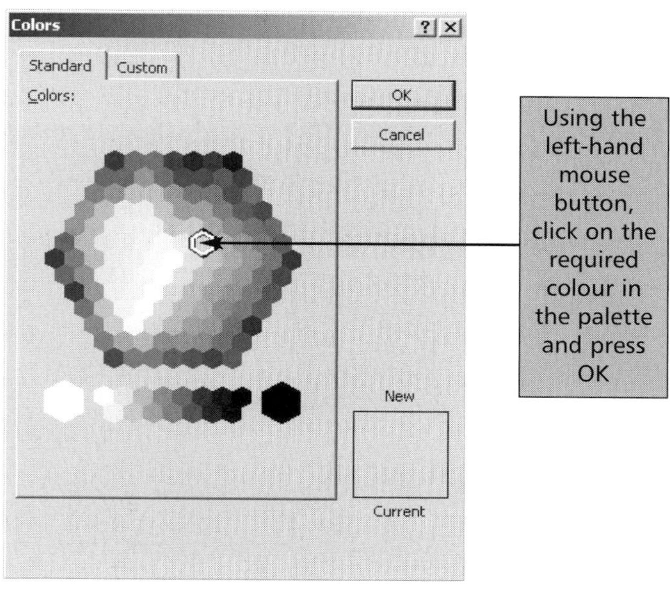

Figure 5.5

Alternatively you can use the Custom tab and either drag the cursor around the palette or enter the desired RGB colour codes (if these are known) as shown in Figure 5.6.

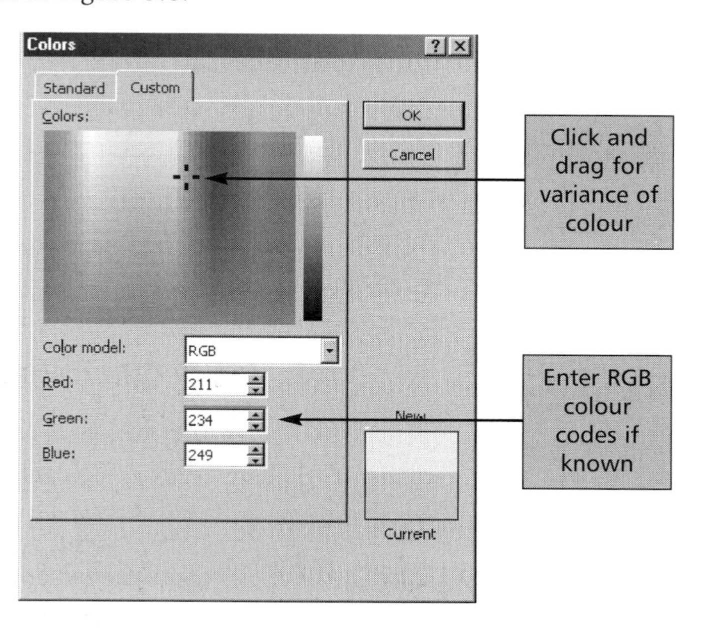

Figure 5.6

Fill effects

If the Fill Effects… option is chosen then another dialogue box appears, as shown in Figure 5.7.

This dialogue box has four tabs each providing a different type of fill effect. Gradient effects can be extremely effective and simple to create. You have the choice of selecting a colour and then customising it as shown above, or alternatively you can use one of PowerPoint's preset colours such as nightfall, daybreak, ocean, fire and so on. Once the two colours have been selected (either using the Two colours or Preset options), there are a variety of shading styles you can choose:

- horizontal
- vertical
- diagonal to 'from corner' and 'from title'.

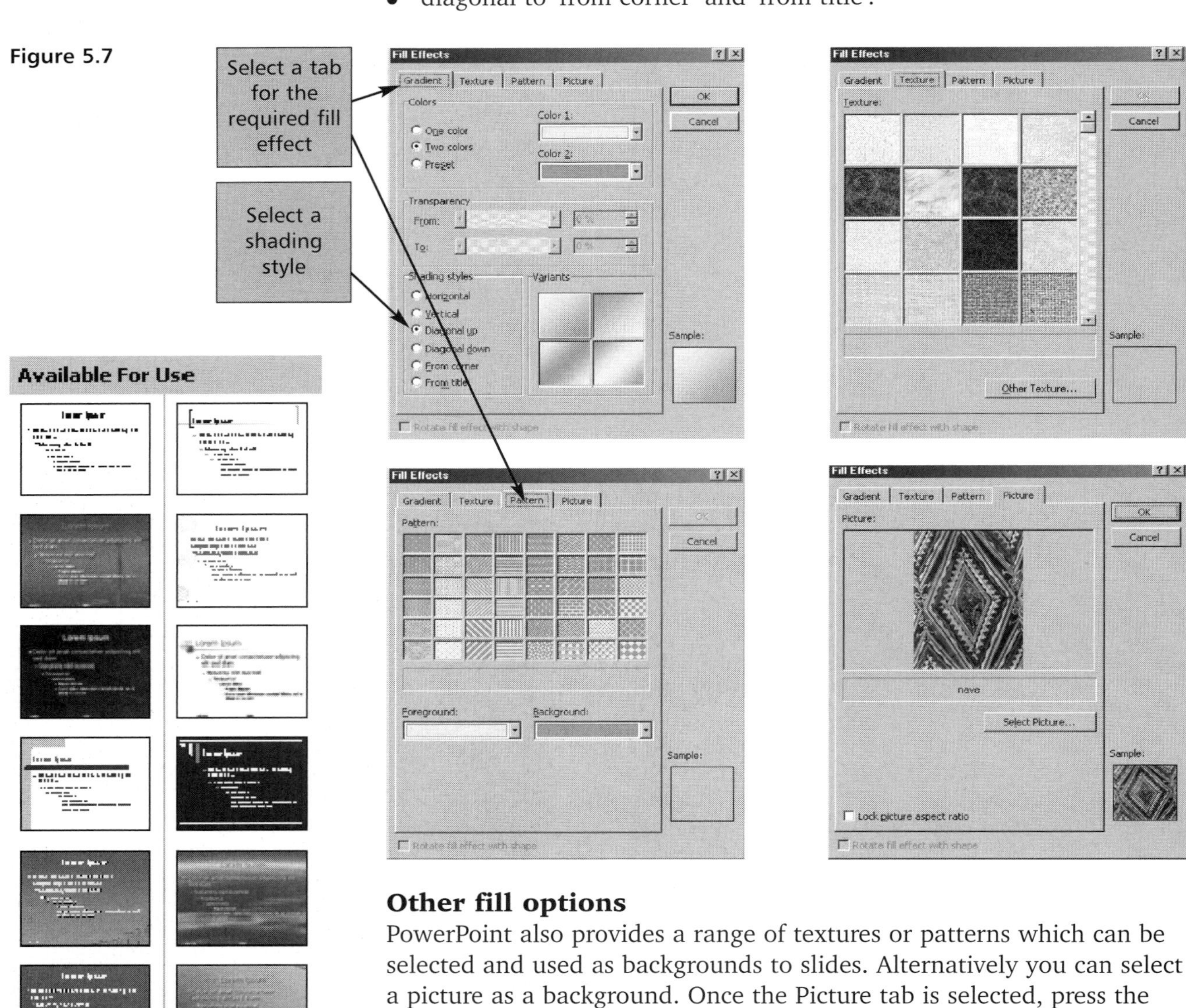

Figure 5.7

Figure 5.8

Other fill options

PowerPoint also provides a range of textures or patterns which can be selected and used as backgrounds to slides. Alternatively you can select a picture as a background. Once the Picture tab is selected, press the Select Picture... button and then choose a picture from the appropriate directory on your disk.

If you choose not to use any of these options you can select one of PowerPoint's built-in slide designs. These are selected by pressing the Design icon Design or selecting Slide Design... from Format on the main menu and then choosing one of the built-in design templates shown in Figure 5.8.

The background you use for a slide is either determined by a specified house style or relies on your skill to make the presentation come alive for the audience. However, for CLAIT Plus the important thing is that your slide background is consistent for all the slides in the presentation. It is also important that the colour chosen does not hinder the viewer's ability to read the information or data on the slides.

Reapplying a style

As you have seen, you can either create your own style template based on a specified house style or you can use one of PowerPoint's built-in styles. You can reapply any of these templates irrespective of the current template in use.

Reapplying styles can, of course, significantly reduce the amount of work needed for a new presentation if such a design template is already available.

To save a file as a template simply select the File and Save As... from the main menu. Once the Save dialogue box appears choose the Design Template (*.pot) in the Save as type: field. Select the folder in which the template is to be saved and give your template a name which will make it easy to locate later on. The template will then be saved for you to re-use at a later date.

Now try to apply the background to the **SafeHome.ppt** file.

Try it out

Open SafeHome if it is not already open.

Select View, Master, Slide Master from the menu.

Select Format, Background from the menu.

Select More Colours... from the drop list.

Select the Custom tab.

Enter Red: 220
Green: 239
Blue: 240

Press OK.

Press Apply.

Select View, Normal from the menu.

Save the presentation.

You should now be able to:

- open a new presentation
- access the Slide Master
- set up fonts as specified in a house style

- set up bullets as specified in a house style
- apply a background to the Slide Master
- create and save a template
- reapply a style.

Build-up Exercise 5: Stage 1

Create a new presentation.

Save the presentation as **First_Aid**.

Setup the Slide Master using the house style shown in Table 5.2.

Style for Master Slide

Table 5.2

Style	Font style	Font size	Font colour (RGB)	Emphasis	Alignment
Title	Serif	40	Dark blue (0, 43, 130)	Bold	Centre
Bullet - level 1	Serif	22	Dark blue (0, 43, 130)	No emphasis	Left
Bullet - level 2	Serif	18	Dark blue (0, 43, 130)	No emphasis	Left
Bullet - level 3	Serif	14	Dark blue (0, 43, 130)	No emphasis	Left
Bullet - level 4	Serif	12	Dark blue (0, 43, 130)	Italic	Left
Background	Colour	Two tone	Top: 255, 255, 255	Bottom: 102, 153, 255	Diagonal up

Return to the Normal view for slides.

Save your presentation.

Importing, inserting and manipulating data, graphics and slides

Inserting and importing data

Having set up the master for a presentation, inserting text and bullet points is straightforward and something you will have already covered if you completed the New CLAIT programme. PowerPoint provides a range of preset slide layouts. These include those that can contain text, objects such as images and charts, or both objects and text. Figure 5.9 shows those that are readily available for you to use.

Most presentations start with a title slide of some description. When you open PowerPoint to start a new presentation the screen will initially show the title slide layout for you to start inputting the title of the presentation. This is the first slide. To the left of the screen are two tabs, one named Outline and the other Slides. These display the contents of each slide and also all the slides in a presentation. The Outline, as the name suggests, simply displays an outline of the text in

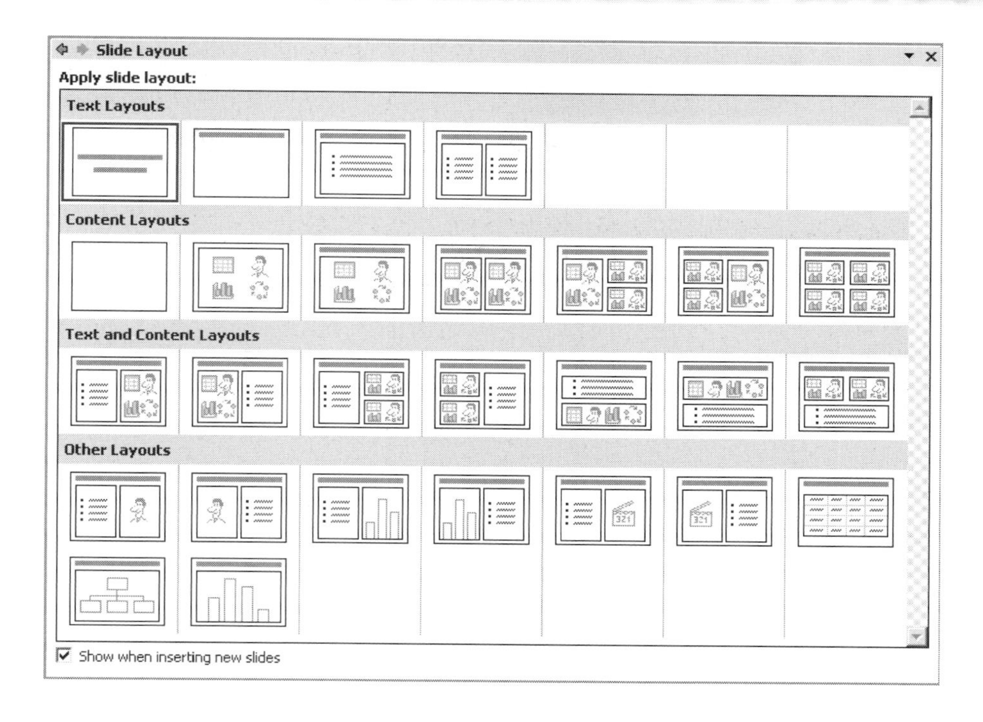

Figure 5.9

a slide, while the Slides tab shows a thumbnail of slide content including charts and images.

Unlike a wordprocessing document, text and objects are inserted into a slide through the use of text and object frames. In the Normal view, and before any text has been inserted, PowerPoint shows the make-up of the slide layout. Have a look at Figure 5.10.

The first slide is designed only to accept text, the middle slide also accepts text, but is formatted so that the second frame is used for bullet text. In the third slide you can select one of the small images to insert that object. Additional text or object frames can be added to a layout at any time. You will be covering these other objects shortly, but for now you are only interested in the slide designed for text. Now try to insert some text and bullet points into a title and bullet slide.

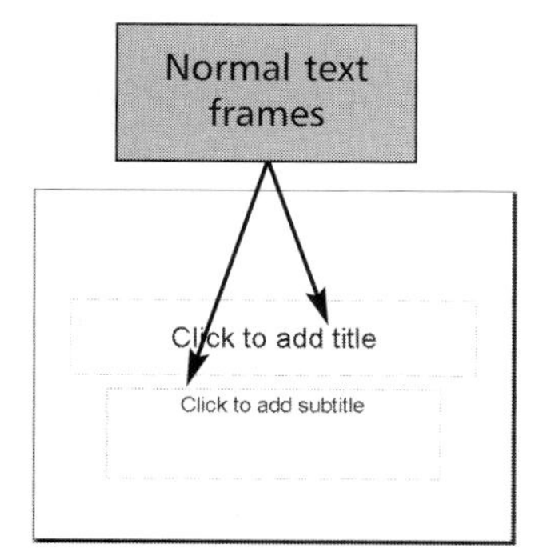

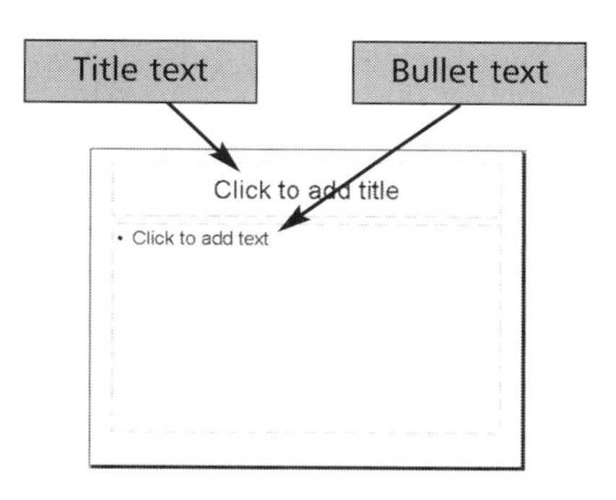

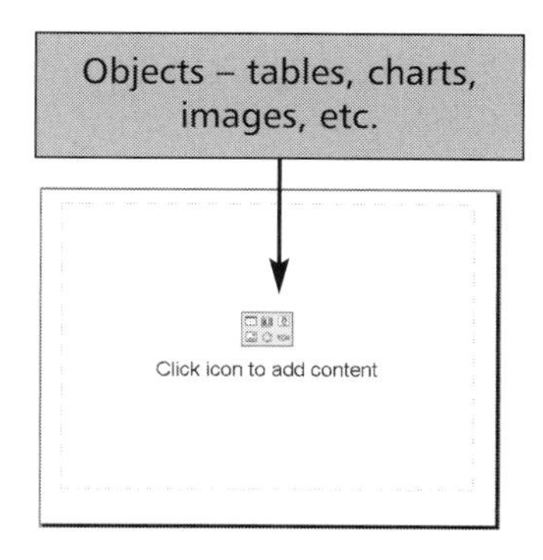

Figure 5.10

Try it out

Open the **SafeHome** presentation.

Click on the first frame, which says 'Click to add title'.

Type 'Make your home safe'.

Notice how the text is automatically formatted to the Slide Master you setup earlier.

Click on the second frame and add your name.

Now click outside the frame for the text to be accepted.

Select Insert, New Slide from the menu. (Alternatively press the new slide toolbar icon New Slide or use the keyboard shortcut Ctrl+M.)

By default, PowerPoint inserts the bullet text slide. If you require a different slide simply select the desired slide from one of the slide layouts shown in the task pane.

Click on the title frame and type 'The basics'.

Click on the bullet frame.

The cursor automatically starts at the top left with a new bullet point, awaiting text. Again, PowerPoint follows the instructions it has been given from the Slide Master. On this occasion, however, you do not want a bullet for the first line. To deselect the bullet, click the bullet icon on the toolbar.

Type 'When you leave your house check:'

Press Enter to insert a new line.

Now you want the second level bullet so:

Click on the bullet icon to reactivate the bullet text.

Press the Tab key to take you to the second level of bullet text. (Alternatively you can click on the promote/demote icon from the toolbar.)

Type 'All non programmed domestic appliances are switched off.'

Press Enter to create a new bullet point line.

Press the Tab key again to demote to the third level of bullets.

Enter the following bullet points:

- Cooker
- Dishwasher
- Washing machine
- Electric fires

Your slide should now look similar to Figure 5.11.

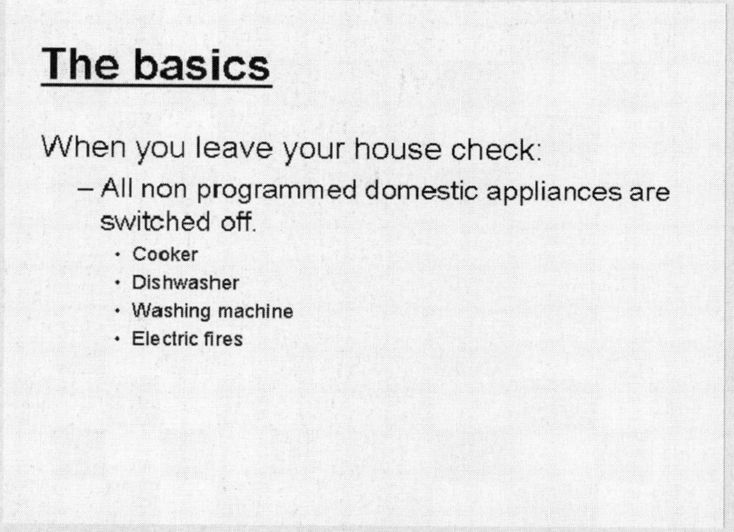

The basics

When you leave your house check:

– All non programmed domestic appliances are switched off.

- Cooker
- Dishwasher
- Washing machine
- Electric fires

Figure 5.11

Save the file.

Inserting images into a presentation

Images of various types can be imported into a slide. Perhaps the four most common image formats are bitmap (.bmp), GIFF (.gif), Windows Metafile (.wmf) and JPEG (.jpg). To insert an image into a slide use the Insert, Picture option on the menu or alternatively click on either the picture or clip art icon on the drawing toolbar. Using Insert, Picture from the menu offers a menu list with a variety of number options. For this unit you will only be interested in those relating to Clip Art... and From File... .

Clip art

Microsoft Office comes complete with a fairly large library of clip art images. The way in which your software was installed will govern how many images are available on your hard disk and how many need to be accessed from the software's installation disks. First try importing an image into your **SafeHome** presentation Slide Master.

Try it out

Open SafeHome if it is not already open.

Open the Slide Master view.

Select Insert, Picture, Clip Art from the menu options.

The first thing that happens is that you will see the Insert Clip Art task pane appear on the right of your screen (see Figure 5.12).

In the Search text: field:

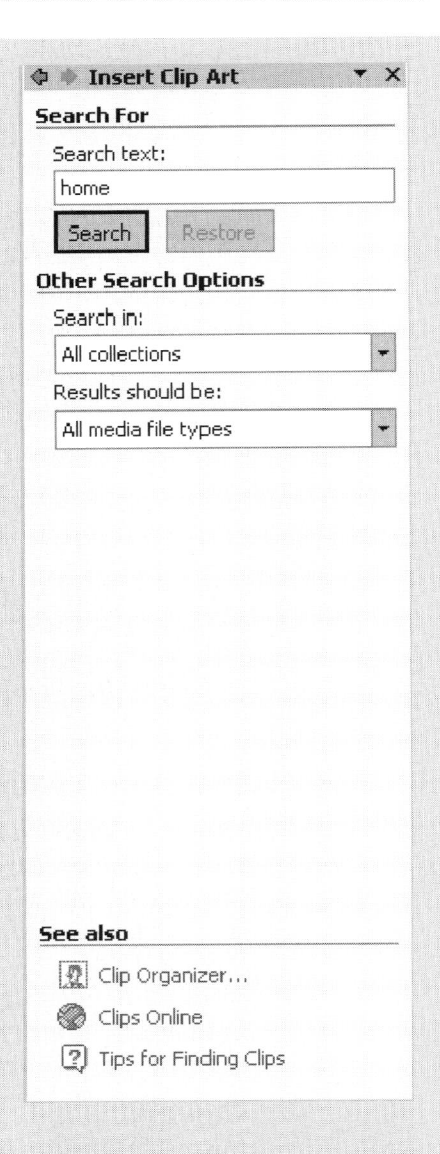

Figure 5.12

Type 'House'.

Amongst the images available you should see one similar to Figure 5.13.

Figure 5.13

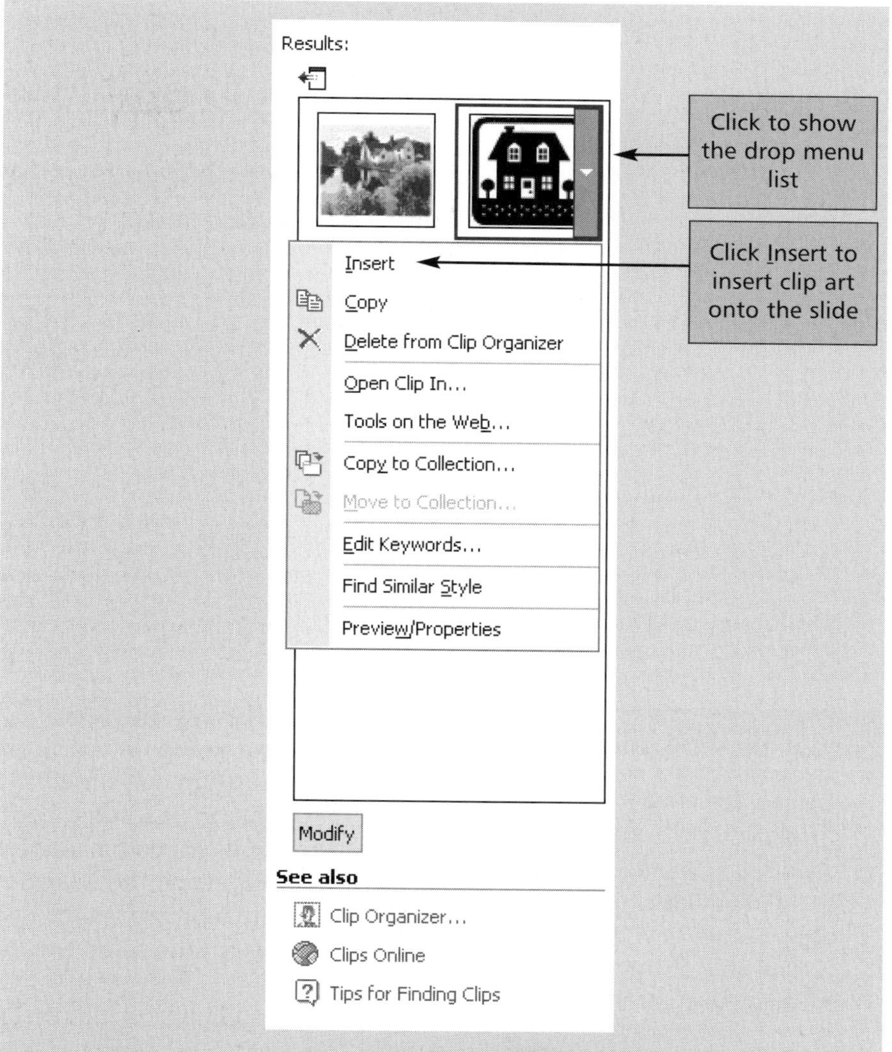

Figure 5.14

By selecting one of the images an arrow will appear to the right of the image. Clicking on the arrow activates the drop menu list as shown in Figure 5.14.

Select the house image (if your library does not have this particular image then select a suitable alternative).

Click on Insert.

The image will be placed on the Slide Master.

With the image selected:

Drag the image to the bottom right of the Slide Master as shown in Figure 5.15.

Save the file.

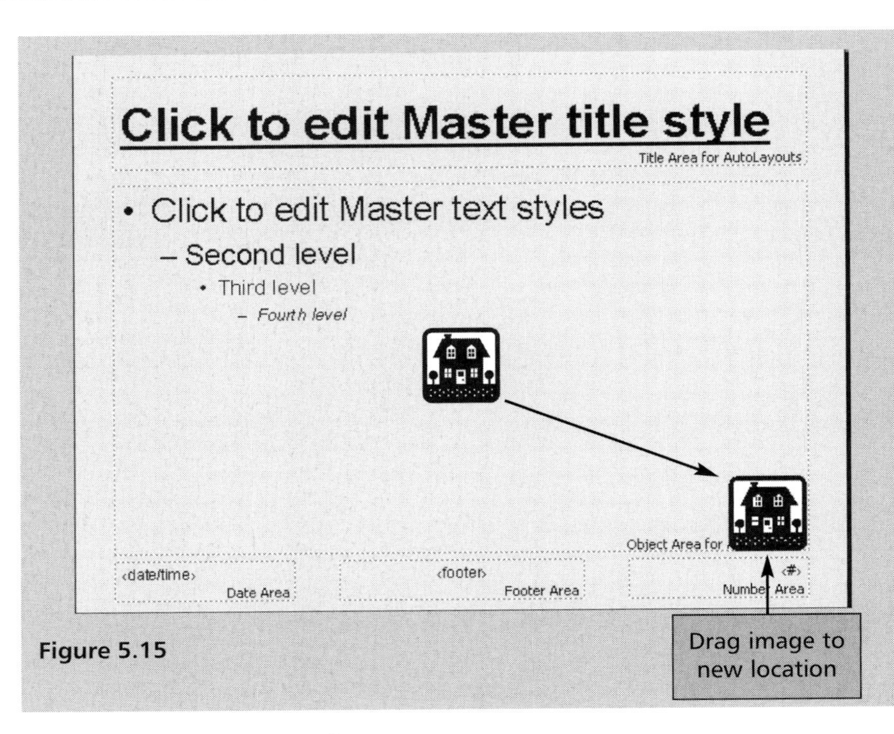

Figure 5.15

> **MOUSE TIP**
>
> As you have found with most options involving objects, an alternative way to insert an object (in this case a picture) is to double-click on it instead of pressing the insert button.

Non clip art library images

To insert an image stored on a disk (floppy, hard or CD) a very similar process to inserting clip art is followed. First select Insert, Picture from the main menu, but instead of selecting Clip Art…, select From File… . The Insert Picture dialogue box appears and using the Look in: field select the folder in which the image is stored. Having found the right folder, click on the required image and press Insert. The image will be placed on the slide in the same way as when you used the insert Clip Art option.

Try inserting an image using the From File... option.

Try it out

Open SafeHome if it is not already open.

Insert a new slide based on title and bullet points.

Enter 'Keys' in the title text box.

Click on the toolbar bullet icon to deselect the bullet format.

Type 'Make sure you':

Press Enter.

Click on the bullet icon.

Enter the following bullet points:

- Keep your keys safely.
- Give a spare set to someone you trust.
- Check that you have keys to all doors and windows.
- Check all keys operate locks properly.

- Put both keys in use and spare keys on a strong key ring.

Save the presentation.

You are now going to place an image into the slide in the Normal view as opposed to the Master view because the image is specific to this slide. If you inserted it on the Slide Master it would appear on all slides in the presentation.

Select Insert, Picture, From File...

Locate the image **Keys.gif** from the folder on the CD accompanying this book.

Click on the image.

Press Insert (or double-click on the image): see Figure 5.16.

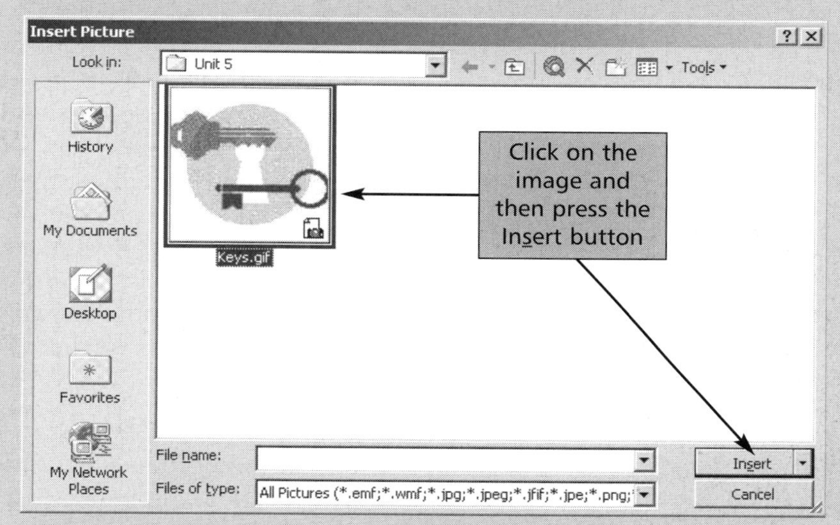

Figure 5.16

The image is inserted into the slide and the bullet text frame has been adjusted to accommodate the picture. Don't worry about the bullet text frame or image's size for now as you will be learning how to resize these in the next section.

Save and close the presentation.

Editing images

You have already seen that all the data in a slide is managed through frames, whether these relate to text or images. Any of these frames can be edited by changing their position, size or other properties such as borders, fill colour and so on. For CLAIT Plus you are expected to know how to import and then edit imported files, whether text or graphic based.

Resizing an image

Except in special circumstances, when you are resizing an image you will normally want to keep the image's original height and width proportional. Have a look at Figure 5.17 on page 228.

Original

Size reduced in proportion

Size reduced not in proportion

Figure 5.17

The first copy (middle image) has been reduced in size in proportion to the original whereas the second copy (on the right) is not in the same proportions as the original.

Images can be resized either by using the mouse and drag technique or setting specific sizes using the Format Picture dialogue box. When using the drag technique, if you want to keep the image's proportions you must use one of the corner drag handles. If you use the handles in the middle of the top, bottom or sides of the image then the image will become distorted from its original proportions.

Rotating an image

In Office XP when an image is selected an additional drag handle appears at the top of the image. This is known as the free rotate handle. It appears from the centre top drag handle with a line to a small green circle. When you place the cursor over this green circle the cursor changes shape to a circular arrow. By clicking and holding down the left-hand mouse button you can rotate the object to any required degree.

If you need to set an image to a specific angle of rotation you will need to use the Format Picture dialogue box (see Figure 5.22). Beneath Height in the Size and rotate section is the Rotation field where you can enter a specified angle of rotation for your image.

Try it out

Open a blank presentation.

Change the title first slide to a blank slide from the Content Layouts selection.

Select Insert, Picture, From File… .

Select the **Bell.jpg** image in Unit 5 from the accompanying CD.

Making sure the image is selected (i.e. the size handles are visible)

Click on one of the corner size handles and reduce the size of the picture in proportion to the original to about half the original's size.

With the image still selected and using right-hand mouse button

Click on the image.

Select Format Picture from the list.

Click on the Size tab.

Making sure the Lock aspect ratio check box in the Scale section is checked

Type '6cm' in the Height field.

The width will automatically change to maintain the ratio.

Click OK to accept the changes.

Move the cursor so that it is positioned over the free rotate handle at the top of the image.

Rotate the image by approximately 180°.

Once you are happy rotating the image using the free rotate handle return the image to its original position. When the image is back to its original position:

Open the Format Picture dialogue box by clicking on the image using the right-hand mouse button and clicking on Format Picture… in the drop menu list.

Select the Size tab on the dialogue box.

Click in the Rotation: field in the Size and rotate section.

Replace 0° with 45°.

Press OK and the image will rotate by 45°.

Close the presentation.

Save your presentation as **Bell**.

Positioning an image

Positioning an image at a specified location is virtually the same as resizing an image. Again, the Format Picture dialogue box is used but instead of the Size tab, the Position tab is selected. There are four fields on view:

Horizontal: From:
Vertical: From:

Enter the relative horizontal position to either the top-left corner or centre of the slide. Then enter the vertical position. The picture will move to the required location after the OK button has been pressed.

Try it out

Open the **Bell** presentation.

Right-click on the bell image.

Select Format Picture.

Select the Position tab in the dialogue box.

Enter the following:

Horizontal: 4 cm
Vertical: 1 cm

Press OK.

The picture has now moved to the new location.

Save the presentation.

Cropping an image

There will be occasions when you have a picture that includes parts that you don't want or need. Cropping allows you to reduce the amount of a picture that is shown on the screen or printed. Cropping does not remove that part of the picture but simply restricts the amount seen and printed. Have a look at Figures 5.18a and 5.18b.

Figures 5.18a and b

The picture on the left is the original and the figure to the right has been cropped to remove the glasses.

To crop a picture first select it so that the drag handles appear. Also by selecting the picture the Picture toolbar shown in Figure 5.19 appears.

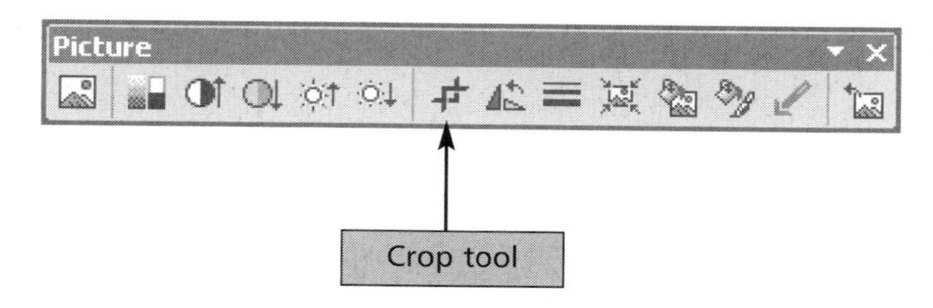

Figure 5.19

Select the crop tool and move it over the drag handle where you want the first crop to take place to reduce the height. Next with the left-hand mouse button held down, drag the crop tool to the point where the picture is to be cropped. Repeat this process for the width: see Figure 5.20.

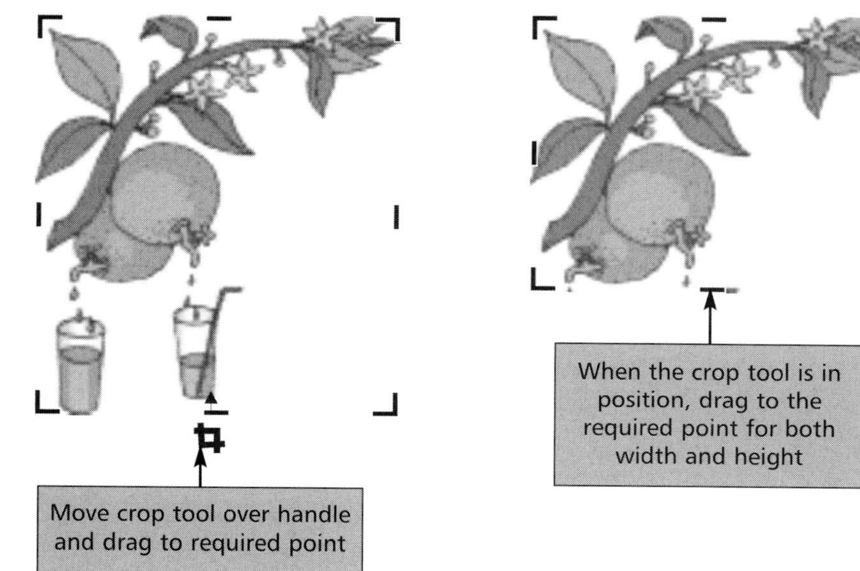

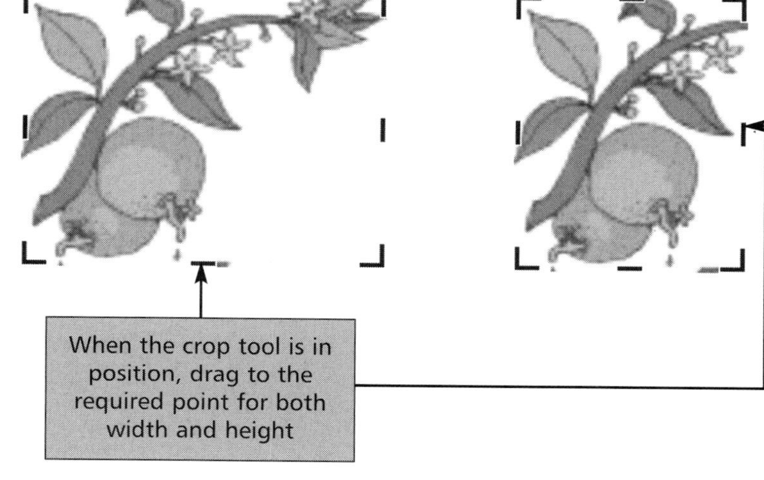

Move crop tool over handle and drag to required point

When the crop tool is in position, drag to the required point for both width and height

Figure 5.20

Remember, cropping the picture does not cut part of the picture, it simply hides that cropped part from view.

Try it out

Open the **SafeHome** presentation.

Option 1 – Using the drag technique

Click on the **Keys.gif** image. You will see eight small white circles appear on the edges and the corners of the picture. From the top-centre white circle there is a short line leading to a green circle. The white circles are drag handles and the green circle is a free rotate handle.

Move the cursor so that it is over the bottom-right white circle. The cursor will change shape to a double-headed arrow.

Note: Moving the cursor over the free rotate green circle will change the shape of the cursor to a circular arrow.

These are both shown in Figure 5.21.

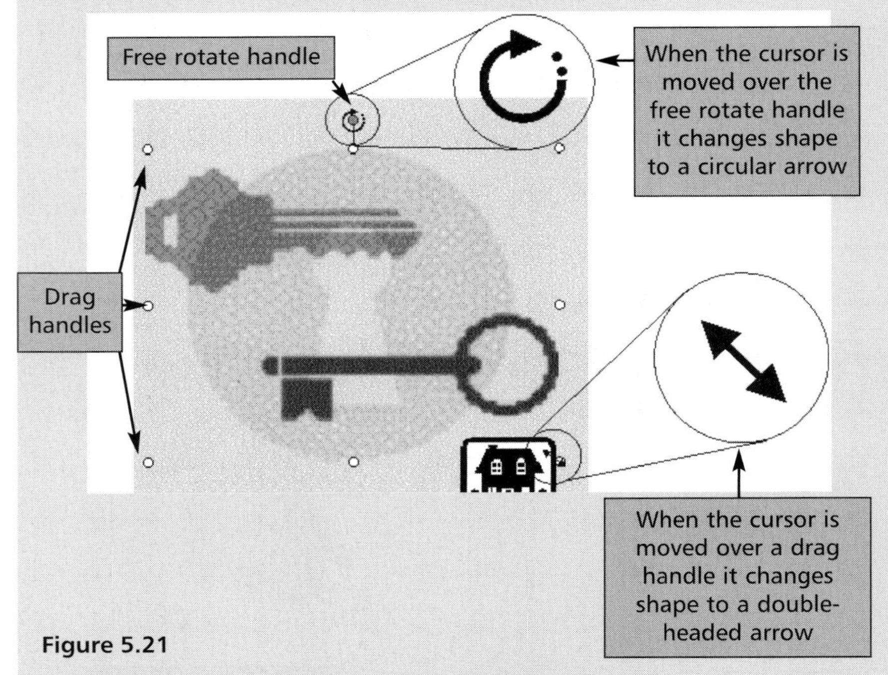

Figure 5.21

Click the left-hand mouse button and while it is still held down, drag the picture inwards to a smaller size – approximately half its original size.

Release the mouse button when you are satisfied with the size of the image.

This is a quick and easy way of adjusting the size of an image. However, resizing images using this method does not allow you to specify the exact size wanted. To do this you will need to format the image using the Format dialogue box.

Before using the second method you will need to undo the changes you have made to the image.

Click on the undo button on the toolbar or select the Undo Resize Object option from the Edit menu item (keyboard shortcut Ctrl+Z).

Option 2 – Using the Format Picture dialogue box

Using the right-hand mouse button:

Click on the **Keys.gif** image to show the drop menu list.

Select Format Picture… .

You will now see the Format Picture dialogue box shown in Figure 5.22.

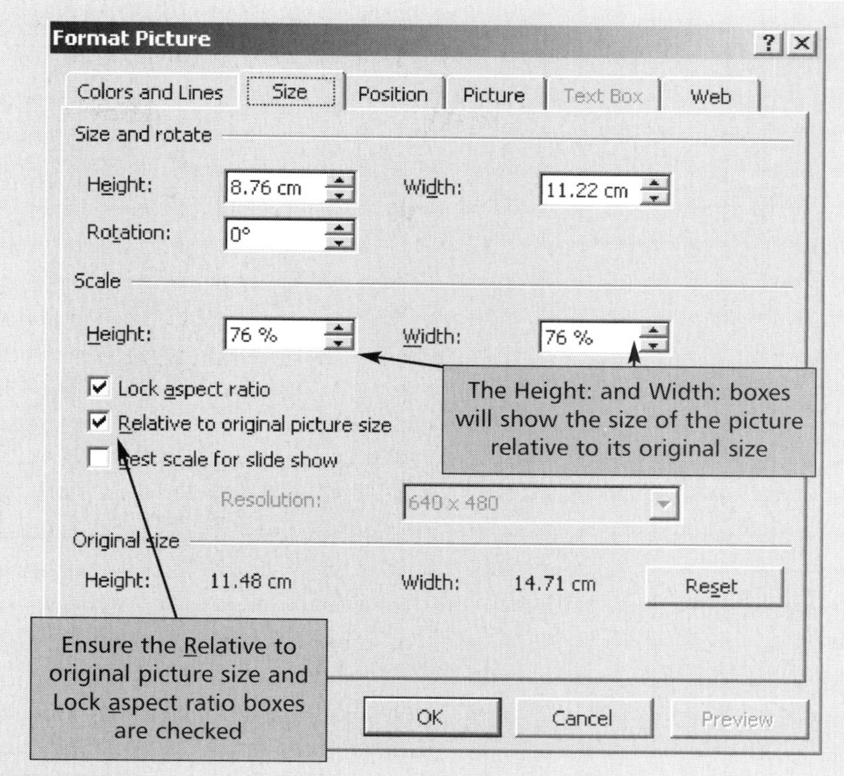

Figure 5.22

Select the Size tab.

In the top section of the dialogue box, Size and rotate, you have the opportunity to insert the actual height and width required for the image. Providing the Lock aspect ratio box is checked when the height is entered, PowerPoint will automatically adjust the width proportionately and maintain the proportional integrity of the picture.

If, on the other hand, you want to change the size of the image by a specific percentage, the Scale section beneath Size and rotate will allow you to do this.

Type '50%' in the Height: box; PowerPoint will assume you want the width also at 50%.

Press OK and the image will change to 50% of its original size.

Drag the image to the top-right of your slide.

Using the Format Picture dialogue options for rotating an image:

Rotate the image by 45°.

Using the crop tool on the picture toolbar (this appears as soon as the picture is selected):

Crop the top and bottom portions of the circle in the image until it looks like Figure 5.23.

Crop to remove top and bottom of circle

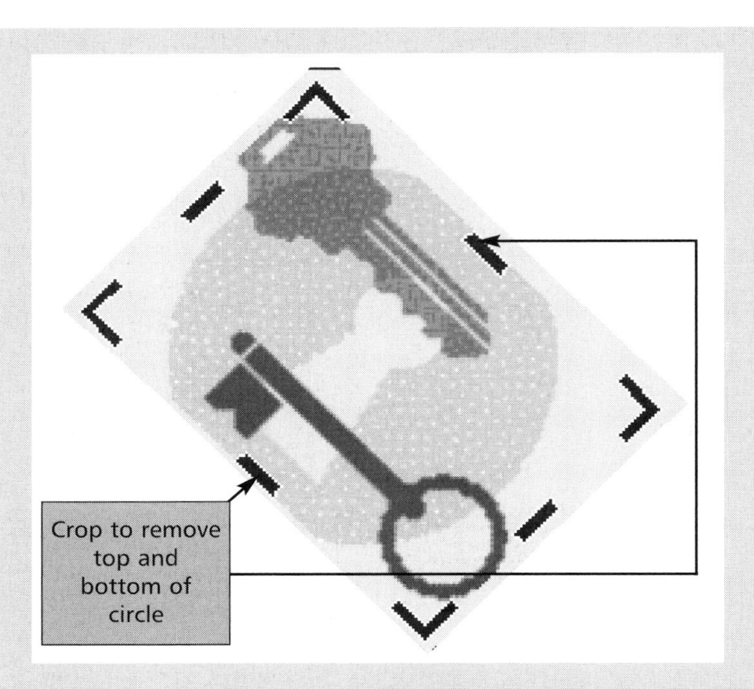

Figure 5.23

You now need to resize the bullet text frame. Unlike image files you can use the centre drag handles and the text will not be distorted. You are simply resizing the frame and the text itself is unaffected.

Click on the bullet text frame to show the drag handles.

Drag the size of the frame out so that it virtually covers the slide.

Your slide should now look similar to Figure 5.24.

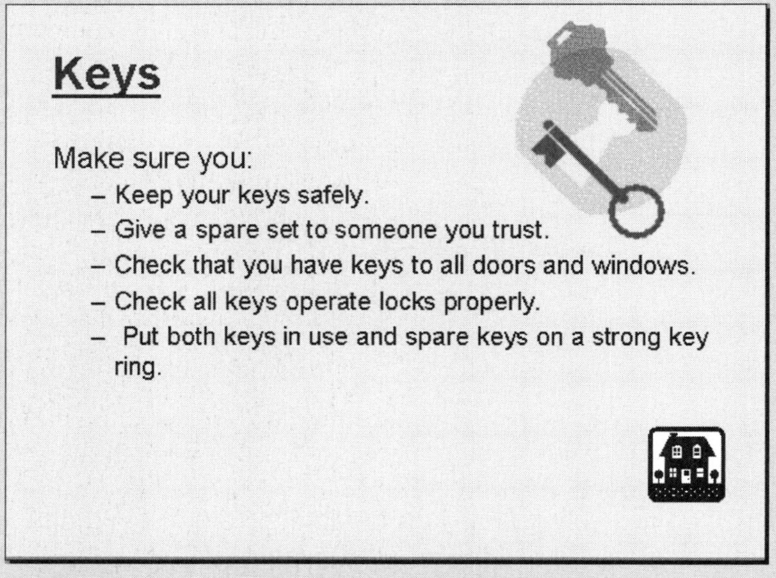

Keys
Make sure you:
– Keep your keys safely.
– Give a spare set to someone you trust.
– Check that you have keys to all doors and windows.
– Check all keys operate locks properly.
– Put both keys in use and spare keys on a strong key ring.

Figure 5.24

Save and close your presentation.

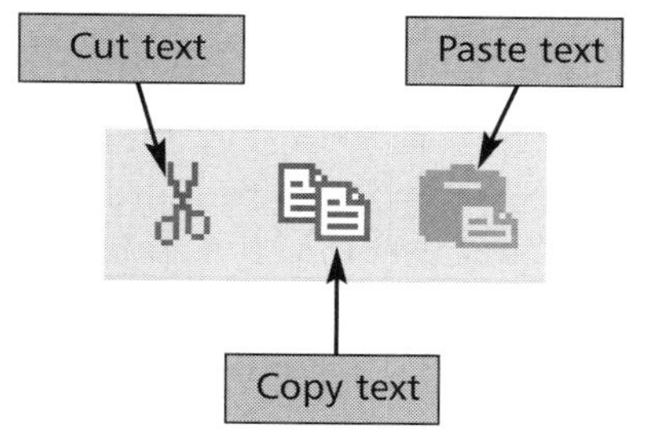

Figure 5.25

Importing text into a presentation

There may well be times when someone other than you prepares a brief or text for a presentation in a different application that you need to import into appropriate PowerPoint slides. In essence the process of using text from, say, a Word document is no different from using the same text in a different Word file. The text is copied from one file and then pasted into the new file. When you complete a CLAIT Plus assignment you will be asked to import text into a PowerPoint slide. The simplest method for doing this is as follows.

First highlight the text in the Word document. Copy the text using either the keyboard option (Crtl+C), the Edit, Copy option from the menu or the toolbar icons shown in Figure 5.25.

Try this out in a simple exercise.

Try it out

Open a new Word document.

Type the text shown below:

Heading:

'IMPORTING TEXT INTO A POWERPOINT SLIDE'

Bullet points:

- Highlight text in Word to be imported in the slide.
- Copy the text using either the keyboard, menu or toolbar option.
- Click on the frame in the slide which is to receive the text.
- Paste the text using either the keyboard, menu or toolbar option.

Note: When the text is pasted into the appropriate frame it will take on the attributes set for that frame. In other words, even if the text in the Word document is, say, Arial 12pt, normal emphasis, if the PowerPoint text frame is set in the Slide Master to Times New Roman, 44pt, bold then the imported text will assume this formatting. If the Slide Master is not set then the frame will take the font type from its original document.

Create a new PowerPoint presentation.

Set the first slide layout to text and bullets.

Highlight the heading IMPORTING TEXT INTO A POWERPOINT SLIDE in your Word document.

Copy the heading using any of the above methods.

Click on the title frame of the presentation slide you have created.

Paste the heading into the frame.

Repeat this procedure for the bullet list created in the Word document.

Applying a bullet style

Earlier in this unit you learnt how to set up the Slide Master to ensure consistency of fonts, style and layout within a presentation. In addition to setting the font type, style, size and colour you can also format the style of bullet to be used when inserting bulleted lists into the slides of your presentation.

First you must decide if the bullet style is to apply throughout your presentation or simply to one particular slide. If the bullet is to be consistent then the style should be set in the Slide Master.

To change the bullet style within the Slide Master open the Slide Master view. Click on the first bullet level Format, Bullets and Numbering from the main menu and the dialogue box shown in Figure 5.26 will appear.

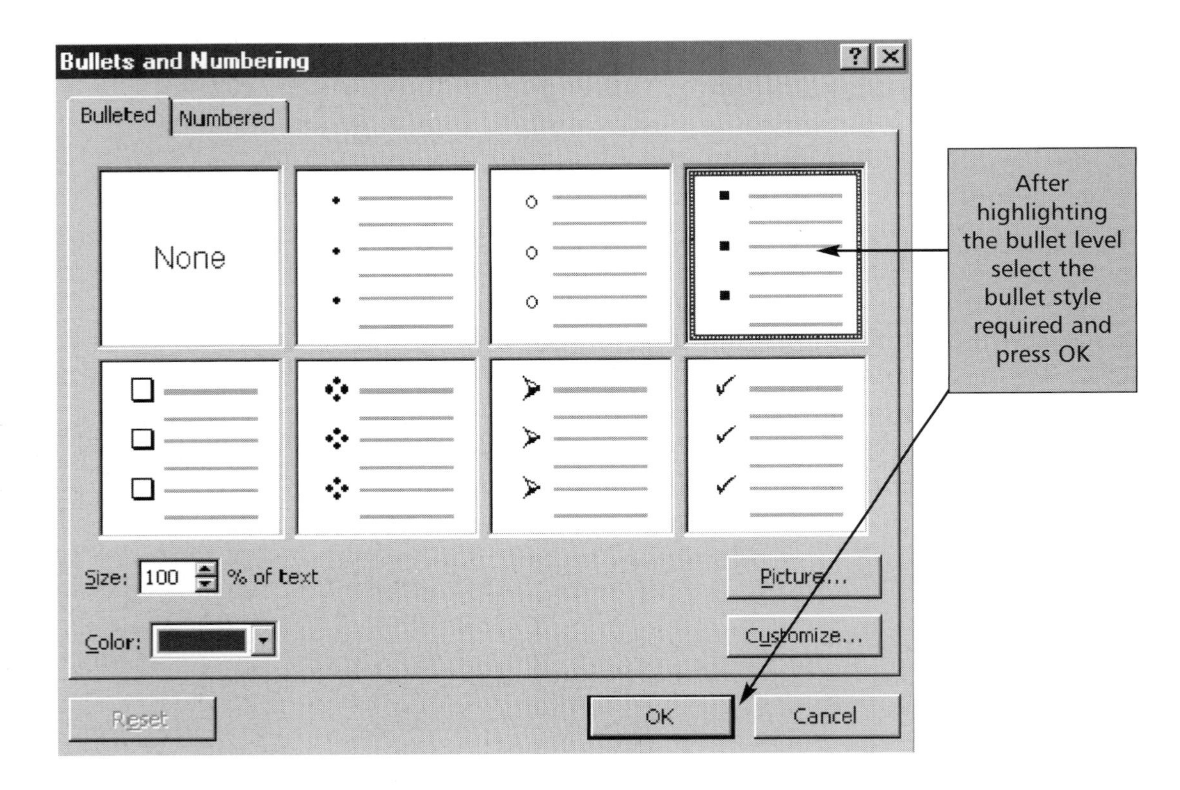

Figure 5.26

PowerPoint has a number of standard bullet styles from which you can choose. Depending on who has used the software and whether the default settings have changed a range of different bullets may be on view. If none of the bullets in the dialogue box are suitable for your needs then you can customise the bullet styles. Pressing the Customize... button will bring the symbols dialogue into view (Figure 5.27).

You can either choose one of these symbols or using the Font: field select a different set of characters or symbols. Alternatively you can use the Picture... button in the Bullets and Numbering dialogue box and select any picture stored on your hard disk.

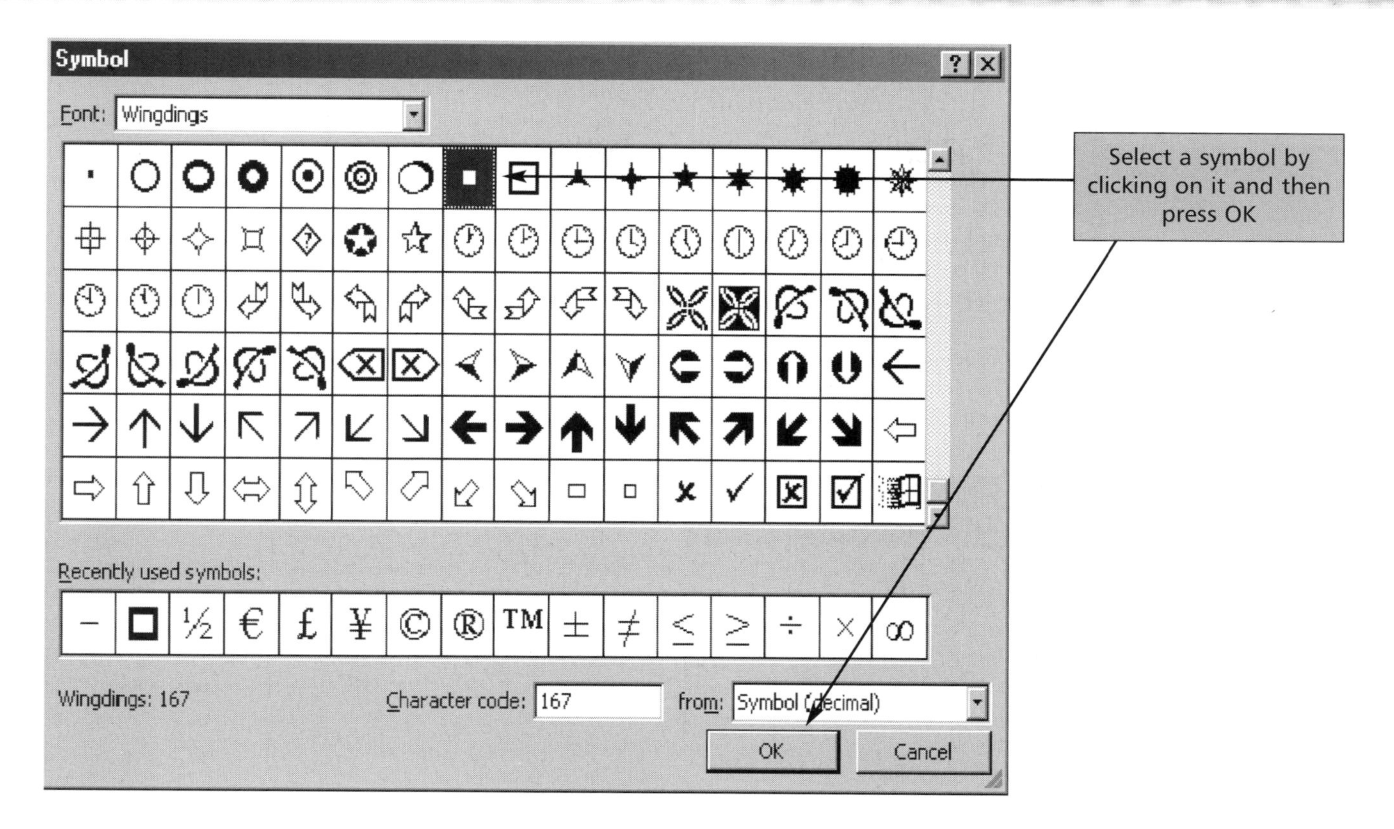

Figure 5.27

Try it out

Create a new PowerPoint presentation.

Set the first slide layout to text and bullets.

Click in the title frame and enter the heading 'CHANGING THE BULLET STYLE'.

Click in the bullet text frame and enter the following bullet points:

- First select Format, Bullets and Numbering on the menu bar.
- In the dialogue box click on the style of bullet you want to use.
- Finally press the OK button to return to the presentation slide.

Select Format, Bullets and Numbering on the menu bar.

Click on a style other than the default style on the slide.

Press the OK button to return to the presentation slide.

Remember that if this style is to be used throughout the presentation then the formatting should be done within the Slide Master view.

You should now be able to:

- insert a clip art image
- insert other image files
- resize and reposition an image
- rotate an image
- crop an image
- resize a text frame
- import text from a Word document into a text frame in PowerPoint
- change the style of bullets.

Build-up Exercise 5: Stage 2

Open your **First_Aid** presentation.

Using the presentation brief named FIRST AID BRIEF from the accompanying CD in folder Unit 5, import each appropriate piece of text from the brief to slides in the presentation.

Change the style of the bullets in the Slide Master as follows:

➢	Level 1	●	Level 3
–	Level 2	■	Level 4

Insert the image **FA_Symbol** so that it is in the bottom left of the Object area for Autolayouts frame of the Slide Master.

Adjust the image size so that it is:

Height 2.5 cm
Width 2.8 cm

Return to Normal view.

Insert the image **Pwr_Line.gif** into Slide 3 – DANGER.

Adjust the image size so that it is:

Height 3 cm
Width 3.68 cm

Move the image so that it is in the top right of the slide, opposite the title DANGER.

Position:

Horizontal 21 cm
Vertical 1 cm

Insert the image **Conscious.gif** into Slide 4 – RESPONSE.

Position:

Horizontal 14 cm
Vertical 4.5 cm

Insert the image **Airway.gif** into Slide 5 – AIRWAY.

Position:

Horizontal 13 cm
Vertical 5 cm

Insert the image **Chk_Breath.gif** into Slide 6 – BREATHING.

Adjust the size of the image so that it is:

Height 8 cm
Width 8.32 cm

Position:

Horizontal 14 cm
Vertical 9 cm

Resize the text frame so that the text in the bullet points is not wrapped.

Insert the image **Pulse.gif** into Slide 7 – CIRCULATION.

Adjust the size of the image so that it is:

Height 10 cm
Width 9.43 cm

Position:

Horizontal 15 cm
Vertical 8 cm

Resize the text frame so that the text in the bullet points is not wrapped.

Select Slide 2.

Insert the image **Ambulance.gif** from the CD.

Crop the image so that the figures to the rear of the vehicle are removed.

Reposition the image so that it is:

Position:

Horizontal 15 cm
Vertical 13 cm

Rotate the image by 45°.

Save your presentation.

The slides in your presentation should now look similar to Figure 5.28.

▶▶

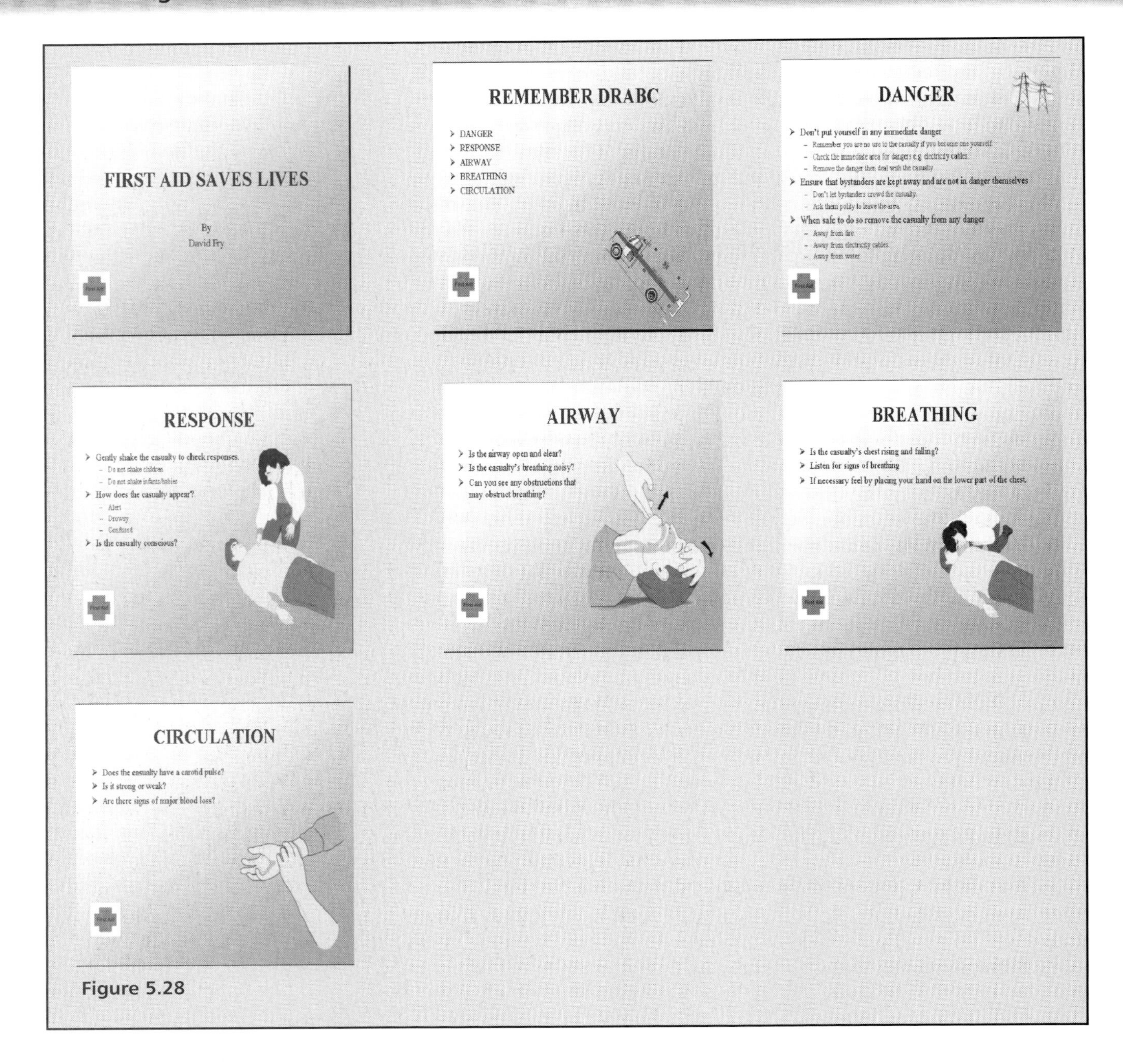

Figure 5.28

Inserting a new slide in a specified location of the presentation

As with any document produced for informational or presentational reasons it is inevitable that you will want to refine the final document by making changes. A typical change you may want to make to a presentation is to insert a slide in the middle of the sequence of slides already created. There are effectively two ways you can achieve this.

Option 1
With the slide presentation in Normal view and the thumbnail views of the whole presentation on the left of the screen, click on the slide under which the new slide will be inserted, or click between two of the slides and a line appears where the new slide will be inserted. Select Insert, New Slide from the menu (alternatively click on the new slide icon New Slide). The new slide will appear below the original slide that was selected: see Figure 5.29.

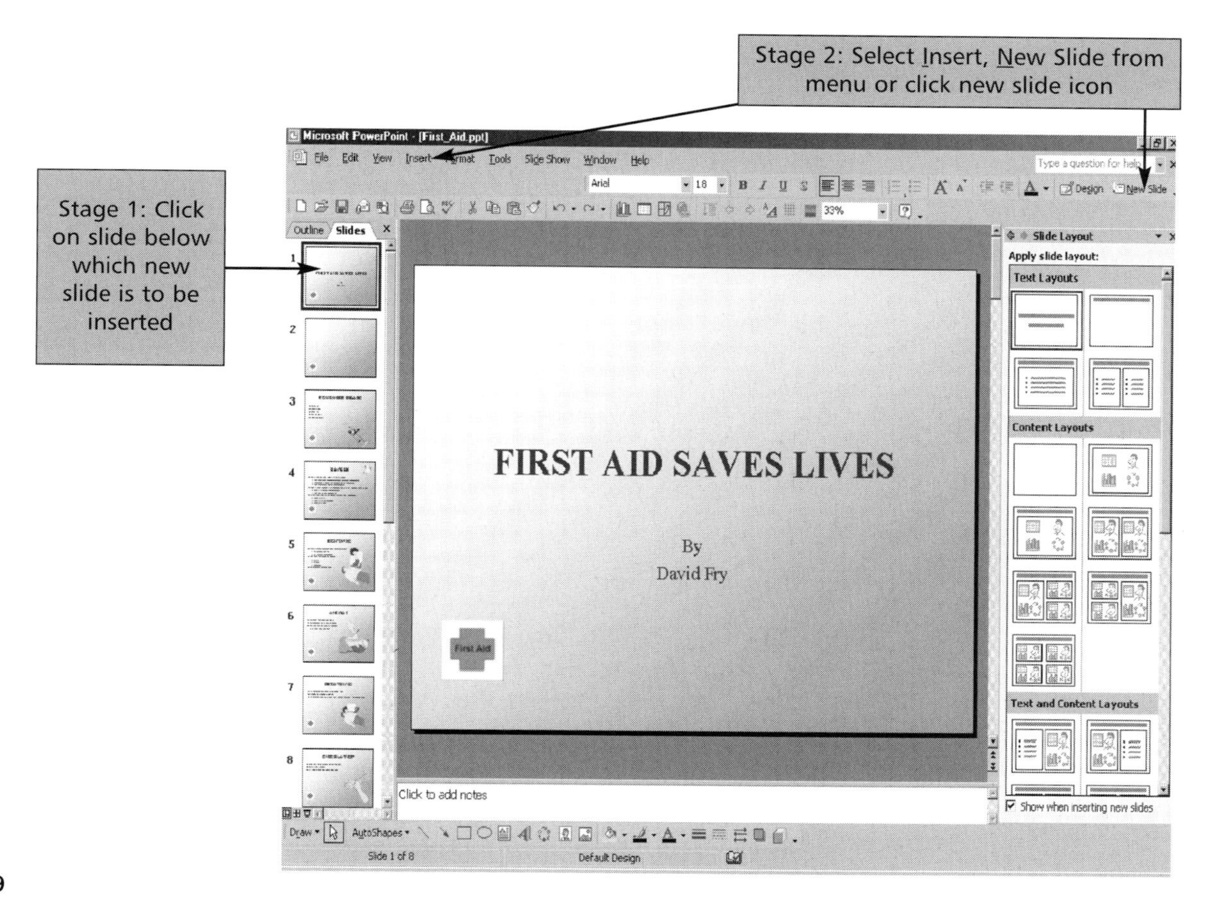

Figure 5.29

Option 2
Select the Slide Sorter view (shown in Figure 5.30); click the cursor at the point in the series of slides where the new slide is to be placed and select Insert, New Slide from the menu, or use the new slide icon.

Using charts and tables in a presentation

Using built-in Wizards

One of the advantages of using the content layout templates provided with PowerPoint is the ease with which you can create a variety of charts and insert tables or images. On page 221 you saw how layouts are divided into frames that can contain either text or objects. Figure 5.31 shows the range of objects available for slides containing objects.

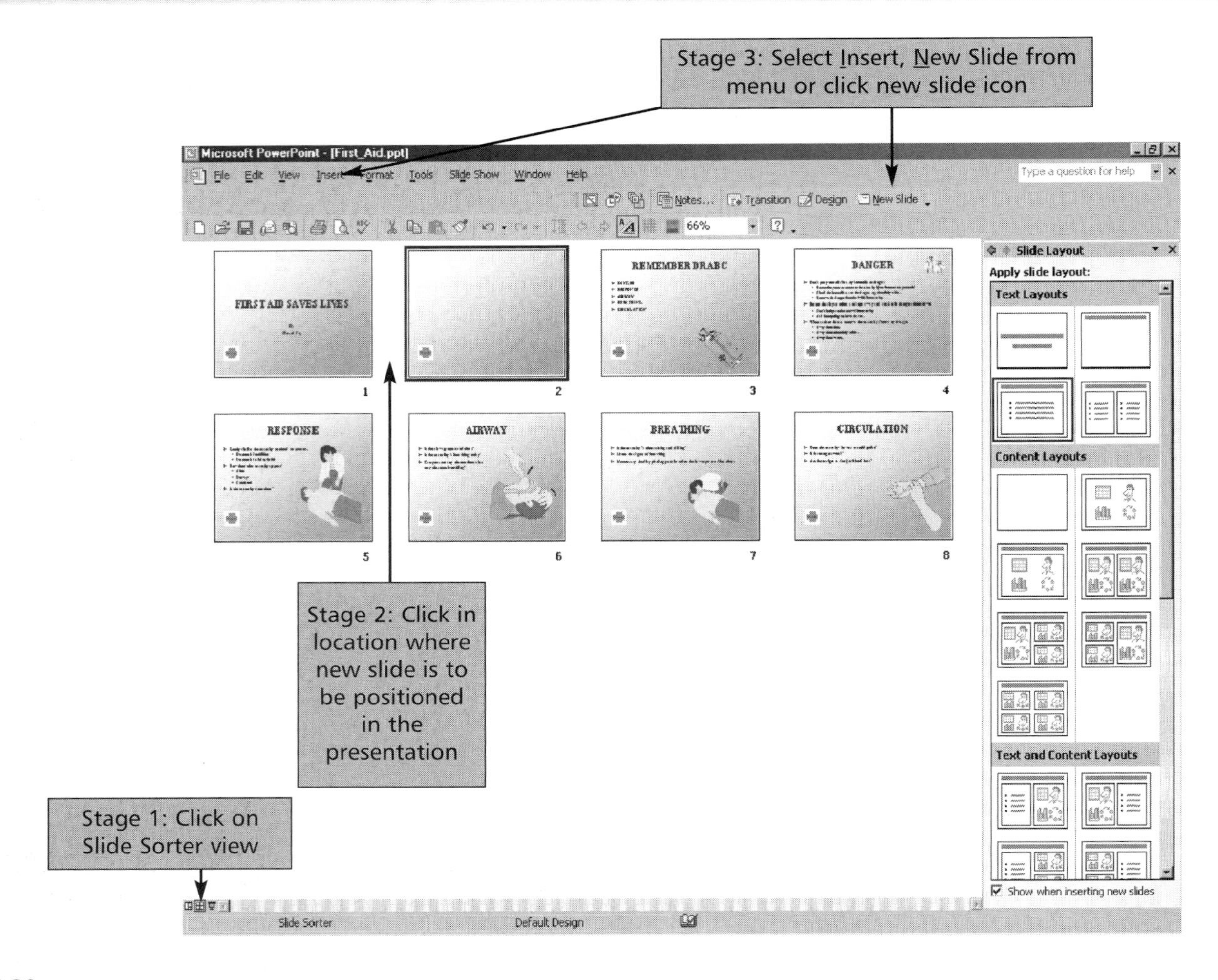

Figure 5.30

So far you have used only the title, and title and bullet, text layouts in a presentation. PowerPoint also provides layouts that allow just objects or a mixture of objects and text. You have already learnt how to insert clip art and pictures using the Insert, Picture option on the menu or using the picture and clip art icons on the drawing toolbar using simple layouts. Other templates include Content layout and Title and Content layout, where you can introduce charts, images, tables or media clips into a slide using the icons shown in Figure 5.31.

In Figure 5.31 you can see the familiar clip art and picture icons. When these are selected in the template of a slide containing objects other than just text, appropriate dialogue boxes are shown for you to locate and/or select clip art and other image files. You will now learn how to insert and use tables in a slide and introduce general numeric data and organisational charts.

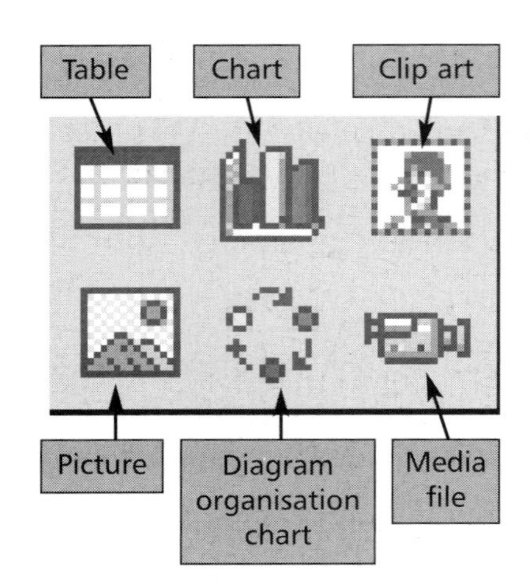

Figure 5.31

Using tables

It is probable that in completing earlier units you will have already come across the use of tables in documents. Using tables in slides is fundamentally no different from using tables in any other application.

In creating lists of data in columns you can, of course, enter data and then use the tab function to start a new column list. Have a look at Figure 5.32.

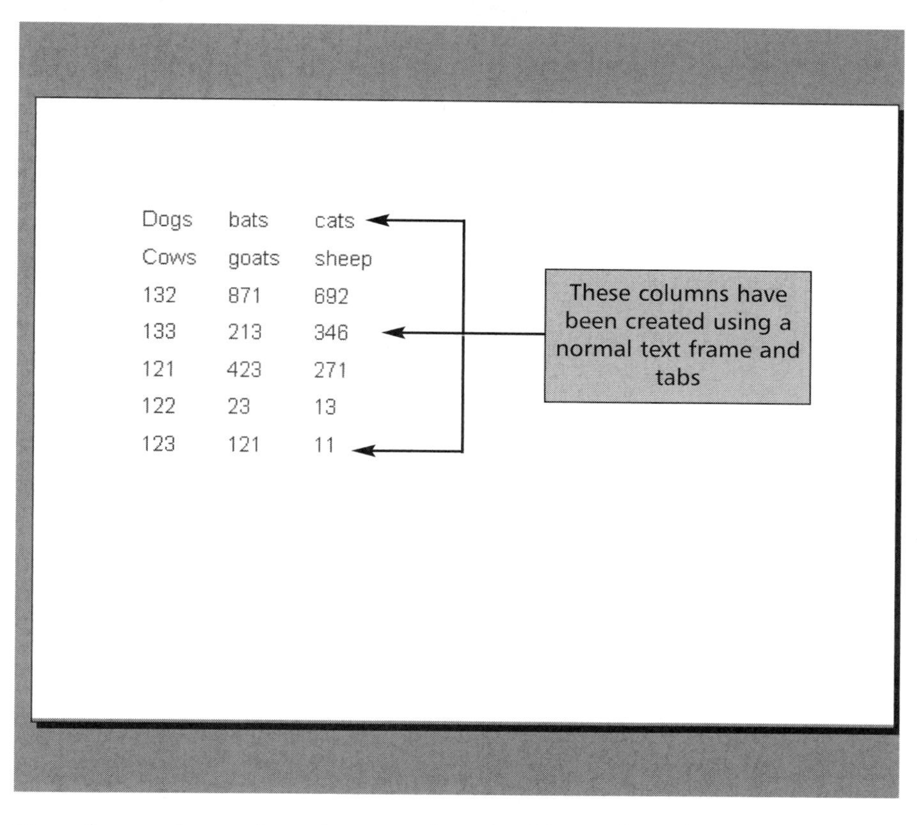

Figure 5.32

Here three columns have been produced with words and numbers. Sometimes this may well be all that you want. However, if you needed to change the alignment of these it would be difficult and fiddly to do so. It is much easier when preparing lists of letters or numbers to use tables. PowerPoint offers a number of ways to create tables within slides.

Option 1

You can create a table by selecting one of the layouts that contains a table placeholder. To insert a table either click on the table icon shown in Figure 5.31 that includes a placeholder for a table, or use the Insert, Table… option from the main menu. Once one of these options has been selected the Insert Table dialogue box shown in Figure 5.33 appears.

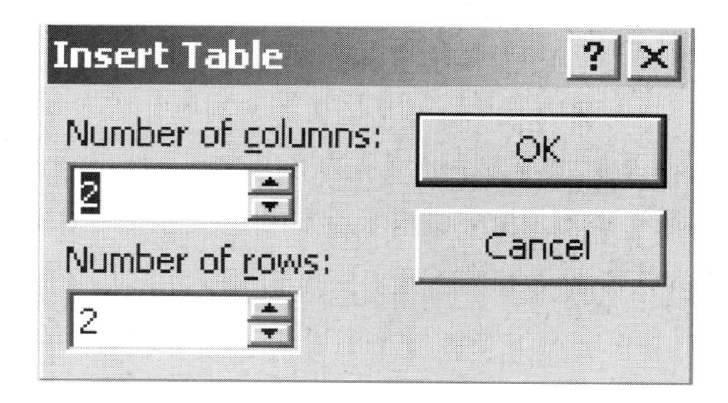

Figure 5.33

Simply enter the required number of columns and rows and press OK. The table will be inserted into the slide and a table formatting toolbox (Tables and Borders) will also appear (see Figure 5.34).

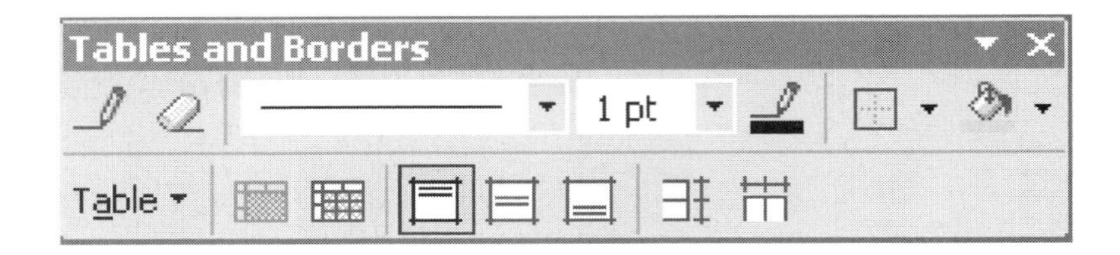

Figure 5.34

This formatting toolbox will be covered a little later.

Option 2
Tables can also be embedded from files created in Word. An embedded object is one that is created in another application and inserted, in this case, into PowerPoint. Whenever the table in Word is changed the object in PowerPoint is automatically updated. For CLAIT Plus you will only be required to create a table in PowerPoint. However, when you learn about charts, later in this unit, you will then cover how to embed an object.

Now try to create a table in PowerPoint.

Try it out

Open the presentation **SafeHome**.

Insert a new slide immediately after the title slide.

Change the default slide to Content layout. (If you need to refresh how to do this review the earlier section on inserting a new slide on page 241.)

Click on the table icon of the placeholder.

Enter Columns: 2 Rows: 5.

Press OK.

Save the presentation.

The table will now appear on the slide.

Entering text into a table

To enter text click in the cell where the text is to be placed and type in the required text. Try entering some text into your new table.

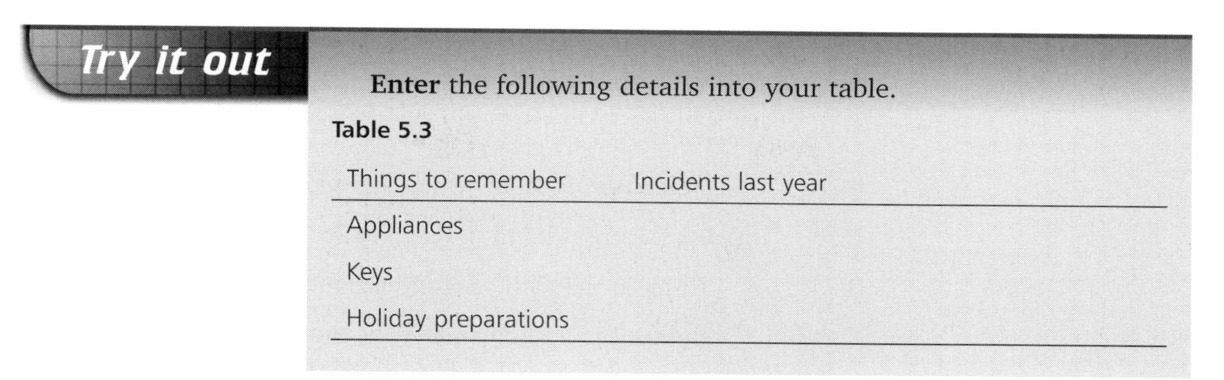

Try it out

Enter the following details into your table.

Table 5.3

Things to remember	Incidents last year
Appliances	
Keys	
Holiday preparations	

Adding and deleting rows and columns

To delete a row or a column simply click in the row or column, press the arrow to the right of Table in the Tables and Borders dialogue box and select the appropriate menu item from the drop menu list shown in Figure 5.35.

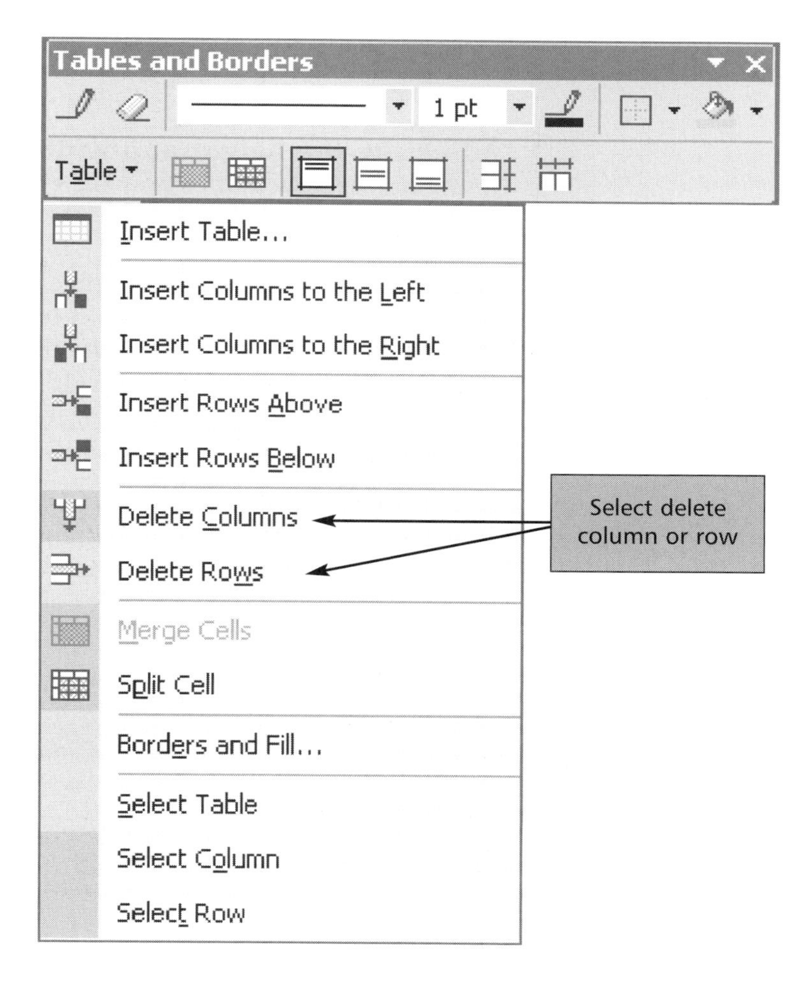

Figure 5.35

To add a column or row, select the appropriate menu item from the same list as shown in Figure 5.35.

Now try deleting a row and adding a column.

Try it out

Open SafeHome if it is not already open.

Delete a row:

Select the slide in which you placed the table.

Using the right-hand mouse button

Click in the fifth row and delete it.

Select Delete Rows from the menu.

Add a column:

Click in the cell that contains the text 'Incidents last year'.

Select Insert Columns to the Right.

Save the presentation.

Adjusting the height and width of columns and rows

In the last exercise notice how the column is inserted but the width exceeds the width of the slide. Unlike tables in Word, PowerPoint does not provide a facility to set the width of columns or the height of rows to a specific size. To change the column width or the row height place the cursor over the column or row boundary that you want to change and when you see the cursor change shape to drag the column or row to the width or height required. You can gauge the width of the column by looking at the ruler at the top of the window of the slide.

Distributing column widths or row heights evenly

To equalise columns or rows, highlight the appropriate columns or rows and then select the Distribute Columns Evenly or Distribute Rows Evenly button on the Tables and Borders toolbox shown in Figure 5.36.

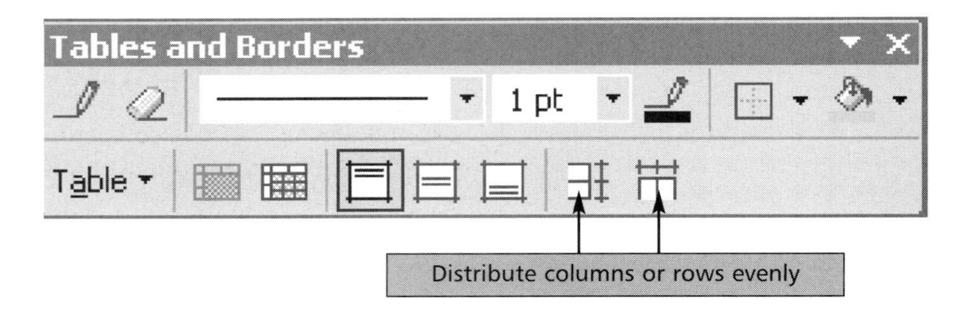

Figure 5.36

Now try altering the width of the new column inserted in the last exercise and entering additional data.

Try it out

Open SafeHome if it is not already open.

Adjust the column widths so that they are roughly 7 cm each. (Use the ruler to judge the width as shown in Figure 5.37. If the rulers are not visible select the Option Ruler from the View option on the main menu bar.)

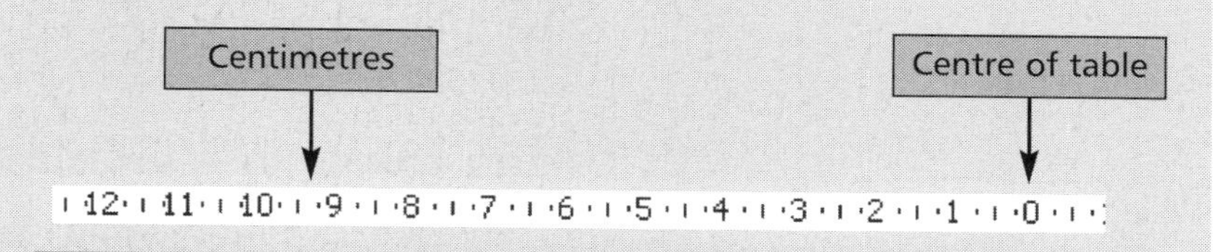

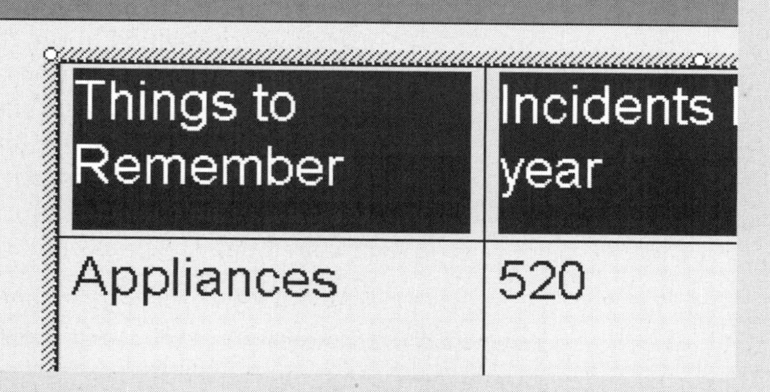

Figure 5.37

Highlight the three columns.

Click the Distribute Columns Evenly button on the toolbox.

Enter the additional data shown in Table 5.4.

Table 5.4

Things to remember	Incidents last year	Costs
Appliances	520	58,000.00
Keys	289	120,000.00
Holiday preparations	600	196,000.00

Aligning data

To align data first select the cell or column that you want to align and then click on the alignment button on the toolbar as shown in Figure 5.38.

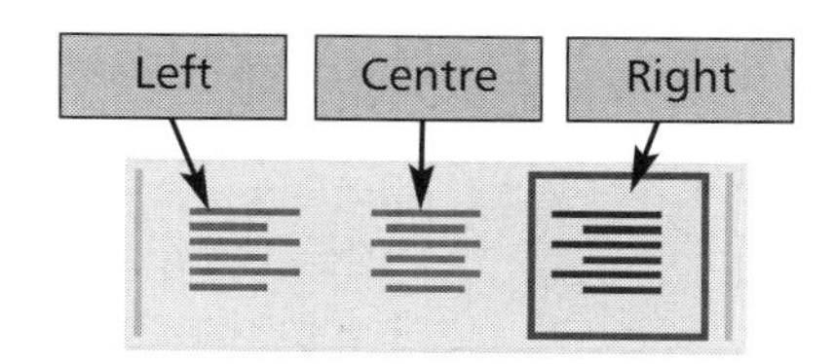

Figure 5.38

Try it out

Open SafeHome if it is not already open.

Select the centre and right hand columns of the slide containing the table.

Click the right-align button from the toolbar.

Save the presentation.

Using charts in a presentation

At the beginning of this section you saw in Figure 5.31 how various objects can be introduced into a slide by simply clicking on the placeholder provided in the relevant slide layout. Having learnt how to introduce and format various aspects of a table you will now see how easy it is to insert a chart that will add impact to the presentation.

To insert a chart choose one of the layout templates provided by PowerPoint that contains placeholders for charts, images, tables and so on. Simply click on the chart icon and you will be shown a simple, pre-prepared datasheet and the associated chart for that data. Have a look at Figure 5.39.

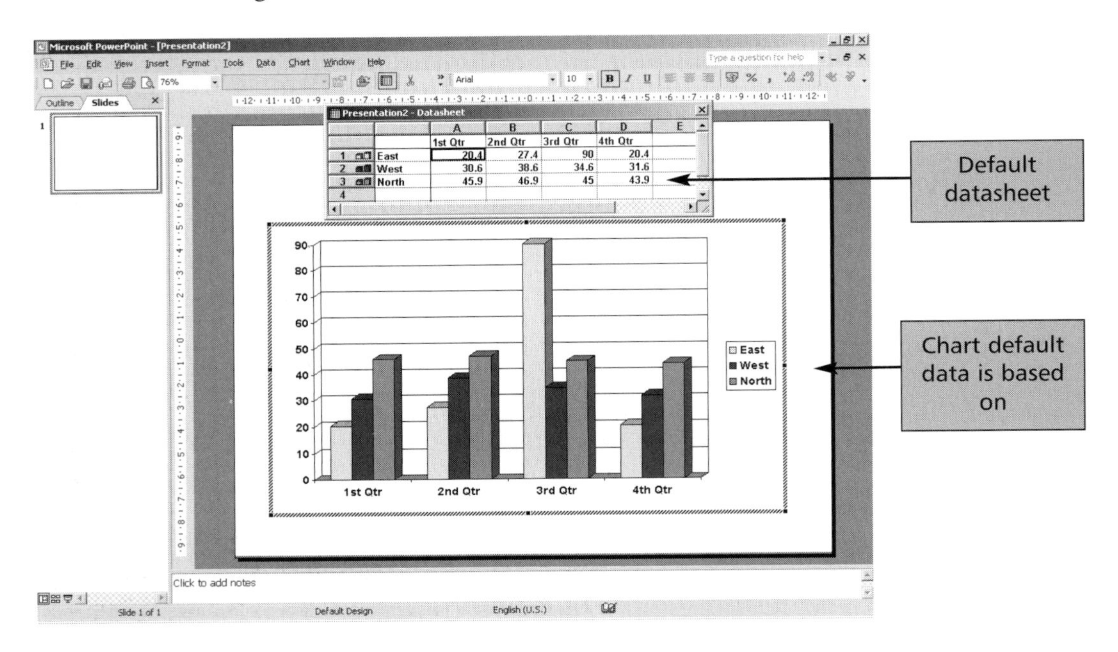

Figure 5.39

PowerPoint automatically prepares a simple datasheet and the underlying chart that represents the data in the datasheet. Both the data and the chart are then fully amendable. In Figure 5.40 the data in the datasheet has been amended and a new line of data added. This is done from the original default datasheet that looks like an Excel spreadsheet. As the data is amended the chart automatically reflects the changes made.

Now have a go at introducing a chart into the **SafeHome** presentation.

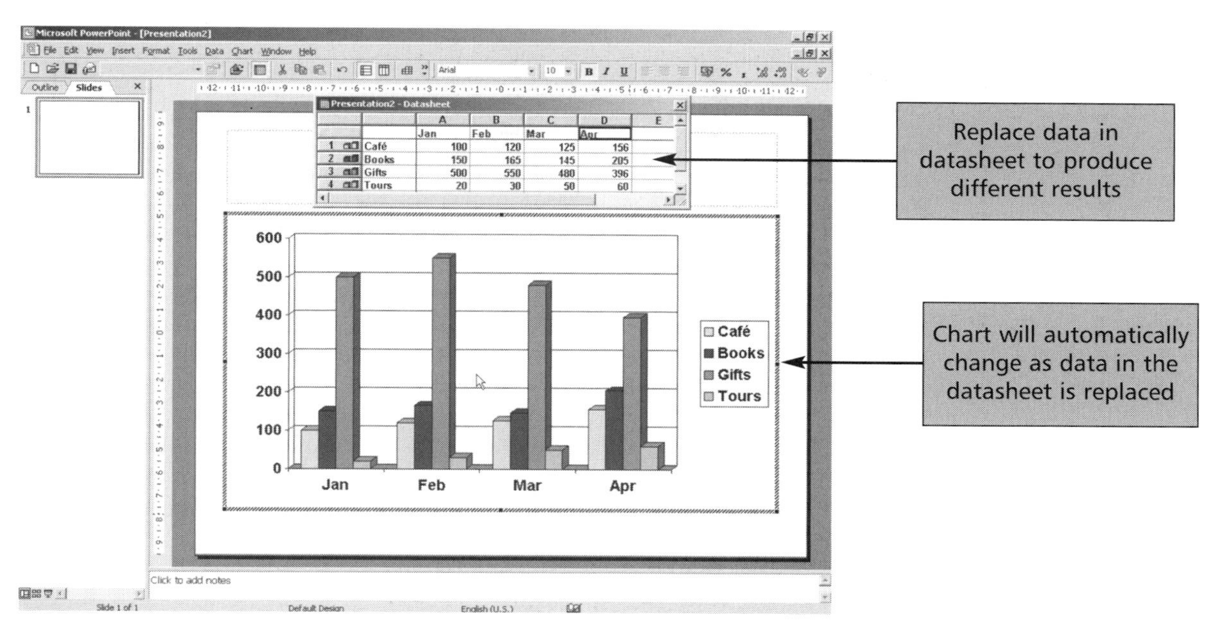

Figure 5.40

Try it out

Open the **SafeHome** presentation if it is not already open.

Insert a new slide based on the Title and Content layout.

Click the chart icon .

Delete the data in columns B and C.

Replace the data in Row Title column A in the datasheet with the data shown in Table 5.5.

Table 5.5

Factors	Incidents
Appliances	520
Keys	289
Holidays	600

With only one series of data it is not very helpful to show the data in a column format. What you want to show is the percentage each factor represents in terms of the overall number of incidents, so you need to change both the chart type and the data series configuration.

Click on the chart so that drag handles are in view.

Select Chart, Chart Type... from the main menu.

The Chart Type dialogue box will appear as shown in Figure 5.41.

On the left of the dialogue box is a list of the chart types available and on the right the sub-types. In this exercise you are going to select the pie chart and the sub-type will be an exploded pie with a 3-D visual effect.

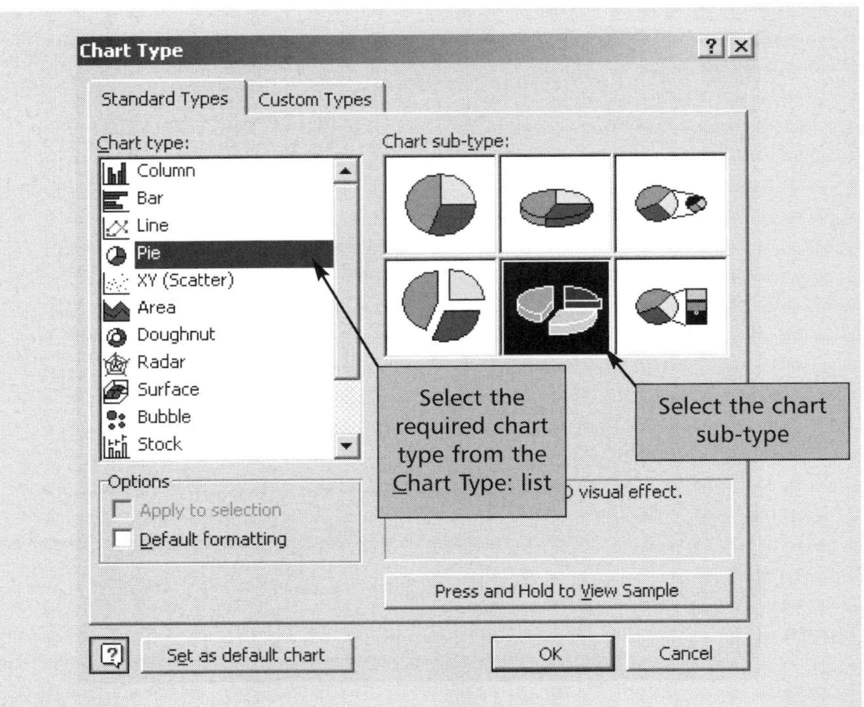

Figure 5.41

Select Pie as the chart type.

Select the exploded pie with a 3D visual effect as the sub-type.

Press OK.

The chart will now change to a pie. However, because the series is currently in rows there is only one segment of data.

Select Data, Series in Columns from the main menu options.

You should now have three segments. The legend appears on the right. By using the right-hand mouse button and clicking on the legend box you are offered the opportunity of formatting the legend.

Click on the legend box using the right-hand mouse button and

Select Format Legend… .

Select the Placement tab in the format dialogue box.

Click in the Bottom check box.

The legend will now be repositioned at the bottom of the chart.

The next stage is to show the percentage for each segment.

Click on the segments of the chart and using the right-hand mouse button:

Select Format Data Series… .

Select the Data labels tab.

You should see the Data label options as shown in Figure 5.42.

Figure 5.42

Click on the Show percent option under the Data labels section.

Press OK.

Finally you will remove the border around the data segments of the chart.

Click on the plot area or border around the segments. Using the right-hand mouse button:

Select None under the Border section of the Format Plot Area dialogue box shown in Figure 5.43.

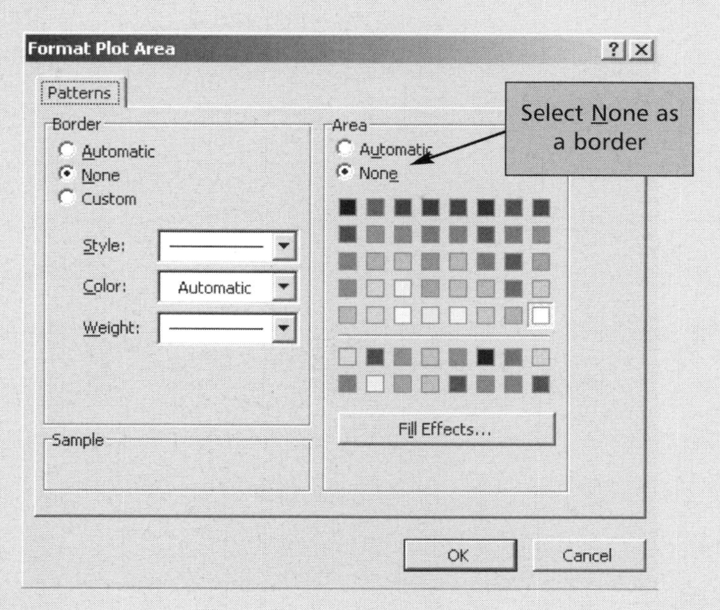

Figure 5.43

Click outside the chart area to accept the selections made.

Your slide and pie chart should now look similar to Figure 5.44.

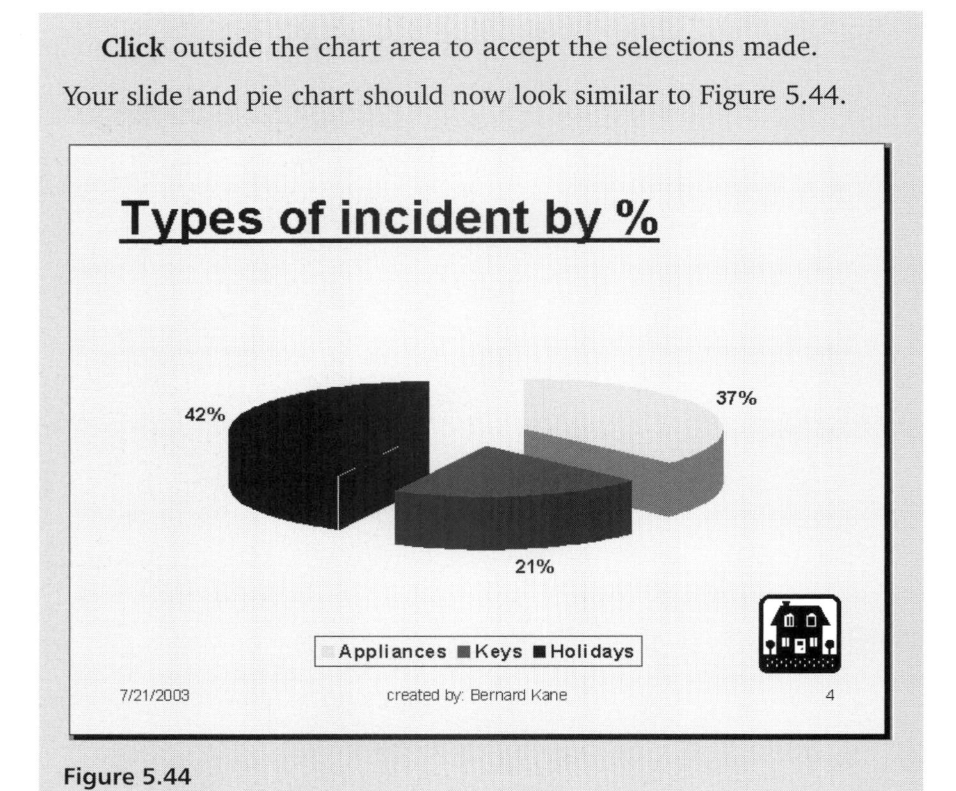

Figure 5.44

Creating organisation charts

In addition to normal charts that are based on numerical data, PowerPoint also provides Wizards that allow you to create other styles of chart and diagram. By pressing the diagram icon the options for different types of diagram or organisation chart are offered in the Diagram Gallery shown in Figure 5.45.

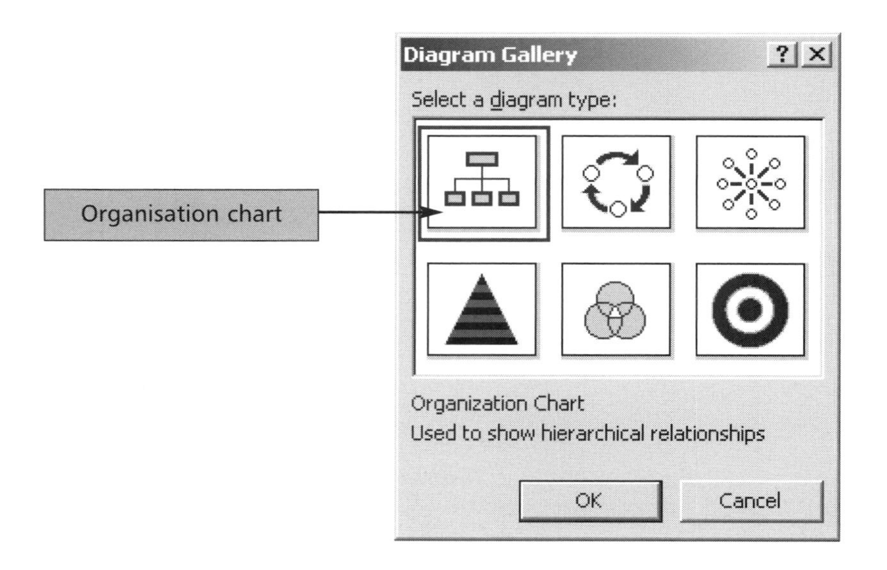

Figure 5.45

For CLAIT Plus you will be required to create and embed an organisation chart. By selecting the organisation chart type from the gallery and the pressing the OK button an organisation frame appears on the slide (or if created in Word, on the page). This is the basic organisational framework with the superior at the top of the chart and three assistants immediately below: see Figure 5.46.

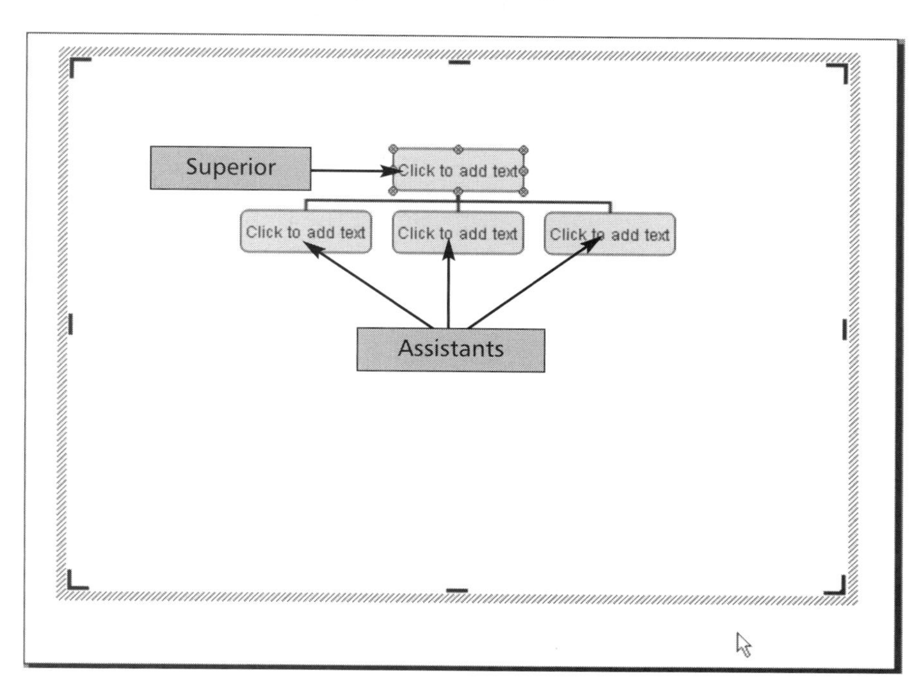

Figure 5.46

Organisation charts in PowerPoint can be modified to suit the organisation. In addition to the superior and assistant hierarchy in Figure 5.46 you can add subordinates and co-workers. You can also change the layout by choosing one of the layout options in the list revealed by pressing the Layout tab on the chart toolbar. Figure 5.47 shows the options available.

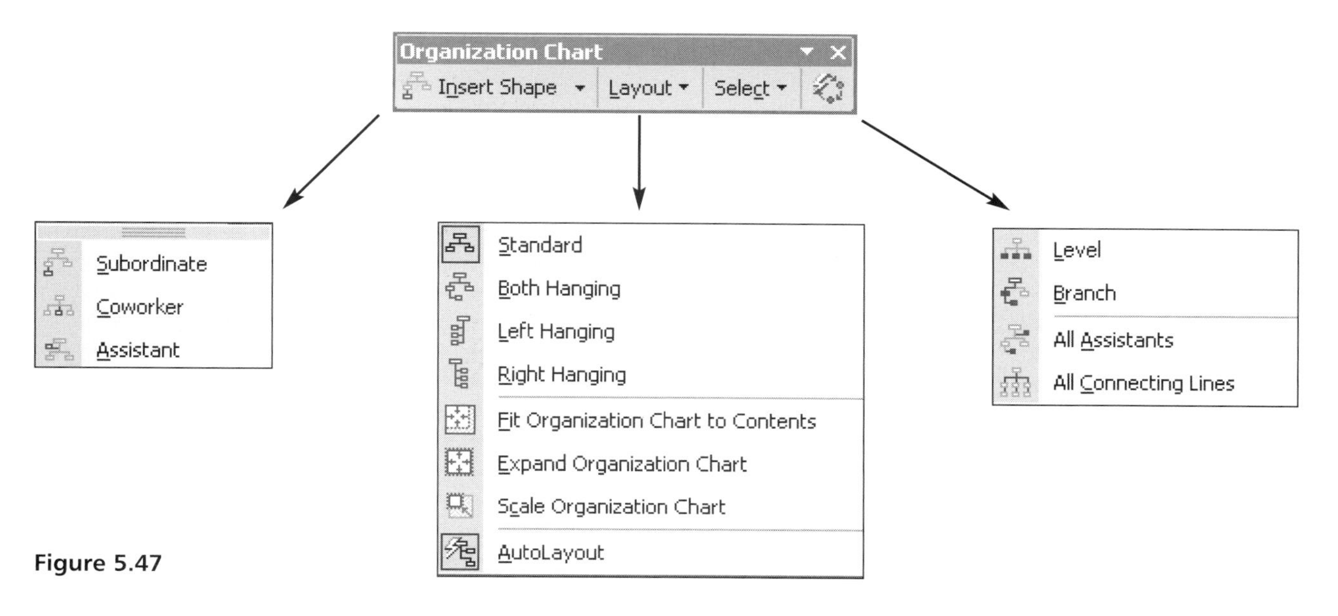

Figure 5.47

To add a co-worker, assistant or subordinate simply click on an existing shape or box to which you want to add, and then select the appropriate new shape from the Insert Shape list.

Try it out

Open SafeHome if it is not already open.

Insert a new slide after the table slide 2.

Set the Content Layout to Title and Content.

Click the Insert Diagram or Organisation Chart icon.

Select the Organisation Chart diagram type.

Click in the superior (top) shape and add the text 'Committee Chairman'.

Click in the first of the assistant (second line) shapes and add text: 'Village Co-ordinator'.

Click in the second assistant shape and add text 'Street Co-ordinator'.

Click in the third assistant shape and add text 'Safe Home Co-ordinator'.

Click on the superior shape (Committee Chairman) and then insert an assistant shape.

Click on the new shape and add the text 'Committee Secretary'.

Click outside the chart frame to accept the changes.

Your chart should now look like Figure 5.48.

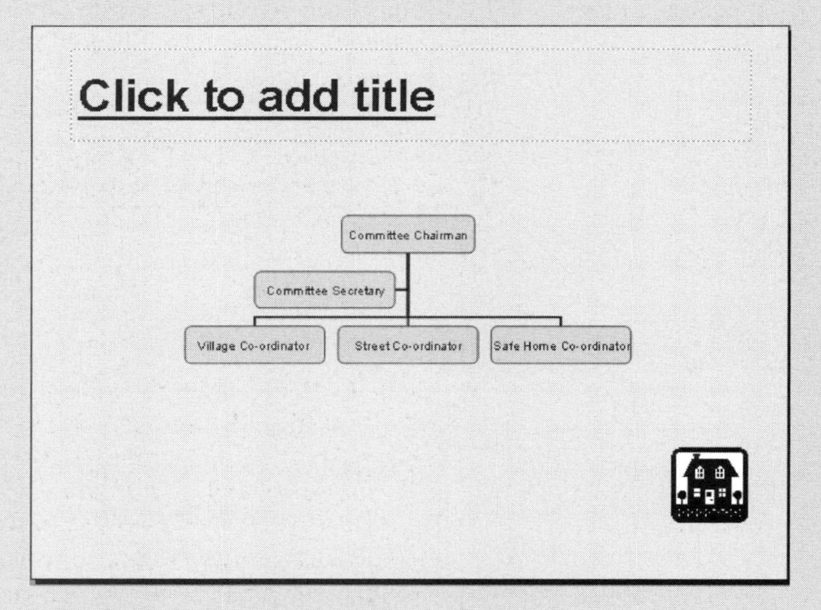

Figure 5.48

Finally add a title to your slide.

In the title text frame of the slide type:

'A Standard Safe Home Village Organisation'.

Embedding and linking data from external charts

Charts can also be created in other applications and then inserted into your presentation. An object, or in this case a chart, that is created in a different application to the one you are using is known as the 'source file'. The application into which the source file is imported is known as the 'destination file'. Inserting an object into the current application is called embedding the object. For example, you can create a similar chart to the one built in the last exercise in a Word document. Once the chart is saved as a file it can be inserted into a PowerPoint slide using the Insert, Object... options on the PowerPoint menu and then, selecting the Create from file... option in the dialogue box, locate the relevant file containing the chart. If you need to update the data in the embedded chart from amendments to the source file you can create a link between the two files. A link can be created between the two charts by clicking in the check box called Link, adjacent to the browse button, as seen in Figure 5.49.

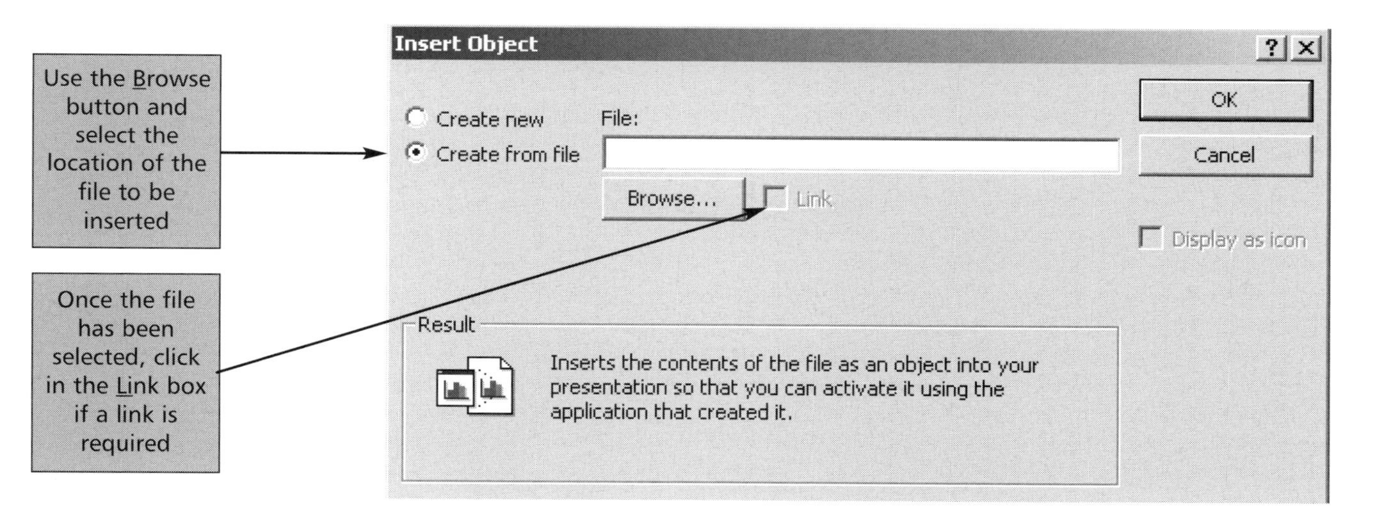

Figure 5.49

When an object is simply embedded any changes in the source file are not reflected in the embedded file once it has been inserted. However, if a link is created you can update the data in the destination file by selecting the linked object (in this case a chart) and using the right-hand mouse button click on Update link.

For CLAIT Plus you are only required to embed a chart, but you may wish to have a go at creating a chart in Word using exactly the same technique as for PowerPoint and then, after saving the file in Word, insert the chart in a PowerPoint slide.

Try it out

Open OrgChart.doc from the accompanying CD.

Save As **OrgChart** on your floppy or hard disk.

Close the file.

Open a new PowerPoint presentation.

Save the presentation as **EmbedExample**.

Type in the main title, 'The Team'.

Type in the sub-title, 'Widgets Incorporated'.

Insert a new slide based on the Title only layout.

Type in the title of the new slide, 'Organisation Chart'.

Click outside the title frame to accept the changes made.

Select Object… from Insert on the main menu.

Click on Create from file.

Locate and select **OrgChart.doc** saved on your floppy or hard disk.

Press OK.

Save your presentation.

Checking the link

Using the right-hand mouse button click on the chart to show the menu list.

Select Linked Document Object, Edit.

The source file will open for you to make amendments.

Click on the Managing Director shape.

Select Insert Shape, Assistant from the Organisation Chart toolbar.

Click on the new shape and

Type 'PA'.

Save the source file when prompted to do so.

Close the source Word file.

Return to the PowerPoint presentation.

Using the right-hand mouse button, click on the chart to show the menu list.

Select Update Link.

Notice how your chart now reflects the changes you made to the chart in the Word document.

Save the presentation.

Close the presentation.

You should now be able to:

- insert a new slide at a specified point in a presentation
- create a table in a slide and enter specified data
- add and delete rows and columns in a table
- adjust the height of rows and width of columns in a table
- align data in a table
- insert and embed charts into a presentation
- modify charts
- create a link between a source and destination file.

Build-up Exercise 5: Stage 3

Open the **First_Aid** presentation.

Insert a new slide based on the Title and Content layout immediately after the title slide.

Type 'A Typical Large Company Safety Organisation' as the slide title.

Create an organisational chart based on Figure 5.50.

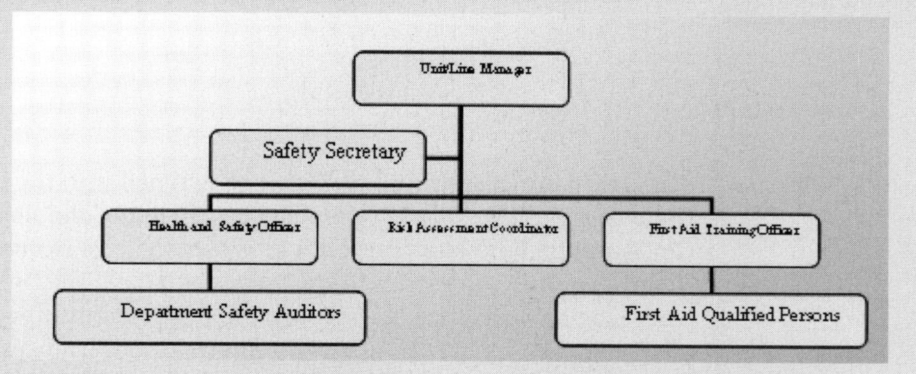

Figure 5.50

Insert a new slide based on the Title and Content layout after slide 8, Circulation.

Create a table based on the information contained in Table 5.6.

Table 5.6

Type	Number
Transport	5210
Falls	15340
Inanimate physical	560
Animate physical	68
Drowning and threats to breathing	1871
Fire, heat and hot substances	24000
Poisoning	32
Other accidents	364
Total (all accidents)	47445

Format the Number column so that it is right-aligned.

Save the presentation.

Using the find and replace function to edit data

If you completed Unit 1 you will already have come across the find and replace facility. The facility offered in PowerPoint is the same. First select Replace... from the Edit option on the main menu (or use the keyboard shortcut key Crtl+H). The dialogue box shown in Figure 5.51 will appear.

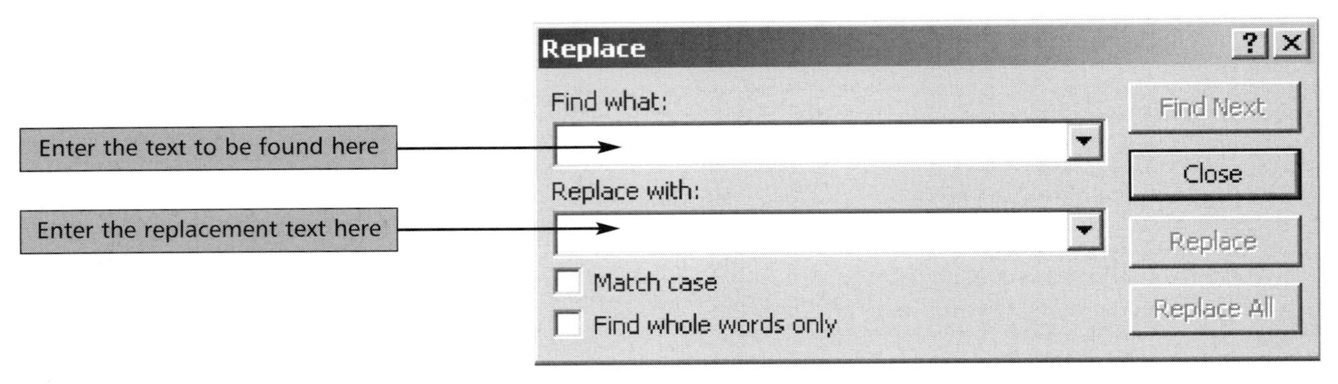

Figure 5.51

The text you wish to find and change is typed into the top Find what: field and the text that is to replace it is typed in the Replace with: field. Pressing the Find Next button will report the first occurrence of the word or phrase you want to find. You then have the option of replacing that single occurrence by pressing the Replace button or, alternatively, pressing the Replace All key will replace all occurrences of the word or phrase in the entire presentation.

Try it out

Open SafeHome if it is not already open.

Select Replace from the Edit option on the toolbar.

Type 'house' in the Find what: field.

Type 'home' in the Replace with: field.

Notice that the two check boxes immediately below the Replace with: field offer you the options of making your search case sensitive (Match case) or finding whole words only.

Press Find Next button.

Press Replace (in this instance you will know that there is only one occurrence of the word).

Press the Close button.

Save the presentation.

Using automatic and custom fields

When you learnt how to set up the Slide Master on page 213 you learnt that text and graphics relied on placeholders, whether in the Slide Master or Normal view of the slide. In addition you saw that custom placeholders can be placed either in the Slide Master or on individual slides. Typical automatic fields are:

- date
- date and time
- slide number.

To insert automatic place holders use View, Header and Footer… on the main menu. The dialogue box shown in Figure 5.52 will appear.

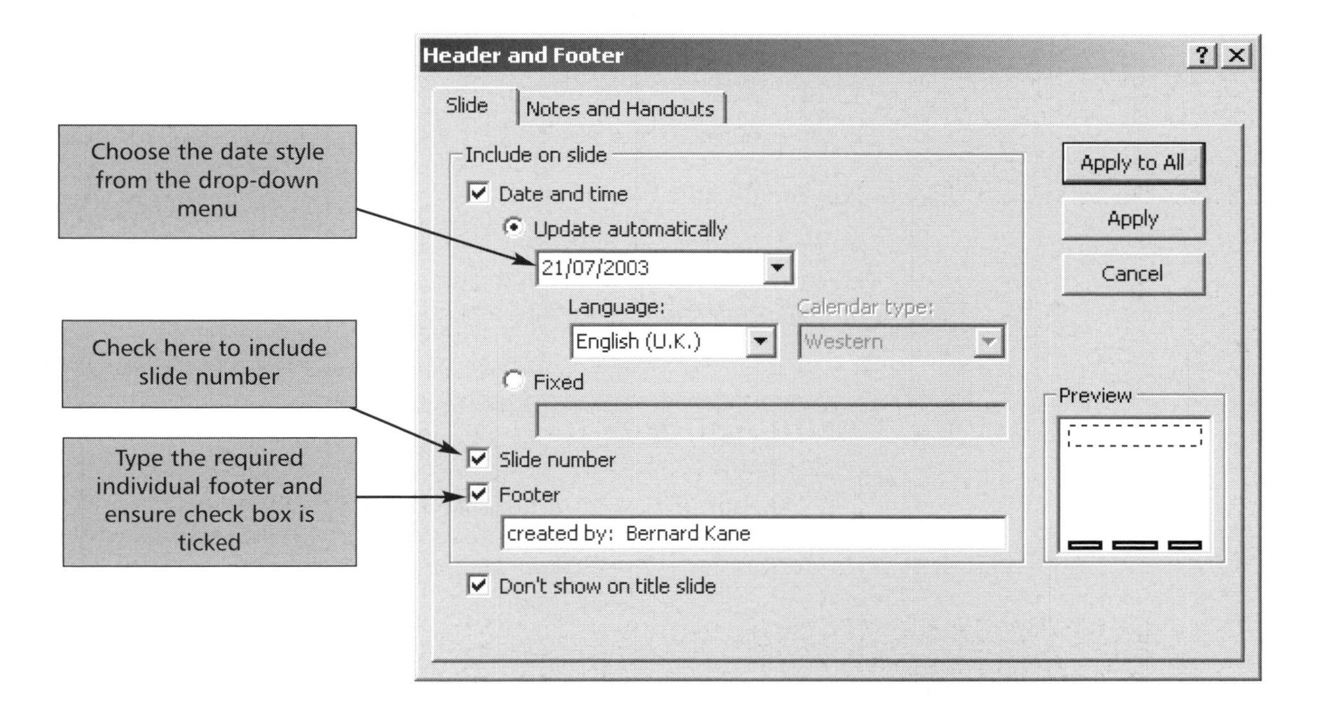

Figure 5.52

If you are inserting a footer in Normal view you can choose whether to apply to the current slide or to all slides in the presentation. You also have the choice at the bottom of the dialogue box to omit the footers from the title slide.

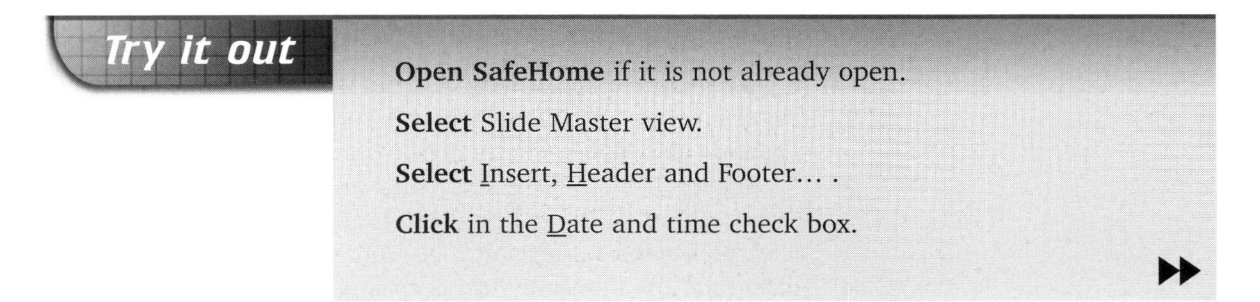

Try it out

Open SafeHome if it is not already open.

Select Slide Master view.

Select Insert, Header and Footer… .

Click in the Date and time check box.

Click on the Update automatically radio button.

Select the short date format (e.g. 3/9/02).

Click in the Slide number and the Footer check boxes.

Type 'created by:' followed by your name.

Click in the Don't show on title slide check box.

Press the Apply to All button.

Select Normal from the View menu to return to the Normal view of your presentation.

You should now see, other than on the first slide, the date on the left of each slide, the slide number on the right and your footer in the centre.

Save the presentation.

You should now be able to:

- find and replace data
- insert automatic fields into a slide
- insert custom footers into a presentation.

Build-up Exercise 5: Stage 4

Open the **First_Aid** presentation if it is not already open.

Select Slide Master view.

Insert the date and slide number on each slide except the title slide.

Insert 'created by:' followed by your name in the bottom centre of each slide except the title slide.

Save the presentation.

Controlling a presentation

Viewing a slide presentation

So far you have learnt how to build individual slides for a presentation using a variety of different types of placeholder. You can view the slide show by clicking on the Slide Show icon in the bottom left corner of the screen or alternatively selecting View Show from the Slide Show option on the main menu. To move through the show simply click on the left-hand mouse button. You will be shown the next slide each time the mouse button is clicked. At the end of the show a black screen will appear with the words 'End of slide show, click to exit'. Once you click you will be returned to the Normal editing view.

PowerPoint also offers other options for viewing the show. Instead of using the mouse button to progress through the show you can select the arrow shown in Figure 5.53.

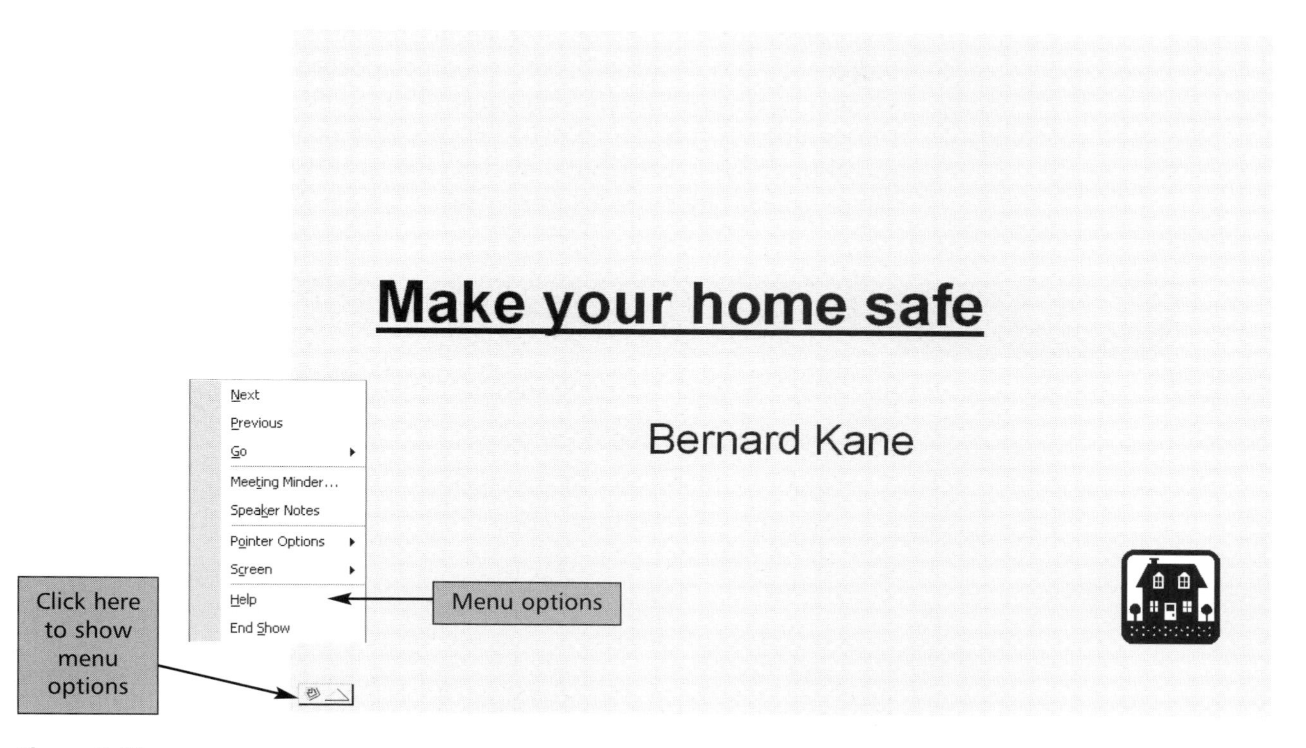

Figure 5.53

You can also move through the presentation by using the Page Up and Page Down keys on the keyboard. Which of these methods you choose is a matter of personal preference.

Controlling a presentation with blank slides

Shortly you will learn how to animate your show and incorporate different settings to move from one slide to another. However, using blank slides can both improve the general view of your presentation and at the same help you mark a particular point in the presentation or indicate that the presentation has concluded without relying on the default blank slide mentioned in the previous section. More often than not you will finish a presentation with a blank slide, or indeed a title slide that defines the end of the presentation. Blank slides can be inserted in any part of the presentation. They can be useful if you want to pause at a particular point or between topics.

Using the build functions

In order to enliven a presentation and make it more interesting to the audience PowerPoint provides a wide range of build functions for animating certain aspects of a slideshow. This is known as the slide build. On the attached CD is a PowerPoint presentation called **Demonstrating**

Build Functions and this provides a brief overview of the type of build facilities that are available. Since the range of these facilities is large the demonstration file can only give a taste of the types of build that can be created. Open the file in PowerPoint and click the Slide Show icon.

Microsoft PowerPoint refers to build facilities as Custom Animations and these provide visual effects to both text and graphics. For example, you can get text to fly from just about any place on the screen in a variety of ways. You can make a graphic appear to move, or in the XP version of PowerPoint you can get the font to change colour as the presentation is run. For CLAIT Plus you are expected to be able to incorporate fairly basic build effects. The easiest way to demonstrate what is meant by build is to carry out a simple Try it out exercise.

Try it out

Create a new blank presentation.

Click on the Title slide frame.

Type 'This is a Build Exercise'.

Click on the border of the Click to add sub-title frame and press the delete button to delete the sub-title frame.

Insert a new slide based on the Title and Text layout.

Click in the Title frame and type:

'Benefits of using the build facility'.

Click in the Click to add text frame and enter the following bulleted points:

- Build effects provide exciting visual effects to a presentation.
- They allow emphasis on important points.
- They create a professional impact.

Click on the Title text frame.

Select Custom Animation… From Slide Show on the main menu.

If you are using PowerPoint XP the Custom Animation task pane will appear to the right of the screen: see Figure 5.54.

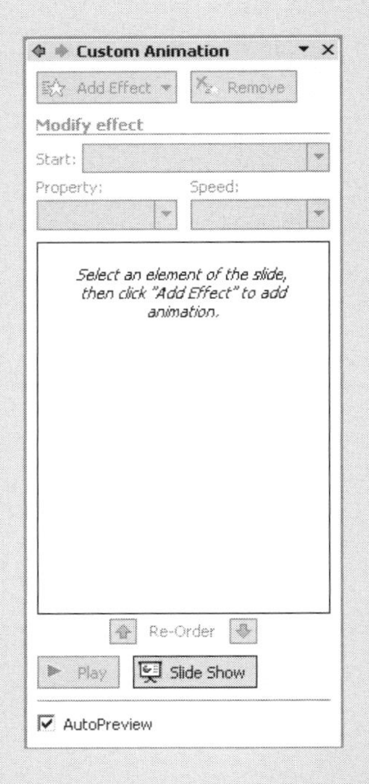

Figure 5.54

When a frame is selected (in this case the title frame) and no previous animations have been added, the only option in the task pane that is available is Add Effect. By selecting this you are then offered a number of options as shown in Figure 5.55.

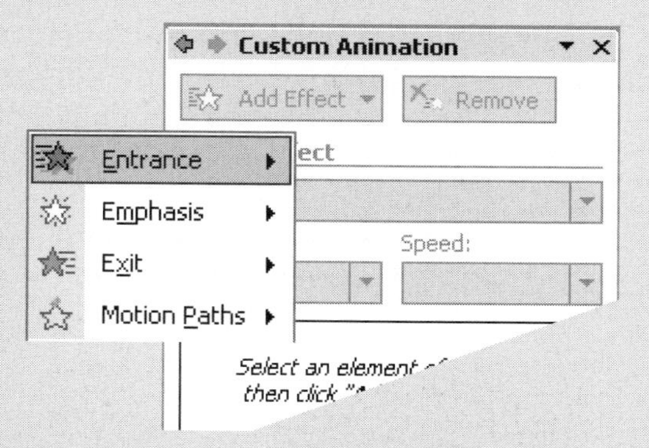

Figure 5.55

At this time you are only interested in the Entrance option. These are the effects that determine how your text is going to appear on the slide. For example is it going to Fly in, Swivel or simply just Appear? Clicking on the Entrance option of the Add Effect list will show you a further list containing a number of entrance effects. If none of these is suitable then you can select the More Effects… option and a further list appears. The two lists are shown in Figure 5.56.

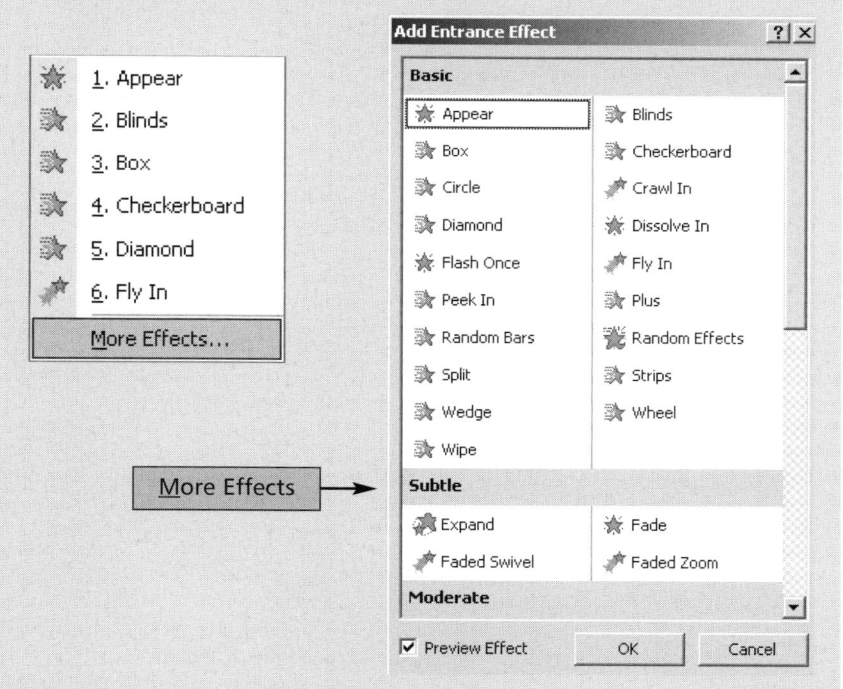

Figure 5.56

In the second options list, the effects (in XP only) are categorised into sub-categories:

- Basic
- Subtle
- Moderate
- Exciting

Select Zoom from the list (which in XP is shown as a Moderate effect); as the choice is selected PowerPoint previews the effect in the background on your slide.

Press OK.

If you now look at the task pane you will notice that a number of further options have been enabled.

Have a look at Figure 5.57.

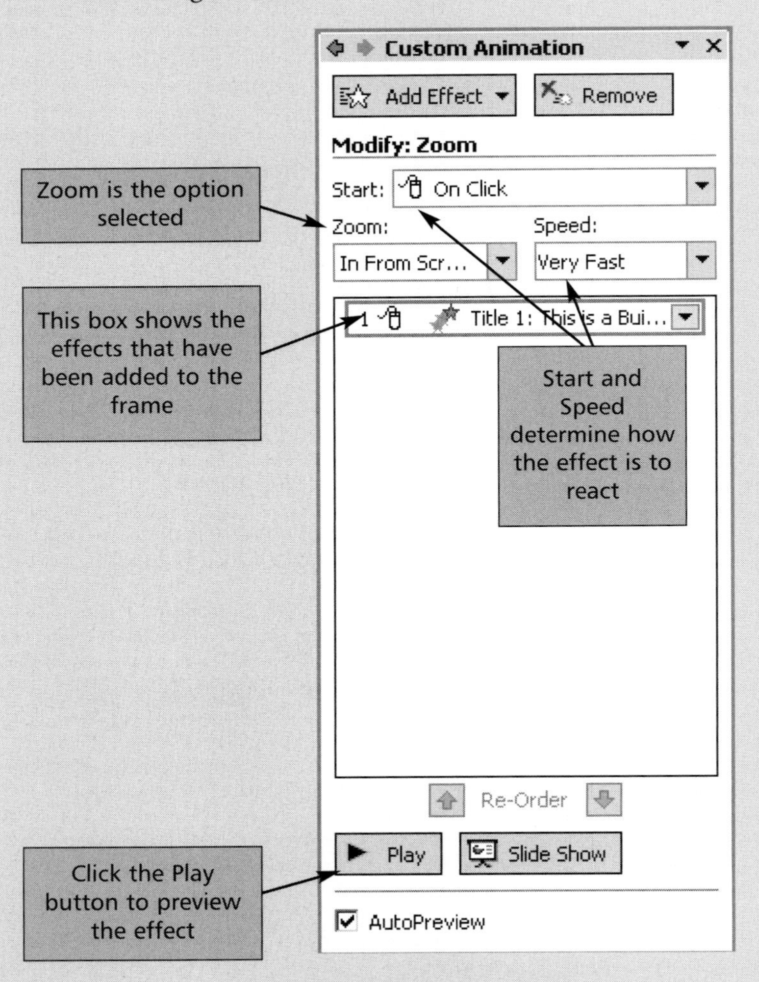

Figure 5.57

In the Start: box PowerPoint indicates, by default, that the animation will start following a mouse click. You can test this by clicking the Slide Show icon in the bottom left of the screen, or by pressing the Slide Show button at the bottom of the animation task pane or finally by pressing the Play button, also located at the bottom of the task pane. If you choose the Slide Show option initially the screen will only display the bullet points you entered earlier. The title is not visible. To view the animated title click the left-hand mouse button and the text appears using the zoom effect. To return to the Normal view press the Esc key on the keyboard.

Save your presentation as **Animate1**.

All text, such as the bulleted points and objects, can be animated using any of the effects provided in the PowerPoint program. The range of effects will vary depending on the version you are using. In the next Try it out exercise you will animate the bullet points on the second slide so that they appear one at a time when the slide show is run.

Try it out

Open Animate1 if it is not already open.

Select the second slide in Normal view.

Click on the bullet list.

Click on the Add Effect button in the task pane and then:

Click on Entrance.

Click on More Effects… .

Select Fade from the list.

Note: if using an earlier version select any suitable effect from those available.

Press OK.

Save the presentation.

Now run the slide show to view the animation effects. As you saw in the previous exercise there are a number of ways you can view the animations set in the slide build. You can either select the Slide Show icon or press the Slide Show button in the task pane or press the Play button, again shown in the task pane. Pressing the Play button will automatically run through each animation in Normal rather than Slide Show view.

Now try introducing some build effects to your **First_Aid** presentation.

Build-up Exercise 5: Stage 5

Open the **First_Aid** presentation.

Select the first slide of the presentation – the title slide.

Using the right-hand mouse button:

Click on the title frame.

Select Custom Animation… from the menu list.

The Custom Animation task pane will appear to the right of your screen.

Click on the Add Effect button in the top left of the task pane Add Effect ▾.

Select Entrance and then Fly In from the list of effects offered: see Figure 5.58.

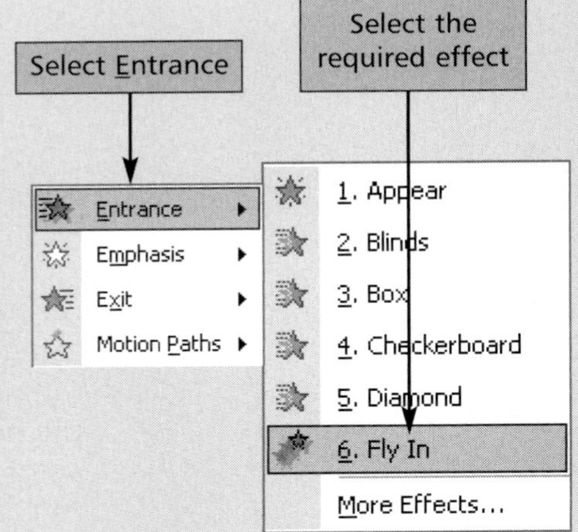

Figure 5.58

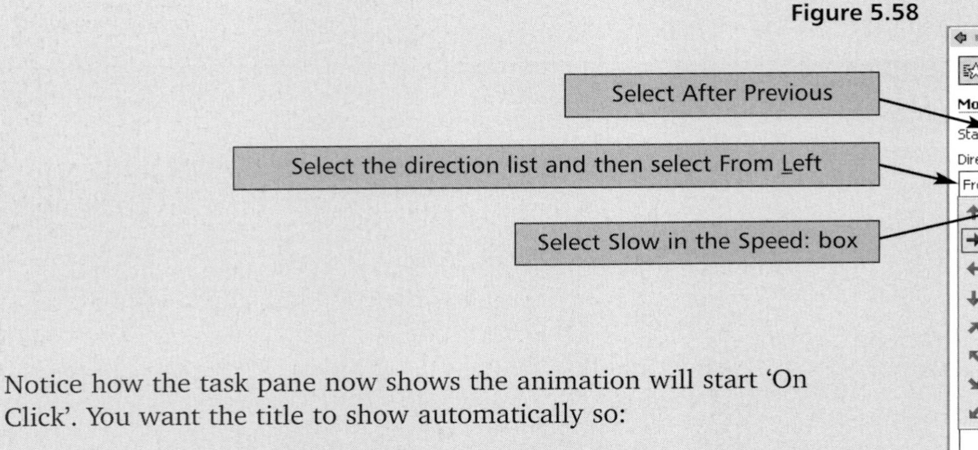

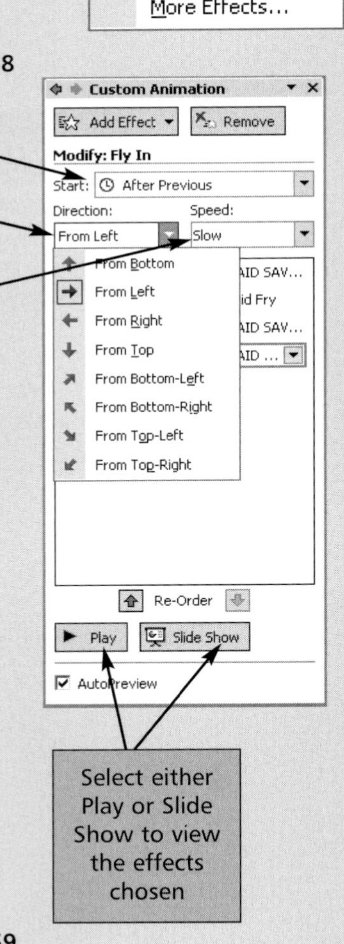

Notice how the task pane now shows the animation will start 'On Click'. You want the title to show automatically so:

Click on the arrow to the right of the Start: field and

Select After Previous from the list offered.

By default PowerPoint selects Fly from the bottom.

Select From Left in the Direction: field.

Set the Speed: field to Slow.

Play the animation using either of the selections at the bottom of the task pane: see Figure 5.59.

Save the presentation.

Figure 5.59

Grouping text

The ability to group text is not specifically a CLAIT Plus requirement. However, understanding build effects is, and the ability to group text at different levels is an extension of the build options.

In the second text box of the title side of the **First_Aid** presentation there are two lines of text. These are not bullet points nor are they separate text boxes. Text can be grouped to enter at different levels. The text can enter all at once, or can be entered by paragraph levels.

In the build-up exercise if you wanted to bring the name text in all at once you would need to understand a little more about the Effect Options… that are available. Have a look at Figure 5.60.

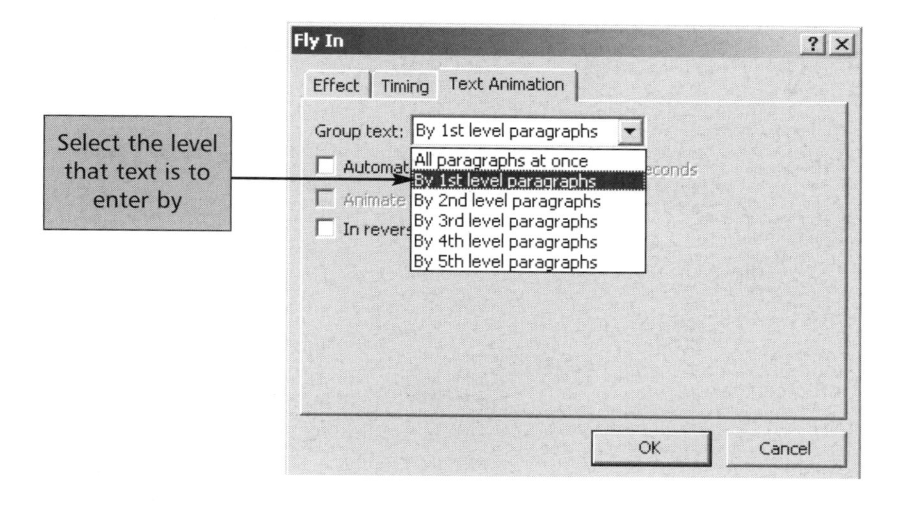

Figure 5.60

The Effect dialogue box is showing that the effect chosen is Fly In. The Text Animation tab is selected and the options available are shown in the drop-down list. If all text is to enter at once then the As one object option should be chosen.

Build-up Exercise 5: Stage 6

Open the **First_Aid** presentation if it is not already open.

Select the second text box in the first slide with the text:

By
David Fry

Select Add Effect, Entrance, Fly In.

Leave the direction as From Bottom.

Change the speed to Medium.

In the lower half of the task pane you will see the new animation effect 'Text 2' listed.

Click on the Text 2 animation in the task pane and then the arrow to the right of the Text 2 box to show the menu options list.

Select Effect Options... (see Figure 5.61).

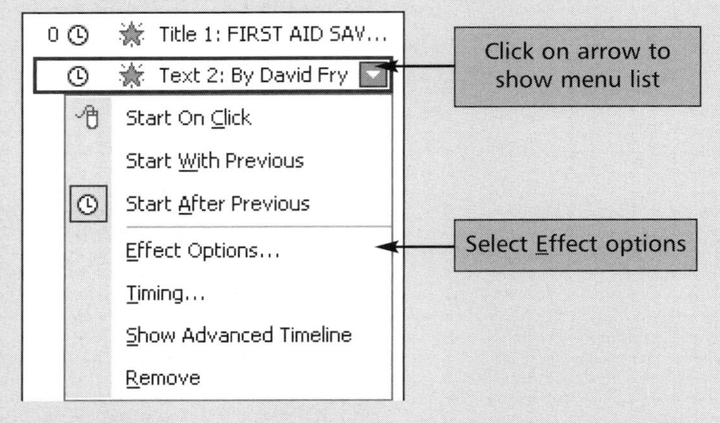

Figure 5.61

Select the text Animation tab.

In the Group text: field:

Select As one object from the list.

Press OK.

Now press the Play button at the bottom of the task pane to check that the effect is what is wanted.

Now introduce animations for the rest of the slides in the presentation. Remember that you can apply effects to picture objects as well as text.

Save the presentation.

Automating build effects

In addition to setting a specified animated effect to text or an object in a slide you can also program the animation to run automatically, as opposed to using a mouse click to activate the effect. Sometimes you will want to use the mouse to move from one point to the next, but on other occasions you may want to have an automated presentation such as the demonstration presentation on the CD accompanying this book. Again, the best way of demonstrating this facility is with a Try it out exercise.

Try it out

Open a new presentation.

Change the opening slide layout to Title and Text.

Type the following as a heading:

'Learning how to animate effects'.

In the second bullet text frame:

Type the following bullet points:

- Click on the frame to be formatted.
- Select Add Effect, followed by Entrance and then choose an effect.
- Click on the appropriate frame in the task pane list.
- Click on the arrow to the right of the list item selected.
- Select Effect Options... .
- Check the 'Automatically after' box.
- Click OK.

> **LAYOUT TIP**
>
> To change the layout, select Format, Slide Layout... from the main menu or using the right-hand mouse button click in a blank area of the slide and from the menu list offered select Slide Layout..., or finally, use the Slide Layout icon from the Formatting toolbar .

Note: As you add an effect to a frame, details will appear in a list of animations in the central part of the task pane. Clicking on a list item will highlight the item and an arrow will appear to the right of the box. Clicking on the arrow will produce a drop-down list of options as shown in Figure 5.62.

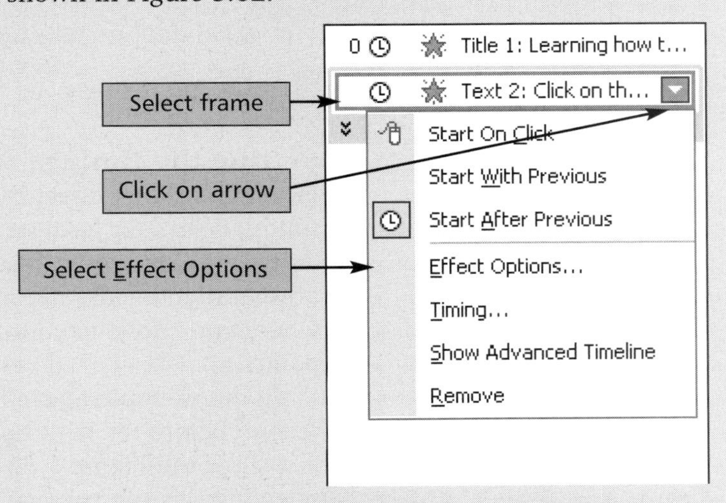

Figure 5.62

On selecting the Effect Options... item from the list the same dialogue box as you saw in Figure 5.60 will appear. However, this time you want each bullet item to appear separately. Being a bullet list PowerPoint assumes this and the 'By 1st level paragraphs' is shown as the default. In this case you want the items to appear without individual mouse clicks so:

Check the Automatically after box.

This will ensure the bullet points will appear automatically without the need to use the mouse to advance each item in the list: see Figure 5.63.

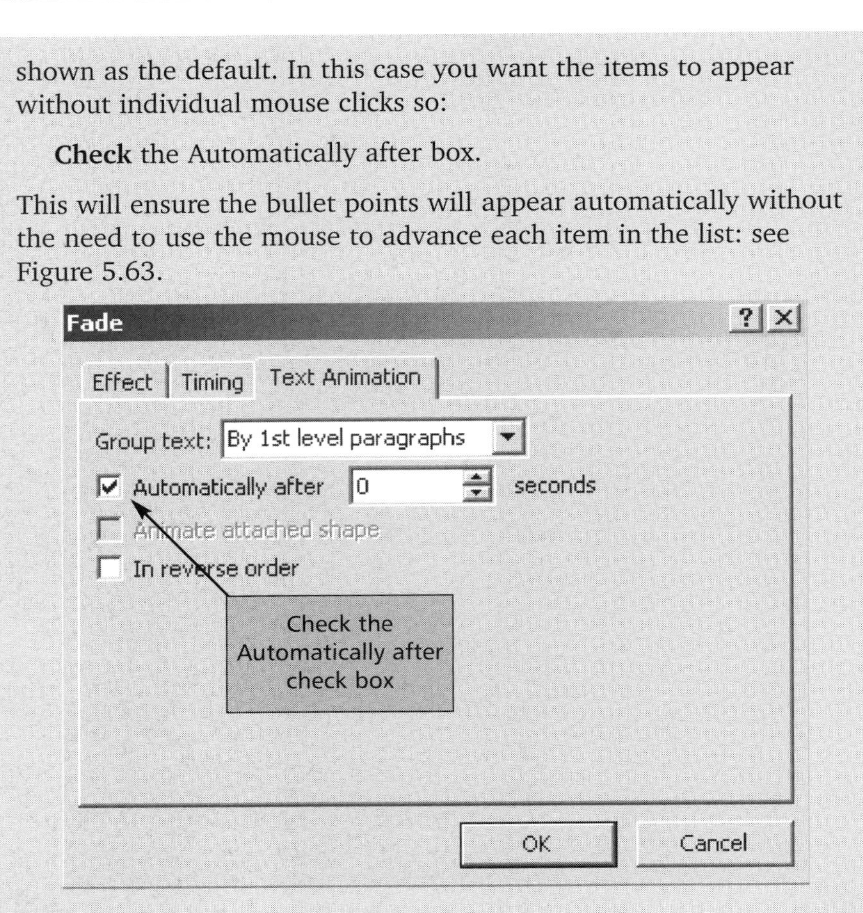

Figure 5.63

Click OK.

Save the presentation as **Timing1.ppt.**

Setting the timings for effects

When you set an effect to run automatically PowerPoint has built-in timing delays for each item. Normally effects will run with virtually no delay at all but you can set the timing controls to meet your own presentation needs. You may, for example, have a prepared script where you know how long you will be talking between each bullet point.

In the example above it may be that you want to talk for one second before the next bullet point comes into view. On the dialogue box shown in Figure 5.63 you will have noticed a Timing tab. By selecting this tab you can choose a range of timing options: see Figure 5.64.

The Start: option will let you select:

- On Click – which means the animation will commence on the click of the mouse button.
- With Previous – to specify that the animation starts at the same time as the previous one.

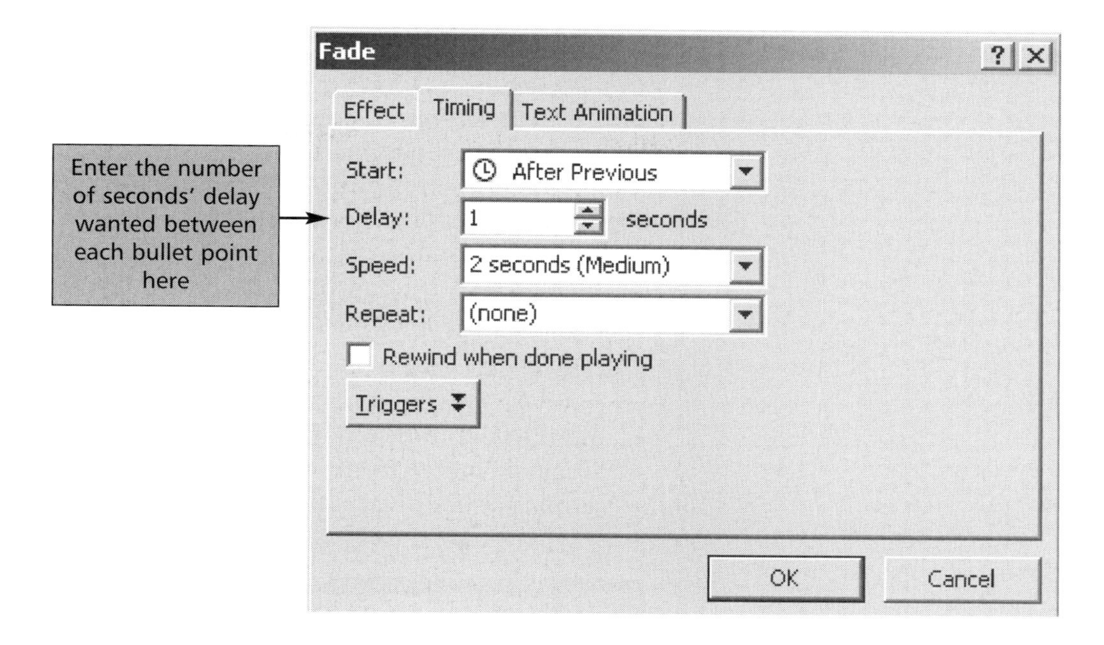

Figure 5.64

- After Previous – to specify that the animation will start immediately after the previous one.

The Delay: field allows you to specify the time delay before the start of the next animation.

The Speed: field allows you specify the speed or length of the animation.

Now try introducing timing between each bullet point.

Try it out

Open your **Timing1.ppt** presentation if it is not already open.

Select the bullet frame in the animations list of the task pane.

Select Effect Options… from the list.

Click on the Timing tab of the dialogue box.

In the Delay: field:

Enter '1' for the number of seconds between each bullet appearing.

In the Speed: box:

Select the '2 seconds (Medium)' option.

Click OK.

Save the presentation.

Run the slide show using any of the techniques previously outlined.

Setting builds in the Master Slide

In the previous section you created build effects in the Normal view of the presentation. Depending on the complexity of your presentation it is often easier to set your build effects in the Master Slide. The process for introducing builds in the Master slide is exactly the same as creating them in the Normal view. This is also true for creating transitions from one slide to another which is covered later in this unit.

You should now be able to:

- view a slide presentation
- control a presentation using blank slides
- use the build function to animate slide objects
- automate build effects
- set timings for build effects.

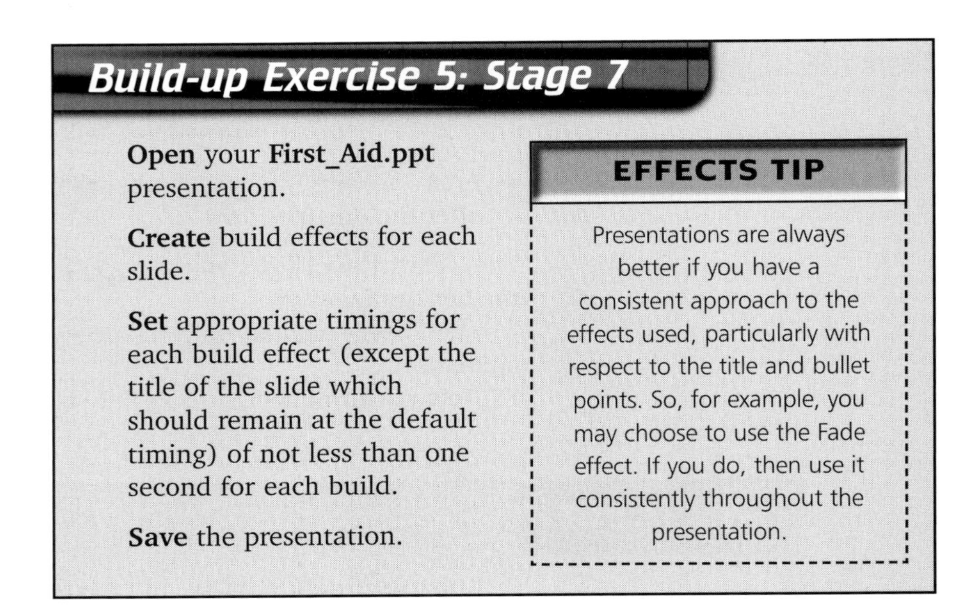

Build-up Exercise 5: Stage 7

Open your **First_Aid.ppt** presentation.

Create build effects for each slide.

Set appropriate timings for each build effect (except the title of the slide which should remain at the default timing) of not less than one second for each build.

Save the presentation.

EFFECTS TIP

Presentations are always better if you have a consistent approach to the effects used, particularly with respect to the title and bullet points. So, for example, you may choose to use the Fade effect. If you do, then use it consistently throughout the presentation.

Modifying presentations

Changing the order of slides in a presentation

Changing the order or position of a slide in a presentation is also a requirement in CLAIT Plus. To change the order or position of a slide, select the Slides tab in the task pane to the left of the screen then click on the slide thumbnail using the left-hand mouse button and with the button depressed drag the slide to the required position as shown in Figure 5.65.

Note: The same procedure can also be carried out using the Outline tab. Hold the cursor over the slide icon next to the slide number and then drag to the new position using the same technique as above.

Notice how the slide number is automatically amended to reflect its new place in the presentation.

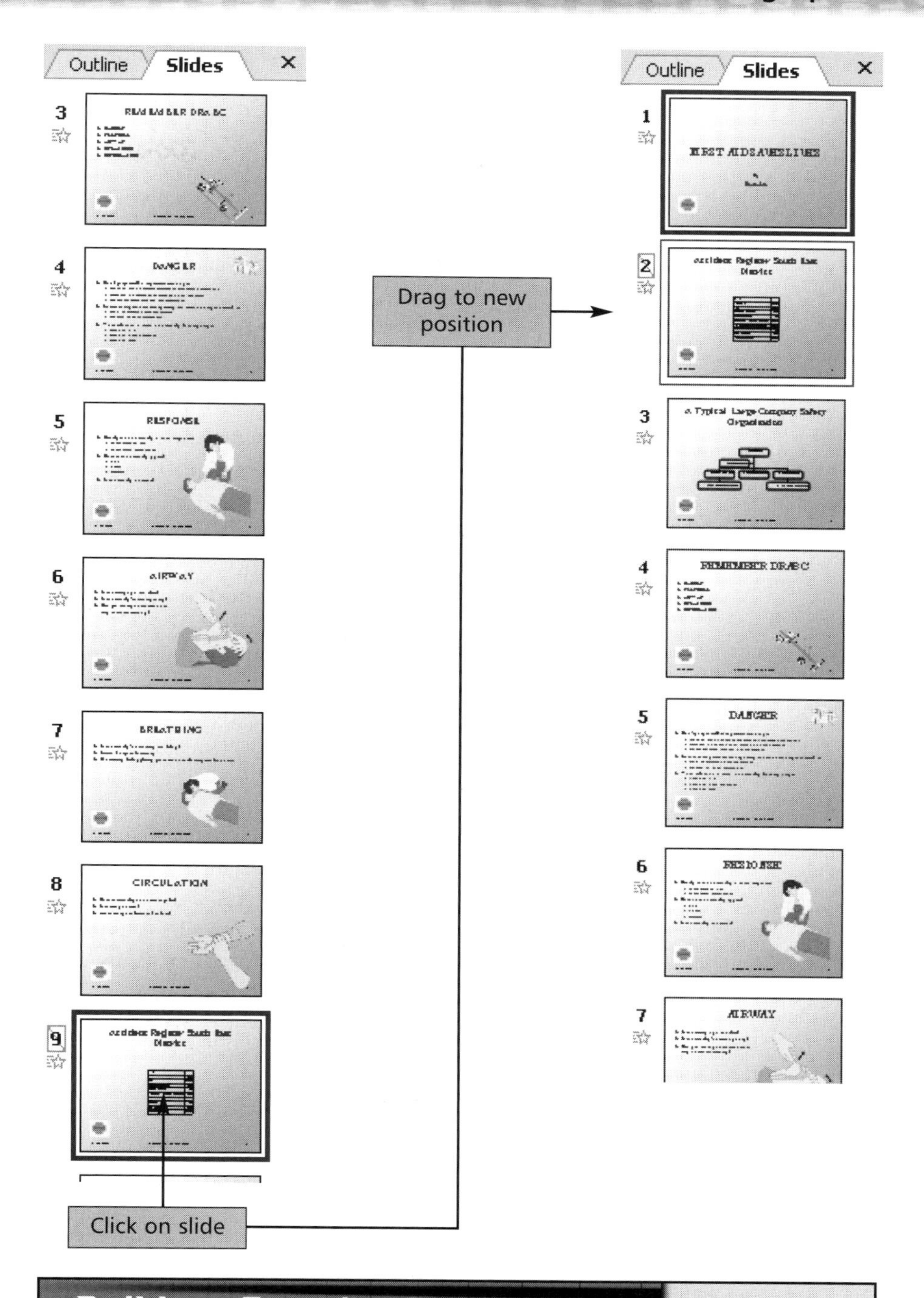

Figure 5.65

Build-up Exercise 5: Stage 8

Open your **First_Aid** presentation.

Move the slide showing the accident register in the South East District from its current position (9) to a position immediately following the first slide.

Save your presentation.

Close the presentation.

For CLAIT Plus you are required to know how to delete and hide slides.

Deleting a slide

To delete a slide simply click on the thumbnail view of the slide you want to delete using the right-hand mouse button and select Delete Slide. To delete more than one slide at a time, press and hold the Crtl key on the keyboard and select each slide to be deleted in turn. Alternatively go to Slide Sorter View by pressing the Slide Sorter View icon and repeat the process outlined above.

Hiding a slide

There may well be times when you prepare a presentation on the same subject but for different audiences. For example, a presentation may be designed for members of your own organisation but could be suitable for external consumption without the information that is specific to your colleagues within the company. You may find that an internal audience needs to know more information on the subject than an external one. Alternatively, you may have confidential information for internal consumption that you would prefer not to show to those outside the organisation. PowerPoint offers you the opportunity to hide slides depending on your audience. To hide a slide select the slide that is to be hidden, in the thumbnails or Slide Sorter view. Now select Hide Slide from the Slide Show menu option.

Creating links to hidden slides

Having hidden slides in the presentation it would be useful if you did not need to amend the presentation to suit the audience. A way of overcoming this is to create a hyperlink to the hidden slide for times when the presentation is to show these. A hyperlink can be created in any part of the presentation, but you would normally create it in the slide immediately before the one that is hidden.

To create a link first:

Open the slide which is to contain the link in Normal view.

Highlight the text or object to which you want to attach the link and either:

Press Insert, Hyperlink from the main menu.

or

Click on the Hyperlink icon from the standard toolbar .

You will be presented with the Insert Hyperlink dialogue box. Don't worry; it is less complicated than it looks in Figure 5.66.

At the top of the dialogue box you will see the text that has been highlighted and which will act as the link text. To the left PowerPoint is asking where you want to link to. In the example you want to link to a slide in the presentation (the hidden Slide 3).

Click on Place in This Document. This tells PowerPoint that the link's address is within the current presentation.

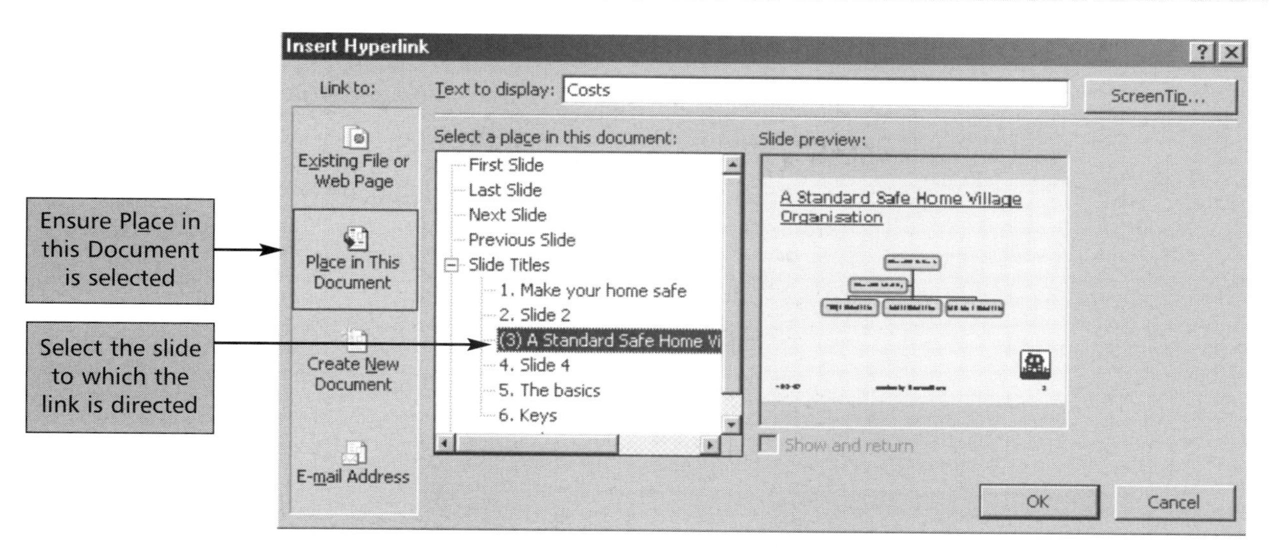

Figure 5.66

In the Select a place in this document: window PowerPoint shows all the places in the document where the link can be made. In this case you are interested in Slide 3 (the brackets around the number three identify this as a hidden slide).

Select Slide No 3 – A Standard Safe Home Village Organisation.

Press OK.

A link has now been created between Slide 2 and Slide 3 using the text 'Costs' in Slide 2. Notice how the text is underlined and the colour of the text has changed to the default colour for showing a hyperlink.

If you want to make the link unobtrusive to the audience, first underline the other headings in the table and then change the colour of the hyperlink through the Design Layout options.

Changing defaults in the design layout

Being able to change the design layout is not a CLAIT Plus requirement but is included here for completeness. To change the hyperlink design colour:

Select Format, Slide design... from the main menu.

In the slide design task pane:

Select Color Schemes (at the top of the task pane).

Select Edit Color Schemes... which can be found at the bottom of the task pane underneath the colour scheme templates.

Under the Custom tab in the Edit Color Scheme dialogue box, amend the colours of:

- Accent and Hyperlink
- Accent followed by Hyperlink

To do this:

Click on the square next to the appropriate scheme colour.

Press the Change Color... button.

Select the colour from the palette by clicking on the colour with the left-hand mouse button.

Press OK.

Press Apply.

Each of the headings will now look the same, even though the Costs heading is a hyperlink to Slide 3.

Try it out

Open SafeHome.ppt.

By following the steps outlined above:

Hide Slide 3.

Create a hyperlink from Slide 2 to Slide 3 using any of the headings in the table in Slide 2.

Insert a blank slide after the last slide of the presentation.

Save the presentation when you have completed this exercise.

Run the slideshow through once to check that Slide 3 is hidden.

Once you have run through the presentation once, start from the beginning again but this time when Slide 2 opens:

Click on the hyperlink you have created and notice how the presentation will go to Slide 3 – the hidden slide. Notice how the cursor changes shape to a hand when it is moved over the word Costs.

Now return to your **First_Aid** presentation in the following build-up exercise and complete the following tasks.

Build-up Exercise 5: Stage 9

Open your **First_Aid** presentation.

Using the techniques outlined above:

Hide Slide 2 (Accident Register South East District).

Create a link from Slide 1 to Slide 2 using the creator's name 'David Fry' for the link.

Optional: if you wish to change the colour scheme of the hyperlink do so.

Save the presentation.

Run the presentation.

Close the presentation.

Using transition facilities

Transitions are another way of making your presentation visually interesting or exciting. Where animated effects have been added to a slide PowerPoint includes a default transition, but these can be fine tuned and enhanced. For example, if your presentation is to run without the use of a mouse to click between slides you could set the slide to advance to the next automatically. This is often done in advertising presentations. Each slide is set to advance automatically and a further facility is also available that allows you to replay (or loop) the whole presentation continuously until it is physically stopped.

Whereas a build effect acts on an object (text, chart picture, etc.) on a slide, a transition applies to the slide as a whole.

Try it out

Open the **SafeHome.ppt** presentation.

Type 'Types of incident by %' as the title for Slide 4.

Insert a blank slide at the end of the presentation.

Create build effects for each of the slides except Slide 7.

You will be unable to create a build effect for the blank slide as there are no text or object frames.

Select Slide Show then Slide Transition from the main menu.

The Slide transition task pane will appear on the right of the screen and is shown in Figure 5.67.

The task pane has three main sections:

- Apply to selected slides:
- Modify transition
- Advance slide

At the bottom of the task pane you also have the opportunity to apply the selected transition to all slides, playing the selected transition in Normal view or in Slide Show view and given the choice whether to preview or not.

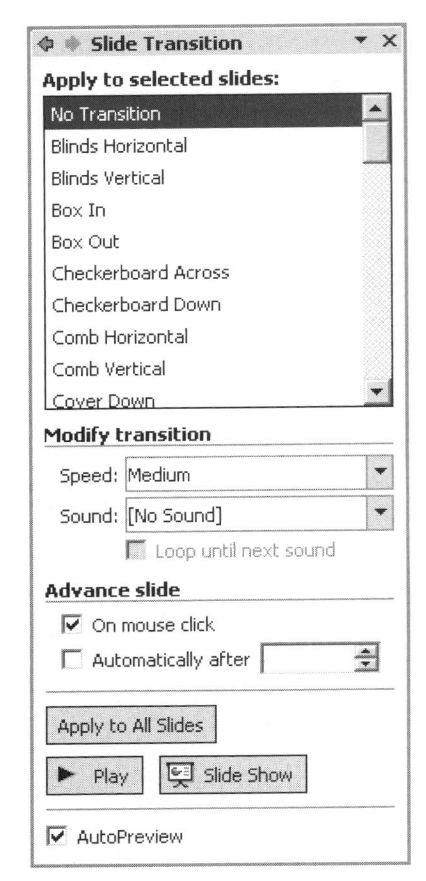

Figure 5.67

Selecting the transition style

PowerPoint offers a range of styles for the transition of a style. To select a style simply scroll down the list in the Apply to selected slides: section and click on one of the styles. If the AutoPreview check box has a tick in it then you will see a preview of the selection as it is made.

Select a transition style from the list.

Modify transition

The second section gives you the option of selecting a speed for the transition – Slow, Medium or Fast – and also selecting a sound from the list provided.

Select Slow for the speed; leave the sound as [No Sound].

Advance slide

In the last of the main sections PowerPoint gives you the option of advancing the slide manually or automatically. Which you choose is determined by whether you want to control the slide advancement or if you prefer the presentation to run through each slide automatically.

Deselect On mouse click.

Select Automatically after.

Underneath the Automatically after option you can enter a delay period.

Enter '2 second' in the Automatically after box.

Note: for the final blank slide leave the option as On mouse click.

Finally you can choose to apply your choices to the current slide or by pressing the Apply to All Slides button your choice is automatically reflected throughout the presentation.

Consistency has been mentioned a number of times in this unit. It can be annoying to the viewer of your presentation to introduce too many styles (either in build effects or transitions).

Note: If you choose Apply to All Slides you will need to manually alter the final blank slide back to the On mouse click option.

Save the presentation.

Close the presentation.

A copy of the presentation can be found in the Unit 5 folder of the accompanying CD.

Remember, as mentioned above, that you can also use the Master Slide to set your transitions between slides. Using the Master Slide helps you to ensure that there is consistency across the presentation.

You should now be able to:

- change the order of slides in a presentation
- delete and hide slides
- create hyperlinks within a presentation
- use the slide transition facility.

Build-up Exercise 5: Stage 10

Open your **First_Aid.ppt** presentation.

Create a transition effect for each slide except the final blank slide.

Brief

- Transition should not advance automatically but only on a mouse click.
- Transition should be consistent throughout the presentation.
- Speed should be Medium.
- No sound is to be applied.

Run your presentation using any of the techniques learnt in this unit.

Save the presentation.

Close the presentation.

A sample file for this presentation called **First_Aid.ppt** can be found on the CD accompanying this book.

Printing presentation support documents

Handouts and presenter guidance notes

Presentations can be used in a variety of ways. There is the type of presentation that simply informs the viewer about a topic or product and runs automatically on a screen. Alternatively, and possibly more usually, there is the type of presentation that is literally presented to the audience slide by slide on a screen, to give information on a specific subject. With the latter type of presentation it is customary to provide 'handouts' that allow the audience to make notes either during the presentation or provide a reminder of the subject matter at a later time. PowerPoint allows you to print off individual slides or a number of slides grouped on a page.

In addition to handouts you can print the presenter's notes for each slide in your presentation. These can be used as an 'aide memoir' to remind the speaker of important points that need be covered for each slide. Have a look a Figure 5.68.

Single slide printout

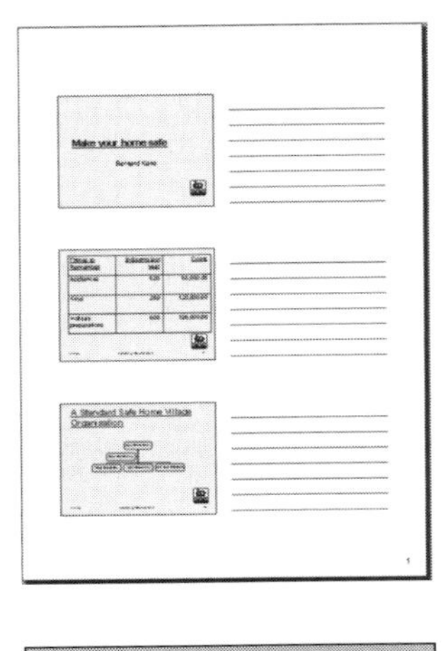

Handout with notes

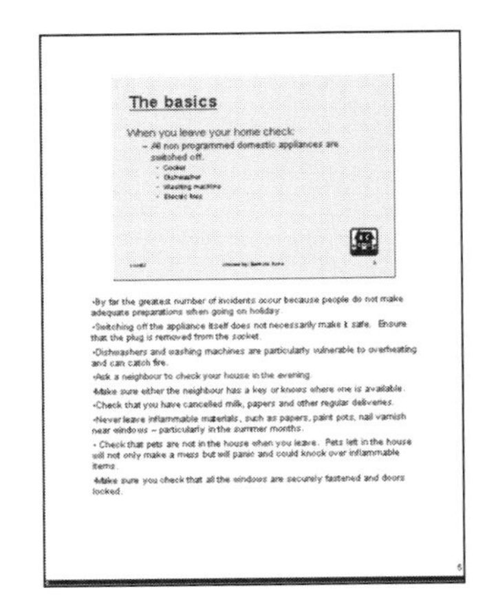

Presenter's notes

Figure 5.68

On the left is a printout of a single slide. In the middle is a handout print with three slides to the page. With the XP version of Office you can print up to nine slides per page (earlier versions only allow you to print six slides per page) but clearly if you use the whole page for slides there will be no room for those watching the presentation to make notes. On the right is a print of an individual slide with speaker notes below the slide to help prompt the speaker with the points he or she wishes to cover.

Printing slides, handouts and speaker notes

To access the print dialogue box select File, Print... from the main menu. The dialogue box shown in Figure 5.69 will appear.

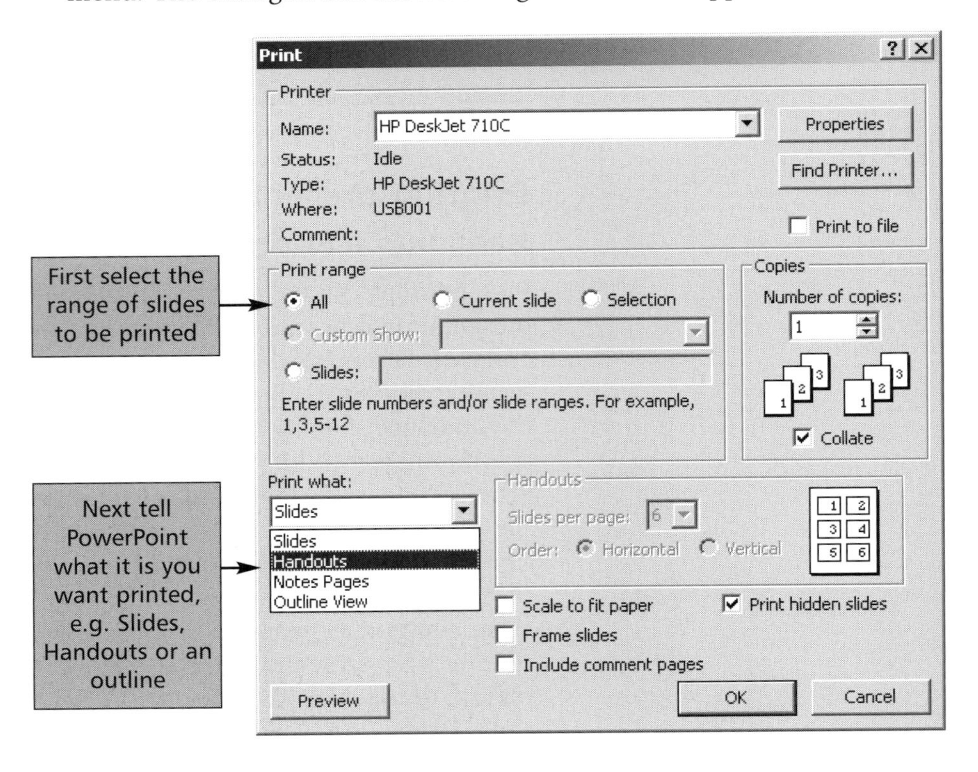

Figure 5.69

If you are familiar with Word you will notice that the Print dialogue box for PowerPoint is not that dissimilar. At the top of the box is information about the printer itself. In the second section you are asked to tell PowerPoint the range of slides to be printed. In the Print what: section you choose the type of print required:

- Slides
- Handouts
- Notes Pages
- Outline View.

By pressing Preview you can see how your print will look. The Preview page menu also allows you to change some of the selections made for that print, such as the number of slides per page, the orientation of the page and aspects such as the order of the slides.

Now try printing each of these options from the **SafeHome.ppt** presentation.

Try it out

Open the **SafeHome.ppt** presentation on the accompanying CD.

1 Print a single slide

Select File, Print... from the main menu.

In the Print range section:

Select Current slide.

In the Print what: section:

Select Slides.

Click on the Preview button to check what will be printed.

Click Print... on the menu bar.

2 Print three slides to a page as handouts

Select File, Print... from the main menu.

In the Print range section:

Select All.

In the Print what: section:

Select Handouts.

In the Handouts section Slides per page:

Type '3'.

Note: the Order: section is automatically disabled as the print will be vertical by default.

Click on the Preview button to check what will be printed.

Click Print... on the menu bar.

3 Print Speaker notes

Speaker's notes have been added to Slide 5 on the CD file.

Select File, Print... from the main menu.

In the Print range section:

Select Slides.

In the adjacent field:

Type '5'.

In the Print what: section:

Select Notes Pages.

Note: the Order: section is automatically disabled as the print will be vertical by default.

Click on the Preview button to check what will be printed.

Click Print... on the menu bar.

4 Print Outline View

Select File, Print... from the main menu.

In the Print range section:

Select All.

In the Print what: section:

Select Outline View.

Click on the Preview button to check what will be printed.

Click Print... on the menu bar.

Using screen prints

Screen prints (sometimes referred to as screen dumps) are the result of a facility whereby you can copy whatever is on the screen to the clipboard and paste the screen as an image in a Word document or other application. On your keyboard you will find a key that has PrtScn and SysRq printed on it. By pressing this button you automatically copy the entire screen view to the clipboard.

For CLAIT Plus you are required to produce a screen print to show the use of special effects and timings in a presentation. When you create an effect or introduce timing for a slide, PowerPoint will indicate that this has been done by showing a small effects icon or the timing used by the thumbnail of the slide. To see these click on the Slide Sorter View icon ⊞ at the bottom of the PowerPoint Screen. Have a look at Figure 5.70.

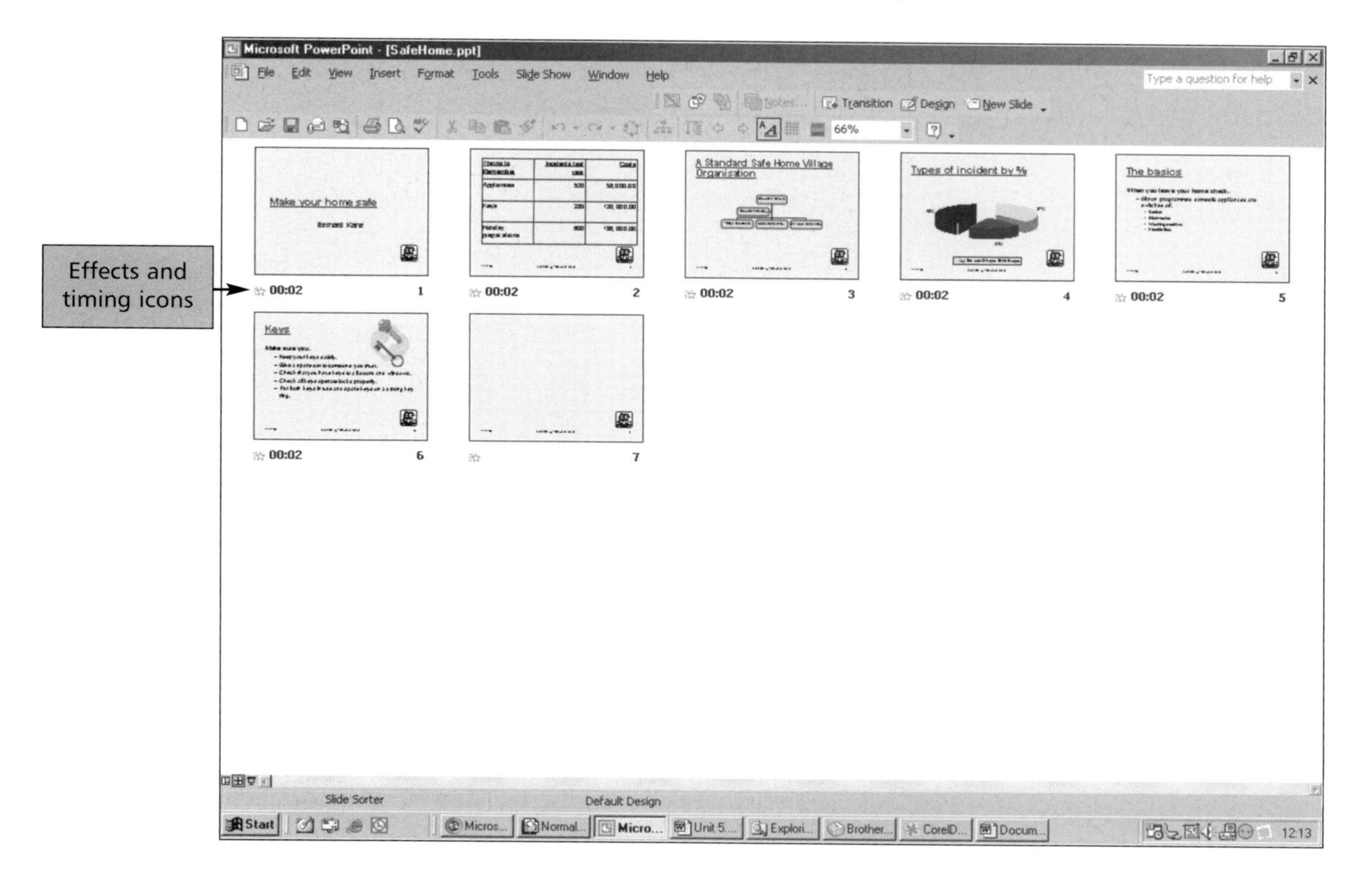

Figure 5.70

This figure was created as a screen print using the PrtScn button and then pasting the contents of the clipboard to a Word document. The small icons and numbers at the bottom of each slide indicate that effects and timing have been used in the slides. Notice how the last slide does not indicate a timing. That is because this was omitted from the last (blank) slide.

You should now be able to understand the use of and print:

- slides
- handouts
- notes pages
- outlines.

You should also be able to:

- create a screen print and paste it to a document for printing.

Build-up Exercise 5: Stage 11

Open your **First_Aid** presentation.

Task 1

Produce the following printouts:

- Single slide prints of Slides 3, 5 and 7.
- Handout prints with three slides per page for Slides 2, 4 and 6.
- Speaker prints for slides 2 and 3 (no notes are attached to these slides so none will show in the printouts).
- An outline print for all slides in the presentation.

Task 2

Create a screen print of all slides from the Slide Sorter view.

Paste the image to a Word (or other application) document.

Print the results.

Save the presentation.

Close the presentation.

You have now covered all the assessment objectives for CLAIT Plus presentation graphics. Now complete the practical assignment below. Solutions for this assignment can be found in Appendix 2.

Presentation graphics

Scenario

You work for a building society that recently changed from being a mutual society to a bank. Your boss has told you that he wants to give a presentation to a selected number of customers to promote the mortgage services the bank offers. He is very much aware that many young couples interested in setting up a home for the first time are unfamiliar with mortgages and how they are financed. He has asked you to prepare a presentation in PowerPoint that gives advice on types of mortgages and the various benefits and disadvantages.

You will need the following files to complete this exercise:

Slide text:	**Mortgages.doc**
Speaker notes:	**Advice_Notes.doc**
Image file:	**Many_Friends.gif**

Task 1

Assessment objectives	**Stage**	
	1	Open PowerPoint. Set up the Master Slide according to the brief on page 286. In this exercise you will: ■ apply a background ■ insert a graphic ■ insert slide numbers ■ insert a name ■ insert a date ■ apply a consistent heading style ■ apply different levels of bullet styles ■ use different font colours.

▶▶

Design brief

House style for master slide

Item	Colour	Style	Position	Guide
Background	Any	Not applicable	Not applicable	A single colour is to be used which may be white
Logo (Many_Friends.gif)	–	–	Top right	Logo must not overlap text and if resized must be kept in proportion
Slide Number	–	–	Bottom right	Do not include on first slide
Name	–	–	Bottom centre	Do not include on first slide
Date	–	–	Bottom left	Do not include on first slide
Builds	–	–	–	At least one effect per slide but no more than two Delay: one second Speed: one second
Transitions	–	–	–	One effect per slide Advance by mouse click
Timings	–	–	–	Two seconds

House style for text

Style type	Font type	Size	Feature	Alignment
Headings	Sans serif	32 points	Bold	Left
Bullets	Sans serif	24 points	Bold and default character is not to be used	Left
Sub-bullet	Sans serif	20 points	Bold/italic	Left

House style for table

Style type	Font type	Size	Feature	Colour	Alignment
Column headings	Serif	20	Bold	Green	Left for text; right for numbers
Text	Serif	20	Normal	Green	Left.
Numbers	–	–	Integer (no decimal places)	–	Right

Task 2

Assessment objectives	Stage	
1b 3a	2	Open the Word file **Mortgages.doc.** Create slides in your PowerPoint presentation based on the information contained in the **Mortgages.doc** file. Save your presentation as **Mortgages.ppt.**
2c 2d 2e 3a 3b 3f	3	Amend the second slide of your presentation to include in a table the information provided below.

MORTGAGE TYPE	RISK LEVEL	PERCENTAGE
PENSION	MEDIUM	5
REPAYMENT	LOW	52
ENDOWMENT	MEDIUM	40
FLEXIBLE	HIGH	3

2a 3a 3d — Stage 4

You want to include a chart that shows the difference in monthly payments on a loan of £50,000 over 25 years between a capitalrepayment scheme and an interest only scheme. Insert a new slide after Slide 6 and create a column chart based on theinformation below:

Rate %	4%	5%	6%	7%	8%	9%
Capital	264	292	322	353	386	420
Interest	167	208	250	292	333	375

Insert a chart heading:

'COMPARISON OF REPAYMENTS BETWEEN CAPITAL & INTEREST ON £50,000'

The chart should have a legend placed at the bottom. Font to be sans serif, bold, size 10 points.

Data labels of monthly payments should be displayed above the relevant columns. Font for labels to be sans serif, bold, size 10 points, colour red.

X axis title: INTEREST RATE. Font for title to be sans serif, bold, size 12 points.

Z axis title (or Y depending on chart style): MONTHLY PAYMENT. Font for title to be sans serif, bold, size 12 points.

Font for Value and Category axes: sans serif, bold, size 10 points.

Ensure that the colour/pattern of the columns is such that they can be readily distinguished.

2c 3e — Stage 5

Insert a new slide after Slide 1. Use the appropriate slide layout to enable an organisation chart to be drawn.
The chart should look like the figure on the next page:

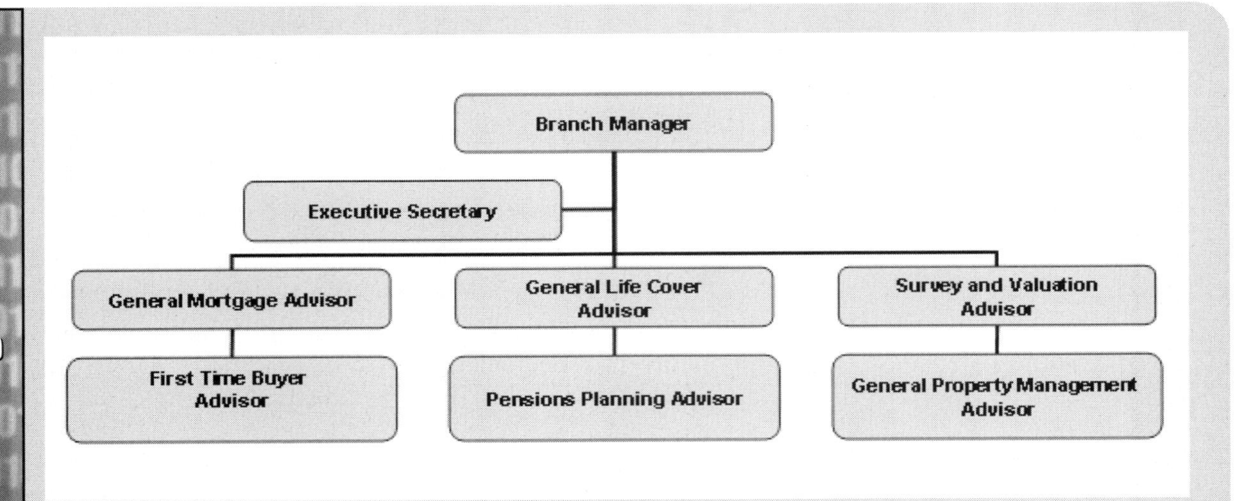

1b 3h		Post names should be sans serif, bold, size 12 points Add a title 'TYPICAL BRANCH ORGANISATION' Once you have completed the chart: Save your presentation. Make this a hidden slide.
3b 3g 2a	6	Make the following amendments to the slides in your presentation. Replace MORTGATE TYPE with MORTGAGE OPTION. On Slide 4, PENSION MORTGAGES: Delete the words in the first bullet point (SELF-EMPLOYED). Make Self-employed a sub-bullet of the first main bullet point. Add another new sub-bullet 'NON COMPANY SCHEME MEMBER'.
4e	7	Create a hyperlink on Slide 1 using the text 'AN INTRODUCTION TO MORTGAGES' to link to Slide 2.
1b 4a 4b	8	Create the build and transition effects for the presentation as indicated in the style brief above. Remember that you can introduce build effects and transitions in the Normal view or the Master Slide view of the presentation. Save your presentation.
5d	9	Produce a single screen print of all slides in the presentation showing the effects you have introduced. **Note:** Timings will only show where these are set in the transition of the slide. Since in this presentation you move from one slide to the next using the mouse click no timings will be shown in the print.
5a	10	Print one copy of 1, 4 and 6.

4d	11	Your manager feels that the order of the mortgage types should be as follows: REPAYMENT ENDOWMENT PENSION FLEXIBLE Re-order the slides so that the current slides 4, 5, 6, 7 appear in the order of the list above.
2a 3a	12	Open the Word file called **Advice_Notes**, which you will find on the accompanying CD. Add the text indicated for each slide as speaker notes. The font for the notes should be sans serif, normal, size 12 points. Print the speaker's notes for slides 6 and 8.
3h	13	Add a blank slide at the end of the presentation.
1b 5e	14	Save and print one outline print showing the text for all slides.

Web page creation

Web page creation for CLAIT Plus builds on some of the skills covered in the level 1 web pages certificate for IT Users – New CLAIT.

Four key assessment objectives

For CLAIT Plus there are four main assessment objectives, each of which contains a number of skills that you will be expected to learn:

- **Create, format and save web pages following a house style**
  - download files
  - create/name a directory/folder/sub-directory/sub-folder
  - create and define web pages
  - use meta tags to describe page content
  - format text, links and background using body tag
  - use standard content
  - save web pages
- **Use and format text, images and tables**
  - insert text and images
  - set image attributes
  - use additional text formatting and special characters
  - insert a table
  - set table dimensions
  - set table/cell alignment
- **Use and format an interactive form**
  - set method and action
  - use common input types
  - set input attributes
  - test a form
- **Link pages to create a website**
  - use images and text as anchors for hyperlinks
  - use hyperlinks to external sites
  - use hyperlinks to local pages
  - use e-mail link

This unit does not assume any prior knowledge of the objectives covered but you may well find it helpful to have completed the level 1 unit in web pages to understand some of the broad concepts of web design and creation. As you go through the unit the relevant knowledge and understanding will be explained. A complete list of the individual skills for each objective, together with the required knowledge and understanding, can be found in Appendix 1.

In this unit you will learn about:

- creating and defining web pages
- inserting text and image files into a web page
- the purpose and use of meta tags
- adding new pages to a website
- formatting an HTML document
- web structures
- standard content
- creating and using tables
- formatting an image's size and position
- using alternative text to describe images
- creating internal, external and e-mail links
- creating and using interactive forms
- testing a form.

Creating and defining web pages

Web pages can be created using a variety of different types of software from basic text editing programmes to sophisticated, specialist web design packages. This book uses Microsoft FrontPage as the web design software. The basic component of any web page is the HTML code on which the page is based. HTML, short for hypertext mark-up language, was developed as a common language which allows text and objects to be viewed consistently, irrespective of the browser being used. Aspects of HTML required for CLAIT Plus are covered a little later in this unit.

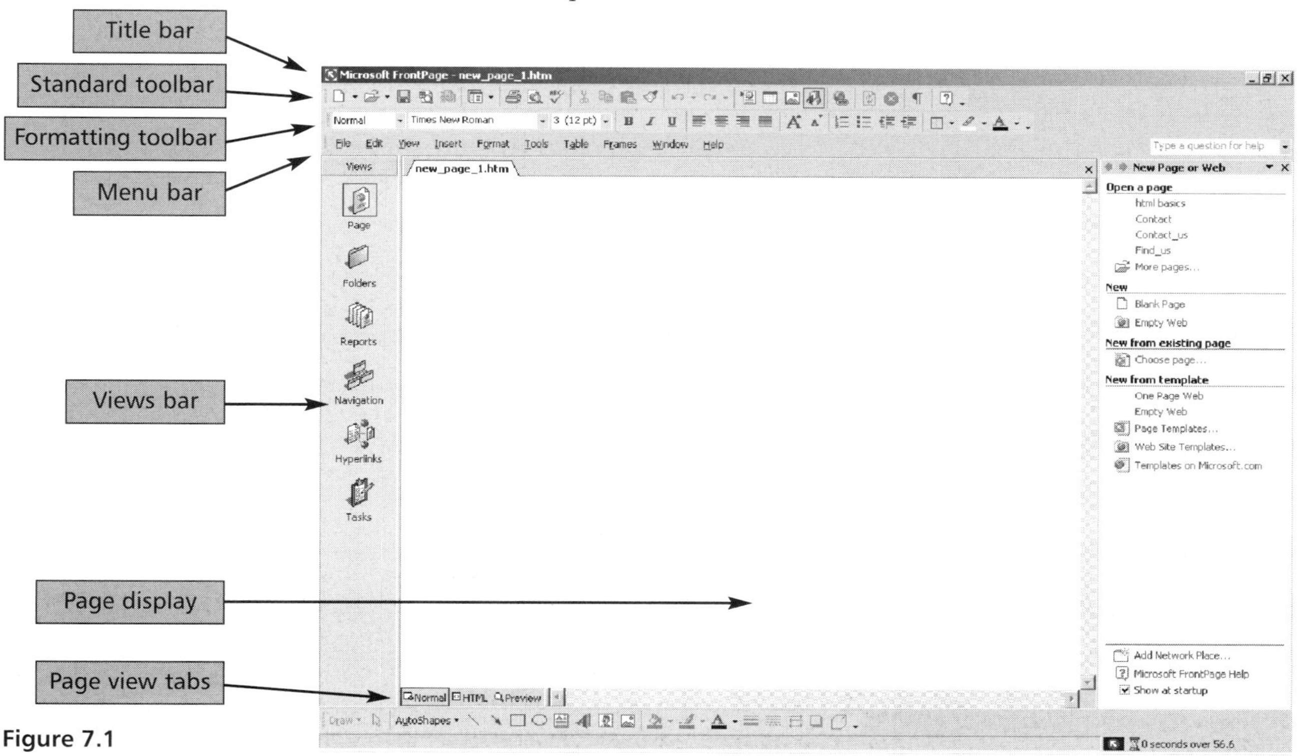

Figure 7.1

To create a new web page in FrontPage, click on the Microsoft FrontPage option from the program list under the Windows Start button. FrontPage will open with a new page ready for you to create the elements of the web page: see Figure 7.1.

If you completed the web pages element at level 1 in New CLAIT and used this software you will be familiar with the FrontPage window. You will also have a broad understanding of the use of HTML code. Figure 7.2 gives a simple example of a web page under construction and the HTML code that FrontPage will automatically generate for you. Every page has compulsory tags, such as </html> … </html>, <head> … </head>, <title> … <title> etc., and other general tags that tell a browser how the text or object is to be handled. In Figure 7.2 you can see that with the HTML code there is a list, identified as <ul>, with the individual items as <li>. This list was typed in the normal page view using the keyboard. FrontPage recognises that for the browser to handle this correctly it must translate it into the appropriate code as seen in the bottom screen of Figure 7.2.

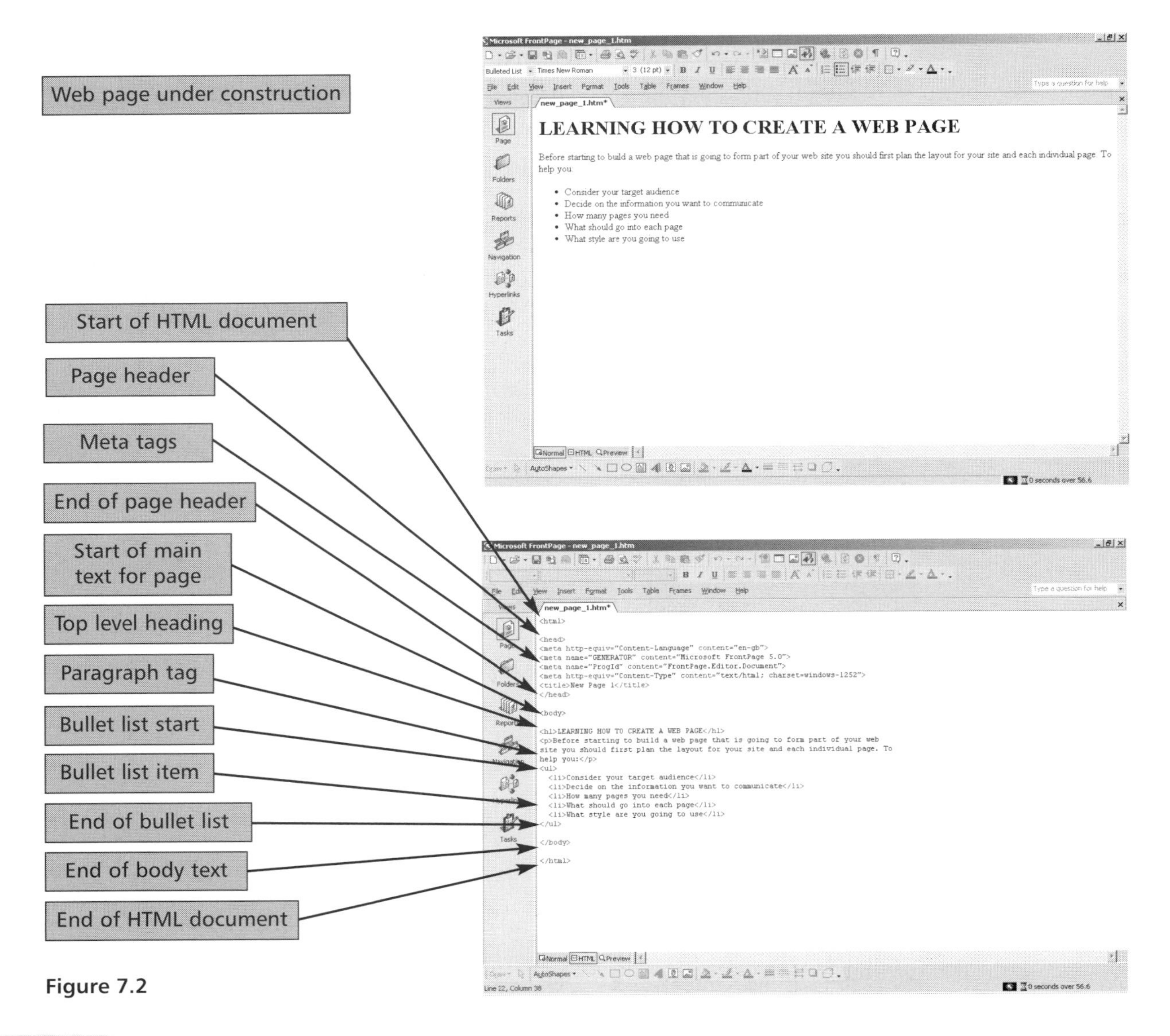

Figure 7.2

For CLAIT Plus you will be expected to have a broad understanding of HTML tags and how they are used to display text, images, links and the background colour of your web page. You will also need to understand how meta tags are used to describe the content of a page. Meta tags are tags that contain, amongst other things, information about the web page that will not be directly displayed to the individual reading the web page. For example, for CLAIT Plus you will be required to insert meta tags that include your name and centre number. Meta tags can also be used to assist browsers to search for keywords. Meta tags will be covered in more detail as you progress through the unit.

As you will have found in other units for CLAIT Plus, very often it is easier to understand the principles and skills needed by completing hand-holding Try it out exercises. In the following exercise you are going to build a very simple web page using text and image files that have been pre-prepared for you.

Try it out

The first thing to do is to create a new web. In this case the term web, with a lower case 'w', refers to a website that is created and managed using the functionality in FrontPage.

Open FrontPage.

Opening FrontPage and creating a new web

To open FrontPage, click the Windows Start button, click Programs (or All Programs if you are using Windows XP), click on Microsoft FrontPage. FrontPage will open with a blank web page called New_Page_1.htm.

Click the down arrow to the right of the create arrow shown in Figure 7.3, and select Web... .

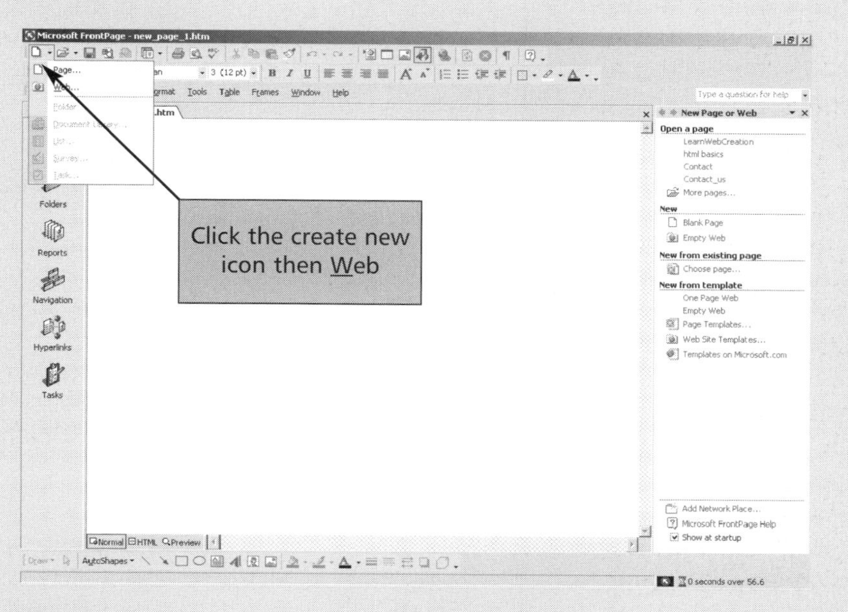

Figure 7.3

The Web Site Templates dialogue box appears as shown in Figure 7.4. On the left of the box FrontPage gives a number of options for the new web, from a one-page website to corporate styled webs and other built-in templates such as Project webs, Customer Support webs and so on. In addition there is an Import Web Wizard option that will be used later. On the right side of the dialogue box FrontPage asks you to tell it where the web is to be located. When FrontPage is installed it automatically sets up a default folder called My Webs. You can choose this folder or create your own. Clicking the Browse... button opens the New Web Location dialogue box in which you can determine where the new web and associated folders are to be placed.

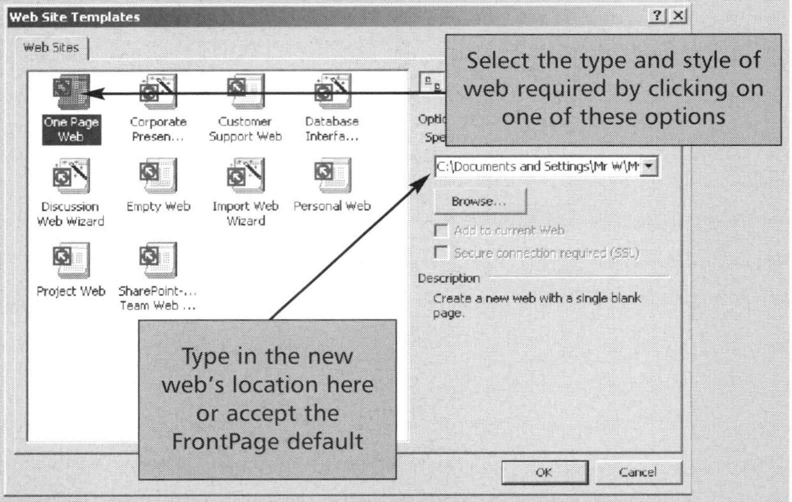

Select the type and style of web required by clicking on one of these options

Type in the new web's location here or accept the FrontPage default

Figure 7.4

When the OK button is clicked FrontPage builds the web, together with a number of folders that are used for managing the site. A web has a home page normally called Index.htm. This page is automatically generated by FrontPage. Have a look at Figure 7.5.

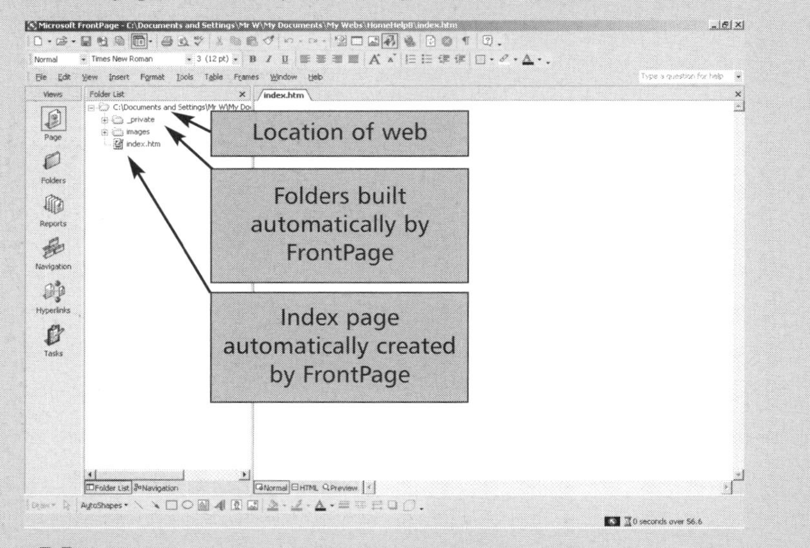

Figure 7.5

TIP

Creating folders

Although FrontPage will create all the folders necessary to build a web, you may wish to create a new folder for holding specific files such as ones you may have downloaded from another location. Creating folders in FrontPage is essentially the same as creating folders in other applications such as Windows Explorer. To create a new folder, using the right-hand mouse button, simply click on the Folder List structure at the place where the folder is to be created, select New and then Folder from the sub-list and a new folder is created. To name the folder overtype the default 'New_Folder' name and insert your own name for the folder.

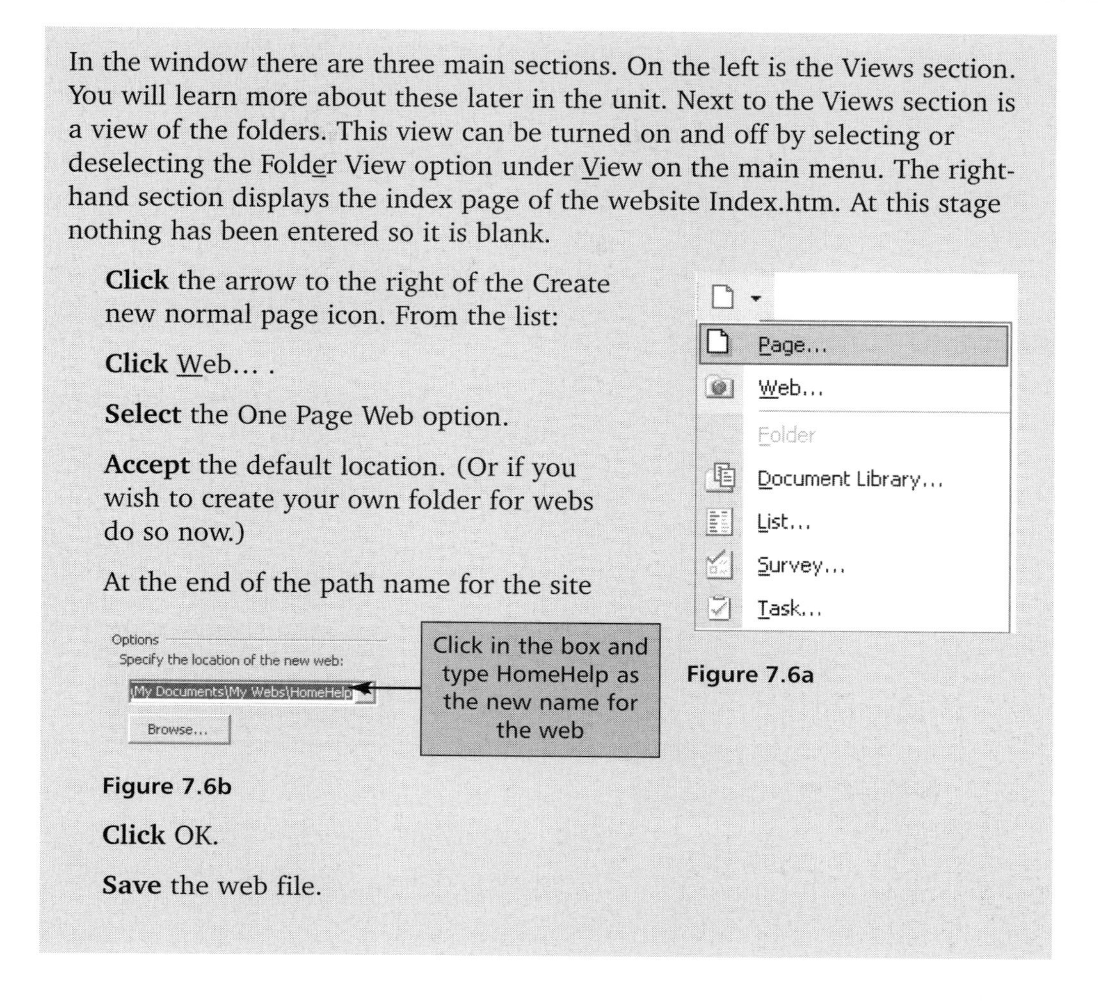

In the window there are three main sections. On the left is the Views section. You will learn more about these later in the unit. Next to the Views section is a view of the folders. This view can be turned on and off by selecting or deselecting the Folder View option under View on the main menu. The right-hand section displays the index page of the website Index.htm. At this stage nothing has been entered so it is blank.

Click the arrow to the right of the Create new normal page icon. From the list:

Click Web… .

Select the One Page Web option.

Accept the default location. (Or if you wish to create your own folder for webs do so now.)

At the end of the path name for the site

Figure 7.6a

Figure 7.6b

Click OK.

Save the web file.

Inserting text files into a web page

Once a web has been created the next stage is to insert the information that is going to tell the viewer what the site is about. Inserting information in the page can be accomplished either by typing text directly onto the page or alternatively by importing pre-prepared files. Inserting text files is very straightforward. First the page in the web that is to receive the text is opened. In a new web you will only have one page – usually the index page. Next File… is selected from Insert on the main menu and the Select File dialogue box shown in Figure 7.7 appears. Make sure the appropriate Files of type: is selected depending on the type of file to be imported. For example, if you are inserting a simple text file 'Text Files [*.txt]' should be selected in the Files of type: field.

Once the Open button is pressed FrontPage gives you a number of options as to how the file should be treated. These are shown in Figure 7.8.

By default FrontPage will select the Formatted Paragraphs option and this is probably what you will need most of the time. Text in a web page can always be reformatted later. Now try inserting a text file into the HomeHelp web created in the last exercise.

Figure 7.7

Figure 7.8

Try it out

Open the HomeHelp web if it is not already open.

Make sure the **Index.htm** file is the current open page.

Click Insert and then File... .

Insert the file **Homepage** from the Web1 sub-folder of Unit 7 on the attached CD.

Click Open.

The file will be inserted into the **Index.htm** page.

Now look at Figures 7.9 and 7.10.

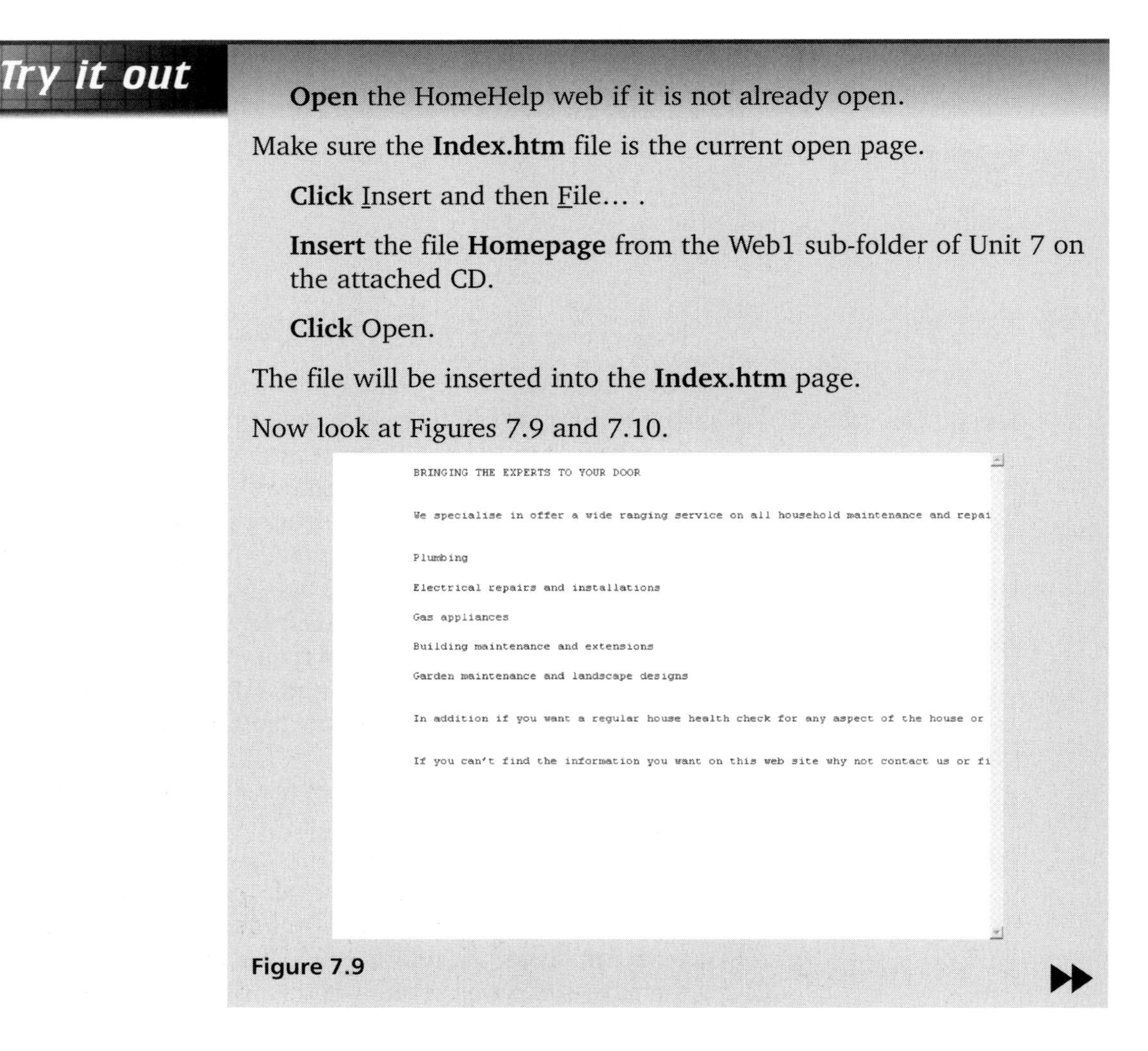

BRINGING THE EXPERTS TO YOUR DOOR
We specialise in offer a wide ranging service on all household maintenance and repai
Plumbing
Electrical repairs and installations
Gas appliances
Building maintenance and extensions
Garden maintenance and landscape designs
In addition if you want a regular house health check for any aspect of the house or
If you can't find the information you want on this web site why not contact us or fi

Figure 7.9

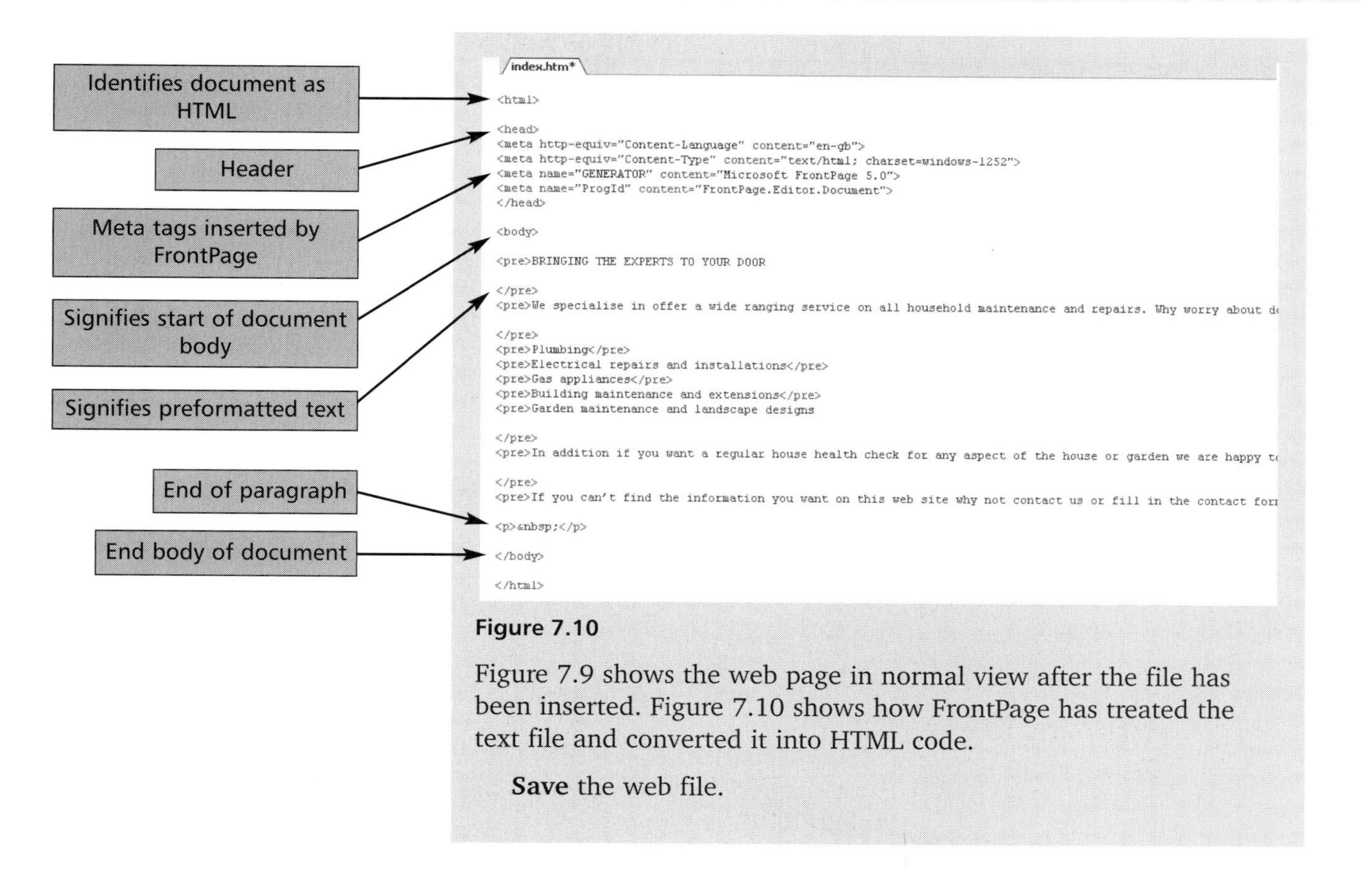
Identifies document as HTML
Header
Meta tags inserted by FrontPage
Signifies start of document body
Signifies preformatted text
End of paragraph
End body of document
index.htm*
<html>
<head>
<meta http-equiv="Content-Language" content="en-gb">
<meta http-equiv="Content-Type" content="text/html; charset=windows-1252">
<meta name="GENERATOR" content="Microsoft FrontPage 5.0">
<meta name="ProgId" content="FrontPage.Editor.Document">
</head>
<body>
<pre>BRINGING THE EXPERTS TO YOUR DOOR
</pre>
<pre>We specialise in offer a wide ranging service on all household maintenance and repairs. Why worry about d
</pre>
<pre>Plumbing</pre>
<pre>Electrical repairs and installations</pre>
<pre>Gas appliances</pre>
<pre>Building maintenance and extensions</pre>
<pre>Garden maintenance and landscape designs
</pre>
<pre>In addition if you want a regular house health check for any aspect of the house or garden we are happy t
</pre>
<pre>If you can't find the information you want on this web site why not contact us or fill in the contact for
<p> </p>
</body>
</html>

Figure 7.10

Figure 7.9 shows the web page in normal view after the file has been inserted. Figure 7.10 shows how FrontPage has treated the text file and converted it into HTML code.

Save the web file.

Using meta tags

As has already been mentioned, in simple terms, meta tags contain information about a web page that is not displayed in the browser. Meta tags are frequently used to insert keywords which are used by search engines and can help them to find specific websites or parts of a site. Meta tags can also be used to present a short description or synopsis of the page. You may well have noticed that when you have used the Search facility in, say, Internet Explorer a short description of the webs listed in the search can be viewed by placing the cursor over the list item. Have a look at Figure 7.11.

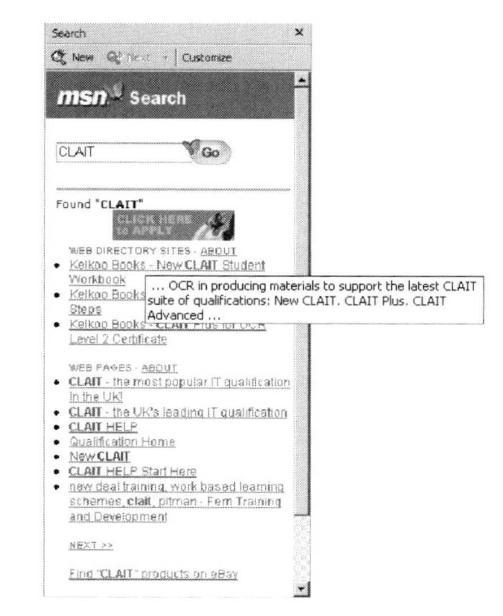
Search
New
Customize
msn Search
CLAIT
Go
Found "CLAIT"
CLICK HERE to APPLY
WEB DIRECTORY SITES - ABOUT
Kelkoo Books - New CLAIT Student Workbook
Kelkoo Books
... OCR in producing materials to support the latest CLAIT suite of qualifications: New CLAIT, CLAIT Plus, CLAIT Advanced ...
Steps
Kelkoo Books
Level 2 Certificate
WEB PAGES - ABOUT
CLAIT - the most popular IT qualification in the UK!
CLAIT - the UK's leading IT qualification
CLAIT HELP
Qualification Home
New CLAIT
CLAIT HELP Start Here
new deal training, work based learning schemes, clait, pitman - Fern Training and Development
NEXT >>
Find "CLAIT" products on eBay

Figure 7.11

Using the word 'CLAIT' the search reported in Figure 7.11 has found a number of sites containing the word CLAIT. CLAIT may well have been a keyword in the sites found. By passing the cursor over the list options you can see a brief description of each site. Descriptions are other meta tag options. For CLAIT Plus you are required to include meta tags in your web giving your name and centre number, keywords used in searches and a description of the site.

HTML has two types of meta tag (or variable); user-defined and system. In this unit you will learn how to add user-defined ('user') variables. To add a user variable you need to be in the normal view of your web page. By clicking on File and then Properties... on the main menu the Page Properties dialogue box shown in Figure 7.12 is displayed. This dialogue box has a number of tabs. Selecting the Custom tab gives access to meta tag information. The top of the dialogue box allows system variables to be added and the bottom user variables.

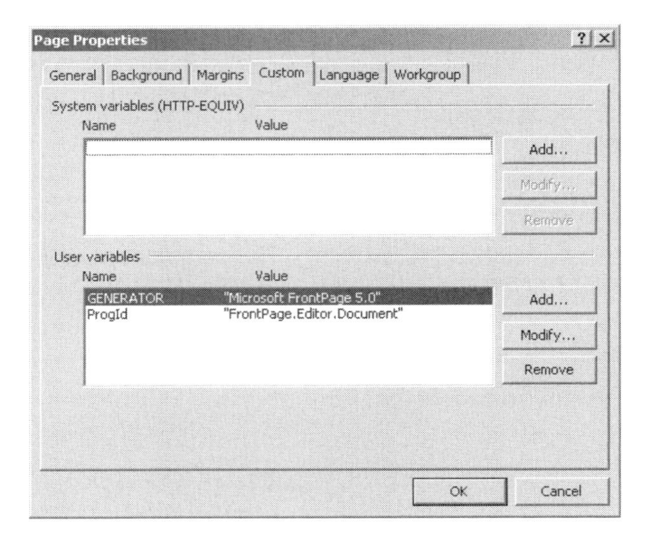

Figure 7.12

If you look back at Figure 7.10 (showing the HTML code generated by FrontPage) you will see the meta tag information for GENERATOR and ProgId. To add a new user variable the Add… button on the Custom tab of the Page Properties dialogue box is clicked, which then brings up the User Meta Variable dialogue box as shown in Figure 7.13.

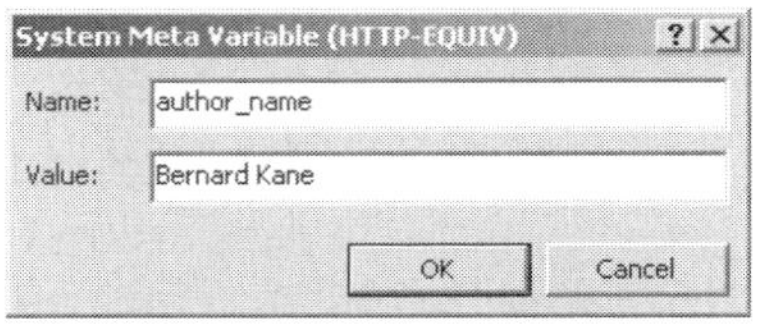

System Meta Variable (HTTP-EQUIV)
Name: author_name
Value: Bernard Kane
OK Cancel

Figure 7.13

In the top field the variable is given a name. In Figure 7.13 this is 'author_name'. Where the name is more than one word use an underscore between the two words, as shown between 'author' and 'name'.

Note: in a scripting language such as HTML or Java, spaces are not permitted between two words so the usual convention is to use an underscore.

The bottom field holds the value of the variable – in this case 'Bernard Kane'. Clicking the OK button of the User Meta Variable dialogue box and then in the Page Properties dialogue box adds this meta tag to the script, as shown in Figure 7.14.

The same process is used for inserting keywords for searches or descriptions for the page. Now try to add meta tags to your HomeHelp web page.

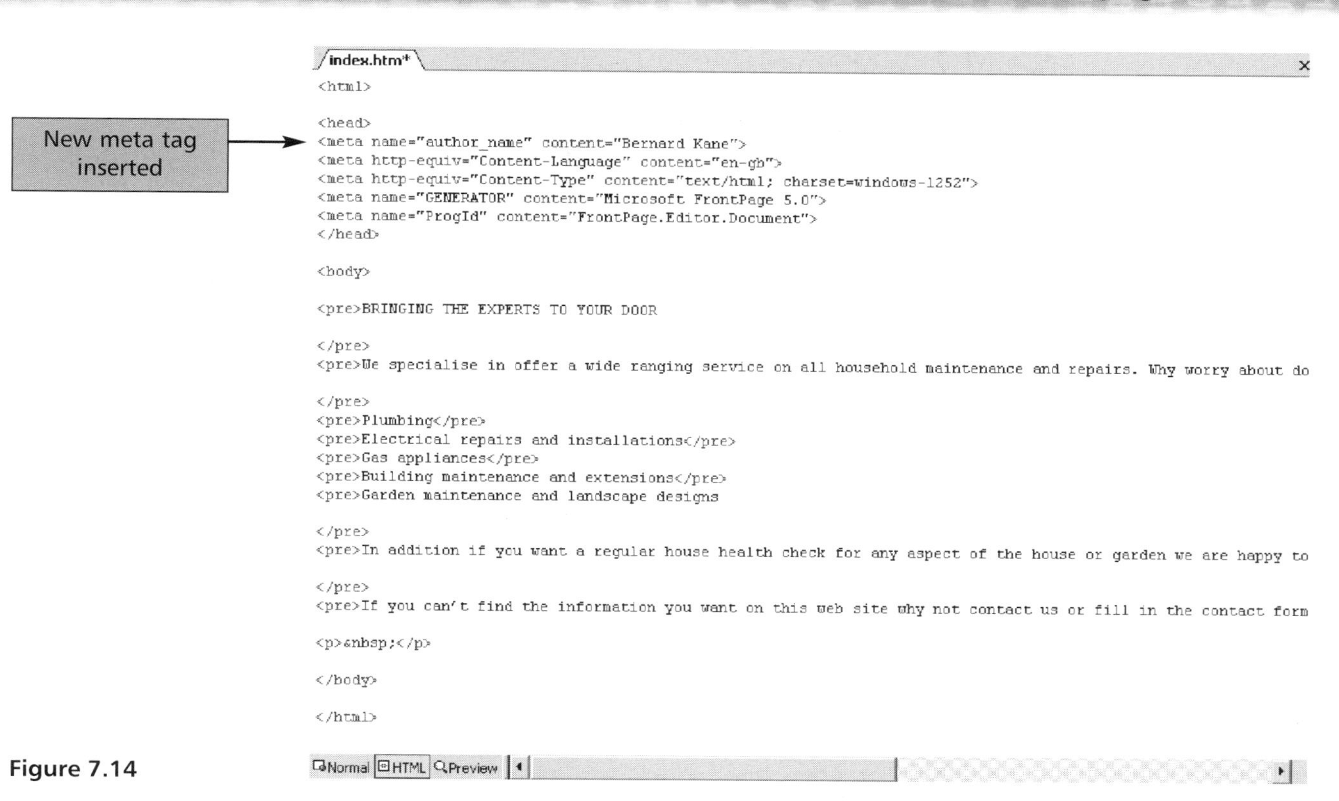
index.htm*
New meta tag inserted
<html>
<head>
<meta name="author_name" content="Bernard Kane">
<meta http-equiv="Content-Language" content="en-gb">
<meta http-equiv="Content-Type" content="text/html; charset=windows-1252">
<meta name="GENERATOR" content="Microsoft FrontPage 5.0">
<meta name="ProgId" content="FrontPage.Editor.Document">
</head>
<body>
<pre>BRINGING THE EXPERTS TO YOUR DOOR
</pre>
<pre>We specialise in offer a wide ranging service on all household maintenance and repairs. Why worry about do
</pre>
<pre>Plumbing</pre>
<pre>Electrical repairs and installations</pre>
<pre>Gas appliances</pre>
<pre>Building maintenance and extensions</pre>
<pre>Garden maintenance and landscape designs
</pre>
<pre>In addition if you want a regular house health check for any aspect of the house or garden we are happy to
</pre>
<pre>If you can't find the information you want on this web site why not contact us or fill in the contact form
<p> </p>
</body>
</html>
Normal HTML Preview

Figure 7.14

Try it out

Open the HomeHelp web if it is not already open.

With the view in Normal:

Click File and then Properties… from the main menu.

Select the Custom tab of the dialogue box.

In the User Variables section:

Click Add.

Type 'author_name' in the Name: field.

Type your own name, followed by a comma and then 'CLAIT Plus Exercise' in the Value: field. The field should then look like this:

Your name, CLAIT Plus Exercise.

Click OK twice to return to the Normal page view.

Click the HTML tab at the bottom of the page.

Notice how your meta tag has now been added to the header section of the HTML code for the page.

Click the Normal tab for the page.

Add a further meta tag as follows:

Name: Description
Value: All your household repair and maintenance needs under one roof

Click OK twice to return to the Normal view of the page.

Click the HTML tab and view the new meta tags.

Save the web file.

Adding new pages to a web

Few websites are single page sites and it is therefore necessary, and indeed a CLAIT Plus requirement, that you create web pages. Pages can be built up by using the content of text files created in more or less any text editor, or they can be built directly onto a new page created in a FrontPage web. CLAIT Plus also requires that you are able to create a new HTML document. When you insert a new page into an existing FrontPage web, or you create a new web page file, you automatically generate a new HTML document.

Adding a new page

To create a new page select the New or Web option from File on the main menu or click the Create a new normal page icon on the toolbar.

Option 1 Menu option

If the menu option is chosen the New Page or Web task pane will appear on the right-hand side of the screen. By clicking the Blank Page option in the new section of the task pane, a new page is inserted into the web. Have a look at Figure 7.15.

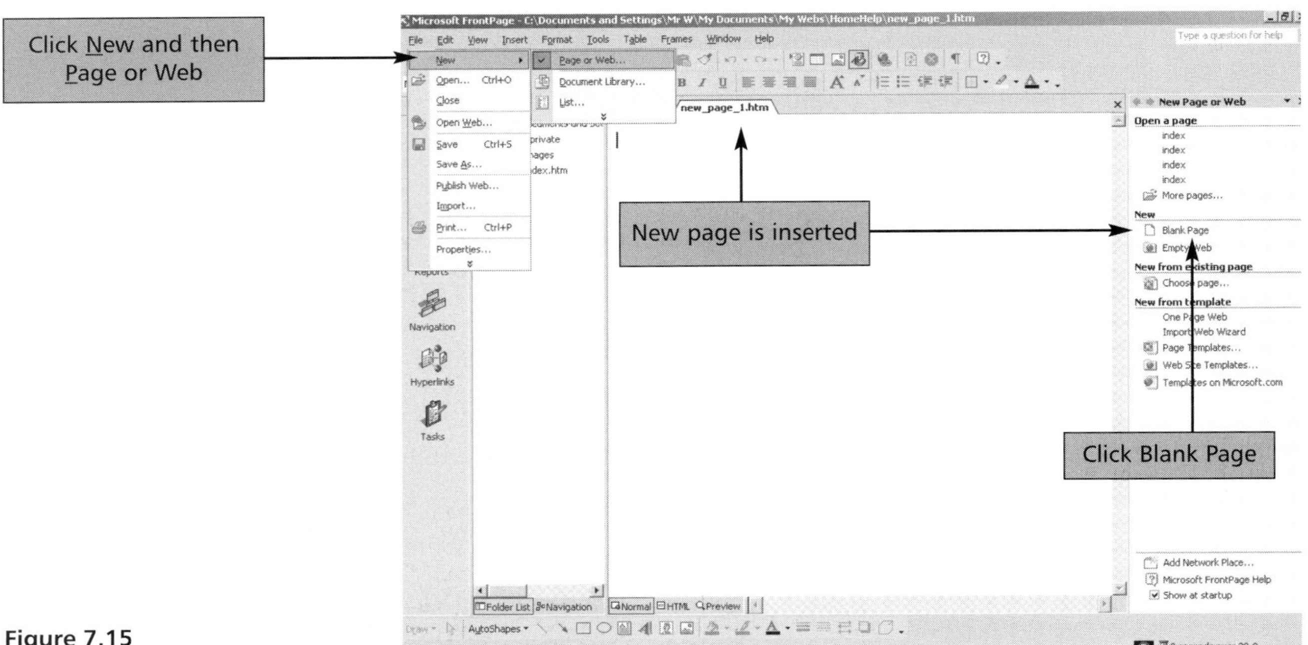

Figure 7.15

Option 2 Toolbar option

By clicking the Create a new normal page icon on the toolbar a new page is automatically inserted into the web.

Once a new page has been created existing files (usually .txt or other HTML files) can be inserted into the new page.

Now you are going to create three new pages for the HomeHelp web using both of the above options.

Try it out

Open HomeHelp if it is not already open.

Using the menu option (Option 1 above) you are going to add a new page to the web and insert a text file from the accompanying CD.

Click File, New, Page or Web from the main menu.

Click Blank Page on the New Page or Web task pane.

Click on the page and

Press Enter to create a new line.

Click Insert, File from the main menu.

In the Look in: field of the Select File dialogue box select the Web1 sub-folder of Unit 7 on the CD. In the Files of Type field select Rich Text Format (*.rtf).

Select Prices.

Click Open.

Click the Save icon on the toolbar and save the new web page as **Prices**.

Your new page should now look similar to Figure 7.16.

Prices.htm | index.htm

Service		Range	Call out Costs per hour
Plumbing		All pipe work, heating systems, bathroom and toilet installations.	£35
Electrical		Circuits, lighting (repair and installation), domestic appliances (including television repairs)	£30
Gas		Boilers and gas fires (maintenance, repair and installations)	£40
Building		Gutters, brickwork, windows, door replacement, floor installations, roof repairs	£35
Construction		Extensions and conservatories	Priced individually
Gardens		Lawn doctor, paving, patios, tree surgery, garden maintenance.	Priced individually
Garden Design		Landscaping – design and construction	Priced individually

Figure 7.16

Click the Create a new normal page icon on the toolbar.

Double-click on the .htm file **The Team** in the Web1 sub-folder of Unit 7 on the CD to open it in the browser. (Alternatively open the file normally in Word.)

Highlight all the text.

Copy and then paste this file into the new_page_1.htm of HomeHelp in FrontPage.

Place your cursor after the colon for each service and before the contact name and tab/backspace so that the services appear as one column and the names as another.

Click the Save icon on the toolbar and save the new web page as **team**.

Your new page should now look similar to Figure 7.17.

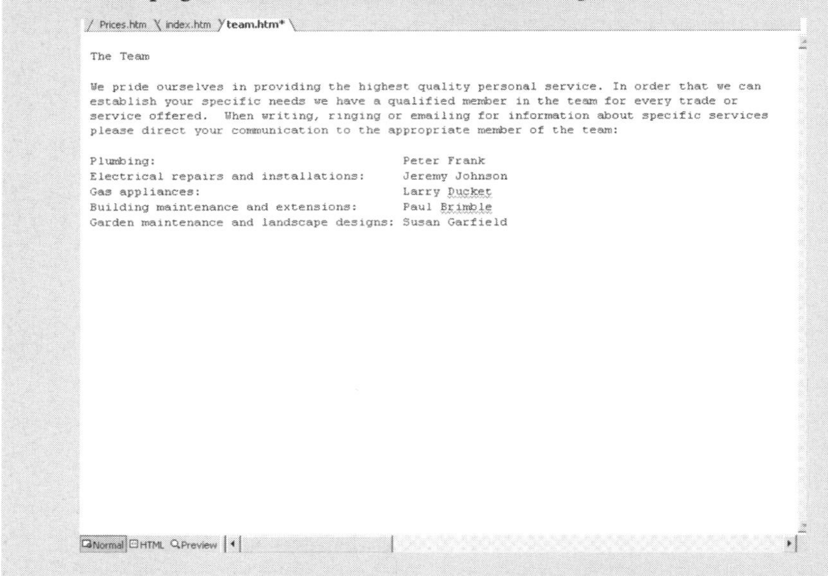

Figure 7.17

Create a third new page and save it as **Contact**.

Formatting an HTML document

Formatting text using styles

You have already seen how HTML tags are used to identify various parts of a document and also how meta tags can be used to set descriptors or identify keywords used in searches. Tags are also used to set the format of text, background colour and other aspects of the web page.

Have a look at Figure 7.18. Here you can see text shown in the normal view of a web page and superimposed is the underlying HTML generated by FrontPage, based on the style instructions given.

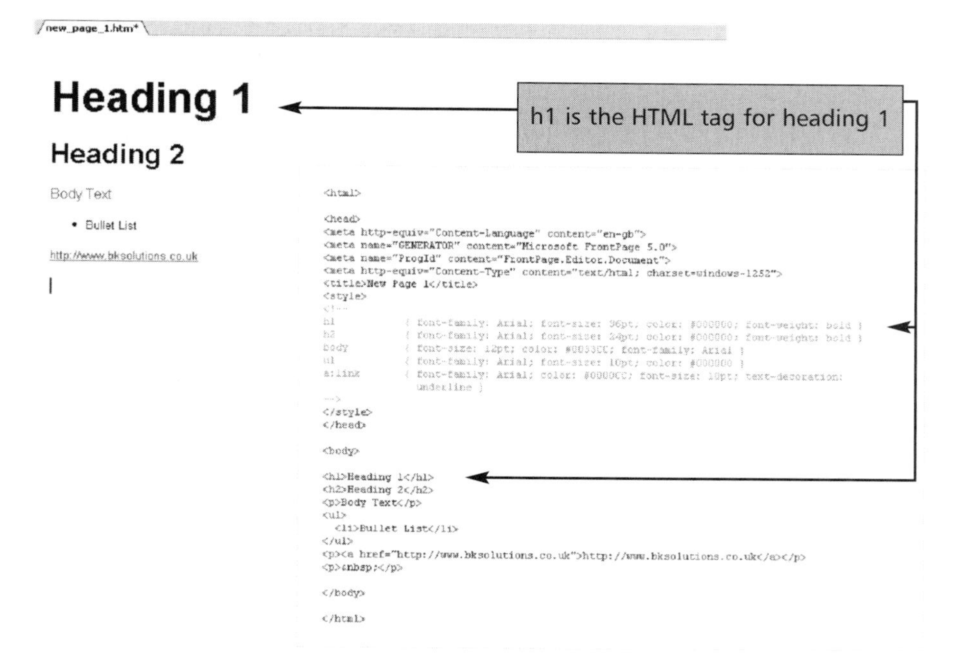

Figure 7.18

In this illustration the <h1>Heading 1</h1> tag has had the style set as:

h1 {font-family: Arial; font-size: 36pt; color: #000000; font-weight: bold}

In simple English this means:

Font	=	Arial
Size	=	36 point
Colour	=	black
Font style	=	bold

You could, of course, have typed the style for the heading directly into an HTML document, but as the old saying goes 'why have a dog and bark yourself?' FrontPage is very capable of interpreting your requirements and converting these into the required HTML code.

You may well have come across house style requirements for other applications in OCR's CLAIT Plus or New CLAIT assessments. To set a style against a pre-set requirement is frankly often much easier than having to originate your own. Say, for example, you had been asked to create a new web page which had to have the following properties:

Text colour	#000000
Background colour	#FFFF99
Font	Arial

Font styles:

Format	**HTML tag**	**Size and style**
Heading 1	(h1)	HTML size 6 (24pt), normal
Body	(body)	HTML size 3 (12pt), normal
Bullet list	(ul)	HTML size 2 (10pt), italic
Link colour	(a:Link)	#0000FF
Visited link colour	(a:visited)	#FF9900

First a new web file is opened using the File, New, Page or Web options on the main menu and then selecting the appropriate choice from the New Page or Web task pane.

Once the new file has been created click on the new page and select Heading 1 from the styles list on the toolbar. Next the main menu Format is selected followed by Style… from the sub-list. The dialogue box shown in Figure 7.19 then appears.

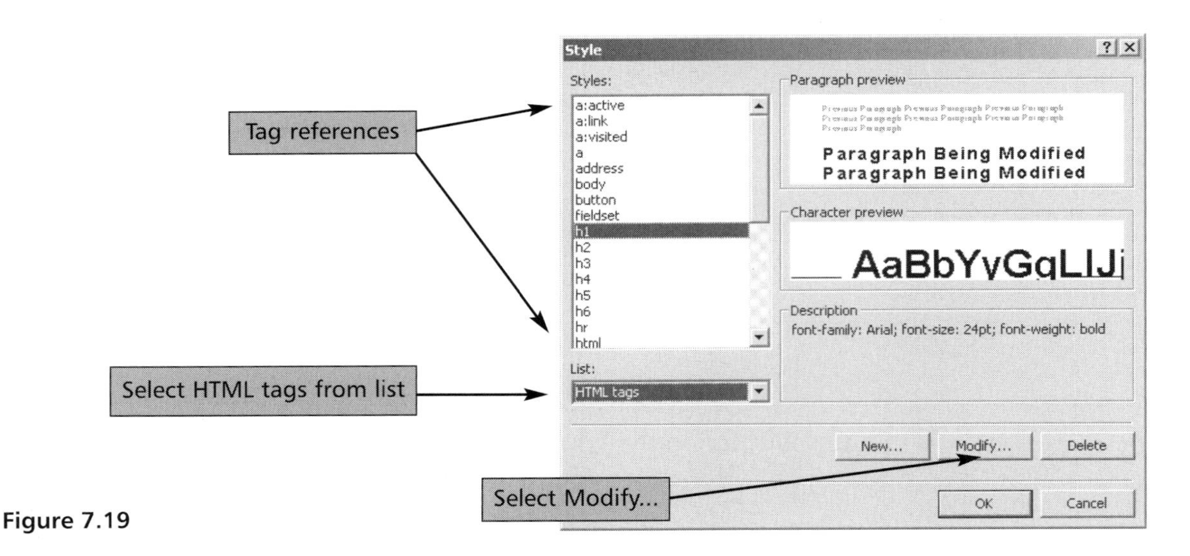

Figure 7.19

The tag referring to the text style you now wish to change is selected, in this example h1 (referring to Heading 1). Clicking the Modify… button allows the Modify Styles dialogue box to appear as shown in Figure 7.20.

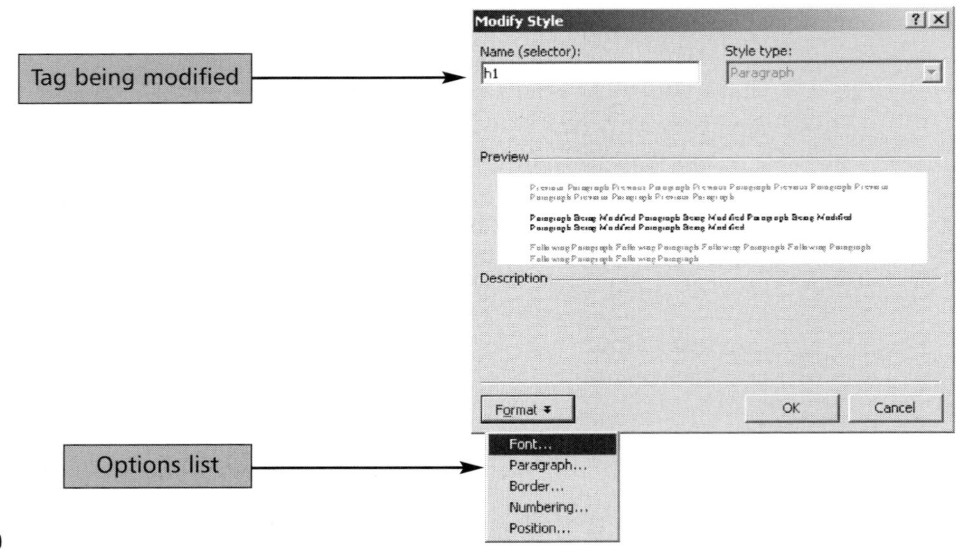

Figure 7.20

On the bottom left of this dialogue box is the Format button. Clicking this button produces the menu list which displays aspects that are available for modification. Clicking the Font… option opens the standard Font dialogue box shown in Figure 7.21.

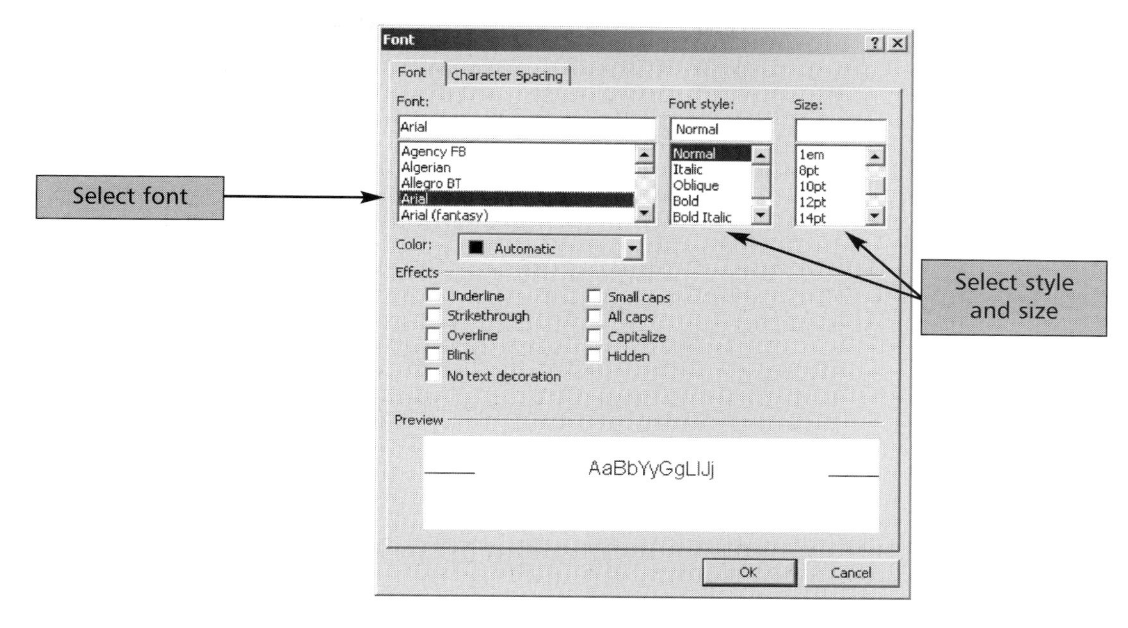

Figure 7.21

Font, font style and size can all be modified as required either by selecting from the appropriate list or typing in the requirements directly via the keyboard. If specific colours are required then it is necessary to enter the hex colour code in the Value: field of the More Colors dialogue box shown in Figure 7.22. In the example above the requirement is for Text Color to be #000000. This can be typed directly into the value box. FrontPage reformats the input as Hex={00,00,00}. For CLAIT Plus you will not be expected to remember colour codes; they are supplied if required.

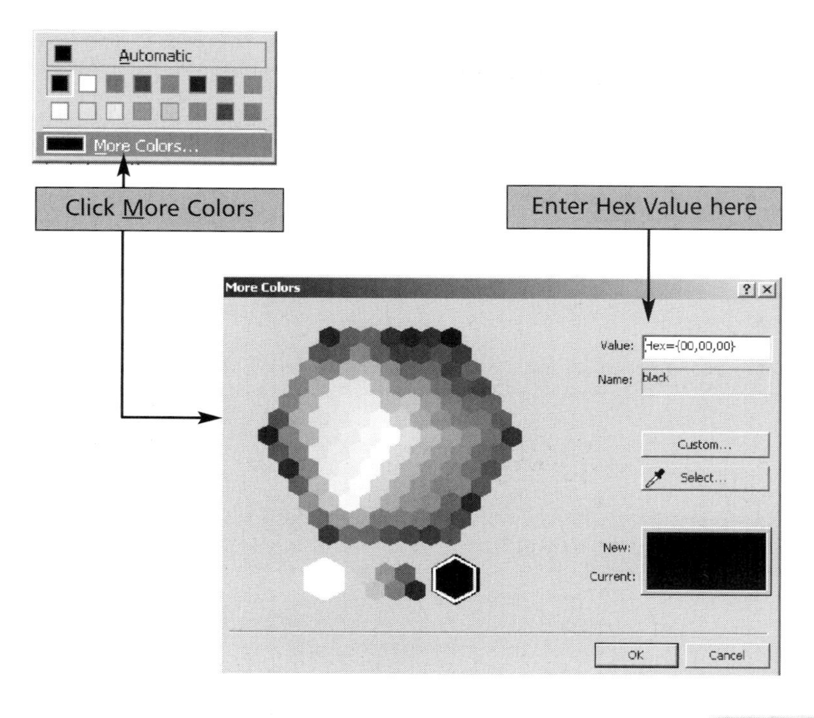

Figure 7.22

Now try to set the styles for your HomeHelp web.

Try it out

Open HomeHelp.

Open the team page.

Click the cursor in front of the T in the heading The Team.

Select Heading 1 from the styles list on the toolbar.

Note: at this stage the heading will pick up the default format for Heading 1.

Click Format, Style… on the main menu.

Select h1 from the HTML tags list.

Click the Modify… button.

Click Format and the Font….

Select Arial as the font, Normal as the style and 24pt as the size.

Click the down arrow to the right of the Color field.

Select More Colors… .

Type '#000000' in the value field.

Click the OK button four times to return to the web page.

Next

Click the cursor in front of the first paragraph, 'We pride…….etc.'

Repeat the above process to relate the Normal style with the HTML tag <p. The font is Arial, style Normal and size 12pt.

Highlight the list which includes both the services and contact names.

Select Bulleted List from the style options on the toolbar.

Click Format, Style… on the main menu.

Select li from the HTML tags list.

Click the Modify… button.

Click Format and the Font….

Select Arial as the font, Italic as the style and 10pt as the size.

Click the down arrow to the right of the Color field.

Select More Colors…

Type '#000000' in the value field.

Click the OK button four times to return to the web page.

If necessary, tidy up the spacing between the service in the list and the contact so that it still appears they have separate columns.

Click the HTML tab.

Notice how the new styles are reflected in the code:

```
h1 { font-family: Arial; font-size: 24pt; color: #000000 }
p  { font-family: Arial; font-size: 12pt; color:#000000 }
ul { font-family: Arial; font-size: 10pt; font-style: italic;
color:#000000 }
```

Notice also how the paragraph tag (<p) has been intermingled with the List item tag (<li) in the list:

```
<ul>
<li>
<p class="MsoPlainText"><span lang="EN-
GB">Plumbing:   Peter Frank</span></li>
<li>
<p class="MsoPlainText"><span lang="EN-GB">Electrical repairs
and installations:     Jeremy
Johnson</span></li>
<li>
<p class="MsoPlainText"><span lang="EN-GB">Gas
appliances:   Larry Ducket</span></li>
<li>
 <p class="MsoPlainText"><span lang="EN-GB">Building
maintenance and
 extensions:      Paul
Brimble</span></li>
 <li>
 <p class="MsoPlainText"><span lang="EN-GB">Garden
maintenance and landscape
 designs: Susan Garfield</span></li>
</ul>
```

Since you are only interested in the HTML code that relates to the list you can clean some of the superfluous code by removing all the <p class .....> elements until your code looks similar to that shown below:

```
<ul>
 <li>Plumbing:     Peter
Frank</span></li>
 <li>Electrical repairs and
installations:    Jeremy
Johnson</span></li>
 <li>Gas appliances:      
Larry Ducket</span></li>
```

```
<li>Building maintenance and
extensions;     Paul
Brimble</span></li>
<li>Garden maintenance and landscape designs:  
Susan Garfield</span></li>
</ul>
```

Note: the   code is generated when inserting blank spaces or tabs. The number present is really determined by the number required to align the names for the services. Normally you would not align using this method. If columns are required then a table would generally be used.

Save your work.

Your page should now look similar to Figure 7.23.

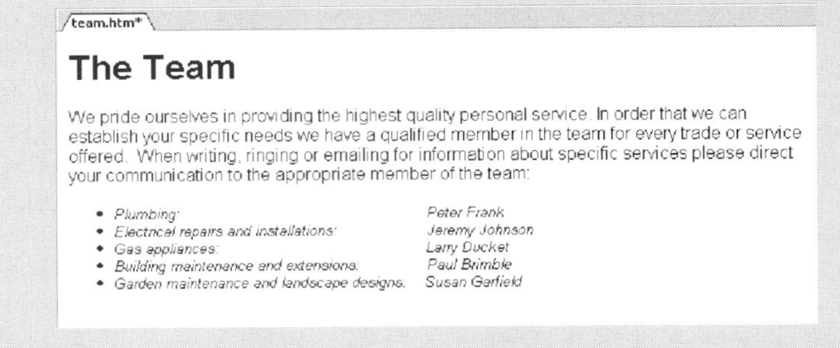

Figure 7.23

Formatting the web page background

The background of a web page can be formatted using a colour scheme, an image or a mixture of both these elements. Alternatively you can use one of FrontPage's many built-in web theme templates. Formatting the background is carried out in much the same way as other formatting tasks. In this case the Page Properties dialogue box provides the facilities to set the background. To access the Page Properties dialogue box click Format from the main menu and then Background... . The Page Properties box appears with the Background tab selected, as shown in Figure 7.24.

You will notice that in the top part of the box the picture can be identified and selected using the Browse... button to locate the image file. The middle section of the dialogue box allows you to select the required colour for the background. The last section allows you to tell FrontPage to use information from another page. Now try formatting the background to the Index page of the HomeHelp web.

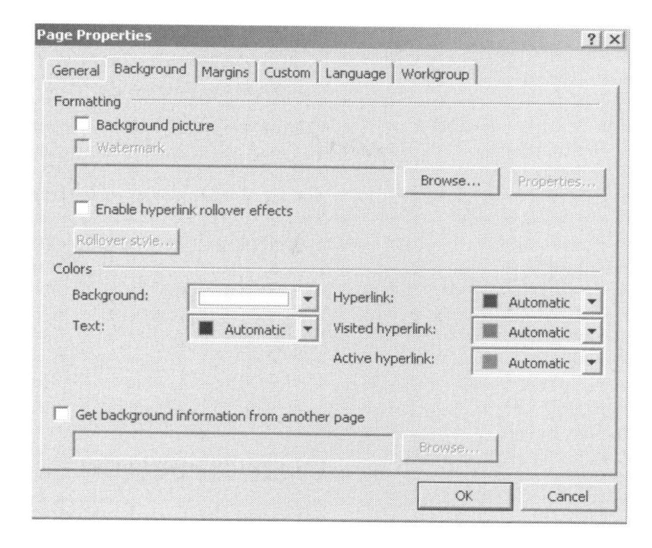

Figure 7.24

Try it out

Open HomeHelp, if it is not already open.

Make sure the Index.htm page is the current page.

Click Format and then Background.

Click on the arrow to the right of the Background: field of the Colors section.

Select More Colors.

In the Value field:

Type '#FFFFCC' (This is simply the hex code 'Hex={FF,FF,CC}' for a pale yellow colour).

Click OK twice to return to the web page.

Save the changes you have made.

Now click on the HTML tab and notice how FrontPage has helpfully included the body tag code for the background colour, <body bgcolor="#FFFFCC">.

Open the page team.htm.

Click Format and then Background.

Click in the check box 'Get background information from another page'.

Click the Browse... button.

In the Current Web dialogue box:

Click Index.htm.

Click OK.

Click OK again to return to the web page.

The page will now reflect that of Index.htm. If you click on the HTML tab, notice that the body tag now shows that the style is taken from Index.htm: <body stylesrc=“index.htm”>.

Now set the background colour for the prices and contact pages using the code #FFFFCC.

Note: you may use either of the techniques shown above.

Save the web.

Web structure

By now you will be more familiar with the general structure of a web page. You have seen that the HTML code separates a page into two main sections, the head and the body. The head contains general information about the page that is not visible to the viewer and the body contains the visible details such as text, images, tables, forms, etc.

Standard content

In the assignments set for CLAIT Plus students are asked to include certain standard contents for each web page. These will form part of the design brief. For example, meta tags containing the author's name, some key words and a description of the page may well form part of this standard content in the <HEAD> section of the page. Other standard content elements can be in the <BODY> of the page and may include navigation buttons containing the links between pages in the web and also e-mail contact back to a specific address.

One of the advantages of using standard contents in a web is that once the content has been created it can be copied and pasted to other pages without the need to recreate the content for each subsequent page.

Creating tables

So far you have learnt how create and format individual pages for a website. However, for those visiting a web they must be able to access each area of the site for it to have any practical value. This is achieved by providing links on each page which allow the visitor to access any area of the site they wish. FrontPage supports a variety of ways by which links can be created. However, for the OCR assignment you will be required to create a navigation table to specific dimensions, with images representing the links to pages. This table will form part of the standard content for each page of the web.

Inserting a table into a web page is similar to inserting a table into a Word document. First the cursor is placed at the point in the page where the table is to be inserted and then Table, Insert, Table... options are selected from the main menu. An Insert Table dialogue box appears as shown in Figure 7.25.

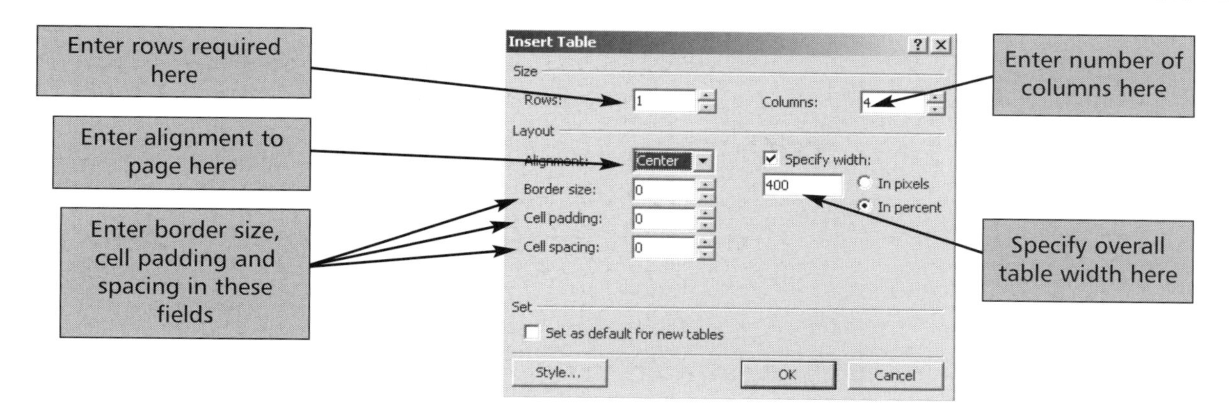

Figure 7.25

Here you can enter the main properties for the table such as the number of rows and columns, the overall width of the table, its alignment to the page and other characteristics such as border size, cell padding and spacing. Clicking the OK button will place the new table on the page. You can change any of the table properties by clicking on the table using the right-hand mouse button and selecting Table Properties... . The dialogue box shown in Figure 7.26 will appear.

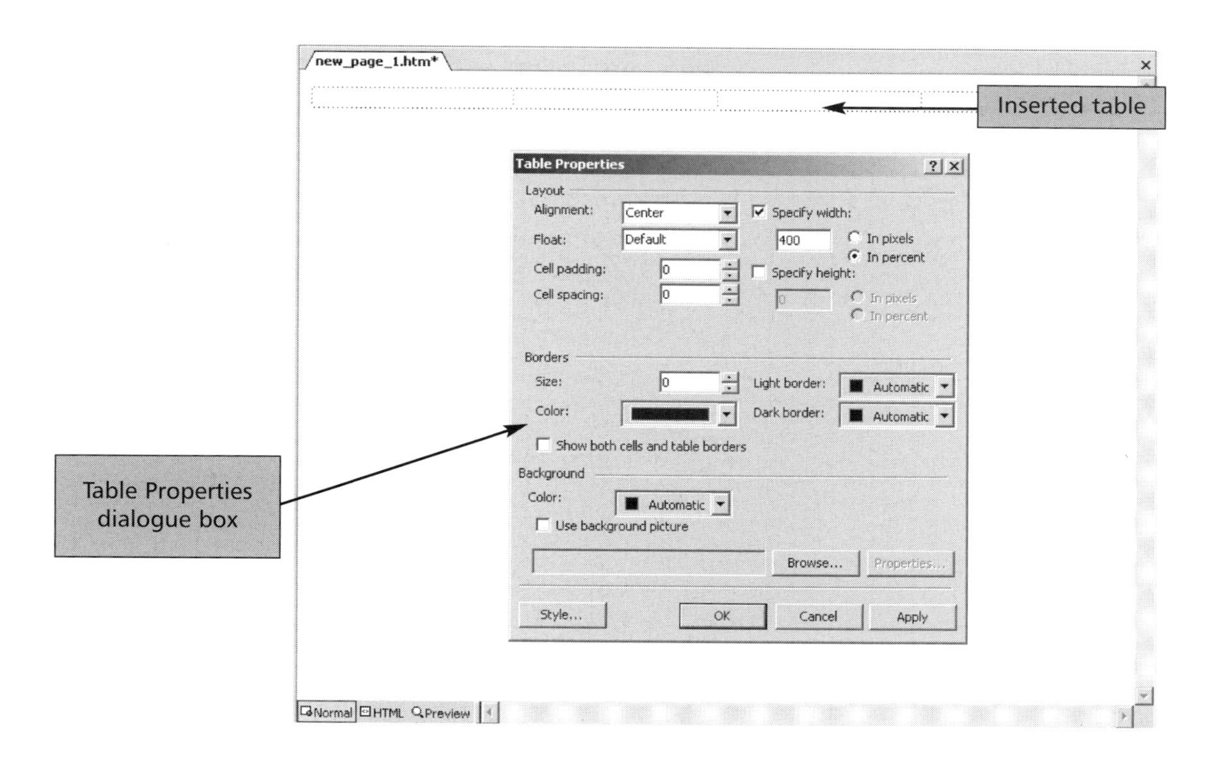

Figure 7.26

To change individual cell properties the same procedure is followed but instead of selecting Table Properties... the Cell Properties... option is selected. The dialogue box shown in Figure 7.27 appears.

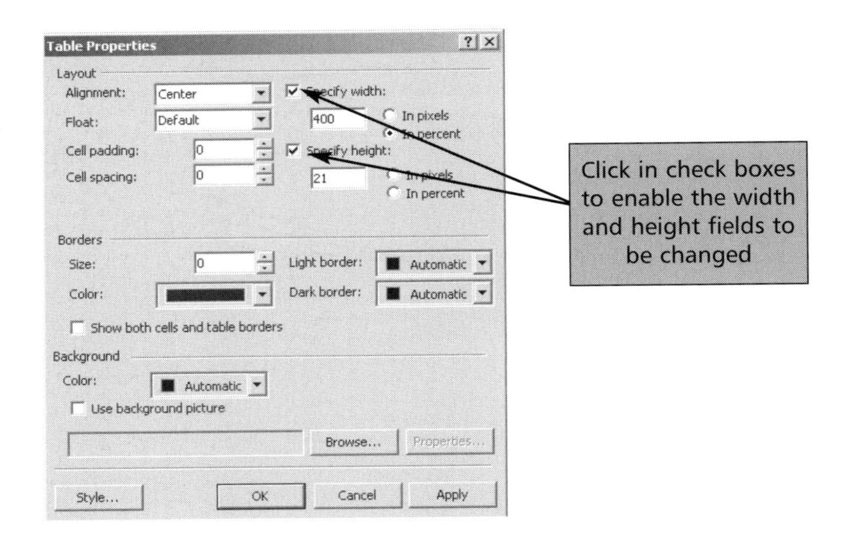

Figure 7.27

Notice how in the bottom of the dialogue box there is a section called Background which gives the option of setting the background colour for the cell or inserting a picture file as the background (using images is covered in the next section). First complete the Try it out exercise to insert a table at the top of each page of the web file.

Try it out

Open HomeHelp if it is not already open.

Place a table for navigation, based on the following dimensions, at the top of the Index.htm page:

Overall width	280
Height	21
Columns	4
Rows	1
Alignment	Centred
Cell spacing	0
Cell padding	0
Border	1

Open Page Index.htm.

Place the cursor in front of the first letter of the page title – 'BRINGING…'.

Press the enter key to create a new line.

Move the cursor to the top of the page.

Click Table, Insert, Table… from the main menu.

Type '1' for rows, '4' for columns.

Enter the remaining table details as shown in the brief above.

Click OK.

The table should now have been inserted at the top of the page as required by the brief.

Save the page.

Using images in web designs

You may well have used images in other applications. Creating web pages that include images is not that dissimilar, but there are some important differences. A website has a wholly independent life, so any files that pages in the site use must be available to the web file as a whole. When you create a new web file in FrontPage it automatically creates a number of folders, including one called images. As long as your web resides on the computer where it was created the web page will be able to locate the image being used, providing the appropriate absolute reference to the file is provided (e.g. C:\My Documents\Images\ball.gif). However, once a web has been published and resides on your provider's server it will not be able to access image files used on any of your pages if they are only present on your computer. For this reason any image files used in the website must be copied to the website's images folder. This way whenever the web is moved to a separate location it can take all the associated files it needs. Files contained in these folders are referred to using relative references.

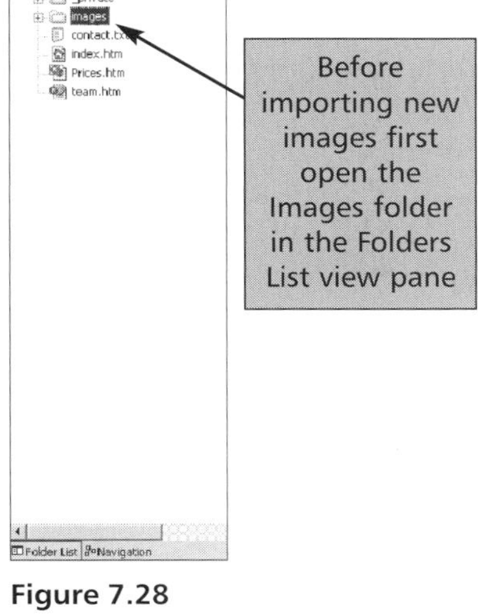

Figure 7.28

Importing to the Images folder

To import an image to the Images folder first open the Images folder in the folders view, see Figure 7.28.

Next, Import is selected from the File main menu options; a new Import dialogue box appears. Clicking the Add File button shows the Add File to Import List dialogue box. Here the required files to import are selected. Once all files have been selected clicking the Open button will transfer them the Import box. Once the OK button is clicked the files are then imported to the Images folder: see Figure 7.29.

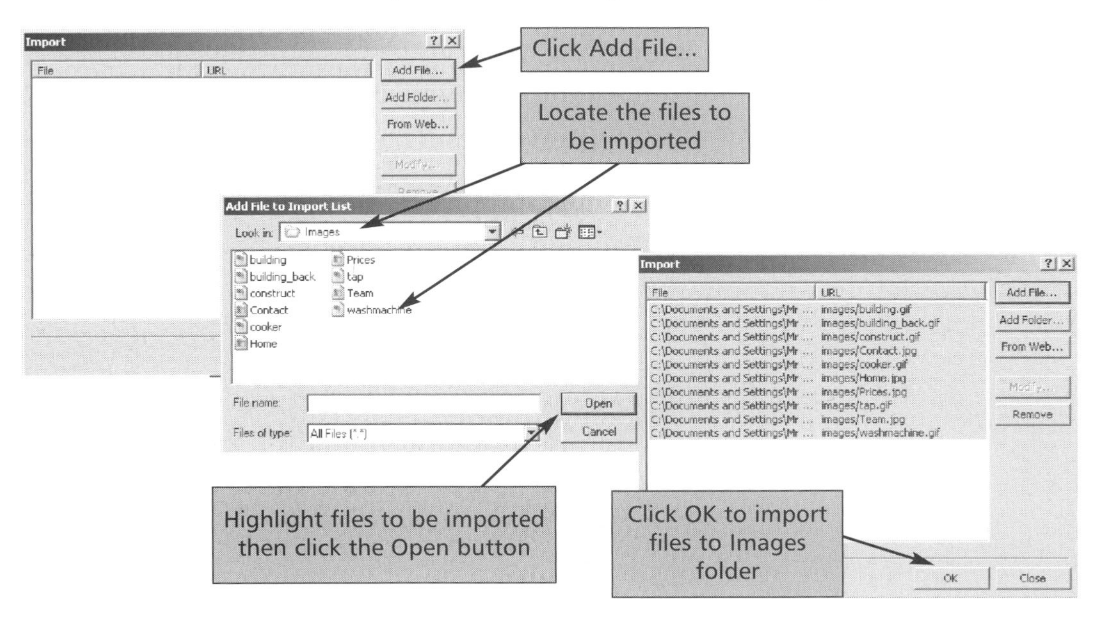

Figure 7.29

When the files have been imported they become an integral part of the web file and will remain with the file when it is published on the Internet. Now try importing some image files to the Images folder of the HomeHelp web.

Try it out

Open HomeHelp if it is not already open.

If the Folder list is not in view:

Click View on the main menu and then Folder List. The Folder view will appear in the window.

Click on the Images folder to open it.

Click File on the main menu and then Import... .

Click Add File.

Locate the Image folder for Unit 7, sub-folder Web1 on the accompanying CD.

Highlight the following files:

Building.gif
Construct.gif
Contact.jpeg
Cooker.gif
Gardening.gif
Garden_Design.gif
Home.jpeg
Iron.gif
Prices.jpeg
Tap.gif
Team.jpeg
Washmachine.gif
Trowel.gif

Click Open.

Click OK.

Your Images folder should now look similar to Figure 7.30.

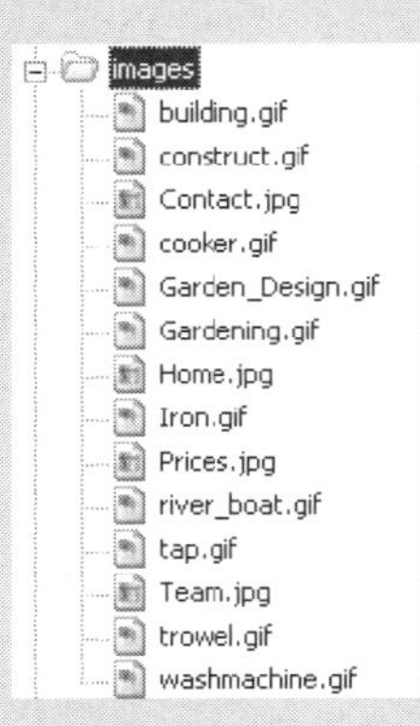

Figure 7.30

Inserting images into a web page

Images can be placed in a frame on a page (such as a cell in a table) or directly into the page itself. The techniques for ensuring the picture is where you want it are slightly different.

Inserting an image into a table cell

To insert an image into a table cell, click in the cell of the table where you want the image to reside. Next click the Insert option on the main menu, followed by Picture. Whether the image required is one stored as a file on your disk or a clip art image will determine whether or not you select 'From File…' or 'Clip Art…' on the menu option list. For the purposes of this unit all image files you need can be found on the accompanying CD. In the next exercise you are going to insert images into the cells of the navigation table you created for the Index.htm page.

Try it out

Open HomeHelp if it is not already open.

Open the Index.htm page.

Click in the first cell of the table.

Click Insert, Picture, From File… .

From the Picture dialogue box:

Highlight Team.

Click the Insert button.

Repeat this process for the images Prices, Contact and Home, placing each image in a separate cell of the table.

When you have finished, your navigation table should look like Figure 7.31.

Team	Prices	Contact	Home

Figure 7.31

Highlight the entire table and copy it, together with the images.

Paste the table and images at the top of each page – Team, Prices and Contact.

Save each of the web pages.

Formatting the size of an image

In the exercise you have just completed the images used were of an appropriate size for the cells in the table. However, there will be times when it is necessary to adjust the size of an image to fit an area. In the next exercise you will insert a number of images into the table on the Prices page and size them according to a design requirement.

To resize an image to a specific size, first, using the right-hand mouse button, click on the image and select the Picture Properties… option from the drop-down menu list. The Picture Properties dialogue box shown in Figure 7.32 will appear.

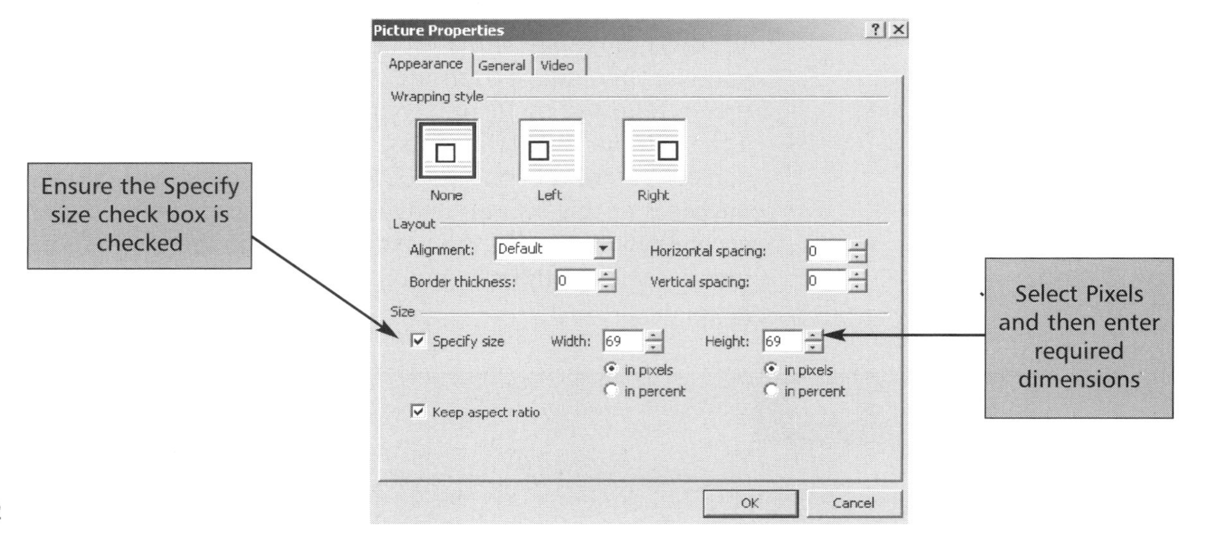

Figure 7.32

In the section of the box marked Size make sure the Specify size check box is enabled and then the appropriate width and height figures can be entered. Try this out.

Try it out

Open HomeHelp if it is not already open.

Open the Prices page.

Insert the pictures as shown in the table below and size them as stated.

Table 7.1

Service	Image	Width (pixels)	Height (pixels)
Plumbing	Tap.gif	62	73
Electrical	Iron.gig	90	46
Gas	Cooker.gif	70	70
Building	Building.gif	60	89
Construction	Construct.gif	70	72
Gardens	Gardening.gif	70	65
Garden Design	Garden_design.gif	70	54

When you have finished your Prices page should look similar to Figure 7.33.

Team | Prices | Contact | Home

Service		Range	Call out Costs per hour
Plumbing		All pipe work, heating systems, bathroom and toilet installations.	£35
Electrical		Circuits, lighting (repair and installation), domestic appliances (including television repairs)	£30
Gas		Boilers and gas fires (maintenance, repair and installations)	£40
Building		Gutters, brickwork, windows, door replacement, floor installations, roof repairs	£35
Construction		Extensions and conservatories	Priced individually
Gardens		Lawn doctor, paving, patios, tree surgery, garden maintenance.	Priced individually
Garden Design		Landscaping – design and construction	Priced individually

Figure 7.33

Positioning images on a page

When you insert an image into a frame such as a table, the position of the image is not really a problem as the table cell itself more or less dictates the image's position. It is then a matter of setting the alignment of the image within the table cell using the Table Properties… dialogue box options. However, images placed directly onto a page operate in a slightly different way.

First the cursor is placed roughly where you want to insert the picture. Insert the picture in the usual way by selecting Insert, Picture, From File… from the main menu. Select the picture from the Picture dialogue box and then click the Insert button.

By using the right-hand mouse button and clicking on the picture, a menu list appears with an option of Picture Properties. Clicking this option will open the Picture Properties dialogue box shown in Figure 7.34.

You will already have seen this dialogue box in Figure 7.32 when you were learning about resizing a picture. As you will see, there are two further sections to the dialogue box – Wrapping style and Layout.

The wrapping style determines how the image will interact with the text. The three options shown in the dialogue box are fairly self-explanatory. The picture is aligned either to the right or left of the text or alternatively has no specific alignment at all.

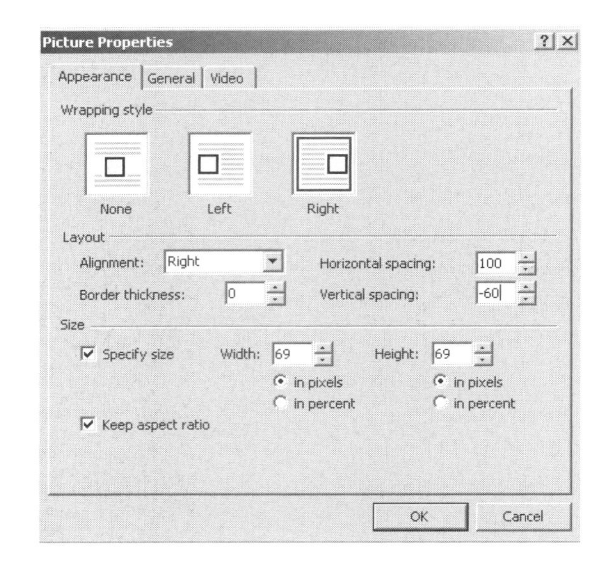

Figure 7.34

More detailed positioning of an image can be achieved by using the position dialogue box with either an absolute or relative reference. Have a look at Figure 7.35.

SELECT FROM A WIDE RANGE OF RIVER CRUISES

- First class accommodation
- Excellent Dining facilities
- Sports facilities to suit all ages
- Regular stops to visit interesting sites

SELECT FROM A WIDE RANGE OF RIVER CRUISES

- First class accommodation
- Excellent Dining facilities
- Sports facilities to suit all ages
- Regular stops to visit interesting sites

Position set 300 pixels from left and 100 pixels from top of page

Position

Wrapping style

None Left Right

Positioning style

None Absolute Relative

Location and size

Left: 300 Width: 100

Top: 100 Height: 61

Z-Order:

OK Cancel

Figure 7.35

Using alternative text to describe images

Alternative text allows FrontPage to display meaningful information about the image as the cursor is passed over the image. Alternative text is also used by Web browsers to display text during image downloads, where the user has graphics turned off, or for users who rely on screen-reading software to convert graphics on the screen to spoken words. To give an image alternative text first, using the right-hand mouse button, click on the image and then select the Picture Properties... option from the menu list given. In the Picture Properties dialogue box click on the General tab and the box shown in Figure 7.36 appears.

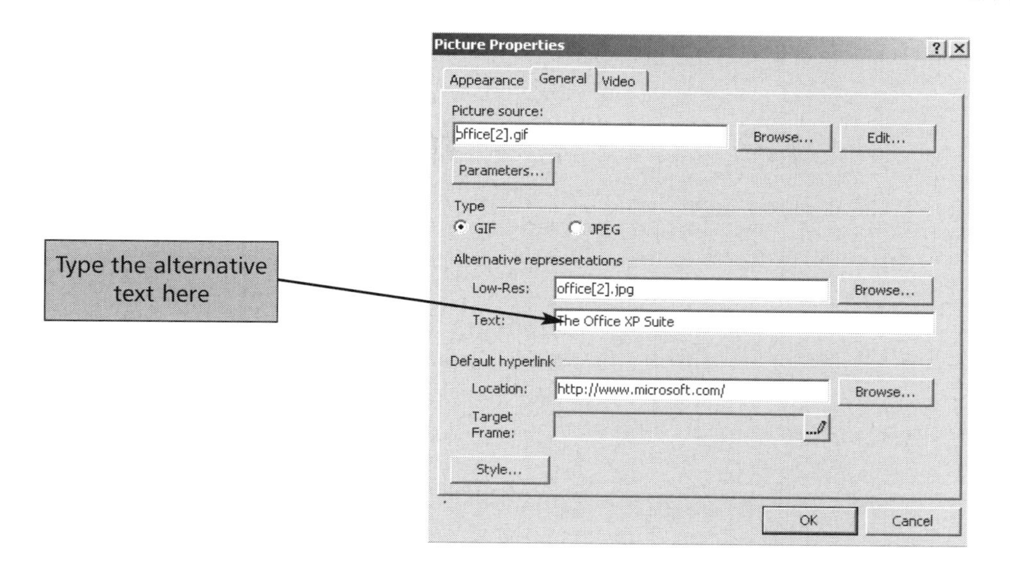

Figure 7.36

Now try to insert an image into the HomeHelp web.

Try it out

Open HomeHelp if it is not already open.

Open the Index.htm page.

Insert the image file **Trowel** from the images folder in your web.

Resize the image so that it is 69 pixels by 69 pixels.

Set the Absolute position as follows: Left 550, Top 225.

Save the web page.

Your page should now look like Figure 7.37.

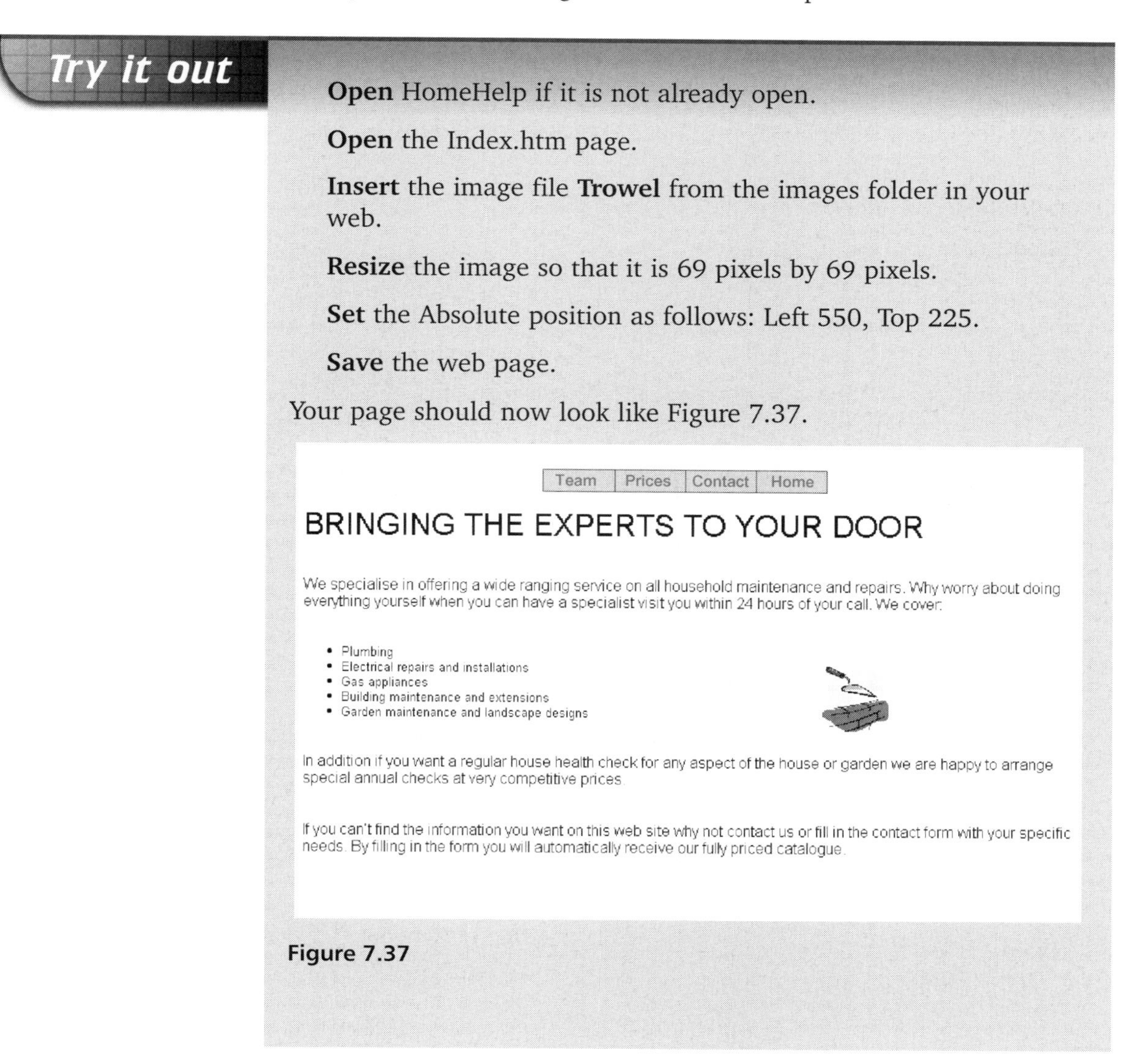

Figure 7.37

You should now be able to:

- create and define web pages
- insert text files and images into a web page
- understand the purpose and be able to use meta tags
- add new pages to a web
- format the web page background
- understand standard content
- create tables
- import to the Images folder
- insert images into a web page
- format the size, position and alternative text of an image.

Build-up Exercise 7: Stage 1

Scenario

You have just been appointed as the office manager of a new ICT training company. The general manager has asked you to prepare a website covering the programmes offered by the company. Since this is the first site you have created the manager has asked you to prepare the work in stages. You have been given the following house style guidelines:

House style guidelines

Structure

- All HTML files for the web should be contained in one directory.
- This directory should contain a sub-directory called Images.
- All image files should be contained in the Images sub-directory.
- All links to files and images on the website should be relative and not absolute.

Note: absolute referencing would include the full path on your machine e.g. c:\My Documents\ My Web...... etc. Your reference to linked pages should only refer to the sub-directory of the web itself.

Standard page properties

- Title as specified for each page brief.
- Background colour Hex={C4,C4,FF}

Standard text properties

- Text colour Hex={00,00,00}
- Link colour Hex={00,00,FF} (Links are covered later in the unit.)
- Visited link colour Hex={FF,CC,66}
- Typeface Sans serif (Arial).
- Text size Heading: HTML size 5 (18pt)
  Sub-heading: HTML size 3 (12pt)
  Body text: HTML size 2 (10pt)

Image properties

- Height and width as specified.

- Border must be set to 0 (zero) for each image.
- Alternative text must be set as specified in the design brief for each page.

Standard content for each page

- Meta tags
- Each page must contain the meta tag information shown in Table 7.2.

Table 7.2

Name	Content
Author	Your name
Keywords	Office, Word, Access, Excel, PowerPoint, Publisher, FrontPage
Description	As specified for each page

Navigation table

The following table of navigation images must be placed at the top of each page. Width 600, Height 37, Columns 4, Rows 1, Alignment centred, Cellspacing 0, Cellpadding 0, Border 0

ABOUT US	FIND US	PROGRAMS	HOME

Copyright notice

Each page must end with the following copyright notice:

Copyright © LearnFast

This notice should be placed right-aligned on the page, and be of body text size.

Design brief for Index.htm

Create a new Web file, initially with a single web page, and name it **LearnFast**.

Insert the standard content as advised in the brief.

Insert the following description as a meta tag:

'Learn about Microsoft Office applications in your own time and at an affordable price'.

Add the text file **LearnFast[1]** and the image file **Office[2]** according to the layout shown in Figure 7.38.

Format the heading 'LEARNING THE SECRETS OF MICROSOFT OFFICE' left-aligned with a font size of 18 point (HTML size 5).

Format the remaining text as body text, font size 10 point (HTML size 2).

Format the **Office[2].jpg** image as:

Width:	100	
Height:	120	
Alignment to text:	Right	
Position:	Left	400
	Top	225
Alternative text:	The Office XP Suite.	

▶▶

[Standard Navigation Table]

LEARNING THE SECRETS OF MICROSOFT OFFICE

LearnFast programmes put you in the driving seat. Learn what you want at your own pace.

What is Covered?

You can learn about any of the following applications selecting the skills you think you might need.

Word
Access
Excel
PowerPoint
Publisher
FrontPage
Outlook

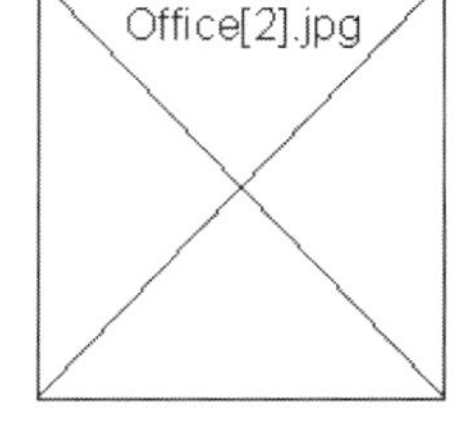

What will it cost?
Each unit costs £150.00 and is designed to be completed over a twelve week programme.
A further two week home support package is provided absolutely free.

[Insert Standard copyright statement here]

Figure 7.38

Design Brief for About._Us.htm

Insert a new web page.

Insert the standard content as advised in the brief.

Insert the following description as a meta tag:

'Find out about the flexibility of LearnFast programmes'.

Add the text file **LearnFast[2]** and format according to the design brief for body text and sub-headings.

Add and format the heading About Us. Text should be left-aligned with a font size of 18 point (HTML size 5).

Add the image file **LearnFast_RegMk.gif** according to the layout shown in the sketch below.

Format the **Office[2].jpg** image as:

Width:	70	
Height:	37	
Alignment to text:	Left	
Position:	Left	10
	Top	500
Alternative text:	The LearnFast Registration Mark.	

▶▶

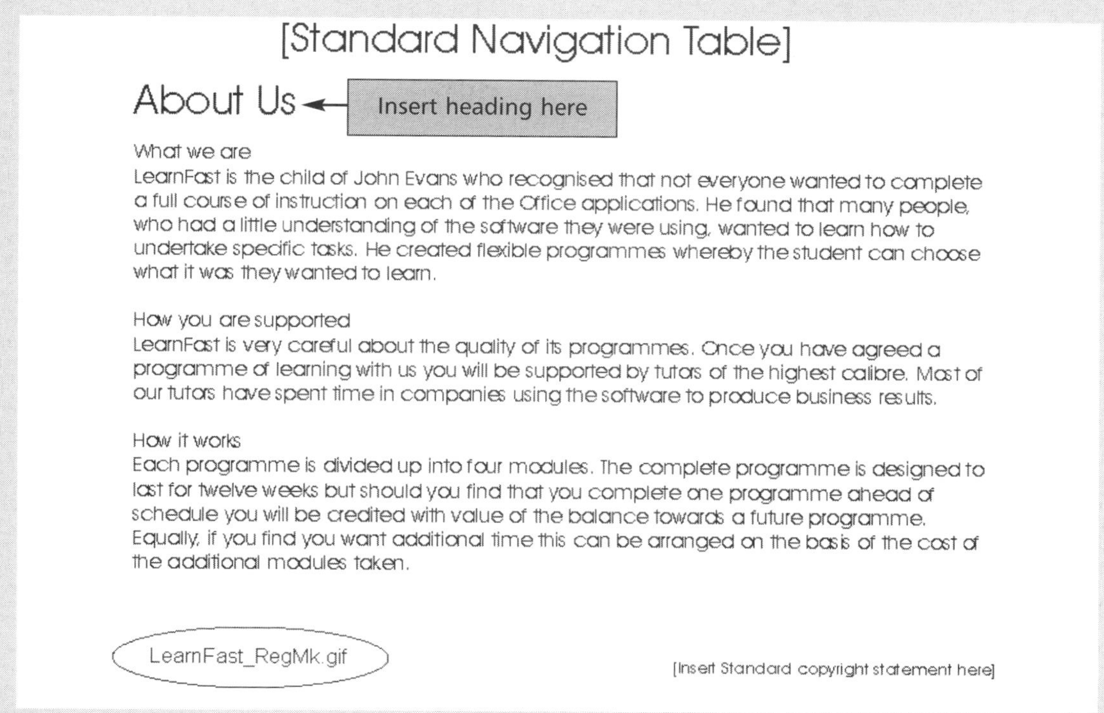

[Standard Navigation Table]

About Us ← Insert heading here

What we are
LearnFast is the child of John Evans who recognised that not everyone wanted to complete a full course of instruction on each of the Office applications. He found that many people, who had a little understanding of the software they were using, wanted to learn how to undertake specific tasks. He created flexible programmes whereby the student can choose what it was they wanted to learn.

How you are supported
LearnFast is very careful about the quality of its programmes. Once you have agreed a programme of learning with us you will be supported by tutors of the highest calibre. Most of our tutors have spent time in companies using the software to produce business results.

How it works
Each programme is divided up into four modules. The complete programme is designed to last for twelve weeks but should you find that you complete one programme ahead of schedule you will be credited with value of the balance towards a future programme. Equally, if you find you want additional time this can be arranged on the basis of the cost of the additional modules taken.

LearnFast_RegMk.gif

[Insert Standard copyright statement here]

Figure 7.39

Remember to import any image files to the image folder of the web file.

Save the web page keeping the name About_Us.htm

Design brief for Programs.htm

Insert a new web page and save it as **Programs.htm.**

Insert the standard content as advised in the foregoing brief.

Insert the following description as a meta tag:

'Office programs offered by 'LearnFast' include both the generic packages and specialist applications such as FrontPage and Publisher'.

Insert a new heading 'THE PROGRAM RANGE'.

The heading should be formatted as follows: Font Arial; Size HTML 5 (18point); Style Bold; Alignment Centre.

Insert a table with the following detail and format.
Format the table as follows:

Width	600 pixels
Height	700 Pixels
Cell padding	2
Cell spacing	2
Border	2
Table alignment	Centred
Cell alignment:	Vertical – top, horizontal columns 1 and 3 left, column 2 centre

Table 7.3

Application	Image	Functionality
Word	Word_2002.jpg	using a wordprocessing application
		building and using tables effectively
		creating data files to use with mail merge
		creating and using forms
		creating computer artwork
Excel	Excel_2002.jpg	understanding what spreadsheets, workbooks and worksheets are
		building a worksheet
		learning about 'what ifs'
		learning useful formulae
		learning about trends, investment appraisals and other available templates
		building charts and graphs
Access	Access_2002.jpg	understanding what databases are and their uses
		understanding how databases are structured
		building simple databases
		building queries, forms and reports
		learning about macros
Publisher	Publisher_2002.jpg	understanding what desk top publishing (DTP) is
		the benefits of DTP over wordprocessing
		creating visually attractive and exciting publications
PowerPoint	Power_Point_2002.jpg	understanding what presentation graphics is about
		creating basic slide presentations for talks and lectures
		learning how to use build and transition techniques
		creating slide notes
FrontPage	Front_Page_2002.jpg	understanding the basics for building web pages
		creating attractive single and multiple page websites
		learning how to amend sites to keep them up to date
		learning about Internet Service Providers and the services they offer
		learning how to publish a website onto the Internet
Outlook	Outlook_2002.jpg	learning about electronic communications
		setting up an e-mail account
		creating e-mail messages
		accessing incoming e-mail messages and learning about attachments

Table 7.4

Column title	Width	Horizontal alignment	Vertical alignment
Application	10%	Left	Top
Image	10%	Centre	Top
Functionality	80%	Left	Top

The following images are placed in the table:

> **Word_2002.jpg, Excel_2002.jpg, Access_2002.jpg, Publisher_2002.jpg, Power_Point_2002.jpg, Front_Page_2002.jpg, Outlook_2002.jpg.**

Each image should be set to:

Width	70 pixels
Height	85 pixels.

Format Column headings as Arial HTML 2 (10 point).

Set the alternative text for each image to be the same as its file name (but without the extension, i.e. the three letters after the full stop).

Format the items in the Functionality column as bulleted lists for each application.

Format table text as: Arial HTML 2 (10 point)

Save the web file.

Your pages should now look like Figures 7.40 to 7.42.

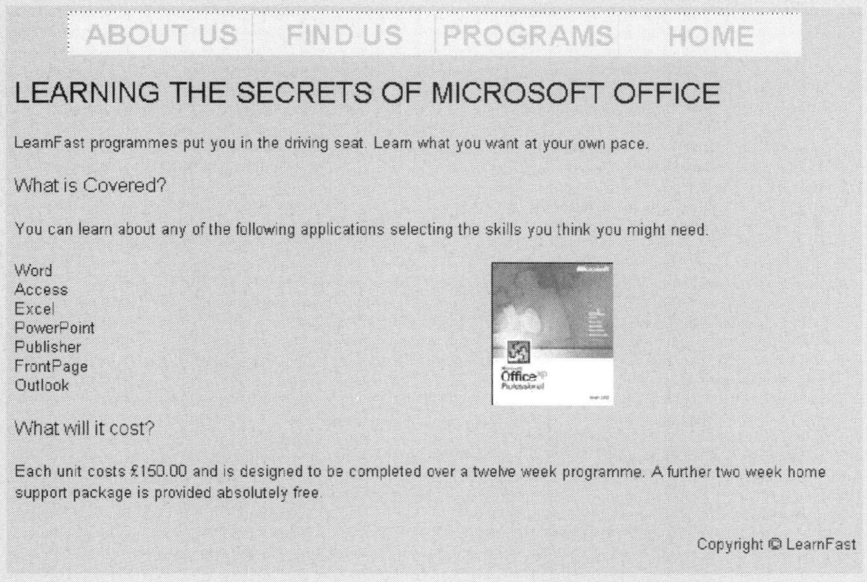

ABOUT US FIND US PROGRAMS HOME
LEARNING THE SECRETS OF MICROSOFT OFFICE
LearnFast programmes put you in the driving seat. Learn what you want at your own pace.
What is Covered?
You can learn about any of the following applications selecting the skills you think you might need.
Word
Access
Excel
PowerPoint
Publisher
FrontPage
Outlook
Office XP
What will it cost?
Each unit costs £150.00 and is designed to be completed over a twelve week programme. A further two week home support package is provided absolutely free.
Copyright © LearnFast

Figure 7.40

ABOUT US | FIND US | PROGRAMS | HOME

ABOUT US

What we are

LearnFast is the child of John Evans who recognised that not everyone wanted to complete a full course of instruction on each of the Office applications. He found that many people, who had a little understanding of the software they were using, wanted to learn how to undertake specific tasks. He created flexible programmes whereby the student can choose what it was they wanted to learn.

How you are supported

LearnFast is very careful about the quality of its programmes. Once you have agreed a programme of learning with us you will be supported by tutors of the highest calibre. Most of our tutors have spent time in companies using the software to produce business results.

How it works

Each programme is divided up into four modules. The complete programme is designed to last for twelve weeks but should you find that you complete one programme ahead of schedule you will be credited with value of the balance towards a future programme. Equally, if you find you want additional time this can be arranged on the basis of the cost of the additional modules taken.

Copyright © LearnFast

Figure 7.41

ABOUT US | FIND US | PROGRAMS | HOME

THE PROGRAM RANGE

Application		Functionality
Word		• using a word processing application • building and using tables effectively • creating data files to use with mail merge • creating and using forms • creating computer artwork
Excel		• understanding what spreadsheet, workbooks and worksheets are • building a worksheet • learning about 'what ifs' • learning useful formulas • Learning about trends, investment appraisals and other available templates • building charts and graphs
Access		• understand what databases are and their uses • understanding how databases are structured • building simple databases • building queries, forms and reports • Learn about macros
Publisher		• understanding what desk top publishing (DTP) is • the benefits of DTP over word processing • creating visual attractive and exciting publications
PowerPoint		• understanding what presentation graphics is about • creating basic slide presentations for talks and lectures • learning how to use build and transition techniques • create slide notes
FrontPage		• understand the basics for building web pages • create attractive single and multiple page web sites • learning how to amend sites to keep them up to date • learning about Internet Service Providers and the services they offer • learning how to publish a web site onto the Internet
Outlook		• learning about electronic communications • setting up an e-mail account • creating e-mail messages • accessing incoming e-mail messages and learning about attachments

Copyright © LearnFast

Figure 7.42

Check the HTML code against Figures 7.43 to 7.45.

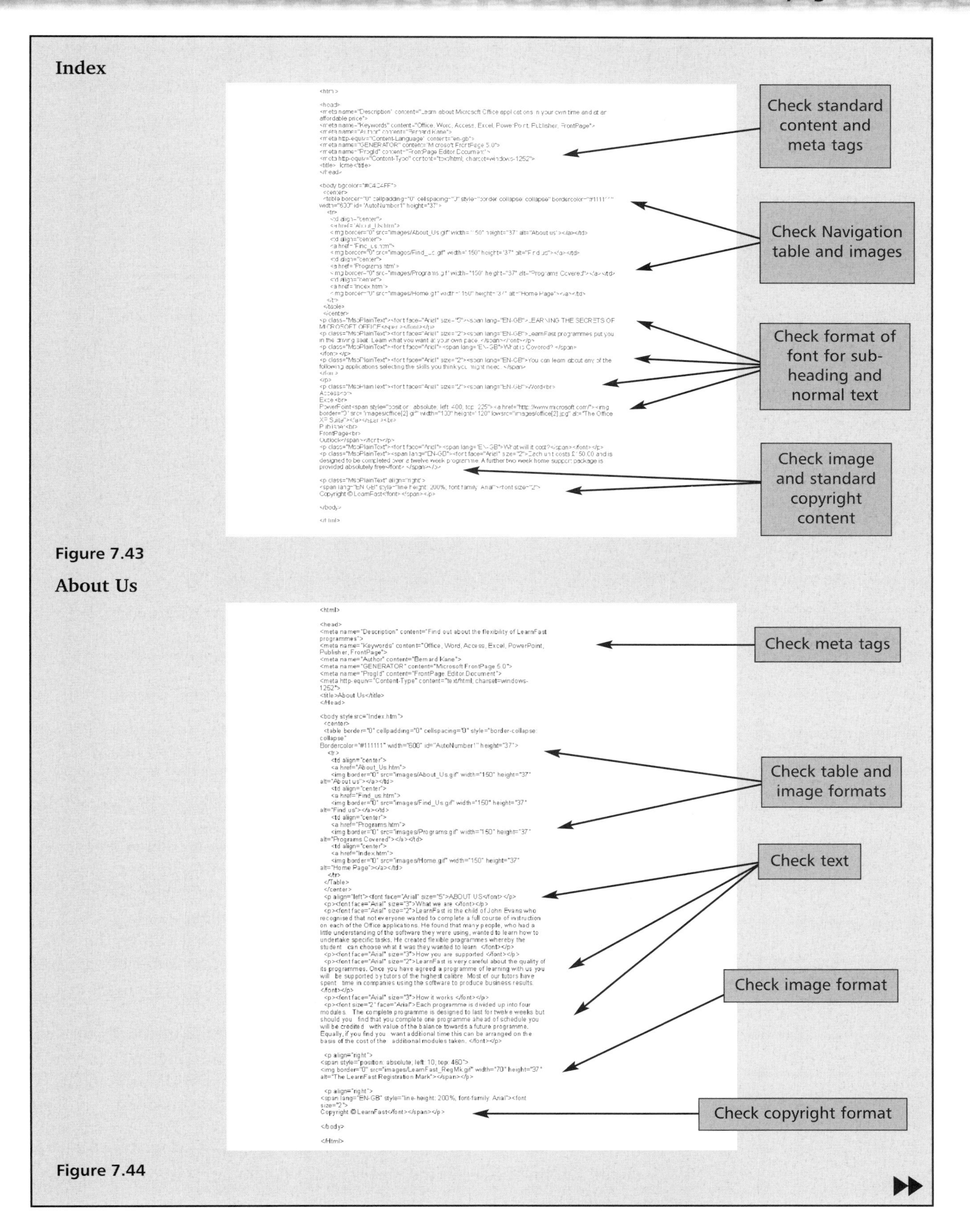

Figure 7.43

Figure 7.44

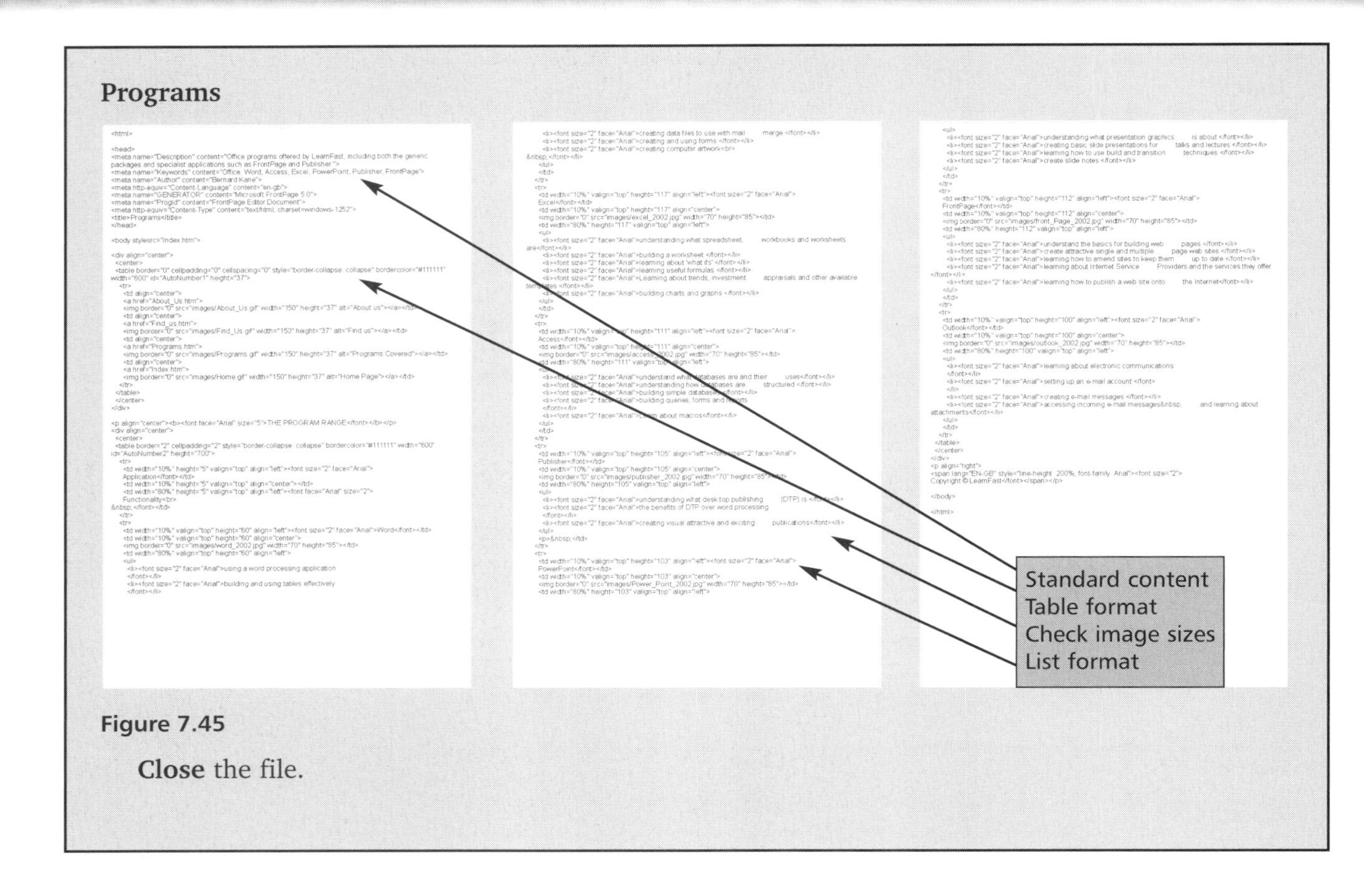

Figure 7.45

Close the file.

Creating links

Internal web links

Links or hyperlinks are an essential function of any web. Links can be either internal to the website itself (known as local links) or external to other sites. Links also provide a way of allowing visitors to your site to e-mail you. Almost any element of a web page (text, image etc.) can be used as the link object. In the previous exercises you created a navigation table with the cells of the table containing images. These will be used to create links to other pages of the web, while other images will be used to provide links to external sites.

To create a link first click on the text or object that will be the link interface using the right-hand mouse button. The menu list offered has an option called Hyperlink… . By clicking this option a dialogue box appears as shown in Figure 7.46.

FrontPage will assume by default that you want to create a link within the current web file. In the example shown in Figure 7.46 you can see that the current web is HomeHelp and that within the main folder there are four pages, of which one (Index.htm) is open. Assuming that the image that will provide the link is the Team button on the navigation bar, selecting the ‘team’ page and clicking OK will create the link between the current page (Index.htm) and Team. Now try this out.

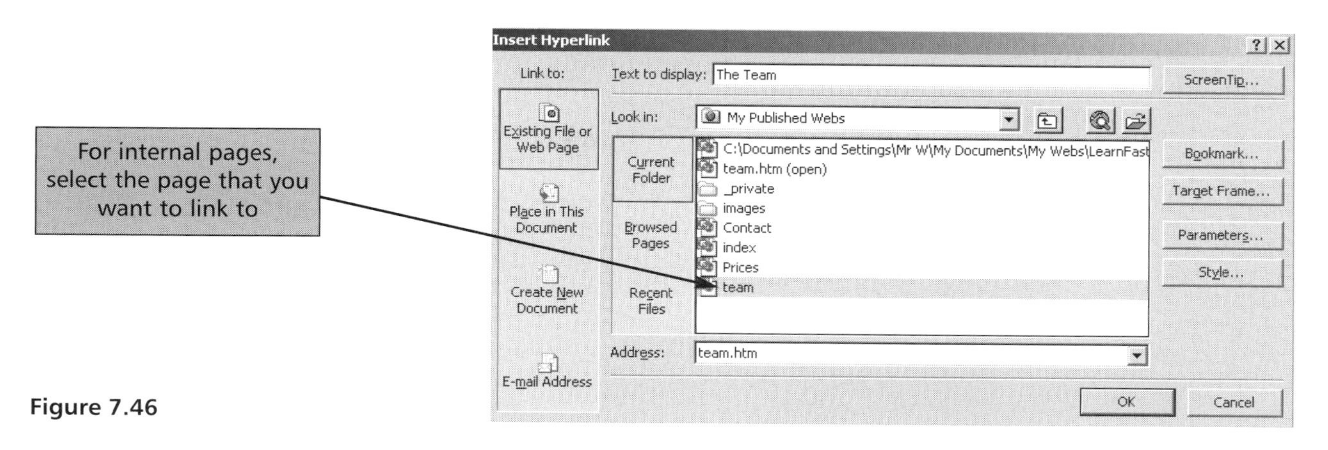

Figure 7.46

Try it out

Open HomeHelp if it is not already open.

Note: remember to open a web file select File, Open Web... from the main menu).

Open the Index.htm page.

Using the right-hand mouse button:

Click on TEAM in the navigation bar and from the menu list select Hyperlink... .

In the Insert Hyperlink dialogue box:

Click team.

Click OK.

Now repeat this process for each of the other images in the navigation bar. Use the Index page in the Insert dialogue box for the Home image.

Once you have created links for each of the buttons on the Index page you will need to repeat the process for each of the other pages in your web. So in the Team page you will need to repeat the 'create hyperlink' process on the navigation bar in that page and similarly on the Prices and Contact Pages.

Once you have created links for each page:

Save and close the pages in turn.

To test your links:

Open the index page.

Click the Preview tab next to the HTML tab.

Click one of the links on the navigation bar and then

Click the HOME link to return to the home (or index) page.

To view your links click on the Hyperlinks icon in the views task pane and the links will appear in the main window. Where there is a '+' you can see further links for that specific page.

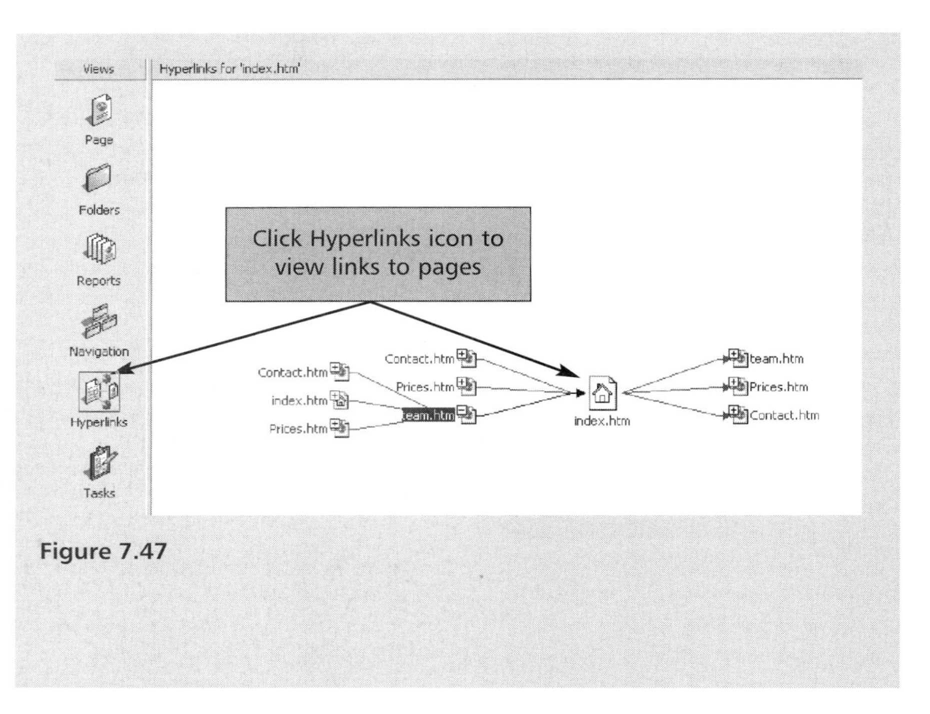

Figure 7.47

External web links

External links are created in much the same way as internal links. However, instead of selecting from the list of pages the URL (universal resource locator) address for the site is entered in the Address: field in the Insert Hyperlink dialogue box: see Figure 7.48.

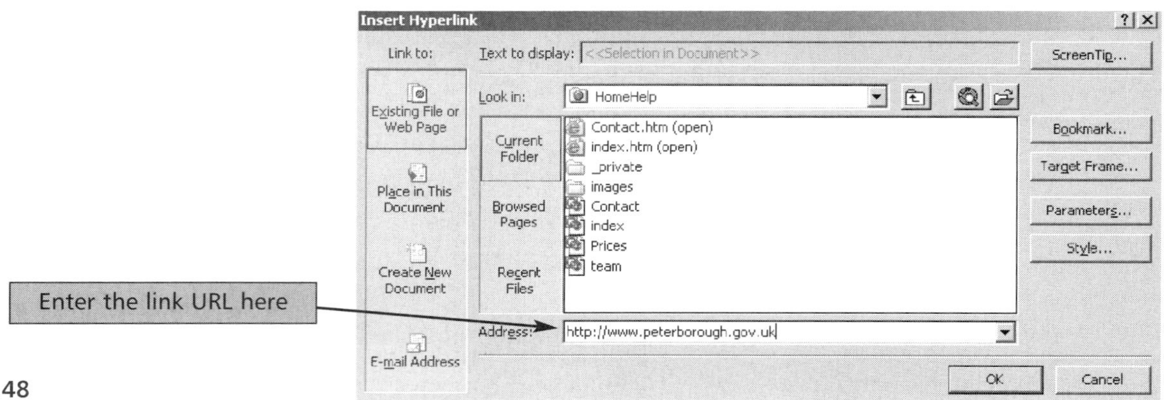

Figure 7.48

Having inserted the link you can view the HTML code that FrontPage has inserted by placing the cursor near the image and then selecting the HTML tab. Figure 7.49 shows the code that has been inserted.

A link can be removed either by deleting it from the actual HTML code or alternatively, using the right-hand mouse button, clicking on the link source (e.g. an image or text) and selecting the Hyperlink Properties... option from the drop-down menu list. The Edit Hyperlink dialogue box will appear. Simply click the Remove Link button to remove the hyperlink from that object. When you do this only the link for the selected object will be removed.

```
<span style="position: absolute; left: 550; top: 225">
<a href="http://www.peterborough.gov.uk">
<img border="0" src="images/trowel.gif" width="69" height="69"></a></span></p>
```

External link ref in HTML code

Figure 7.49

Now try using an image as an anchor for an external hyperlink.

Try it out

Open HomeHelp if it is not already open.

Open the Index.htm page.

For the purposes of the exercise you are going to link the page with the Microsoft Network web page (http://www.msn.com) using the **trowel.gif** image.

Using the right-hand mouse button:

Click on the trowel image.

Click on the Hyperlink... option.

In the Address: field of the dialogue box

Type 'http://www.msn.com'.

Click OK.

Save the web.

If you now preview your web in the browser you can check the link by clicking on the trowel.

Note: to open your web in the browser click on the Preview in Browser icon on the tool bar.

Using e-mail links

The e-mail link is a third type of hyperlink that you can introduce using the same Insert Hyperlink dialogue box. Using an e-mail link allows you to invite the site visitor to contact you or someone else via e-mail without their having to set the e-mail address up. As you will have often found while working through these units, the easiest way to understand how to set up such a link is by trying it out for yourself.

Try it out

Open HomeHelp if it is not already open.

Open the page team.htm.

Place the cursor on a new line after the end of the last item in the bullet list.

Type 'Plumbing:' and press tab.

Click Insert, Hyperlink... from the main menu to bring up the Insert Hyperlink dialogue box.

Click the E-mail Address option in the Link to: section and then

Type the e-mail address, 'peter.frank@homehelp.co.uk', in the field as shown in Figure 7.50.

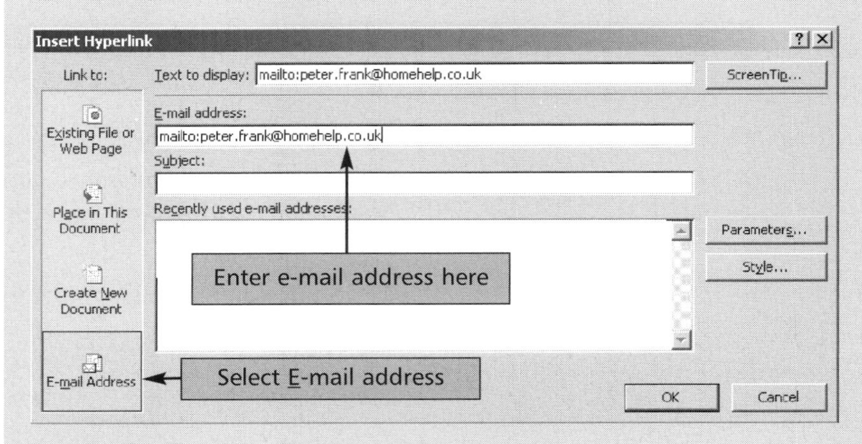

Figure 7.50

Click OK.

Now repeat this process for each of the contacts in the list using their 'firstname.surname@homehelp.co.uk' as the address. Each address should be preceded by the remaining services: Electrical, Gas, Building, Gardens.

Your page should now look similar to Figure 7.51.

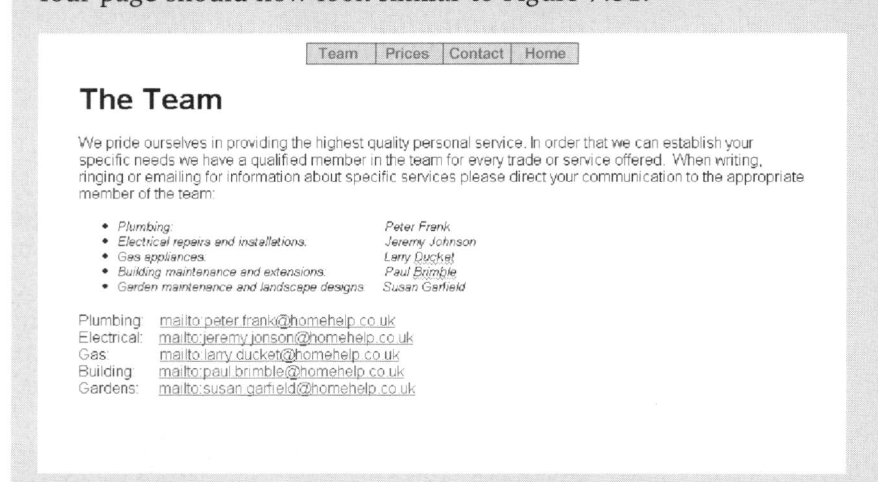

Figure 7.51

As these are not real e-mail addresses you would not be able to send an e-mail using these addresses, however, they are technically correct and therefore you can see how FrontPage treats the Mail to: option.

Click the Preview tab.

Click the Peter Frank mailto address.

The e-mail editor will open with Peter Frank's e-mail address ready for the user to type his request, as shown in Figure 7.52.

Figure 7.52

You should now be able to:

- create internal web links
- create links to external webs
- create e-mail links.

Build-up Exercise 7: Stage 2

Open LearnFast.

Using the information contained in Table 7.5

Create the links to the pages shown, and insert the appropriate alternative text.

Table 7.5

Page	Navigation bar	Alt text	Link to
Index.htm	About Us	About us	About_us.htm
	Find Us	Find us	Find_us.htm
	Programs	Programs Covered	Programs.htm
	Home	Home Page	Index.htm
About_us.htm	About Us	About us	About_us.htm
	Find Us	Find us	Find_us.htm
	Programs	Programs Covered	Programs.htm
	Home	Home Page	Index.htm
Find_us.htm	About Us	About us	About_us.htm
	Find Us	Find us	Find_us.htm
	Programs	Programs Covered	Programs.htm
	Home	Home Page	Index.htm
Programs.htm	About Us	About us	About_us.htm
	Find Us	Find us	Find_us.htm
	Programs	Programs Covered	Programs.htm
	Home	Home Page	Index.htm

Save each page of the web.

Link the Office XP image on the Index.htm page to http://www.microsoft.com.

Open the Find_us.htm page.

Immediately under the navigation bar:

Type 'Contact us:' (text should be formatted as per the standard text properties for body text).

Insert an e-mail hyperlink after the Contact us: text to Support@LearnFast.co.uk.

Save the amended pages.

Creating and using interactive forms

Most websites set aside a page or an area of the site to receive visitor feedback. This can be for ordering goods, seeking general information or providing the company with details of your requirements in respect of services offered. FrontPage provides three ways to create interactive forms. First you can use the form page Wizard, secondly you can use the form page template and thirdly you can build a form from scratch. You can, of course, also build a form simply using HTML. FrontPage is excellent in helping you build both simple and complex forms. The one drawback in using FrontPage for building interactive forms is that your web has to be published with an ISP with FrontPage extensions before you can test the form, or alternatively you will need to make some amendments to the HTML generated by FrontPage. This is really not as complicated as it sounds; here you will learn how to use FrontPage to build your forms and then modify the HTML so that your form can be tested.

For the assessment in CLAIT Plus you will be given a design brief similar to other pages but with specific fields that should be contained within the form.

There are two parts to this section. The first is building the form and the second is modifying the HTML so that you can test it.

Creating a form from scratch

When creating a form from scratch first insert a form area on the page by clicking Insert, Form and Form from the main menu. This places the form area which includes a Submit and Reset button as shown in Figure 7.53.

Submit | Reset

Figure 7.53

The form area can be expanded by clicking in the form area box and pressing the enter key: see Figure 7.54. The cursor can be placed either in front of the default Submit and Reset buttons, or after them.

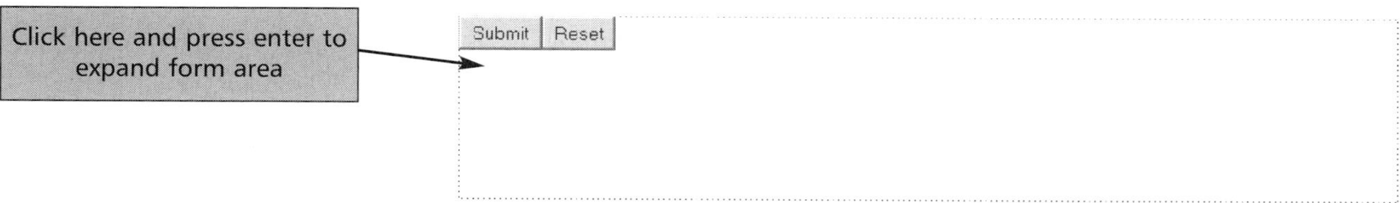

Figure 7.54

Form fields

FrontPage provides a range of fields that can be used in its forms. Figure 7.55 shows the fields available.

Some of the fields provide for single line entries, such as the Textbox field, whereas others allow a virtually limitless amount of text to be entered, such as the Text Area field. You can also provide the user with choice boxes such as the Drop-Down box where you can insert any number of options for the user to select from.

Now create a simple interactive form for the HomeHelp web.

Try it out

Open HomeHelp if it is not already open.

Open the Contact.htm page.

Click on the page just below the navigation bar.

Click Heading 1 from the Styles option on the formatting toolbar.

Type the heading, 'How you can help'.

Press Enter on the keyboard to create a new line.

Click Insert, Form and select Form from the sub-menu list.

With the cursor in front of the Submit button:

Press enter four or five times.

At the top of the form:

Note: all label text is to be formatted as Arial HTML 2 (10 point).

Type 'Please provide your contact details:'

Press Enter.

Type 'Title'.

Press the keyboard Tab key three times.

Click Insert, Form, and select Drop-Down Box from the menu list.

You can now put any titles into the box using the Form Field properties… option.

Using the right-hand mouse button:

Click on the Drop-Down box and select the Form Field properties… option from the menu list. The dialogue box shown in Figure 7.56 will now appear.

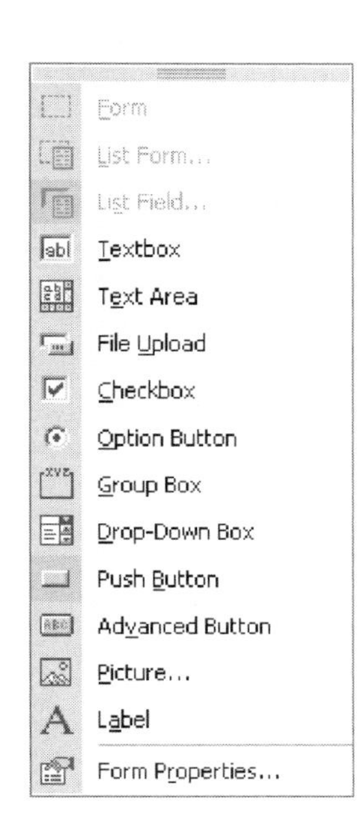

Figure 7.55

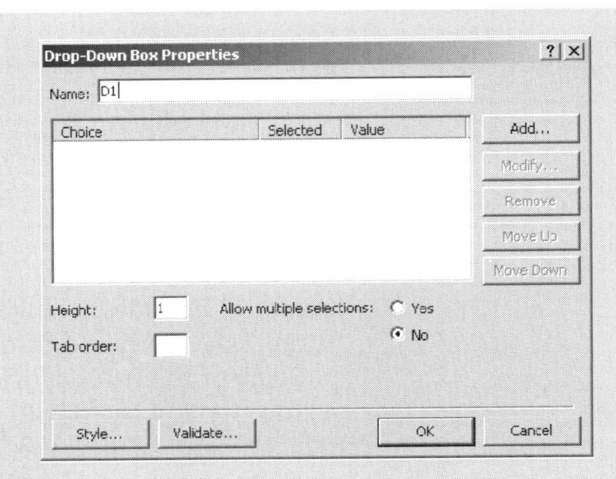

Figure 7.56

In the top of the box you can give the form field a name or accept the FrontPage default name.

Type 'Title' as the field name.

Click the Add… button.

A new dialogue box appears as shown in Figure 7.57.

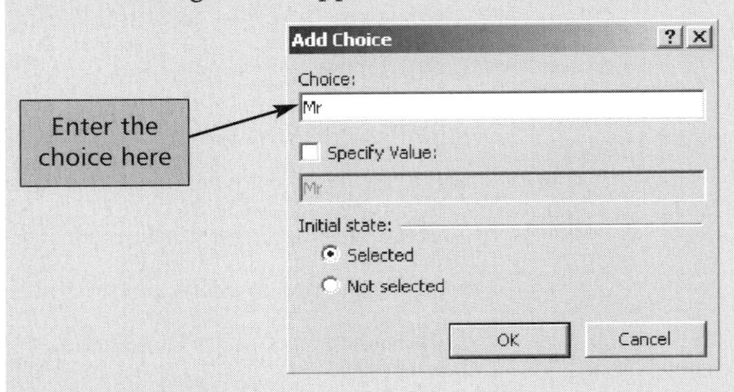

Figure 7.57

Type 'Mr' in the Choice: field.

Click the Selected radio button.

Click OK.

Now enter the following additional values:

Mrs
Miss
Ms
Dr

For each of these the Not Selected radio button should be clicked.

Click OK to return to the web page. You can return to the field at any time to make additions or changes.

To view the field:

GENERAL TIP

Choice Field

In the Choice: field the value for the list is entered (e.g. Mr, Mrs or Miss).

You can also determine the initial state of the choice. So for example if 'Mr' was in the list and the Initial State was 'Selected', this would be the default value for the drop box. To change the value you would need to click on the drop arrow and make a further choice from the list.

Click Preview.

Your form should now look like Figure 7.58.

Figure 7.58

Now enter the fields with the appropriate field properties as shown in Table 7.6.

Note: to set the field properties use the right-hand mouse button and click on the field and select the Form Field Properties… option from the menu list.

Table 7.6

Label	Form Field	Properties
First Name	Textbox	Name: First_Name Width in Characters: 20 Tab order: 2
Surname	Textbox	Name: Surname Width in Characters: 20 Tab order: 3
Address	Text area	Name: Address Width in Characters: 28 Tab order: 4 No of Lines: 4
Help Required	Text area	Name: Help_required Width in Characters: 50 Tab order: 5 No of Lines:4
Yes	Check Box	Name: Email_Yes Value: On Initial State: Not Checked Tab order: 6
No	Check Box	Name: Email_No Value: On Initial State: Not Checked Tab order: 7

continued

Label	Form Field	Properties
Email:	Textbox	Name: Email Width in Characters: 35 Tab order: 8

Your form should look similar to Figure 7.59 when complete.

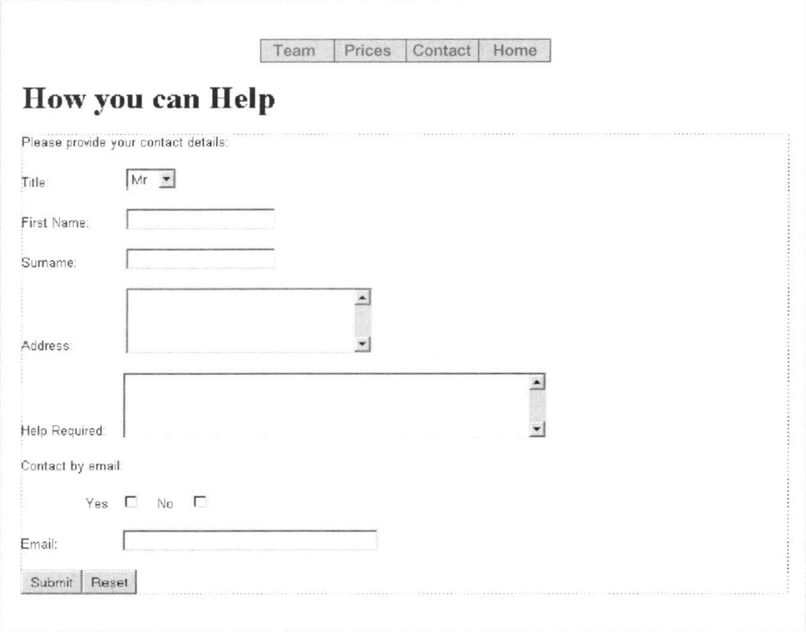

Team | Prices | Contact | Home

How you can Help

Please provide your contact details:

Title: Mr

First Name:

Surname:

Address:

Help Required:

Contact by email:

Yes No

Email:

Submit Reset

Figure 7.59

Save the form and file.

Understanding method and action

So far you have seen how FrontPage and other HTML editing programs can create the necessary HTML code to make your pages work. But until you start to develop web forms the information flow is all one way – i.e. to the visitor of the website. The purpose of creating forms is so that any visitor to the site can send data back to you for analysis or indeed to make a request. The way in which the information from a form is sent is very largely dependent on the purpose of the form.

Authors of forms can choose how they want to receive the input from those visitors using the website. The simplest way is where the data is e-mailed back to the author directly from the viewer's browser. The more usual method is by sending data back via the author's web server, where it can be processed using CGI (common gateway interface) programs. A CGI script is a program run on a web server, activated by input from a browser. Quite often a CGI script is linked to other programs such as a database.

Every form on a web has two parts: the code that is part of the form itself and the script which processes the contents of the form. These are linked through the HTML code and are associated with two attributes: method and action. For CLAIT Plus you are expected to understand these two attributes.

As you have already seen in this section, the <Form> tag defines the area where the HTML contents are placed to create the elements such as textboxes, text areas, radio buttons, check boxes, and so on. Tags allowed inside the <Body> of a page are also allowed inside a form. So various formatting lists may all be found inside the form tag.

Method and action are attributes that are only allowed to exist inside a form and must be used if the form is to be employed correctly. In the simplest terms 'method' identifies the way the form's data will be sent from the browser being used to input to the server housing the script where the data will be processed. Method has two values: get and post. Action provides the name of the server and script.

If you were to look at the HTML for the form you created earlier you would see that FrontPage automatically inserted both method and action attributes:

The FrontPage-generated HTML for method and action were:

```
<form method="POST" action="—WEBBOT-SELF—"
onSubmit="location.href='_derived/nortbots.htm';return false;"
webbot-onSubmit>
<!—webbot bot= "SaveResults" u-file="_private/form_results.csv" s-
format= "TEXT/CSV" s-label-fields="TRUE" b-reverse-
chronology="FALSE" s-email-format="TEXT/PRE" s-email-
address="bernard.kane@bksolutions.co.uk" b-email-label-
fields="TRUE" s-builtin-fields startspan —><strong>[FrontPage Save
Results Component]</strong><!—webbot bot="SaveResults"
endspan i-checksum="6561" —><p>
```

Note: The method and action attributes have simply been emboldened to make them easier to identify.

Don't panic! You will not be expected to know or understand the HTML statements created here by FrontPage. However, had this web been published to a server supporting FrontPage extensions, visitor inputs would have returned data to a form called 'form_results.csv' which resides in the private folder of the web server.

Since you will not be publishing the web you will need to modify the action attribute in order to test your form. To do this you will replace the FrontPage code with details of the server and script that will process the form:

```
<form method=POST action="http://www.progress-
webmail.co.uk/cgi-bin/webmail.cgi" name="Contact">
```

The action contains the URL (universal resource locator) of the CGI program (in this case 'http://www.progress-webmail.co.uk/cgi-bin/webmail.cgi').

When you are completing your assignment you will be given the exact form action to include in your HTML code.

Hidden fields

In the changes to the HTML code generated by FrontPage shown above, the form indicates where the CGI script is located, and the method and action to be taken. What is missing is an instruction of where to post the results. Clearly the form needs to tell the web server holding the CGI script where the post is to be delivered to – namely your e-mail address. Such instructions are known as 'hidden fields' since they are not visible on the form.

> ***Hidden elements look like the HTML shown here:***
>
> <input type= "hidden" name="thename" value= "the value">
> Translated as an e-mail address this would appear as:
> <input type=hidden name=recipient
> value=bernard.kane@bksolutions.co.uk>

Now amend the HTML code of your form so that it can be tested.

Try it out

Open HomeHelp if it is not already open.

Open the page Contact.htm.

Click the HTML tab to show the HTML code.

Highlight the lines starting '<form method="POST"...........', and finishing '<!—webbot bot="SaveResults" endspan i-checksum="6561" —><p>'.

Type the replacement code: '<form method=POST action="http://www.progress-webmail.co.uk/cgi-bin/webmail.cgi" name="Contact">'.

Add a new line of code immediately below this:

'<input type=hidden name=recipient value= Your email address>'.

Where the '=' is your own e-mail address.

Save the changes you have made to the page.

Testing the form

Having made the necessary changes, testing the form is very straightforward. First a connection is made to the net and the form page is opened using the Preview in Browser icon . The details requested on the form are completed and the Submit button clicked.

The host server produces a new page indicating that the information has been received and checked and that an e-mail with the relevant details has been sent to the relevant e-mail address.

On checking the e-mail a new e-mail will have been received from the host server www.progress-media.co.uk containing all the details of the form from the HomeHelp web. Try it out.

Try it out

Make a connection to the Internet using Internet Explorer or your personal browser.

Open HomeHelp if it is not already open.

Open the page containing the form, then on the toolbar click the Preview in Browser icon .

Enter details into the form giving:

- Your name.
- Address.
- Help required (this is free text so you can write whatever you wish).
- Whether you can be contacted by e-mail.
- Your e-mail address.

Click the Submit button.

You will receive confirmation similar to that shown in Figure 7.60 from the server that your request has been received and that an e-mail has been sent with the details you submitted.

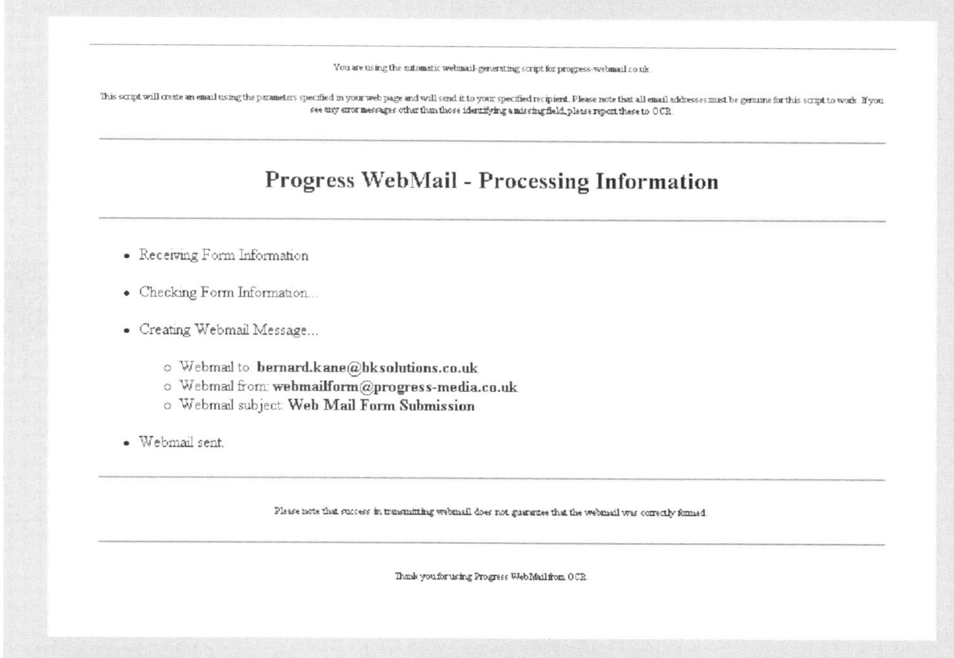
You are using the automatic webmail-generating script for progress-webmail.co.uk
This script will create an email using the parameters specified in your web page and will send it to your specified recipient. Please note that all email addresses must be genuine for this script to work. If you see any error messages other than those identifying a missing field, please report these to OCR.
Progress WebMail - Processing Information
Receiving Form Information
Checking Form Information...
Creating Webmail Message...
Webmail to: bernard.kane@bksolutions.co.uk
Webmail from: webmailform@progress-media.co.uk
Webmail subject: Web Mail Form Submission
Webmail sent.
Please note that success in transmitting webmail does not guarantee that the webmail was correctly formed.
Thank you for using Progress WebMail from OCR.

Figure 7.60

If you check your e-mail you will find an e-mail, similar to the one shown in Figure 7.61, has been sent with the details of your submission to the server.

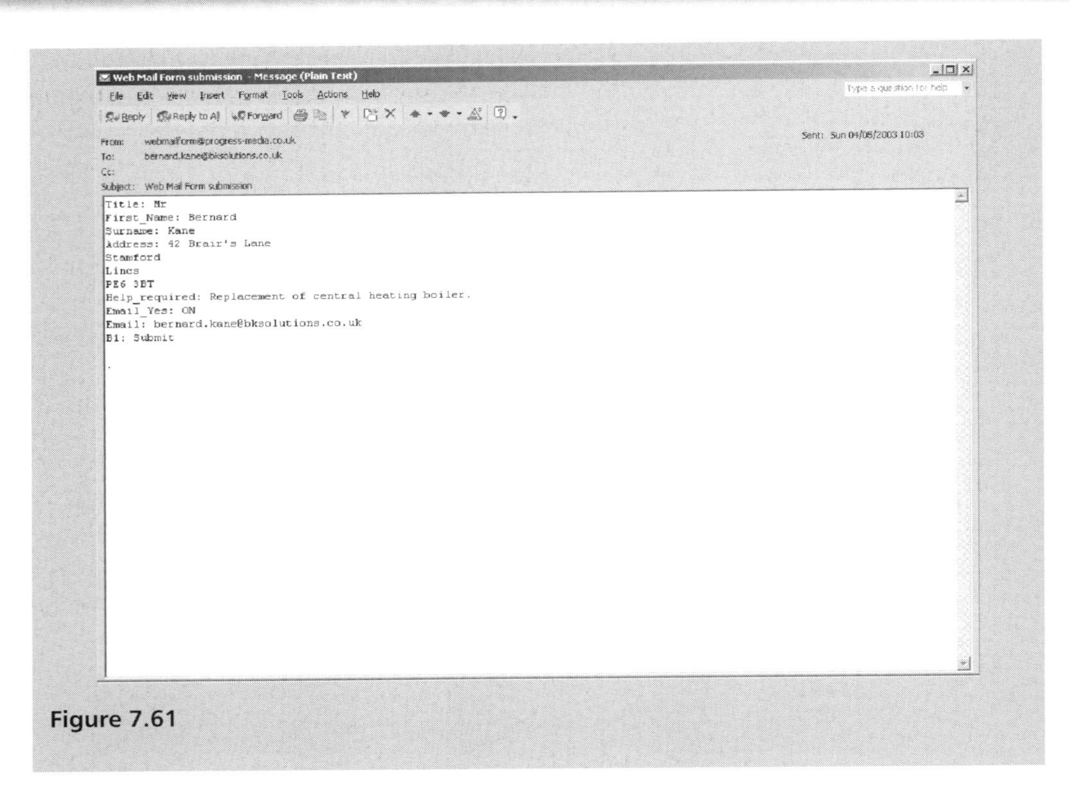

Figure 7.61

You should now be able to:

- create a form from scratch
- understand form fields
- understand method and action
- test a form.

Build-up Exercise 7: Stage 2

Open LearnFast.

Create a new page.

Save the page as **Contact_us**.

Insert the standard content meta tags for author and keywords.

Insert a description meta tag as follows:

Name: Description
Value: Tell us how we can help you?

Set the background as for the other pages in the site (Background Hex ="#C4C4FF">).

▶▶

Insert standard navigation bar and provide links to each of the pages in the web.

Insert the heading 'Let us know how we can help you'.

Format the heading as Arial HTML 5 (18 point).

Create an interactive form as follows:

Table 7.7

Type	Name	Settings	
Hidden Field	recipient	Your e-mail address	
Drop-down box	Title	Name:	Title
		Height:	1
		Tab Order:	1
		List Content:	
		Mr, Mrs, Miss, Ms, Dr, Rev	
Textbox	Initial	Width:	5
		Tab Order:	2
Textbox	Surname	Width:	20
		Tab Order:	3
Textarea	Address	Width:	30
		No of Lines:	5
		Tab Order:	4
Textbox	Home_Phone	Width:	20
		Tab Order	5
Textarea	Applications	Width:	30
		No of lines:	2
		Tab Order:	6
Checkbox	Phone_Yes	Not checked	
		Value:	On
		Tab Order:	7
Checkbox	Phone_No	Not checked	
		Value:	On
		Tab Order:	7
Submit	Submit	Tab Order:	8
		Value:	Submit
Reset	Reset	Tab Order:	9
		Value:	Reset

Replace the FrontPage-generated method and action with:

Method= POST
Action= http://www.progress-webmail.co.uk/cgi-bin/webmail.cgi
Name= "Contact"

(Remember the input for the hidden field: <input type=hidden name=recipient value=Your email address>.)

Insert the standard copyright notice after the form.

Your form should now look similar to Figure 7.62.

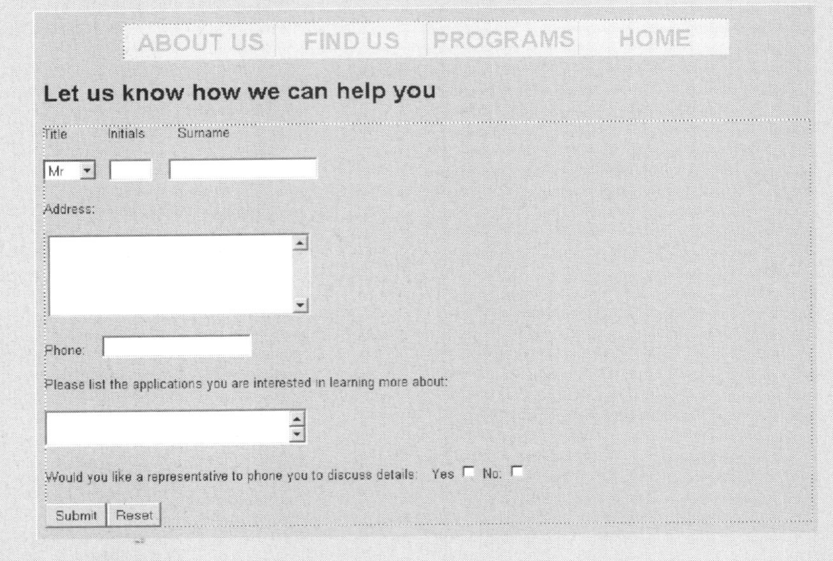

Figure 7.62

Save the web page and form.

Build-up Exercise 7: Stage 3

Open the Index.htm page.

After the last sentence and before the copyright statement:

Type 'To let us know what your needs are click here: Please complete our order form'.

Insert a link using the text 'Please complete our order form', that opens the contact page with the form you have just created.

Save your web file.

Click the Preview in Browser icon and test the new link.

Close the Browser.

Open the Find_us.htm page.

Insert image file **Map.gif**.

Format the image so that its absolute position is: Left 60, Top 100.

Save the web page.

Now open your web in the browser (either Internet Explorer or your personal browser) and test the links and the form.

Downloading files from the web

For CLAIT Plus you will need to be able to download files from an OCR designated website. To download a file first

Click on the folder in the folders list in your web (or create a new folder and call it downloads) and then

Select Import from the File option on the main menu. The Import dialogue box will appear.

Click the 'From Web…' button and FrontPage will ask you where you want to import the file from.

Click the 'From a World Wide Web site' radio button and in the location field enter the URL for the required site.

Click the Next button and you will be given the choice of limiting what is to be downloaded.

Deselect the 'Limit to this page plus' and the 'Limit to' file size check boxes.

Click the 'Limit to text and image files' check box.

Click the Next and then Finish buttons and the Dial Up Connection box will appear.

Note: If you are permanently connected to the web then FrontPage will go straight to the selected site.

FrontPage will then automatically download all the files on the web selected and you will be able to view them in the folder the files were downloaded to in your FrontPage web.

That completes all the objectives you will need to know for CLAIT Plus in web page creation. Now try and put the skills you have learnt in this unit into practice by completing the practical assignment below. Solutions to this exercise can be found in Appendix 2.

Web page creation

Scenario

You have just created a new company called PlayGolf. The company is geared towards helping people find affordable golfing holidays and arranging golf tuition.

You decide you need a website that will be accessed by people picking up your literature and marketing material.

You are to set up a website according to the following information:

- The site map
- The house style guidelines below.
- The standard content for each page
- The design brief for each page.

All text and graphics you will need to build the basics of the site are contained on the CD accompanying this book.

Site map

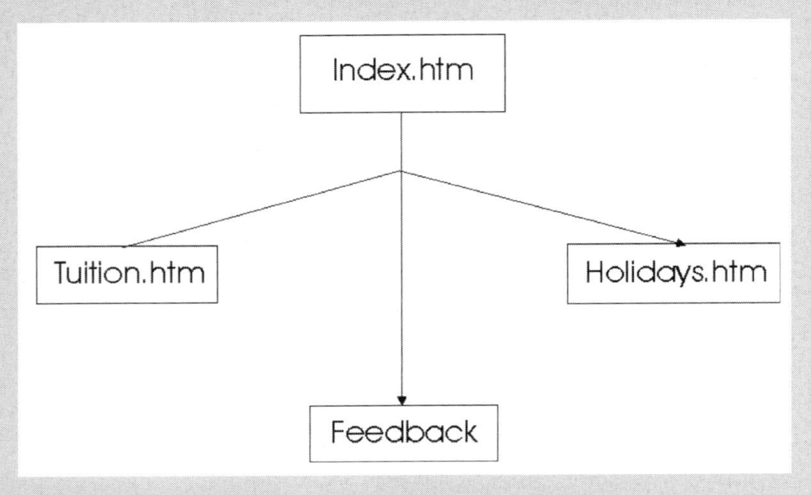

House style guidelines for the PlayGolf website

Site structure

- All HTML files for the website should be contained within the same directory.
- The main directory should contain a sub-directory called Images.

(**Note:** if you are using FrontPage, this will be generated automatically.)

- All image files that will be used in the site must be contained within the Images sub-directory.
- All links to files and images must be relative and not absolute.

Standard page properties

- Title – as specified in each page design brief.
- Background colour for all pages – Hex={E2,FE,CF}

Standard text properties

- Text colour – Hex={00,00,00}
- Link colour – Hex={00,66,FF}

- Visited link colour – Hex={C8,ED,F9}
- Typeface – Sans serif arial
- Text sizes: Heading – HTML Size 5 (18pt)
  Sub-heading – HTML Size 4 (14pt)
  Body text – HTML Size 2 (10pt)

Image properties

- Height and width must be specified accurately for each image.
- Border for each image must be set to 0 (zero).
- Text must be as specified in the design brief for each page.

Standard content for each page

The following must appear on every page of the website.

Meta tags

Each page must contain the following meta tag information:

Name	Content
Author:	Your full name
Keywords:	Tuition, Holidays, Offers, Breaks
Description:	As specified in the design brief for each page

Navigation table

The following navigation images must be placed at the top of each page:

Width: 470 (pixels); Height: 22 (pixels); Columns: 5; Rows: 1; Alignment: Centred; Cellspacing: 0; Cellpadding: 0 Border: 1

Images

Holiday_Button.bmp Tuition_Button.bmp Offers_Button.bmp Contact_Button.bmp Home_Button.bmp

The images all have a width of 94 pixels and a height of 22 pixels and are to be formatted as follows:

Image/cell	Alt text	Link to:
Holiday_Button.bmp	Holidays	Holidays.htm
Tuition_Button.bmp	Tuition details	Tuition.htm
Offers_Button.bmp	Current Offers	Offers.htm
Contact_Button.bmp	Contact Us	Contact_Us.htm
Home_Button.bmp	Home Page	Index.htm

Copyright notice

Each page must end with the following copyright notice:

Text	Format
Copyright©PlayGolf	Right-aligned Body text size

Design brief for Index.htm

Assessment objectives	Stage	
1c, 1d, 1e, 1g 2a, 2b, 2d 2e, 2f, 4a, 4b, 4c, 4d	1	Create a new web file using FrontPage. Format the page according to the house style guidelines and insert the standard content – (meta tags, navigation table and copyright notice). Save the web page created as **Index.htm.**
	2	Insert a heading for the Index.htm page: PLAYING GOLF FOR FUN AND ENJOYMENT
1d	3	Insert the following description in the appropriate meta tag: How we help you get the most out of your golf.
2a 2b	4	Add the text file **Home_Page.txt** and the image file **Golf_Logo.gif** in the layout shown in the sketch below.

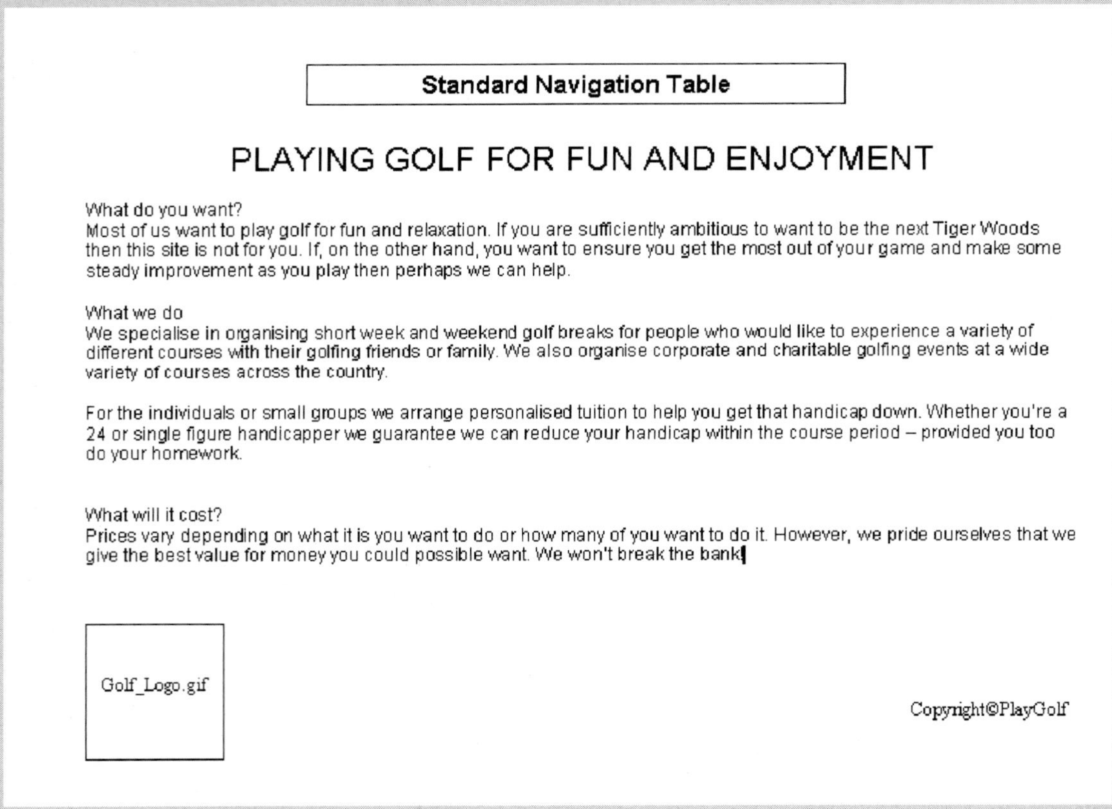

Standard Navigation Table

PLAYING GOLF FOR FUN AND ENJOYMENT

What do you want?
Most of us want to play golf for fun and relaxation. If you are sufficiently ambitious to want to be the next Tiger Woods then this site is not for you. If, on the other hand, you want to ensure you get the most out of your game and make some steady improvement as you play then perhaps we can help.

What we do
We specialise in organising short week and weekend golf breaks for people who would like to experience a variety of different courses with their golfing friends or family. We also organise corporate and charitable golfing events at a wide variety of courses across the country.

For the individuals or small groups we arrange personalised tuition to help you get that handicap down. Whether you're a 24 or single figure handicapper we guarantee we can reduce your handicap within the course period – provided you too do your homework.

What will it cost?
Prices vary depending on what it is you want to do or how many of you want to do it. However, we pride ourselves that we give the best value for money you could possible want. We won't break the bank!

Golf_Logo.gif

Copyright©PlayGolf

Figure 7.64

Stage		
5	Format the image Golf_Logo as follows:	
	Width:	70
	Height:	84
	Position:	Left-aligned
	From Left:	10
	From Top:	480

2c	6	The heading should be centred and in the heading house style. Sub-headings should be left-aligned and in the house style. Remaining body text as per the house style guidelines ensuring that there are no line spaces between the sub-heading and paragraph text but there is at least one line space between paragraphs.
1g	7	Save the web page keeping the filename **Index.htm**.

Design brief for Holidays.htm

1c, 1d, 1e, 1g **2a, 2b, 2d** **2e, 2f** **4a, 4b, 4c, 4d**	1	Create a new web page. Save the page with the name **Holidays.htm** Insert the standard content for web pages – (meta tags, navigation table and copyright notice). Insert a new description meta tag: 'A small selection of short break golf holidays'. Insert the Rich Text Format table file from the CD named 'Breaks'.
	2	Type 'Short Break Holidays' as the heading for the page. **Format**: Alignment: Centre Font: As per standard text properties
2e, 2f	3	Format the table as follows: Table alignment: Centre Cell alignment: Columns Location and Break: Left-aligned Columns Nights and Cost: Centre-aligned Width: 340 pixels Cell padding: 2 Cell spacing: 0 Border Size: 1 Table background colour: Hex={00,FF,FF}
2a, 2c	4	Leaving a space after the table, Insert the text file **included.txt**. Format the lines after 'What is included' as a bullet list.
2a	5	Import the image **Airplane_1** to the Images folder and Insert the image on the page as follows: **Size**: Width: 190 pixels Height: 54 pixels **Position**: Left: 480 Top: 370
1g	6	Save the web page keeping the filename **Holidays.htm**.

Design brief for Tuition.htm

1c, 1d, 1e **2a, 2b, 2d** **2e, 2f** **4a, 4b, 4c, 4d**	**1**	Create a new web page. Save the page as **Tuition.htm**. Insert the standard content for web pages – (meta tags, navigation table and copyright notice). Insert a new description meta tag: 'Tuition options and costs'.
	2	Insert the following heading for the page: TUITION - OPTIONS AND COST The format for the heading is as per the standard text properties.
2a	**3**	Insert the text file **Options.txt** immediately below the heading but leaving a space between the heading and first line of text. Sub-headings should be left-aligned and in the house style format. The remaining body text is as per the house style guidelines ensuring that there are no line spaces between the sub-heading and paragraph text but there is at least one line space between paragraphs.
2d, 2e 2f	**4**	Insert the file **Table_options** below the COSTS paragraph. Format the table as follows: Width: 400 pixels Cell padding: 4 Cell spacing: 4 Border: 4 Table alignment: Centred Cell alignment: See table below:

Table 7.8

Column title	Width	Horizontal alignment	Vertical alignment
Advice & Guidance	25%	Left	Middle
Image	25%	Centre	Middle
Cost per hour	15%	Centre	Middle
Other benefits	35%	Left	Middle

2a, 2b	**5**	The table contains the following images: Ballanddriver.gif Ball.gif Silhouette2.gif The relative sizes of these images should be: Ballanddriver.gif width: 100 Height: 77 Ball.gif width: 50 Height: 50 Silhouette2.gif width: 75 Height: 115 Ensure that each of the images is clearly visible in the table.

Set the alternative text for each image as follows:

Ballanddriver.gif – Ball and Driver
Ball.gif – Ball
Silhouette2.gif – Silhouette

Save the file as **Tuition.htm.**

Design brief for Contact_Us.htm

1c, 1d, 1e, 1g 2a, 2b, 2d 2e, 2f 4a, 4b, 4c, 4d	1	Create a new web page. Save the page as **Contact_Us.htm.** Insert the standard content for web pages – (meta tags, navigation table and copyright notice). Set background colour as per standard page properties. Insert a new description meta tag: 'Give us your feedback'.
2a	2	Insert the following heading for the page: HOW CAN WE HELP?
3b, 3c, 3d	3	Set up the page including an interactive form as shown in Figure 7.65.

Insert Standard Navigation Table

HOW CAN WE HELP?

1. Please enter your name and address:

Insert Textbox — Name

Insert Text Area — Address

Insert Text Box — Telephone Number

2. Please tell us which of our services you are interested in receiving details about:

Check box — Holidays
Check box — Clubs
Check box — Analysis
Check box — Lessons

3. Would you like us to contact you to discuss the options you may be interested in?

Check box — Yes
Check box — No

4. Please enter your e-mail address in the box provided — Insert Textbox

5. Please indicate the age group you are in from the list below:

Radio button — 20 - 30
Radio button — 31 - 40
Radio button — 41 - 50
Radio button — 51 - 60
Radio button — Over 60

Thank you for providing this information. We will contact you shortly.

Submit button — Reset button

Standard copyright notice

Figure 7.65

Set the form field properties as shown in Table 7.9.

Table 7.9

Type	Name	Field settings
Hidden field	Recipient	Your e-mail address
Textbox	Name	Width: 25
Text area	Address	Width: 25 Lines: 5
Textbox	Telephone	Width: 25
Checkbox	Holidays	Initial state: Not checked
Checkbox	Clubs	Initial state: Not checked
Checkbox	Analysis	Initial state: Not checked
Checkbox	Lessons	Initial state: Not checked
Checkbox	Contact_Yes	Initial state: Not checked
Checkbox	Contact_No	Initial state: Not checked
Radio button	Age_1	Initial state: Not selected Value: V1
Radio button	Age_2	Initial state: Not selected Value: V2
Radio button	Age_3	Initial state: Not selected Value: V3
Radio button	Age_4	Initial state: Not selected Value: V4
Radio button	Age_5	Initial state: Not selected Value: V5
Submit button	Submit	Value=Submit
Reset button	Reset	Value=Reset

2c	4	The format for the heading is as per the standard text properties. Format the body text for the form as for standard body text properties.
3a	5	Set Method="POST" Set Action=http://www.progress-webmail.co.uk/cgi-bin/webmail.cgi name="Contact_Us"> <input type=hidden name=recipient value=your email address>
1e	6	Save the page.
3d	7	Make a connection to the Internet using your browser. Open your form using the Preview in Browser icon on the toolbar. Type appropriate responses into your form. Click the Submit button.

Open your e-mail software and you should receive an e-mail in response to your form submission.

Design brief for Offers.htm

1c, 1d, 1e, 1g 2a, 2b, 2d, 2e 2f, 4a, 4b 4c, 4d	1	Create a new web page. Save the page as **Offers.htm**. Insert the standard content for web pages – (meta tags, navigation table and copyright notice). Set background colour as per standard page properties. Insert a new description meta tag: 'Current Offers'.
2a	2	Insert the following heading for the page: TAKE ADVANTAGE OF SEASONAL OFFERS
2a, 4d	3	Insert the text file **Offers** beneath the main heading. Insert an e-mail link to sales@playgolf.co.uk after the text 'Please contact us:"
2c	4	The format for the heading is as per the standard text properties. Format the body text for the form as for standard body text properties.

Graphs and charts

Graphs and charts for CLAIT Plus builds on some of the skills covered in the level 1 graphs and charts certificate for IT Users – New CLAIT. If you have completed the level 1 certificate you will find that some of the objectives reinforce what you learnt at level 1 whilst others help you develop additional skills, including using scatter and line–column graphs, trend lines, formatting graphs and charts and a number of other useful functions available within the software.

Five key assessment objectives

For CLAIT Plus there are five main assessment objectives, each of which contains a number of skills that you will be expected to learn.

- **Select and control data source**
  - open a data file
  - select a single set of data
  - select comparative data sets
  - select sub-sets of large data sets
  - select data from non-adjacent rows and columns
- **Present data using charts and graphs**
  - use an exploding pie chart
  - emphasise pie chart segments
  - use column and bar charts for large comparative data sets
  - use line–column graphs
  - use x–y scatter graphs
- **Set parameters of graphs and charts**
  - select and enter titles, sub-titles and axis titles
  - select and display data labels
  - apply and remove a legend
  - set the upper and lower limits and intervals on axes
  - insert trendlines
  - insert a trendline equation
  - insert and position text boxes
- **Format graphs and charts**
  - follow a house style
  - apply super- and sub-script effects
  - apply specific numeric formatting on axes
  - apply and remove background fill to/from the plot area
  - apply fill to bars in data series
  - join scatter points together in a line
  - set the style and weights of lines
  - apply and remove line markers

- **Print graphs and charts**
  - print graphs and charts in landscape format
  - print graphs and charts in portrait format

This unit does not assume any prior knowledge of the objectives covered, but you may well find it helpful to have completed the level 1 unit in graphs and charts to understand some of new skills at level 2. As you go through the unit the relevant knowledge and understanding will be explained. A complete list of the individual skills for each objective, together with the required knowledge and understanding, can be found in Appendix 1.

In this unit you will learn about:

- selecting and controlling data sources
- types of charts and graphs and when they are used
- selecting a single data range and creating a pie chart
- selecting data sets for comparative analysis using column charts
- creating line and column charts
- creating X–Y scatter graphs
- selecting sub-sets of data and non-adjacent columns and rows
- setting the parameters for graphs and charts
- formatting aspects of graphs and charts
- printing charts and graphs.

Selecting and controlling data sources

Opening a data file

For the purposes of this unit you will be using Microsoft Excel as the preferred application for producing graphs and charts. Since OCR does not set any specific criteria for software to use in completing certification in graphs and charts (or indeed any of its units), comma separated value (.csv) files are provided in the exercises for this unit. You can open csv files in any compatible software since the data for each field is separated by a comma. The csv format is used in much the same way as Rich Text (.rtf) and text only (.txt) files are, when the originator is not sure what particular wordprocessing software the recipient is using. Generally speaking, modern spreadsheet software will recognise and convert from most proprietary packages. You do not need to worry about the format of the file as Excel will open csv files as if they were Excel files with an .xls extension. The main difference between an Excel and csv file is that the csv file will not save any formatting, functions or formulae. Because of this you will be asked to save the .csv file as an Excel file before starting the exercise being undertaken. Once opened the file can be saved either as .csv or .xls by clicking Save As... from the File option on the main menu and ensuring that the Save as type: field in the Save As dialogue box has Microsoft Excel Workbook selected.

Now try opening a .csv data file and saving it as an Excel workbook.

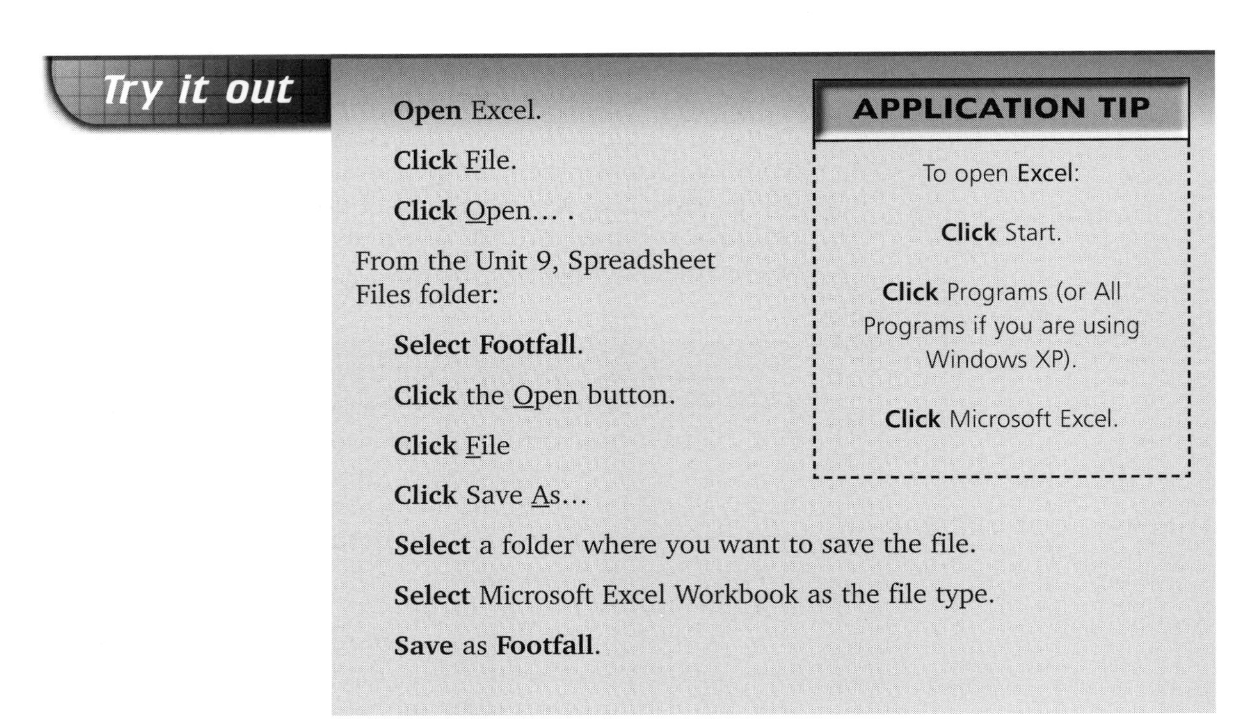

Try it out

Open Excel.

Click File.

Click Open... .

From the Unit 9, Spreadsheet Files folder:

Select Footfall.

Click the Open button.

Click File

Click Save As...

Select a folder where you want to save the file.

Select Microsoft Excel Workbook as the file type.

Save as **Footfall.**

APPLICATION TIP

To open **Excel**:

Click Start.

Click Programs (or All Programs if you are using Windows XP).

Click Microsoft Excel.

Types of charts and graphs and their uses

Excel supports a wide variety of charts and graphs to display data in an informative and interesting way. For CLAIT Plus you will need to know and understand how to create exploding pie, bar/column charts, line–column and X–Y scatter graphs. Table 9.1 on the next page gives an example of each of these and their use.

Selecting a single data set and creating a pie chart

Before you can create a chart or graph you need to select the data that will be used to build it. Selecting single sets of data is straightforward and will be something you covered if you have completed a level 1 programme for charts and graphs. Have a look at Figure 9.1 on the next page.

The spreadsheet has a simple, single range of data showing the value of sales for various fruits. These values are represented in a pie chart which is in the process of being created using the Chart Wizard. However, although you can start using the Wizard before creating a chart it is far simpler to identify the range of data to be used before launching the Wizard.

Now have a go at building a simple pie chart from a single range of data.

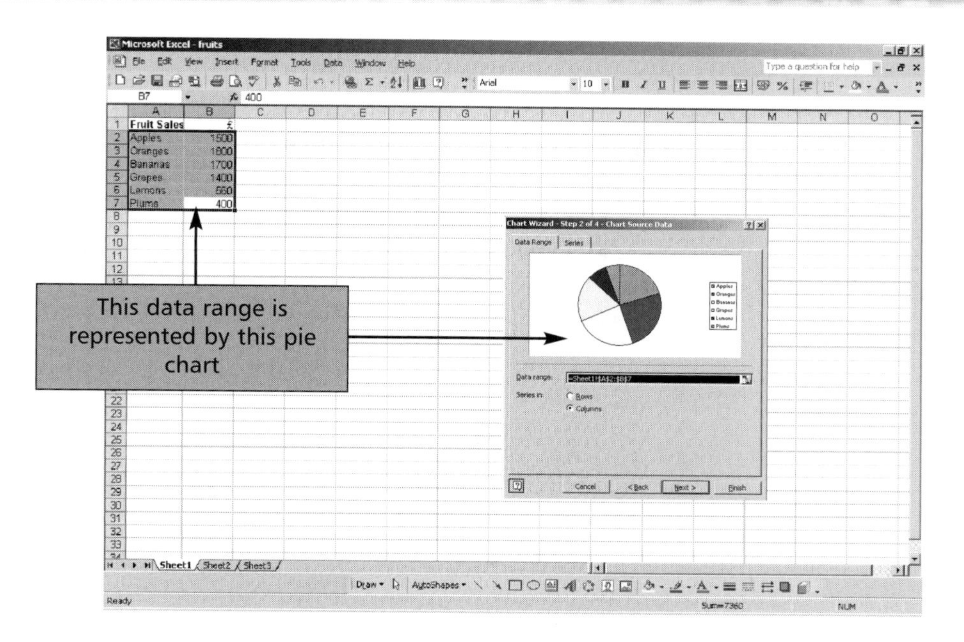

Figure 9.1

Table 9.1 *Types of graphs and charts and their uses*

Chart type	Used for:	Example
Exploding pie	showing the proportion of specific data in relation to the whole	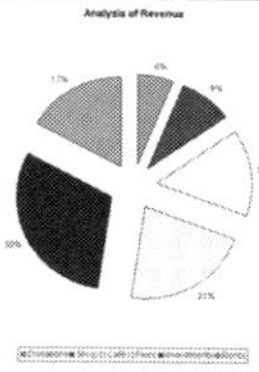
Column	a vertical comparison of data in a series to each other.	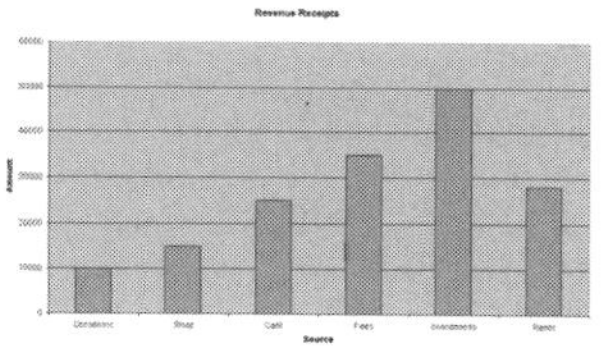
Bar	a horizontal comparison of data in a series to each other.	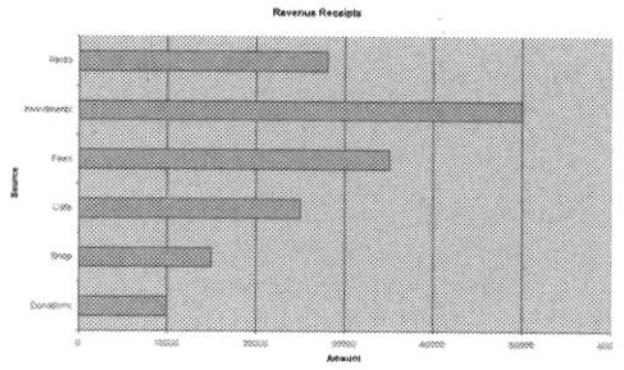
Line–column	where a line series and a column series are plotted on the same axis.	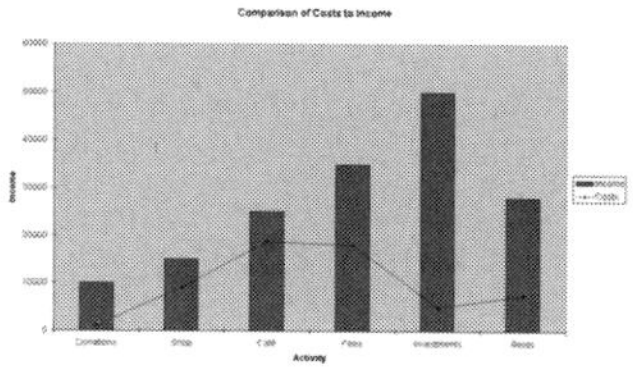
X–Y scatter	identifying trends or defining relationships between two data sets.	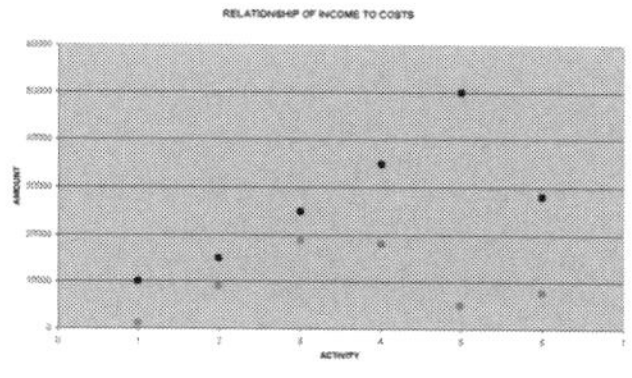

Try it out

Open Excel.

Note: To open Excel click on the Start button on the bottom left of window, click on Programs (or All Programs if you are using Windows XP). Click Microsoft Excel.

Open the .csv file **Animals** in the Spreadsheet sub-folder of Unit 9 on the accompanying CD.

Save the file to your hard disk as an Excel workbook using the file name **Animals**.

Select the data range A3 to B8.

Click on the charts icon on the toolbar .

The dialogue box shown in Figure 9.2 will appear.

Click on Pie as the type of chart required.

Click on the exploded pie chart in the Chart sub-type: panel.

EXCEL TIP

To save the file click File and then Save As... on the main menu. Select the folder where the file is to be saved in the Save in: field. In the Save as type: field select Microsoft Excel Workbook (or .xls). Click the Save button.

EXCEL TIP

To select the range click on the cell A3 and, with the left-hand mouse button held down, drag the cursor to cell B8. Release the mouse button and the highlighted range will be selected.

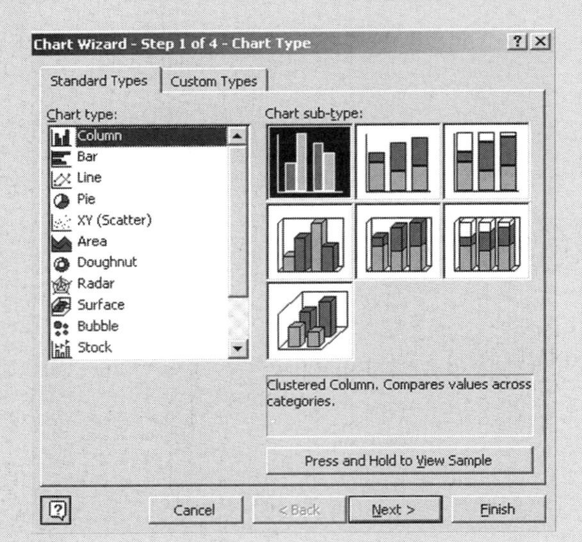

Figure 9.2

Click Next >.

The dialogue box shown in Figure 9.3 will now appear.

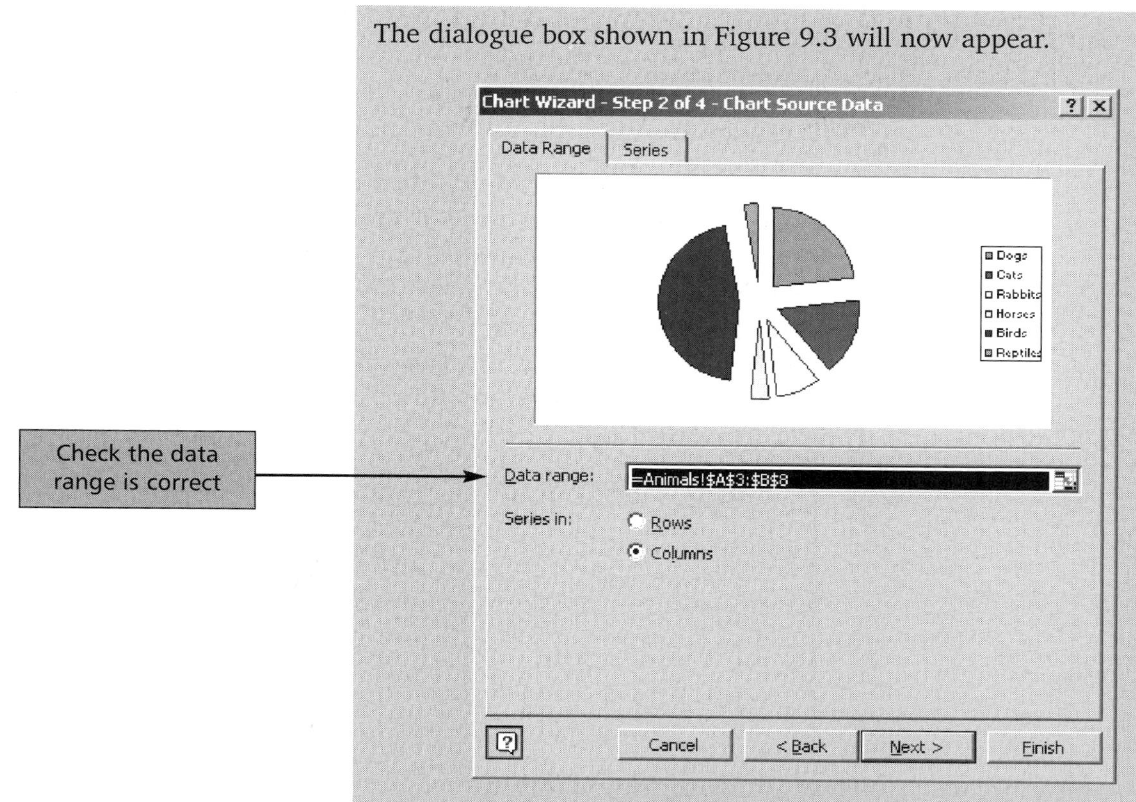

Figure 9.3

Check the data range is the one you want. Don't worry about the Series tab at this stage.

Click Next >.

The next dialogue box allows you to give your pie chart a title. See Figure 9.4.

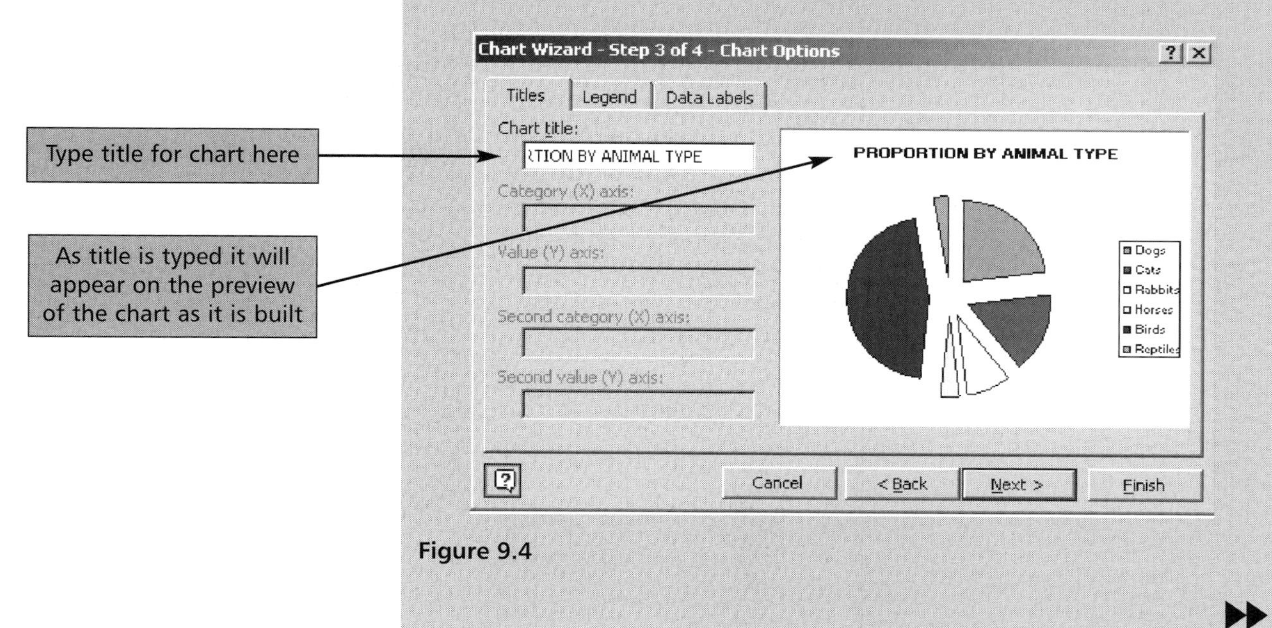

Figure 9.4

Type 'PROPORTION BY ANIMAL TYPE' in the Chart title: field.

Note: the Axis fields are disabled. This is because there are no X and Y axes in a pie chart.

Click on the Legend tab. Here you are given the option of repositioning the legend or not having a legend at all. By selecting one of the options the legend will move according to the option selected, or will disappear altogether if the Show legend check box is deselected.

Click on Bottom as the placement section of the dialogue box and the legend will move to the bottom of the chart as shown in Figure 9.5.

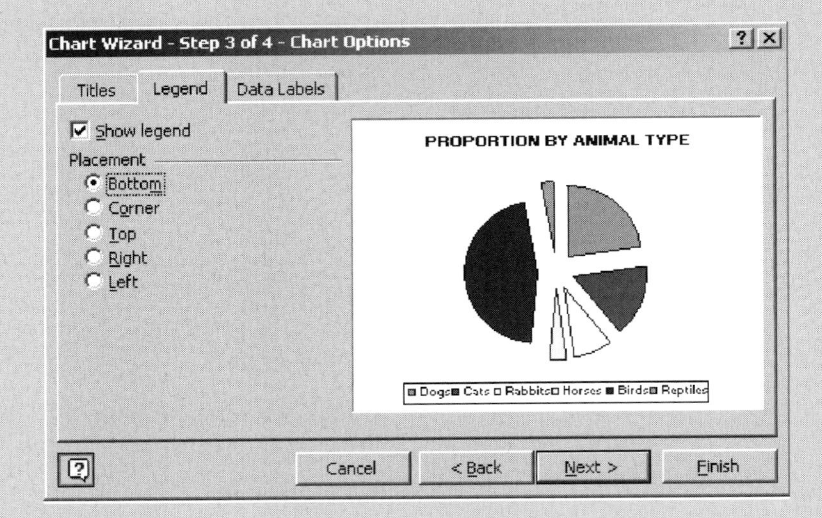

Figure 9.5

Click on the Data Labels tab.

Here you can choose what text is actually shown on the segments of the pie chart. You can choose one or all the options. Clearly, if you are using a legend it would not make a lot of sense to duplicate the Category name for each segment as well as having a legend. In this case you are going to show the percentage of each category.

Click the Percentage check box and you will see, as in Figure 9.6, the percentages for each animal appear in the preview.

PIE CHART TIP

Emphasising the segments

If you want to emphasise a particular segment of a pie chart you can do this by clicking once on a segment. This will select all segments. Next click on the segment again and only that particular segment will be selected. By clicking and holding down the left-hand mouse button you can then drag the segment away from the centre to add emphasis to it.

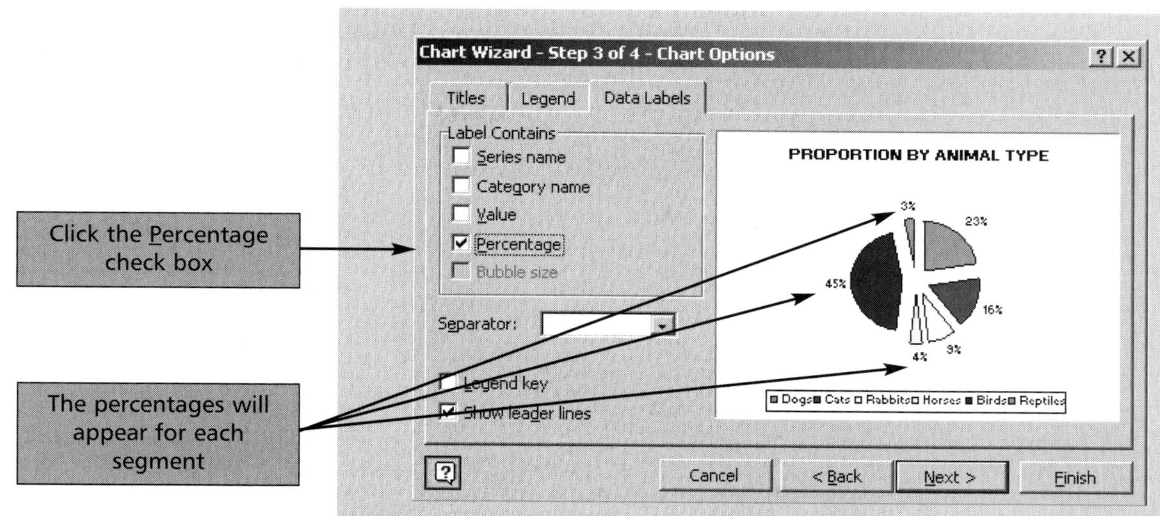

Figure 9.6

Click Next >.

Finally Excel gives you the choice of placing your new chart either in the current workbook sheet or in a separate sheet.

Click As new sheet: and

Type 'Animals by Proportion' as the name of the new sheet: see Figure 9.7.

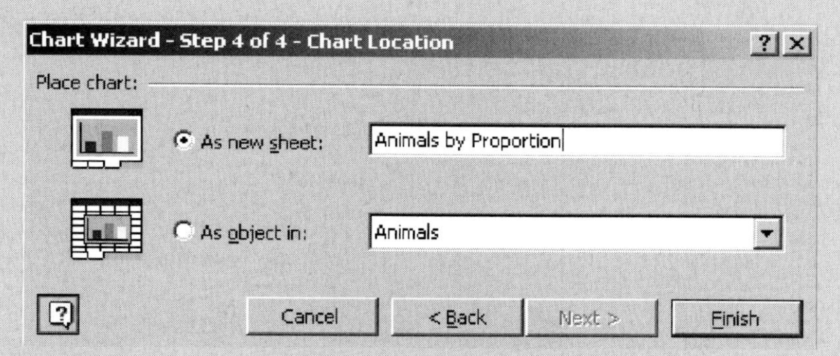

Figure 9.7

When you have finished:

Click Finish and Excel will create the new chart and place it in a new sheet with the name you have given it.

Now you are going to emphasise the Birds (45%) segment.

Click on the Birds segment.

Click a second time and, whilst still holding down the left-hand mouse button, drag the segment to the left, away from the other segments.

Save your file and chart.

Your pie chart should now look like Figure 9.8.

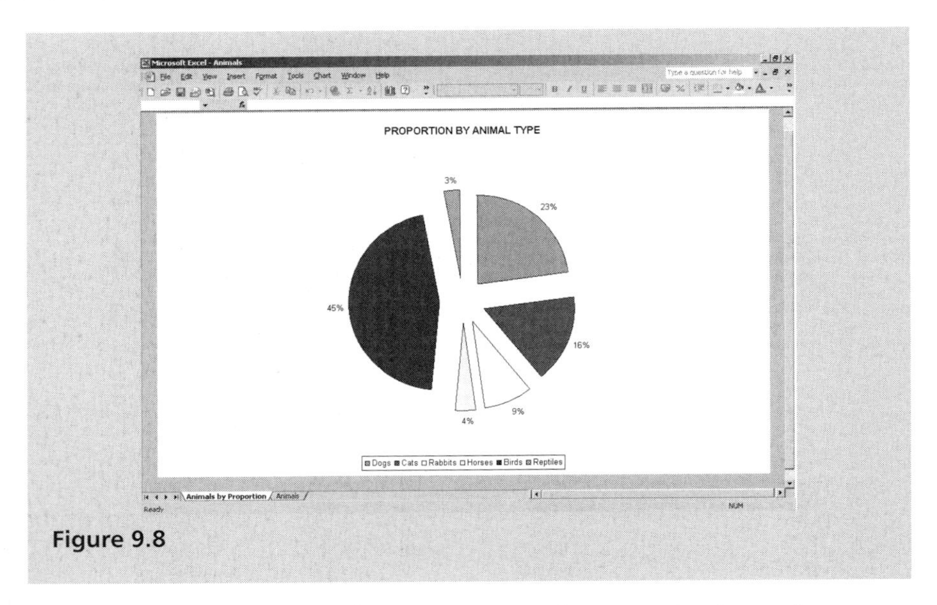

Figure 9.8

Selecting data sets for comparative analysis using column charts

As you saw in the previous section, pie charts are extremely useful for painting a simple picture of a single set of data. However, more often than not you will want to show comparisons between two data sets – for instance sales over two years. Pie charts would be unable to show this type of information and therefore a different type of chart is used. As shown in Table 9.1, column and bar charts are particularly suited to this type of comparison.

Figure 9.9 shows a data set depicting the number of book sales by type and region.

	A	B	C	D	E	F
1	**Book Sales by Type and Region**					
2	**Book Type**	**Region 1**	**Region 2**	**Region 3**	**Region 4**	**Region 5**
3	**Fiction**	5621	3362	1251	1055	3698
4	**Biographical**	1051	1250	1478	995	2451
5	**Historical**	561	418	336	584	568
6	**Practical**	6897	3658	2510	2144	3214
7	**Gardening**	1025	4258	2145	1447	2547
8	**Politics**	1451	987	899	659	445
9	**Totals**	16606	13933	8619	6884	12923

Figure 9.9

For the sake of argument say you wanted to compare book type sales by region rather than region sales by type. This data set lends itself to a column or bar type of chart. First the data is selected. Note that this workbook includes the total sales for each region. If these were included in the data set for the chart you would get an inaccurate picture of the information. The data to be selected is only the raw data for the sales and the relevant axis headings, as shown in Figure 9.10.

The chart icon is clicked and the same dialogue box appears as shown in the pie example. However, this time the column chart type must be selected and, to make the chart a little more interesting, the 3-D sub-type is also selected as shown in Figure 9.11.

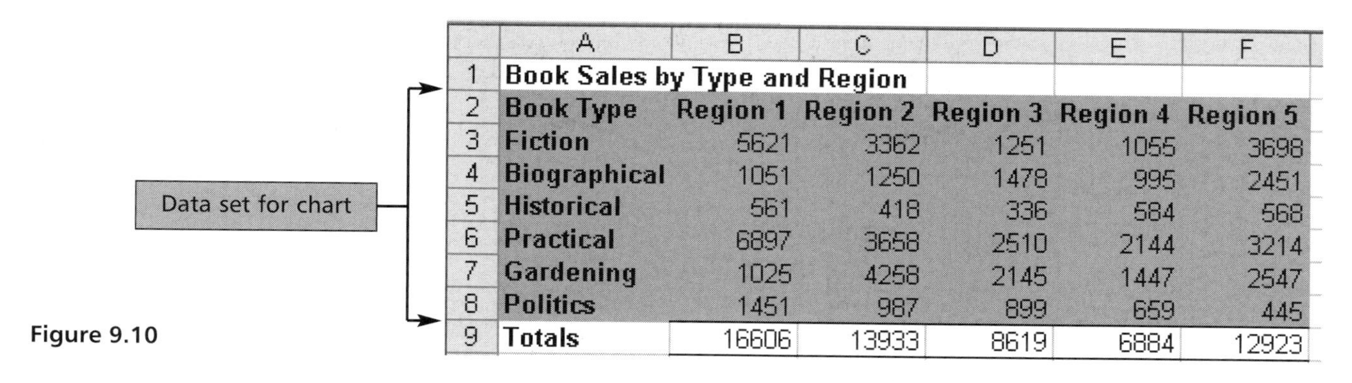

	A	B	C	D	E	F
1	**Book Sales by Type and Region**					
2	**Book Type**	**Region 1**	**Region 2**	**Region 3**	**Region 4**	**Region 5**
3	**Fiction**	5621	3362	1251	1055	3698
4	**Biographical**	1051	1250	1478	995	2451
5	**Historical**	561	418	336	584	568
6	**Practical**	6897	3658	2510	2144	3214
7	**Gardening**	1025	4258	2145	1447	2547
8	**Politics**	1451	987	899	659	445
9	**Totals**	16606	13933	8619	6884	12923

Figure 9.10

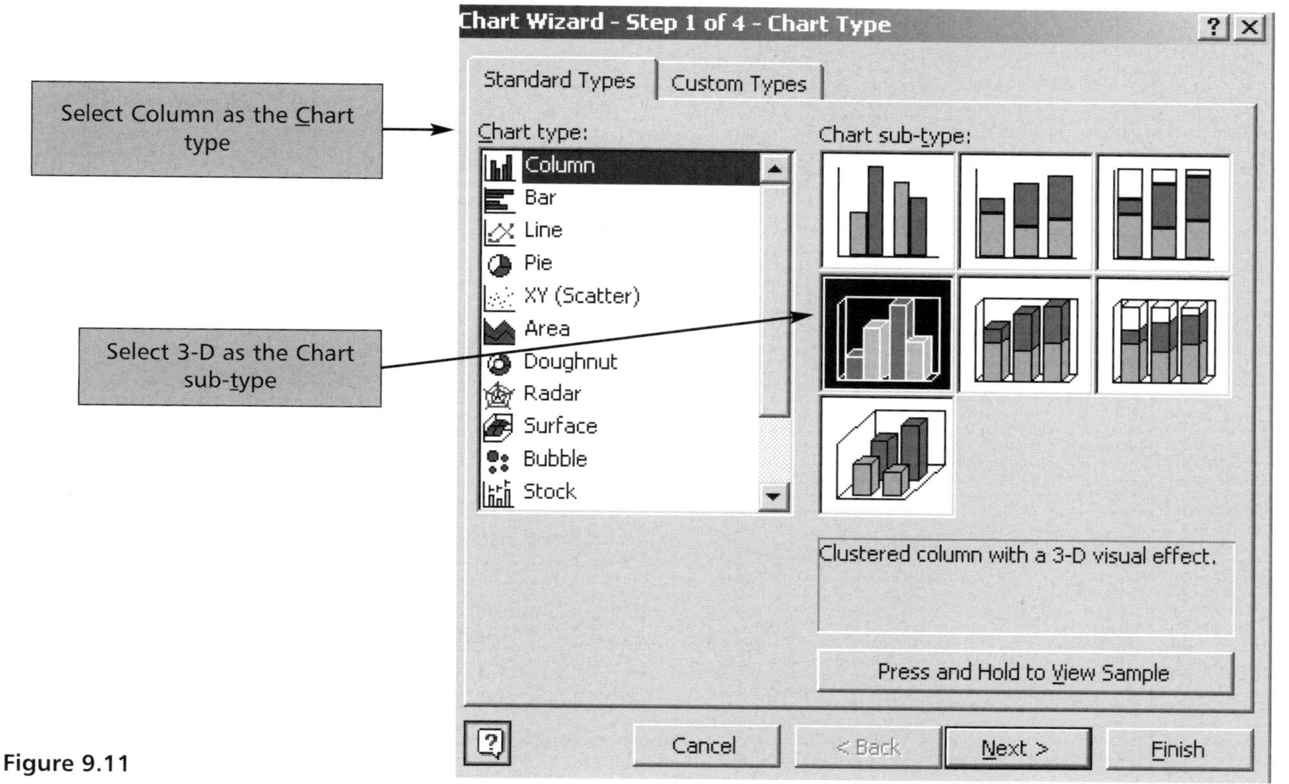

Figure 9.11

After clicking the Next > button Excel previews the chart and by default shows the data Series in: by Columns. This would be fine if you wanted the X-axis to show the book type. However, in this case you want the X-axis to be the region. Figure 9.12 perhaps demonstrates this a little clearer in graphical form.

After clicking on the Next > button a similar dialogue box to that seen in Figure 9.4 appears although in this case there are more tabs and you will see under the Titles tab that both the X and the Z axes options for titles are enabled. Had this been a simple 2-D chart only the X and Y options would have been available: see Figure 9.13.

After the titles have been inserted into the relevant fields and the Next > button clicked Excel again asks if the chart is to be placed in the current worksheet or in a new separate sheet. The final result will then look like Figure 9.14.

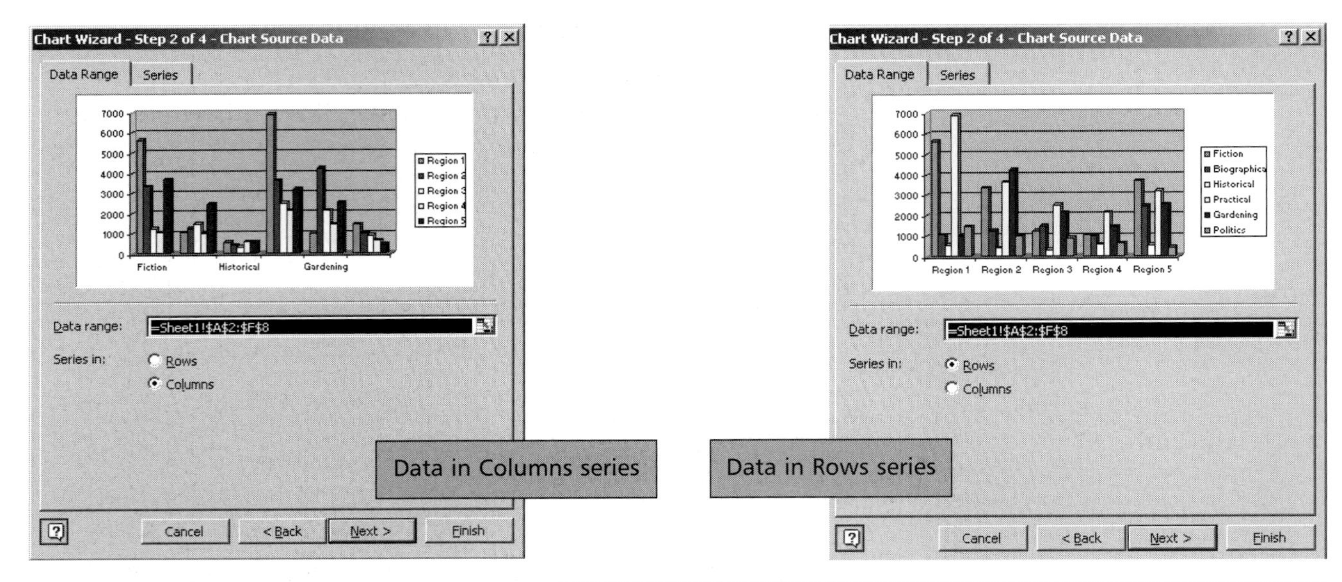

Figure 9.12

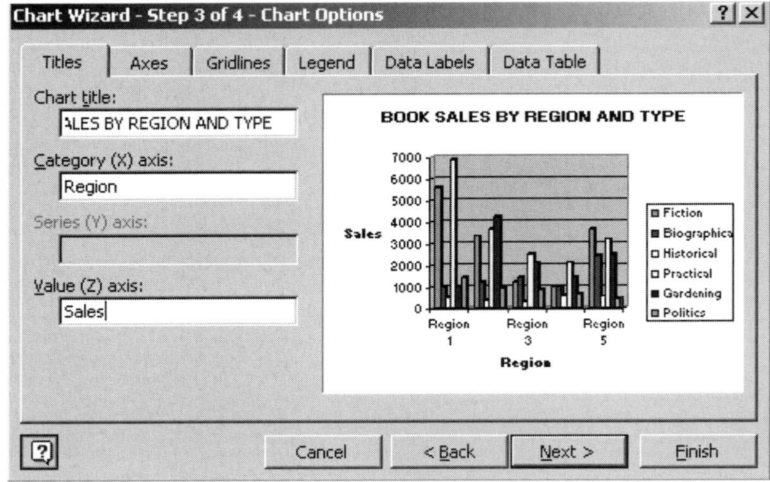

Figure 9.13

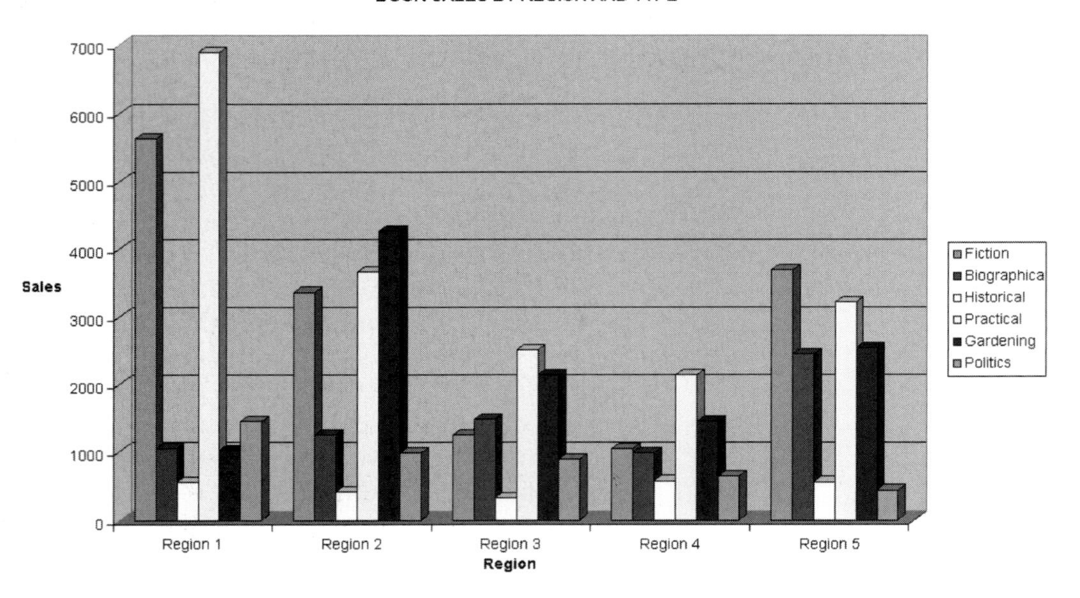

Figure 9.14

Creating line and column charts

Line and column charts are another way of comparing data where there are two sets of data that may be significantly different in terms of size, volume or scale. Have a look at Figure 9.15.

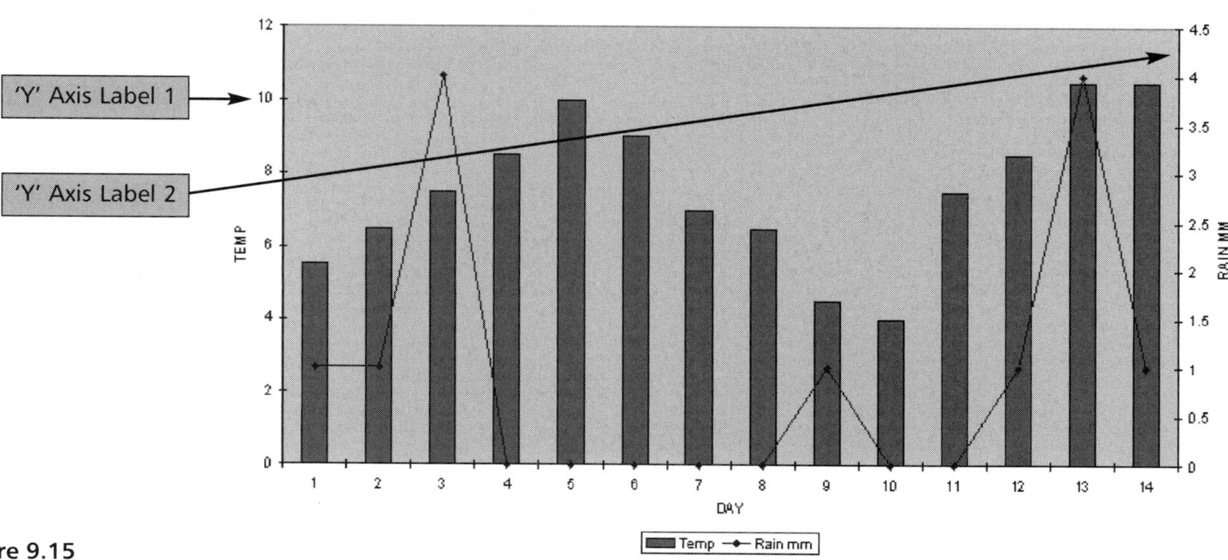

Figure 9.15

Here you can see a chart that maps both the maximum rainfall for January and the temperature. Using a second Y-axis scale allows a better view of the second data set relating to temperature. Had the values of the two data sets been very similar in terms of spread or if the second value had been constant and within the range of values, both sets of data could have simply been plotted using a line–column graph with one Y-axis scale. It is very much a case of 'horses for courses'. Now have a go at building a line–column chart.

Try it out

Open the file **Weather_2002.csv** in the sub-folder Spreadsheets of Unit 9 on the accompanying CD.

You are going to create a line–column chart with two axis labels, using the data from the spreadsheet.

Highlight the data range A2:C13.

Click the chart icon on the toolbar.

Select the Custom Types tab.

Select Line – Column on 2 Axes as the type of chart.

Click Next >.

Click the Series tab.

With the Series2 highlighted, in the Name: field,

Type 'Temp'.

Click on Series1 to highlight it and then in the Name: field,

Type 'Rainfall mm'.

Notice how in the preview the new names are shown.

Click Next >.

Click the Titles tab if it is not already the default tab.

Type 'MIN TEMPERATURE AND RAINFALL 2002' in the Chart title: field.

Click in the Category (X) axis: field and

Type 'Month' for the X-axis title.

Click first Value (Y) axis: field.

Type 'Minimum Temp'.

Click in the Second value (Y) axis: field.

Type 'Rainfall mm'.

Click on the Legend tab.

Click the Bottom radio button in the Placement section.

Click Next >.

Click the As new sheet: radio button.

Type 'MINTemp of Rainfall 2002'.

Click the Finish button.

Save the file and chart as a Microsoft Excel Workbook with the name **Weather_2002**.

Your chart should look similar to Figure 9.16.

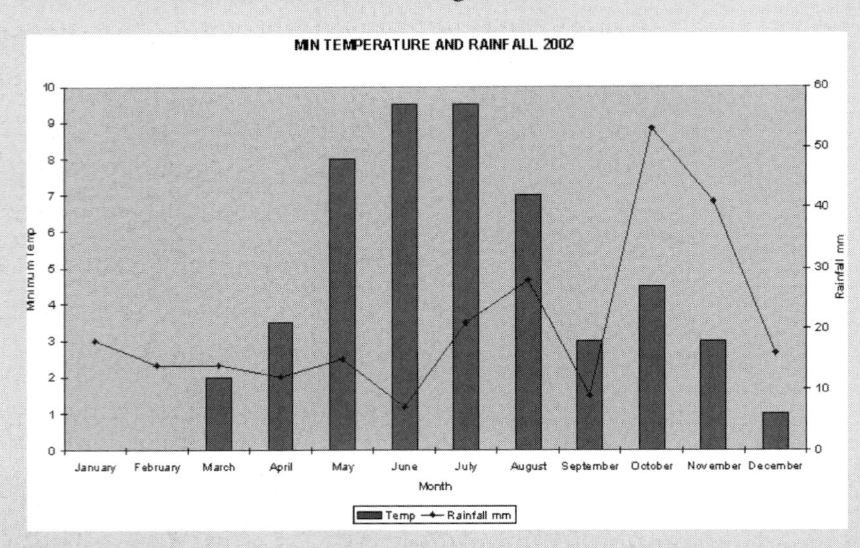

Figure 9.16

Creating X–Y scatter graphs

As we saw on page 357, X–Y scatter graphs allow comparison between two sets of data and the correlation of data to be assessed. Figure 9.17 is a scatter graph comparing the actual level of the Footsie index for a series of months with the predicted values of the same months.

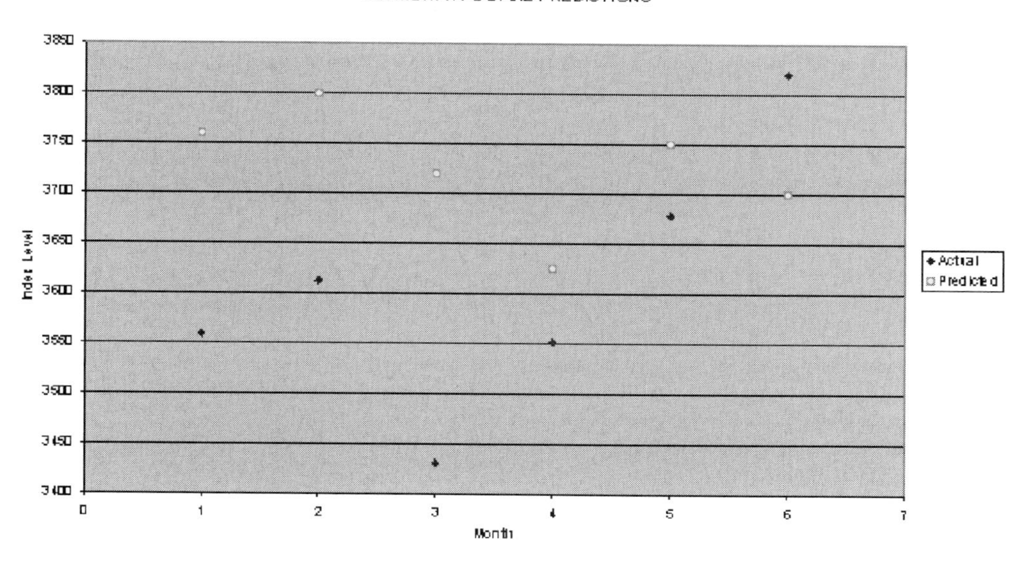

Figure 9.17

Here you can see that for the first five months of the period the prediction was higher than the actual performance of the index. In the sixth month the prediction was lower than performance.

Scatter graphs are produced in much the same way as any other graph or chart. As it is often easier to learn through practice, try creating a simple X–Y scatter graph for yourself.

Try it out

Open Excel if it is not already open.

Open the file **Forecast.csv** which can be found in the Spreadsheets sub-folder of Unit 9 on the accompanying CD.

Save the file as an Excel workbook with the same name.

Highlight the data range A2:C11.

Click on the Chart Wizard icon.

Click on XY (Scatter).

Accept the default Scatter: compares pairs of values.

Click Next >.

Check that you are happy with the preview and the data series are shown correctly. When you are satisfied:

Click Next >.

Make sure the Titles tab is selected.

Type 'COMPARISION OF ACTUAL RAIN TO FORECAST' in the Chart title: field.

Type 'Month' for the X-axis title.

Type 'Rainfall (mm)' for the Y-axis title.

Click Next >.

Click the As new sheet: radio button.

Type the new sheet's name as 'Rain_Forecast'.

Click the Finish button.

Your finished graph should look similar to Figure 9.18.

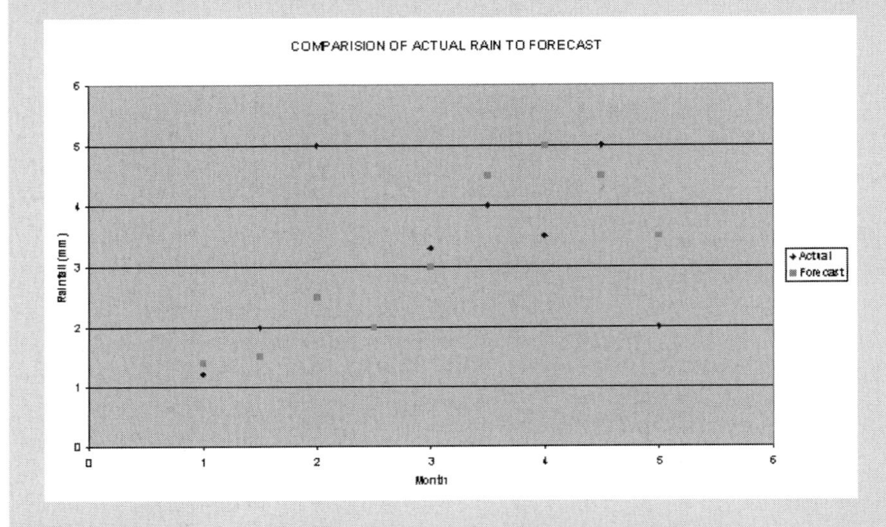

Figure 9.18

Selecting sub-sets of data and non-adjacent columns and rows

Selecting sub-sets of data

So far the charts and graphs you have created rely on a complete set of data and also data ranges that are adjacent to one another. However, life is not always that simple and it may well be that you are asked to provide charts or graphs on specific parts of a spreadsheet. This requires that you are able to select sub-sets of data or data in columns and rows that are not necessarily adjacent to each other. The principles for selecting non-adjacent sets or sub-sets of data are basically the same. Have a look at Figure 9.19.

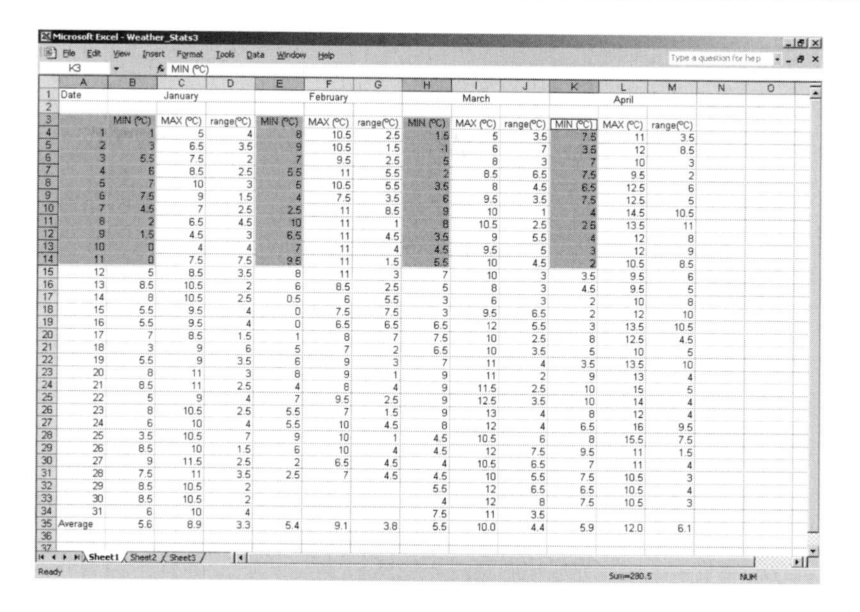

Figure 9.19

Here, as you can see, the cells containing minimum temperature for the first 14 days of each month in the quarter have been selected.

To select sub-sets of data the first cell in the range of data is clicked as normal; in this case the Date column – cell A3. Then using the left-hand mouse button the range for the first series is highlighted using the drag method. Here it would be A3:B17 as the A and B columns are adjacent. Next, holding down the Ctrl key on the keyboard, the first cell in the second series is clicked and the mouse dragged to the end of that series; here it would be E17. This process is then repeated for each sub-set in the series. See Figures 9.19 and 9.20.

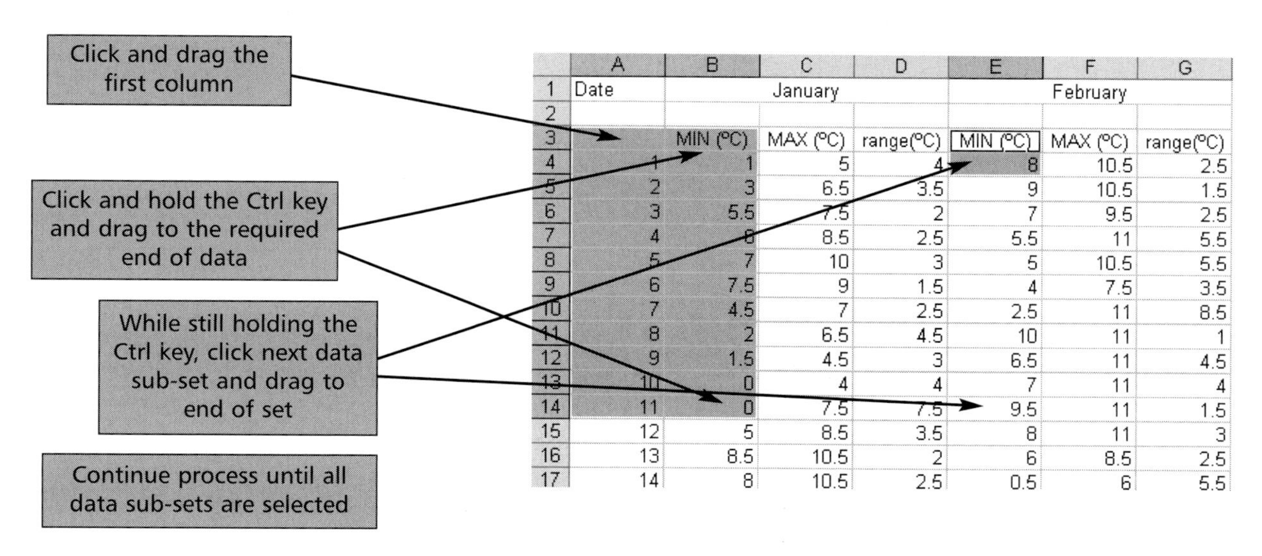

	A	B	C	D	E	F	G
1	Date		January			February	
2							
3		MIN (°C)	MAX (°C)	range(°C)	MIN (°C)	MAX (°C)	range(°C)
4	1	1	5	4	8	10.5	2.5
5	2	3	6.5	3.5	9	10.5	1.5
6	3	5.5	7.5	2	7	9.5	2.5
7	4	6	8.5	2.5	5.5	11	5.5
8	5	7	10	3	5	10.5	5.5
9	6	7.5	9	1.5	4	7.5	3.5
10	7	4.5	7	2.5	2.5	11	8.5
11	8	2	6.5	4.5	10	11	1
12	9	1.5	4.5	3	6.5	11	4.5
13	10	0	4	4	7	11	4
14	11	0	7.5	7.5	9.5	11	1.5
15	12	5	8.5	3.5	8	11	3
16	13	8.5	10.5	2	6	8.5	2.5
17	14	8	10.5	2.5	0.5	6	5.5

Figure 9.20

Selecting data sets by rows is carried out in exactly the same way by selecting cells in the first row and then using the Ctrl key to select non-adjacent rows as required.

Now try selecting a sub-set of data and then non-adjacent sets of data.

Try it out

Open Excel if it is not already open.

Open the file **Weather_Stats.csv** from the Spreadsheet Files sub-folder of Unit 9.

Exercise 1 – sub-set

Select the sub-set of data for the range A3:B17.

Click the Charts Wizard icon from the tool bar.

Select Bar as the type of chart from those offered under Standard Types in the Wizard.

Click Next >.

Click Next > again.

Type 'MINIMUM AND MAXIMUM TEMPS - 1-14 JANUARY' as the chart title.

Type 'Temperature' as the X-axis label.

Type 'Day' as the Y-axis label.

Click Next >.

Click the As new sheet radio button.

Type 'MIN MAX 1-14 JANUARY' as the sheet name.

Click Finish.

Save the workbook as an Excel file **Weather_Stats1** on your hard or floppy disk.

Figure 9.21 shows the chart and sub-set of data on which the chart is based.

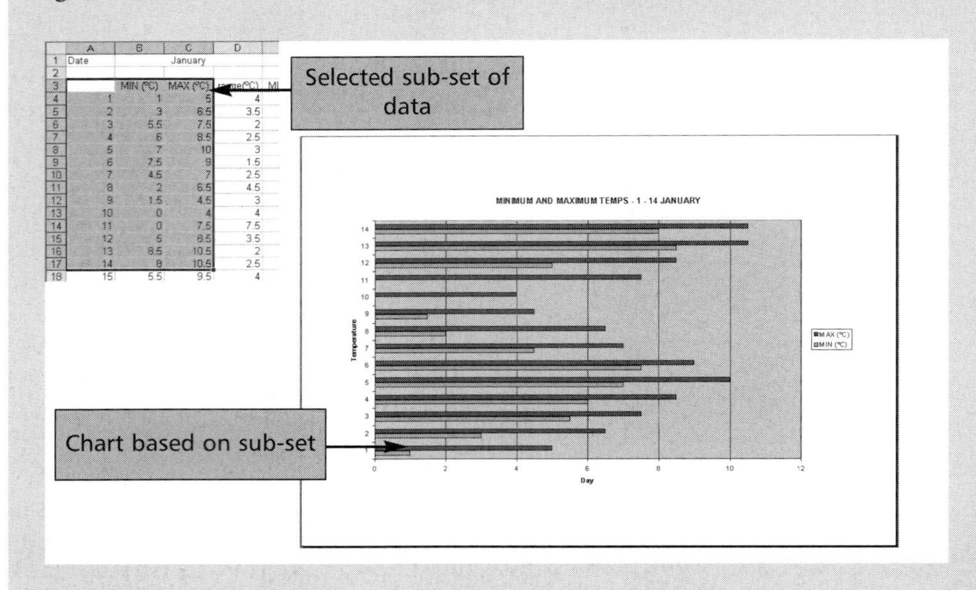

Figure 9.21

Exercise 2 – non-adjacent data

This exercise uses the file that was saved above.

Click a blank area of the spreadsheet to deselect the sub-set of data used in the above exercise.

Select the data range A3:C17.

Click and hold down the Ctrl key on the keyboard.

Click on the cell E3 and drag to highlight the range E3:E17.

Whilst still holding the Ctrl key down:

Click cell H3 and then highlight the range H3:H17.

Repeat this process and highlight the range K3:K17.

Your spreadsheet should now look like Figure 9.22.

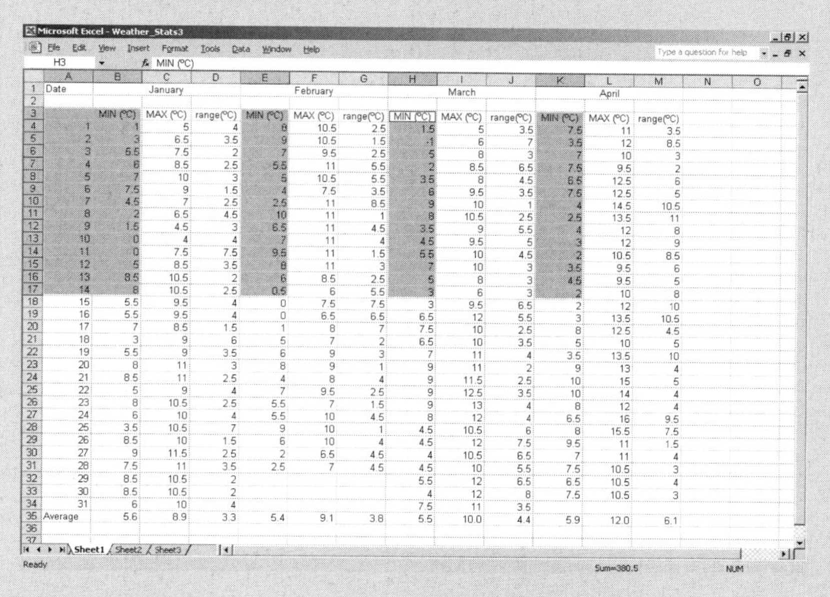

	A	B	C	D	E	F	G	H	I	J	K	L	M
1	Date		January			February			March			April	
2													
3		MIN (ºC)	MAX (ºC)	range(ºC)	MIN (ºC)	MAX (ºC)	range(ºC)	MIN (ºC)	MAX (ºC)	range(ºC)	MIN (ºC)	MAX (ºC)	range(ºC)
4	1	1	5	4	8	10.5	2.5	1.5	5	3.5	7.5	11	3.5
5	2	3	6.5	3.5	9	10.5	1.5	-1	6	7	3.5	12	8.5
6	3	5.5	7.5	2	7	9.5	2.5	5	8	3	7	10	3
7	4	6	8.5	2.5	5.5	11	5.5	2	8.5	6.5	7.5	9.5	2
8	5	7	10	3	5	10.5	5.5	3.5	8	4.5	6.5	12.5	6
9	6	7.5	9	1.5	4	7.5	3.5	6	9.5	3.5	7.5	12.5	5
10	7	4.5	7	2.5	2.5	11	8.5	9	10	1	4	14.5	10.5
11	8	2	6.5	4.5	10	11	1	8	10.5	2.5	2.5	13.5	11
12	9	1.5	4.5	3	6.5	11	4.5	3.5	9	5.5	4	12	8
13	10	0	4	4	7	11	4	4.5	9.5	5	3	12	9
14	11	0	7.5	7.5	9.5	11	1.5	5.5	10	4.5	2	10.5	8.5
15	12	5	8.5	3.5	8	11	3	7	10	3	3.5	9.5	6
16	13	8.5	10.5	2	6	8.5	2.5	5	8	3	4.5	9.5	5
17	14	8	10.5	2.5	0.5	6	5.5	3	6	3	2	10	8
18	15	5.5	9.5	4	0	7.5	7.5	3	9.5	6.5	2	12	10
19	16	5.5	9.5	4	0	6.5	6.5	6.5	12	5.5	3	13.5	10.5
20	17	7	8.5	1.5	1	8	7	7.5	10	2.5	8	12.5	4.5
21	18	3	9	6	5	7	2	6.5	10	3.5	5	10	5
22	19	5.5	9	3.5	6	9	3	7	11	4	3.5	13.5	10
23	20	8	11	3	8	9	1	9	11	2	9	13	4
24	21	8.5	11	2.5	4	8	4	9	11.5	2.5	10	15	5
25	22	5	9	4	7	9.5	2.5	9	12.5	3.5	10	14	4
26	23	8	10.5	2.5	5.5	7	1.5	9	13	4	8	12	4
27	24	6	10	4	5.5	10	4.5	8	12	4	6.5	16	9.5
28	25	3.5	10.5	7	9	10	1	4.5	10.5	6	8	15.5	7.5
29	26	8.5	10	1.5	6	10	4	4.5	12	7.5	9.5	11	1.5
30	27	9	11.5	2.5	2	6.5	4.5	4	10.5	6.5	7	11	4
31	28	7.5	11	3.5	2.5	7	4.5	4.5	10	5.5	7.5	10.5	3
32	29	8.5	10.5	2				5.5	12	6.5	6.5	10.5	4
33	30	8.5	10.5	2				4	12	8	7.5	10.5	3
34	31	6	10	4				7.5	11	3.5			
35	Average	5.6	8.9	3.3	5.4	9.1	3.8	5.5	10.0	4.4	5.9	12.0	6.1
36													
37													

Figure 9.22

Click on the Charts Wizard icon.

Select Column with 3-D visual effect.

Click Next >.

Click on the Series tab.

Click to highlight Series 1, and in the Name field type 'Jan'.

Click to highlight Series 2, and in the Name field type 'Feb'.

Repeat this process until each series has been renamed.

Click the Next > button.

Type 'MINIMUM TEMPERATURES – JAN-APR' as the chart title.

Type 'Day' as the X-axis label.

Type 'Temperature' as the Z-axis label.

Select the Legend tab and

Click Bottom for the position of the legend.

Click Next >.

Click the As new sheet radio button.

Type 'MIN TEMPERATURES JAN-APR' as the sheet name.

Click Finish.

Save the workbook.

Your chart should now look like Figure 9.23.

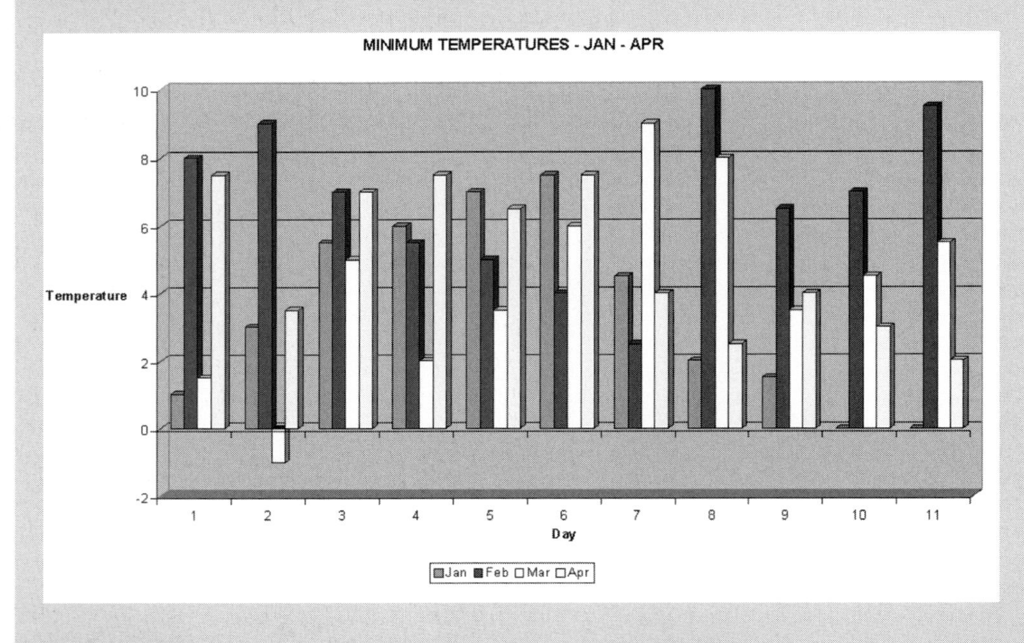

Figure 9.23

You should now be able to:

- open a data file
- select and control the data sources
- understand the various types of charts and graphs and when they are used
- select a single data range and create a pie chart
- select data sets for comparative analysis using column charts
- create line and column charts
- create X–Y scatter graphs
- select sub-sets of data and non-adjacent columns and rows.

Build-up Exercise 9a: Stage 1

Scenario 1

In the first stage you will create a comparative column chart that compares the capital value of a series of properties with their rental value.

Open Excel if it is not already open.

Open the file **Property.csv** from the Spreadsheet Files sub-folder of Unit 9 on the CD.

Save the file as an Excel (.xls) spreadsheet to your hard or floppy disk.

Use the data provided to build a column chart that compares the capital value for each property with its rental value.

The following titles should be included in the chart:

Chart title: COMPARISON OF CAPITAL AND RENTAL VALUES
X-Axis title: Property
Y-Axis title: Value

Format the legend so that it appears at the bottom of the chart.

Create a new worksheet for the chart and name the new worksheet 'Column Comparative'.

Save your workbook and chart.

Your chart should look like Figure 9.24.

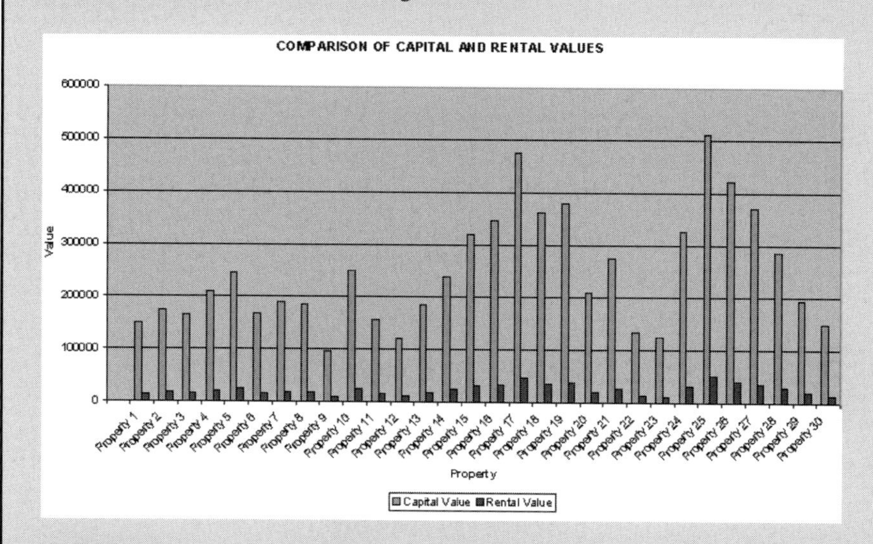

Figure 9.24

Build-up Exercise 9a: Stage 2

Scenario 2

Next you will create a line–column chart that plots the actual lease period for a selected commercial range of properties (the columns) and the remaining length of time the lease has to run for each of these properties (the line).

Open the file **Property.xls** if it is not still open from the previous exercise.

Select the following data ranges, being the properties for which the chart is to be created:

A9 and H9:I9
A11 and H11:I11
A16 and H16:I16
A20 and H20:I22
A24 and H24:I26
A28 and H28:I28
A31 and H31:I31

Click the chart icon.

Select the Custom Types tab.

Click Line – Column as the chart type.

Click Next >.

Click the Series tab.

Highlight Series 2 and in the Name: field

Type 'Years'.

Click and highlight Series 1, and in the Name: field

Type 'Property'.

Click Next >.

Type the title of your chart, 'REVIEW OF LEASE AND REMAINING YEARS (COMMERCIAL)'.

Type the X-axis label as 'Property'.

Type the Y-axis label as 'Years'.

Select the Legend tab and place the legend at the top of the chart.

Click Next >.

Click the As new sheet: radio button.

Type 'Commercial Years Remaining' as the new sheet's name.

Click the Finish button.

Your chart should now look like Figure 9.25.

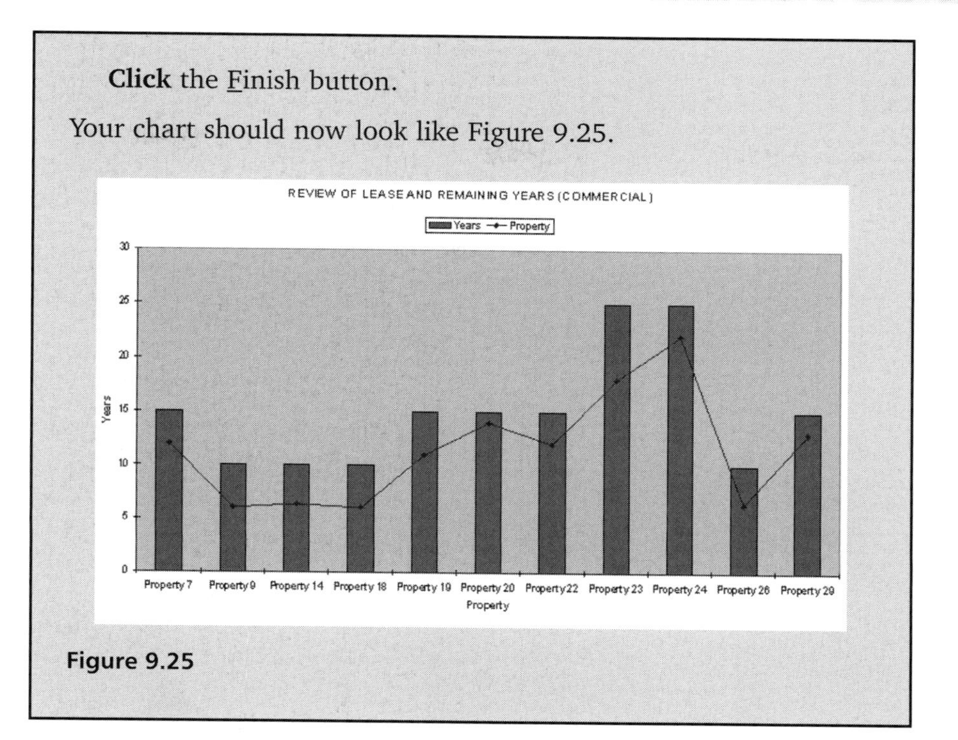

Figure 9.25

Build-up Exercise 9a: Stage 3

Scenario 3

Create an exploding pie chart to demonstrate the percentage capital value for each group of properties (i.e. commercial, residential and company use).

Open Excel if it is not already open.

Open the file **Property2.csv** from the Spreadsheet sub-folder of Unit 9 on the accompanying CD.

Save the file as an .xls file on your hard or floppy disk using the same name as the .csv file.

Highlight the range A2:B4.

Click the chart icon.

Select Pie as the chart type.

Select the exploded pie as the chart sub-type.

Click Next >.

If you are satisfied with the preview of the chart and data range:

Click Next >.

Give your chart the title 'PROPERTY VALUE BY PERCENTAGE'.

Click the Legend tab and deselect the Show legend check box.

Click the Data Labels tab and select the Category name and Percentage check boxes to show the data on the segments.

Click Next >.

Select As new sheet: and give the sheet the name 'VALUE BY PERCENT'.

Click the Finish button.

Your chart should look like Figure 9.26.

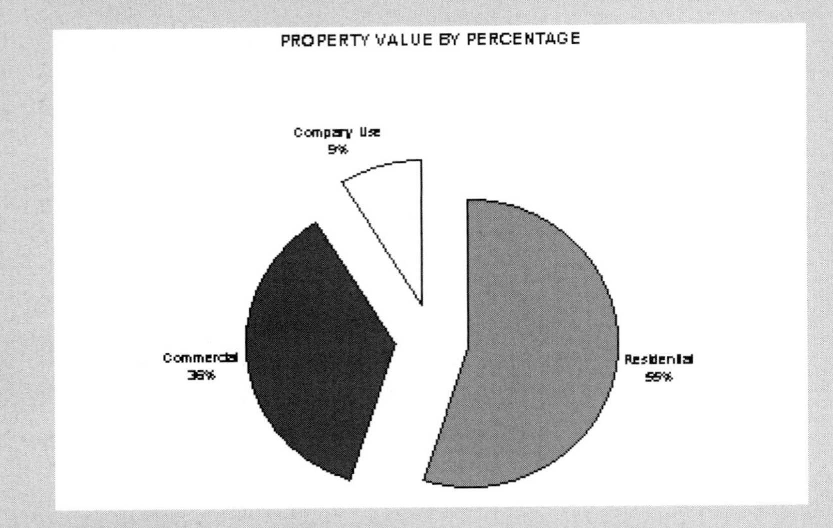

Figure 9.26

Build-up Exercise 9a: Stage 4

Scenario 4

Create an X–Y scatter graph to show the actual values of all properties in 2003 and their predicted values in 2004.

Open Excel if it is not already open.

Open the file **Property3.csv** from the Spreadsheet sub-folder of Unit 9 on the accompanying CD.

Save the file as an .xls file on your hard or floppy disk using the same name (**Property3**) as the .csv file.

Highlight the ranges:

A3:A32

G3:H32

Click the chart icon on the toolbar and

Select XY (Scatter) from the standard types.

Click Next >.

Click the Series tab.

Rename Series 1 '2003 Values'.

Rename Series 2 '2004 Predictions'.

Click Next >.

Type 'ACTUAL VALUES FOR 2003 AND PREDICTIONS FOR 2004' as the main title for your graph.

Type 'Property' as the X-axis label.

Type 'Values' as the Y-axis label.

Place the legend at the bottom of the graph.

Click Next >.

Type 'VALUE PREDICTIONS' in the As new sheet: field.

Click Finish.

Save your spreadsheet and graph.

Your graph should look like Figure 9.27.

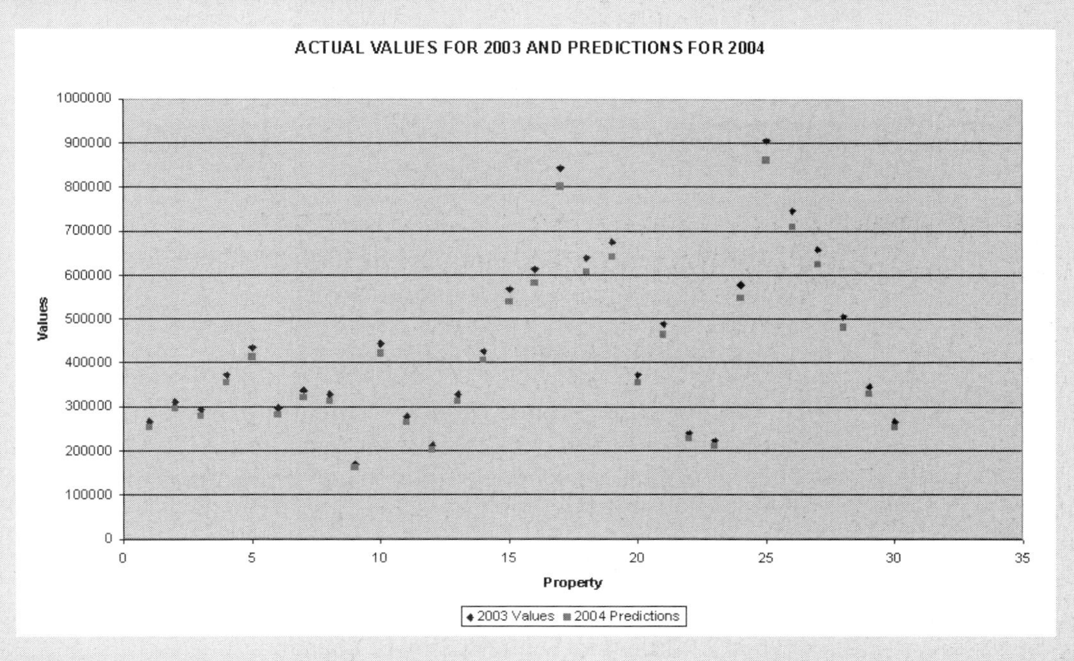

Figure 9.27

Setting the parameters of graphs and charts

For CLAIT Plus you will need to be able to set certain parameters for your charts and graphs. Some of these you may have already covered if you completed New CLAIT at level 1 and this section may act as something of a refresher. For example, you have already learnt in this unit how to create titles for the main chart and also the axis titles. Similarly you have learnt how to set legends and remove them. Excel makes editing these features very easy. For CLAIT Plus you will need to understand the differences between titles, sub-titles, axis titles, labels and legends.

Have a look at Figure 9.28 which shows the various components of a simple chart.

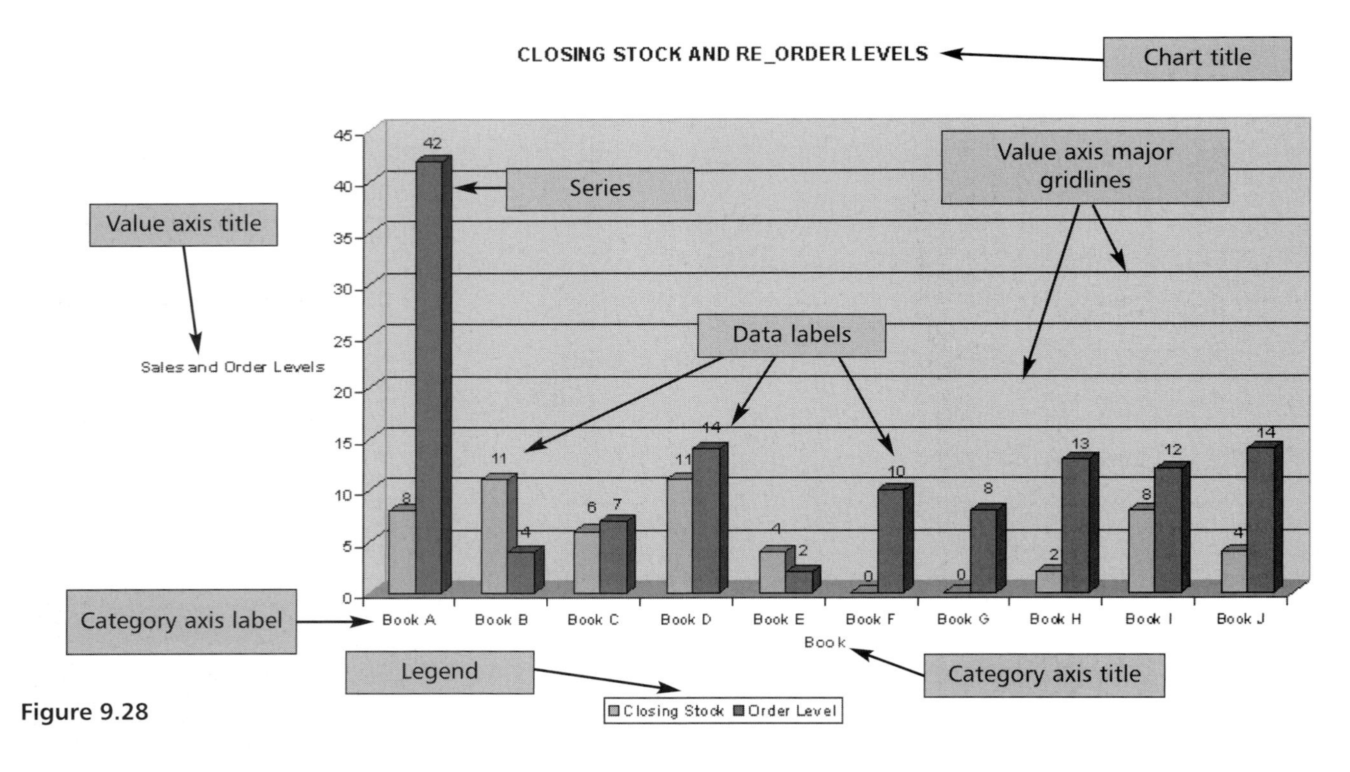

Figure 9.28

Each of these components can be formatted to suit specific requirements or a general house style.

Formatting titles and labels

As is the case with all Windows formatting options, there is usually more than one way to achieve the same result. To format a title in a chart double-click on the title to show the Format Chart Title dialogue box shown in Figure 9.29.

Alternatively you can click on the title using the right-hand mouse button which will bring up a menu list: see Figure 9.30.

By clicking on the Format Chart Title… option the same dialogue box as shown in Figure 9.29 will appear.

The dialogue box has three tabs: Patterns, Font and Alignment. Exactly which aspect of the title you wish to format will determine

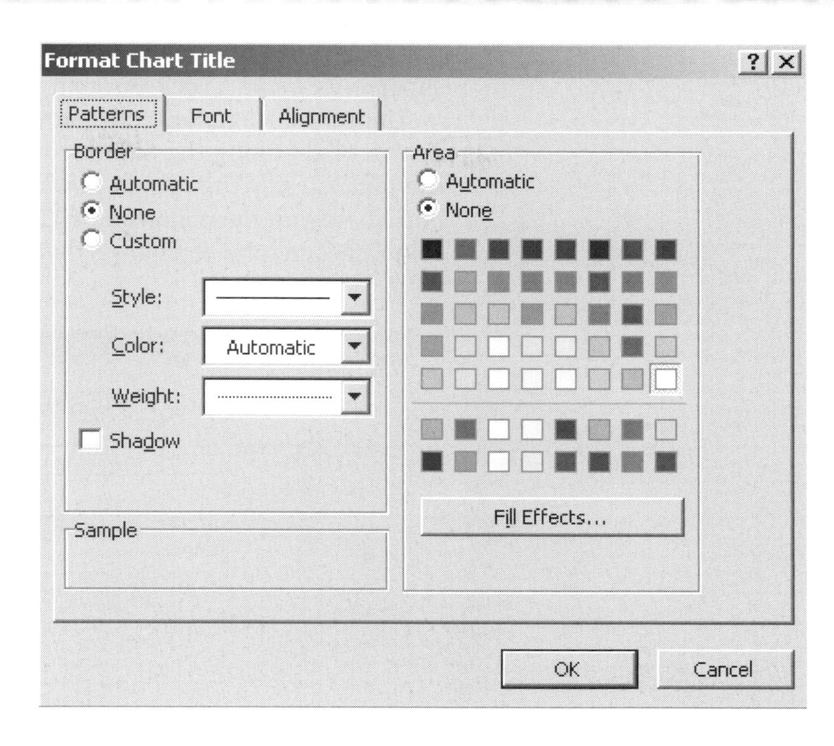

Figure 9.29

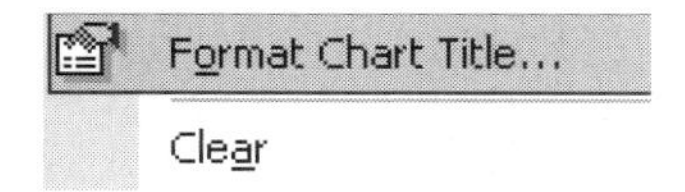

Figure 9.30

which tab should be selected. To change the font for the title the Font tab is selected as shown in Figure 9.31.

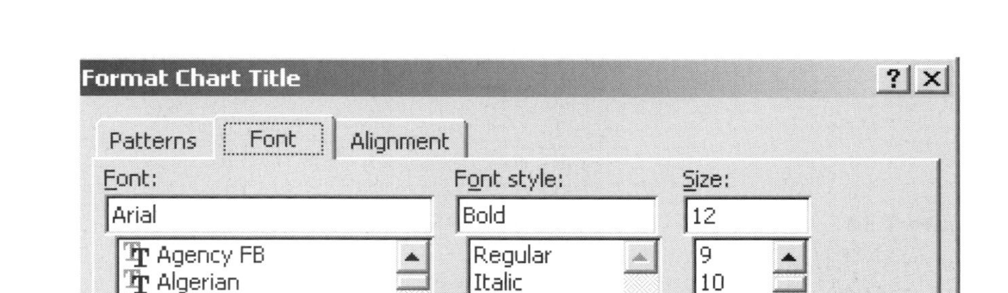

Figure 9.31

In the top part of the box you are able to change the font type, style and size. In the middle the title can be underlined if required, the font colour changed and the background to the text box made opaque or transparent. In the Effects section the text can be changed to subscript, superscript or be struck through.

Under the Alignment tab (shown in Figure 9.32), you have the option of changing the alignment in the text box and the orientation of the text. Clearly this would not normally be relevant with a main title but where you have many axis labels with fairly lengthy names it is sometimes helpful to change their alignment to make them easier to read.

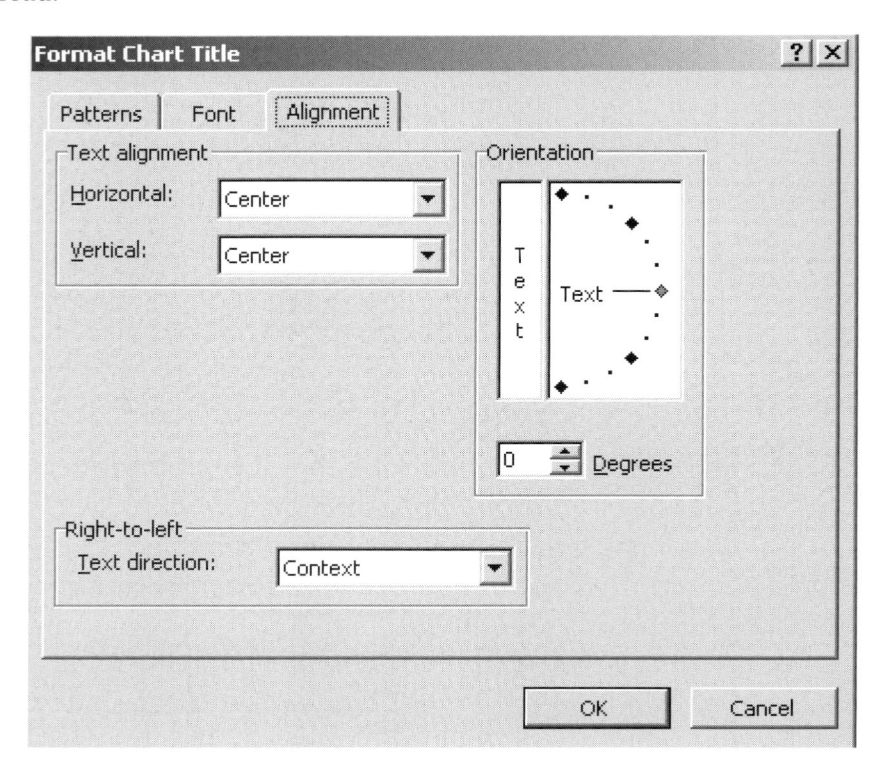

Figure 9.32

Finally the Patterns tab shown in Figure 9.33 on the next page allows you to format the actual box that contains the text.

Have a look at Figure 9.34. The text box containing the title text on the left has the default formatting while that on the right has been formatted so that the box has both a border and a two-tone fill effect.

Now have a go at formatting some main and axis titles.

Try it out

Open Excel if it is not already open.

Open the file **Weather_Stats** you created earlier.

Click the chart sheet named MIN TEMPERATURES JAN-APR.

Click on the chart title and using either of the options mentioned above bring up the Format Chart Title dialogue box.

Click the Font tab.

Select the Size: of the font as 16.

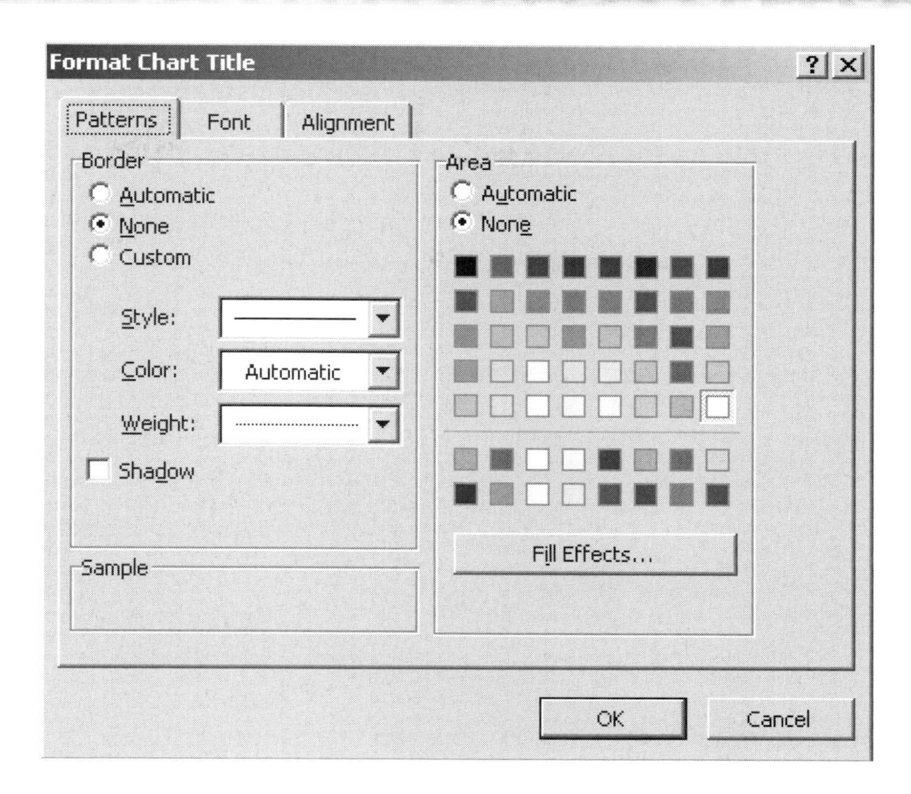

Figure 9.33

CLOSING STOCK AND RE_ORDER LEVELS

CLOSING STOCK AND RE_ORDER LEVELS

Figure 9.34

Select the Font style: as Bold Italic.

Click the Patterns tab.

For the Border:

Select Automatic.

Click the Shadow check box to enable the shadow.

In the Area section:

Click the Fill Effects… button.

In the Color: section:

Click the Two colors radio button.

Select White as Color 1: and a grey shade for Color 2:.

In the Shading styles section ensure the Horizontal radio button is selected.

Click OK twice.

The title should now look like Figure 9.35.

MINIMUM TEMPERATURES - JAN - APR

Figure 9.35

Using exactly the same technique format the X- and Y-axis labels (Day and Temperature) as follows:

Font: Arial
Font size: 12
Font style: Italic
Font colour: Dark blue

Save the file.

Your chart should now look like Figure 9.36.

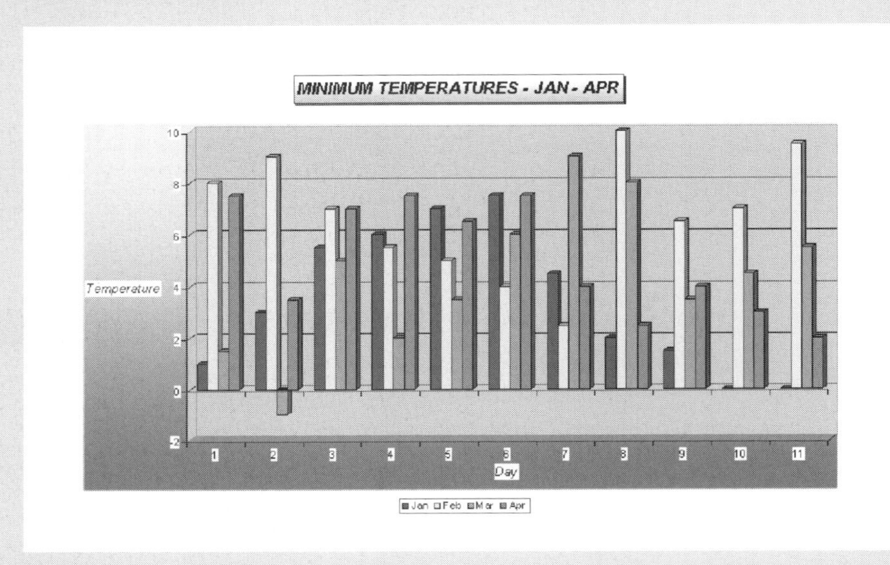

Figure 9.36

Displaying data labels to a series

On page 360 you saw how easy it is to include data labels for segments in a pie chart. The amount of data you display and the level of detail for any particular chart will depend largely on the reader/recipient's requirements. If the aim is to give only a general impression of trends or information to the recipient then the fine detail is probably not necessary. However, where the graph or chart is complex, or the actual figures in each series are required, it is easy to attach the relevant data to the chart. Now try adding data labels to a chart.

Try it out

Open the Excel file **Animals** you saved on page 359.

If you did not save this file then open the **Animals.csv** file on the attached CD.

Click the worksheet containing the raw data for the Animal Welfare Centre.

Highlight the range A3:B8.

Note: if you move the data to a different range, then highlight all the data for the Centre but not the heading Animal Welfare Centre.

Select a standard column chart using the chart icon on the toolbar.

Click Next >.

Click the Title tab.

Type the following:

Chart Title: 'ANIMALS HELD AT CENTRE-AUG 04'
X-axis title: 'Animal Type'
Y-axis title: 'Animal Nos'

As there is only one series of data in this worksheet there is no need for a legend.

Click the Legend tab.

Deselect the Show legend: check box.

Click the Data Labels tab.

In the Label Contains section:

Click the Value option.

Notice how in the preview window the actual number for each animal is shown above the column for that animal type.

Click Next >.

Click the As new Sheet: option and

Type 'Animals by Number' as the sheet name

Click Finish.

Save the workbook.

Your chart should now look like Figure 9.37.

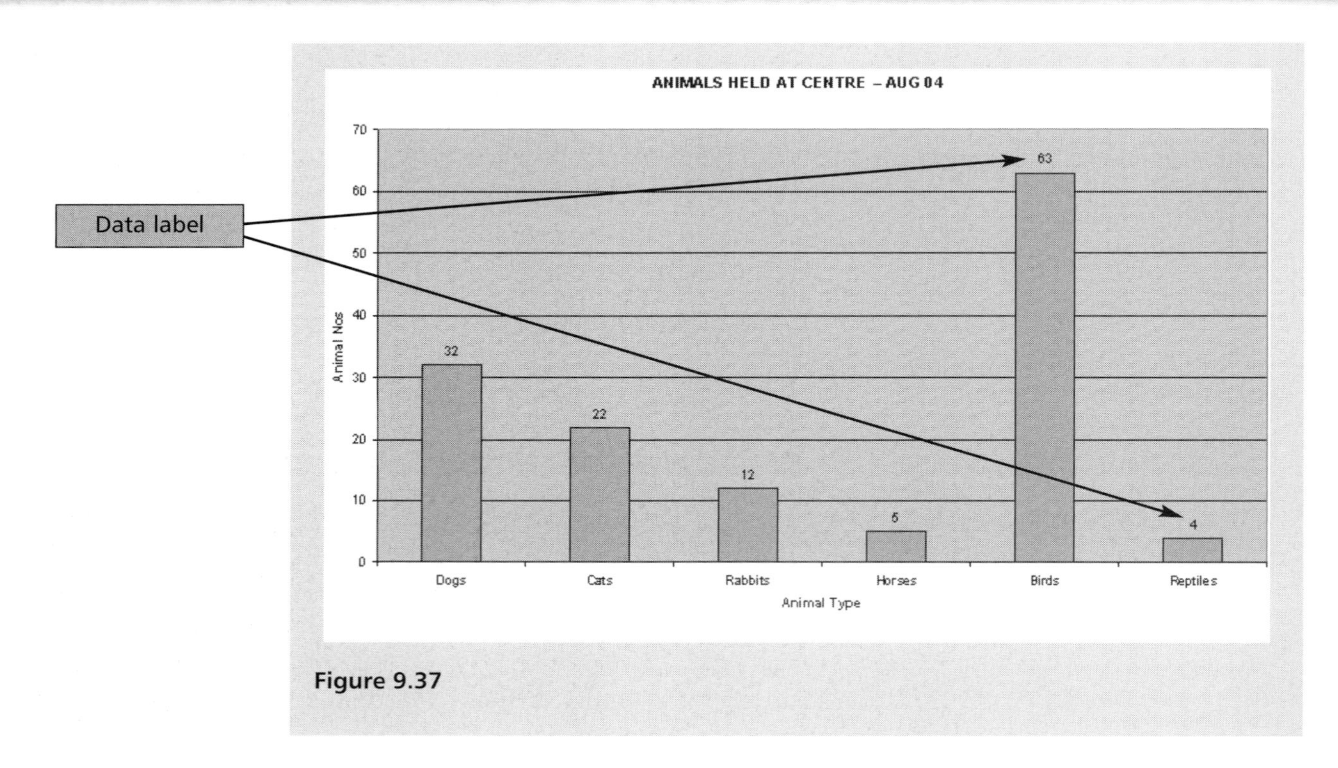

Figure 9.37

Formatting data labels

Data labels can be formatted in very much the same way as any other text object such as a main title and axis titles. To format a data label the cursor is placed over one of the labels in the series and by double-clicking on the number, all the labels in the series are selected and the Format Data Label dialogue box appears as shown in Figure 9.38.

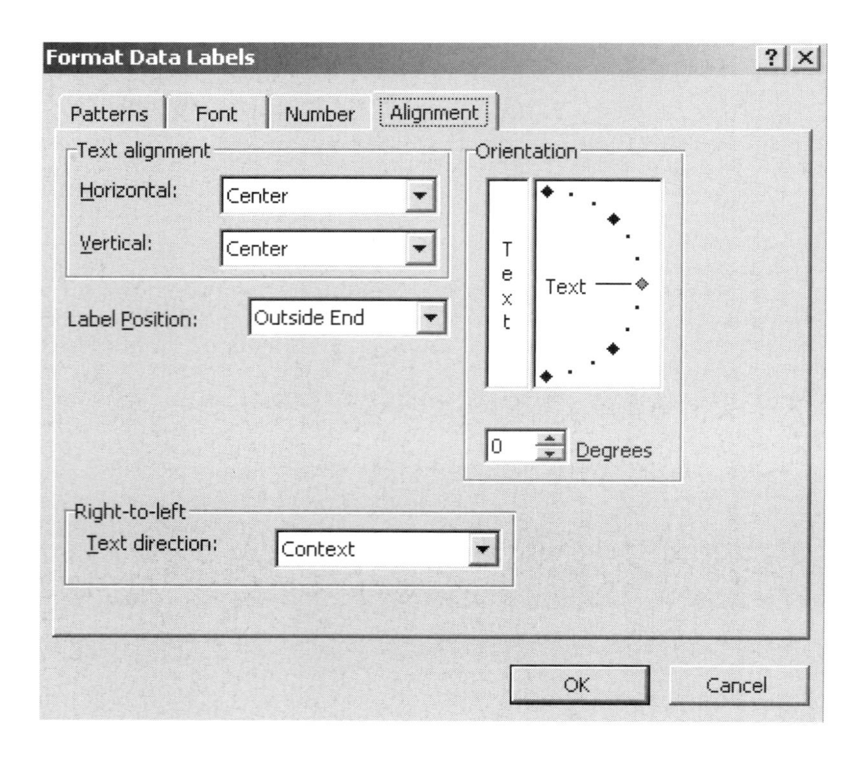

Figure 9.38

This dialogue box is very similar to the Format Axis Title and Format Chart Title boxes but it has an additional tab labelled Number. The font, alignment or pattern options are exactly the same as when formatting any other text or number. Numerical data on a chart or graph can be formatted in the same way as the worksheet containing the raw data. Numbers can be formatted to a specified number of decimal places, as currency, accounting, percentages, fractions and so on.

Have a look at Figure 9.39.

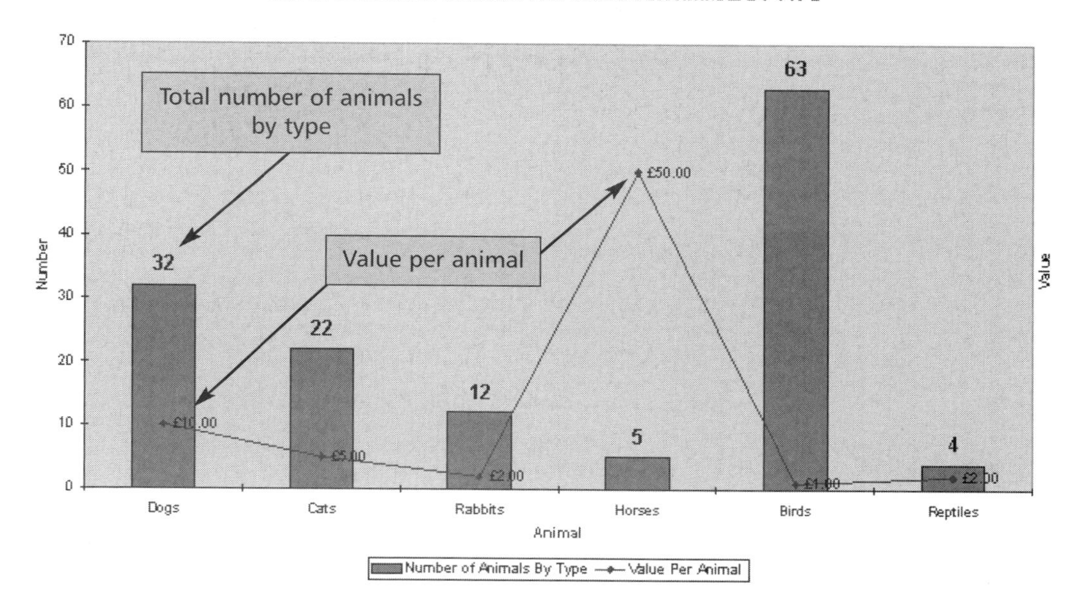

Figure 9.39

Here there are two series of data in the line–column chart. The columns represent the total number for each type of animal, whereas the line shows the relative value for each type of animal. The total number is formatted as a general number and the value is formatted as currency to two decimal places. Also, the size of the font has been increased for the column figures to distinguish them more easily from the value numbers.

In the next Try it out exercise you will create a line graph and display and format the data labels.

Try it out

Open the .csv file **Portfolio** from the Spreadsheet sub-folder of Unit 9 on the attached CD.

Save the file as an Excel workbook using the same name, **Portfolio.**

You are going to create a line graph that compares the cost price of each stock to its current price.

Highlight the following ranges of data:

A2:A6, C2:C6, D2:D6.

Click on the chart icon from the toolbar,

Select Line from the standard types of graph.

Click Next > twice.

Type the following chart and axis titles:

Chart title: 'COMPARISON OF COST PRICE TO CURRENT VALUE'
X-axis title: 'Stock'
Y-axis title: 'Price'

Format the chart legend so that it is at the bottom of the chart.

Click the Data Labels tab.

Click the Value check box.

Click Next >.

Click As new sheet: and

Type the new sheet name as 'Price Comparisons'.

Click Finish.

Your chart worksheet should now look like Figure 9.40.

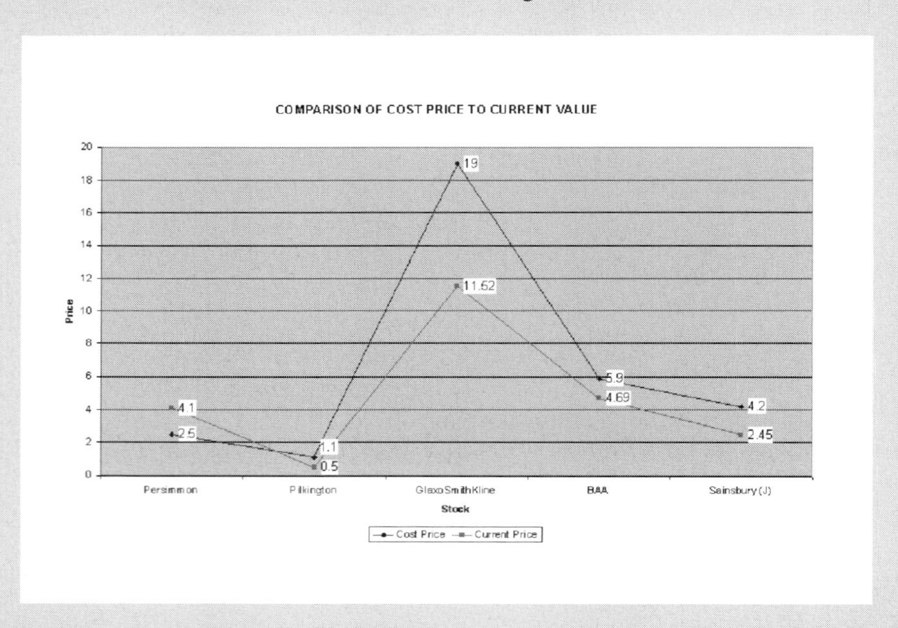

Figure 9.40

Double-click on the Cost Price data series so that the Format Data Labels dialogue box appears.

Click the Font tab.

Amend the font so that it is Arial, Bold and size 14 point.

Repeat this process for the Current Price series.

Using the same technique:

Format both axis labels as size 16 point in the same font type and bold.

Format the Category axis labels so that they are in italic using the same technique as above.

Format the chart title so it is 22 point and underlined; use the same technique again.

Note: to underline the title select Single from the Underline: combo box list.

Now format the axis numbers:

Double-click on any of the Y-axis numbers to show the Format Axis dialogue box.

Click the Number tab.

On the left of the box you will see the Category list ranging from a General number to Custom.

Click Currency as the category.

Click in the Decimal places: field.

Type '0'.

Click OK.

Your chart should now look like Figure 9.41.

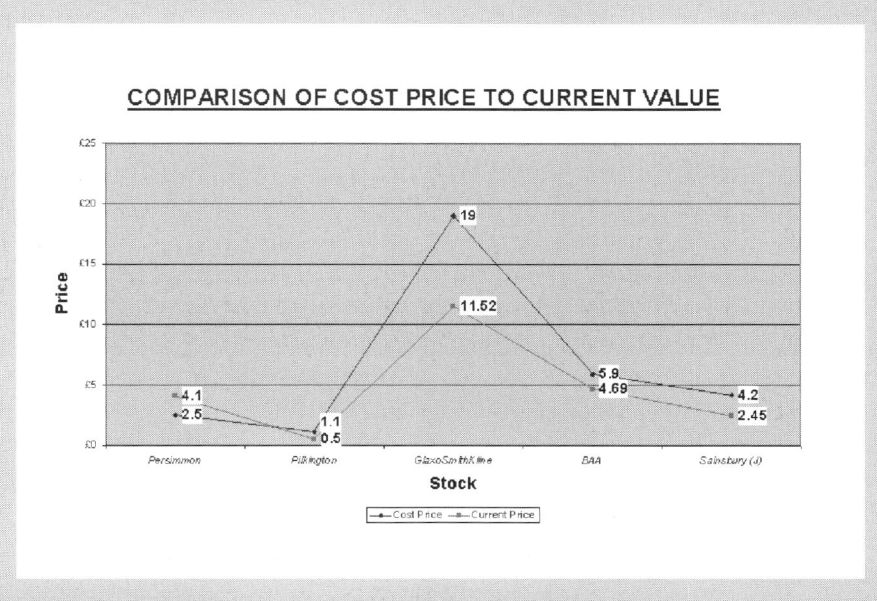

Figure 9.41

Save the workbook.

Setting the upper and lower limits on axes

You will have noticed that as Excel builds a graph or chart on a specific range of data it automatically makes assumptions regarding the upper and lower limits for each axis. So, for example, in the exercise you just completed you can see from Figure 9.41 that Excel detected that the range of data was no greater than 19 and no lower than 0.5. In creating the Value axis Excel therefore made 0 the lowest point in the scale and 20 the highest, with intervals of 2 (i.e. 0, 2, 4, 6, 8, etc.). However, in this example you are including the actual data as a label on the graph, so you may not want the graph to look so busy. To do this you could increase the intervals or indeed change the range of values altogether.

To change the upper and lower limits and intervals of the axes an actual value on the axis itself is double-clicked to access the Format Axis dialogue box. The Scale tab is then selected as shown in Figure 9.42.

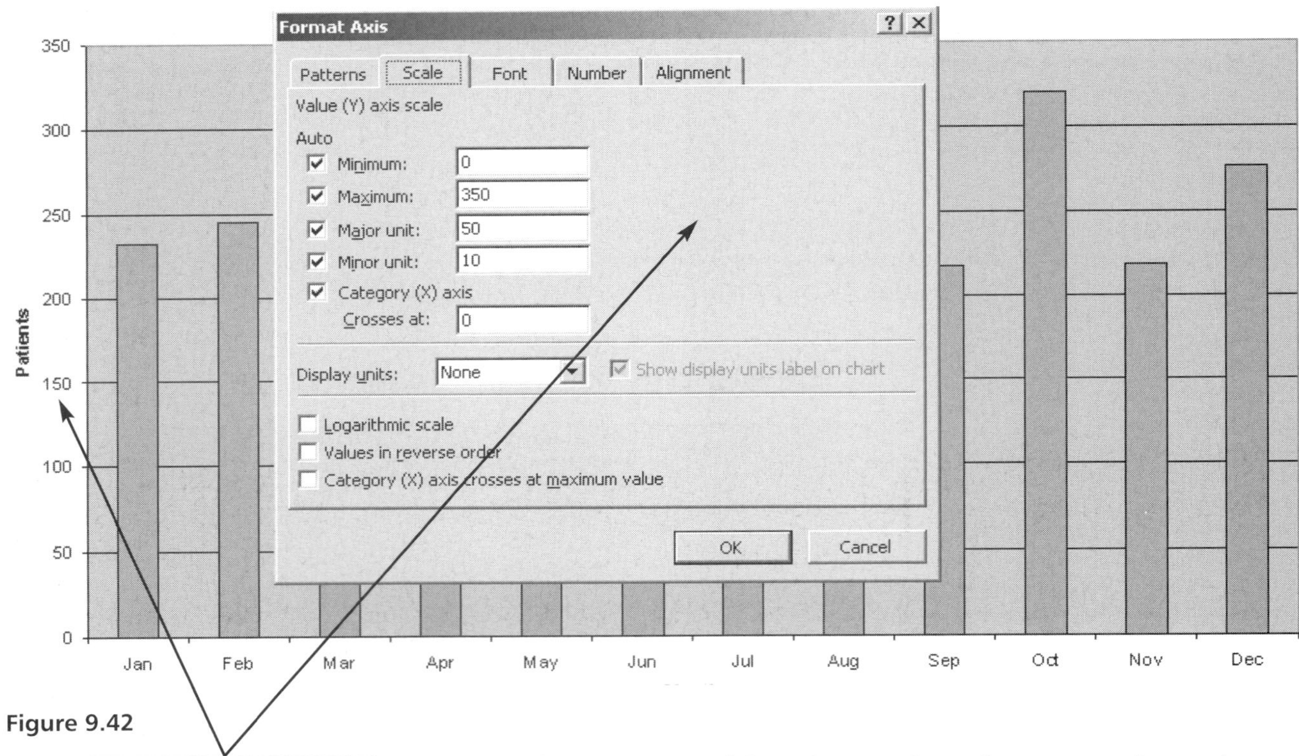

Figure 9.42

In the 'Value (Y) axis scale' section you have the opportunity to change the Minimum: and Maximum: limits of the scale (here they are 0 and 350) and also major and minor units for the scale. At the moment the major unit is 50. If, for the sake of argument, you want to change the maximum upper limit to 400 and the major interval to 100 then the dialogue options would be changed as shown in Figure 9.43. The effects of these changes are also shown in Figure 9.43. There would be no point in changing the lower limit as there would never be an occasion where there were fewer than zero patients in the surgery.

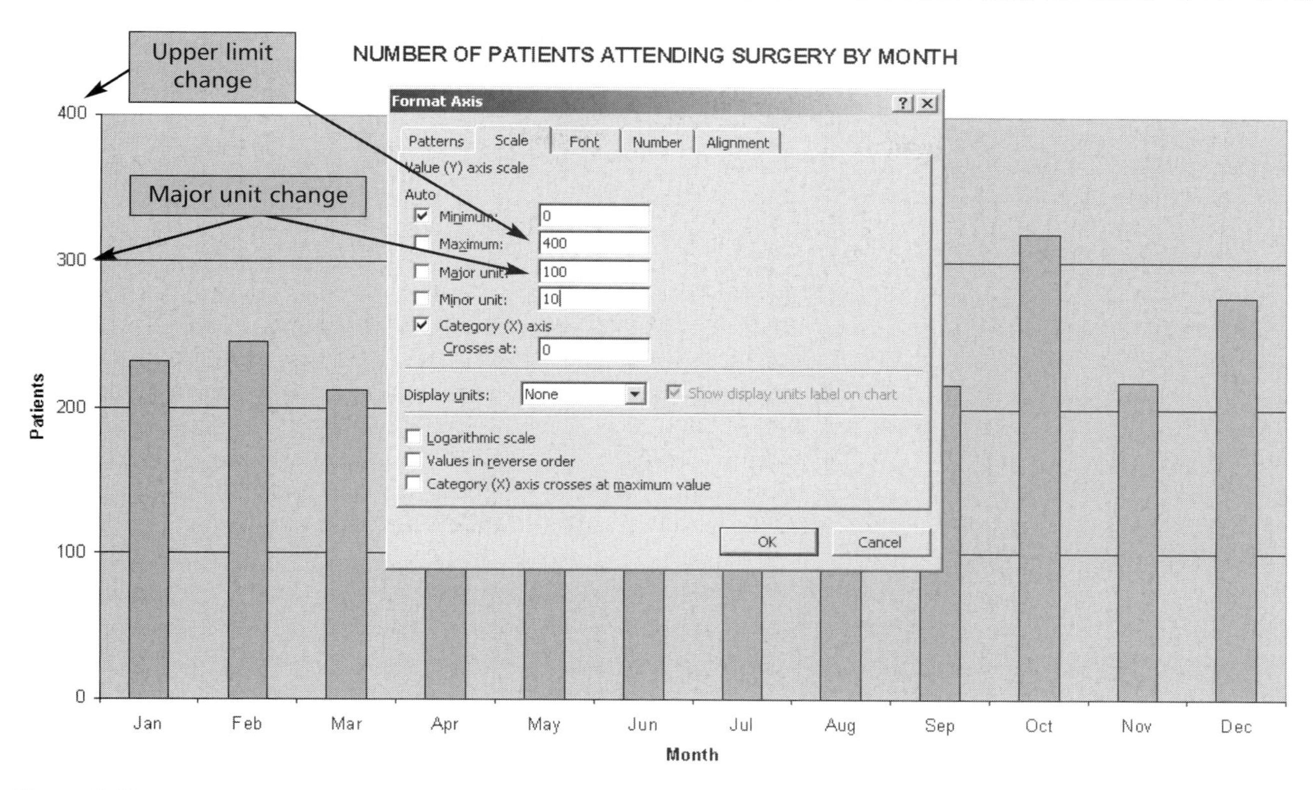

Figure 9.43

In the next Try it out exercise you are going to change the Y-value axis scale so that the scale goes up in steps of five and you are going to change the upper limit to 25.

Try it out

Open the file **Portfolio.xls** in Excel if it is not already open.

Select the Price Comparisons sheet with the line graph.

Double-click on the Y-axis value to show the Format Axis dialogue box.

In the Maximum: field for the limits:

Type '25'.

In the Major unit: field:

Type '5'.

Click OK.

Save the workbook.

Your line graph should now look like Figure 9.44.

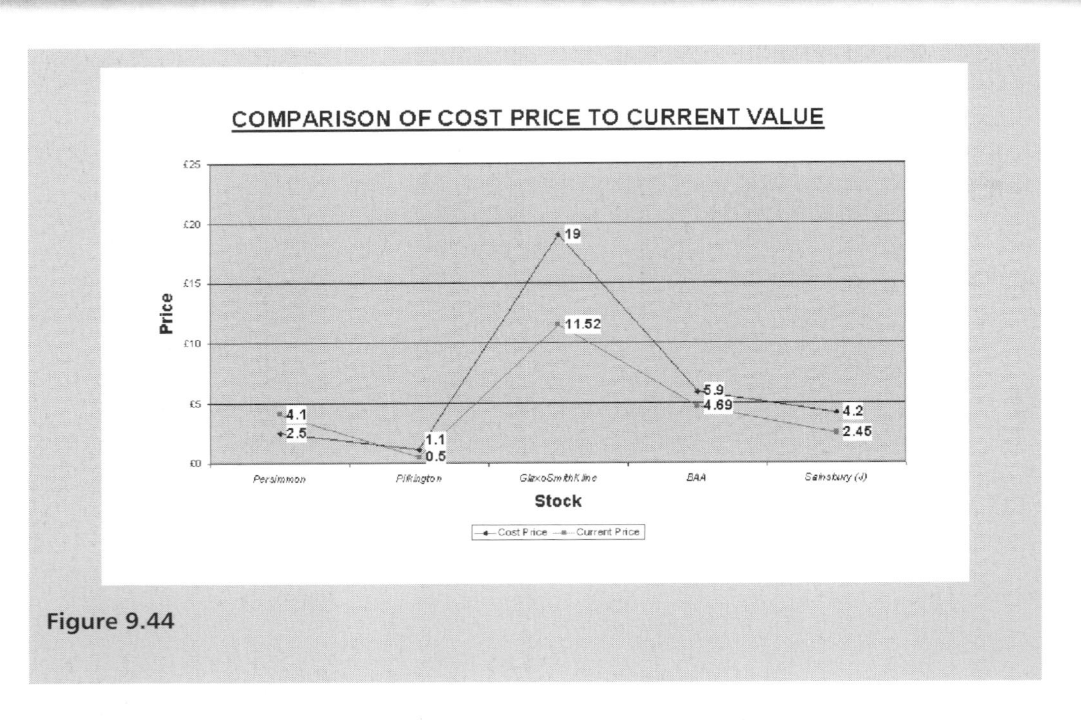

Figure 9.44

Inserting trendlines and trendline equations

Trendlines are used to display graphically trends in data and allow you to analyse potential problems with predictions made. For example, you could add a trendline to a sales chart or graph to predict when your sales might reach a certain level, and this might then be built into a business plan. You may need to do this for example, if you are predicting a major expense for a new piece of equipment and you want to assess whether the sales are likely to be at the level where such expenditure is justified.

Excel will generate a variety of different types of trendline. For CLAIT plus you need to understand how to apply a linear trendline to a scatter graph and also how to display the related equation.

Adding trendlines and the related equations is very straightforward. First the graph or chart is created. Next the Add Trendline... option is selected from the Chart option on the main menu. You will then see the Add Trendline dialogue box shown in Figure 9.45.

The dialogue box has two tabs, Type and Options. For now you are only interested in the linear type of trendline. On the Options tab shown in Figure 9.46 you can give the trendline a name and also the degree of forecasting required.

In the lower section of the dialogue box there are three check boxes. The only one you will need to be aware of is the one which says 'Display equation on chart'.

In Figure 9.47 you can see that in this example a forward projection of three months has been added and also the equation relating to the trendline displayed.

Now have a go at this yourself.

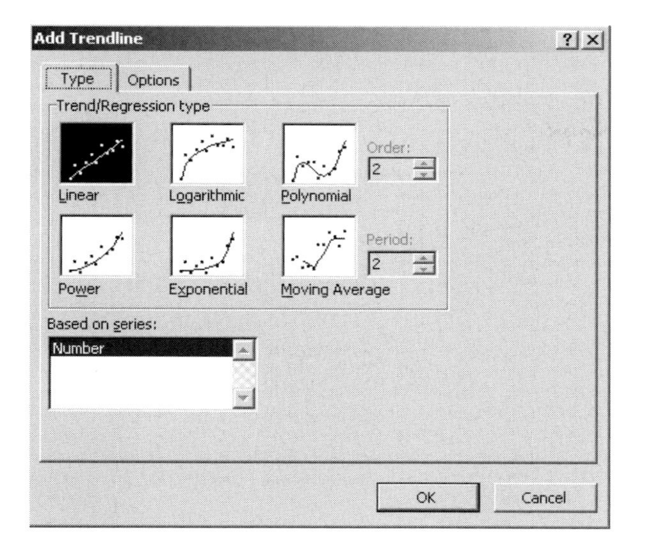

Figure 9.45

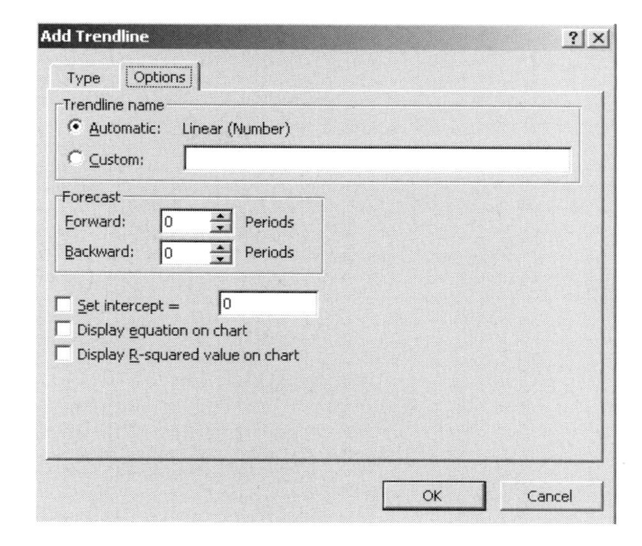

Figure 9.46

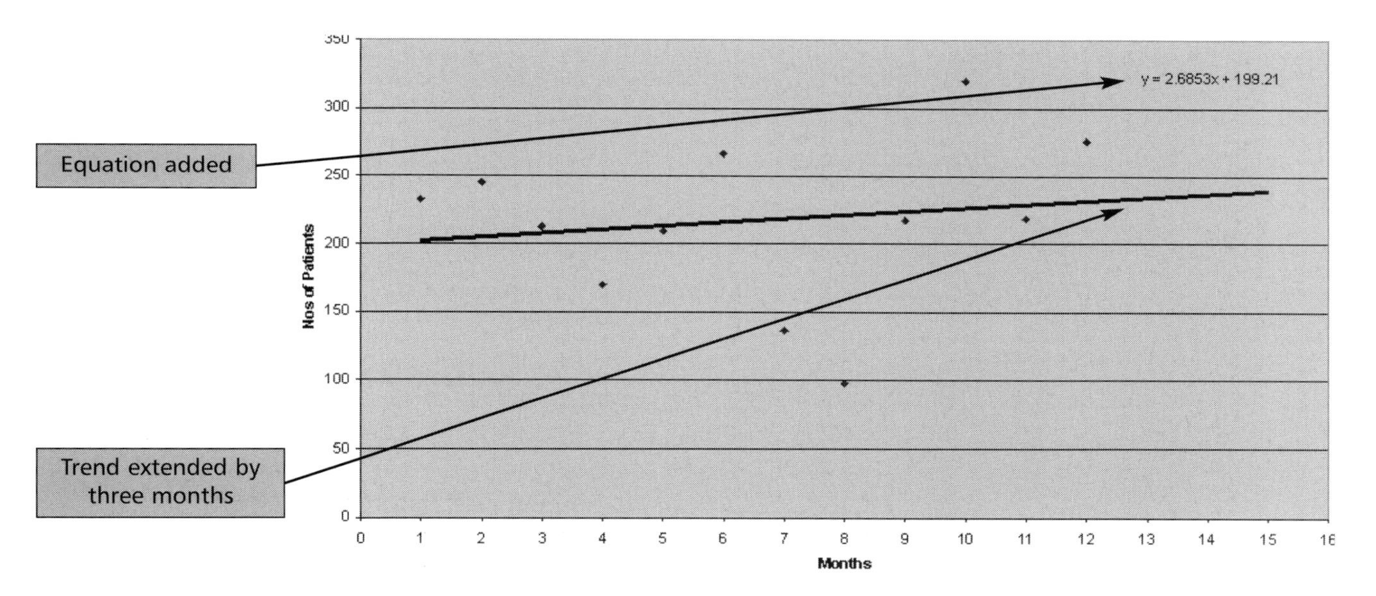

Figure 9.47

Try it out

Open Excel if it is not already open.

Open the file **Student_Averages.csv** from the Spreadsheet sub-folder of Unit 9 on the CD.

Save the file as an Excel workbook (.xls) using the same name as the .csv file.

Create a scatter graph with Age Group on the X-axis and Average score on the Y-axis. Range = B2:C9.

Name the sheet containing the graph 'Average_Score_By_Age'.

Display the Y-axis labels on the graph.

Once you have completed the scatter graph:

Click Add Trendline… from the Chart option on the main menu.

Click Linear as the trendline type.

Select the Option tab.

Click Display equation on chart.

Click OK.

The trendline will appear on the chart, together with its associated equation.

Notice how the equation straddles the trendline itself. To move the equation click on it to select it. Now the equation can be dragged to your preferred position on the graph.

Click the equation.

Drag the equation box so that it is in the top-right corner of the graph.

Save the workbook.

Your graph should look like Figure 9.48.

> **TIP**
>
> **Scatter chart tip**
>
> To change the axis values of the X and Y ranges, select the Series tab and click on the box to the right of the X Values: field. This will return you to the data. Using the drag technique drag the cursor over the data for the X-axis and then repeat the process for the Y-axis. After each range has been highlighted click the icon to return to the Series tab in the dialogue box.

Average Score By Age Group

Age Group	Average Score
1	89
2	91
3	75
4	58
5	79
6	88
7	83
8	96

y = 0.8214x + 78.679

Figure 9.48

Inserting text boxes on a chart or graph

You will see from the graph you have just completed that it would be difficult to identify which class each point represented. One way round this is to add text boxes to the graph to illustrate individual or all data points. You can always identify a specific data point by placing the cursor over it on the chart or graph. A box will appear showing which data the point relates to, as shown in Figure 9.49.

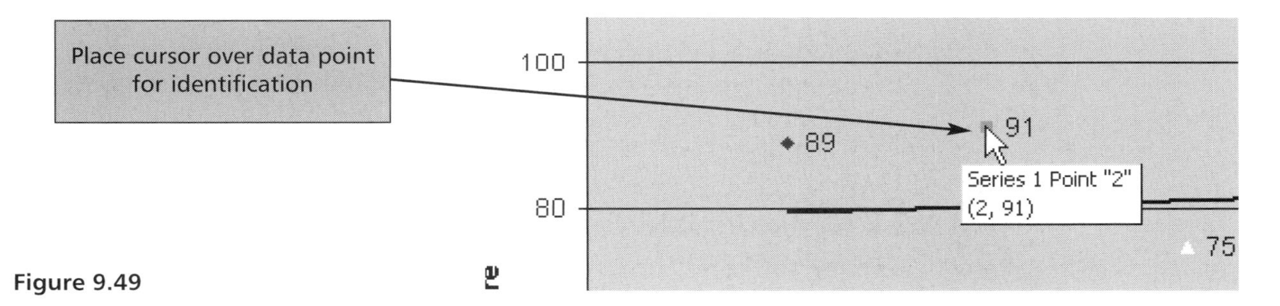

Figure 9.49

Alternatively you can go back to your main spreadsheet containing the raw data and identify the point by looking at the data itself.
Once you have identified the data you can use the drawing toolbox shown in Figure 9.50 to add a text box.

Text box icon

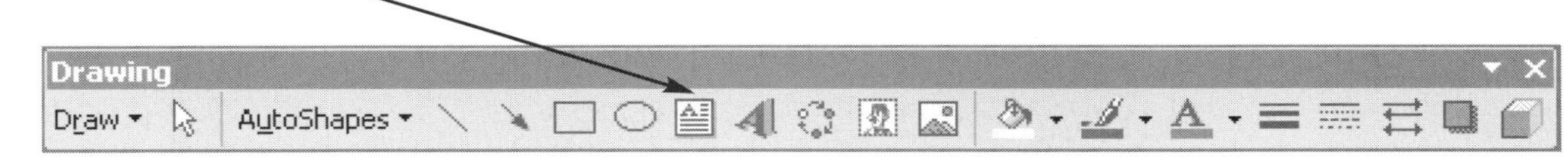

Figure 9.50

If you look at Figure 9.51 you will see this is a scatter graph showing the forecast rainfall for the year, against the actual rainfall. Without the text boxes it would be diffcut to identify the month to which the data relates.

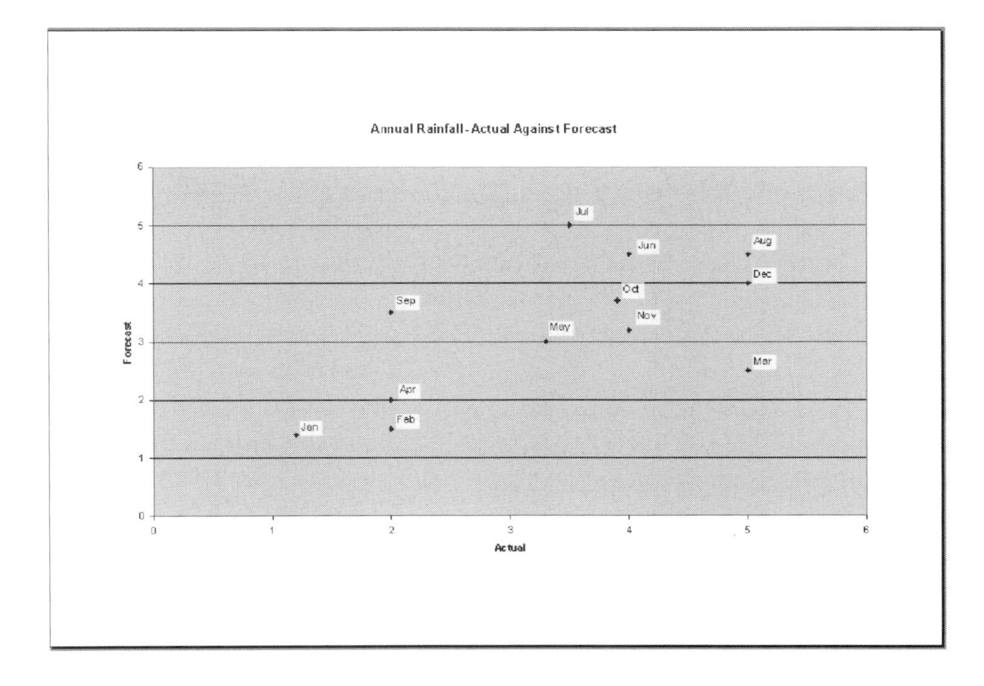

Figure 9.51

Now try to add text boxes to your **Student_Averages** X–Y scatter graph.

Try it out

Open Excel and the **Student_Averages.xls** file if it is not already open.

Click on the sheet containing the X–Y scatter graph Average_Score_By_Age.

If the drawing toolbar is not enabled then:

Click Toolbars from the View option on the main menu.

Click Drawing and the drawing toolbar will appear, normally at the bottom of the main screen window.

Click the text box icon and then move the cursor over the first data point.

Click on the graph to create a text box.

Type 'Class A'.

Insert similar text boxes for each of the other data points.

DATA POINT TIP

If you are not sure which is the appropriate data point for the text box name move the cursor over the actual data point on the graph and note the series values. Relate this to the raw data in the spreadsheet. In the Try it out exercise the values follow each other, so for example, the first data point shows Series 1 Point "1" (1,89), where 1 is the first age group and 89 the average score.

Your graph should look like Figure 9.52 when you have inserted all the text boxes.

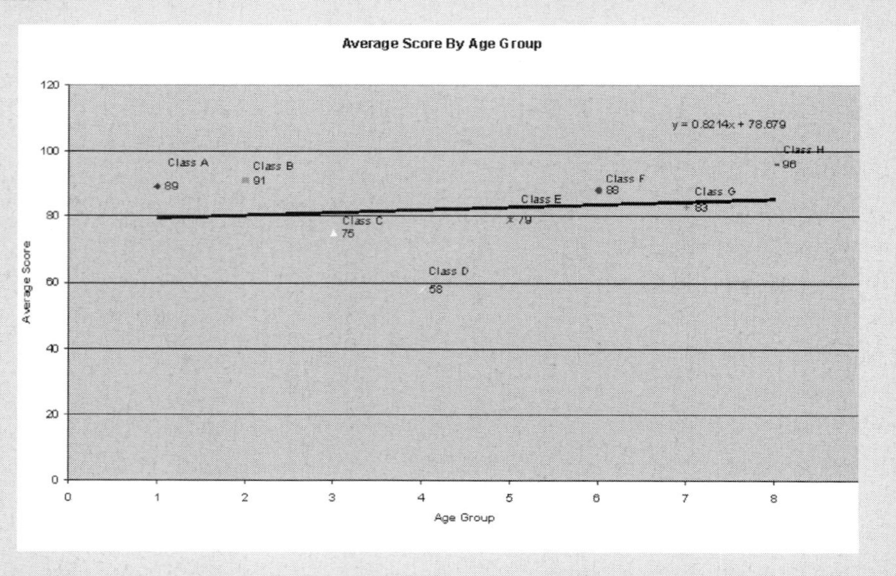

Figure 9.52

You should now be able to:

- format titles and labels
- display data labels to a series
- format data labels
- apply numeric formatting to an axis
- set the upper and lower limits on axes
- insert trendlines and trendline equations
- insert text boxes on a chart or graph.

Build-up Exercise 9b: Stage 1

Open Excel and the file **Paint.csv**.

Save the file as an Excel workbook using the same name, **Paint**.

Create a new X–Y scatter chart to analyse the correlation of temperature with drying time.

Use the following information to create the graph:

Main Title: Effects of Temperature on Drying Time
X-axis title: Temperature
Y-axis title: Time (Minutes)

Format the main title in the graph so that it is:

Font: Arial
Font Size: 14
Font Style: Bold italic
Underlined with a single line

Format the axis titles:

Font: Arial
Font size: 12
Font style: Bold italic

Display the X-values for the data points on the graph.

Format the data labels as:

Font: Arial
Font size: 10
Font style: Bold

Insert a text box at the point where the optimum drying temperature is 22°C and the drying time 14 minutes. The text for the text box should read:

'Optimum temperature for a 14 minute drying time'.

Save the workbook and graph.

Format the X-axis as follows:

Scale: Minimum value 5, maximum value 32, interval 2.

▶▶

Format the Y-axis as follows:

Scale: Minimum value 5, maximum value 55, interval 5.

Move the text box so that the 'O' of Optimum is immediately below the '22'.

Your graph should now look like Figure 9.53.

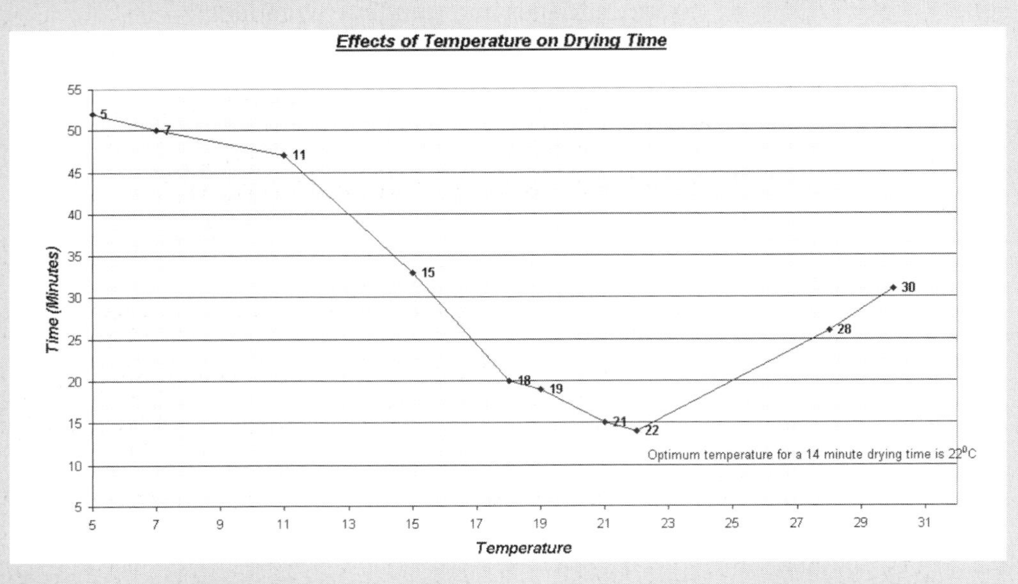

Figure 9.53

Formatting graphs and charts

Adding headers and footers to a chart or graph

If you have completed previous units for either CLAIT Plus or New CLAIT you will know that following house styles is a requirement when presenting your work for assessment. The charts and graphs part of CLAIT Plus is no different, and you will need to know how to insert your name and centre number as a header or footer on each chart you are asked to create. Inserting a header or footer is done through the Page Setup... option which can be found under File on the main menu. Clicking on Page Setup... will make the Page Setup dialogue box appear. This dialogue box has four tabs: Page, Margins, Header/Footer and Chart.

By clicking on the Header/Footer tab you will be offered the opportunity to insert one of the default headers or footers, such as the page number or file path: see Figure 9.54.

By clicking on the Custom Header... or Custom Footer... buttons a further dialogue box appears shown in Figure 9.55.

Figure 9.55 box shows the options for a custom header but both the custom header and footer dialogue boxes are the same. To insert a custom header or footer, simply click in the appropriate box Left section:, Center section: or Right section: and then either type in the required text or use one of the buttons above the section boxes to insert page numbers, date, time, etc. Now try this out.

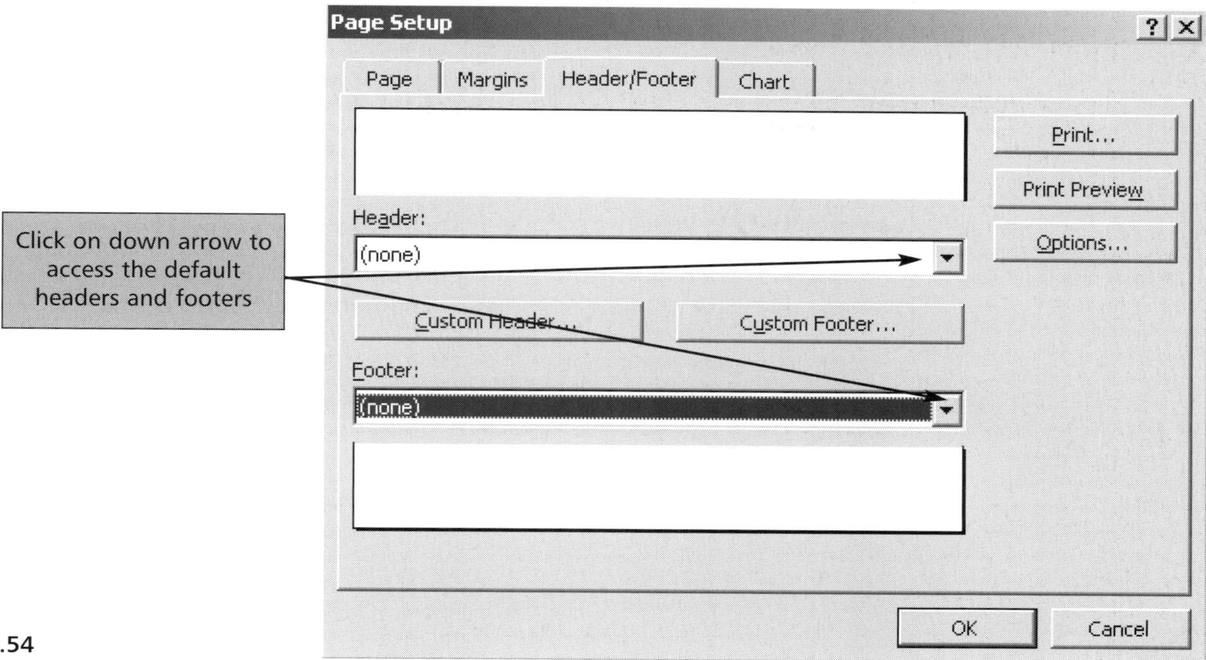

Figure 9.54

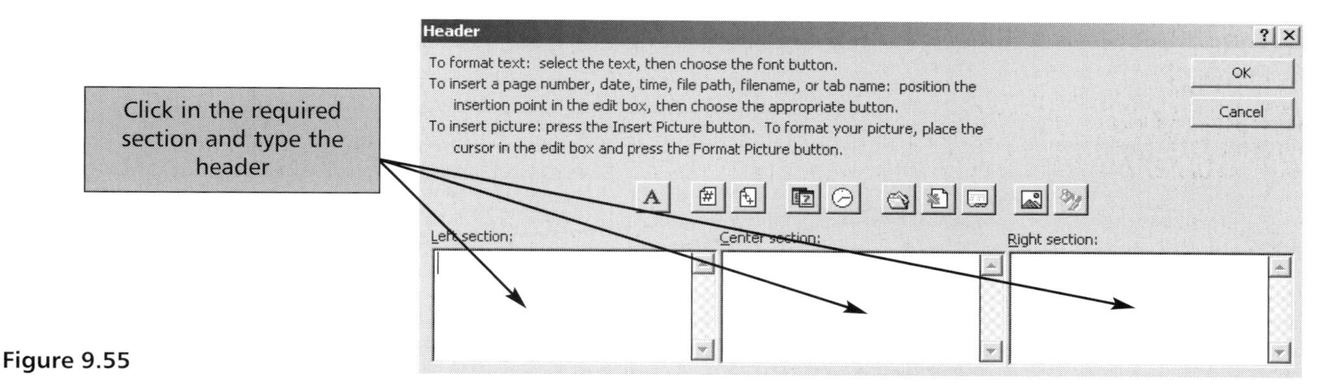

Figure 9.55

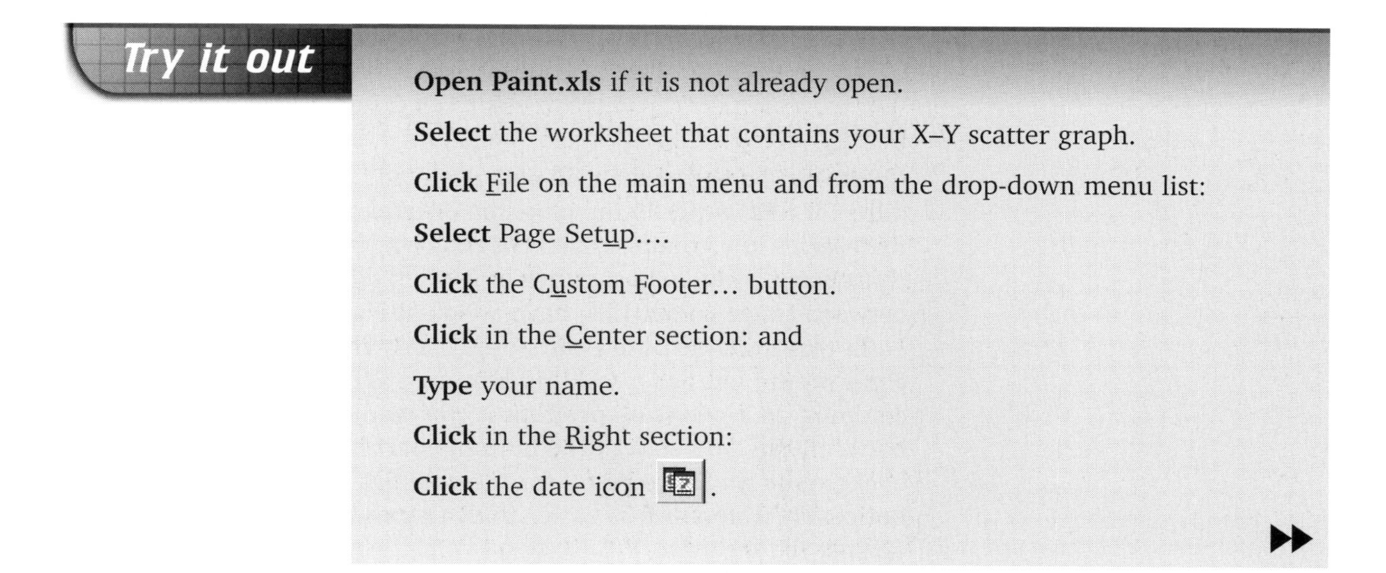

Try it out

Open Paint.xls if it is not already open.

Select the worksheet that contains your X–Y scatter graph.

Click File on the main menu and from the drop-down menu list:

Select Page Setup....

Click the Custom Footer... button.

Click in the Center section: and

Type your name.

Click in the Right section:

Click the date icon.

Click OK.

Notice how you are now given a preview of the header or footer in the Page Setup dialogue box.

Click OK again to return to your chart.

To see how the header or footer will look in a printed version:

Click Print Preview from File on the main menu and you will see a print preview of your chart, complete with footer: see Figure 9.56.

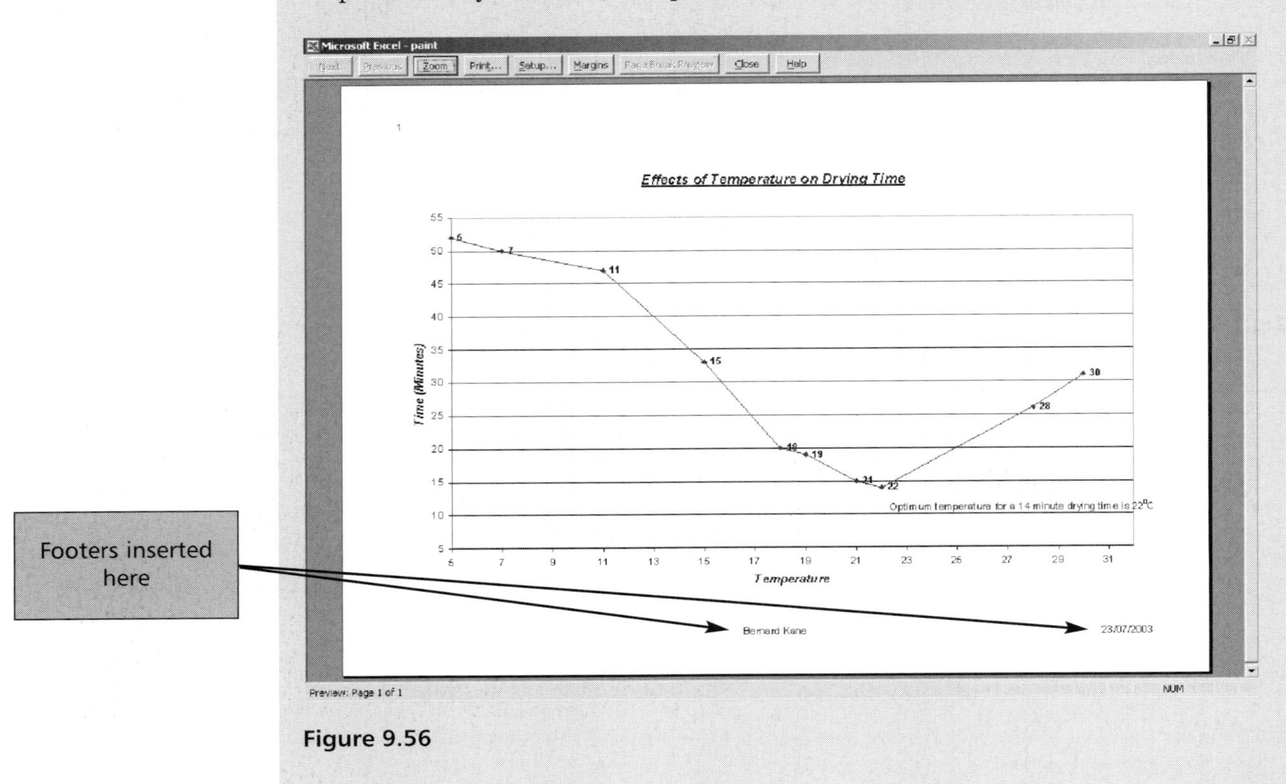

Figure 9.56

Applying fills to plot areas and bars in a data series

Charts can be both enhanced and also made easier to read by applying different fills, either to the plot area or indeed to the actual bars themselves in a column chart. For example, if you are reproducing a chart using a non-colour printer it is often difficult to distinguish between single colour fills; have a look at Figure 9.57.

In this example both charts use exactly the same raw data. The chart on the left has a solid fill plot area and solid fill for the actual columns. In a greyscale printout it can be difficult to distinguish between the data series. The bottom chart has a texture fill background and pattern fill for the columns. As the patterns are noticeably different it is easier to distinguish the various columns against the legend.

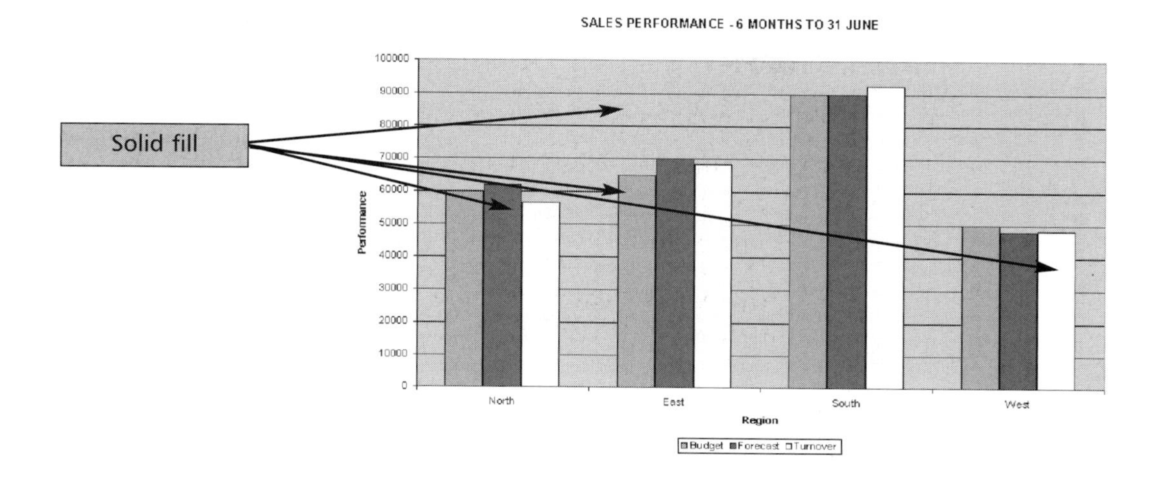

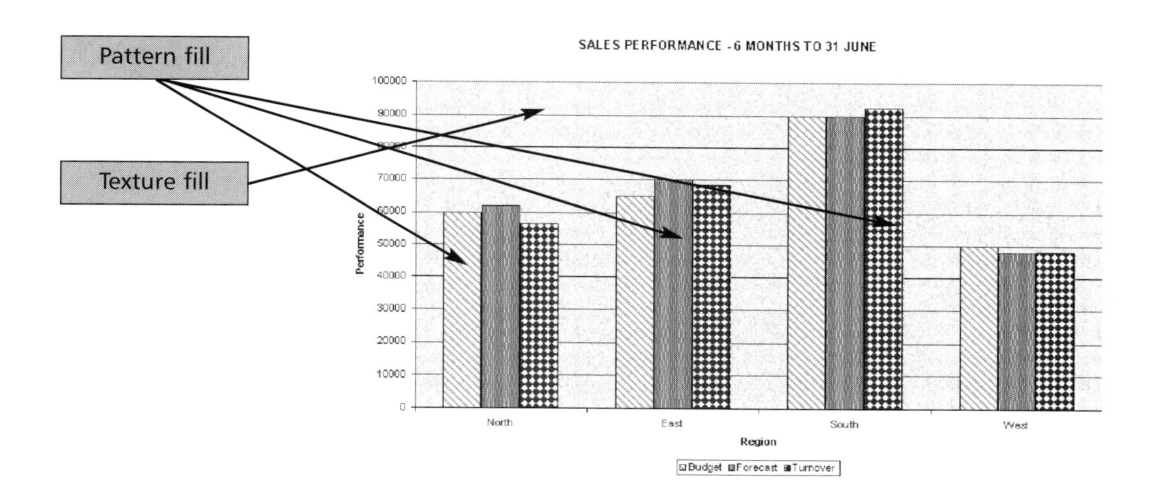

Figure 9.57

Now try changing the background fill and the column fill in the next hand-holding Try it out exercise.

Try it out

Stage 1: Apply a fill to the plot area

Open the file **Weather_Stats** you saved earlier in this unit.

Select the worksheet called MIN TEMPERATURES JAN–APR.

Using the right-hand mouse button:

Click on the white plot area just outside the chart itself and from the menu list offered:

Click on Format Plot Area.

Note: For non 3-D charts the plot area is actually the grey area on the chart. If you are not sure which part of the chart you are on, simply leave the cursor stationary for a second and a small information box will appear that will tell you if you are on the plot area or chart area and so on.

The dialogue box shown in Figure 9.58 will appear.

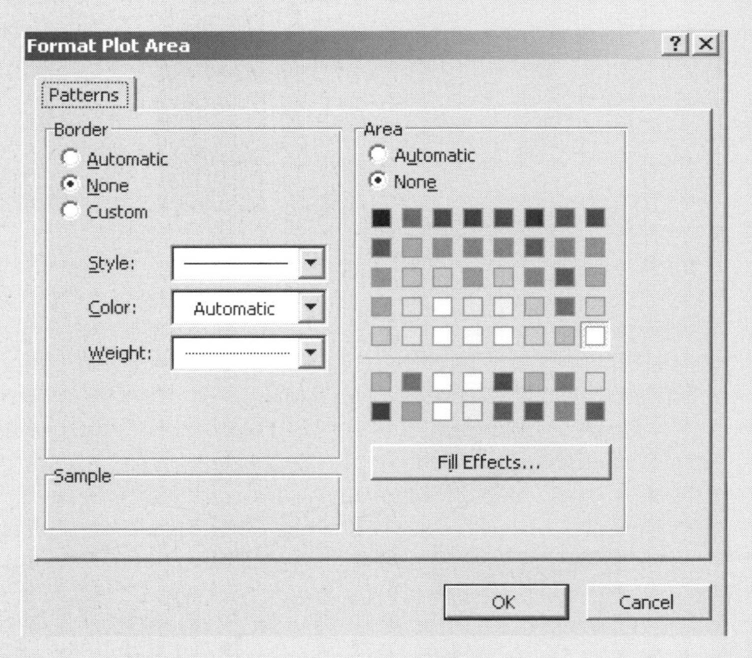

Figure 9.58

The dialogue box has two sections; one for formatting the border and one for the area fill.

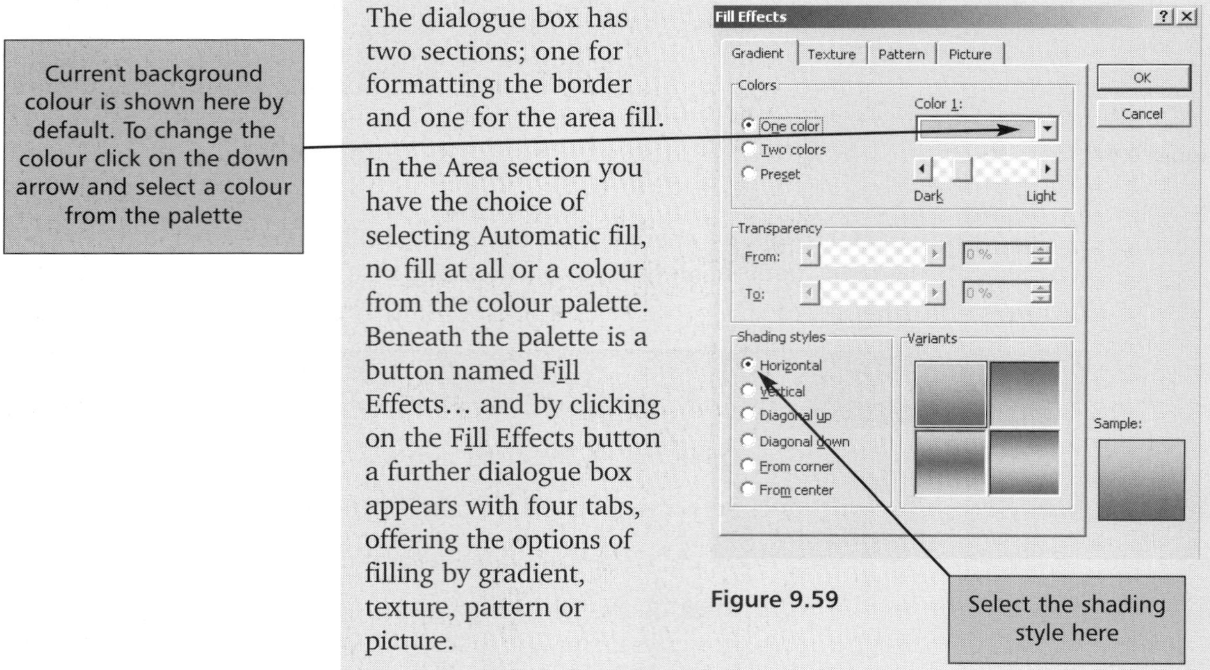

Current background colour is shown here by default. To change the colour click on the down arrow and select a colour from the palette

In the Area section you have the choice of selecting Automatic fill, no fill at all or a colour from the colour palette. Beneath the palette is a button named Fill Effects... and by clicking on the Fill Effects button a further dialogue box appears with four tabs, offering the options of filling by gradient, texture, pattern or picture.

Figure 9.59

Select the shading style here

This dialogue box is shown in Figure 9.59.

In this example you are going to apply a gradient fill to the plot area.

Click the Fill Effects... button.

Make sure the One color radio button option is selected.

Click on the arrow to the right of the Color 1: box.

Click on a pale yellow colour from the palette.

Click on the Horizontal radio button for the shading style (if this is not selected by default).

Click OK twice to return to the chart.

Save the workbook.

Stage 2: Apply a fill to the data series

Again using the right-hand mouse button:

Click on the first data point column in the chart, as shown in Figure 9.60.

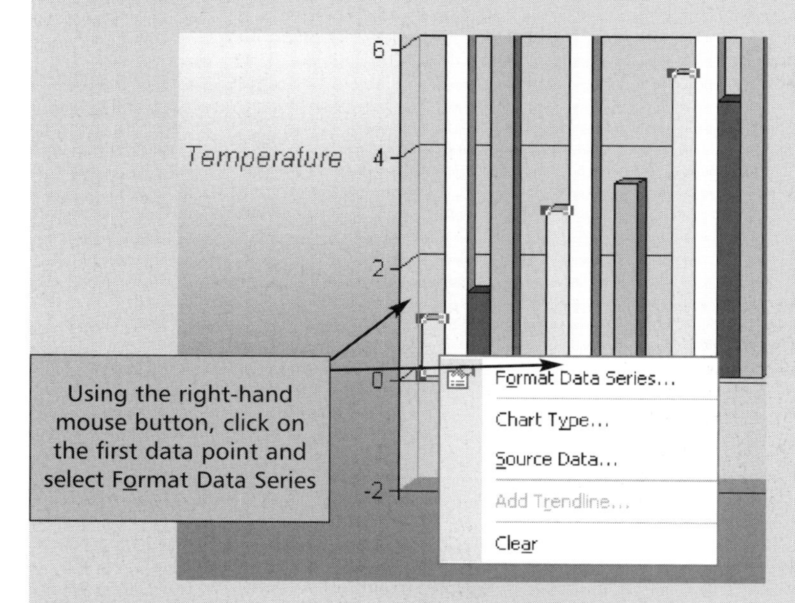

Figure 9.60

The Format Data Series dialogue box will now appear as shown in Figure 9.61.

Notice how this dialogue box is very similar to the one used to format the background fill but instead of four tabs this has five.

Click Fill Effects... .

Click the Patterns tab if it is not already showing.

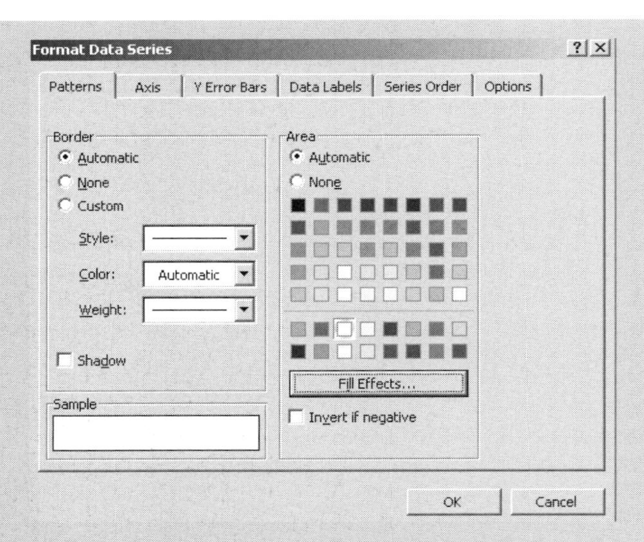

Figure 9.61

In Figure 9.62 you can see the various patterns that are available.

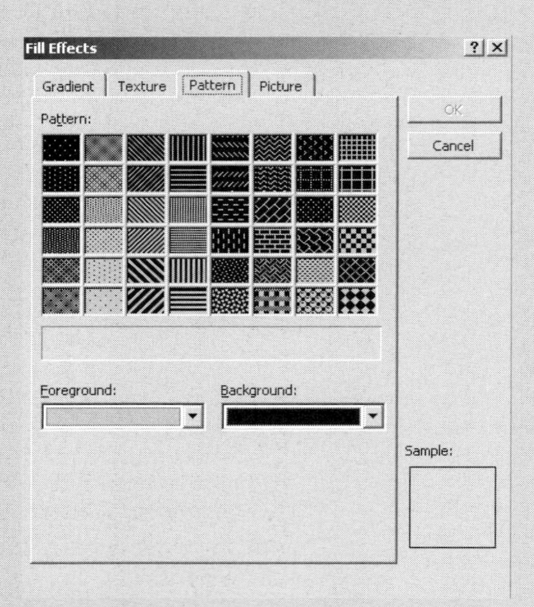

Figure 9.62

Click on one of the patterns to select it.

Click OK twice to return to the chart.

Note: at this stage you can also change both the foreground and background colours if this is necessary by clicking on the arrow for Foreground: or Background, and then selecting a colour from the colour palette. You may find that where the data series colour is very pale, or even white, it will be necessary to change the foreground to a darker colour to see the patterns clearly.

Now repeat this process for each of the data points choosing colours and patterns that allow the columns to be easily distinguished from each other.

Your chart should now look similar to Figure 9.63.

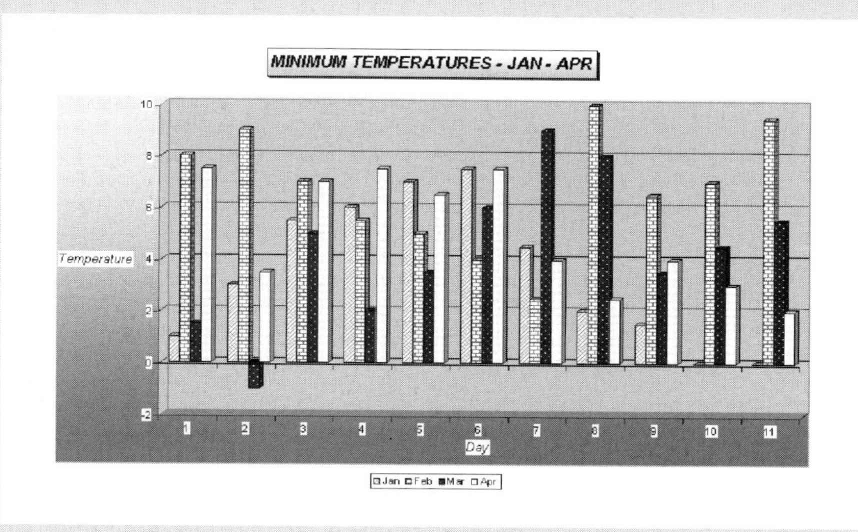

Figure 9.63

Save the chart.

Close the file.

To remove a background or plot fill, open the appropriate dialogue box and in the area section click the None radio button.

Applying and removing lines and data point markers

You will have already seen that when creating a scatter graph the data points are represented by a series of markers. Sometimes you may wish to join these markers with a line or indeed simply use a line and leave out the markers altogether. Joining lines between markers is not the same as adding a trendline which relies on an equation to generate the trend. Markers joined together are simply that; there is no implied significance in respect of the line between the marker points. For CLAIT Plus you will need to be able to add lines to connect markers and also to remove markers from lines.

To add a line so that it connects markers the Format Data Series dialogue box is used. When used in conjunction with scatter graphs it is slightly different to the Format Data Series dialogue box used for other charts and graphs. Have a look at Figure 9.64.

The first thing you will notice is that there are seven tab pages as opposed to the five for other charts. For CLAIT Plus you will only need to use the tabs for Patterns and possibly Data Labels.

Accessing the Format Data Series dialogue box for scatter graphs is undertaken in exactly the same way as that for other charts and graphs. First move the cursor over one of the data points and, using the

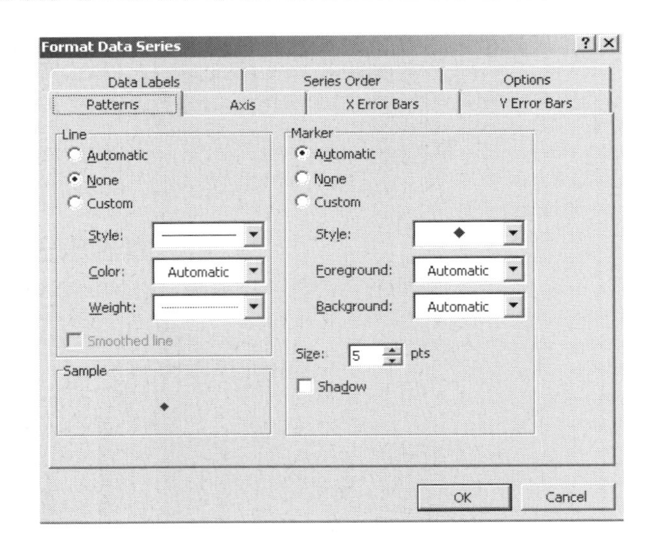

Figure 9.64

right-hand mouse button, click on the data point and select Format Data Series... from the menu list. To join the data points with a line, click on the Patterns tab (if it is not already in view). On the left of the page is the Line section offering a number of options: Automatic, None or Custom.

By selecting the Automatic option and clicking OK, a single line will be created joining each of the data points in the series. This line can be removed by selecting the None option and clicking the OK button. If the line is to be formatted the Custom option is used. Using the Custom option allows the style, colour and line weight (thickness) of the line to be formatted.

On the right-hand side of the dialogue box in the Marker section, the style of marker can be formatted. Again the Automatic and None options are available and the Custom option allows the Style, Foreground and Background colours to be formatted. In addition the size of the marker can be adjusted by using the Size: field and a shadow can be added to the marker by clicking in the Shadow check box.

To remove a marker once it has been created simply select the None option in the Marker section of the Format Data Series dialogue box.

In the next Try it out exercise you will create a scatter graph and format it as indicated. You will then join the data points together.

Try it out

Open the file **Detectors.csv** in Excel.

Save the file as an Excel (.xls) workbook.

Using the data range A3:B12:

Create an X–Y scatter graph with the following information and styles:

Graph title:	EFFECTIVENESS OF DETECTORS IN BAND 2
Font:	Times New Roman
Font style:	Bold
Font size:	14
Underline:	Single
Value (X) axis title:	Depth (Inches)
Font:	Times New Roman
Font style:	Bold
Font size:	12
Value (Y) axis title:	Effectiveness
Font:	Times New Roman
Font style:	Bold
Font size:	12
Maximum value (Y) axis scale:	11
Minimum value (Y) axis scale:	0
Marker style:	Square
Marker size:	Size 6
Plot area colour:	Light blue

Using the right-hand mouse button:

Click on one of the markers, and

Select Format Data Series… .

Click the Patterns tab.

In the Line section of the dialogue box:

Click the Automatic radio button.

Make sure the Smoothed line check box is unchecked.

Save As new sheet: named 'Effectiveness'.

Save your chart and workbook.

Your graph should now look similar to Figure 9.65.

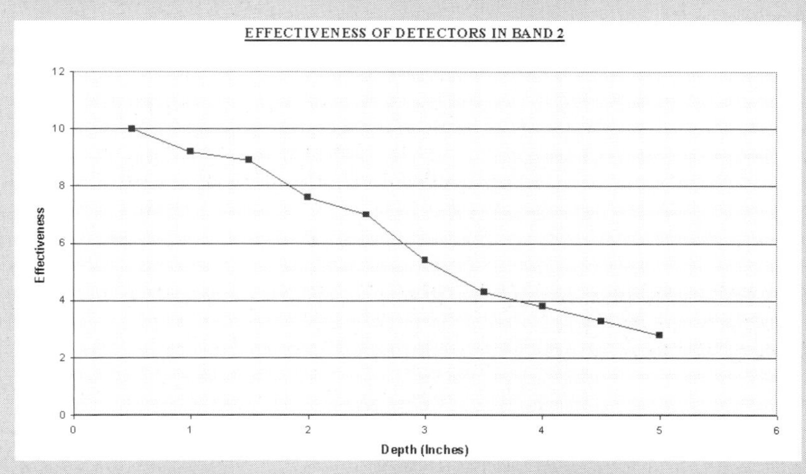

Figure 9.65

Close the file.

Setting the style and weight of lines

There will be times when it is necessary to add emphasis to a chart or graph and changing the style or weight of lines is a way of achieving this. When connecting the marker points in the previous Try it out exercise the Automatic option for creating the line was used. Two other radio button options in the Line section of the dialogue box are also available: None and Custom. Under the Custom option are a further four options for formatting the connecting line: Style, Color: Weight and Smoothed line.

The line can be reformatted by clicking on the data points using the right-hand mouse button, clicking the Format Data Series... option to show the dialogue box and selecting the formats required from the options available in the Style, Color and Weight lists. The Smoothed line check box allows the line to be smoothed as opposed to a series of straight sections (the default). Now try formatting the connecting line in the chart created in the previous Try it out exercise.

Try it out

Open the **Detectors.xls** file from the previous exercise.

Click the Effectiveness worksheet containing the scatter graph.

Using the right-hand mouse button:

Click on one of the data points.

Click Format Data Series... .

Select the Custom radio button.

Keep the line style as a solid, single line.

Select a dark blue (or any colour of your choice) from the colour palette.

Select the thickest line available.

Click OK.

Your graph should now look like Figure 9.66.

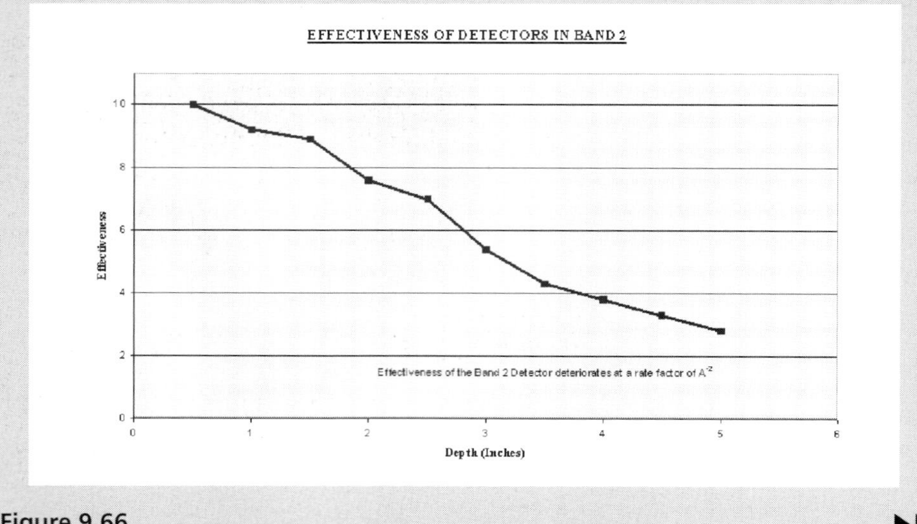

Figure 9.66

Save the workbook.

Close the file.

Applying superscript and subscript effects

Superscripts and subscripts are additional aspects of formatted text. Below are a number of examples of text containing superscripts and subscripts.

Superscript	Subscript
24°	12_1
23rd	R_{a1}
$Note^1$	$STD_{®}$
R^2	X_k

Changing a text box character to superscript or subscript in an Excel chart or graph is accomplished using the Format Text Box. First the text or symbol to be formatted is highlighted and then the dialogue box is accessed by clicking Format on the main menu and then Selected Object from the list options. The Format Text Box shown in Figure 9.67 then appears.

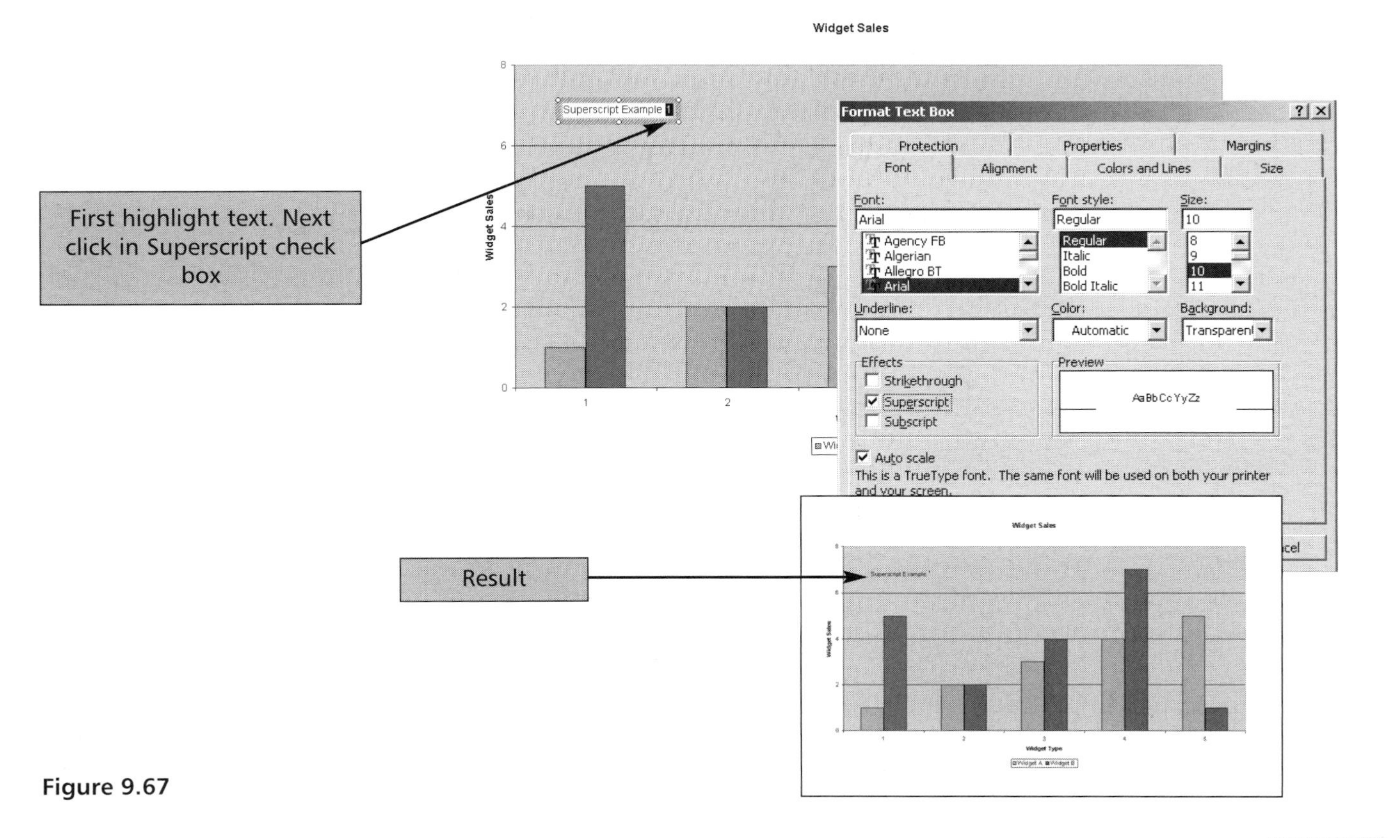

Figure 9.67

After the text has been highlighted clicking in either the Superscript or Subscript check box will format the text according to the choice made. Remember that having made the choice superscript will remain the format option until the check box is unselected. So, for example, were you to type something else after the '1' in the example in Figure 9.67 it would also be in superscript. To revert to normal text the Format Text Box dialogue box is opened again and the check box is cleared to remove the superscript formatting.

Try it out

Open the **Detectors.xls** file in Excel.

Create a new text box with the following text and place the box below the graph data points:

'Effectiveness of the Band 2 Detector deteriorates at a rate factor of A-2'.

Highlight '-2' at the end of the text you have just typed.

Click Format and then Selected Object.

Click in the Superscript check box.

Click OK.

Your text box text should now show '-2' as a superscript, thus: Effectiveness of the Band 2 Detector deteriorates at a rate factor of A^{-2}.

You should now be able to:

- add headers and footers to a chart or graph
- apply fills to plot areas and bars in a data series
- apply and remove lines and data point markers
- set the style and weight of lines
- apply superscript and subscript text.

Build-up Exercise 9c: Stage 1

Open Gardens.csv from the Spreadsheet files sub-folder of Unit 9 on the CD.

Create a line–column chart on two axes showing the size of each garden and the relative price per weekly cut.

Series 1 name:	Garden Size
Series 2 name:	Price per cut
Main Title:	RELATIVE COSTS PER GARDEN PER WEEK

X-axis title: Garden
First Value Axis title: Size
Secondary Value Axis title: Price per week

Use the default font styles and sizes.

Create the chart as a new worksheet with the name 'Garden Prices'.

Format the alignment of the category X-axis labels so that they are at an angle of 45 degrees.

Format the columns in the chart with a pattern rather than solid colour fill.

Format the plot area of the chart so that it is pale yellow.

Format the line connecting the data point markers so that it is solid and thick.

Remove the data point markers from the line.

Insert a text box with the following text:

'Price based on £1.25 per mtr2'

Format the '2' in 'mtr2' as a superscript.

Save the workbook to your hard or floppy disk in Excel format using the name 'Gardens'.

Close the file and the application.

Your chart should look like Figure 9.69.

FORMATTING TIP

To format the angle of text double-click on the text to be formatted or, using the right-hand mouse button, click and select the Format Axis... option. In the dialogue box click on the Alignment tab, and in the Orientation section of the box either type the number of degrees required or alternatively click and drag the text symbol shown in Figure 9.68.

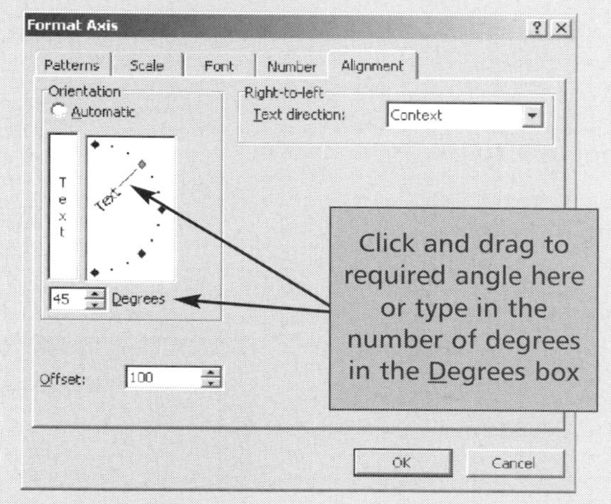

Figure 9.68

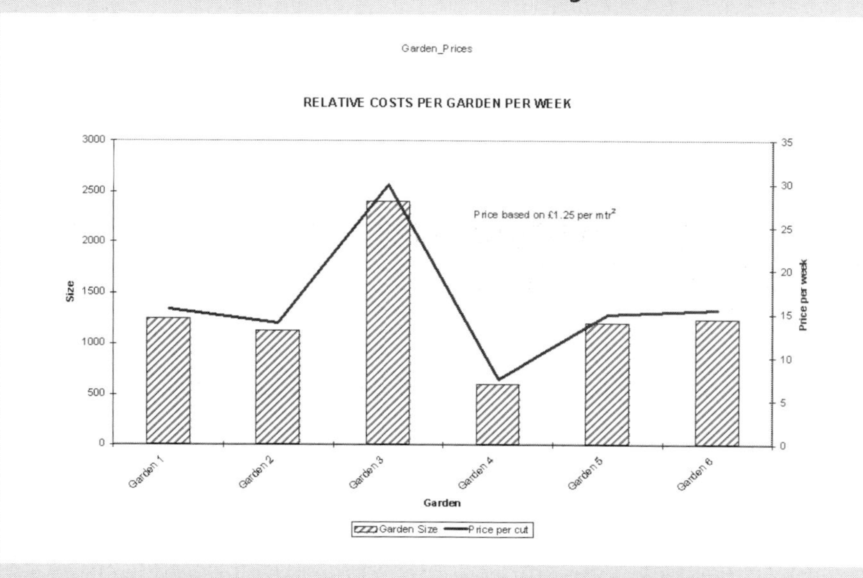

Figure 9.69

Printing charts and graphs

Charts can be printed using the normal Print... option from File on the main menu, but if the page, orientation or other settings need to be changed before printing it is better to use the options available from Print Preview, also found on the File main menu list. For CLAIT Plus you are required to able to distinguish between portrait and landscape printing and understand how to set the orientation before printing. Figure 9.70 shows the difference between portrait and landscape orientations.

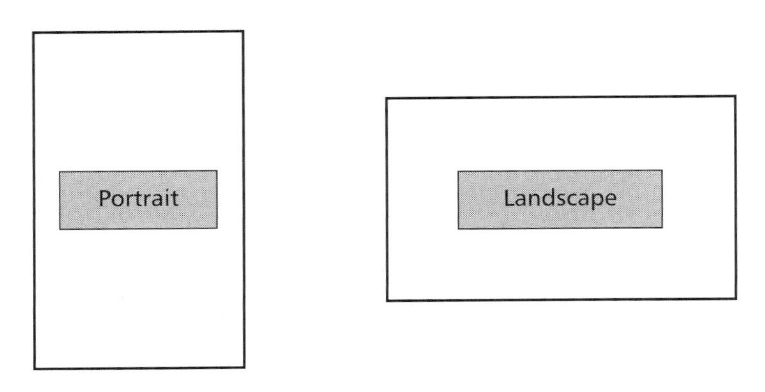

Figure 9.70

To change the settings select Print Preview from the File option on the main menu. You will see a screen similar to Figure 9.71.

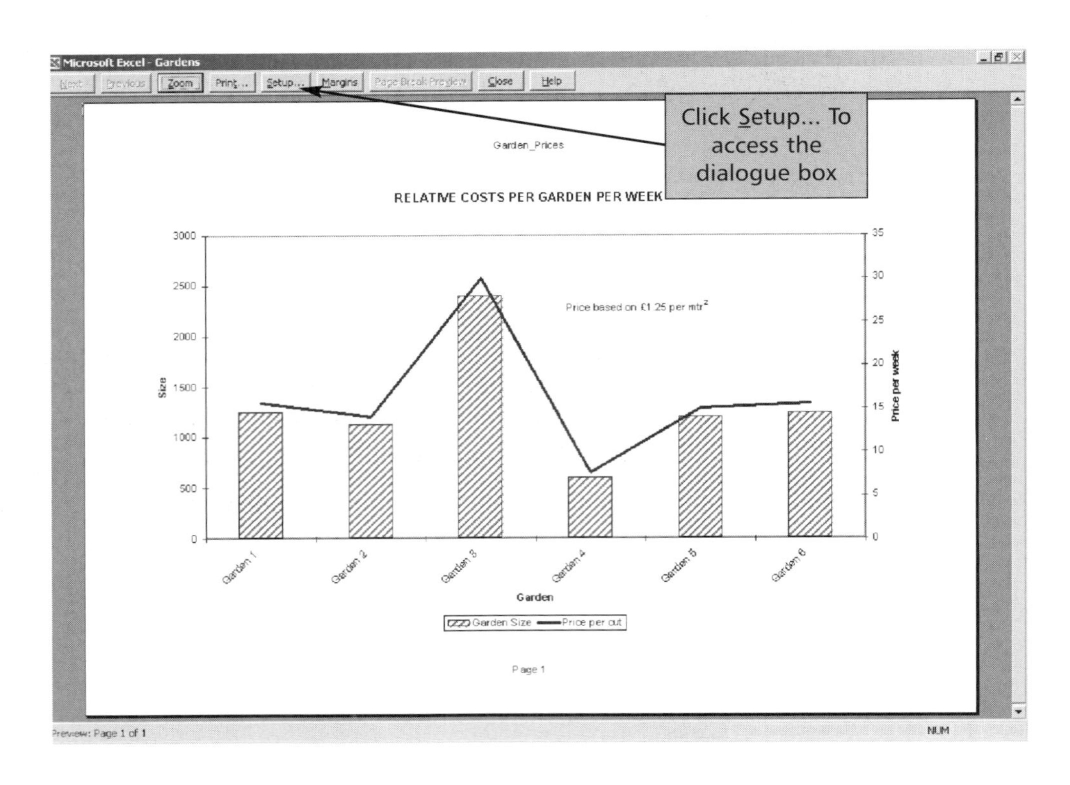

Figure 9.71

Clicking on the Setup... button will open the Page Setup dialogue box shown in Figure 9.72.

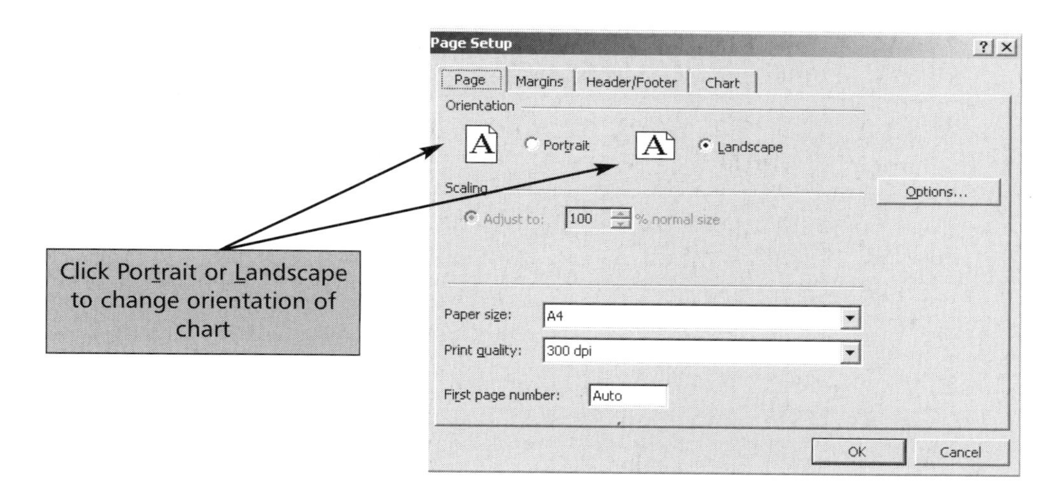

Figure 9.72

Selecting either the Portrait or Landscape options and clicking OK will return you to the Print Preview window, where clicking the Print... button will open the Print dialogue box shown in Figure 9.73.

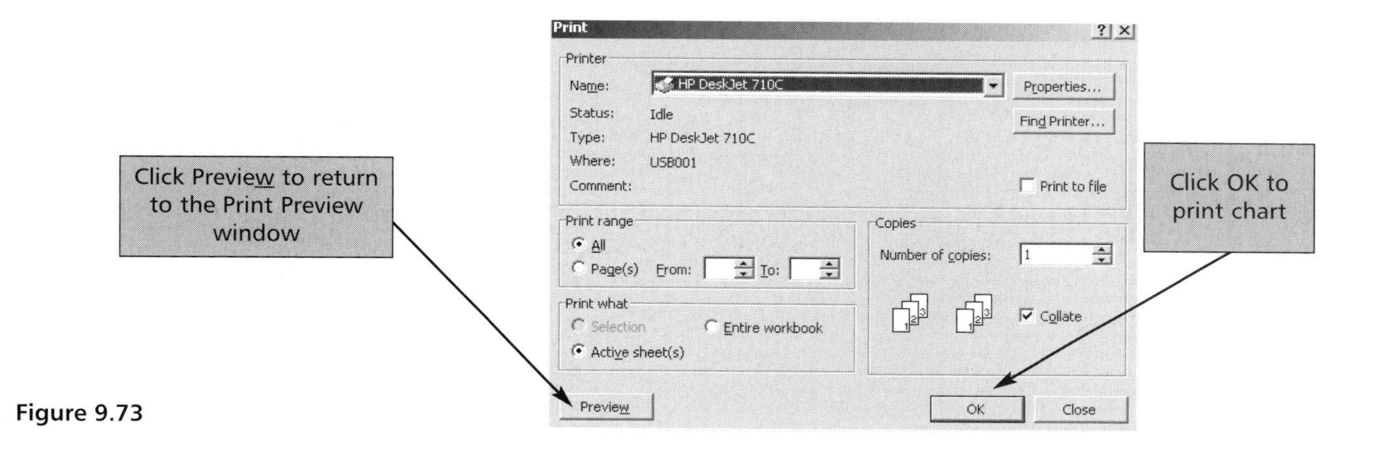

Figure 9.73

If you are satisfied that the correct page settings have been applied to the chart then clicking OK will print the chart. If further changes are needed then click the Preview button and return to the Print Preview window where further changes can be made.

Note: In the Page Setup dialogue box you can also change the margins, the scale of the chart and also insert headers and footers.

Build-up Exercise 9c: Stage 2

Open Gardens.xls.

Click File and then Print Preview.

Click Setup....

Click the Page tab if it is not already selected by default.

Check the radio button for Landscape printing is selected.

Click OK.

Click the Print... button in the Preview window.

Click OK to print your chart.

Save the workbook.

Close the file.

You have now covered all the assessment objectives and the associated knowledge and understanding for CLAIT Plus in graphs and charts. Now try and put the skills you have learnt in this unit into practice by completing the practical assignment below. Solutions to this assignment can be found in Appendix 2.

Graphs and charts

Scenario

You are the business manager for a fitness centre in the Midlands called Bycroft which is part of a regional group of small centres. The area manager is reviewing the performance of centres and has asked you to provide a number of charts and graphs for a presentation to be given by the managing director.

You will use the following files:

Fitness Usage

PercentByGender

UsageByAge

Inc_Exp

You must create the charts and graphs requested using the house style guidelines and the specified types of charts or graphs.

House style guidelines

Pie charts

Typeface	Sans serif (Arial)
Text sizes	
Title	Font size 16 point, bold italic
Sub-title	Font size 16 point, bold italic
Data labels	Font size 14 point, bold
Legend	Font size 12 point, bold

Column charts, line graphs and X–Y scatter graphs

Typeface	Serif (Times New Roman)
Text sizes	
Title	Font size 16 point, bold italic
Sub-title	Font size 16 point, bold italic
X-axis title	Font size 14 point, bold
Y-axis title	Font size 14 point, bold
Text or numbering on X-axis	Font size 12 point, bold
Text or numbering on Y-axis	Font size 12 point, bold
Legend	Font size 12 point, bold
Text box labels	Font size 12 point, single, solid border
Trendline equations	Font size 12 point
Headers and footers:	Each chart must display your name and page number

Practical assignment 9

Scenario

First you have been asked to produce two pie charts showing the use of each facility by sex.

Task 1

Assessment objectives	Stage	
1a	1	Open the file **PercentByGender.csv** and save it, using the same name, as an Excel file.
2a	2	Create two exploding pie charts displaying the percentage use by males and females for all facilities.
3a	3	Type the main titles of your charts as: 'Percentage of Females Using Facilities' 'Percentage of Males Using Facilities' Add a sub title for both charts: 'All Facilities'
3b	4	Display data labels as a percentage for each facility.
3c	5	Use a legend and position it at the bottom of each chart.
2b	6	The management is particularly interested in the use being made by spas as these are expensive to maintain. Emphasise this segment by pulling it away from other segments.
4a 5a	7	Display both charts in landscape orientation. Format the charts according to the house style. Save and print a copy of both charts.

Scenario

You have been asked for the second graph to produce a comparison vertical bar chart showing the usage by gender and age for each facility in the centre.

Task 2

1a	1	Open the file **UsageByAge.csv** and save it as an Excel (.xls) workbook.
2c 3a	2	Create a comparative vertical bar chart with a legend to plot the lower and upper age limits for each facility in the centre. Type the following titles for the chart: Main title: 'AGE LIMIT COMPARISONS - MALE - FEMALE BY FACILITY' Category X-axis: 'Facility' Value Y-axis: 'Age'
3b	3	Align the X-axis labels so that they are at 45 degrees. Ensure all labels can be read clearly.
3d	4	Format the Y-axis scale as follows: Minimum: 1 Maximum: 81 Major unit: 20

4e	5	Apply a different fill effect to each of the four series so that they are clearly distinguishable when printed.
1a 4a 5a	6	Display the vertical bar chart in landscape orientation. Format the chart according to the house style guidelines. Save the chart. Print the chart in landscape orientation.

Scenario

The third chart requested is for a scatter graph showing the correlation between the income generated and the net profit obtained.

Task 3

1a	1	Open **Inc_Exp.csv** and save it as an Excel .xls file using the same name.
1c 3a 2e	2	Create an X–Y scatter graph showing the income required to produce the net profit levels for each year of operation. Title: 'Income Levels for Net Profit' X-axis title: 'Income' Y-axis title: 'Profit' Ensure the data used is: Income Net Profit
3d 4c	3	Format the X-axis as follows: Scale Minimum value: 180,000 Maximum value: 300,000 Numbers formatted as currency to 0 decimal places.
3d 4c	4	Format the Y-axis as follows: Scale Minimum value: 10,000 Maximum value: 32,000 Numbers formatted as currency to 0 decimal places.
4f 4g 4h	5	Join the points on the line using a solid, thick line. Remove all markers.
4d	6	Format the plot area so that it is pale blue.
3g	7	Insert a text box at the end of the line and above the line with the following text: 'Target Profit for 2004'
4a 5b	8	Display the scatter graph in landscape orientation and ensure that the house style guidelines have been adhered to. Print the graph.

Scenario

For the fourth chart you are asked to create a line–column chart showing the actual usage of facilities against total membership.

Task 4

1a	1	Open file **FitnessUsage.csv** and then save it as an Excel .xls file using the same name.
2d 3a 3c	2	Create a line–column graph of the total number of members against those who actually use the facility. Main title: 'Analysis of Total Membership Compared to Actual Usage' X-axis label: 'Facility' Y-axis label: 'Membership' Set the legend, using Total membership and Membership Usage, at the top of the line–column graph.
4c	3	Format the X-axis as follows: X-axis labels: alignment 45 degrees
3d	4	Format the Y-axis as follows: Scale: Minimum value 100 Maximum value 1,700 Data labels: Total Membership: Red, bold Actual Users: Blue, bold
4d	5	Apply a two-colour pattern fill to the plot area ensuring the two fills are distinguishable on a non-colour printout.
4a	6	Display the line–column graph in landscape orientation. Format the line–column graph according to the house style.

Scenario

The final graph you have been asked to produce compares the use of the centre by male and female members against the average temperatures for each month of the year.

Task 5

1a	1	Open file **UsageByTemp.csv** and then save it as an Excel .xls file using the same name.
2e 3a	2	Create an X–Y scatter graph to plot use of the centre by male and female members against the average monthly temperature. Main title: 'Monthly Comparision of Centre Use By Male and Female Members' Value X-axis title: 'Temp' Value Y-axis title: 'Centre Visits'
3e 3f 3g	3	Add trendlines for both male and female member usage and display the equations of the trendlines. Position the equations at the top of the plot area. Insert a text box to the left of each equation identifying the appropriate equation as either Male Members or Female Members.

4g	4	Format the trendlines as thick lines of long dashes. Each trendline should be colour coded to distinguish between male and female trends.
4h	5	Format the male marker as a solid circle.
3d	6	Format the Y-axis as follows: Scale Minimum value: 400 Maximum value: 1800 Major unit: 250 Format the X-axis as follows: Scale Minimum value: 0 Maximum value: 18 Major unit: 1 **Note:** after setting the scale for the axes you will need to adjust the alignment of the equation and associated text boxes.
4a	7	Display the X–Y scatter graph in landscape orientation.
5b		Format the scatter graph according to the house style (except for the equations which should be formatted as per the labels associated with them, but without the border). Save and print the graph retaining the landscape orientation.

Index

Note: Page numbers preceded by CD are to be found on the CD which accompanies the book. Page numbers which have no prefix are to be found in the book.